Asian American Religious Cultures

Jonathan H. X. Lee, Fumitaka Matsuoka, Edmond Yee, and Ronald Y. Nakasone, Editors

Volume I

Essays and A–H

American Religious Cultures

 ABC-CLIO™

An Imprint of ABC-CLIO, LLC
Santa Barbara, California • Denver, Colorado

Library of Congress Cataloging-in-Publication Data

Asian American religious cultures / Jonathan H.X. Lee, Fumitaka Matsuoka, Edmond Yee, and Ronald Y. Nakasone, editors.

    volumes cm .– (American Religious Cultures)
  Includes bibliographical references and index.
  ISBN 978-1-59884-330-9 (alk. paper) – ISBN 978-1-59884-331-6 (ebook)
1. Asian Americans–Religion–Encyclopedias. 2. Asian Americans–Social life and customs–Encyclopedias. 3. United States–Religion–Encyclopedias. I. Lee, Jonathan H. X., editor. II. Matsuoka, Fumitaka, editor. III. Yee, Edmond, 1938- editor. IV. Nakasone, Ronald Y., editor.
  BL2525.A845   2015
  200.89′95073–dc23   2014046610

ISBN: 978-1-59884-330-9
EISBN: 978-1-59884-331-6

19 18 17 16 15   1 2 3 4 5

This book is also available on the World Wide Web as an eBook.
Visit www.abc-clio.com for details.

ABC-CLIO, LLC
130 Cremona Drive, P.O. Box 1911
Santa Barbara, California 93116-1911

This book is printed on acid-free paper ∞

Manufactured in the United States of America

Contents

Preface

Asian American Religious Cultures is a two-volume encyclopedia designed to be user friendly and informative for high school students, college undergraduates, and interested nonspecialist readers. The entries in the work are grounded on the perspective that Asian Americans are continuously (re)shaping their religious beliefs, practices, lifeways, communities, identities, and understanding of self in relation to others and the cosmos. The entries also reveal a transnational relationship, historically and in the present moment, between and among Asians and Asian Americans, Asian religions and their manifold manifestations in the United States, and their influence in and contribution to the American mosaic.

Contributors to these volumes are faith practitioners, religious leaders, community elders, and academics who bridge the emic-etic division in the study of religions to provide a complete kaleidoscopic presentation of Asian American religious cultures. The volumes include 19 alphabetically arranged thematic essays on topics that cover theories and methods, and critical topics in the study of Asian American religious cultures. Each of the more than 200 individual entries, like each thematic essay, concludes with a bibliography of additional print or electronic information resources and a listing of cross-references to related entries in a "See also" line at the end of the entry text. A Guide to Related Topics breaks the essays and entries into topic categories that trace broad ideas and themes across the two volumes. These volumes also offer a general introduction placing the topic of the encyclopedia into broad historical context, a select bibliography of important general information resources, and a detailed subject index. The essays and entries were authored by over 100 contributors, the majority with advanced graduate degrees, or people of faith who wanted to share their religious communities with a wider audience.

While we employ the panethnic umbrella classification of "Asian American," we acknowledge the competing, more "inclusive" categories of "Asian Pacific American" or "Asian Pacific Islander," which include the diverse Pacific Islander ethno-religious communities and faith traditions. "Asian Pacific American" and

"Asian Pacific Islander" are controversial panethnic classifications; together with "Asian American" none of the panethnic references are accepted wholeheartedly by the folks that these three classifications wish to embrace. Although there are entries that represent Pacific Islander religious cultures, we include them with the expressed awareness that many wish—taxonomically—to divorce Asian Americans from Pacific Islanders as an ideological, political, economic, and social discourse. We support the right of Pacific Islanders to self-determination and look forward to the future when Pacific Islander studies develop into an autonomous discipline, and when panethnic umbrella classifications are no longer considered progressive. We also support the wish of Pacific Islanders to not be subsumed under the umbrella category of "Asian Pacific" American. We hope we do not offend our Pacific Islander allies by including coverage of Pacific Islander religious cultures in these volumes. We do so humbly, respectfully, and with utmost care.

This project could easily be doubled, if not tripled in size—there are many topics that we wished to include, but could not do so because we could not locate a qualified specialist. This tells us that there is a need for more studies on Asian American religious cultures, which we hope these volumes will assist in promoting. Although the field of Asian American religious studies has seen healthy growth since the 1990s, much more work is needed to document the rich, diverse, and dynamic histories, developments, and transformations of the religious cultures of Asian Americans. The volumes of *Asian American Religious Cultures* constitute a drop in the bucket for what is yet to come.

Acknowledgments

We all wish to acknowledge all the contributors who have made these volumes enriching and encompassing. In addition, we all wish to thank our families for their continued support and understanding, as well as acknowledge our respect and gratitude for one another. We extend appreciation especially to devotees of the respective faith traditions, who, in addition to sharing their most cherished beliefs, voiced their deepest yearnings and highest aspirations. We also wish to acknowledge the early contribution of Jane Naomi Iwamura, who used her social and academic connections to bring in contributors. Jonathan H. X. Lee wishes to thank the College of Ethnic Studies at San Francisco State University for funding that provided time to work on this project. Lee also wishes to acknowledge support from his students and colleagues in the Asian American Studies Department, and his research assistant, Sidney C. Li.

Introduction

"Asian American" refers to an American—both foreign and American born—of Asian descent. The term "Asia" was derived from the Greek word *Asianos*, which some scholars believe originated from the Assyrians who used the word *asu* to mean "east": the first occurrence or origin of this word would date back to 1000 BCE if not earlier. The ancient Greeks used this term to designate an area east of the principal Greek world. The expression came to embrace a greater geological area when Alexander the Great (356–323 BCE) began his wars against the Persian Empire. Subsequently, the Romans used the term "Asia" to include the lands given to them by Attalus III in 133 BCE. In short, "Asia" was invented by the ancient Greeks and Romans, and expanded by Western geographers to include the land mass east of the Ural Mountains and Ural River, even extending to Japan and Java. Within this vast region there is no common "Asian" culture. It is this distinct diversity and heterogeneity that makes studying Asian American religious cultures dynamic. As an overarching designation, as a reference, and as a category "Asian American" is, therefore, composed of many groups differing in national origin, ethnicity, language, and length of residence in the United States.

Asian American Religious Landscapes

Demographically speaking, East Asian Americans (Chinese, Japanese, Korean) and Vietnamese are formed by Mahāyāna Buddhism, Daoism, Confucianism, and Christianity. Southeast Asian Americans (Cambodian, Laotian, Thai, Burmese, and so forth) identify more with Theravāda Buddhism. While South Asian Americans are largely Hindu, among this group are many Jains, Zoroastrians, Muslims, Sikhs, and Orthodox Christians. Pakistanis and Afghans are predominantly Muslim. Pacific Islanders and Filipinos have very high Christian affiliation, the latter predominantly Roman Catholic. The tremendous growth and diversity of Asian Americans today is largely a result of the Hart-Celler Act of 1965 that liberalized U.S. immigration policy. This act sets the dividing line between two waves of Asian American immigration.

First Wave. The landscape of Asian American religions is closely tied with the geopolitical history of Asian America and Oceania. The settlement of Asian Americans first occurred in 1763 with the establishment of a community by Chinese and Filipinos in Louisiana. Some American Protestant churches recruited Native Hawaiians and Chinese immigrants to be sent to their homelands for mission purposes. These churches also assisted the U.S. government and U.S. companies in the promotion of a capitalistic and colonial system of government and commerce in Hawai'i and Asia.

At the same time, Asian Americans also relied on religions to survive in the harsh environment of the new land and to maintain their dignity. The result was cultural blending among Asian American religious groups. In Hawai'i the native Hawaiians and Asian immigrants accepted the Christianity that was introduced by Protestant Congregationalist churches in the mid-19th century. At the same time, they also brought into their new faith the non-Christian religious practices and values of their background. The early Asian American Protestants in Hawai'i brought with them a strong nationalism.

Hostility toward Asian immigrants steadily grew in the United States. The Chinese Exclusion Act (1882), the proscription of Japanese, Indian Asian, and all Asian immigration (1924), and the immigration ban on Filipinos (1934) effectively closed the door to Asian migration. In 1870, Asian immigrants were deemed ineligible for American citizenship. The Cable Act of 1922 revoked the citizenship of any American woman who married an alien ineligible for citizenship. The following year, the U.S. Supreme Court upheld the constitutionality of the alien land laws of several western states that denied aliens ineligible for citizenship the right to own property. An estimated 120,000 Japanese nationals and Japanese Americans were placed in internment camps during World War II. The Chinese Exclusion Act was finally repealed in 1943, but many discriminatory laws remained in effect during the middle decades of the 20th century.

In spite of the hostile and discriminatory environment in which Asian immigrants had to live and work, remarkably, they were able to contribute to U.S. society in many ways. The early Asian immigrants strived toward better working conditions and fought against racial discrimination. Japanese Americans sacrificed their lives as U.S. soldiers during World War II despite their families being placed in internment camps. Religions played a significant role in Asian Americans' efforts to be solid members of U.S. society. In addition to those who joined Protestant churches in Hawai'i and the American West, the early immigrants created and maintained their own faith organizations. The Buddhist Church of America, for example, rooted in Jōdo Shinshū (Pure Land) Buddhism in Japan, is the predominant tradition among Japanese Americans in the continental United States and Hawai'i. Chinese Americans established numerous temples and shrines in 12 states. The first Asian Indian immigrants from Punjabi built a Sikh *gurdwara* in Stockton, California, in 1915. Filipino immigrants, predominantly Catholic, established various social organizations in the continental United States and Hawai'i, and other Pacific Islanders have undergone tremendous religious transformations. Christian mission schools improved literacy and brought Westernization. Protestantism became the dominant religion of Hawaiians by the end of the 19th century (Roman Catholicism became dominant in Guam and Tahiti). Hawaiian and Pacific Islander Christianity, however, creatively blended indigenous traditions with Christianity even while professing orthodox Christian commitments.

Second Wave. The religious landscape of Asian Americans has become more diverse and complicated since the Immigration and Nationality Act (Hart-Celler Act) of 1965. The number of those who embrace non-Abrahamic faiths has increased greatly, particularly Buddhists and Hindus. According to Pew Research, Buddhists and Hindus today account for roughly the same share of the U.S. public as Jews (roughly 2 percent). Most Asian Americans belong to the two largest U.S. religious groups: Christians and those who have no particular religious affiliation. Asian American adult Christians occupy 42 percent, whereas the unaffiliated Asian Americans are 26 percent. The third largest group is Buddhists, roughly one in seven Asian Americans (14 percent), followed by Hindus (10 percent), Muslims (4 percent), and Sikhs (1 percent). Those who profess other religions make up 2 percent of Asian Americans.

Each of the six largest Asian American ethnic groups contributes to the complexity of religious affiliations. Filipinos are largely Catholic, Koreans tend to be Protestant. Approximately half of Indian Americans are Hindu; half of Chinese Americans are unaffiliated. Japanese Americans are a mix of Christians, Buddhists, devotees of new religions, and the unaffiliated. Vietnamese Americans tend to belong to various traditions of Buddhism. Therefore, religious cultures in Asian American communities are an equally complex affair and include all the major world faith traditions, as well as new religious movements (e.g., Soka Gakkai, Falun Gong, Caodai) and folk religions. Given the countless variations that exist, Asian Americans must be viewed as a group whose identity is necessarily heterogeneous, hybrid, and multiple. Very few assumptions can be made about Asian Americans' religious affiliations, and attention must be paid to the sociohistorical differences that are the hallmark of Asian American religious cultures.

Words Matter: "Religion" and/or "Spirituality"

The expressions "religion" and "spirituality" have been a major difficulty in compiling and editing this encyclopedia. The current dictionary definitions of "religion" are fashioned to encompass the variety of cultural and world views concerning the meaning and purpose of human life. These definitions primarily reflect current Western perceptions of what constitutes a faith tradition, namely a written canon that articulates its beliefs, an institution that gives form to its yearnings and aspirations, and a priesthood that transmits its beliefs and aspirations by living and sharing its ideals. "Religion" also encompasses doctrines, values, rituals, and the arts.

As a conceptual template "religion," derived from the Latin *religiō*, refers to a covenant that entails obligations between individuals and communities and their God, a mutuality that is fundamental to Abrahamic faith traditions. But Anthony C. Yu, Julia Ching, and others have expressed reservations about the appropriateness of this notion of "religion" to a tradition like shamanism, for example, that is bereft of an institution or a canon or priesthood; or to Confucianism that has a canon, but without a highly structured organized institution and an ordained priesthood. While the Buddhist tradition has a canon, institution, and priesthood, it does not posit a personality—god or divinity—with whom the devotee can establish a covenant.

Additionally, objections have been raised. "Religion" and its adjectival "religious" give form to codified beliefs and expression, and do not account for the full range of the ineffable aspects of the human experience. In their stead, "spirituality" and its adjectival "spiritual" have emerged as alternative expressions in research, clinical settings, and reflection. Thus, in an effort to lend some clarity, the following paragraphs review the expressions "religion" and "spirituality" and a few of their respective implications in the lives of Asian Americans and their communities.

"Spiritual" and "Spirituality." The expressions "spiritual" and "spirituality," in contrast with "religion" and "religious," are more fundamental and expansive. The Latin root *spīritus* means "to breathe"; it refers to the vital principle or animating force that quickens sentiency and life. The importance of "breath as life" or "life-breath" is evident in early Indian earth deity *yaksha* and *yakshi* sculptures with their inflated lower abdomens, a motif that appears in South and Southeast Asian Buddhist sculpture. The notion present in the Old Testament and Babylonian myths also appears as *qi* in Daoist and Confucian thought.

"Spiritual" and "spirituality" accommodate a variety of faith traditions and personal experiences that address concerns that animate life, more specifically the human experience. As a concept "spirituality" is a hermeneutic bridge between Christianity and its varied denominations and nontheistic faith traditions. "Spirituality," for example, can accommodate the nontheistic Confucian-inspired understanding vision of reality, including aging and old age, that inspire and give meaning and purpose to future elders. This distinction was not lost to the early Catholic missionaries, who questioned whether Confucianism can be correctly labeled a "religion." During the late 19th and 20th centuries, Chinese intellectuals, who considered "religion" to be superstition, thought Confucianism to be a philosophy, a view that is still held in the People's Republic of China.

"Spiritual" and "spirituality" are appropriate for shamanic experiences that have no formal institutions and are also applicable to the absence of a self-conscious and independent "self" in traditional Polynesian cultures, where an individual's identity is determined by his or her place in the family lineage, community, and the natural world. Within the Samoan-Polynesian context, for example, "spirituality" is a communal experience that is guided by a shared vision of the world—seen and unseen—that is manifested through a lifestyle and affirmed through ritual, architecture, the arts, and other modalities. Intriguingly, pre-European-contact Samoans did not build places of worship or give form to Tagaloa, their highest deity; rather, the sacred was and still is embodied in *vā tapuia*, the covenantal relationships between and among people and with the natural world.

"Spiritual" also embraces mystical experiences within a tradition and outside its confines. As noted in the essay on "Spirituality," the authors of *The Study of Spirituality* traced the expression to the 15th- and 16th-century European Christians who were interested in transcendental mystical experiences. These experiences were pursued primarily by clerics through established communal practices and supported by theology. Lay seekers, in contrast, cultivated these quests through individual avenues outside the established formats, moving beyond the confines of "religion" and its institutional notions of faith and meaning. These explorations allowed for the experience of alternative realities, practices, beliefs, and spiritualities. There can be as many "spiritualities" as there are "spiritual" persons.

The proliferation of "private spiritualities" and their accompanying experiences give rise to many academic and practical questions. This is not to say that "private spiritualities" are any less genuine; personal experiences are meaningful. Appreciated only by the individual and perhaps by a few of his or her cohorts, the absence of coherent doctrinal support, a shared ritual expression, and the gravitas of history, "private spiritualities" are suspect. How can the validity of an inner or transcendental experience be ascertained? Another question pertains to the method or methods that lead to an "authentic" experience. Are individual methods universally applicable? These and other questions are beyond the scope of this introduction. In addition, "private spiritualities" pose many problems for caregivers and caregiving facilities. Without shared cohort experiences, activity directors struggle to plan meaningful programs.

Asian American History, Religion, and Race

The racial landscape of the United States has profoundly changed since the enactment of the Immigration and Nationality Act (Hart-Celler Act) of 1965 that abolished the previous national origins formula. This landmark act opened the door to immigrants from previously restricted regions of the world such as Asia, Africa, and the Middle East. The Latin American population in the United States also increased dramatically even though such an increase was not intended by this act. By the 1990s, the U.S. population had grown more than one-third, driven by both legal and illegal immigration. Ethnic and racial minorities, as defined by the U.S. Census Bureau, rose from 25 percent of the U.S. population during the year 1990 to 30 percent in the year 2000 and then to 36.6 percent in 2010. The Census Bureau estimated in 2012 that nonwhite groups, led by Hispanic Americans, black Americans, Asian Americans, Native Americans, and Pacific Islander Americans would together outnumber non-Hispanic white Americans by the decade of 2040. Most of the growth is taking place in major metropolitan areas such as Chicago, Los Angeles, Miami, New York City, and the San Francisco Bay Area. The concentration of populations in these areas is already having a major impact on local as well as national politics and foreshadows the future of American race relations. The shift in the population makeup of the United States is also impacting the religious landscape as well.

Race as Positioning. The definition and meaning of race have been changing in accordance with the demographic change of the U.S. population impacting Asian Americans. The Americans of Asian descent alone increased by 43 percent from 2000 to 2010 and the Asian Americans-in-combination population grew 46 percent during the same period. These populations grew more than any other American race group during the period. The multiple-race Asian American population also experienced considerable growth, increasingly by 60 percent. The 2010 U.S. Census reports that leading this growth was the Asian and white population, which grew by 87 percent. The report also highlighted results for "detailed" Asian groups, indicating that the Chinese American population was the largest detailed group. For the Asian alone-or-in-any combination population, Filipinos and Asian Indians were the second- and third-largest detailed Asian groups. Another noted finding is that among the detailed Asian groups with alone-or-in-any-combination populations of one million or more, the Japanese population had the highest proportion that identified with multiple detailed Asian groups and/or another race(s) (41 percent). After Japanese, Filipinos had the next highest proportion of respondents who identified with multiple detailed Asian groups and/or another race(s) (25 percent).

This rapidly changing racial landscape of Asian Americans caused some scholars to suggest that Asian American racial identity is increasingly "heterogeneous, hybrid, and multiple." Lisa Lowe says this fluid and complex picture of racial identity of Asian Americans is "not the 'free' oscillation between or among chosen identities." Rather, it "is the uneven process through which immigrant communities encounter the violence of the US state, and the capital imperatives served by the United States and by the Asian states from which they come, and the process through which they survive this violence by living, inventing, and reproducing different cultural alternatives." In other words, a fixed notion of racial identity is illusionary today. Racial identity for Asian Americans is not a stable essence but a *positioning*, manifesting itself in politics at local, regional, national, and transnational levels.

Racism: A Contradictory Struggle for Membership in U.S. Society. Despite the rapid increase in the variety of racial and ethnic populations largely resulting from the enactment of the 1965 Immigration and Naturalization Act as well as the Civil Rights Act of the same year, what is persistent is racial discrimination and racism. Asian Americans along with people of other racial groups are consistently subject to racism even in the present time. Race for Asian Americans is indispensably related to their experiences of racism. Racism manifests itself in various levels of politics. Lowe says, "the history of the nation's attempt to resolve the contradictions between its economic and political imperative through laws that excluded Asians from citizenship—from 1790 until the 1940s—contributes to our general understanding of *race* as a contradictory site of struggle for cultural, economic, as well as political membership in the United States." Michael Omi and Howard Winant also make a similar point in their book *Racial Formation in the United States.*

Racism is furthermore exacerbated by the often assumed notion of being "American" as being "white." This assumption is a sociological construct in which people from diverse European backgrounds were assimilated into an identity that conferred privilege and segregated their poor members from nonwhites. Because "whiteness" became so firmly rooted in the American subconsciousness, even many well-intentioned Euro-American civil rights activists could not see that their visions of an integrated society meant conformity to these "norms."

"America represented liminality," says historian Ronald Takaki. Asian immigrants in their journey across the Pacific Ocean crossed boundaries that are not delineated in space. These immigrants were placed in the ambiguous and unfamiliar situation betwixt and between anything familiar and comfortable points of reference. They found themselves in a marginal place culturally and religiously as well as geographically where they could also experiment and improvise something anew. Burdened by racism, nevertheless, Asian immigrants created a pattern of life beyond the familiar and traditional and paved the way for the present-day life of Asian Americans that is fluid, complex, and contradictory to the often assumed norms of white Americans. And yet, the present-day Asian Americans continue to bear the historical stigma of "strangers from a different shore." Simultaneously, the myth of the "model minority" still persists.

Asian American Race and Religion. The religious lives of Asian Americans are closely tied to the demographic shifts taking place in the United States and the complexity of what constitutes "Asian Americans." Race, ethnicity, cultural identities, and the historical predominance of Christianity are the key factors to be considered in order to describe Asian American religions. For Asian Americans the term "religion" is not readily agreed upon. For the purpose of the introductory chapter of this encyclopedia, the term "religion" is used to describe what is commonly termed "institutionalized religion" embraced by Asian Americans, both the new immigrants and those who have lived in this land over several generations. However, this description itself is subject to debate just as the terms "Asian Americans" and "race" cannot be singularly defined. For one thing, the borders and boundaries of "religions" are constantly remade among and within Asian American institutionalized religions.

Unlike the Abrahamic theistic religious traditions (Judaism, Christianity, and Islam), many of the Asian American "religions" are nontheistic. Therefore, a relatively clear boundary set among the Abrahamic traditions does not describe the state of the religious experiences of many Asian Americans. This is to say that the epistemological framework used by the traditional study of comparative religions in the West is not helpful to understand Asian Americans' religions and religious experiences. There are Asian American "Buddhist-Christians," just as in the case of other institutional religions. The formative experiences of religions by the first wave of Asian immigrants upon those who are born later are likely to leave a deep impression for what is the self-understanding and confession of the current generation Asian Americans. Conversion is not the only means of embracing a new faith for Asian Americans. The familial religious experiences and the cumulative traditions are just as powerful as their embracing a new faith that often originates in the European American religions.

Furthermore, Asian American religious institutions of immigrants tend to emphasize doing rather than believing, that is, doing of ritual, worship attendance, and charity, whereas the offspring of immigrants are influenced by the American culture of radical individualism and often experience religion as authentic self-expression and religious community as a locus of identity politics. Timothy Tseng notes that the "neglect of Asian American religions throughout much of the twentieth century was due, in part, to the concentration of Asian Americans in the American West, a region that has only recently engaged the attention of American historians."

"Asian Americans: A Mosaic of Faiths"—Pew Research Religion & Public Life Project

The second wave of the Asian American religious scene is indeed distinct among all the religious groups in the United States. One distinct mark of Asian Americans is that they are more religiously diverse than the U.S. population. Americans in general are overwhelmingly Christian (75 percent). There are substantial differences in religious affiliation among Asian Americans. Those who are unaffiliated tend to express lower levels of religious commitment than unaffiliated Americans in the general public. Seventy-six percent say religion is not very important or not at all important in their lives, compared with 58 percent among unaffiliated U.S. adults as a whole. However, evangelical Protestants among Asian Americans rank among the most religious groups in the United States, going beyond white evangelicals in weekly church attendance (76 percent vs. 64 percent). The second wave of Asian American religion points to wide variations within the highly diverse Asian American population.

There are many differences among Asian Americans about the importance of religion in their lives. Asian American Buddhists and Asian American Hindus are much less inclined than Asian American Christians to say that religion plays a very important role in their lives. The percentage of Asian American Buddhists who say they believe in God or a universal spirit is 71 percent compared to those non-Buddhist Asian Americans (80 percent) and the U.S. public (92 percent). The number of Asian American Christians who attend religious services occasionally or regularly is higher than for Asian American Buddhists and Hindus, but many of the Buddhists and Hindus report that they maintain religious shrines in their homes.

Sociological studies of second-wave Asian American religions have increased markedly in the past 20 years. These are influenced by racialization, postcolonial, diasporic, and transnational theories. A number of studies of intergenerational transition or second-generation Asian American religions have also been published very recently. Collectively, they provide a wealth of data for historians of Asian American religions. Nevertheless, there have been very few historical studies of the second-wave communities. Historians can contribute to the study of second-wave Asian American religions by emphasizing continuity and change in religious communities and organizations as well as developing biographical studies of significant individuals. They can also highlight the interactions of these communities with broader American, Asian, and, indeed, global historic movements and contexts. Finally, they can offer comparative frameworks that help track the similarities and differences among second-wave Asian American religious communities. Historical research on Asian American religions holds great promise.

Finally, it is worth speaking about those Asian Americans who seem to have no religious affiliation at all. Asian Americans are twice as likely to describe themselves as "secular" in comparison with members of other racial-ethnic groups. This is not surprising. Other factors aside, "religion" is a more alien concept, that is, less intuitive, for many Asian Americans, especially those of the immigrant generation, than it is for the majority of the American public. Americans usually conceive of religion as an allegiance to a particular faith, a belief in God or a similar higher power, or something that is dependent on regular church attendance. Religion and spirituality in Asia, and by extension, Asian America, often fits none of these requirements. Asian American religiosity, by its very nature, is syncretic and draws from folk stories, cultural beliefs, community wisdom, and personal invention as well as from the various faith traditions. It is difficult for certain Asian American religious practitioners (such as Hmong, Buddhists, and Hindus) to envision an anthropomorphized, all-powerful God with whom one has a personal relationship. And for many Asian Americans, spirituality is philosophically informed (such as in Confucianism), rather than divinely inspired, and religious faith is often indistinguishable from secular interests.

Hence, understanding religion among Asian Americans requires a new lens—one that takes into account the porosity of Asian American life. Instead of the term "religion," which does not fully capture the richness of an Asian American spiritual sensibility, it is perhaps better to conceive of Asian American religions as "spiritual cultures" in which the sacred takes more fluid and unconventional forms. Through this new lens, we might be better able to see, appreciate, understand, and analyze what continues to serve as the main sources of spiritual strength (the significance of family, food, and community gatherings, for example) and spiritual witness (Asian American arts and literature, storytelling, clothes, and the like) and to discern the lively traces of religious presence that the lives of Asian Americans elegantly bear.

Asian American Religious Studies and Asian American Studies Matter(s)

According to the 2012 (revised and updated in 2013) Pew Research Center report, "The Rise of Asian Americans," Asian Americans are the "fastest-growing racial group in the United States." Asian American religions and religiosities can be taught as a stand-alone course, or as a part of other courses, specifically Introduction to World Religions, which takes a diasporic approach and emphasizes religious encounters. Religious Studies and Asian American Studies are both inherently interdisciplinary and multi-methodological disciplines. Both disciplines pay careful consideration to emic-etic boundaries. However, Asian American Studies promotes and condones experimentation with personal experience in research and teaching.

It is important to note that the history of Asian American Studies as an academic discipline is relatively short: 45 years. Asian American Studies was born on March 20, 1969, when a contract was signed at San Francisco State College (now University) to establish the country's first and still only School (now College) of Ethnic Studies. This was one of the results of the Third World Liberation Front strike that began on November 6, 1968. This legacy informs Asian American Studies' raison d'être—its pedagogy and research—inside and outside of the classroom. Asian American Studies is founded on the dual principles of self-determination and social justice. Asian American self-determination is expressed—individually and collectively—from the demand of Asian American subjectivity, as knowing Asian Americans through history, art, literature, social sciences, and education, but also as subjects of research. Early on, a penchant for Marxian revolutionary class critique of Asian American Studies during this period ignored questions of religions and religious beliefs. However, the quotidian experiences of Asian Americans revealed a deep enchantment with religion. The study of Asian American religions and religiosities gained momentum in 1996, when *Amerasia Journal* published the first special issue on Asian American religions. Eighteen years later, the legacy of that first special issue is incontestable as the field of Asian American religious studies has grown, as indicated by the incorporation of the Asian North American Religion and Society Group at the American Academy of Religion, and the development of the Asian Pacific American Religions Research Initiative, not to mention the growing single-authored and -edited volumes dealing with Asian American religiosities.

Since the birth of Asian American Studies, matters of subjectivity are still central to Asian American lives—inside and outside of academe. In particular, many Asian American youth express frustration with their inability to articulate—clearly and decisively—their entanglement with existential questions about their subjectivity apropos their ethnic, national, religious, and cultural self-awareness. Asian American students must also reconcile their identity against popular racialized stereotypes of Asian Americans as "model minorities" who are math and science wizards, or Asian American women as submissive yet hypersexual dragon ladies, and Asian American men as submissive and asexual or effeminate. As teachers and students who study Asian religions in America, one must temper the inclination to Orientalize the subjects and their religiosities. This perennial tussle with self-awareness, being, existence, and form is a central matter of subjectivity. Subjectivity mattered then, and it matters today, and will matter in the future. The study of Asian American religions and religiosities offers fertile ground for explorations of Asian American subjectivity that is a primary concern for Asian American students who grow up American. Besides the focus on Asian American subjects, Asian American Studies provides a model to examine different constructions of the "Oriental" as a means to recognize larger systems of power and hierarchy. It is grounded in postcolonial methodologies, discursive analysis, and allows the observed to become observers. More importantly, Asian American Studies is founded on a social justice praxis that celebrates scholars who are also activists. Asian American Studies provides a theoretical and methodological approach for emancipatory teaching and learning that puts, at the center of study, voices of subjects historically marginalized and starts with the premise that education is political by nature. At this juncture, critical consciousness is possible, or as Kathleen Weiler says, coming to a realization of "consciousness of oppression" requires a commitment to end oppression.

When Religious Studies intersects with Asian American Studies, there are potentials and problems. Religion is not examined as a priori, just as race is not innately biological. Both religion and race are examined as historical social constructions. Religion and race intersect in people's lives and inform their perceptions of the world and how they live, interact, and learn. The merger of Asian American Studies with Religious Studies allows for teaching and learning that focuses on the lived experiences of Asian Americans and requires that Asian American religiosity be investigated in relation to political, social, economic, and historical forces: religion is embedded in everyday life and experience. Asian American Studies scholars and students who study religion will be challenged to observe *epoché* (suspension of judgment), with the radical belief that one's life experience and background are important to their academic work, which is guided by a social justice praxis that seeks to improve the community and the lives of people in them.

Coda

Finally, how do we envision Asian American religious cultures? The sheer diversity of ethnic communities and religious traditions that fall under the rubric of "Asian American" make the landscape of religious cultures quite chaotic. The epistemological differences in defining religion and culture among different faith traditions further complicate an analysis of the religious landscape. However, this much can be said: the study of Asian American religious cultures is inextricably bound to the material contexts of labor, racism, stereotyping, and social history. Asian American religious cultures refuse to be subsumed under the dominant methods and approaches of either religious studies or Asian American studies as they have developed. As such, the study of Asian American religious cultures needs to acknowledge the constellation of relationships among colonialism, marginality, liminality, and "amphiboly." The study is not simply "theological" but what Bernard Faure terms "performative" scholarship where the object of study "to project its structures onto the theoretical approach" as a way to avoid closing off other, new ways of viewing religion. "Ultimately, revealing is always hiding; any insight generates its own blindness; any deconstruction is always already a reconstruction."

Jonathan H. X. Lee, Fumitaka Matsuoka, Edmond Yee, and Ronald Y. Nakasone

Further Reading

Burns, Jeffrey, Ellen Skerrett, and Joseph M. White, eds. *Keeping Faith: European and Asian Catholic Immigrants.* Maryknoll, NY: Orbis Books, 2000.

Cadge, Wendy. *Heartwood: The First Generation of Theravāda Buddhism in America.* Chicago: University of Chicago Press, 2005.

Carnes, Tony, and Fenggeng Yang, eds. *Asian American Religions: The Making and Remaking of Borders and Boundaries.* New York: New York University Press, 2004.

Ecklund, Elaine Howard. *Korean American Evangelicals: New Models for Civic Life.* New York: Oxford University Press, 2006.

Fenton, John Y. *Transplanting Religious Traditions: Asian Indians in America.* Westport, CT: Praeger, 1988.

Guillermo, Artemio R., ed. *Churches Aflame: Asian Americans and United Methodism.* Nashville: Abingdon, 1991.

Hawley, John Stratton, and Gurinder Singh Mann, eds. *Studying the Sikhs: Issues for North America.* Albany: State University of New York Press, 1993.

Hayashi, Brian. *"For the Sake of Our Japanese Brethren": Assimilation, Nationalism, and Protestantism among the Japanese of Los Angeles, 1895–1942.* Stanford, CA: Stanford University Press, 1995.

Iwamura, Jane Naomi, and Paul Spickard, eds. *Revealing the Sacred in Asian and Pacific America.* New York: Routledge, 2003.

Jeung, Russell. *Faithful Generations: Race and New Asian American Churches.* New Brunswick, NJ: Rutgers University Press, 2005.

Jones, Cheslyn, Geoffrey Wainwright, and Edward Yarnold, eds. *The Study of Spirituality.* New York: Oxford University Press, 1986.

Joshi, Khyati Y. *New Roots in America's Sacred Ground: Religion, Race, and Ethnicity in Indian America.* New Brunswick, NJ: Rutgers University Press, 2006.

Kim, Jung Ha. *Bridge-Makers and Cross-Bearers: Korean American Women and the Church.* Atlanta: Scholars Press, 1997.

Kim, Rebecca Y. *God's New Whiz Kids?: Korean American Evangelicals on Campus.* New York: New York University Press, 2006.

Kurien, Prema A. *A Place at the Multicultural Table: The Development of an American Hinduism.* New Brunswick, NJ: Rutgers University Press, 2007.

Lee, Jung Young. *Marginality: The Key to Multicultural Theology.* Minneapolis: Fortress Press, 1995.

Lee, Timothy S. "In View of Existing Conditions: A Brief History of the North American Pacific/Asian Disciples, 1891–2010 (From the Margins to the Mainstream)." *Discipliana: A Journal of Stone-Campbell History* 71, no. 1 (2012): 6–26.

Leonard, Karen Isaksen. *Muslims in the United States: The State of Research.* New York: Russell Sage Foundation, 2003.

Lowe, Lisa. *Immigrants Acts: On Asian American Cultural Politics.* Durham, NC: Duke University Press, 1996.

Mann, Gurinder Singh, Paul David Numrich, and Raymond B. Williams. *Buddhists, Hindus, and Sikhs in America: A Short History.* New York: Oxford University Press, 2007.

Mark, Diane Mai Lin. *Seasons of Light: The History of Chinese Christian Churches in Hawai'i.* Honolulu: Chinese Christian Association of Hawai'i, 1989.

Matsuoka, Fumitaka. *Out of Silence: Emerging Themes in Asian American Churches.* Cleveland: United Church, 1995.

Min, Pyong Gap, and Jung Ha Kim, eds. *Religions in Asian America: Building Faith Communities.* Walnut Creek, CA: Altamira, 2002.

Nakasone, Ronald Y., ed. *Reflections on the Okinawan Experience: Essays Commemorating 100 Years of Okinawan Immigration.* Fremont, CA: Dharma Cloud, 1996.

Ogawa, Dennis M. *Kodomo no tame ni—For the Sake of the Children: The Japanese American Experience in Hawai'i.* Honolulu: University Press of Hawai'i, 1978.

Phan, Peter C. *Christianity with an Asian Face: Asian American Theology in the Making.* Maryknoll, NY: Orbis Books, 2003.

Phan, Peter. *Vietnamese-American Catholics.* Mahwah, NJ: Paulist Press, 2005.

Takaki, Ronald. *Strangers from a Different Shore: A History of Asian Americans.* Rev. ed. Boston: Back Bay Books, 1989.

Tatla, Darshan Singh. *Sikhs in North America: An Annotated Bibliography.* Westport, CT: Greenwood Press, 1991.

Tseng, Timothy. "Asian American Religions." *The Columbia Guide to Religion in American History.* Paul Harvey, Edward J. Blum, eds. New York: Columbia University Press, 2012.

US Catholic Historian. Theme: Asian American Catholics 18, no. 1 (2000).

Weiler, Kathleen. "Freire and a Feminist Pedagogy of Difference." *Harvard Educational Review* 61 (1991): 449–74.

Williams, Raymond Brady. *Christian Pluralism in the United States: The Indian Immigrant Experience.* New York: Cambridge University Press, 1996.

Williams, Raymond Brady. *Religions of Immigrants from India and Pakistan: New Threads in the American Tapestry.* New York: Cambridge University Press, 1988.

Yang, Fenggang. *Chinese Christians in America: Conversion, Assimilation, and Adhesive Identities.* University Park: The Pennsylvania State University Press, 1999.

Yoo, David K., ed. *New Spiritual Homes: Religion and Asian Americans.* Honolulu: University of Hawai'i Press, 1999.

Yoo, David K. *Growing Up Nisei: Race, Generation, and Culture among Japanese Americans of California, 1924–49.* Urbana: University of Illinois Press, 2000.

Yu, Henry. *Thinking Orientals: Migration, Contact, and Exoticism in Modern America.* New York: Oxford University Press, 2001.

Guide to Related Topics

ESSAYS

Arts and Cultural Production
Bible and Asian Americans
Care and Service
Catholics
Christian Fellowships
Gender and Sexuality
Immigration
Interpretation
Islamophobia
Jews
LGBT Asian Americans and Christianity
Muslims
Panethnic Religious Institutions
Politics and Religion
Religion and Law
Religion, Race, and Orientalism
Secularization and Asian Americans
Spirituality
Theological Construction

ENTRIES

Canonical Literature

Confucian Canon
Daoist Canon
Hindu Canon
Islamic Canon
Sikh Canon
Tripiṭaka (Buddhist Canon)

Ethnic Religious Communities

Afghan American Religions
Burmese Americans
Cambodian American Religions
Cambodian Americans and
　Mormonism
Cham Americans
Cham Muslims
Chamorro Spirituality
Chinese American Religions
Filipino Protestants
Hawaiian Religion
Hezhen (Nānai) Shamanism
Hmong American Religions
Hmong Shamanism
Indian American Christians
Indian American Muslims
Indian American Sikhs
Indonesian American Muslims
Indonesian American Religions
Iu Mien
Japanese American Christianity
Japanese American Internment,
　Remembrance and Redress

Japanese American Mortuary and
  Memorial Rituals
Japanese American Religions
Korean American Religions
Korean Buddhism
Korean Shamanism
Laotian American Religions
Marshall Islands, Religion in
Micronesian and Polynesian Traditional
  Religions
Mongolian American Religions
Nepali American Religions
Okinawan (Ryūkyūan) Spiritual
  Culture
Pacific Islander Religious Cultures
Pakistani American Religions
Samoan Spirituality
Taiwanese American Religions
Thai American Religions
Thai Buddhist Immigrant Culture
Thai Buddhist Immigrant Spirituality
Tibetan American Religions
Tongan Spirituality
Vietnamese American Buddhists
Vietnamese American Catholics
Vietnamese American Religions
Yamato Colony

Religious Arts and Music

Aikidō
Arabic (Islamic) Calligraphy
Buddha Image
Butoh
Chanoyu
Chinese Drama and Religion
Classical Indian Dance
Hindustani Classical Music
Japanese Gardens
Shin Buddhist Music
Sho, Calligraphy

Religious Concepts, Deities, Ideas, and Symbols

Aloha Spirit
Dragons
Guangong
Guanyin
Han
Kava
Lotus Flower
Nāga
Reincarnation in Dharmic Religions
Sikh Gurus
Sovereignty
Swastika
Tianhou, Empress of Heaven
Yinyang

Religious Denominations, Sects, and Traditions

Asiamericans in the Episcopal Church
Caodaism
Confucianism
Daoism
El Shaddai
Falun Dafa/Falun Gong
Filipino Protestants
Gedatsu-kai
Higashi Honganji
Hoa Hao Buddhism
Iglesia Ni Cristo (INC)
Ijun
Jainism
Jehovah's Witnesses
Jōdo Shū (Pure Land Sect)
Konkōkyō/The Konko Faith
Lutherans
Mahikari (True Light)
Malaysian American Religions
Mormons

Nichiren Shōshū
Nichiren Shū
North American Pacific/Asian Disciples (NAPAD)
Presbyterian Churches of Japanese Heritage
Reiyūkai
Rinzai Zen
Risshō Kōsei-kai (RKK)
Santo Niño
Seichō no Ie (SNI)
Sekai Kyūsei-kyō Izunome (Church of World Messianity)
Selma (California) Japanese Mission Church
Seventh-day Adventist Church
Shamanism, Modern
Shingon
Shinnyo-en
Shinrankai
Shintō
Soka Gakkai
Sōtō Zen
Tendai Shū
Tenrikyō
Theravāda Buddhism
United Church of Christ (UCC)
United Methodism

Religious Festivals

Chinese New Year
Duanwu Festival
Eid al-Adha, Festival of Sacrifice
Ghost Festival/Zhongyuan Festival
Indian Festivals
Matsuri
Mid-Autumn Festival
Obon (Urabon)
Qingming Festival
Ramadan
Songkran

Ullambana Assembly
Vesākha (Vesak)

Religious Figures

Aglipay, Gregorio (1860–1940)
Bhante Dharmawara (Bellong Mahathera) (1889–1999)
Chan, Wing-tsit (1901–1994)
Choy, Wilbur W. Y. (1918–)
Estrella, Julia Keiko Higa Matsui (1940–)
Henepola Gunaratana (1927–)
Hsuan Hua (1918–1995)
Imamura, Yemyō (1867–1932)
Kagiwada, David (1929–1985)
Kubose, Gyomay (1905–2000)
Mahā Ghosananda (1929–2007)
Matsushita, Eiichi (1930–1984)
Morikawa, Jitsuo (1912–1987)
Nakamura, Paul T. (1926–)
Rajan, Frederick E. N. (1949–)
Ratanasara, Havanpola (1920–2000)
Sano, Roy I. (1931–)
Shunryū Suzuki (1904–1971)
Swami Prabhavananda (1893–1976)
Swami Vivekananda (1863–1902)
Tarthang Tulku (1935–)
Thich Duc Niem (1937–2003)
Thich Thien An (1926–1980)
Trungpa, Chögyam (1939–1987)
Tu Weiming (1940–)
Wake, Lloyd K. (1922–)
Wangyal, Ngawang (1901–1983)
Yee, James J. (1968–)

Religious Institutions and Organizations

Bala Vihar
Berkeley Buddhist Monastery

Religious Rituals and Practices

Part 1

Essays

Arts and Cultural Production

Asian American artists create complex and multilayered art because of their multilayered histories and hybrid cultures. In the United States and its territories, Asian Americans have consciously chosen parts of their cultures to preserve and parts of other cultures to adopt. These changes reflect the variety of cultures, political contexts, and religions in Asia as well as in the

M.I.A. attends the Elle Style Awards 2015 at Sky Garden at The Walkie Talkie Tower on February 24, 2015, in London, England. (David M. Benett/Getty Images)

United States. This essay focuses on the hybridity that is employed and expressed among Asian American artists, highlighting individual artists with unique styles, missions, and histories.

It is important to mention some of the major events that shape arts and cultural production among Asian Americans. The process of migration transforms and transplants the arts from other countries. Some immigration factors that affect the arts are origin, destination, age of immigrants, time period, means (e.g., by invitation, physical displacement, and Asian funding), status (e.g., undocumented, transnational, and refugee), and duration or periodicity of immigration (e.g., temporary work and forced exile). Take a brief illustrative comparison: Shuye Sonoda was a Japanese Buddhist missionary, funded by Japanese and Japanese American organizations to proselytize to the United States, who arrived in 1898 without the possibility of gaining American citizenship; M.I.A. is a transnational Sri Lankan, a popular hip-hop artist who maintains homes in several countries, including the United States, and who is not currently an American citizen.

Events that affect the relationship of the United States to Asian countries include war, economic globalization, and ideological conflicts, and this relationship shapes the American popular image of the countries of origin. This image varies by time period and region in the United States and affects the reception of arts and religion linked to that country.

An open question regarding Asian American arts and cultural production is whether the produced art is a product of latent Orientalism or peripheral Orientalism. This is a question of the means of production (how are arts produced and for what socioeconomic benefit) and a question of cultural authenticity. This essay describes some influences on the arts—personal, cultural, economic, discursive, and regional—without assessing the amount of Orientalist influence.

In this essay, arts are categorized according to how they relate to the body. This categorization more clearly illustrates the arts that influence each other, both within each category and across categories. For the purpose of this essay, an art is considered any practice that is cultivated and passed on and any product that appeals to aesthetics.

Internal Arts

The internal arts cultivate the body and mind. Meditative arts are practiced by many groups and often reflect religious heritages. For example, sitting meditation, or *zazen*, is a form of Chinese and Japanese Chan and Zen Buddhist meditation taught to Asian American and non-Asian convert Buddhists. *Vipassanā* meditation is frequently practiced in countries where Theravāda Buddhism is prevalent such as in Sri Lanka and Thailand. Buddhists who teach these arts come from a variety of socioeconomic backgrounds, such as well-educated Japanese and refugee Vietnamese Buddhists. In addition, non–Asian American Buddhists often sponsor teachers from Asia to teach in the United States. In a Buddhist context these arts teach one not to accumulate *karma*, which ties one to the cycles of rebirth, in addition to teaching concentration, awareness, clarity of thought, and mental relaxation. Meditative arts are frequently taught in Buddhist temples and "wellness" programs.

Another popular internal art is *hatha yoga*. *Hatha yoga* is from India and comes to the United States in similar ways as the Buddhist meditative arts. In a Hindu context, *hatha yoga* is the physical exercises that help one to reach higher mental and spiritual states of being, and hence it is united with meditation, spiritual education, and medicine. Outside of the Hindu context, *yoga* is considered an exercise that helps to develop mental awareness, spiritual knowledge, and wisdom.

Body Art

Body art is done to the skin and other parts of the body, such as the ears, mouth, and tongue. In traditional contexts, body art is often part of rituals, such as puberty rites and warrior commendations. Important to its significance is the pain that the body endures while making the art. Some body art takes multiple sessions to complete and the body often requires time to heal. For example, in traditional Filipino culture, one tattoo illustrates a young woman's ability to withstand the pain of childbirth. The art also represents the body artist—his or her artistic and religious lineage—and thus the art connects the recipient of body art to an artistic and religious community. In these ways, body art is part of oral culture; it is a symbol that can be used to recite personal and cultural history.

Outside of traditional contexts, body art retains the connection to oral culture with its ability to incite the telling of one's personal story. However, because it takes place outside of traditional gift exchange, the relationship of artist to recipient is closer to a client relationship than a traditional master–disciple relationship. For this reason, getting body art can come from an individual's choice to externalize the emotions of a life transition. Similarly, the style of body art represents an individual's choice to connect to a particular culture, and in some cases this is a reconnection to the individual's own culture or to a culture lost in the process of colonialism. Some people get body art that is not from their own culture to represent their sense of connection to other cultures. Similarly, contemporary tattoo artists create decontextualized art to connect to modern culture and new senses of self. For example, Hawai'i-born Filipino American Leo Zulueta is well known for his "tribal style" tattoos that use traditional Polynesian lines in large modern shapes. Also involved in body art is the technology of creating the art. The artist may use traditional instruments to remain close to the traditional process or may use new technology to be more contemporary. Some contemporary tattoo technology can make the tattoo lines cleaner and appear more modern. In addition, new technology leads to new possibilities for body alteration.

Arts in Everyday Ritual

This category spans the arts that are practiced routinely to maintain a sense of community and family. For artistic families, all of the arts mentioned in this essay may be part of family tradition, but this category is meant to encompass "common arts." For example, many practice Asian religious rituals in the home. These rituals may involve the creation and maintenance of altars, the recitation of sacred stories, dancing, adopting sacred postures, wearing cultural clothing, and cooking special foods. In many Japanese American homes, there are Buddhist and Shintō altars that require daily offerings of food and flowers and the recitation of mantras (sacred verses). This practice is an art in itself, but also requires more intricate items created by Japanese American artists. Woodworkers create the wooden altars and figurines, weavers create the clothing, and chefs create the desserts and other offerings. Vietnamese American Catholics often have altars in their homes, and worshipping at these altars can connect them to the daily routines of their families in other countries, which may foster a sense of closeness to them. Many of the items for Catholic altars can be purchased from artists of non–Asian American descent because other Catholic groups create and sell them. Some Asian American Protestant Christians practice Bible readings, and these meetings often involve traditions of reciting scripture, interpreting the stories of scripture in the context of one's own life story, creating sacred and communal food, and singing Christian songs.

These arts in everyday rituals have been used to create signature styles. For example, Japanese American origami artist Linda Mihara, well known for her connected crane art, has combined her family's origami tradition with her fashion experience to create Japanese-style dresses made of folded paper.

Martial Arts

The martial arts are those that train the body to connect the mind to the body to experience life fully. The traditions of training and coping with violence can be highly ritualized and stylized. These may be linked to religion, such as training to embody the personality and agility of spirits, and commemorating deceased warriors with religious rituals and symbols. The public aspects of the rituals are linked to acting because the martial arts train the body for public display and can include performing mythology. Martial arts are also related to body art because the completion of training may lead to a rite of passage that includes body art, and the symbols of valor and pain endurance can make demonstrations of prowess more intimidating. The private practices of martial arts are often linked to the internal arts, such as those that maintain health and those that maintain mental clarity. Implicit throughout the martial arts are ethics and proper conduct. This can be seen in combat rules and combat etiquette as well as

Domo owner and *Aikidō* instructor Gaku Homma Sensei flips an advanced *Aikidō* student during a seniors class he teaches at his *Aikidō* center, adjacent to his restaurant in Denver, March 24, 2014. Homma has shaped the Domo into a place where you can immerse yourself in Japanese culture, by visiting a museum that evokes a northern Japanese farmhouse, strolling in a garden studded with Buddha statues, or even taking a martial arts class in the converted former warehouse where the restaurant compound is located. Homma uses the profits not to enrich himself financially, but instead funds orphanages around the world. (AP Photo/Brennan Linsley)

more broadly in the conception of the proper place of violence in a society. Some martial arts have become more well known through sports. Japanese judo and Korean tae kwon do are Olympic sports. In recent times, jiujitsu has become popular through the popularity of mixed martial arts sports.

Martial arts have a film history for Asian Americans, most notably the presence of Chinese American Bruce Lee in films such as *Enter the Dragon* and *Fist of Fury*. Bruce Lee's charisma has led to the spread of his martial art, Jeet Kune Do, which is a flexible and dynamic martial art that developed from Lee's understanding of other martial arts and Chinese religious philosophy. Another well-known Asian American martial artist is Filipino American Ernie Reyes Jr., who has had film roles since the age of 12. Due to the association of martial arts and film there are many martial arts training schools that focus on noncombative, acrobatic, and musical performances. The current mixture of performance, tradition, and philosophy along with mutually influencing martial arts from a variety of Asian cultures has led to a unique hybrid of religious and charismatic martial arts. The popular image of martial arts has influenced hip-hop competitions, and many Asian American dancers, emcees, graffiti artists, and deejays adopt a martial arts persona while competing.

Music

Asian Americans perform music in Western, non-Western, and hybrid styles that reflect their history. Filipino Americans continue to express the multilayered history of the Philippines and relate this to their experience in the United States. This hybridity contributes to the success of Filipino Americans in hip-hop, which is a bricolage art form rooted in African styles of hybridity. Hip-hop is also popular among other Asian American youth groups, and this often relates to the proximity to other minorities in the United States, similar experiences of racial marginalization as expressed by African Americans and Latinos, and hip-hop's ability to express Asian American hybridity of the traditional and modern using layered music samples and multilingual lyrics. Asian Americans have excelled at all areas of hip-hop, including the notable presences of mixed-race Filipino American turntablist DJ QBert and mixed-race Japanese American emcee Mike Shinoda, both of whom express the creativity and history of Asian American life.

Similar to their connection to hip-hop, Asian Americans have identified with jazz. For example, vocalist Pat Suzuki was at the forefront of commercial jazz and Broadway theater, and saxophonist Fred Ho has united the passions of jazz with radical movements for racial justice. Asian Americans have also excelled at Western classical music. This relates to the upward mobility of some Asian Americans; Western classical music has an air of class and respectability that can be beneficial to some Asian Americans seeking to prove their belonging in higher-class circles and to others as an extension of their Western education. The latter relates to a history of colonialism in Asian countries, where education was demonstrated by the ability to perform Western arts and classical music, such as opera. Transnational Chinese

American cellist Yo Yo Ma was born in Paris and raised in New York City. He has used his success in classical music to promote international cultural exchanges, as demonstrated by his musical collaborations and philanthropic foundation. He represented his transnational identity in his performance for the movie *Crouching Tiger, Hidden Dragon* that featured Asian actors and martial artists, a transnational Taiwanese American director, Ang Lee, and a transnational Chinese American musical director, Tan Dun.

Performance Arts

Performance arts are staged arts that include musical performances. They are closely linked to religion in many Asian cultures. Chinese Daoist plays involved mythology, music, dance, and acrobatics. Japanese traditions of parades, or *matsuri*, are rooted in local and national religions. In the United States, many of the traditions have been transformed in a few key ways. At least from the 1930s onward, ethnic enclaves, such as Chinatowns, have frequently developed themselves as destinations for American tourism. Part of this transformation was the creation of sectors of the enclaves—such as nightclubs, shopping malls, and Westernized restaurants—where tourists could observe and sample parts of ethnic culture that were considered non-threatening. Special events in the enclaves have involved performances of cultural arts. Notable examples of this phenomenon include hula performances in Waikiki, New Year parades in Chinese American and Vietnamese American communities, and Cherry Blossom festivals in historic Japa-

nese American neighborhoods. Filipino Americans continue the tradition of the *Santacruzan*, a Catholic procession celebrating la Reyna Elena, and some Filipino Americans have queered the procession by including cross-dressing men.

Some performance arts maintain a tension between the more commercially viable art forms made popular in ethnic-tourist enclaves and the larger mission of maintaining traditional culture. The National Asian American Theatre Company fosters writers and actors who express a hybridity between Asian American and non-Asian cultures found in the United States. Many well-known actors and writers have been associated with these movements, such as playwright Philip Kan Gotanda and film actor Victor Wong. Avant-garde dancers Eiko and Koma are also examples of artists who engage non–Asian American art communities with Asian American issues, such as the aftermath of the Cambodian genocide.

Performance art is influenced strongly by music, internal arts, martial arts, and flat arts. The mutual influence brings about performances with a hybridized spiritual experience consisting of visual images of gods and communal unity, bodies with emotion and personality, and sounds that call to communal history and traditional religion. Contemporary examples of this are hip-hop artists who combine artistic training, cultural knowledge, and community outreach with African American styles of hybridity and religious experience. While Asian Americans have been in early hip-hop movements, in recent years they have been champion dancers, such as several winning teams on the MTV show *America's Best Dance Crew*, and mixed-race Filipino Daniel "Cloud" Campos who is part of the champion b-boy team Skill Methodz Crew.

Environmental Arts

Several Asian cultures have highly developed traditions of environmental design, such as Chinese Daoist geomancy and Japanese gardens for strolling and meditation. The principles of environmental art are related to architecture and interior design. Chinese Americans, for example, may design the interiors of their homes based on *fengshui*, geomancy, whether or not they hold Daoist beliefs. Japanese Americans also may carry the aesthetics of interior and landscape design—such as the use of *shoji* screens and strolling paths near colorful trees—whether or not they hold Shintō or Buddhist beliefs.

There is a long history of using Asian design by Asian nations to promote themselves internationally and by Western people to express their sense of cosmopolitan style. For example, Japan has used art exhibitions, such as the Columbian Exposition of 1893, to promote the image of being both modern and traditional. This image was further promoted in cultural exchanges when Japanese designers would help Europeans and Americans develop gardens in public parks and private businesses. The exchange of ideas as well as Asian Americans taking advantage of the demand for artists with expertise in Asian design has led to Asian American artists with a variety of artistic skills developed from family tradition, conceptions of the ancient world, and contemporary art. Transnational artist Isamu

Noguchi took family traditions and art education in the United States and Japan to create a unique blend of environmental art, such as his use of boulders, water, and etched concrete to create a *Zen*-inspired courtyard in Chase Manhattan Plaza in New York.

Language Arts

The language arts include literature, poetry, and graphic design. Asian Americans have traditions of language arts in English, other languages, and mixtures of languages reflecting their hybridity. Some works have become standard reading in Asian American studies programs, such as Filipino American Carlos Bulosan's *America Is in the Heart* and Chinese American Maxine Hong Kingston's *The Woman Warrior*. These arts have been influenced by other arts, but most notably by performance arts and music because of these arts' use of mythology, colorful imagery, and the emotion of hybridity. Poetry and songwriting have also been present since the first arrival in the United States. In the Japanese American community, songwriting is linked directly to poetry because poetry forms are song forms, and poetry clubs (*haiku* and *tanka*) have been popular. This is also linked to religious traditions such as Obon (Festival for the Dead), which includes singing and dancing to celebrate with ancestors and unrested souls.

Graphic design has been influenced by Asian and European calligraphy, and by Asian American and American imagery. This has led to the production of children's books, mixed-media art, and poster art. Asian Americans have created comics and comic books in both American style and Japanese style (*manga*). For example, Henry Yoshitaka Kiyama used an American comic style and Japanese American mixed language to illustrate his and friends' experiences of the years between 1904 and 1922 in America in *The Four Immigrants Manga*.

Contemporary language arts often mix the use of different Asian American traditions of language art. This mixture of arts often represents the pains and pleasures of Asian American life. For example, Korean American Theresa Hak Kyung Cha's *Dictee* traces her spiritual and physical journey of hybridity using multiple languages, mythologies, images, Catholic catechism assignments, poetry, and graphic art spacing. Asian Americans in hip-hop also have mixed traditions, such as the graffiti art of David Choe and the spoken word poetry of Denizen Kane, both of whom mix Protestant Christianity, cultural traditions and music, and American popular culture.

Plastic Arts

Asian Americans have been at the forefront of the plastic arts, such as sculpture, furniture design, and toy design. Traditions of sculpture in rock, wood, and metal can be traced to ancient times. Many of the ideas of traditional sculpture can be linked to environmental art. For example, the form and function of Hawaiian sculpture are related to the construction of objects in religious ritual sites. Many ancient forms of Polynesian religions were tied to family traditions of specific trades, such as canoe construction, and each tradition held religious rites

for different stages of construction. In contemporary plastic art, the lines are often influenced by the lines of traditional sculpture. For example, Japanese American George Tsutakawa used the lines found in traditional Japanese rock and wood sculpture, Japanese calligraphy, and northwest Native American wood sculptures to create water fountains that flow like brushstrokes.

Contemporary toys call to the images of popular culture, most notably those of Asian science fiction films, action films, and American cartoons. Asian American science fiction may mix contemporary fears, ancient traditions, and icons of a bygone America. Put into toys, the future fears become miniaturized, while the past becomes consumable and kitschy. It is this play with past and present that Asian Americans excel at depicting, especially considering that they have been represented as a threat to America and as diminutive, innocuous, and cute, while their hybridity is rooted in the Asian American and American past and present. The magazine *Giant Robot*, founded by Martin Wong and Eric Nakamura, reports on Asian American popular culture and represents this culture with its image of the robot that comes to save or destroy the world, an image found in science fiction and animation. Thus, contemporary Asian American plastic arts display a transnational consciousness that is influenced by ancient traditions, contemporary aesthetics, and American hybridity.

Flat Arts

Asian Americans have traditions traced to ancient times of using brushes, pencils, and woodblocks to create art on paper and canvas. Chinese calligraphy has been linked to prehistoric pictographs, and this form of writing has influenced writing across East Asia where China's intellectual accomplishments have spread. Ancient Polynesian cultures painted symbols onto functional objects. South Asians have long traditions of printing mantras and other sacred writings on paper and textiles using woodblocks. Japanese ukiyo-e is a print tradition of multiple woodblocks that relates to Japanese traditions of paper and color creation. We should also consider some forms of body art as the painting of symbols onto a "canvas" of the skin. Due to colonialism and Westernization, many Asian American countries have learned Western styles of painting and drawing that have been adopted whole and in hybrid forms, such as some Japanese *ukiyo-e* that used single-point perspective.

Watercolor is an art that expresses the hybridity of Asian Americans well because it allows for the use of Asian brushstrokes in a Western medium. Chinese American Dong Kingman, born in Oakland, California, was a watercolorist who painted American cityscapes using Chinese landscape brush techniques learned as a college student in China. Today, Chizuko Judy Sugita de Queiroz, who was trained in American universities and was influenced by her world travels, uses watercolors to illustrate her internment memories.

Asian Americans have embraced nearly every branch of photography, from the avant-garde to men's magazines. Toyo Miyatake photographed the Manzanar internment camp using a secret camera, which was confiscated, and then he photographed Manzanar under strict supervision. A contemporary example is Corky Lee, a Chinese American photojournalist who has documented Asian American historical events, such as the protests surrounding the Vincent Chin case.

High-Tech Arts

New technology expands the possibilities to create art. In recent decades, due to preferences in immigration policy, many Asian Americans have immigrated to the United States based on their having technological skills. In addition, some American-born Asian Americans have desired to integrate a transnational image of Asian technological superiority into their identity through the use of hip, high-tech art. The technological achievements of Asian Americans and transnational identities have influenced nearly every form of Asian American art created in recent decades. For example, Sanjay Patel illustrated the vibrant stories of the *Ramāyaṇa* using his training in sketch art and Adobe Illustrator. Tibetan and Japanese Buddhists have been working with neuroscientists to discover the brain's role during meditation. The art of deejaying relies on the technology of the turntable, and in recent years mixing technology has exploded due to music compression technology and the ability to share music quickly over the Internet. The Internet has also helped Asian Americans share and teach their art, such as DJ QBert's online deejay school. Performance arts have also incorporated high-tech arts, such as film clips and lighting that responds to music.

Other arts rely on high-tech arts. Asian Americans have become known for their skills at building and racing Japanese import cars, called "tuners." This culture was captured in *The Fast and the Furious* film series, which was adapted from the *Vibe* magazine article "Racer X" written by Chinese American Ken Li about two Chinese American racers. The third film, *The Fast and the Furious: Tokyo Drift*, was directed by, starred, and had stunt driving performed by Asian Americans. The import tuner racing culture integrates the ingenious, independent, and masculine image of American cars with the image of Asian technological superiority, and with African American, Latino, and early Asian American car subcultures.

Asian Americans are at many levels of the video game industry. This industry has spawned new forms of community and friendship, including new identities and ideals. Many of the fantasies, heroes, and religions played in the games and acted out in video gaming cultures come from popular culture, such as the game *Dungeons and Dragons*, spy films, Orientalist fantasies, and American sports. Asian Americans form communities with other Asian Americans and non–Asian Americans as they play and reenact these domestic games and games from Asia. They also design websites and other online worlds, such as those in *Second Life*. Many of these artistic websites illustrate Asian American entrepreneurship, such as the website of the magazine *Giant Robot* and the website of mixed-race Japanese American pornographer Asia Carrera. Other Asian Americans are involved in many levels of digital film art. Japanese American comedian and actor Masi Oka starred in the technological and animation-savvy

television series *Heroes* and did digital artwork for Industrial Light and Magic, which is George Lucas's digital art and film company.

Brett Esaki

See also: Entries: Aikidō; Arabic (Islamic) Calligraphy; *Āyurveda*; Buddha Image; Buddhist Education; Buddhist Meditation; *Butoh; Chanoyu;* Chinese Drama and Religion; Chinese Medicine; Chinese New Year; Classical Indian Dance; Confucian Rituals; Daoist Rituals; Duanwu Festival; Eid al-Adha, Festival of Sacrifice; *Fengshui*; Ghost Festival/Zhongyuan Festival; Hezhen (Nānai) Shamanism; Hindu Education; Hindustani Classical Music; Indian Festivals; Japanese American Internment, Remembrance, and Redress; Japanese American Mortuary and Memorial Rituals; Japanese Gardens; *Matsuri*; Mid-Autumn Festival; Obon (Urabon); Qingming Festival; Ramadan; Shin Buddhist Music; *Sho*, Calligraphy; *Songkran*; *Taiji Quan;* Thai Religious Foodways; Tule Lake; Ullambana Assembly; Vesākha (Vesak); *Yoga*

Further Reading

Brown, Kendall H. "Performing Hybridity: Wedding Rituals at Japanese-Style Gardens in Southern California." In Michel Conan, ed. *Performance and Appropriation: Profane Rituals in Gardens and Landscapes.* Washington, DC: Dumbarton Oaks, 2007, pp. 133–52.

Hamamoto, Darrell, and Sandra Liu, eds. *Countervisions: Asian American Film Criticism.* Philadelphia: Temple University Press, 2000.

Ho, Fred Wei-han. *Wicked Theory, Naked Practice: A Fred Ho Reader.* Edited by Diane Fujino. Minneapolis: University of Minnesota Press, 2009.

Ling, Amy, ed. *Yellow Light: The Flowering of Asian American Arts.* Philadelphia: Temple University Press, 1999.

Lowe, Lisa. *Immigrant Acts: On Asian American Cultural Politics.* Durham, NC: Duke University Press, 1996.

Nakano, Jiro, and Kay Nakano, eds. and trans. *Poets Behind Barbed Wire.* Honolulu: Bamboo Ridge Press, 1983.

Nguyen, Mimi Thi, and Thuy Linh Nguyen Tu, eds. *Alien Encounters: Popular Culture in Asian America.* Durham, NC: Duke University Press, 2007.

Shimizu, Celine Parrenas. *The Hypersexuality of Race: Performing Asian/American Women on Screen and Scene.* Durham, NC: Duke University Press, 2007.

Wong, Deborah Anne. *Speak It Louder: Asian Americans Making Music.* New York: Routledge, 2004.

Yano, Christine Reiko. *Crowning the Nice Girl: Gender, Ethnicity, and Culture in Hawai'i's Cherry Blossom Festival.* Honolulu: University of Hawai'i Press, 2006.

Bible and Asian Americans

How do Asian Americans interpret the Hebrew and Christian Bible? Do they differ in their interpretations from other Americans? The Pew Research's Religion and Public Life Project in 2012 provides the following data: Asian Americans are less likely than the U.S. public overall to say the Bible and other works of scripture are the word of God and should be taken literally, word for word. But here again, Asian American Christians tend to resemble Christians in the general public. Seven in 10 Asian American Catholics say the Bible is the word of God, whereas 86 percent of Asian American Protestants view it

the same. Twenty-nine percent of Asian American Catholics say the Bible should be interpreted literally. For Asian American Protestants, the figure is 26 percent. These figures compare with 36 percent of Asian American Hindus who consider their holy scripture is the word of God. Among Asian American Buddhists 24 percent say their holy scripture is the word of God and 10 percent of them say their sacred texts should be taken literally. The Pew Research survey notes that differences in responses among these religious groups may reflect different understandings of "holy scripture" as a collective term for multiple texts. Younger Asian Americans (ages 18 to 34) appear to see scripture as written by religious figures compared to older generations and also are likely to say that scripture should be interpreted literally.

It can be said that those who stress the importance of the various methods of interpreting the Bible are being self-critical and systematic about the way they are reading the Bible. *Biblical exegesis* is the critical interpretation and explanation of the meaning of the biblical texts. The word *critical* in critical interpretation involves critical thinking, that is to say, considering all the evidence and different arguments, not criticizing something or putting something down. Biblical interpretation is necessary for a number of reasons. First, the Bible needs to be translated into the language of the reader or hearer. Translation from one language to another is necessarily interpretation. It is the taking of the meaning from the words of one language and putting it in the words of another language. There are never words that are exactly equivalent in two different languages. Furthermore, biblical interpretation is necessary to convey the meaning of ancient texts to contemporary readers or hearers. One can understand the Bible better if one has some basic knowledge of the historical, cultural, and social contexts of the Bible.

There are a number of different approaches to interpreting the Bible. These methods for biblical interpretation can be grouped according to whether they focus on the world of the author, the world of the text, or the world of the reader.

There are various approaches to biblical interpretation such as historical criticism, social-scientific criticism, genre analysis, narrative criticism, rhetorical criticism, feminist criticism, and so on. A recently emerging approach of Asian North American interpretation of the Bible is what is called postcolonial/global perspectives. This approach of biblical interpretation is based on the interpreter's particular social, cultural, and racial background as an Asian American. Contrary to such critical method of interpretation as canonical criticism that looks at the meaning of a biblical text in relation to the other texts in the Bible, Asian American scholars shift the historical center in interpretation of the Bible from the North Atlantic perspective and move it to the academic periphery in their considerations of the ideologies, sociocultural boundaries, and identity formations that inform biblical interpretations. They shift the focus from the traditional European interpretations to the Asian American context. Tat-Siong Benny Liew in his book *What Is Asian American Biblical Hermeneutics?: Reading the New Testament* (Intersections: Asian and Pacific American Transcultural Stud-

ies), for example, locates the central principles of Asian American biblical hermeneutics and their dilemmas, the processes of consent and dissent for example, within the Gospel of John's inclusiveness, the work of reading and interpreting in and for Chinese America, applying the concept of diaspora and immigration, and dealing with poetics, politics, and endless paradoxes that are key topics within Asian American ethnic and cultural studies.

Asian American biblical hermeneutics as a whole affirm Asian America as a panethnic coalition, at the same time acknowledging the differences that exist within that very same coalition. The question of Asian American panethnicity and heterogeneity—or that of balancing identity politics and coalition building—tends to frame the raison d'être of Asian American biblical studies. Asian American biblical scholars argue that the Bible and Asian America should come together in order to counter racist assumptions of Western biblical scholars who use the Bible to racialize and colonize Asians as a race of "heathens." Moreover, they insist that Asian Americans need to honor the ethnic and cultural diversity that exists within the panethnic unity. A significant reason for Asian Americans' reading of the Bible is that Asian American communities, despite the "race of heathens" construction imposed from outside cultures, are not only mutually inclusive but also actively overlapping. In other words, Asian American communities and contexts have been institutionally or socioculturally insisting that they are "legitimated" to read the Bible. These communities and their scholars feel the "right" to patrol the boundaries and demand from others an explanation of their use of the Bible. At the same time, they acknowledge that there is no racial/ethnic and/or disciplinary monopoly over the Bible and its interpretation. Asian American Jews and Christians have their own legitimate reasons to read the Bible in the ways that speak to their lives. Despite the discomfort and/or disorientation on the part of those who have been historically and academically legitimated to read the Bible, biblical interpretation does come from multiple, internally diverse, and externally traversing communities. Questions of canon are important because what one reads helps construct who one is. There are relations between "reading" of the Bible and "being" as Asian Americans that go both ways, as Mary F. Foskett, Jeffrey Kah-Jin Kuan, and John Ahn suggest in their edited work, *Ways of Being, Ways of Reading: Asian American Biblical Interpretation.* Different ways of being may lead to alternative ways of reading, and readers are never passive reflections of what they read. Literature scholar David L. Eng implores us not to underestimate the "interpellative" or "performative" force that one's reading might have on the development of a reader's subjectivity and identity. If Asian Americans are reading the Bible, then they must talk about not only the implications of what they read, but also how they read.

Asian American biblical scholars also recognize that their biblical hermeneutics is an expression of the globalized world. Benny Liew argues that biblical hermeneutics is a form of "talking back" to the historically colonial postures and assumptions behind the biblical scholarship. Precisely by putting together what many might see as "disparate" elements, Asian American biblical hermeneutics has the positive potential and purpose to interrogate many previously assumed understandings and practices, whether they concern biblical hermeneutics or Asian America. In other words, assembling the Bible and Asian America is an intentional attempt to appropriate a cultural canon in order to re-create and transform multiple cultures through a form of multicultural critique. The Bible is particularly good for this purpose not only because of its canonical status, but also because it is a collection of texts that was first written by the colonized but then has become instrumental for colonization. Asian American biblical scholars maintain that the Bible is a fascinating library of texts that pose issues and raise questions concerning multiple and interlocking differential relations of power. Given its status and history, the Bible is therefore particularly good to "think with," argues Liew. "Thinking with" the Bible means not only that the Bible in no way determines or dictates one's thought, but also that the Bible itself remains open because of the points of departure that it provides for its readers. The Bible in this sense becomes "an open text, and hence a text we are obliged to go on working on, working with."

Just as "Asian American" threatens the apparent divide between "Asia" and "America," Asian American biblical hermeneutics might put into crises more "binary assumptions," "purity obsessions," and "unity illusions." Asian American biblical scholars question both the historical colonial treatments surrounding the ownership of the Bible and also those about origins. While it is standard to situate the Bible in Palestinian soil and within the

Jewish heritage, the very word "Asian" uncannily brings back echoes of referring to the so-called biblical land—for instance, by Greeks and Romans between fifth century BCE and fifth century CE— as "Asia" or "Asian." Just as Egypt is often separated from its North African location, so Asia is now generally considered to be apart from rather than a part of the biblical landscape. Perhaps herein lies the heart or the threat of Asian America in general and Asian American biblical hermeneutics in particular: both gesture toward an "other" who might also be part of the self. It challenges closure by stirring up forgotten histories or stories, and/or by shaking up what has long been accepted as self-evident.

The issues surrounding the biblical canon, for Asians, are related to the unequal power dynamics of race/ethnicity and other interlocking power differentials and/ or help construct a different reading of the Bible. The Bible's canonical status and contents in general, and its history within and crossings into Asian America in particular, make it one potentially provocative and productive site of intervention. This issue is expressed in Asian American biblical scholars' challenge to the historical assumptive interpretations of gender and sexuality in the Bible. In his *What Is Asian American Biblical Hermeneutics?*, Liew examines how Paul's as well as Jesus's masculinity is linked to Paul's status as a diasporic and colonized Jew under the Roman empire. Paul's masculinist positions are read anew alongside his own "feminization" as a colonized Jew. Liew observes that in Paul's time, "race/ethnicity and religion were 'constitutively interrelated.'"

By reading Paul's masculinist positions in 1 Corinthians in relation to his "feminization" as a colonized Jew whose body was inscribed as "feminine" by the dominant Roman ideologies, Liew seeks to contextualize Paul's text, not to justify Paul's masculinist biases toward women and other "sexual dissidents," but to refuse any attempt to essentialize a minority person or culture as simply patriarchal or homophobic in relation to certain problems of gender and sexuality. By arguing that racial/ethnic persons experience what he terms "status inversion" in the larger sociopolitical world, Liew notes the significance of increased and intensified anxiety and aggression in such persons and how they in turn target misplaced aggression toward smaller groups even more marginalized within their group, especially in religious settings. Liew also suggests that in order for racialized and de-masculinized Paul to remasculinize himself, he deflects his racial/ethnic abjection to female bodies as well as homoerotic bodies. In making the argument that similar logic appears in the context of white supremacy in the United States, Liew contends that the privilege of patriarchy is not extended to those who are racialized and demasculinized. Furthermore, Liew points to Frank Chin's remasculinization efforts, apparent in his attacks on Maxine Hong Kingston's *Woman Warrior* as well as in his targeting Fu Manchu as a "homosexual menace" and Charlie Chan as an "effeminate closet queen." These attacks resonate with what Jasbir K. Puar and others are consistently recognizing, that is, that racialization, sexuality, religion, and gender are often simultaneously deployed to work against people. In the context of heteronormativity and patriarchy, then, those who are racialized and experience gender failure (demasculinization/feminization) will project their ambivalence and anxiety onto others, such as women and sexual dissidents. For Liew, such essentializing moves only provide more excuses to the dominant and imperial cultures for continuing their hegemony.

The current and emerging scholarships of biblical hermeneutics among Asian American Christians and Jews serve as powerful forces for legitimizing their efforts and make them compelling voices for the scholarly world of biblical studies. This is so because when Asian American communities and Bible-reading communities are recognized as mutually complementary in the world of biblical scholarship, then "reading" of the Bible and "being" of Asian Americans are also recognized as mutually constitutive of each other.

Fumitaka Matsuoka

See also: Essays: Interpretation

Further Reading

Cheng, Patrick S. "Multiplicity and Judges 19: Constructing a Queer Asian Pacific American Biblical Hermeneutic." *Semeia* 90–91 (2002): 119–33.

Fernandez, Eleazar S. "From Babel to Pentecost: Finding a Home in the Belly of the Empire." *Semeia* 90–91 (2002): 29–50.

Foskett, Mary F. "The Accidents of Being and the Politics of Identity: Biblical Images of Adoption and Asian Adoptees in America." *Semeia* 90–91 (2002): 135–44.

Foskett, Mary F., Jeffrey Kah-Jin Kuan, and John Ahn, eds. *Ways of Being, Ways of Reading: Asian American Biblical Interpretation.* Indianapolis: Chalice Press, 2006.

Kim, Eunjoo Mary. "Hermeneutics and Asian American Preaching." *Semeia* 90–91 (2002): 269–90.

Kim, Eunjoo Mary. "Home as Memory, Metaphor, and Promise in Asian/Pacific American Religious Experience." *Semeia* 90–91 (2002): 87–104.

Kim, Uriah (Yong-Hwan). "Uriah the Hittite: A (Con)Text of Struggle for Identity." *Semeia* 90–91 (2002): 69–85.

Liew, Tat-Siong Benny. *What Is Asian American Biblical Hermeneutics?: Reading the New Testament.* Intersections: Asian and Pacific American Transcultural Studies. Honolulu: University of Hawai'i Press, 2008.

Reitz, Henry W. "My Father Has No Children: Reflections on a *Hapa* Identity toward a Hermeutic of Particularity." *Semeia* 90–91 (2002): 145–57.

Sano, Roy I. "Shifts in Reading the Bible: Hermeneutical Moves among Asian Americans." *Semeia* 90–91 (2002): 105–18.

Care and Service

Definitions and Historical Context

Within the experiential context of Asian Americans and their religious cultures, the terms *care* and *service* refer to the approaches, strategies, and skills through which persons who represent a specific faith community—whether they be ordained, commissioned, monastic, or laity—offer emotional, spiritual, and occasionally material support and assistance to persons in crisis or need. This definition encompasses what the Western Christian tradition has named *cura animarum*, the cure/care of souls or, more technically, pastoral care. Historically the discipline of pastoral care can be traced back to the treatise *Liber Regulæ Pastoralis* of Pope Gregory I in the sixth century CE, but practitioners have been intentional in addressing the needs of Asian American populations only within the past three decades. While the functions of pastoral care have been described classically as healing, sustaining, guiding, and reconciling, this essay follows the lead of pastoral theologian Carrie Doehring, who proposes three interrelated criteria for intentionally offering care and service: (1) attending to the health, safety, and security of those seeking care; (2) addressing issues of grief, loss, and transition in careseekers' lives; and (3) helping people to reconnect with their sense of ultimate meaning and with the ordinary goodness of life. After stating some initial cautions, this essay will explore each of these dimensions with a focus on salient dynamics for Asian American populations, and then conclude with two general suggestions for caregivers.

The following paragraphs employ the terms "spiritual caregiver" and "pastoral care provider," both of which imply that trained professionals are offering a range of formal caring interventions. Although such a connotation certainly holds much truth, and this essay strives to add to the knowledge base of those professionals, readers are advised to notice that a great deal of pastoral care occurs informally. Often simple kindnesses and acts of hospitality can convey a powerful message of companionship, hope, and meaning to persons who are in crisis. Examples would include Taiwanese Buddhist laypeople organizing relief efforts for hurricane victims, elderly Japanese Americans delivering Meals on Wheels or volunteering with young children, guests at a Sikh *gurdwara* receiving both the ritual *prashad*

food during a service and a feast afterwards, and Theravādin monks visiting Thai adult caregivers of their stroke-affected relatives at their homes to offer encouragement, advice, and traditional healing rituals. In these situations and countless others, pastoral caring—as defined above—is happening, even if it does not closely resemble the Western-influenced counseling paradigm that is usually seen as normative.

Dynamics and Practices

Caveats. A key principle in providing competent and compassionate pastoral care is that caregivers must acknowledge and respect the particularity of the persons whom they are serving. While this essay seeks to honor that principle by illuminating specific themes in Asian Americans' lives, the principle is simultaneously jeopardized by the artifice of grouping them together—risking the threats of stereotyping, reinforcing hegemonic assumptions, and eliding antagonism between ethnic groups. Hence caregivers must recognize the tremendous variety of peoples within the grouping—in terms of racial and ethnic identity as the U.S. Census Bureau reports, for instance, as well as in religious affiliation as the Pew Forum notes; avoid presupposing cultural homogeneity, that everyone who identifies with a cultural group avows the same constellation of values, beliefs, and practices; and exercise both an empathic curiosity and a humility that will sensitize caregivers' discernment and help facilitate careseekers' expression of their unique stories and convictions.

Attending to Health, Safety, and Security

As with any effective outreach to persons in crisis, pastoral care and service providers must ensure that the persons seeking help are not confronting immediate threats to their physical, emotional, or spiritual health and well-being. On some occasions these concerns may be the "foreground" and lie at the core of the situation for which a careseeker requests assistance; in other instances they form part of the "background" that requires a caregiver's intervention before the careseeker's assessed spiritual needs can be addressed. Within the broad population of Asian Americans, some issues relevant to the health, safety, and security of careseekers would include the following concepts.

Face, Shame, and Reluctance to Seek Help. A pervasive theme in East Asian, South Asian, Southeast Asian, Hawaiian, and Samoan cultures is the understanding that one's personal identity is rooted in a collectivist, relational, familial orientation: a "we-self" rather than an individually focused "I-self." This orientation finds voice, for example, in the Hawaiian term *nā 'ohana* (family), the Korean idea of *jip-an* (within the house), and the Japanese distinction between *tatemae* (what can be revealed publicly) and *honne* (what one shares only with intimates). In many of these cultural contexts, this collectivist emphasis is buttressed by a drive to seek harmony (even if it means sacrificing one's needs for the common good), a desire to maintain face or family honor, and a corresponding avoidance of any circumstance that might provoke shame. Shame is perceived as a custodian of relatedness with others, employed to socialize children to cultural norms and then internalized as a function of the superego.

This cluster of values has led many members of Asian American groups to underutilize mental health services and, to an extent, spiritual care. In many cases, seeking assistance outside the family is an embarrassment, and having a family member with a psychiatric illness is especially stigmatizing because that person's illness often implies weakness or a lack of discipline and endurance. Consequently, families frequently attempt to resolve difficulties within their own ranks, occasionally aggravating the ill member's condition by delaying treatment. Yet because many Asian Americans will turn to their religious authorities or cultural group elders if internal family efforts do not work, pastoral caregivers can heighten their effectiveness by building connections with local religious and cultural leaders to facilitate collaborative intervention and referral.

Emotional Restraint and Somatization of Distress. As implied by the section above, Asian Americans can tend toward developing what psychoanalyst Alan Roland names a "dual self" structure, in which one self observes the formal etiquette required in a hierarchical, emotionally interwoven relational web, while most thoughts, feelings, and fantasies are contained in a private self that provides a sense of personal space. This structure often means that Asian Americans practice a form of affective restraint, especially around matters of family and vocation, which enhances group solidarity and is prized as a mark of maturity. However, if parents do not express affection and affirmation, it can lead to Asian American children feeling a lack of confidence and esteem and can prompt those who are more Westernized to assume that Asian Americans do not have an emotional life. Correlative with emotive reticence is the pattern of Asian Americans with emotional difficulties to present somatic complaints, particularly among Southeast Asians and others with a shorter immigration history in the United States and less exposure to Western medical modalities. In *Handbook of Asian American Psychology*, public health scholars Lawrence Hsin Yang and Ahtoy Won Pat-Borja theorize that bodily complaints are culturally mediated metaphors that allow Asian Americans to convey a message parallel to an affective message and thus obtain help without incurring stigma. Given this set of meanings, psychologists Derald Wing Sue and David Sue advise caregivers to inquire about somatic symptoms while gently probing about psychosocial dynamics, for example, "Dealing with headaches can be troublesome; how are these affecting your mood these days?"

Discrimination, Injustice, and Trauma. Caregivers need to recognize that the histories of most Asian American groups' immigration to the United States have their origins in economic exploitation, and that Asian Americans endure persistent discrimination, injustice, and trauma to various degrees. The racial construction of Asian Americans as a "model minority" and as "perpetual foreigners"

and of native Hawaiians as shiftless exacerbates tensions. In addition, specific events in U.S. history—the internment of Japanese Americans during World War II, the enforcement of anti-immigration and antimiscegenation laws, some Hawaiians' resistance to U.S. annexation and statehood and their desire to reclaim sovereignty, and Indonesians' sense of *malu* (shame) over being mistaken as Muslim extremists in the wake of the September 11, 2001, terrorist attacks—continue to provoke very painful feelings for many Asian Americans. For recent immigrants, trauma may have occurred prior to relocating, as with Cambodians who fled the genocides of the Khmer Rouge regime, but then recur after migration. Some of the resulting difficulties faced by Asian Americans include posttraumatic stress disorder; adults compelling their children to acculturate more rapidly, to "fit in"; and intergenerational transmission of the psychological effects of trauma. Effective pastoral intervention in these cases involves not only assessing the level of trauma and caring for individuals and families in crisis, but also requires that caregivers become engaged activists who seek to improve or eliminate the unjust conditions that created the crisis.

Gender Inequalities. Another dynamic affecting many Asian Americans involves a hierarchical social order symbolized by the Confucian "three obediences," which dictates that a woman should be obedient to her father until marriage, to her husband while married, and to her son when widowed. While migration patterns, globalization, and cross-cultural interactions have resulted in some structural loosening, patriarchy still has an effect, as when women are limited to traditional roles in congregational settings. Caregivers should also note that there are exceptions to this pattern: Rhea Almeida notes in *Ethnicity and Family Therapy* that Indian Muslim feminists consider gender segregation to be less serious than class inequality; and Hawaiian culture illustrates a transformation of gender norms, with women gradually being perceived as more equal in influence and with kinship determined ambilineally. Gender norms have been imposed externally as well: Asian American women have been culturally constructed as subservient and docile, as erotic and exotic, or as sexless "worker bees," while Asian American men have been perceived either as asexual overachievers or deviant sexual aggressors. Yet even with the combined normative pressures within and without, flexibility in gender roles is still possible, as when Chinese men submit to their elderly mothers because of the overarching Confucian ideal of filial piety and when native Hawaiians espouse a more accepting attitude toward *māhū* (transgendered persons) than is usually experienced among other cultural groups. Spiritual caregivers can model equality and mutuality through gender-inclusive language, being conscious of power differentials in relationships, and interpreting sacred texts in empowering ways for women as well as "racialized" minorities—thus reflecting on one's faith from the side of the oppressed.

Domestic Violence. Like other U.S. population groups, Asian Americans tend to underreport incidents of domestic violence. Asian American women may be more reticent in reporting and seeking help because of sexual-economic commodification, an internal desire or external pressure to save face, or a culturally influenced mindset that does not recognize or define victimization, while Asian American male batterers may consider abusive behaviors as an appropriate reinforcement of patriarchal norms and structures. Pastoral caregivers need to view Asian American abuse survivors within the context of their cultural groupings and encourage flexibility in implementing family- and community-based interventions.

Addressing Grief, Loss, and Transition

Grief is commonly defined as the emotional, cognitive, and spiritual process through which persons react to an experience of loss. As the Buddhist tale of Kisagotami illustrates—to heal her dead child, she is commanded to beg poppy seeds from a home where death has never entered, which she is unable to find—it is a universal human experience, with multiple variations of affective tone and expression based on personal temperament, sociohistorical context, familial norms, and cultural values and practices. While grief is readily recognized following a person's death, pastoral caregivers and other helping professionals have learned to identify it in other contexts as well, including the loss of significant objects (e.g., in a house fire) or status (e.g., job loss) as well as during transitions, even if welcomed (e.g., graduating, beginning a career, marrying, or giving birth). For Asian Americans, some contexts of loss and transition that could prompt grief responses are discussed in the following paragraphs.

Death and Dying. A current trend in the medical, nursing, and human services literature involves devoting much deserved attention to end-of-life care issues. Generally Asian American families prefer to mediate news of a loved one's terminal illness, sometimes filtering a poor prognosis to protect that person, maintain her or his hope, and ensure a good death that preserves the family's face; how closely any particular family follows this trend will vary to some extent with acculturation. Nursing professor Marjorie Kagawa-Singer and bioethicist Leslie Blackhall contend that caregivers must navigate cautiously between the poles of stereotyping (i.e., withholding diagnoses from Asian American patients *because* they are Asian American) and of cultural imperialism (i.e., insisting on disclosure of health information, even if it means ignoring the patient's and family's express wishes). They also suggest that caregivers in end-of-life cases directly address trust and suspicion issues; work to improve access and reduce inequities; offer informed refusal as a possibility; identify and include key family members as decision makers; and emphasize hospice care as a supplement to, and not a replacement for, family care.

Because of the diversity of Asian American cultural customs and religious traditions, a summary of practices in the event of a loved one's illness and death is beyond this essay's scope. Several helpful comparative resources exist, and caregivers would do well to familiarize themselves with them to glean clues about how a particular family might be using rituals and beliefs to cope with its crisis.

Acculturation Stress. For more recent Asian American immigrants, the stress of moving to the United States and facing multiple layers of cultural disconnection—in language, norms, values, and socioeconomic status, among other variables—is disorienting and can be debilitating. Such stress can affect both ends of the life cycle. Elderly Asian Americans might believe that their children and grandchildren are not paying sufficient filial respect, and that the cultural skills and knowledge they possess are meaningless because they are not situated in their ethnic enclave. Meanwhile, Asian American children may feel caught in a cultural double bind: asked by their elders to be successful in a competitive school environment while remaining respectful and humble at home. In addition, some mainstream social time markers may not have equivalents in Asian Americans' developmental experience. In *Ethnicity and Family Therapy* Almeida observes, for example, that neither the concept of adolescence nor of adult children leaving home have matching phases in the extended life cycles of Asian Muslim and Hindu families. Further, the level of acculturative stress will vary by group and will affect why help is sought: U.S.-born Asian Americans usually are concerned about racial discrimination, mental health, family conflicts, self-realization, and intergenerational communication while Asian-born immigrants and refugees may struggle with economic survival concerns, sociocultural transition and adjustment issues, daily living skills in a new country, interracial dating and marriage issues, cultural uprootedness, and separation from homeland ties.

Complicated Intergenerational Relationships. Beyond the examples detailed immediately above, there are other avenues for intergenerational tension. In some Asian American populations there is a high degree of differentiation of generations— Koreans distinguishing between 1.5 and 2nd generations, and Japanese naming each generation separately (Issei, Nisei, Sansei, etc.), for instance—and these distinctions can come to symbolize levels of adherence to, or modification of, traditional cultural values. An older generation might hew more closely to a Confucian ideal of filial piety and familial obligation, while later generations might espouse a more individualist ethic; younger Asian Americans might prefer a direct style of engaging conflict, while their parents might lean toward an indirect, "face-saving" approach (e.g., Korean *chae-myun*); and older members of an ethnic religious institution might use the ancestral language in discussing congregational decisions, to the frustration of younger English-speaking members. Noticing these generational dynamics can be useful in providing appropriate care interventions.

Depression and Suicidality. According to data from the U.S. Department of Health and Human Services (2009), the prevalence of major depressive disorders among Asian American adults is less than the national average (3.6 percent vs. 7.5 percent). However, native Hawaiians and mixed-race persons were diagnosed at

rates well above the national average (11.6 percent and 13.3 percent, respectively), and all Asian American populations at higher percentages than their counterparts in Asian countries. The risk for suicide is similar, with Asian Americans attempting at a lower rate; elderly persons, especially women, and Hawaiian and Micronesian adolescents are the exceptions. Pastoral caregivers should be prepared to listen for clues about depressive episodes and suicidal ideation and be prepared to make appropriate referrals while assuring care-seekers of their continued presence and care. It is also worthwhile to observe for symptoms of neurasthenia, a disorder similar to chronic fatigue syndrome that is described in the World Health Organization's *International Classification of Diseases*, 10th revision (*ICD-10*), and commonly diagnosed in Asian American patients.

Internalized Racism. For many Asian Americans this dynamic is very subtle. Social worker Maria P. P. Root in *Ethnicity and Family Therapy* calls it "colorism" and pastoral theologian Greer Anne Wenh-In Ng declares it a "hierarchy of color," by which they mean an unconscious privileging of majority-race norms and values. Assisting people as they confront microaggressions and insults as people of color, helping them to recognize their complicity in benefiting from such hierarchies, and standing with them as they expose the injustices such hierarchies generate are three critical pastoral tasks.

Mixed-Race Dynamics. Interracial marriages and intimate partnerships are giving rise to a rapidly growing number of Asian

American mixed-race children (often designated by the Hawaiian word *hapa*, meaning "half"), whom as they age experience at least four interwoven internal and social dynamics: fluid self-identity definitions, uncertainty about whether they belong within a given community, tension while negotiating how they define their group identity to others, and the difficulty of coherently integrating multiple heritages, parental values, and individual and social meanings. Spiritual caregivers are encouraged to listen empathically to the pain and alienation that mixed-race persons may express, while equipping them to embrace the richness and resiliency that their multiplicity affords them.

Reconnecting with Ultimate Meaning and Ordinary Goodness

This criterion is where pastoral care distinguishes itself most clearly from other forms of human service provision, although in recent years psychotherapists, social workers, nurses, physicians, and others have demonstrated a growing interest in the linkages between spirituality and health. Offering spiritual care to people in crisis entails helping them to tap into and gain strength from the values, ideals, teachings, practices, and communities that can yield a sense of meaning and a capacity for hoping, as well as a perspective on life itself that invites and embraces its ordinary goodness. When caregivers facilitate this task skillfully and compassionately, they succeed in helping people reconnect (or in the Latin, *re-* + *ligio*) with whom and what they care most deeply about. Some of the avenues by which this kind of reconnection

can be facilitated in the lives of Asian Americans include the following concepts.

Acknowledging the Horizontal and the Vertical Aspects of Life. Roland (2006) maintains that, to understand Asian Americans' self-concepts, one must be aware of both their horizontal and vertical orientations. Horizontal refers to the linkages between the self and family, community, or group; vertical refers to the linkages with the cosmic, religious, sacred, and ultimate. Caregivers who are trained in Western therapeutic or religious modalities may be surprised by the syncretism of many Asian Americans; yet careseekers' reported experiences with the world of personal destiny, past lives, and ancestral spirits need to be welcomed into conversation. If an Asian American careseeker discerns that a caregiver is not open, these topics will be omitted from counseling and a vital dimension of that person's life will remain unexplored.

Folk Medicine and Indigenous Rituals. A corollary to the above is that Asian Americans commonly combine Western therapies with indigenous treatments and rituals. Examples include the use of Chinese herbs, *qigong*, and acupuncture, Indian Ayurvedic medicine, Hawaiian *lomilomi* massage, Filipino *hilots* (unlicensed chiropractors), and Pakistani Muslims wearing *tawiz* amulets with Qur'anic verses and consulting with *pir* (living or dead spiritual leaders) in times of need. Even though well-intentioned caregivers and careseekers can disagree about whether and how these modalities interact, sometimes with tragic results, this blending has become more prevalent beyond Asian American groups and is now practiced by the larger U.S. population and categorized as complementary and alternative medicine.

Far from adopting either an adversarial or condescending perspective, spiritual caregivers can learn from the wisdom that lies within indigenous ritual practices. One prominent example is described by social worker Valli Kalei Kanuha in *Ethnicity and Family Therapy* and the native Hawaiian *ho'oponopono* (to make right) family healing ritual. It begins with *pule weke* (an opening prayer) and then proceeds through *'oia'i'o* (truth-telling), *mahiki* (a process of forgiving, releasing, and resolving conflicts), *pule ho'opau* (a closing prayer), and *pani* (an ending ritual with food for the gods and all participants). The ritual operationalizes a number of principles that are helpful in offering sensitive pastoral care and service: (1) problems reside in relationships with people and the spiritual world (*mana*); (2) harmony and balance in the family and nature are desirable; (3) healing must involve the group; (4) spirituality (*ho'omana*) and ritual are crucial aspects of healing; (5) respected elders (*haku*) must guide the process in their prescribed role as mediators (i.e., the negative psychodynamic connotations of triangulation often do not apply); and (6) healing methods must be indigenous to the culture.

The Caregiver's Flexibility. The previous two paragraphs foreshadow this section: When engaged in caring, the spiritual caregiver must provide both structure and interrelational flexibility. This entails providing a clear description of what will be offered and a willingness to step beyond "normal procedure"—meeting careseekers outside of one's office, or scheduling one longer session rather than several shorter hourly sessions—to explicitly demonstrate personal concern and accommodate cultural distinctiveness. Doing so fulfills two conditions that Root names as essential for Asian American individuals and families to seek aid: (1) a sense that the caregiver understands and accepts their reasons for distress, and (2) a caregiver who is actively helping them to make sense of the counseling situation and to have positive expectations of it. It will likely mean that an Asian American care recipient will demonstrate greater dependency and positive transference with the caregiver, and it may mean that the caregiver is expected to take a more directive approach in counseling situations. Yet the balance is delicate: too much assertiveness can exacerbate deference and reticence, so with some Asian Americans it is wiser to present options rather than "homework." Utilizing a Rogerian stance of unconditional regard in tandem with cognitive-behavioral or other action-oriented, problem-solving methods seems particularly useful, while approaches that explore psychodynamics in depth may heighten individual shame if a careseeker feels that her or his parents' shortcomings are being revealed.

Clinicians and spiritual caregivers may need to be less confrontational and work more slowly, particularly when engaging traditionally taboo subjects like sexuality, discrimination, or death, because as Asian Americans reveal more, they may feel more vulnerable to shame. Patience is worthwhile, and assurances of confidentiality are crucial. As social worker Tazuko Shibus-awa states in *Ethnicity and Family Therapy*, it may even be strategic to simply acknowledge that a secret is present, but not probe further unless the situation warrants legal action because that move honors *fumon ni fusu* (Japanese for "keeping things unquestioned") while allowing careseekers the choice of when and how to engage the details of the secret.

The Caregiving Context. Social worker Evelyn Lee and psychologist Matthew Mock in *Ethnicity and Family Therapy* give several insights in counseling Asian American families: Initial appointments should be made with the family's decision maker (often the father) and made convenient for work schedules; address the family politely and formally at first, offering verbal and nonverbal expressions of welcome, and be prepared to "shoot the breeze" and answer some personal questions as a way of establishing trust; show interest in and an appreciation of Asian American cultures; empathize with careseekers about their ambivalence and possible shame in seeking counseling, while reframing that they are courageous and loving in asking for help so as to fulfill their family obligations; and realize that family members may not possess the communication skills to discuss problems and express themselves openly in a group setting. In those cases, a staging approach can be employed—beginning with one or two individuals and gradually building up to a meeting with the whole family.

Emphasizing Cultural Assets and Familial Strengths. Key to effective caring of Asian Americans is the caregiver's ability to focus on the family's resiliency, creativity, and strengths and reframing conflicts in ways that draw upon those assets. Caregivers can supplement this stance by embodying the role of a teacher about American customs, behavior, and values, and empowering Asian American careseekers to teach them about Asian American folkways in *Ethnicity and Family Therapy* and *Counseling the Culturally Diverse: Theory and Practice*. One suggestion in this regard involves simply asking careseekers if they know of cultural metaphors or proverbs that describe their presenting problem more accurately.

Two cautions seem relevant here. One involves asking younger family members to serve as translators. It appears to draw on a familial strength and can bolster those children's pride at being able to assist their families, yet it can upset a family's authority structure and increase the stress that the translating person feels, so it is not recommended. The second caution concerns an apparent fatalism that is often heard among Asian Americans in phrases such as the Japanese *shikata ga nai* (it cannot be helped), the Korean *pal-ja* (immutable destiny), the Tagalog *Bahala na* (leave it to God), Asian Muslims' use of *inshallah* (if Allah wills), and native Hawaiians saying "Ain't no big thing." Rather than interpreting these expressions as a form of despair, it is more helpful to consider these as adaptive strategies for coping with political and socioeconomic systems over which Asian Americans historically have had little influence.

Celebrating Interdependence. One of the enduring assets that Asian American families have at hand is their interdependence, and spiritual caregivers do well to capitalize on that asset in their plans of care. Recognizing the restorative power of rituals can be a powerful step: when Japanese American Christians and Buddhists alike share in the bazaar during the season of Obon, the time of remembering the dead; when Indian Hindu brothers and sisters participate in the *rakhi* festival and celebrate their bond as siblings, which can symbolize the healing of family conflicts; and when Cambodians celebrate the *chol chnam* New Year ritual, fostering a solidarity that counters the alienation and terror of the Khmer Rouge.

Numerous voices have suggested that human services need to be tailored to meet the needs of an Asian American community, or else they will falter due to underutilization. Such tailoring efforts usually include hiring ethnically similar service providers, designing culturally specific programs, and assessing needs and interventions that would be appropriate for the population's dynamics. These are all laudable. Yet it is equally important that these populations exercise as much mutual empowerment as possible. If programs are designed to give clients a variety of services, but control is vested entirely in professionals (and decision making is taken out of local hands), then they may fall prey to paternalism and disuse. In contrast, business associations, clan societies, Korean "ricing" communities, and ethnic religious organizations are exemplars of self-empowering interdependence—with congregational structures serving as acculturation agents, as resources for preserving culture and ethnic identity, as adaptations to a society where religion is voluntary and pluralistic, and as a strategic means to allay the majority's suspicions about the minority group.

Establishing Credibility and Providing Gift-Giving. Essential to an effective care strategy is the issue of credibility, which psychologists Stanley Sue and Nolan Zane define as the careseeker's perception of the caregiver as an effective and trustworthy helper. Such credibility is initially given to the caregiver because of the careseeker's perception of the helper's age, education, gender, and social status, particularly if the caregiver is seen as authoritative. Yet this ascribed credibility lasts only briefly and must be supplemented quickly by achieved status if the intervention is to continue. If a caregiver is perceived as skillful in conceptualizing a problem in a manner consistent with a careseeker's belief systems, in offering culturally compatible means to resolve it, in formulating mutually defined goals for the caring encounter, and in embodying warmth, competence, and maturity, then the care recipient's confidence will persist and the possibility of a healing event increases dramatically. Sue and Zane assert that if careseekers feel a direct and immediate benefit from a caregiver's work, it is seen as a gift from the caregiver that establishes rapport, trust, and a relationship in which hope can blossom.

Concluding Suggestions

Self-Awareness. The caregiver's self-knowledge is extremely important in any caring encounter, and thus sensitive spiritual care with Asian Americans demands an undying curiosity about one's life and ministry. As American author James Baldwin once said in another context, "The questions which one asks oneself begin, at last, to illuminate the world, and become one's key to the experience of others," so good questions for spiritual caregivers to consider about their actions might include: "What is in my head and heart? What are my attitudes, values, and assumptions about the world? How do I behave around others? What messages am I sending others?" These questions can be the starting point for acquiring what Sue and Sue call "multicultural counseling competencies," a set of attitudes and beliefs, knowledge bases, and skills that enable care providers to be aware not only of their own values and biases, but also of careseekers' worldviews and of culturally appropriate interventions. In nurturing these competencies, caregivers will strengthen their sensitivity and desire to help, even as they set aside their value judgments and unconscious defense mechanisms about cultures—such as color blindness, cultural countertransference, and overidentification with the careseeker.

Consultation. Effective pastoral care and service providers, like other practitioners in the helping professions, rely not only on their own self-reflection but also on the wisdom of a community of colleagues with whom they can receive consultation about their work. Learning how to solicit and absorb honest, caring confrontation, clarification, and support about one's pastoral functioning is an art that requires patience and diligence. Persons interested in cultivating this art are strongly encouraged to enroll in a training program accredited by the Association for Clinical Pastoral Education (ACPE). Even with CPE's cultural limitations, these training programs consistently structure a fertile educational milieu wherein spiritual caregivers can practice and hone their cultural humility.

Peter Yuichi Clark

See also: Entries: Japanese American Mortuary and Memorial Rituals

Further Reading

Akutsu, Phillip D., and Joyce P. Chu. "Clinical Problems That Initiate Professional Help-Seeking Behaviors from Asian Americans." *Professional Psychology: Research and Practice* 37, no. 4 (2006): 407–15.

Asian & Pacific Islander Institute on Domestic Violence and the U.S. Department of Health and Human Services, Administration for Children and Families. *Domestic Violence in Asian & Pacific Islander Communities National Summit 2002: Proceedings.* San Francisco: Authors, 2002.

Augsburger, David W. *Pastoral Counseling across Cultures.* Philadelphia: Westminster Press, 1986.

Barnes, Patricia M., Barbara Bloom, and Richard L. Nahin. "Complementary and Alternative Medicine Use among Adults and Children: United States, 2007." *National Health Statistics Reports*, no. 12. Hyattsville, MD: National Center for Health Statistics, 2008.

Braun, Kathryn L., and Rhea Nichols. "Death and Dying in Four Asian American Cultures: A Descriptive Study." *Death Studies* 21, no. 4 (1997): 327–59.

Chen, Moon S., Jr. "Informal Care and the Empowerment of Minority Communities: Comparisons between the USA and the UK." *Ethnicity and Health* 4, no. 3 (1991): 139–51.

Clark, Peter Yuichi. "*Biblical Themes for Pastoral Care* Revisited: An Asian American Re-reading of a Classic Pastoral Care Text." *Semeia* 90–91 (2002): 291–14.

Clark, Peter Yuichi. "Exploring the Pastoral Dynamics of Mixed-Race Persons." *Pastoral Psychology* 52, no. 4 (2004): 315–28.

Clark, Peter Yuichi. "Tending to Trees of Life . . . and Hope." *Journal of Supervision and Training in Ministry* 26 (2006): 103–32.

Doi, Takeo. *The Anatomy of Dependence.* Revised ed. Translated by John Bester. Tokyo: Kodansha, 1981.

Fujii, June S., Susan N. Fukushima, and Joe Yamamoto. "Psychiatric Care of Japanese Americans." In Albert C. Gaw, ed. *Culture, Ethnicity, and Mental Illness.* Washington, DC: American Psychiatric Press, 1993, pp. 305–45.

Hughes, Dora L. *Quality of Health Care for Asian Americans: Findings from the Commonwealth Fund 2001 Health Care Quality Survey.* Publication 525. New York: The Commonwealth Fund, 2002.

Jullamate, Pornchai, Zaida de Azeredo, Constança Pául, and Rachaneeporn Subgranon. "Thai Stroke Patient Caregivers: Who They Are and What They Need." *Cerebrovascular Diseases* 21, nos. 1–2 (January 2006): 128–33.

Kim, Stephen K. "Pastoral Care to Asian American Families." *Military Chaplains' Review* [U.S. Army publication 16-92-3] (Summer 1992): 19–28.

Lester, Andrew D. *Hope in Pastoral Care and Counseling.* Louisville, KY: Westminster John Knox Press, 1995.

Lipson, Juliene G., Suzanne L. Dibble, and Pamela A. Minarik, eds. *Culture and Nursing Care.* San Francisco: UCSF Nursing Press, 1996.

McGoldrick, Monica, Joe Giordano, and Nydia Garcia-Preto, eds. *Ethnicity and Family Therapy.* 3rd ed. New York: Guilford Press, 2005.

Schwartz, Pamela Yew. "Why Is Neurasthenia Important in Asian Cultures?" *Western Journal of Medicine* 176 (September 2002): 257–58.

Shim, Steve Sangkwon. "Pastoral Counseling with Asian Americans." In Robert J. Wicks, Derald Wing Sue, and David Sue. *Counseling the Culturally Diverse: Theory and Practice.* 4th ed. New York: John Wiley and Sons, 2003.

U.S. Department of Health and Human Services, Substance Abuse and Mental Health Services Administration, Office of Applied Studies. *The NSDUH Report: Treatment of Substance Use and Depression among Adults, by Race/Ethnicity.* Rockville, MD: Author, 2009.

Wicks, Robert J., Derald Wing Sue, and David Sue. *Counseling the Culturally Diverse: Theory and Practice.* 4th ed. New York: John Wiley and Sons, 2003.

Catholics

Asian American Catholics comprise a small but significant group within the wider world of Asian American Christianity, which is broadly Protestant and Evangelical in character. For a long time, Asian American Catholics were hidden in the background of the broader United States Catholic Church. The United States Conference of Catholic Bishops (USCCB) publicly acknowledged for the first time the presence of the Asian American Catholics and the rich diversity of cultures, traditions, and gifts that they bring to the United States Catholic Church in its landmark pastoral letter, *Asian and Pacific Presence: Harmony in Faith* (2001). In this pastoral letter, the United States Catholic bishops concede that Asian Americans, be they newly arrived immigrants or native-born whose roots in the United States extend

Bishop Ignatius Wang adjusts his collar prior to the movement of a procession leading to his ordination at St. Mary's Cathedral in San Francisco, January 30, 2003. Looking on at left is Father Didacus Ma. Wang, the first Catholic Bishop of Chinese or Asian ancestry to be appointed in the U.S. (AP Photo/Eric Risberg)

many generations, "have remained, until very recently, nearly invisible in the Church in the United States." *Asian and Pacific Presence* estimates that some 83.0 percent of Filipino Americans (1.54 million), 29.0 percent of Vietnamese Americans (0.33 million), 17.0 percent of Indian Americans (0.29 million), 12.3 percent of Chinese Americans (0.30 million), 7.0 percent of Korean Americans (0.07 million), 4.0 percent of Japanese Americans (0.03 million), 84 percent of Guamanian (Chomorro) Americans (48,921), 22.3 percent of Samoan Americans (20,290), and 14.4 percent of Tongan Americans (4,000) are Catholics.

Most Asian American Catholics are Roman Catholics, that is, they belong to the Roman Catholic (Latin Rite) Church that is one of the 23 autonomous Catholic churches, of which 22 are Eastern and 1 is Western, that are in communion with the bishop of Rome. A small but significant minority of Asian American Catholics hail from the Eastern Catholic churches. For example, a minority of Indian American Catholics are Saint Thomas Christians who belong to the Syro-Malabar and Syro-Malankara Catholic churches, both of which trace their historical lineage from the ancient Saint Thomas Christians of India, who embraced Christianity from as early as the first and second centuries CE.

Among the Indian Americans who are Eastern Catholics, about 85,000 Indian Americans belong to the Syro-Malabar Catholic Church and 10,000 Indian Americans belong to the Syro-Malankara Catholic Church in the United States. Within the Syro-Malabar community in the United States, around 9,000 are Knanaya Catholics who trace their unique ethnic and religious heritage to the Assyrian Christian refugees from Edessa led by Knai Thomman (Thomas of Cana), who arrived in Kodungalloor (Cranganore) in Kerala, India around the year 345. The Knanaya Catholics are distinct from other Indian American Catholics by their continued practice of endogamy in the United States. Notwithstanding their small numbers, Indian American Syro-Malabar Catholics can proudly attest to the fact that they have their own eparchy (diocese) in the United States, the Syro-Malabar Eparchy of Saint Thomas that was established in 2001 in Chicago with Mar Jacob Angadiath (b. 1945) as bishop. In addition, many Syro-Malabar Catholic missioners have answered the call of the United States Catholic Bishops to minister in Roman Catholic parishes throughout the United States. In 2010, Pope Benedict XVI established an exarchate for the Syro-Malankara Catholic community in New York with Thomas Mar Eusebius (b. 1961) as exarch (bishop).

Beginnings and Growth

The Asian American Catholic community traces its beginnings to the arrival of Filipino sailors during the Spanish colonial era. The earliest known presence of Asian Catholics on U.S. soil occurred in 1587, when "Luzon Indians" on the Spanish galleon *Nuestra Senora de Buena Esperanza* accompanied Captain Pedro de Unamuno ashore when he landed at Morro Bay on the California coast. Filipino sailors who deserted ashore in the United States to escape the harsh realities of the Spanish galleon trade established the Filipino settlement of Saint Malo in Saint Bernard Parish of Louisiana in 1763. Although the Saint Malo settlement was eventually destroyed in 1915 by the New Orleans Hurricane, the Filipino historical presence on the United States soil, albeit as a small but thriving community, is an important testimony to the fact that Asian American Catholics have been part of the religious landscape of the United States since the mid-18th century.

The massive influx of Asian immigration to the United States since the passage of the Immigration and Nationality Act of 1965 (Hart-Celler Act), which abolished the restrictive measures that limited Asian immigration, has contributed significantly to the diversity of the United States Catholic Church. Many Filipino, Indian, Chinese, and Korean Catholics and their families took advantage of the 1965 immigration reforms to immigrate to the United States in search of a better future for themselves and their families. A significant number of Vietnamese American Catholics in the United States fled their homeland because of persecution by the Communist regime that seized power in 1975. Recent decades have witnessed a number of mainland Chinese Catholics fleeing from Communist harassment by seeking refuge and sanctuary in the United

States. As a result, persecution and martyrdom are contemporary experiences, rather than historical footnotes for many Asian American Catholic communities.

Church Life

Within the broader ecclesiological framework of the United States Catholic Church, Asian American Catholic communities may be organized as (1) one of many diverse ethnic communities within a large multicultural parish, (2) a territorial parish, or (3) a personal parish. In the first scenario, a typical multicultural parish often offers special liturgical services and programs for different ethnic communities, including various Asian American communities. This is by far the most common setup in many parts of the United States. Among the Asian American Catholic communities, the territorial parish is common for Vietnamese American Catholic communities in those areas with sufficiently large numbers of Vietnamese American Catholics, for example, in New Orleans, Louisiana and Orange County, California. As for the third option, many United States bishops have established personal parishes for specific Asian American communities. A personal parish is an extraterritorial parish within a diocese that may be created to minister to the particular needs of a specific community because of language, nationality, or liturgical rite, for example, Eastern Catholic personal parishes. In this regard, many Vietnamese American territorial parishes also function as personal parishes for other Vietnamese living outside their geographical confines. The personal parish setup is common for Vietnamese American, Korean American, Chinese American, Syro-Malabar, and Syro-Malankara Catholic communities, where there is a pastoral need for liturgical services and other church-based programs but where the numbers do not justify the establishment of a territorial parish for those groups.

While Asian American Catholics consider themselves as members of the universal Catholic Church, they also perceive their own distinctive religious worldviews, traditions, and practices as integral to their ethnic and sociocultural identities. In this respect, their Catholic faith often becomes the focus of minority ethnic identification, providing the framework for addressing life issues, as well as assisting to preserve, negotiate, and perpetuate their distinctive ethnic identities and cultural traditions in the wider mainstream of contemporary U.S. society. This situation is further accentuated in the daily life experiences of first-generation Asian immigrants to the United States because of language barriers, cultural differences, and other adjustment issues.

An important development that flows from the foregoing point is the centrality of the local parish church as a hub for communal fellowship and mutual support in many Asian American Catholic communities. For example, first-generation Asian immigrants in the United States often rely on their local parish church as a community center that provides social, welfare, and other support services, for example, English literacy classes are offered to adults, immigration services and citizenship classes are offered to new immigrants, and job opportunities are advertised. Many Asian American Catholics also perceive the local parish church as the venue for all traditional cultural festivities and community-centered activities. For example, the Catholic parish church is often the most important ethnic institution serving various sociocultural roles in addition to the usual religious functions in many Vietnamese American communities. Hence, Vietnamese American Catholic parishes typically organize community-based New Year and other cultural celebrations, as well as offer classes in the mother tongue and cultural heritage to the American-born children of first-generation Vietnamese immigrants to the United States. Not surprisingly, many Vietnamese Americans often view the church as the preserver of their language and cultural traditions as they struggle to preserve their distinctive social, cultural, and religious traditions in contemporary U.S. society.

Many Asian American Catholic communities have active national parachurch organizations such as lay associations, youth groups, Bible study groups, charismatic prayer groups, and Cursillo groups for communal fellowship and empowerment. In addition to national organizations, they have also established ethnic-based parachurch organizations, for example, the Eucharistic Youth Society of the Vietnamese American Catholics, which is an organization for young Vietnamese American Catholic boys and girls that is modeled after the Boy Scouts. Other examples of prominent Asian American Catholic organizations include the National Filipino Ministry Council, the Hmong American Catholic National Association, the Federation of Vietnamese Clergy, Religious, and Lay Leaders in the United States, the Korean Priests Association of America and

Canada, the Indian American Catholic Association, the Knanaya Catholic Congress of North America, and the Knanaya Youth League of North America.

Interestingly, the most common and prominent lay association in many Vietnamese American, Korean American, Chinese American, and Filipino American Catholic communities is the Legion of Mary. While the Legion of Mary may be moribund in white American suburban Catholic parishes, nevertheless it is thriving and growing in Asian American Catholic communities. This is because the Legion of Mary enables and empowers Asian American Catholic women to take on public leadership and service roles within the context of these traditional patriarchal Asian cultures that typically do not have public space for such roles. Through the Legion of Mary, many Asian American Catholic women who are otherwise marginalized in a traditional patriarchal communal structure and male-oriented clerical parish framework are now able to participate actively in their parish and community life.

One silver lining in the declining rate of religious vocations in the United States Catholic Church is the significant growth of Asian American priestly and religious vocations in general, and the Vietnamese American Catholic community's significant contribution to priestly and religious vocations in particular. The Vietnamese American Catholic community also stands out with its many indigenous religious congregations from Vietnam that have taken root in the United States. This includes the Congregation of the Mother Co-Redemptrix (*Dòng Đông Công*) a male religious order based in Carthage, Missouri, and the Lovers of the Holy Cross (*Dòng Mên Thánh Gia*), the oldest and largest of the Vietnamese female religious congregations in Vietnam and the United States. Other indigenous Vietnamese American Catholic religious congregations include the Congregation of Mary, Queen (*Trinh Vuong*), a female religious order that is an offshoot of the Lovers of the Holy Cross (headquarters in Springfield, Missouri), and the Vietnamese Dominican Sisters (headquarters in Houston).

Within the United States Catholic Church, Bishop Ignatius Chung Wang (b. 1934) was the first Asian American and Chinese American to become a bishop in the United States Catholic Church when he served as auxiliary bishop of the Archdiocese of San Francisco from 2002 to 2009. Bishop Dominic Mai Thanh Lương (b. 1940) became the second Asian American and first Vietnamese American bishop when he was appointed as auxiliary bishop of the Diocese of Orange, California, in 2003. In 2004, Oscar Azarcon Solis (b. 1953) became the first Filipino American to become bishop when he was consecrated as auxiliary bishop of the Archdiocese of Los Angeles in 2004. The Pacific Islander Catholics in the United States were justifiably proud when Pope Benedict XVI appointed Guamanian American Randolph Roque Calvo (b. 1951) as bishop of Reno in 2005.

Asian American Catholic Popular Devotions

In the case of many first-generation Asian American Catholics who are immigrants themselves, it is inevitable that their various Asian racial-ethnic identities are indelibly imprinted in their lives and brought by them from their ancestral lands to the United States. For them, the age-old sociocultural traditions, religious customs, pious and devotional practices, as well as theological perspectives that they brought with them from their ancestral lands are given pride of place and juxtaposed with new traditions, customs, and practices that they encounter in the United States. Asian American Catholic theologians use terms such as "contextualization," "inculturation," "interculturation," and "dialogue" to describe the foregoing process. In doing so, traditional Asian sociocultural and religious understandings are retrieved, reenvisioned, and reformulated in response to the call to shape emerging Asian American identities.

As a result, a distinctive trait of Asian American Catholic communities that sets them apart from other Asian American Christians is the prominence that they give to popular devotions. For example, Filipino American Catholics are deeply attached to their favorite devotions, such as the Black Nazarene, Santo Niño, and *Simbang Gabi* (a novena of masses in the octave before Christmas). Popular devotions to the Blessed Virgin Mary feature prominently in many Asian American Catholic communities, having taken root and demonstrating a remarkable growth in the United States. The dedication of the shrines to Our Lady of Antipolo (June 7, 1997) for the Filipino American Catholics, Our Lady of Velankanni (August 16, 1997) for the Indian American Catholics, Our Lady of China (August 3, 2002), Our Lady of La Vang (October 21, 2006) for the Vietnamese American Catholics, as well as Our Lady of the Korean Martyrs and

Our Lady of Korea at Cana (September 22, 2007) in the Basilica of the National Shrine of the Immaculate Conception in Washington, DC, together with the annual pilgrimages by various Asian American Catholic communities to these shrines bear testimony to the vibrancy of Asian American Catholic devotional piety.

At the same time, Asian American Catholic devotional piety goes beyond mere informal home-based daily or weekly rituals. In several instances, popular devotions also serve important identity formation and maintenance roles. The annual Marian Days (*Ngày Thánh Mẫu*) in honor of Our Lady of La Vang in Carthage, Missouri, every August since 1978 draws more than 70,000 Vietnamese American Catholics, making it not only an important Marian festival and pilgrimage, but also a public celebration of Vietnamese American Catholic identity and pride.

More importantly, traditional Asian popular devotions also have a strong transnational character, originating from the Asian milieu, brought over by the immigrating generations, as well as transplanted and nurtured by subsequent generations. Moreover, many Asian American Catholics continue to maintain and practice the popular devotions that they brought with them from their ancestral lands in part because these devotions not only nurture their faith and spiritual life, but also enable them to extend and maintain continuous transnational ties with their kinfolk or communities from their ancestral lands in an increasingly globalized world. For many Asian American Catholics, the close identification between faith, ethnicity, and culture is so entrenched that when Asian Americans participate in popular devotional practices, they are asserting their religious, cultural, and transnational identities simultaneously.

Jonathan Y. Tan

See also: Entries: Maryknoll Catholic Missionaries; Vietnamese American Catholics

Further Reading

Bautista, Veltisezar. *The Filipino Americans from 1763 to the Present: Their History, Culture, and Traditions*. Midlothian, VA: Bookhaus, 1998.

Burns, Jeffrey M., Ellen Skerrett, and Joseph M. White, eds. *Keeping Faith: European and Asian Catholic Immigrants*. Maryknoll, NY: Orbis Books, 2000.

Phan, Peter C. *Vietnamese-American Catholics*. New York/Mahwah, NJ: Paulist Press, 2005.

Tan, Jonathan Y. *Introducing Asian American Theologies*. Maryknoll, NY: Orbis Books, 2008.

Tan, Jonathan Y. "Asian American Marian Devotions as Ritual Practice." *New Theology Review* 23, no. 3 (2010): 35–44.

United States Conference of Catholic Bishops. *Asian and Pacific Presence: Harmony in Faith*. Washington, DC: USCCB, 2001.

Williams, Raymond B. *Christian Pluralism in the United States: The Immigrant Experience*. Cambridge: Cambridge University Press, 1996.

Christian Fellowships

The historical roots of Asian American Christian fellowships date back to a multiplicity of origins. In the late 20th century, as ties to traditional denominations began to wane, Americans witnessed the revitalization of Christianity through revivalist figures like Billy Graham and the growth of parachurch ministries outside of the denominational structure. That is, with the increasing secularization of higher education, college campuses were no longer intimately tied to denominational campus ministries; instead, university ministry became a place where independent parachurches increasingly entered the religious marketplace to form the religious sensibilities of American students. Two of the largest student parachurch ministries, Campus Crusade for Christ (Cru) and Intervarsity Christian Fellowship (IVCF), entered American universities during this time: Cru was founded in 1951 on the University of California, Los Angeles (UCLA) campus and IVCF just one decade before in 1941 on the University of Michigan campus (though its origins date back to 1877 at the University of Cambridge, England).

Coinciding with this shift in American denominational history, the post-1965 wave of Asian immigration to the United States and the increasing Christianization of Third World nations (including Asian nations) changed the landscape of the primarily white American or European composition of these parachurch ministries. The Asian American population in IVCF, for instance, grew nationwide by 267 percent over a 15-year period from 992 to 3,640 students. By 2011, IVCF's Asian American Ministries counted 5,639 students, one of the largest contingencies among parachurch ministries and a record number for the organization. IVCF has made a concerted effort to include "racial reconciliation" as a key aspect of their min-

istry, and the organization has been noted for conducting racially integrated Bible studies as early as the 1940s and giving Asian Americans leadership opportunities since 1979. A prime example of the organization's effort to develop culturally relevant leadership material is the tract *Invitation to Lead: Guidance for Emerging Asian American Leaders*, written by Paul Tokunaga, a member of the executive team.

While IVCF's success highlights the Asian Americanization of parachurch ministries in recent decades, the history of Cru reveals the multiple origins from which Asian American Christian fellowships emerged. In 1951, Bill Bright, the founder of Cru, left his studies at Fuller Theological Seminary to found the evangelical student ministry, which began at UCLA and grew into a global movement, especially with its first international partnership with South Korea in 1958. Korea Campus Crusade for Christ, led by Joon Gon Kim, became an influential organization in South Korea, leading millions of people at revivals, trumping the numbers that even the American chapter of Cru could gather on its domestic soil.

Ultimately, it was through these Korean roots that a ministry for 1.5 and second-generation Korean Americans was first established. Cru had historic challenges with racial inclusion, and Kim found few resources for Korean immigrants in the 1980s. Thus, in 1982 he reimported the Korean version of Cru into the United States, creating "Korea Campus Crusade for Christ *in America*." Epic Movement, a Cru ministry specifically devoted to Asian Americans, later developed in the 1990s alongside other ethnic-specific ministries, but it was rooted in a separate stream of Asian American culture and history. Cru's history shows how Asian American Christian fellowships have formed out of inter-weaving narratives of racial exclusion, transnational ties to the Asian homeland, and the need for culturally sensitive and culturally relevant religious communities.

In addition to IVCF and Cru's influence, parachurch ministries with Asian American founders also emerged in the late 20th century, such as Asian American Christian Fellowship (AACF), the college ministry arm of the Japanese Evangelical Missionary Society. There are numerous churches, ranging from nondenomina-tional church plants to ethnic churches af-filiated with Methodist or Presbyterian denominations, that are highly college ministry–focused (though they are not technically parachurches). These church-based ministries reveal the way in which the Asian American Christian fellowship experience is also deeply tied to the larger immigrant church and second-generation panethnic religious communities.

Race, Identity, and Evangelical Theology

While various Asian American Christian fellowships have distinct histories and cul-tures, it is largely assumed that their com-mon conservative evangelical theology binds them together. The Great Commis-sion (Matthew 28:16–20) to "make disci-ples of all nations" is a central mission for many of these ministries. Evangelical the-ology has traditionally prioritized the uni-versal rather than the particular contextual elements of the Christian faith, so the role of racial/ethnic identity formation within evangelical circles has been a point of debate.

Scholars have made attempts to under-stand the impact of evangelical theology upon Asian American identity. Rudy Bus-to's study on Asian American evangelical college students suggests that evangelical-ism actually reinforces the stereotype of the Asian American as a "model minority," or rather, a "model *moral* minority," prevent-ing Asian Americans from enacting agency and self-determination. On the one hand, as D. Michael Lindsay suggests, Asian Ameri-cans have made it into the halls of power through attaining elite education. However, this upward mobility carries with it the bur-den and tax of the stereotype of the "model *moral* minority." This stereotype exoticizes Asian American evangelicals as it uplifts (and therefore dehumanizes) them to an idealized standard. Yet another "trap," as Busto shows, evangelicalism "reinforces" the pressure of moral performance on Asian American evangelical college students. As much as Asian American college students are influencing evangelicalism in the ranks of elite higher education, the evangelical tradition is also impacting their Asian American subjectivity.

Evangelical theologian Soong-Chan Rah uses a similar rhetoric of "captivity" to interrogate the racial bias in the contem-porary American evangelical tradition. Rah diagnoses "Western cultural captiv-ity" as bondage to Western notions of indi-vidualism, consumerism, racism, and cultural imperialism. With the rapid growth of ethnic minorities in global and local evangelicalism, Rah envisions the "next evangelicalism" in which the church is released from such captivity. He critiques the dominant discriminatory culture of North American evangelicalism by differentiating between "cultural norms" and "biblical [norms]." He calls ethnic minorities to the center, prioritizing the marginalized Asian American experience to release evangelicalism from the trend of unbiblical cultural captivity.

While Busto diagnoses the problematic trappings of an evangelical theological orientation for Asian American identity, Rah suggests returning back to biblical orthodoxy to release Asian American evangelicals from captivity. Though different diagnoses and critiques, Busto and Rah share in common the angst-ridden task of understanding Asian American religious and ethnic identity in a tradition that has traditionally been steeped in Western theology and culture.

Yet practitioners within Asian American Christian fellowships continue to define the parachurch ministry experience as crucial contexts for Asian American identity formation and leadership development. Melanie Mar-Chow, an American Baptist minister and a long-time member as well as leader of AACF, states that the fellowship was a place where Asian Americans could belong, for the AACF provided not only a context for religious development, but also a place for ethnic identity formation. Indeed, according to Rebecca Kim, Korean American college students will choose an ethnic-specific campus fellowship over a white-dominant or even multicultural campus fellowship because of these strong common cultural bonds. Furthermore, Tommy Dyo suggests that ministry in an Asian American context also

transforms leadership development strategies: Cru has traditionally asked individual people to give their lives up to God in 20 minutes, but from doing Asian American ministry, one learns the concept of being group-oriented and that community experience is key in Christian ministry.

These leaders continue to testify to the fact that the Asian American Christian fellowship experience provides an outlet for ethnic expression that would not otherwise happen in a more white-dominant setting; but the extent to which evangelical theology and evangelical culture—as suggested by Busto and Rah—are responsible for perpetuating the racial exclusion of these minorities is an issue worth further pondering. Scholars of biblical studies and theology are increasingly developing an Asian American hermeneutic from which to engage the Christian tradition; further engagement with liberationist, intercultural, and postcolonial theologies may provide new avenues for developing Asian American Christian identity for these parachurch communities.

As scholars and practitioners continue to understand the dynamic life of the Asian American Christian fellowship, there are a few areas of it that remain understudied. For example, while many have theorized how racial identity is formed through these fellowships, few have studied the intersection of race and gender. The parachurch experience may be an invigorating context for women outside of the trappings of the traditional church, but the more conservative theological proclivities of many of these organizations may also prevent women from fully exercising leadership. Further study would be helpful to investigate these potential hypotheses. In addition to gender identity formation, these religious communities likely have a strong influence on Asian American college students' understanding of sex and sexuality, which is yet another area for potential study.

Conclusion

Indeed, Asian American Christian fellowships have had and continue to have a deep impact on the religious lives of Asian Americans, providing an important window into the changing landscape of American religion. Rooted in multiple, interweaving histories of immigration, the development of the second generation, the restructuring of American religion, and the increasing development of Christianity in Asia, these parachurch ministries provide a critical lens through which scholars and practitioners may reevaluate their paradigms of understanding religion. To consider the history and sociology of the American Christian tradition without understanding the role of the Asian American parachurch life would be to miss a deeply influential experience in American religious life.

Helen Jin Kim

Further Reading

Busto, Rudy. "The Gospel According to the Model Minority? Hazarding an Interpretation of Asian American Evangelical College Students." In David Yoo, ed. *New Spiritual Homes: Religion and Asian Americans.* Honolulu: University of Hawai'i Press, 1999.

Kim, Rebecca. *God's New Whiz Kids?: Korean American Evangelicals on Campus.* New York: New York University Press, 2006.

Rah, Soong Chan. *The Next Evangelicalism: Freeing the Church from Western Cultural Captivity.* Downers Grove, IL: IVP Books, 2009.

Toyama, Nikki A., et al. *More Than Serving Tea: Asian American Women on Expectations, Relationships, Leadership and Faith.* Downers Grove, IL: IVP Books, 2006.

Gender and Sexuality

Scholars in the fields of women's studies, progressive gender studies, and lesbian, gay, bisexual, and transgender (LGBT)/queer studies agree that both sexuality and gender are socially constructed, thus historically and culturally variable. Gender as an "objective" or discrete category that sustains the notion of universal patriarchy has been critiqued by feminist scholars from early on. Sexuality has also been construed and theorized in varied ways, spanning from the site of male domination and violence to sexual desires, from reproduction to exploitation of sexual labor, from sexual identities to sexual behaviors, and so on. Neither gender nor sexuality can be analyzed in a vacuum or in isolation, but in a particular context as constitutive of each other and/or interacting with other categories of social relationships. Thus, there are multiple notions, practices, and effects of gender and sexuality, such as masculinities, femininities, transgender, gendering activities, gendered racialization, gendered socialization, and multiplicity of sexualities.

The critical survey provided here will highlight some major themes, patterns, and foci that have emerged in the Asian American religious and theological scholarship on gender and sexuality. This, in turn, will shed light on the areas that require more attention and research in future studies. Given the complexity and the interdisciplinary nature of the field of Asian American religious and theological studies, the survey does not cover the whole range of Asian American religious and theological scholarship on gender and sexuality. Moreover, it is best to remember that studies of gender and sexuality constitute a newly emerging field of discourse and even more so when this discourse is examined through the particular lens of racial/ethnic (Asian American) theories and in the discipline of religious and theological studies.

Gender as an analytic category has been deployed in multiple ways in Asian American religious and theological studies, ranging from a focus on gender roles, gender identities, gender stereotypes, gendered symbols and images of the divine, and gender relations to treatments of gender ideology, gender hierarchy, gendered division of labor, and gendered activism in relation to various aspects of diverse religious traditions, including their belief systems, practices, institutional structures, and faith communities. Compared to gender, discussion around sexuality has been limited to certain aspects of sexuality in Asian American religious and theological studies. The mutually constitutive relations of gender, sexuality, race, ethnicity, class, and religion have also been less theorized in Asian American religious and theological studies and are in need of more analysis, particularly on the question of why these constitutive relations are rarely examined together.

Gender and Asian American Theological and Biblical Discourses

One of the earliest Asian American theological/biblical studies that has incorporated gender as an analytic category is found in the work of feminist scholars affiliated with the organization Pacific, Asian, and North American Asian Women in Theology and Ministry (PANAAWTM). Starting with 13 Asian and Asian North American women in 1984, PANAAWTM has grown into a significant grassroots movement, with a network and scholarship that is interdisciplinary, transnational, cross-generational, and interreligious. The majority of its members are affiliated predominantly with Christianity. Since its inception PANAAWTM members, who are from diverse social locations, have recognized the historical and cultural specificities of gender and thus have analyzed divergent gender-related struggles within and across different Asian American religious communities. As the founding or early members of PANAAWTM, scholars such as Kwok Pui-Lan, Nantawan Boonprasat Lewis, Hyung Kyung Chung, Rita Nakashima Brock, Jung Ha Kim, and Gale Yee have integrated gender as an analytic category into their work, drawing from varied feminist theories that construe gender differently. Many of these leading Asian American feminist scholars have criticized not only "malestream" theology for its lack of gender analysis but also feminist theology that deploys gender as the fundamental organizing concept, discounting other constitutive categories such as race, ethnicity, class, and nation-state. Like many other feminist scholars who have criticized gender, when taken as a universal and ahistorical concept, PAN-AAWTM scholars have cautioned against losing sight of the different historical and cultural contexts in which social categories are produced and interact with one another. Thus, the ways in which PANAAWTM scholars use gender as an analytic category vary, for their analysis of gender is done contextually and in interactions with race, ethnicity, class, sexuality, and neo/colonial status. Sixteen essays included in the first PANAAWTM anthology, *Off the Menu* (2007), are a case in point.

One of the earlier feminist works that treats gender in relation to Christology is Rita Nakashima Brock's *Journeys by Heart* (1988). From the outset, Brock clearly identifies two sources that shape her journey in this work—one is her Japanese heritage and the other is feminism. Drawing on feminist psychoanalysis and object-relations theory, Brock criticizes classical christologies, especially atonement christologies, which have focused on the life of one heroic male figure, Jesus. Brock expands Christ beyond Jesus of Nazareth to what she calls Christa/Community. Christa/Community is the community of life-giving power where the true power of the redemption of human life can be found. For Brock, such life-giving power of community is erotic power. She also critiques male dominance not just as the actions of individual men, but as an entire system of patriarchy. Brock's work is significant in that it challenges some feminist christologies that are built on the model of Jesus as the individual male hero and liberator without connecting his power

to the community that has experienced his power. Such community is a nonpatriarchal community where women and men equally participate.

Another attempt to articulate Asian American feminist christology is *The Grace of Sophia* (2002) by Grace Ji-Sun Kim, a second-generation Canadian theologian. She explores a meaningful way to relate Christ to Korean American women who suffer from racism, sexism, and classism, and proposes that a liberating and healing christology for immigrant Korean women can be found in the biblical figure of Sophia.

Asian American feminist theologians have contributed to the unraveling of the conjunctions of feminism, postcolonialism, and theology in the interests of social justice and transformation. Kwok Pui-lan, in her *Postcolonial Imagination and Feminist Theology* (2005), contends that the most "hybridized concept in the Christian tradition is that of Jesus/Christ." Through her critique of gender binarism and sexual ideology, with the support of scholars like Susanna Heschel and Marcella Althaus-Reid, Kwok wonders how an "indecent Christ" or Bi-Christ or transvestite Christ can challenge "the conventional norms of masculinity and heteronormativity" so that we may reconfigure our thinking about Christ and salvation. W. Anne Joh's *Heart of the Cross* (2006) continues along similar theological reflections on salvation and Jesus/Christ. By using the feminist psychoanalytic category of abjection and with the help of Grace Jantzen's work, Joh suggests that redemption, particularly for much of Christian tradition, has operated as a masculinized and hierarchicalized way through its valorization of heteronormativity and sexism. She argues that destabilization of the gendered understanding of redemption can take place through the use of the psychoanalytic category of semiotics.

Challenging the unexamined use of the homogeneous category of "Asian women" and the unifying category of "Asian," Nami Kim's "My/Our Comfort Not at the Expense of Somebody Else's" (2005) calls for doing Asian feminist theology as a critical global feminist theology that is not based on the limited analysis of sex/gender nor on the essentialized notion of Asian. Kim argues that it is crucial to take into account differences among women in/from Asia if feminist theology wants to claim its relevance for women whose lives are shaped under the global capitalist economy. Asian American Muslim feminist scholar Aysha Hidayatullah's brief but important piece "Inspiration and Struggle" (2009) examines an emerging body of Muslim feminist theology in North America that engages developing feminist reinterpretations of Islam's sacred texts. Like Kim, Hidayatullah considers taking differences among Muslim women as one of the challenges for Muslim feminist theology in North America.

Gale A. Yee's *Poor Banished Children of Eve* (2003) is a feminist investigation of the symbolization of women as evil in biblical tradition, such as Eve in Genesis, Gomer in Hosea, and the "strange woman" of the Proverbs. Her work is a clear example of analyses that deploy gender in relation to race, class, and colonial status, demonstrating that women do not experience gender in the same way. Yee takes a further step, drawing a link between the cultural construction of "Asian women" as highly sexualized/eroticized throughout different historical periods in the United States, on the one hand, and the dominant culture's ideological resolutions for racist anxieties and fears in dealing with Asian immigrants beginning in the late 1800s, on the other (2003: 159).

In his *What Is Asian American Biblical Hermeneutics?* (2008), Tat-Siong Benny Liew examines how Paul's as well as Jesus's masculinity is linked to Paul's status as a diasporic and colonized Jew under the Roman empire. Paul's masculinist positions are read anew alongside his own "feminization" as a colonized Jew. Liew observes that in Paul's time, "race/ethnicity and religion were 'constitutively interrelated.'" By reading Paul's masculinist positions in 1 Corinthians in relation to his "feminization" as a colonized Jew whose body was inscribed as "feminine" by the dominant Roman ideologies, Liew seeks to contextualize Paul's text, not to justify Paul's masculinist biases toward women and other "sexual dissidents" but to refuse any attempt to essentialize a minority person or culture as simply patriarchal or homophobic in relation to certain problems of gender and sexuality. By arguing that racial/ethnic persons experience what he terms "status inversion" in the larger sociopolitical world, Liew notes the significance of increased and intensified anxiety and aggression in such persons and how they in turn target misplaced aggression toward smaller groups even more marginalized within their group, especially in religious settings. Liew also suggests that for racialized and demasculinized

Paul to remasculinize himself, he deflects his racial/ethnic abjection to female bodies as well as homoerotic bodies. In making the argument that similar logic appears in the context of white supremacy in the United States, Liew contends that the privilege of patriarchy is not extended to those who are racialized and demasculinized. Furthermore, Liew points to Frank Chin's remasculinization efforts, apparent in his attacks on Maxine Hong Kingston's *Woman Warrior* as well as in his targeting Fu Manchu as a "homosexual menace" and Charlie Chan as an "effeminate closet queen." These attacks resonate with what Jasbir K. Puar (2007) and others are consistently recognizing, that is, that racialization, sexuality, religion, and gender are often simultaneously deployed to work against people. In the context of heteronormativity and patriarchy, then, those who are racialized and experience gender failure (demasculinization/feminization) will project their ambivalence and anxiety onto others, such as women and sexual dissidents. For Liew, such essentializing moves only provide more excuses to the dominant and imperial cultures for continuing their hegemony.

Gender Identities and Gender Relations in Asian American Religious Communities

Scholars in Asian American religious and theological studies have examined the importance of religion in forming gender identities and gender relations in Asian American communities. In her book *When Women Come First* (2005), which studies transnational migration of Kerala Indian Christians, Sheba Mariam George examines how gender relations are organized in three different social spheres: work, home, and community. Her study of different gendered spheres was suggestive in showing how Kerala Indian Christian men actively sought to create an alternate space where they were provided with the status that they lost during the transition to the United States. In other words, Kerala Indian Christian men, who have experienced racialized (and classed) marginalization, utilized their immigrant congregations so as to support their own patriarchal privilege. Immigrant Christian churches become the main source of community life, and that role is intensified due to the lack of other options for social life for immigrant Kerala Christian men. When immigrant Kerala Christian males looked to the immigrant Christian congregation to compensate for the losses in autonomy and patriarchal status, immigrant Kerala Christian women often turned to other spheres where they could assert themselves. George argues that men and women, both as couples and as a community, attempted to maintain balance through a strategy of "complementary gender relations" in the different spheres. What her study illuminates is that the reproduction of patriarchy as a set of social relations is negotiated within and across different gendered spheres, and gender and class relations are bound together in that process.

Another work that illuminates gendered characteristics of immigration and the racialized (and classed) nature of marginalization in the United States is found in a work that addresses a Korean American Buddhist community. Sharon A. Suh's

"'To Be Buddhist Is to Be Korean'" (2003) demonstrates how an ethnic religious organization plays a key role in sustaining Korean male identity, primarily as Korean, even after immigration to the United States. Through her field study of Sa Chal, a Buddhist temple located in Los Angeles, and of its male practitioners, Suh finds that a transition to the United States has a tremendous impact on Korean men's self-esteem, especially if their social status and professional positions were high while living in Korea. Korean men's assertion of maintaining a transnational Korean identity by participating in the academic lectures and transnational political activities sponsored by the temple is a direct response to their downward status as an ethnic minority in the United States as well as their religious minority status within the broader Korean American community, whose members are predominantly Christian. Maintaining a transnational identity, then, becomes one type of "coping mechanism and method of adaptation" for Korean men who have experienced downward mobility in their immigration to the United States, and the temple becomes "the symbol of home" for them. In her more comprehensive work *Being Buddhist in a Christian World* (2004), Suh suggests that the Buddhist temple she studied tends to be more gender egalitarian than Korean immigrant churches primarily for two reasons: first, it has not created lay positions comparable to the position of elders in churches that can give power and authority to men, and second, unlike evangelical Christianity, Buddhism does not justify subordination of women to men doctrinally.

Unlike George and Suh, who have focused primarily on the role of religious institutions in sustaining immigrant male identities in immigrant Indian churches and in a Buddhist temple, respectively, Jung Ha Kim explores what it means to be a woman in the context of the Korean American church that is a gendered and racially/ethnically conditioned place in her book *Bridge-Makers and Cross-Bearers* (1997). Viewing churched Korean Americans as still powerfully influenced by Confucian gender ideologies and norms, Kim argues that churched Korean American women's "learned silence" and their embrace of traditional gender ideology are not acts of submission, but survival strategies. Kim's work highlights the limits of an either/or choice between gender and race/ethnicity, which is often imposed on women of color in forming their identities, and demonstrates that churched Korean American women often see themselves as "both/and." As in many other racial/ethnic minority groups, Kim shows that cross-gender solidarity between Korean American women and men in the church is crucial for group survival. Yet, such solidarity, as Kim notes, often functions to silence concerns over sexism that churched Korean American women experience every day. Kim's work is significant in that it does not prioritize gender but looks at how gender is constructed in relation to representations and practices of race/ethnicity, class, national origin, and religion, thus avoiding an essentialist understanding of gender.

If cross-gender solidarity between Korean American women and men operates to suppress concerns over sexism, which affect the everyday life of Korean

American women, sexism also functions to consolidate patriarchal and hierarchical church leadership in immigrant Korean churches in the United States. In his 2006 comparative study of Korean Christian women in church leadership in churches in South Korea and the Korean immigrant churches in the United States, Pyong Gap Min provides a gloomy picture of women's leadership status in immigrant Korean churches. His study shows the division of labor in ministry as women's leadership is still limited to the areas related to education for children and youth, music, elderly care, visitation, and mission activities. Min argues that Korean women's subordinate status in Korean churches cannot be simply understood based on evangelical theology alone. Instead, it should be viewed as a result of both biblical interpretation and the Confucian gender ideology that justify women's lower status in the church structure. Min further argues that patriarchal cultures in the Korean immigrant community in general and Korean immigrant churches in particular are stronger than those in their home country. Immigrant Korean male pastors' and elders' resistance to changing the gender hierarchy are due to their lost status during the immigration process, which they seek to compensate for by maintaining hierarchical gender structures and relations within the immigrant congregation.

Carolyn Chen's "A Self of One's Own" (2005), a comparative study of the use of Buddhism and Christianity to construct a sense of self by Taiwanese immigrant women as religious converts, shows that Buddhism and Christianity offer alternative conceptions of the genderless self, thus enabling Taiwanese immigrant women to contest traditional gender roles. What sets Chen's work apart from other studies of immigrant women and religion is that while other studies pay attention to the construction of gender in male-led immigrant congregations, her study focuses on how immigrant women themselves interpret and practice religion in their everyday lives. Such an analytical shift that focuses on individual interpretations of religious teachings on gender in women's daily lives, contends Chen, shows a more complex relationship between religion and patriarchy.

Racialization of Gender, Sexuality, and Religion

Understanding identity as intersectional or even as assemblage, scholars are examining the interplay of race, sexuality, gender, and religion as constructing identities in various ways. Not only does racialization of gender take place but racialization of sexuality also takes place in a direct link with racialization of religion. Jasmin Zine, a Canadian feminist scholar, articulates Muslim women's struggles for identity and liberation in her "Creating a Critical Faith-Centered Space for Antiracist Feminism" (2004). By critically examining the construction of Muslim women, both within particular Islamic discourses and in Western liberal secular feminist discourses, Zine explores a new discursive space where Muslim women who are spiritually dedicated to Islam can ground their "theoretical and praxis-oriented projects." Such an alternative space is also where Muslim women can express a new understanding of their own subjectivities.

Likewise, Jasbir K. Puar, in *Terrorist Assemblages* (2007), argues that often whiteness is identified as a queer norm and straightness as a racial norm. Puar further offers a cogent analysis of gender by noting that white heteronormativity shores up its identity through "virile masculinity" while constructing the sexuality of the other as "failed and perverse masculinities," as emasculated bodies that always have femininity as their reference point for malfunction. Heteronormativity also views these projected "failures" and "perversions" as signals also of a whole set of pathologies of the mind and body, for example, homosexuality, incest, pedophilia, madness and disease. This dynamic produces particular ways in which identity becomes a negative register. It is nearly impossible to ask, in a positive register, what it would mean, for example, to be a practicing queer Muslim. Moreover, it is nearly impossible to negotiate and navigate the complex construction of identity positively, when identity comes at the intersection of gender, sexuality, and religion, and when these dimensions are often pitted against each other in various racialized formations.

In examining how other religions have been constructed through a process of racialization, *Living Our Religions* (2008), an anthology co-edited by Anjana Narayan and Bandana Purkayastha, offers a critique of "Western" feminist perspectives by using the capital "W" to problematize the ways in which women's experiences have been universalized by the West, at the risk of essentializing non-Western women and non-Western religious traditions. This essentializing process became more intense after the emergence of the U.S. "war on terror." This anthology then resonates with works by Puar and Zine in that a similar question is raised: "What does it mean to be raced and gendered, and to practice religious traditions that are often demonized by the dominant powers?" As Purkayastha notes, "where 'American' continues to be defined as primarily white and Christian," it is an "uphill battle" for women to identify themselves as, say, an American Muslim, or even for that matter as an American queer Muslim. *Living Our Religions* lifts up what South Asian American women of Indian, Pakistani, Bangladeshi, and Nepali origin say about their experiences by challenging the Orientalist and fundamentalist claims and constructions of Hindu and Muslim women as subordinate. In criticizing the dominant construction of ethnic women as more "subordinate" by her "dominant" tradition and culture, this anthology argues that ethnic women are often constructed as victims of their religions and cultures. This volume joins those few recent studies that have moved beyond the discussion on the representation of women in temples or *mosques*. Raising critical questions about how traditions affect women and how gender differences between diverse women and men are constructed and sustained, the essays in this anthology demonstrate the ways in which South Asian American women through their everyday practice define their religions, negotiate boundaries, and sustain changes. This collection also seeks to provide a counter narrative to the way that religion has been defined always in relation to Christianity as the norm. In doing so, the authors provide salient and compelling narratives and analyses of how religious practices are heterogeneous and fluid, thus blurring religious boundaries, while at the same time bringing about cohesive communities through this very fluidity and heterogeneity. Moreover, it is not just that people embrace differing religious practices, but that some even embrace and practice a plurality of differing religious traditions.

Sexual Labor and Sexual and Gendered Violence within and across Asian American Communities

Due to the ongoing presence of sexual violence against women and children, exploitation of women's sexual labor, and gendered violence against sexual minorities within and across Asian American communities, Asian American religious and theological studies need to continue to provide critical analyses on these issues. Yet, as many Asian American scholars have cautioned, any effort to bring justice to sexual and gendered violence within Asian American communities should be done carefully in ways that do not reinscribe and reproduce the racist and colonialist constructions of racial/ethnic minority groups and religious traditions other than Christianity as "inherently patriarchal," "more violent," "more homophobic," and/or "less to no resistant." One way of combating such constructions is to provide a more nuanced analysis of patriarchy not as a fixed hierarchical gender relation but as a set of negotiated social relations in which gender and class are inextricably implicated. This kind of analysis will illuminate how patriarchal relations are negotiated, mediated, contested, and/or reproduced in different Asian American religious communities. It will also help Asian American communities understand and explore various alternatives for immigrant men who have opted for violence as a way of compensating for any status losses they experienced during the immigration process.

By far one of the most consistent themes evident among Asian American religious and theological studies in relation to sexuality is sexual violence and exploitation of women's sexual labor. Sexual exploitation and violence that Asian American feminist scholars investigate are often examined in relation to colonial history and/or continuing neocolonial relations between various Asian societies and the United States. For instance, Nantawan Boonprasat Lewis has long been working on the issues related to sexual violence against women, trafficking in women, and sex work in Asia. Her piece "Religion, Colonization and Sexual Violence" in her co-edited volume with Marie M. Fortune, *Remembering Conquest* (1999), is one such example. Lewis assesses Thai feminists' stance on the role of religion both as a source of moral ambiguity and of liberation in the context of sexual violence against women in Thailand in relation to U.S. colonization of Thailand. Rachel Bundang's "Scars ARE History" (1999) in the same volume presents a Filipina American immigrant's perspective on the intersection of religion, colonization, and sexual violence in the building of modern Philippine society. Through the examination of icons, such as the *babaylan*, Maria Clara, and Miss Saigon, which lay bare the Philippines' colonial history under Spain and ongoing neocolonial relations with the United States, Bundang provides a critical view of the development of Filipina womanhood. Rita Nakashima Brock and Susan Brooks Thistlethwaite's co-authored *Casting Stones* (1996) is another work that examines the exploitation of women's sexual labor in five Asian countries as well as in the United States. It is a cross-cultural field work that critically looks at various religious perspectives and attitudes toward sexuality, gender, and prostitution/sex work.

Hypersexuality, Virginity, and Marriage/Reproduction

While gender as one of the main analytical concepts has been discussed in multiple ways in Asian American religious and theological studies, sexuality has been less prominent. In her keynote speech at the 19th PANAAWTM conference, Kwok Pui-Lan (2004) calls attention to the lack of engagement among Asian American feminist scholars in religious and theological studies on the issue of sex and sexuality. As Kwok points out, however, it is not that sexuality has not been discussed or written about by Asian American scholars, but that their scholarship has remained focused on certain aspects of female sexuality. In other words, discussion of female sexuality is clustered around three themes: sexual violence and sexual exploitation, reproduction and marriage-related issues, and the perceived notion of the hypersexuality of Asian women. More often than not, heterosexuality has been assumed in the discussions on sexuality.

One of the explanations Kwok provides regarding Asian American women's tendency to refrain from speaking about sexuality in public is due to the prevailing representations of "Asian women" as hypersexual in the dominant U.S. culture, including the media. The cultural construction of Asian women's racialized sexuality has revolved around various sexual stereotypes, oscillating from hypersexual Dragon Lady to dominatrix Pearl, from sexually sophisticated Suzie Wong to Miss Saigon. In contrast to such construction of hypersexual "Asian female" sexuality, "Asian male" sexuality has been constructed based on the notion of the asexual or desexualized male, often in comparison not only to white European male sexuality but also to black male sexuality.

Kwok (2004) also mentions that one of the "relatively safe ways" of addressing female sexuality among Asian and Asian American feminist theologians is to discuss the notions of virginity in relation to more liberating depictions of Mary, the mother of Jesus. As Kwok puts it, however, a new understanding of virginity that highlights Mary's independence and her ability to reproduce new humanity without men's cooperation precludes discussion of the sexuality of women who enter into intimate relations with men or other women. Moreover, such discussion of virginity is still premised on the assumption that virginity matters, whether positively or negatively, which may require a further scrutiny as to whether the notion of virginity/chastity is a useful concept at all when discussing female sexuality. From a biblical studies perspective, Mary F. Foskett has examined varied representations of virginity in the New Testament in her *A Virgin Conceived* (2002).

Another common theme in sexuality is marriage and its related issues, such as family, divorce, and reproduction. Canadian religious educator Greer Anne Wenh-In Ng's edited volume *Tales of Interracial Marriage with Study Guide* (1993), evangelical theologian Young Lee Hertig's *Cultural Tag of War* (2001), and biblical scholar Seung Ai Yang's "Has Jesus Ever Condemned Divorce?" (2007) are some of the examples that have focused on the issues related to marriage. Rita Nakashima Brock's "Marriage Troubles" (2003) challenges and deconstructs a common Christian understanding of family as a "God-given" or "natural" order that is transhistorical.

Taboo of Female Sexuality and HIV/AIDS

One of the most undertheorized dimensions to sexuality is the HIV/AIDS crisis in Asian American religious and theological scholarship. Such noticeable absence is not a significant indicator of the absence of this crisis in Asian American communities but that HIV/AIDS is often racialized to the extent that people identify this crisis with Africa and/or African American communities and not with anywhere else. One of the few published works on the issue of sexuality in relation to HIV/AIDS is "No Garlic, Please, We Are Indian" (2007) by PANAAWTM scholar Anne Dondapati Allen. In this essay, Allen brings together female sexuality, the HIV/AIDS crisis in India, and Indian Christian theology's silence around these issues. Addressing the epidemic of HIV/

AIDS and its devastating impact on women and children in India, Allen examines the social and political processes that contributed to this situation. Tracing the origin of establishing sexual activity as a taboo for Indian women during colonial India in the 1800s and 1900s, Allen discusses dominant constructs of female sexuality in India. She stresses that Indian Christian theology's silence around issues of female sexuality will only reinforce negative images and attitudes about female sexuality, which impact every aspect of Indian women's life including the dehumanizing treatment of women diagnosed with AIDS.

LGBT Identity Formation and Activism in Asian American Religious Communities

Contrary to common perceptions, there has been a growing LGBT activism in Asian American religious communities, especially among Christian communities. However, as Kwok (2004) has rightly pointed out, it has been underreported. One of the few essays that address LGBT activism and the translesbigay identity is PANAAWTM scholar and activist Rose Wu's "A Story of Its Own Name" (2007). Wu's essay explores the power of self-naming and representing within Hong Kong's sexual minority community and sheds light on the possibility of not simply adopting the Western translesbigay movements' strategies and terminologies as universal but rediscovering the cultural roots of homo-, bi-, and trans-sexuality within Chinese heritage and traditions. As she emphasizes, such rediscovery should be accompanied by a critical examination.

Wu also stresses the importance of creating global networks such as the Global Chinese Tongzhi Annual Conference.

Patrick Cheng is another Asian American scholar whose work highlights the identity formation of queer Asian Pacific Americans. Using the acronym QAPA (Queer Asian Pacific American), Patrick Cheng argues that being queer and being Asian Pacific American poses a complex set of markers that are often posed in contradiction to each other in QAPA's identity formation. QAPA then refers to a wide range of sexualities, gender identities, and ethnicities. In his article "Reclaiming Our Traditions, Rituals, and Spaces" (2006), Cheng points to two major themes that are experienced by QAPAs: that of metaphorical homelessness and alienation from the body. Cheng suggests three ways by which these fractured and painful experiences of exclusion may find healing. His suggestions include (1) reclaiming the Asian spiritual traditions of one's ancestors; (2) reclaiming rites and rituals that affirm our bodies and sexualities; and (3) reclaiming the idea of sacred space to include those sites and spaces where communities are formed and able to flourish.

Recent data released by the Asian Pacific American Legal Center (APALC) (2009) reveals that age, English proficiency, and religiosity were the three determining factors in voting on California's Proposition 8 (a proposed ban on same-sex marriage) across ethnic groups among Asian Pacific Americans. According to APALC (2009), while older Asian and Pacific Americans in every ethnic group tended to vote for Proposition 8, Korean American voters were more likely to support Proposition 8 by a wide margin than any other ethnic groups among Asian Pacific Americans. Among those who rallied *for* Proposition 8 were evangelical Christians, including Christians in the communities of color, who were successfully mobilized by various Christian Right organizations such as Focus on the Family, Concerned Women for America, and the Family Research Council. Asian American religious studies scholar Russell Jeung attests to this as he states that it is plausible that nonreligious Asian Americans opposed Proposition 8, while Asian American church attendees voted similarly to the weekly church attendees in general in California, 84 percent of whom voted yes on Proposition 8. As Jeung and other Asian American scholars and activists note, however, passage of Proposition 8 requires a more comprehensive analysis. Such analysis may include an in-depth analysis of various factors, such as strategies of Christian Right activism, their use of media in racial/ethnic minority communities, and shortcomings identified within the "No" campaigns by various LGBT organizations and their supporters, along with age, language, and theological and religious underpinnings for its pass.

For instance, support of Proposition 8 by the majority of the immigrant Korean churches cannot be sufficiently explained by literalist biblical interpretations and/or evangelical theology alone, which are often provided as the primary cause of homophobia in evangelical churches, including Korean American churches. The critical and nuanced analysis of the complex interplay between homophobia, heteronormativity, and heteropatriarchy in evangelical

Christianity will assist Asian American communities that are interested in promoting sexual justice in both their religious institutions and the larger society. Unraveling the complexity of this issue will further help people in the Asian American religious communities, who have been actively working for sexual justice, to become more strategic about building alliances with different groups of people who do not necessarily share the same sexual identities. This will also help break the silence around HIV/AIDS and its stigmatization that affects Asian American communities. Moreover, while Proposition 8 generates conversations about equal rights for same-sex marriage and the role of religion, such discussions require open and constructive discussions about gender, sexuality, sexual justice, and religion in relation to what it means to be human in all its complexity.

Conclusion

While it is crucial not to conflate gender with sexuality, it is important to understand gender and sexuality as mutually constitutive. As one is gendered and racialized in a context, sexuality is also racialized and mediated by class in the current national and transnational economy. In other words, how one is sexualized should not be construed as a separate process nor be given priority over other categories. As scholars have argued, gender binary understood as gender inequality not only normatizes heterosexual desire but also legitimizes gendered division of labor. Although Asian American religious and theological studies have foregrounded the ways in which religion, race, ethnicity, and theological studies have foregrounded the ways in which religion, race, ethnicity, gender, nation, and sexuality are interconnected from the vantage points of various Asian American communities, it seems necessary to underscore the salience of such interconnection in future studies.

As scholarly attention to sexuality has been uneven, and nearly absent, in the field of Asian American religious and theological scholarship, it may need to expand its scope and extent in the area related to sexuality in general and female sexuality in particular. This will include but not be limited to (1) theorizing the ways in which gender, sexual, racial, ethnic, and religious identities of Asian American women are contested, negotiated, and mediated; and (2) redefining sexuality, including "race positive sexuality" and "perverse sexuality" that has often been classified as nonnormative sexual identities/acts, queer sex, and practices that "do not demand morality, chastity, and modesty that discipline women." It will also include, to draw on Kwok's suggestions, articulating Asian American women as sexual subjects without reifying sexual identities narrowly or rigidly, using sexual stories as resources for Asian American feminist theology, recovering the sexual pleasure of (oppressed) women, and entering into deeper dialogue with Asian cultural and religious traditions to reclaim female embodiment and sexuality in Asian cultures and communities. Resources including sexual stories can be drawn from literature, cultural texts including popular culture, ethnographic fieldwork accounts, interviews, media, and the combination of any or all of these sources and methods.

Nami Kim and Wonhee Anne Joh

See also: Essays: LGBT Asian Americans and Christianity; Religion, Race, and Orientalism

Further Reading

Brock, Rita Nakashima. *Journeys by Heart: A Christology of Erotic Power.* New York: Crossroad, 1991.

Brock, Rita Nakashima, Jung Ha Kim, Pui-lan Kwok, and Seung Ai Yang. *Off the Menu: Asian and Asian North American Women's Religion and Theology.* Louisville, KY: Westminster John Knox, 2007.

Brock, Rita Nakashima, and Susan Brooks Thistlethwaite. *Casting Stones: Prostitution and Liberation in Asia and the United States.* Minneapolis: Augsburg Fortress, 1996.

George, Sheba Mariam. *When Women Come First: Gender and Class in Transnational Migration.* Berkeley: University of California Press, 2005.

Joh, W. Anne. *The Heart of the Cross: A Postcolonial Christology.* Louisville, KY: Westminster John Knox, 2006.

Kim, Grace Ji-Sun. *The Grace of Sophia: Korean North American Women's Theology.* Eugene, OR: Wipf & Stock, 2002.

Kim, Jung Ha. *Bridge-Makers and Cross-Bearers: Korean-American Women and the Church.* American Academy of Religion Academy Series. New York: Oxford University Press, 1997.

Kwok Pui-lan. *Postcolonial Imagination and Feminist Theology.* Louisville, KY: Westminster John Knox, 2005.

Liew, Tat-Siong Benny. *What Is Asian American Biblical Hermeneutics?: Reading the New Testament. Intersections: Asian and Pacific American Transcultural Studies.* Honolulu: University of Hawai'i Press, 2008.

Puar, Jasbir K. *Terrorist Assemblages: Homonational in Queer Times.* Durham, NC: Duke University Press, 2007.

Suh, Sharon. *Being Buddhist in a Christian World: Gender and Community in a Korean American Temple.* Seattle: University of Washington Press, 2004.

Immigration

Setting Asian religions in America in the context of immigration risks engaging some misperceptions—especially in our current early 21st-century context. Immigration and assimilation are highly contested realities today, and the racialization of Asian people in American society, as it was a century ago, is wrapped up in the perception of Asian American people as those who have come from somewhere else, those whose homes are not "here"—that is, immigrants. It also necessarily risks giving centrality to the United States in the narrative. It is the United States that created the framework of immigration and naturalization laws that we discuss here, and without attention to globalization and migration and their particular histories, we risk creating a sense of powerlessness of Asian Americans, religions, and cultures before this disconnected and often arbitrary set of laws.

To counteract this idea that Asian American religious cultures are particularly "immigrant" in nature, with all that that might imply, I want to begin therefore by stating explicitly that, among scholars of American religious history in general, it is not uncommon to approach religious life through the lens of immigration. Only Native Americans can claim a nonimmigrant religious history. Every religious group, denomination, and demographic in the United States has been shaped by the legal and practical realities of immigration; the time, place,

Buddist clerics bless members of the Japanese American and local communities during an interfaith religious service at the cementery of the Manzanar National Historic Site, April 24, 2004, in Independence, California. Manzanar is the best preserved of the camps where thousands of Japanese Americans and citizens of Japan were held during World War II. (AP Photo/Damian Dovarganes)

and manner of entry of groups and individuals; and the ways in which certain groups have been favored or disfavored in legal immigration regimes. Asian Americans and their religious cultures are not unique in this respect, and taking this approach to understanding the religious lives and histories of Asian Americans should not be understood as emphasizing "foreignness."

Asian immigrants, however, beginning with the Chinese in 1882, have borne the burden of specific exclusionary immigration and naturalization legislation earlier, more frequently, and more drastically than any other ethnic or racial group in the United States. Like immigrants throughout the world, they have responded to a history and experience of exclusion and persecution with determination and creativity, and they have experienced suffering that has been woven into the memories and religious lives of the communities in later generations.

The immigration laws that have affected Asian Americans have frequently been based on racial concerns, but these concerns have often been interpreted religiously in the U.S. context. The question of what race, and what religion, an Asian immigrant "is" has left its mark in American legal history, and often one was answered by the other—that is, an immigrant's religion was held to mark his or her race, and vice versa.

Thus, the relationship between immigration, religion in America, and Asian American communities has three aspects. The religions of Asians and Pacific Islanders in the United States have been shaped by the history of immigration law. Immigration law has often been based on perceptions of the race and religion of Asian Americans. And the American religious landscape as a whole has been deeply formed by Asian American immigration and their religious lives.

Colonial and Missionary-Sponsored Immigration

During the colonial era and after the Revolutionary War, the United States had no specific immigration legislation whatsoever. The need was for more people to till and cultivate the "empty" lands taken from Native Americans and to defend the new, weak nation militarily. Asian American immigration during this period was relatively rare, as relationships with Asia and the Pacific were just being established through increasing European colonization and the earliest modern missionary efforts.

The founders of the United States did not wish to discourage any potential immigrants, but in 1790, Congress passed its first naturalization law, known later as RS 2169. This statute specified that U.S. naturalization was open to "free white men." Naturalization was the process whereby immigrants became citizens—those born on U.S. soil were already, by constitutional guarantee, citizens. After the Civil War, the Naturalization Statute was amended to include "those of African descent," thus granting naturalization rights to future African immigrants.

In later years, the question of whether Asians could be included or excluded from citizenship would become crucial in legal court cases and in immigration law.

Properly speaking, Asian immigration to the North American continent predated the United States or any immigration regime thereof. Filipino sailors on Spanish galleons escaped from the harsh shipboard life to the shores of California and Louisiana in the 18th century. In Louisiana, 40 years before the United States made the Louisiana Purchase, Filipinos established an isolated bayou community that persevered until the great hurricane of 1915.

Early missionaries from Massachusetts established the cultural hegemony of the fledgling United States over the Sandwich Islands early in the 19th century, working to convert native Hawaiians to a congregational Protestant faith. Missionary converts came to New England for training and education. The Hawaiian Islands were not at that time U.S. soil, but were an independent kingdom. This was one of the first real efforts to convert Pacific Islanders, but certainly not the last. In a sort of inverted immigration, multiple generations of missionary families from New England spread throughout the Pacific, working to convert the Pacific Islanders in many cultures to a very culture-specific Christianity, one that involved a New England Protestant lifestyle of private property ownership, literacy for Bible reading, "modest" clothing, household habits, sexual mores, and gender roles.

Missionaries continued to sponsor their converts throughout the 19th century. The famous American missionary Adoniram Judson began his work in Burma in 1812.

From the Burma mission came some of the earliest Burmese converts and immigrants, including San C. Po, whose application for American citizenship appeared in an Albany, New York courtroom in 1894. A member of the Karen ethnic group, Po came to the United States under the auspices of missionaries seeking to create an educated "native" class of pastors, doctors, and teachers for the mission field. And like many others, Po desired to stay in the United States as a citizen after his education—a pattern that continues in the 21st century.

However, Po encountered RS 2169 in his efforts to become an American citizen. It was necessary for the court in Albany, New York, to decide whether a Burmese man was "white." In Po's case, the court decided that a Burmese man was not "white," and therefore was not eligible to be a U.S. citizen. This was the first of a long series of court cases about the race categorization of Asian immigrants and the corresponding rights of naturalization.

Po returned to Burma as a physician and wrote one of the first books in English on the Karen people. The phenomenon of immigrants "sponsored" by American religious organizations continued throughout the 20th and into the 21st century, particularly regarding refugees sponsored by congregations and religious professionals such as pastors, who have always constituted a special legal immigration category.

Early Chinese Immigration and the Chinese Exclusion Act

Though individual Asians had entered the United States as merchants, students, or immigrants from the earliest colonial eras, the first mass Asian immigrant wave to the United States was of Chinese men to the West Coast of the United States in the 1840s and 1850s. California had only recently been wrested from Mexico and added to the United States when gold was discovered at Sutter's Mill. Hearing the vastly inflated stories of streets paved with gold, Chinese men—like men throughout the Americas, Europe, and Australia—flocked to search for Gold Mountain.

Like most immigrants, the Chinese expected to return home with their newfound wealth. And like most immigrants, the Chinese discovered that the streets paved with gold were paved only with hard work and suffering. Unlike the immigrants from Europe and the eastern United States, the Chinese immigrants also discovered racial antipathy and economic exploitation far beyond their expectations, a legal regime that excluded and oppressed them because of their race, physical abuse and arson, a hatred of their religion and language, and eventually the loss of hopes of establishing families as they were sequestered in "bachelor Chinatowns."

At this time, Christian missionaries had been working in China for over two decades, but the vast majority of Chinese were non-Christian. Traditional Chinese religious life, with Confucian, Buddhist, animist, and Taoist elements, was deeply intertwined with medicine, belief in spirits both good and evil, veneration of the ancestors, and particularly with generating a family. "Joss houses" or temples were built in Chinatowns to burn incense before deities and benevolent spirits, and Chinese immigrants did their best to provide ceremonies and burials for their countrymen that would care for their spirits in the afterlife.

As anti-Chinese sentiment grew in California, Christian missionaries based in San Francisco and the eastern United States worked to protect the rights and safety of Chinese immigrants. They established Sunday schools to teach English to the Chinese and acted as cultural brokers in advocating for their needs with the city and state. However, their advocacy failed, and in 1882 Congress passed the first Chinese Exclusion Act, the first race-based immigration restriction law.

The Exclusion Act denied the rights of immigration to Chinese laborers and women, but gave extremely limited rights to wealthier Chinese merchants, their wives, and their families. The earlier Chinese immigration had been highly skewed toward men, so there were no Chinese women available for a large number of the Chinese who were already present in the United States. For many Chinese men who immigrated before the Exclusion Act, who had been unmarried at that time, this meant that they were effectively condemned to lifelong bachelorhood.

In addition to its effects on American immigration history, setting the stage for increasing exclusion on racial grounds, the Exclusion Act shaped the religious lives of Chinese immigrants. Those men who remained unmarried and without sons could not achieve the expected religious goals in the Chinese religious system—they could not provide sons to perform the rites for the ancestors, or for themselves when they died. Chinese Christian converts, forming their own churches, were similarly bachelors. These churches became fraternal associations, encouraging the men to find spiritual worth in different goals—of contributing to the community, developing relationships and friendships with one another, supporting relatives in China, and working for Chinese nationalism. Until the second generation of Chinese immigrants grew up and had their own families, the children of those relatively few men who were lucky enough to have wives, Chinese-American religious life was truncated by the Exclusion Act.

Japanese Immigration and the Gentlemen's Agreement

When the influx of Chinese "cheap labor" dried up, employers looked for another source of workers. The Japanese immigration had begun around the same time as the Chinese, but until after the Exclusion Act, it was relatively small. Enough Japanese immigrants had converted to Christianity to found the first Japanese American Christian congregation in San Francisco in 1877, but most of the Japanese were Buddhists. Some were Zen Buddhists, others belonged to the Jōdo Shin branch of Buddhism.

The Japanese immigrants faced hostility similar to the Chinese, and Christian missionaries again tried to advocate for their rights, unsuccessfully. But because Japan was perceived as a stronger nation that would respond badly to an insult, no "Japanese Exclusion Act" was passed. Instead, in 1907 President Roosevelt negotiated a face-saving deal with the Japanese government called the Gentlemen's Agreement. This agreement stated that the Japanese government would not provide passports for any laborers intending to come to the United States.

The agreement, however, did not cover women—and for a brief period, Japanese in the United States were able to send home for "picture brides." The Japanese therefore did not experience the enforced bachelorhood of many Chinese immigrants, but were able to start families. The first immigrant generation, called the Issei, gave birth to the second, the Nisei. As immigration from Japan ceased after the Issei, the Nisei and Sansei (third generation) experienced a closed, age-stratified Japanese American culture for several decades.

There were many schools to train Japanese Christian pastors, but finding Buddhist priests in this early period was more difficult. Buddhist priests from Japan who had immigrated as Issei worked to teach the Dharma, but suffered from the same oppression as all other Japanese—including, eventually, internment during World War II. Some of these Buddhist teachers, such as D. T. Suzuki, became known for bringing Zen Buddhism to white America, but the new converts rarely had fellowship with Japanese immigrants or Japanese American Buddhists. Similarly, the Japanese Christians found themselves socially isolated from the white Christian churches. Japanese Nisei Christians established parallel "YMCA" structures for Japanese Christian young people, and Japanese Nisei Buddhists did the same.

1917 Barred Zone Act

Japanese immigration in the form of "picture brides" continued for a few years after the 1907 Gentleman's Agreement, much

to the dismay of anti-Asian legislators and organizations. In 1917, immigration law was adapted again, this time to bar immigration from any nation within a "Barred Zone" that included all of Asia—those regions that had not yet been specifically restricted by the Chinese Exclusion Act and the Gentleman's Agreement, including Southeast Asia and the Indian subcontinent. (The Philippines presented a special case, as explained below.)

The main Asian immigrant group affected by the 1917 Barred Zone Act were Indians. Indians had been entering the United States for many years in small numbers, but as general anti-Asian prejudice rose, even the small number of Indian migrants attracted legal and popular hostility. Most of the West Coast Indian immigrants were male Sikhs from the Punjab in Northern India, and most were not able to bring wives with them. When the 1917 act cut off further immigration, many of these immigrants were isolated in the Central Valley of California, where some married Mexican American women to create a unique Sikh-Mexican subculture.

Asian Immigrants and Citizenship: Takao Ozawa and Bhagat Singh Thind

The "problem" of Asian citizenship and RS 2169 was finally resolved in two Supreme Court cases during these years of heightened anti-Asian racism and general American isolationism after the First World War. The question of citizenship touched on immigration rights and other civil rights, as laws such as the 1913 Alien

Land Act denied the right to own land to those "ineligible for citizenship."

Takao Ozawa, a Japanese immigrant in Hawai'i, petitioned the courts for legal citizenship and was denied on the basis of his race—according to general interpretations, Japanese were not "white" and therefore not eligible for citizenship according to RS 2169. Ozawa appealed his case all the way to the Supreme Court, and lost. He argued that although he was Japanese in origin, he was American in culture—that he was Christian, spoke English, and taught his children to speak only English, keeping them away from the Buddhist-run Japanese language schools in Hawai'i. While acknowledging that Ozawa might, in fact, make an ideal citizen, and might even deserve citizenship, the Supreme Court nonetheless ruled that according to the law, he was ineligible.

That same year, 1922, the Supreme Court ruled that an Indian immigrant, Bhagat Singh Thind, was ineligible for citizenship on just the opposite grounds—that while Thind was ethnologically "white," his "Hindu" religion meant that he was unable to assimilate into the "civilization of white men" intended to be protected by RS 2169. Thind's case is especially interesting due to the layers of racial and religious interpretations dealt in by the Court. Most courts up to that time had accepted Northern Indians as "white" because, according to the ethnology of the time, they were categorized as "Aryan." In particular, the usual argument ran that the caste system of Hinduism protected the racial purity of upper-caste Northern Indians. Thind had already received citizenship on these grounds, as had many other Indian immigrants before him.

However, Thind's citizenship was stripped from him on appeal of the immigration and naturalization lawyers to the Supreme Court. The Court ruled that because Hinduism's caste system and general religious practices were completely incompatible with "the civilization of white men," Thind could not be considered "white" and therefore did not have eligibility for citizenship within the meaning of RS 2169.

Leaving aside the irony that Thind was Sikh, not Hindu (as were most Indian immigrants of that era), these two court cases taken together show that underlying all the immigration legislation of this time is a racism blended with religious prejudice, aiming to exclude and to harass Asian immigrants to the United States. However, there was no serious political effort to take away the constitutional right of birthright citizenship from the children of Asian immigrants. Regardless of their parents' struggles against discrimination and injustice, the children of these immigrants entered the world as American citizens. Undoubtedly their parents thought this would protect them from further incursions upon their rights and dignity; but, unfortunately, this proved not to be the case.

1924 Reed-Johnson Act

The patchwork of existing immigration and naturalization laws was overhauled completely in 1924 with the Reed-Johnson Act, also known as the National Origins Act or Quota Act. This law codified immigration rights according to small "quotas" given to different countries, based on the 1890 census of those already in the United States. Using the 1890 census as a base ensured that the numbers of Asian immigrants would always be small, even for those who still could emigrate—the Barred Zone and the Chinese Exclusion Acts remained in effect.

Ironically, the Reed-Johnson Act had its roots in the ideas of a defender of Asian immigration rights, Christian missionary to Japan Sidney Gulick. Gulick had grown up as the child of missionaries in Micronesia and spent his adult life arguing for the rights of Asian immigrants to the United States. He argued that American immigration law should be based on "assimilability," rather than race or national origin per se, and that the numbers permitted to enter the United States should be based on the 1910 census. This would have restricted Asian immigration, of course, but would have set Asian nations on the same par as other countries. The anti-Asian animus behind the 1924 act, however, joined with other fears of the high immigration from Southern and Eastern Europe to ensure that the 1890 census was used as a base for the national quotas. The end result was that immigration from all regions except Northwestern Europe was drastically reduced.

The one loophole in Reed-Johnson was that it did not restrict or monitor any immigration from the Western Hemisphere. A continuing trickle of Asian immigration continued during these years via Mexico and Canada. And Chinese immigrants continued to bring in "family members," one by one, as "paper sons."

Filipino Immigration: The Spanish-American War to 1934 Tydings-McDuffie Act

After the United States "liberated" the Philippine Islands from Spain in 1898 during the Spanish-American War, the Philippines held a unique place in American legal status. It was part of the territories of the United States, and therefore Filipino immigrants were not affected by laws about immigration. As other Asian immigration dried up due to restrictive laws, Filipinos came to fill the gaps in labor in the fields and farms and to study in American universities. Most of these immigrants came from the northern island of Luzon and spoke the Ilocano language. While most Filipinos were Catholic, some belonged to the Aglipayan church, a revolutionary protest movement; others were leaving the Catholic church to join the churches of American Protestant missionaries, or found new spiritual homes in the United States. All of these immigrants held in common a cultural language of mystical practice, prayer, and devotion to the saints, as well as deep veneration for the ties of family and godparenthood. Many settled in Hawai'i and in California's farming areas, with thriving communities in Stockton and Los Angeles.

The continued immigration of Filipinos to the United States was not very popular among anti-Asian organizations, and it was one of the reasons that the Philippines, unlike Guam and Puerto Rico, did not become a permanent American territory. The Filipino people were also agitating for independence. The U.S. Congress gave the islands limited independence in 1934 with the Tydings-McDuffie Act, but retained extensive control over the archipelago's economy and military. The main immediate result of Tydings-McDuffie was that Filipinos no longer had the right to enter the United States freely as American nationals and were reclassified as aliens subject to the restrictive immigration laws. Filipino immigration therefore decreased after 1934.

War and Immigration Legislation

During and after World War II, several pieces of war-related immigration legislation had a special effect on Asian immigration. War created a new identification of allies and enemies. The first effect was the repeal of the Chinese Exclusion Act in 1943, intended as recognition of China's role as an ally in the war. The quota given to China was almost infinitesimally small, but the importance of the repeal of the Exclusion Act had an effect on the ways in which Chinese could now understand their role in the United States. During this same time, of course, Japanese immigrants and their American-born citizen children and grandchildren were being herded into the internment camps.

The effect of the camps on Japanese American religious life has echoes down through today. Both Buddhist and Christian Japanese were torn between trying to prove their fidelity to American authorities, or turning away from attempts at integration into American society. Japanese who were interned, and their descendants, relive and reinterpret their deep losses during this time with pilgrimages to Manzanar, one of the camps located in eastern Oregon. These pilgrimages, organized by a Japanese Methodist church, are open to those of all faiths.

Second, the War Brides Act was passed in 1945. This act was the first move in American immigration legislation to prioritize "family reunification" rather than national origins as the deciding factor in immigration rights. American military members who married women from any nation received a special waiver to bring their fiancées and wives and children to the United States, without counting against their nation's quota. While the war brides came from all over the world, this led to extensive new immigration by Asian women, including Filipino women after World War II, Korean women during and after the Korean War, and Vietnamese women during the Vietnam War.

In 1952, the McCarran-Walter Act removed the category of "alien ineligible for citizenship" from American legal language, thus enabling Japanese immigrants to naturalize. It also removed the "barred zone" of the 1917 legislation, replacing it with the term "Asia-Pacific Triangle." Although this at last brought Asian immigrants into legal parity with non-Asians, it made little practical difference, as the quota system was retained— and the total quota of Asian Pacific immigrants permitted under the new act was only 2,000 per year from all 19 countries involved. It also counted Asian immigrants against their country's quota regardless of the country they actually immigrated from; someone of Japanese descent who emigrated from England would be counted against the Japanese quota for that year.

In 1953, the Refugee Relief Act enabled Chinese citizens fleeing Communist persecution to enter the United States. This began a slow growth in the Chinese-American community. In general, however, large flows of new immigrants waited until the laws changed completely in 1965.

1965 Hart-Celler Act and the Refugee Acts of 1975, 1980, and 1987

Like 1882 and 1924, 1965 is a watershed date in American immigration history. The Hart-Celler Act completely reorganized the structure of U.S. immigration law to center around employment and family, rather than race or national origins. While quotas remained in terms of total immigration and for particular kinds of visas, many categories were exempt from the quotas. Family reunification, with descending categories of preferences for different kinds of relatives, meant that chain migration could take place—one immigrant could bring immediate and eventually extended family, who could sponsor others.

Post-1965 immigration has been extraordinarily diverse, bringing immigrants from every country in Asia and the Pacific, with widely varying economic and education backgrounds. Particular employment needs in the United States have led to intense job-specific flows at different times—for instance, a shortage of nurses has brought large numbers of Filipina and Indian Keralite nurses to the United States. As family members followed the employed immigrant, religious institutions could be established.

Since 1965, Korean Presbyterianism, for instance, has become an important part of the American Christian scene, as have Filipino and Vietnamese Catholic parishes. Indian Orthodox, Indonesian Lutherans, Filipino Aglipayan and Iglesia Ni Cristo, Tongan and Samoan Methodists, Chinese and Japanese churches, and dozens more denominations and cultural groupings have challenged the American Christian churches and denominations to widen their conception of the Christian faith. Among second-generation immigrants, pan-Asian ethnic churches have sprung up, often without definite ties to traditional denominations.

Large numbers of highly educated Indian immigrants, often Hindu but also Muslim and Sikh, entered the United States using employment-based visas. These immigrants have often concentrated in high-paying professions, and thus have been able to begin building large religious structures—temples, *gurdwaras*, and *mosques*. Often these groups have faced prejudice and difficulty from local communities in their efforts to build their religious institutions, and extensive local legal battles have ensued, ostensibly over issues of zoning and traffic, but often experienced as racism and religious prejudice.

In 1975, a new gate for Asian immigration was opened, also as the result of war. As the United States left Vietnam, those who had supported the United States (or who were suspected of doing so) were left unprotected in the violent aftermath in Vietnam, Laos, and Cambodia. In an effort to provide some care for those who had lost everything in the American war, Congress passed a law opening the gates to these refugees. This act was amended and widened in 1980, and another Southeast Asian

Refugee Act in 1987 gave greater attention to the needs of these refugee communities once they entered the United States.

For the first time, significant numbers of Southeast Asians entered the United States as a result. The upheavals in their home countries meant that all classes, education levels, and ethnic groups were cast on the waters. Chinese Vietnamese merchants, wealthy urban leaders, impoverished Laotian farmers, Cambodians fleeing the killing fields, and Hmong people of the mountains all established communities in the United States, often sponsored by church groups and congregations. Their religions were as diverse as their experiences and languages. Hmong came from an animist, shamanistic culture, while many Vietnamese were Catholic; Cambodians and Laotians might be Buddhist, but might also find Christianity compatible with their lives in the United States.

Refugees of all sorts suffered immense culture shock in the United States, but perhaps none more so than members of minority ethnic cultures such as the Hmong. Isolated even within their home country of Laos, with a shamanistic religion tied to the land, the Hmong struggled to find a meaningful place in the urbanized United States. Cambodians fleeing the Khmer Rouge and Laotian farmers also struggled with poverty and violence in the United States, but eventually succeeded in setting up temples and gradually created their own communities.

All of these groups have contributed to the great ethnic, religious, and cultural diversity of the American Asian community. Post-1965 immigration has led to over 17 million Asians in the United States, according to the 2010 census. Chinese is now the third most commonly spoken language in the United States (after Spanish and English), while Tagalog, Vietnamese, and Korean are each spoken by over 1 million Americans.

Post 9/11 Immigration

American immigration entered a new phase after 9/11, the date in 2001 when the Twin Towers were bombed by terrorists and the United States declared "war on terror." Much of this war included suspicion of Muslims and suspicion of foreigners, which spilled over into Asian immigrant life even without great changes in actual immigration law.

Even before 9/11, the immigration process for many had become a broken process. The system was overwhelmed and experienced as arbitrary and punitive by many of those who intended to enter the United States legally and remain as residents. Waiting lists for some "preferences" (the legal levels of family reunification or employment visas) stretched for 15 or 20 years.

After 9/11, all of this became much more difficult, particularly for those from countries with large Muslim populations, such as Malaysia, Pakistan, and Indonesia. American Sikhs also found themselves under attack, as a religiously observant Sikh man, who wears a turban and a beard, looks "Muslim" to some Americans. (Again, this is a particularly ironic turnaround given that for most of American Sikh history, Sikhs were confused with Hindus in the larger American culture.) Muslims and Sikhs alike faced popular prejudice and even violence during the immediate aftermath of 9/11.

The general tenor of American politics post-9/11 has become much more isolationist, similar to the years just after World War I, and this has been reflected in the debate over immigration, including the debate about "illegal" or undocumented immigrants. While popular debate currently focuses on Latinos as the main source of "illegals," in fact many Asian immigrants are also undocumented. American Asian immigrants have experienced midnight raids, indefinite detention, endless court cases, and deportation just as the larger immigrant community has, and American Asian American young people have also come forward in support of the DREAM Act, an act that would give rights of residency to those undocumented young people brought to the United States as children and who have completed either college or military service.

In 2012, as the current immigration system struggled under the weight of complexity, numbers, and uncertainty, it seemed likely that new immigration legislation would eventually be passed. While the DREAM Act would give relief to some Asian immigrants, the system as a whole requires change. There is increasing debate about how and when to recast the immigration legislation wholesale, as in 1924 and 1965. Whatever occurs, it will surely affect the lives of Asian immigrants and their communities in the United States.

Jennifer Snow

See also: Essays: Religion and Law

Further Reading

Fadiman, Anne. *The Spirit Catches You and You Fall Down: A Hmong Child, Her American Doctors, and the Collision of Two Cultures.* New York: Farrar, Straus and Giroux, 1998.

Iwamura, Jane Naomi, and Paul Spickard. *Revealing the Sacred in Asian and Pacific America.* New York: Routledge, 2002.

Odo, Franklin, ed. *The Columbia Documentary History of the Asian American Experience.* New York: Columbia University Press, 2002.

Salyer, Lucy E. *Laws Harsh as Tigers: Chinese Immigrants and the Shaping of Modern Immigration Law.* Chapel Hill: University of North Carolina Press, 1995.

Snow, Jennifer. *Protestant Missionaries, Asian Immigrants, and American Ideologies of Race, 1850–1924.* New York: Routledge, 2007.

Tan, Jonathan. *Introducing Asian American Theologies.* Maryknoll, NY: Orbis Books, 2008.

Yoo, David K. *New Spiritual Homes: Religion and Asian Americans.* Honolulu: University of Hawai'i Press, 1999.

Interpretation

Broad Description and History

In its broadest sense, interpretation refers to the act of explaining or elucidating the meaning of something (we shall broadly call it a "text" here) by someone (referred to here as the interpreter) in the way that the interpreter understands it and wants it to be understood by the recipient. A more technical term in various academic disciplines used to refer to interpretation is hermeneutics (interpreter = hermeneut). "Hermeneutics" is derived from the name of the Greek messenger god Hermes. In that derivation, we can read several important nuances that carry great import, particularly for Asian American religions. First of all, the message that a messenger delivers is rarely a word-for-word transcript or a recording that can be played back exactly as the message-sender stated it. Rather, it usually involves the mediation of the messenger who acts as a bridge between the source and recipient of the message. This messenger, therefore, plays a crucial role in the process because he or she has to understand the message and then convey that message to the intended recipients. "Understanding" and "communicating a message" are phases in which the nature and process of interpretation are more clearly in evidence. First, the messenger's mind is not a *tabula rasa* (Latin, "blank slate"). Rather, the messenger understands a message, in the words of the theologian David Tracy, "bearing the history of the effects, both conscious and unconscious, of the traditions to which [he or she] ineluctably belong[s]." In short, whatever the messenger understands is already a product of the interaction between the message and the messenger's "pre-understandings." That important term, taken literally, refers to the ideas about the matter that the messenger already has in his or her mind when confronted with the message. More broadly defined, pre-understandings can include all the factors—such as history, social location, culture, personality, and so on—that influence how a messenger understands a message. Pre-understandings play a crucial role in identifying a peculiarly Asian American approach to interpretation. They are what influence and qualify the mode in which Asian Americans understand and interpret any text.

A second factor to point out is that what the messenger conveys to the intended recipients of the message is what he or she has understood of the message. As mentioned, this is not usually a word-for-word account but is itself *already an interpretation*. It should also be noted that the quality of the communication of the message to its intended recipients depends on the medium by which the messenger communicates the message. It is also possible that a given messenger can either consciously or unconsciously alter the message itself.

In the academic disciplines, hermeneutics refers to the general theory and practice of interpretation. In the Christian theological tradition, hermeneutics began as an important subfield of biblical studies because the Bible, as the foundational Christian text that carries a crucial and normative meaning for the whole Christian tradition, was deemed a text that needed to be interpreted correctly and validly. Hence, hermeneutics dealt with the method and conditions of valid biblical interpretation. In light of this origin, hermeneutics, narrowly understood, still means how we understand written texts, particularly texts that readers somehow consider distant from themselves (such as the Bible) due to factors such as history, social location, ideology, geography, culture, and so forth. From being a subfield of biblical studies, the discipline of hermeneutics moved into the broader area of general textual interpretation. At present, the term encompasses a wide range of meanings and applications. "Text," as the object of the activity of hermeneutics, has often come to be understood very broadly as practically any manifestation with a more or less coherent set of symbols that has a message and can be read or understood. At present, hermeneutics is, therefore, considered a crucial part of almost all disciplines spanning from those it has been traditionally linked with such as theology and philosophy to various other disciplines such as literary criticism, rhetoric, cultural studies, anthropology, the social sciences, and many others. Discussions within the general field of hermeneutics cover a wide range of topics including understanding, interpretation, analysis, meaning and meaningfulness, textuality, language, and historicity, among others.

History of Hermeneutics: The Western Tradition. As a general philosophical enterprise, hermeneutics can be traced to Aristotle (d. 322 BCE) who, in his *Peri Hermeneias* (On Interpretation), dealt with interpretation under the topic of logic and explained the relationship between language and logic. Early Christian and later scholastic thought continued to link hermeneutics with logic and its related disciplines of rhetoric and grammar. Of course, Christians were concerned above all with the interpretation of scripture. Thus, interpretation in Christianity centered on principles and methods by which scripture could be and should be validly interpreted. Illustrative of this tendency was the contrast between the theological school of thought centered in Antioch, which emphasized the literal interpretation of scripture, and the one in Alexandria, which tended to use more allegorical ways of interpretation. With Augustine, we can say that early Christian hermeneutics reached a significant stage of development

because he drew both from Antiochene (more literal) and Alexandrian (allegorical and spiritual) principles and methodologies. He also maintained that the "rule of faith" (i.e., the living tradition of the Christian community) is the necessary context for the valid interpretation of scripture.

However, it is only with the Christian theologian Friedrich Schleiermacher (1768–1834) that a more philosophical theory of hermeneutics emerged. He is thus considered one of the founding figures of modern hermeneutics. Schleiermacher shifted the focus from principles and methods of textual interpretation to the conditions that make the human faculty of understanding possible and to the person of the interpreter him- or herself. For him, the task of hermeneutics was to help the interpreter reproduce the meaning of the messenger-sender in his or her consciousness. In a famous adage, he suggested that the interpreter should understand the text "as well as and then even better than its author." Schleiermacher divides interpretation into two parts: grammatical and psychological. The former requires familiarity with the linguistic and syntactical structures of the text. The latter has to do with the interplay between the reader and the text. Grammatical interpretation is merely a preparation for technical or psychological interpretation, which, for Schleiermacher, is understanding in the full sense of the word. Schleiermacher underlined the creative dimension of interpretation as evidenced in his famous position that reading should be an art.

Wilhelm Dilthey (1833–1911), another foundational figure in the history of hermeneutics, anchored hermeneutics firmly in historical consciousness and tradition by positing "lived experience" (in German, *Erlebnis*) as a foundational category for the hermeneutical enterprise. For Dilthey, to understand and interpret a text basically meant the ability to bring oneself out of one's present time and relive or reexperience (in German, *Nacherleben*) the original *Erlebnis* referred to therein. Thus, although the interpreter is always codetermined by his or her own particular historical context, the determinant of valid interpretation is found in a serious effort to overcome historical distance to have access to the original experience in life that brought a particular text into being, in short, interpreting the text while respecting its historical integrity. The text, therefore, is not only a piece of linguistic communication. It is actually a part of humanity's whole cultural heritage in history.

Martin Heidegger (1889–1976) is particularly significant in the history of hermeneutics, first, for situating the problem of interpretation as constitutive for being itself. In Heidegger's scheme, a person's existence is in effect realized by an act of interpretation. Furthermore, it was Heidegger who referred to human understanding (and, hence, also interpretation) as circular in nature. This is known as the "hermeneutical circle," a concept that has become one of the key characteristics for understanding the nature of the human activity of interpretation. According to this notion, interpretation is circular in structure because it does not begin with a clean slate. Instead, the interpreter begins the activity of interpretation by bringing his or her pre-understandings to the process. In the course of trying to interpret something, the interpreter may have to revise those pre-understandings when new information and data warrant change. These modified understandings in turn become the elements that the interpreter brings to the next phase of interpretive work. In short, interpretation consists of a circle of understandings (or interpretations) in the interpreter: pre-understandings that become new understandings, which, in turn, become the starting points of understanding for a new phase of trying to grasp the object of scrutiny better.

Hans Georg Gadamer (1900–2002) explained hermeneutics as a dialogical process between present and past ("tradition" has a prominent place in his thought), as well as between text and interpreter, each with its own "horizon." The goal of this dialogue is what Gadamer called a "fusion of horizons," and the medium through which dialogue happens is language.

Other names worthy of mention here are the following. As a reaction to Gadamer's acceptance of tradition as authoritative in the hermeneutical enterprise, thinkers such as Karl-Otto Apel and Jürgen Habermas developed a critical hermeneutics marked by suspicion with regard to the truth claims of tradition. Paul Ricoeur (1913–2005) can be seen as a mediating figure between a hermeneutics marked by suspicion and one characterized by trust or retrieval. He has written numerous works that describe hermeneutics as understanding the past and its relevance for the present, as well as hermeneutics as directed toward the future while working for change in the present. Ricoeur is also notable for his works dealing with biblical hermeneutics and how a metaphorical approach to an analysis of narratives can open up new and relevant insights into texts. Jacques Derrida (1930–2004) was instrumental in developing the critical theory known as deconstruction, which seeks to expose oppositions, paradoxes, and hierarchies in texts. His work has influenced hermeneutics in our postmodern world in a major way. Last but not least, David Tracy is also significant as a theologian who has emphasized (arguably more than any other contemporary theologian) the radical and all-encompassing hermeneutical nature of the whole enterprise of Christian theology.

Points of Broad Agreement about the Nature of Interpretation. The result of this history of interpretation or hermeneutics as a discipline in the Western tradition can be expressed in the following points below. They reflect a broad consensus about the nature of human understanding and interpretation or hermeneutics in academic circles and serve as a springboard to reflect on what is peculiar to Asian American contextual interpretation.

- Interpretation is an all-pervasive factor in human life because all human understanding is fundamentally interpretive in nature. Tracy even extends the role of hermeneutics to *all* human activity, saying, "We need to reflect on what none of us can finally evade: the need to interpret to understand at all. . . . Every time we act, deliberate, judge, understand, or even experience, we are interpreting. To understand at all is to interpret."

- The term "hermeneutic circle" mentioned above is a good way to describe the ubiquitous nature of interpretation in any human effort to understand anything. The process starts already with initial interpretations (pre-understandings) in the interpreter's mind and moves to revised interpretations, which, in turn, serve as the understandings that drive the process of interpretation forward. A second dimension of the hermeneutic circle is the principle that humans can only understand a whole by understanding its constituent parts. At the same time, humans can understand the smaller parts only if they have some idea of the greater whole. This makes another circle composed of whole and parts. An arguably better term suggested by Grant Osborne is "hermeneutical spiral" because it denotes a movement that goes upward and is more constructive in that earlier rather naive pre-understandings develop into understandings that are more focused and mature.

- Human understanding and interpretation are historically, culturally, and linguistically conditioned. An interpreter is often confronted by an object from a historical epoch, culture, or language considered an "Other," which he or she endeavors to understand better and to interpret. Interpretation then involves the effort to bridge the gap between present and past, between one culture and another, between one language and another. In this case, interpretation involves the serious work of acquiring the necessary historical, cultural, or linguistic knowledge so that an interpreter can comprehend the object of scrutiny better. On the other hand, history, culture, and language are also the existential conditions that radically mark interpreters, who cannot delude themselves into believing that they can be completely neutral and objective. For our purposes here, these existential conditions of the interpreter have to do with Asian American histories, cultures, and languages. Hence, interpreters would do well to keep in mind the limitations as well as the richness that their own contexts have.

• The term "text" best describes the object of interpretation. This refers first and foremost to written texts, but it can be extended to mean anything that has some meaning and that can be read or understood. When a particular text becomes vitally significant to a group of persons because of a clear expression of truth widely acknowledged to be present in it—a particular expression of truth that transcends its historical setting, defies any definitive interpretation, and requires a continual reinterpretation by each succeeding generation—then that text can be considered a "classic." Classics are the privileged objects of interpretation.

The Rise of Contextual Theologies. The recent history of different general approaches to interpretation can be delineated from a survey of trends in biblical studies because the Bible has been and continues to be the text *par excellence* in the Christian religious tradition. Hence, hermeneutics in Christian circles is arguably still primarily focused on this text. In a survey of trends in biblical studies, Fernando Segovia observes that traditional historical criticism broadly conceived was the dominant interpretive paradigm in the discipline through the mid-1970s. This approach was characterized by an emphasis on the text as a means to access either the real author of the text or the world in which a text was born. It can also be described as a model centered on the so-called "world behind the text." It stressed a radical contextualization of the text using historical-critical methods. The underlying principle here was that the true significance of the text lies in the intention of the author or the intended message to the original audience located in a particular world.

However, beginning from the mid-1970s, an interpretive paradigm that can be labeled as literary criticism broadly conceived was able to dislodge the hitherto dominant historical criticism and establish itself as an alternative approach to the biblical text through the 1980s and into the 1990s. Approaches such as narrative criticism, structuralism, rhetorical criticism, deconstructionism, among others, are included in this interpretive paradigm. This paradigm centered on the text itself as a medium and attempted to put the spotlight on the communication that occurred between implied author and implied reader with the intention of delineating the real meaning of the text. Hence, this paradigm can still be described as being characterized by a search for the objective meaning of the text-message. It can also be styled as focused on the so-called "world in or of the text."

Alongside the development of text-centered approaches, an interpretive paradigm that can be styled as cultural criticism broadly conceived also began to make its presence felt. Included in this category are methods that put a premium on sociological, anthropological, ideological, and cultural analysis. These cultural approaches are, in a sense, similar to the traditional historical criticism in that they stressed the importance of gaining a better access to the original world of the text. However, compared to historical criticism, cultural approaches were generally more sophisticated in different areas. They stressed the broader social, economic, and cultural aspects of the world in which a particular text was produced. They undertook more penetrating ideological analyses of the text's sociological contexts. They also underlined the radical differences between the world of the text and the present (world of the) reader of the text.

With the loss of historical criticism's dominance, a different identifiable paradigm began to take shape. This new approach, in a way, spurned the notion of a neutral and disinterested reader (put forward as the ideal reader by historical and literary approaches) and made, as its focus, the real, flesh-and-blood readers of the texts and their particular contexts (the "world in front of the text"). The development of liberation theology in Latin America undoubtedly played a major part in the rise to prominence of this interpretive approach. Liberation theology takes "location in life" or context as its starting point. Since the Latin American context was (and

is) characterized by endemic and systemic poverty and oppression, liberation theology's hallmark, identified as its basic interpretive stance, became the concept of God's "preferential option for the poor." It followed then that the church should make God's priority its own, especially at the existential level.

In other parts of the world, particularly areas that once formed part of the British Empire, a new mode of analysis that came to be known as postcolonial thought began to take shape. It made its focus the study and analysis of the nature and effects of imperialism and colonialism both in the colonizer and the colonized. As in liberation theology, postcolonial thought put a spotlight on the reader of the text, particularly on this reader's social location as within oppressive, imperial, and hegemonic structures, if not physically, then psychologically. It suggested ways by which readers could resist and free themselves from hegemonic oppression. This confluence of approaches that underlined the state and context of the flesh-and-blood reader began to be felt in the academy in general and in those involved in interpretation in particular.

From the 1990s (up to the present), there has virtually been an explosion of material on or utilizing contextual approaches to biblical and other religion-related texts. The aim of such approaches, as summarized by Segovia, is to make the discipline of biblical studies (we can apply this, however, to interpretation in general)—broadly described—postcolonial, that is, less Eurocentric or Western. This was to be done by bringing the voices of groups hitherto considered marginal into greater prominence. It is in this wave of an ever-increasing and continuing awareness in the academy of the importance of contextual approaches that we find ourselves at present. It is also there in which we can contextualize Asian American interpretive approaches.

Explicit Asian American theologizing and interpretive reflection can be traced to the early trailblazing efforts of theologians such as Roy Isao Sano, Sang Hyun Lee, Jung Young Lee, and David Ng among others in the 1970s and 1980s through the 1990s. It was in the 1990s, we can say, that what was up to that point a trickle became a regular flow, which became, at the turn of the century, a virtual explosion of explicit Asian American theological and hermeneutical reflection. A number of significant studies done either by single authors or by a community of Asian American authors have and continue to advance the state of Asian American theology in general and Asian American hermeneutical reflection in particular.

Asian American Characteristic Traits and Interpretive Styles

What we have discussed thus far can be considered important traditions regarding interpretation/hermeneutics. These hermeneutical traditions have a direct bearing on Asian American interpretive approaches and practices because, as we have seen, interpreters go about the task of interpretation bearing the traditions of which they are part. As the Hermes metaphor for interpretation suggests, the dynamics involved between message (text) and intended recipient are centered on the messenger-in-

terpreter. In this case, the messenger has a personality that can be broadly described as Asian (with its specificity such as Chinese, Filipino, etc.) or Pacific (again with its specificity such as Samoan, Fijian, etc.) hyphenated with North American. This Asian-Pacific-North American personality gives a specific character to the interpretive work that is undertaken and to its results. To understand how Asian American contextual interpretation is done and what the role of the Asian American interpreter is in the process, David Tracy's description of steps for interpretation can be used with much profit.

Steps in Interpretation. Tracy proposes the following as steps in the interpretive enterprise: (1) First, interpreters enter the act of interpreting "bearing the history of the effects of the traditions to which they ineluctably belong." (2) Second, interpreters confront a "classic." (3) Third, interpreters engage this classic text in a hermeneutical conversation.

Applying these steps to Asian American interpretation, the first step refers to the specific Asian American "personality" of the one engaged in interpretation. This includes the whole composite of history, country of origin, cultural traits, the mixture of cultural worlds that is present in the interpreter's self, race, ethnicity, dominant experiences of joy, historic injuries suffered, present realities, and so forth. Consulting the specific entries of this encyclopedia on constituencies that fall under the umbrella term "Asian American" will give one a clearer picture of what comprises step one. In step two, interpreters confront "texts" that they consider classics.

There are many classics that interpreters can confront. Classics can range from dominant religious beliefs such as Jesus's uniqueness or even divinity, the nature of salvation and wholeness, and so on, to cultural mores or practices such as the notion of shame, the ethos of individuality, patriarchal cultural patterns, and so forth. In step three, interpreters endeavor to converse with the classic they have chosen to interpret with a genuine openness to what the classic attempts to say while, at the same time, making their own Asian American traits part and parcel of the conversation, not to impose but to open oneself up to new ways of being and understanding as a result of the conversation.

In the remaining space, we will attempt to delineate more clearly some dominant traits that Asian Americans bring to the table of interpretation because those traits form the specific character of the Asian American interpreter, a character that, we have seen, is of utmost important in a peculiarly Asian American interpretive process.

Typical Characteristics of Asian American Interpreters. From a close analysis of common Asian American experiences (to a certain extent, these can be applied to Pacific Americans' experiences as well), one can say that the following factors characterize many Asian Americans: First, many Asian Americans have experienced a kind of diaspora, that is, they have been uprooted either willingly or unwillingly from a place in Asia or the Pacific Islands they regarded as home and transplanted to this continent and this Western society. Such an experience decisively shapes particularly the first generation of immigrants

(still a significant portion of Asian American populations) but also later generations, those who were born and/or raised in North America. That last statement should include the caveat that one must endeavor not to equate the different Asian American generations as if they were the same because their experiences can be very different. Nevertheless, the experience of uprooting and replanting or, for those born and raised in North America, the experience of being more radically in contact with two (or more) cultural worlds since childhood creates in many individuals an identity that can be described as hybrid. This hybrid identity is often marked by a sense of standing betwixt and between two (or more) very different cultural worlds and an effort to find one's place while being situated at the margins of those intersecting/overlapping worlds.

Another typical characteristic of Asian American experience is the frequent yet subtle marginalization to which Asian Americans have been and continue to be subjected in North America, particularly by the dominant groups. Such social marginalization is often accompanied by a growing alienation that Asian Americans feel from their (or their forebears') original homelands.

A third factor is the process of continual social "positionings" or "posturings" that Asian Americans have to undertake to survive, flourish, and find a certain measure of integrity in North American society. A fourth factor is the sense of being privileged or blessed found in many more integrated Asian Americans because they are able to be present in multiple worlds at the same time and to call these worlds "home" in some way. Finally, there is also the effort on the part of many Asian Americans to find integrity and transcendence in their liminal, betwixt and between state by trying to hold the different worlds that coexist in themselves in a relation of dynamic tension with each other.

The above-mentioned characteristics, it can be argued, make up the general contours of Asian American identity. One can use the expression "diasporic hybridity" to describe such identities. The "diasporic" part refers to a complex of experiences involving being uprooted from a homeland and moving to a new, often inhospitable place. The "hybridity" part refers to life in the North American location where one acquires a hybrid identity over time due to one's location "in between and in both" two (or more) cultural worlds to which one can claim some affiliation. Hybridity can also be described as a mixture of phenomena: in particular, phenomena related to culture, tradition, race, ethnicity, or religion that have been commonly considered heretofore to be self-standing, reasonably definable, and distinct from others. The mixture sometimes occurs to such an extent that a *tertium quid* (Latin, "a third factor") results. This resulting mix, this *tertium quid*–like identity in many Asian Americans carries traits in unequal measures from all the parent ingredients of the mixture. Many Asian Americans can, therefore, identify at least in some way with their "parent ingredients." At the same time, Asian American identities cannot be *exclusively* identified with any one of the parent ingredients.

With the above factors in mind, an Asian American interpretive paradigm can be described as a way of looking at life or at different texts while firmly rooted in the consciousness that one is standing at the interstices of multiple worlds. Alternatively, an Asian American interpretive paradigm can also be depicted as rooted in a consciousness that one's identity is made up not of one monolithic, monocultural world but rather of hybridity, that is, multiple worlds that intersect, coexist, and mix in one's very being.

Asian American Interpretation. It is his or her identity traits or pre-understandings that the Asian American interpreter carries to the metaphorical table of interpretation. There, the interpreter encounters many works that can be deemed classics. Since one cannot converse with everything one finds fascinating, the Asian American interpreter has to choose which classics to confront. When the choice has been made, the phase of interpretive conversation begins. This conversation has been described using various expressions such as "looking at" ("reading," "seeing," etc.) "name of classic" (e.g., John's Gospel or the notion of salvation) with "Asian American eyes" and other similar expressions. Some of these expressions are arguably better than others. It is safe to say, though, that an interpretation that does not result in the give and take of true conversation but remains at the level of imposing "my or our own" agenda upon the classic to be interpreted somehow lacks integrity as an activity. Gadamer and Tracy described the interpretive enterprise as a game. A game is characterized by "movement" and a good game is one in which the players "lose themselves" in the movement of the game. "Games liberate our ability to understand ourselves by facing something different, other, and sometimes strange." The same principles should be present in authentic hermeneutical conversations conducted by Asian American interpreters with classics they have chosen to (re)interpret. As mentioned, there should be a genuine openness to and respect for the otherness of the classic in such a way that the Asian American interpreter really allows the classic to speak for itself. This is the first mark of a genuine hermeneutical conversation.

However, there is another side to hermeneutical conversations that shows the particularity and value of an Asian American interpretive style. As pointed out, Asian American interpreters bring a set of peculiarly Asian American traits (pre-understandings) to the hermeneutical table. Without prejudice to the importance of genuine openness to the Other advocated earlier, an Asian American interpretive style is nevertheless also convinced that Asian American pre-understandings carry such an immense value that *they have to be brought to bear on the interpretation of classics*. To give concrete examples, the historic injuries suffered by Asian Americans can uncover deep injustices that are still latent in, say, official policies toward minority groups in North America; the common Asian American experience of hybridity, of trying to hold simultaneously very different worlds in dynamic tension, can uncover some scandalously exclusionary elements in certain Christian beliefs about Jesus's uniqueness; many Asian American women's struggles with deeply embedded patriarchal structures in their cultures can be helpful to resist the subtle patriarchy that still exists in North American society or even in church communities; the common Asian American context of interreligiosity can suggest important ways by which different faith traditions can live with each other. These are just a few ways that suggest how Asian American interpretive styles can contribute to the wider society. This is why it is equally important to maintain firmly one's typical Asian American traits in any hermeneutical conversation.

If one surveys the plethora of works produced in the fields of Asian American religions and theology, one can note that many, perhaps the majority of these works, roughly follow the steps for interpretation outlined above. The works or studies produced by Asian American authors are often the result of a hermeneutical conversation. For example, a recent collection of various studies on different topics by Asian/Asian American women is a case in point. Even a cursory review of the different studies in the book shows that many, if not all of them are the results of the kind of hermeneutical conversations described here. Some articles there are: "Ancestral Returns: Reexamining the Horizons of Asian American Religious Practice"—an Asian American hermeneutical conversation with the practice of ancestor veneration; "Violence and Asian American Experience: From Abjection to *Jeong*"—a hermeneutical conversation with the phenomenon of violence, approaching it from the perspective of the Korean notion of *Jeong*; "Bitter Melon, Bitter Delight: Reading Jeremiah, Reading Me"—a hermeneutical conversation with the biblical figure of Jeremiah through Asian American interpretive lenses.

Conclusion

An important phase in the methodology of liberation theology is what it calls *compromiso*, a Spanish word that refers to a commitment to the process of liberation. One can argue that there is also a similar defining commitment in an Asian American hermeneutical style. Different Asian American thinkers refer to it in various ways. It may be described as a kind of renunciation of the logic of the center ("center myopia") and a commitment to view reality from the margins. It can be identified with the act of embracing what can be called "holy insecurity," understood as an act of surrender to "who one is" as an Asian American, to one's marginal state. It can be expressed furthermore as "interstitial integrity," that is, Asian Americans are not incomplete, half-way beings as considered in the recent past. As people living simultaneously in many worlds, they have an integrity all their own. They do not have to depend on the powers-that-be (either in America or in Asia or in other "centers") to affirm them according to monocultural standards or binary modes of thinking. They have every right to affirm their own integrity.

Such a commitment results in fundamental attitudes toward the world that are characteristic of Asian American life: the acceptance, embrace, and commitment to live fully the pain and pathos, the insecurity, the ambiguity of being an Asian American, not merely as an exercise of what can be expressed as *gaman* in Japanese (just gritting one's teeth and stoically putting up with life's sorrows), but as the very *michi* (Japanese, "path") that transforms one's way of understanding life. Of course, the Asian American interpreter cannot forget the promise of interstitial integrity—the exhilaration of being present in multiple worlds at the same time and finding integrity in who one is. Embracing one's Asian American identity also produces in oneself a compassion that can reach out to others. It can bring one the strength and courage to continue the struggle, both to resist the unjust hegemony of the powers-that-be and to achieve a fuller humanity for all, especially those who are subjected to any kind of injustice. The Asian American interpreter who journeys on the hermeneutical *michi* discovers in a deeper way who he or she really is, what his or her identity as an interpreter is—one that is comprised of complexity, fluidity, multiplicity, heterogeneity, and hybridity. And the interpreter can rightly be proud that this Asian American identity is a veritable well of immense richness for the interpretive enterprise.

Julius-Kei Kato

See also: Essays: Bible and Asian Americans

Further Reading

Bevans, Stephen. *Models of Contextual Theology*. Revised and expanded ed. Maryknoll, NY: Orbis Books, 2002.

De La Torre, Miguel, ed. *Handbook of US Theologies of Liberation*. St. Louis: Chalice Press, 2004.

Fernandez, Eleazar, and Fernando Segovia, eds. *A Dream Unfinished: Theological Reflections on America from the Margins*. Maryknoll, NY: Orbis, 2001.

Foskett, Mary, and Jeffrey Kah-Jin Kuan, eds. *Ways of Being, Ways of Reading: Asian*

American Biblical Interpretation. St. Louis: Chalice Press, 2006.

Kato, Julius-Kei. *How Immigrant Christians Interpret Their Religion: Asian American Diasporic Hybridity and Its Implications for Hermeneutics.* Lewiston, NY: Edwin Mellen Press, 2012.

Kwok Pui-lan. *Discovering the Bible in the Non-Biblical World.* Maryknoll, NY: Orbis, 1995.

Kwok Pui-lan. *Postcolonial Imagination and Feminist Theology.* Louisville, KY: Westminister John Knox Press, 2005.

Lee, Jung Young. *Marginality: The Key to Multicultural Theology.* Minneapolis: Fortress Press, 1995.

Liew, Tat-Siong Benny. *What Is Asian American Biblical Hermeneutics?* Honolulu: University of Hawai'i Press, 2009.

Liew, Tat-Siong Benny, and Gale A. Yee, eds. *The Bible in Asian America.* Semeia 90–91. Atlanta: Society of Biblical Literature, 2002.

Matsuoka, Fumitaka. *Out of Silence: Emerging Themes in Asian American Churches.* Cleveland: United Church Press, 1995.

Matsuoka, Fumitaka, and Eleazar S. Fernandez, eds. *Realizing the America of Our Hearts: Theological Voices of Asian Americans.* St. Louis: Chalice Press, 2003.

McCarthy, Joseph. "Hermeneutics." In Donald W. Musser and Joseph L. Price, eds. *Handbook of Christian Theology.* Nashville: Abingdon, 2003, pp. 231–37.

Nakashima Brock, Rita, Jung Ha Kim, Kwok Pui-Lan, and Seung Ai Yang, eds. *Off the Menu: Asian and Asian American Women's Religion and Theology.* Louisville, KY: Westminster John Knox Press, 2007.

Osborne, Grant. *The Hermeneutical Spiral: A Comprehensive Introduction to Biblical Interpretation.* Downers Grove, IL: InterVarsity, 1991.

Phan, Peter. *Christianity with an Asian Face: Asian American Theology in the Making.* Maryknoll, NY: Orbis, 2003.

Segovia, Fernando. "Pedagogical Discourse and Practices in Contemporary Biblical Criticism." In Fernando Segovia and Mary Ann Tolbert, eds. *Teaching the Bible: The Discourses and Politics of Biblical Pedagogy.* Maryknoll, NY: Orbis, 1998, pp. 1–28.

Tan, Jonathan. *Asian American Theologies.* Maryknoll, NY: Orbis Books, 2008.

Thiselton, Anthony C. *Hermeneutics: An Introduction.* Grand Rapids, MI: Eerdmans, 2009.

Tracy, David. *The Analogical Imagination: Christian Theology and the Culture of Pluralism.* New York: Crossroad, 1981.

Tracy, David. *Plurality and Ambiguity: Hermeneutics, Religion, Hope.* Chicago: The University of Chicago Press, 1987.

Yamada, Frank. "Constructing Hybridity and Heterogeneity: Asian American Biblical Interpretation from a Third-Generation Perspective." In Mary Foskett and Jeffrey Kah-Jin Kuan, eds. *Ways of Being, Ways of Reading: Asian American Biblical Interpretation.* St. Louis: Chalice Press, 2006, pp. 164–77.

Islamophobia

The term "Islamophobia" has gained widespread circulation in Western political, public, and academic discourses in recent years. While the concept generally refers to anti-Islamic and anti-Muslim sentiment, there is little consensus regarding its exact definition. It is perhaps more useful to approach Islamophobia as a multiple and diverse phenomenon linked to specific histories and contexts. For example, anti-Muslim sentiment has a long history in Europe, reaching as far back as the Crusades. In the United States, however, the events of 9/11 and its aftermath facilitated

Sauleha Husain, foreground left, joins other students with the Muslim Consultative Network's summer youth program, as they gather on the steps of New York's City Hall, August 14, 2013, to speak out against Islamophobia and profiling by the New York City Police Department. (AP Photo/ Richard Drew)

an abrupt rise in Islamophobic sentiment. Because the perpetrators of 9/11 identified as Muslim, and because the media and political actors emphasized a link between Islam and terrorism, Islam became an object of fear and hostility in a way that it had never been before in the American context.

What Is Islamophobia?

Islamophobia as an analytic concept has been used to describe a broad spectrum of attitudes and behavior, ranging from religious intolerance to antiterrorism. A widely accepted definition from a report entitled "Islamophobia: A Challenge for Us All" outlines eight components that encapsulate Islamophobia. These include the belief that Islam is a monolithic bloc, that it is separate and "other," that it is unresponsive to change, and inferior to the West. Furthermore, Islam is seen as a political ideology that is violent, threatening, and supportive of terrorism. Finally, anti-Muslim hostility is not only seen as normal or natural, but is used to justify discriminatory practices against Muslims. Often, some or all of these assumptions are projected onto all followers of Islam, regardless of the sheer diversity of Muslims across the globe.

Other attempts to understand and define Islamophobia have compared sentiments based on fear, intolerance, and racism. Maussen groups together numerous forms of discourse, speech, and acts as Islamophobic by suggesting that they all stem from "an identical ideological core, which is an 'irrational fear' of Islam." This irrational dread, based on the belief that Muslims are trying to "take over" the Western world, emanates from a long history of Christian-Muslim tension in Europe, as we will see below. Alternatively, others argue that Islamophobia is an intolerance to Muslims' religious practice and behavior. Because their beliefs and customs are often visibly different from the Judeo-Christian mainstream, Muslims are seen as rejecting the norms and values of the larger society. Here, Islamophobia is based on an aversion toward difference, whereby the "Other" is both essentialized and seen as a threat to the purity of the nation or community. More recent approaches to Islamophobia in the West consider it to be a new form of racism linked to a shift in geopolitics, appearing in the public sphere with the rise of Muslim immigration to Europe and intensifying after the September 11 attacks.

The Rise of Islamophobia in the West: Historical and Global Context

Europe. Unique forms of Islamophobia have developed in response to particular historical and social contexts in the West. The case of Europe differs from that of the United States, although Islamophobic perspectives on both sides of the Pacific have certainly influenced one another through media and other channels. While various countries in Europe have had their own iterations of discrimination against Muslims, fear and hatred of Islam on the continent can be traced back through multiple confrontations between the Muslim world and Europe from the Crusades to colonialism. While the Crusades served to establish Islam as the foremost enemy to Christian Europe, Western imperialism garnered anti-Muslim sentiment as a racist tool for colonial endeavors. Muslim cultures were deemed barbaric and primitive in comparison to European civilization, and thus justified and even glorified imperial conquest.

Decolonization and Muslim immigration to the West has spurred new forms of Islamophobic sentiment in the public sphere, raising questions of integration and national sanctity. Muslims in various European countries face discrimination and cultural racism, targeted as a result of their skin color, their non-European descent, and an imagined Islamic culture. This perceived "culture" is seen as monolithic, oppressive, and antithetical to such European ideals as equality, liberty, and democracy. As a result, Islamic cultural symbols such as the headscarf are selectively interpreted to represent a threat to the European way of life, generating moral panic and fear.

United States. Historically, Americans have had little direct contact with Muslim cultures and people until relatively recently. While Muslims from Arab and South Asian countries did migrate to the

United States as early as the 1900s, they were racialized in a way to fit preexisting ethnic or racial categories rather than identified by religious affiliation. For example, prior to the events of 9/11, most Arab immigrants were racially categorized as "white" and were thus ethnically "invisible." Despite the lack of reference to Islam in American public culture, the vilification of Arabs and the Middle East became a common trend in the American media starting in the mid-to-late 1900s. Subtle and sometimes overtly distorted portrayals of Arab villains pitted against the often white American protagonist served to validate everything from domestic racial inequality to international foreign policy and war. This racist portrayal of a minority group allowed for the creation of a convenient image of the "Other" against which a dominant American self was defined. Fear of the "Other," whether it be African Americans, Communists, or Asians, is tied to a long history of racism and racialization in the United States, whereby aspects of social personhood (such as class, ethnicity, and religion) are essentialized and naturalized.

Islamophobia and Global Politics. Anti-Arab and anti-Asian xenophobia in the West gradually transitioned to anti-Muslim sentiment in response to changes in identity politics linked to globalization. New global hegemonies supported by powerful media networks asserted forms of racism that demonized Muslims and their religion. This transition was reflected in the way people responded to global media coverage of such events as the Rushdie affair, the Iran hostage crisis, the Oklahoma City bombing, and the first Gulf War. Rather than considering the historical and political circumstances around which these major events occurred, politicians and the media invoked cultural difference, demonizing and blaming Islam. For example, coverage of the Rushdie affair, in which Muslims protested the publication of a book by Salman Rushdie that demeaned an Islamic holy figure, focused on angry Muslim mobs and sweeping religious decrees. In doing so, the Western public was led to believe that all Muslims were "irrational" fanatics that responded to provocation in violent ways. Similarly, during the Iran hostage crisis and the first Gulf War, the figure of the Muslim fundamentalist leader was depicted as an enemy and a threat, justifying military intervention and resulting in the belief that Islam was the root cause of global society's ills. Thus, for many Americans, "Islam became synonymous with the Middle East, Muslim men with violence, and Muslim women with oppression." Islamophobic sentiment flourished through the conflation of histories, politics, and societies, and the essentialization of Islam as a "culture" considered antithetical to the West.

Post-9/11 Islamophobia in the United States

It was the events and aftermath of 9/11 that took the growing suspicions and fears that many Americans had developed against Islam to a new level. Anti-Muslim sentiment prior to 9/11 ranged from general distaste and ignorance to intolerance. However, September 11 marked a dramatic shift in the social and political landscape of the

United States. In the days and weeks following, the U.S. government's response and extensive media coverage produced and circulated narratives of the tragedy as well as images and stereotypes of the men responsible for the attack. In the face of the panic and uncertainly that resulted, discourses emerged that invoked oppositions between "us" (the freedom-loving, civilized West) and "them" (the barbaric, violent followers of Islam). Drawing on the notion of a "clash of civilizations," political pundits and the media marked an insurmountable divide between Islamic culture and "Western civilization." No longer was the feared "Other" defined primarily based on racial or ethnic background, but rather through a racialized religious identity that constructed "the Muslim as terrorist." Mainstream American media repeatedly showcased images of angry, bearded men in turbans laced with guns and bombs. The term "Islamic" was used to characterize "terrorism" such that the two became interlinked in the mind of the public, and Islamic culture was not only deemed barbaric and primitive but also immediately threatening to the West.

This form of racism based on cultural difference served three agendas. First, it justified the declaration of a war on terror that led to aggressive and militaristic foreign policy in the Middle East and later South Asia. Second, in labeling Islamic civilization as inferior, it allowed for attempts to understand the culture and religion of the "Other" in a way that conveniently left out politics, history, and the diversity of Muslim identities. Thus, difference was both created and erased as all Muslims were deemed the same. Finally, such racialization allowed for the creation of a kind of second state under the auspices of the U.S. federal government— the homeland security state. Under this regime, measures were put into place that allowed for the establishment of Guantanamo, extraordinary rendition, the authorization of domestic spying, and very explicit forms of racial profiling, challenging the very essence of liberal democracy and human and civil rights. The main target of the U.S. security state was the Muslim population. Legislation in the name of homeland security exacerbated Islamophobia, with security discourses such as "If you see something, say something" encouraging a witch hunt against "suspicious-looking" Muslims. Such anti-Muslim sentiment was coupled with a rise in American patriotism, reminding some of the mutual crafting of ethnic and American identity in the shadow of the internment of Japanese Americans during World War II.

Post-9/11 security discourses and the right-wing political agenda advocated suspicion and hatred of Muslims and Islam. As a result, Muslims in the United States experienced multiple levels of discrimination—as immigrants, as people of color, as non-Christians, and as potential suspects. In their day-to-day lives, Muslims watched as their religion was constantly associated with terrorism and violence in the media. Mainstream news channels such as Fox News broadcast images of Palestinian children allegedly dancing "in celebration" of the attacks on America, as well as images of "Muslims" around the world burning American flags and chanting anti-American slogans. Political cartoons and the print media, both liberal and conservative, increasingly demonized and de-meaned Islam. Hollywood and television, now more than ever, depicted themes where Muslim characters were portrayed as enemies of the United States. Further-more, mutually reinforcing public images and policies motivated hate crimes against Muslims and people that "looked like" Muslims. Muslim women wearing head-scarves had them pulled off, a Sikh man donning a turban was mistaken for a Muslim and murdered, and *mosques* were desecrated. In an attempt to proactively challenge the rise in Islamophobia in America, Muslim organizations and groups such as Islamophobia Watch have begun to document and report instances of anti-Muslim bigotry and anti-Islamic ideology.

Islamophobia Today

Over a decade after the 9/11 attacks, Mus-lims continue to be perceived as the ulti-mate alter to being American, facing discrimination and racism. The ongoing misrepresentation of Islam in the media of-fers insight into American national identity and the strategic ways in which images of the "Other" are used for political gains. A central aspect of American cultural poli-tics, Islamophobia has given rise to such recent conflicts as the Ground Zero *mosque* controversy, the Qur'an-burning debacle in 2010, and the coining of the phrase "Sharia creep" to denote growing fears of Islamic law "creeping" its way into American life. One of the effects of such mediated inci-dences is that Muslim American identities and forms of belonging are reduced to "a few reactionary cultural practices," leaving

them misunderstood and marginalized. As Muslims tackle these challenges, they are engaging in various debates and discourses in an attempt to take a stand against Islam-ophobia and its various iterations in the West.

Rabia Kamal

See also: Essays: Muslims; Religion, Race, and Orientalism; *Entries:* Yee, James J.

Further Reading

Agamben, Giorgio. *State of Exception.* Trans-lated by K. Attell. Chicago: University of Chicago Press, 2005.

Esposito, John L., and Ibrahim Kalin. *Islamo-phobia: The Challenge of Pluralism in the 21st Century.* New York: Oxford University Press, 2011.

Gottschalk, Peter, and Gabriel Greenberg. *Is-lam: Making Muslims the Enemy.* Lanham, MD: Rowman & Littlefield, 2008.

Jamal, Amanay, and Nadine Naber, eds. *Race and Arab Americans Before and After 9/11: From Invisible Citizens to Visible Subjects.* Syracuse, NY: Syracuse University Press, 2008.

Kalkan, Kerem O., Geoffrey C. Layman, and Eric M. Uslaner. "'Bands of Others'? Atti-tudes toward Muslims in Contemporary American Society." *The Journal of Politics* 71, no. 3 (2009): 1–16.

Kamal, Rabia. "Reimagining Islam: Muslim Cultural Citizenship in the Post-9/11 Amer-ican Public Sphere." Dissertation, Univer-sity of Pennsylvania, 2012. Ann Arbor: ProQuest/UMI.

Kaplan, Jeffrey. "Islamophobia in America? September 11 and Islamophobic Hate Crime." *Terrorism and Political Violence* 18, no. 1 (2006): 1–33.

Poynting, Scott, and George Morgan. *Global Islamophobia: Muslims and Moral Panic in the West.* Farnham, UK: Ashgate, 2013.

Omi, Michael, and Howard Winant. *Racial Formation in the United States: From the 1960s to the 1990s*. New York: Routledge, 1994.

Runnymede Trust. "Islamophobia: A Challenge for Us All." London: Runnymede Trust, Commission on British Muslims and Islamophobia, 1997.

Said, Edward W. *Covering Islam: How the Media and the Experts Determine How We See the Rest of the World*. New York: Vintage, 1997.

Salaita, Steven G. "Beyond Orientalism and Islamophobia: 9/11, Anti-Arab Racism, and the Mythos of National Pride." *The New Centennial Review* 6, no. 2 (2006): 245–66.

Sheehi, Stephen. *Islamophobia: The Ideological Campaign against Muslims*. Gardena, CA: SCB Distributors, 2011.

Werbner, Pnina. "Islamophobia: Incitement to Religious Hatred: Legislating for a New Fear?" *Anthropology Today* 21, no. 1 (2005): 5–9.

Jews

In the United States, Jews are commonly thought, both by Jews and non-Jews, to be individuals of Eastern European or Central European (Ashkenazic) descent. This has resulted in a limited understanding of what constitutes Jewish food, music, language, and even forms of Jewish worship and synagogue design. In fact, Jews in America, as well as the world, have always been diverse, with, for example, the nation's first Jews being of Sephardic origin, that is, descendants of Spanish and Portuguese Jews who were forced to flee the Iberian Peninsula with the reign of Queen Isabella and King Ferdinand in 1492. This article introduces the Asian American Jewish population, a community that is commonly overlooked both by Jewish American scholars and by Asian American scholars.

History

Asian American Jews are defined in this essay as American Jews who have origins in East, South, or Southeast Asia. Migration and diaspora play a key role in the history of the Jews. Both symbolically and literally, its origins are in two countries and four communities. These are the Chinese Jews and in India, the Cochin Jews, Bene Israel, and Baghdadi Jews. (Note:

Rabbi Angela Buchdahl, Senior Rabbi of Central Synagogue, the 13th senior rabbi in its history since 1839, and the first woman to lead the congregation, left, and U.S. President Barack Obama following his remarks at the second of two Hanukkah receptions in the Grand Foyer of the White House, December 17, 2014, in Washington, D.C. (Ron Sachs-Pool/Getty Images)

Jewish scholars often refer to Jews with Middle Eastern and Central Asian origin, except for Iran, as "Oriental Jews" or "Mizrahi [Eastern] Jews," but they are not included in this discussion.)

Chinese Jews. Jews have lived in China for at least 1,000 years. Most researchers believe the community resulted from Jewish merchants from Persia (present-day Iran) who traveled along the Silk Road to China for business. The Persian Jews (whose community had existed since 600 BCE.) first arrived by the eighth century CE, settled, and became integrated into the native Chinese population while retaining and passing along to subsequent generations their traditions and faith. These were peoples that very clearly looked Chinese and yet practiced Judaism. The most well-known of these Chinese Jewish communities were the Jews of Kaifeng. Kaifeng in central China served as the country's capital during the Song dynasty (960–1127 CE). Other Chinese Jewish communities existed in Hangzhou, Ningbo, Yangzhou, Ningxia, and elsewhere. In general, Chinese Jews were not discriminated against. Indeed, they were allowed to take the rigorous imperial exams whose content was based on the Chinese classics, and the passage of which would result in becoming one of the country's few mandarins and appointment to a much desired position in the civil service. Many Chinese Jews successfully passed these wholly merit-based exams, thus entering the elite of society, and received appointments to offices throughout the country.

Under the rule of Genghis Khan during the Yuan Dynasty (1271–1368 CE), however, Jews could not keep *kashruth* nor could Muslims honor *halal*, and circumcision was forbidden. Moreover, during the following Ming Dynasty (1368–1644), an emperor assigned the Jews seven surnames to use by which they are still identifiable today—Ai, Shi, Gao, Jin, Li, Zhang, and Zhao. These are the Sinification of the seven Jewish clan names— Ezra, Shimon, Cohen, Gilbert, Levy, Joshua, and Jonathan.

Despite the many political changes and wars, the Kaifeng Jews, in particular, were well supported by officials. The community was located in a city that was not only the country's capital but also an economic and cultural center of international renown. The community received special permission to build a synagogue in 1163 and to rebuild it after the floods of the nearby Yellow River in 1421, 1461, 1489, and 1642. Ming emperor Chen Zu's brother sponsored the first reconstruction and donated imperial funds. Among the community documents extant from the Kaifeng community are a Memorial Book with the names, written in both Mandarin and Hebrew, of the more than 1,000 community members who died between ca. 1400 CE and 1670 CE. The Kaifeng community continued into the early 20th century despite additional floods and the Taiping Rebellion (1850–1854), under which they greatly suffered and had to disperse. At its height, the Kaifeng Jewish community had numbered 6,000.

By the early 20th century, the Kaifeng community had almost completely assimilated, but they continued to practice different burial practices than the broader population and to retain their own burial ground. They also continued to follow the dietary laws of not eating pork or shellfish, and in the case of some men, wearing a blue *kippah* (skullcap). With the political opening of China in 1980, the liberalization of laws on religion, tourism from Western Jews, and information about the community written in Mandarin by native scholars, potential descendants of Chinese Jews have eagerly explored their roots. Some have made *aliyah* after undergoing conversion, deemed necessary because Jewish identity in China was passed down via the patrilineal line.

Jews in India. Jews have been present in India for thousands of years and in distinct communities. The oldest community was the Cochin Jews, located on the Malabar Coast in southwest India, which formed and grew as a result of three migrations. First was the arrival of traders from Judea in 562 BCE in Cochin (Kochi), Kerala; second was an influx of refugees as with the destruction of the Second Temple in 70 CE; and finally, the arrival at the end of the 15th century of Sephardi Jews who fled the Iberian Peninsula. These last arriving Jews were known as the Paradesi Jews and did not fully integrate with the Cochin Jews. Visually, the Cochin Jews were not distinct from other Indians. They also benefited greatly from a supportive relationship with India's rulers. Laws were codified in 1065 CE that granted the community special privileges including permission to live freely, own synagogues, and own land without any restrictions. In the eighth century, a Jewish merchant was given the rank of prince of the Jews of Cochin and given the authority of a principality. At present

less than 100 remain while approximately 4,000 reside in Israel.

The Bene Israel community is also very old. There are several theories about its origins with some claiming that they are one of the 10 "lost" tribes of Israel. Others believe that their community originated from those who escaped by sea from Israel during the reign of Antiochus Epiphanes in 175 CE. During their voyage, it is believed, the Bene Israel ancestors were shipwrecked and washed ashore on the Konkan coast, south of Bombay. The survivors were assisted by locals and they settled in the villages of Konkan, adopting Hindu first names that corresponded to their Biblical names and as local practice adopting surnames that were the village name appended by "kar."

Many Bene Israel became oil pressers and they were known as Shanwar Telis or Shabbat-observing oilmen. They adopted the local language and soon became physically indistinguishable from the surrounding villagers but continued to observe Shabbat and most festivals, circumcise their sons, perform offerings outlined in the Torah, and recite the Shema. There was a religious revival as early as 1000 CE or as late as 1800 CE with the arrival of Cochin Jews, who trained the community leadership and served as cantors, teachers, and ritual slaughterers. The community was loyal to the British colonizers, with some Bene Israel serving in high ranks of the colonial forces in the 19th century, and by the late 19th century community members who had moved to Bombay were regularly serving in white-collar jobs, eventually achieving prominent posts as doctors, lawyers, and government officials. By the 20th century, members of the community had established synagogues in Poona, Ahmedabad, and New Delhi. At its height in 1948, the Bene Israel population totaled 20,000. Currently there are less than 5,000 Bene Israel. Many made *aliyah* post-independence such that there are more than 60,000 Bene Israel living in Israel, including both those who immigrated and their Israeli-born children.

Finally, there is the community of Baghdadi Jews. Despite their name, these Jews have origins not only in Iraq, but also Iran, Afghanistan, Syria, and Yemen. These were thus Mizrahi Jews who were moving to India, fleeing persecution and seeking opportunities. The first groups emigrated to Surat (Gujarat) in 1730. There the community established a synagogue, but eventually most moved to Bombay, where community members become prominent traders, society members, and philanthropists. Some moved elsewhere in India, including Calcutta, and became prominent in the jute and tea trades. Prominent families include the Sassoons, whose merchant empire eventually spread throughout Asia. At its height the community numbered 7,000, but fewer than 50 exist today. Despite the small numbers of Indian Jews, the country is served by a number of clergy from the Orthodox to Progressive (Reform) movements.

Asian American Jews: Contemporary Experience

There is as yet no comprehensive study of Asian American Jews, but a review of existing literature as well as interviews and communication directly with many of these Jews provides a preliminary picture. Currently, the Asian American Jewish population is small, at approximately 0.6 percent (40,884) of the total Jewish population, and relatively young, with most in the ages of infancy to forties. It is diverse and composed of Asians who were adopted by Jewish American parents, children of relationships between Asians or Asian Americans and Jewish Americans, Asian Americans who have converted to Judaism, and a very small number of Indian Jews who have immigrated to the United States. The population is expected to grow as overseas adoption, mixed-race marriage, and conversion continue, and the offspring of today's Asian American Jews attain childbearing age.

The most common Asian American Jewish ethnicity is Chinese. Others are Korean, Vietnamese, Indian, and otherwise Asian. Conversion for Asian Americans is no different than for any individual born outside the community and usually involves at least a period of study of Jewish rituals, traditions, and history; study of Hebrew; questioning by a *bet din* (rabbinic court); and in Orthodox, Conservative, and many Reform communities, submersion in the *mikveh* (ritual bath). While it is not necessarily a requirement depending on the denomination of their synagogue, many adoptive parents will submerge their adoptive child in the *mikveh* to forestall any problems about the child's Jewishness in the future.

Most young Asian American Jews, following the adherence of their parents, are spread among different religious denominations, including Reform, Conservative, and Orthodox, as well as those who express their Jewishness primarily in a non-religious, cultural manner. As such there is a range of observance of the *mitzvoth* (commandments) in the Torah, including the observation of *kashruth*, the dietary laws, as well as those Jews who count themselves as secular. Membership in the Reform community seems most common among Asian American Jews and their families, not surprisingly considering it was the first denomination to wholeheartedly embrace diversity, racial, ethnic, and otherwise, but there is definitely membership in synagogues of the other, more observant, denominations. Like other young Jews, Asian American Jews receive a range of Jewish education from no formal training, to religious and Hebrew school, to Jewish day schools. Many young Asian American Jews have had a *bar* or *bat mitzvah,* some have attended Jewish summer camp, and some have traveled to Israel.

Asian American Jews are already starting to reach positions of religious leadership, including Rabbi Cantor Andrea Warnick Buchdahl, who serves a Reform synagogue in New York City and is the daughter of a Korean mother and an Ashkenazi Jewish father, and Rabbi Jaqueline Mates-Muchin, who serves a Reform synagogue in the San Francisco Bay Area. Rabbi Mates-Muchin is the daughter of a Cantonese–Jewish American physician who is an authorized *mohelet* (performer of religious circumcisions) who converted to Judaism and an Ashkenazi Jewish father.

The existence of the Asian American Jewish population was made possible only through the passage of civil rights–related laws and policies during the 1950s and 1960s. Specifically, the McCarran-Walter Act of 1952 overturned race as the basis for determining eligibility for citizenship (race-based eligibility determination had only been applied to Asians, not Europeans). Especially important was the passage of the Immigration Act of 1965 that eliminated immigration quotas by ethnicity and nationality. These previous quotas were significantly lower for Asian than for European countries, such that each Asian country only had about 100 spaces allotted for immigration per year. The new quotas were based on familial relationships and work skills that the potential immigrant could bring to the United States. Thanks to these new laws many more Asians successfully immigrated to America, and Asian Americans referred by the government as "aliens ineligible for citizenship," including thousands of Japanese Americans, finally obtained the rights they had long deserved to be citizens.

The final civil rights action that was vital to the creation of the Asian American Jewish population was the unanimous decision in 1967 by the U.S. Supreme Court in *Loving vs. Virginia,* which declared that all interracial marriage bans were unconstitutional. While antimiscegenation laws are commonly thought to have only applied to black-white relationships, in fact in many states they had also long applied to Asian-white relationships and other nonwhite-white relationships as well. At the time of the court decision, four states, Missouri, Georgia, South Carolina, and Texas, considered Asian-white relationships to be a felony. Not many years before the decision, California, Oregon, and eight other states still prohibited Asian-white relationships. The California law had been enforced for some 100 years.

The changes in immigration and naturalization laws made it possible to have significantly more non-Jewish Asians immigrate to the United States and opened the doors to Indian Jews. These new immigrants increased the likelihood that there would be interactions with Jews of European descent, for example at work, and the possible establishment of lifelong relationships, which thanks to the 1967 Supreme Court decision was not something that would have to be carefully hidden at all times, lest one receive a punishment that had immediate as well as lifetime negative repercussions. In addition, the larger numbers of non-Jewish Asian immigrants increased the likelihood that they or some of their children, in the course of growing up in America, might become interested in the Jewish religion and explore conversion. Conversion is commonly thought of as primarily in relation to marriage or long-term partnership, but some Asian American Jews have converted because of spiritual and community reasons not related to any relationship.

Finally, the increase in adoption from Asia particularly from the 1970s onward has been a significant contributor to the increase in Asian American Jews. While it was previously common for American Jews to look toward Russia and the former Soviet republics after deciding on international adoption, concerns about health problems among prospective adoptees, including fetal alcohol syndrome, led prospective parents to look elsewhere. In total, the number of children adopted by Ameri-

cans from Asia is very large, with data from the U.S. State Department revealing that more than 92,000 children were adopted from South Korea between 1948 and 2000 and a current estimate of Korean American adoptees between 110,000 and 150,000 and ranging in age from infancy to their fifties. Statistics from 1989–2008 reveal that China, which began permitting adoption in the early 1990s, is the birthplace of many American adoptees, at over 66,000 total and nearly 6,000 per year. South Korea continued to be an important source at more than 34,000 in total and more than 1,000 per year. Vietnam sent some babies abroad, with more than 6,000 total and more than 750 per year. These numbers are significantly impacted by societal conflict, instability, and poverty.

Jewish parents from all backgrounds are adopting Asian children. They include heterosexual couples who are unable to have biological children, lesbian or gay couples, straight or gay singles, or couples of any background who believe that becoming a parent through international adoption best fits their values. In Asia, they found generally healthy children who were in orphanages because of familial poverty or the country's one-child policy, which led to the abandonment of otherwise healthy baby girls.

While the pathway to Judaism and the Jewish community of Asian American Jews is diverse, once officially part of the community, some experiences are shared by all. Unlike other religions, Jewishness is both a faith and an ethnicity. Once one is accepted into the community one is not required to believe in God, but to join the community, one must undergo a religious conversion. The ethnic definition of Jewishness can present a conflict when Asian American Jews encounter those who are not fully knowledgeable about the Jewish experience, including the diverse communities in history.

Because of the stereotype that all Jews are of Ashkenazi descent and look "white," it is not uncommon for adult Asian American Jews, even in cosmopolitan areas, to enter Jewish institutions and be assumed to not be part of the community because they "don't look Jewish," while a white non-Jewish companion is assumed to be Jewish. For adopted Asian American Jews and those born to Asian and European Jewish parents, this is usually not significant during childhood, because their parents and the family are known to the community. However, some youths have encountered some questions when first attending Jewish events or institutions, such as Jewish camp or Jewish day school, on their own.

The period after leaving home, usually for college, and into early adulthood is usually challenging. Many begin or continue to truly engage with all of their identities, religious and ethnic. How do they balance their Asian and Jewish identities? What does it mean for them personally to be Asian and Jewish? Can one balance these identities? Do they feel welcomed by the Jewish communities? How about by Asian Americans? Some Jews have found that despite their strong Jewish faith, practice, and knowledge, they were treated as an outsider by synagogues they were exploring.

While their children were young, many parents, especially of Asian American Jews by adoption, made extra effort to expose them to their Asian culture, seeking to avoid the unfortunate experiences of the first Korean American adoptees. This included enrolling them in language and culture schools, or in some cases bilingual day schools. For interracial children of Asian and European Jewish couples, this was usually easier as they had at least one parent, and possibly grandparents and other extended family who could directly share Asian traditions and culture, and at least one parent and possibly extended family who could share Jewish rituals and cultures. Once they reached adulthood, it was up to these Asian American Jews themselves to determine how and the extent to which they fit into the Asian American and, largely, Ashkenazi Jewish communities.

The coming years will be important ones in determining whether Asian American Jews will desire to remain in the community after entering adulthood. Important steps have been taken by the Jewish community to help them in their questioning. It is commendable that Reform Judaism and individual Reform synagogues have embraced diversity, publishing and exhibiting photos and personal experiences of Asian American Jews and integrating the many diverse Jewish communities extant in history into their religious school curriculum. New organizations have also been created to facilitate interaction between Jews of color including Asian Americans, African Americans, and Hispanics. These actions are important because it shows Asian American Jews that they are not alone, and that there have been others who looked like them in history. However, considerably more will have to be done to ensure the continuity and growth of the Asian American Jewish community in the long term. More Jewish denominations, institutions, and individuals need to truly embrace the racial and ethnic diversity of the Jewish community, a diversity that has truly existed for thousands of years.

Patricia Y. C. E. Lin

Further Reading

Ehrlich, M. Avrum, ed. *The Jewish-Chinese Nexus: A Meeting of Civilizations*. London: Routledge, 2008.

Hunter, Manfred, ed. *Between Mumbai and Manila: Judaism in Asia since the Founding of the State of Israel.* Proceedings of the International Conference, held at the Department of Comparative Religion of the University of Bonn, May 30 to June 1, 2012. Goettingen, Germany: Vandenhoeck & Ruprecht, 2013.

Jen, Gish. *Mona in the Promised Land*. New York: Alfred A. Knopf, 1996.

Kim, Helen K., and Noah S. Leavitt. "The Newest Jews? Understanding Jewish American and Asian American Marriages." *Contemporary Jewry* 32 (2012): 135–66.

LGBT Asian Americans and Christianity

Lesbian, gay, bisexual, and transgender (LGBT) Asian American Christians experience many challenges in terms of integrating their sexualities and gender identities with their racial/ethnic identities and their religious identities. Since at least the late 1960s, LGBT Asian American Christians have been telling their stories of multiple marginalization within different communities. Since at least the early 2000s, they have founded organizations to support their existence at the intersections of queerness, race, and religion.

LGBT Asian American Christians often experience a profound sense of metaphorical homelessness—that is, not belonging fully to the communities of which they are a part—as well as a deep alienation from their bodies. This is because many LGBT Asian American Christians experience racism from the LGBT community, queerphobia from the Asian American community, and both racism and queerphobia from their churches and other communities of faith.

Not surprisingly, LGBT Asian American Christians have sought to heal these wounds by telling their stories and by reclaiming their spiritual traditions, rituals, and spaces. For example, many of them have experienced a greater sense of wholeness and community through their involvement with organizations such as Queer Asian Spirit and the Network on Religion and Justice for Asian American LGBTQ People. These organizations not only support the spiritual growth of LGBT Asian American Christians, but they also advocate for justice and social change within the broader LGBT, Asian American, and Christian communities.

LGBT Asian American Christian Voices

LGBT Asian American Christians have been telling their stories of multiple marginalization since at least the late 1960s. For example, Lloyd Wake, a Japanese American Methodist minister and LGBT ally, recalls meeting with a number of LGBT Asian

Rev. Dr. Jonipher Kupono Kwong of the First Unitarian Church of Honolulu stands along several others of Hawai'i's clergy and speaks to attendees at an All You Need is Love rally at the Hawai'i State Capitol in Honolulu, Hawai'i, October 27, 2013. Hawai'i, which had a pioneering role in the acceptance of same-sex matrimony in the United States two decades ago, could become the 15th state to extend marriage rights to gay couples when state lawmakers met for a special session in 2013. (Marco Garcia/Reuters/Corbis)

American couples—mostly lesbian Filipina Americans—after he joined the staff of Glide Memorial Church in San Francisco in 1967. Wake conducted "covenant friendship" ceremonies for such couples after they told him about their experiences of being excluded from their racial/ethnic and religious communities of origin.

It was not until the 1990s, however, that LGBT Asian Americans started to document their experiences more widely. A number of secular anthologies—including *Asian American Sexualities: Dimensions of the Gay and Lesbian Experience* (Leong, 1996); *Q&A: Queer in Asian America* (Eng

and Hom, 1998); and *Embodying Asian/ American Sexualities* (Masequesmay and Metzger, 2009)—have been published since the mid-1990s about the experiences of LGBT Asian Americans at the intersections of queerness and race. With the exception of a handful of essays, however (Lim, 1998; Shrake, 2009), these works have been largely silent about the lives and spiritual experiences of LGBT Asian American Christians.

An important event for the LGBT Asian American Christian movement occurred in 1993 when Hong K. Tan, a gay MCC minister of Chinese descent from the United

Kingdom, was elected an elder of the Metropolitan Community Churches (MCC), an LGBT-positive Christian denomination. Following his election, Tan helped to develop networks of LGBT Asian American Christians and allies within the United States. One such network was the MCC API Institute, which met in Los Angeles in 1999 and in Toronto in 2001. As a result of these networks, greater numbers of LGBT Asian American Christians began telling their stories.

During the late 1990s, a number of LGBT Asian American Christians began writing theologically about the joys and challenges of integrating their sexualities and gender identities with their racial/ethnic identities and religious identities. For example, Eric H. F. Law, a gay Chinese American Episcopal priest, wrote an essay, "A Spirituality of Creative Marginality" (1997), in which he compared the tension between his sexuality and his racial/ethnic identity to the traditional Christian theological understanding of the two natures (that is, human and divine) of Jesus Christ. Law's essay was one of the earliest christological reflections on the LGBT Asian American experience.

Leng Lim, also a gay Chinese American Episcopal priest, wrote in his essay "The Bible Tells Me to Hate Myself" (2002) about how the fundamentalist biblical theologies of many Asian American ministers are deeply hurtful to LGBT Asian American Christians. Lim noted that many LGBT Asian American Christians, including students and young adults, have internalized a message of self-hate that is antithetical to the loving principles of Christianity.

Beginning in 2004, during the aftermath of the issuance of same-sex marriage licenses by the city of San Francisco, many LGBT Asian American Christians began to "come out" about their stories. These individuals sought to counter the vocal and public opposition by conservative Asian American churches to the marriage equality movement. In 2007, the documentary film *In God's House: Asian American Lesbian and Gay Families in the Church* was released. The film featured stories of LGBT Asian American Christians, including Oneida Chi, who was a lesbian Chinese American lay leader with the GRACE community, a faith-sharing group for LGBT Asian American Christians and their allies.

A key event for LGBT Asian American Christian scholarship occurred in 2011 with the publication of a special issue of the journal *Theology and Sexuality* on queer Asian theologies. In that issue, six Asian and Asian American queer theologians and scholars of religion—Michael Sepidoza Campos, Patrick S. Cheng, Min-Ah Cho, Joseph N. Goh, Gina Masequesmay, and Su Yon Pak—contributed articles on the experiences of queer Asian people of faith, including LGBT people of Chinese, Filipino, Japanese, Korean, Malaysian, and Vietnamese descent.

Also in 2013, Patrick S. Cheng, a gay Chinese American theologian and professor at the Episcopal Divinity School in Cambridge, Massachusetts, published a genealogy of queer Asian theologies in his book *Rainbow Theology: Bridging Race, Sexuality, and Spirit* (2013). In that book, Cheng argued that writings by LGBT Asian American Christians share certain themes relating to multiplicity, middle spaces, and mediation. Specifically, Cheng noted a number of common themes in such writings, including experiences of exclusion by Asian American churches, racism within the LGBT community, and concerns for transnational and cross-border issues.

LGBT Asian American Christian Organizations

In addition to voicing and writing about their experiences, LGBT Asian American Christians have founded a number of organizations since the early 2000s to network with—and to provide pastoral care to—one another, to facilitate spiritual growth, and to advocate for greater acceptance within the broader LGBT, Asian American, and Christian communities. One such organization is Queer Asian Spirit (QAS). QAS was originally founded in 2000 as a local email listserv by Patrick S. Cheng and Susie Chin, a bisexual Chinese American lay leader with MCC. QAS now has an international online presence, including a website with resources for queer Asian people of faith, as well as an online interfaith magazine, the *QAS E-Zine*, which is published twice a year. The *QAS E-Zine* is edited by Joseph N. Goh, a queer-gay Malaysian theologian and ordained minister with the North American Catholic Ecumenical Church, and it features voices of queer Asian persons of faith from around the world.

Another such organization is GRACE, a faith-sharing group for LGBT Asian American Christians and allies that was founded in April 2000. GRACE was founded several months after a groundbreaking workshop, "Opening the Gates of Heaven: Asian Pacific Gay and Lesbian Christians and Our Churches," was held in October 1999. The workshop was sponsored by the Pacific Asian Center for Theology and Strategies (PACTS) of the Graduate Theological Union in Berkeley, California. Both PACTS and a successor organization, the PANA Institute, played important behind-the-scenes roles in terms of supporting the ministry of LGBT Asian American Christians in the 2000s.

The Asian Pacific Islander Roundtable (API Roundtable) at the Center for Lesbian and Gay Studies in Religion and Ministry in Berkeley, California, is another resource for LGBT Asian American Christians. Originally convened in 2003 by Kyle Miura, a gay Japanese American graduate of the Pacific School of Religion, the API Roundtable sponsors ecumenical and interfaith programs for queer Asian people of faith and their allies. Coordinators of the API Roundtable have included Elizabeth Leung, a lesbian Chinese American minister with the United Church of Christ, and Jess Delegencia, a gay Filipino American minister and educator.

The Network on Religion and Justice for API LGBTQ People (NRJ) was founded in 2005 to provide respect and justice for LGBT Asian Americans within various communities of faith. NRJ currently seeks to create safe spaces for LGBT Asian American Christians, to educate and support Asian American church communities that wish to become open and affirming of LGBT people, and to develop resources for queer Asian communities of faith. In

2007, NRJ produced *In God's House*, the documentary film about LGBT Asian American Christians. Leaders of NRJ have included Elizabeth Leung; Deborah Lee, an LGBT ally and Chinese American minister with the United Church of Christ; Sharon Hwang Colligan, a bisexual and biracial social activist of Chinese and Polish descent; and Lauren Quock, a queer Chinese American artist and educator.

The Emerging Queer Asian Pacific Islander Religion Scholars organization (EQARS) was founded in 2009 to support the religious studies and theological scholarship of queer Asian people of faith, including LGBT Asian American Christians. EQARS consists of queer Asian and allied scholars from around the world, including Michael Sepidoza Campos, Patrick S. Cheng, Joseph N. Goh, Elizabeth Leung, Hugo Córdova Quero, Miak Siew, Yuenmei Wong, Lai-shan Yip, and Junehee Yoon. Its members meet virtually via Skype to discuss issues of concern.

LGBT Asian American Christians have been involved with ministries not just in the United States, but also around the world. Boon Lin Ngeo, a gay Malaysian American minister with MCC, has been involved with ministries to LGBT Christians in Asia, including China and Malaysia. In the summer of 2013, Ngeo and Patrick S. Cheng were keynote speakers at the Amplify conference in Hong Kong, a gathering of over 300 LGBT Asian Christians from across Asia. Another leader with respect to queer Asian global ministries is Stedney Phillips, a lesbian Asian American MCC minster and former chair of the MCC Asia Pacific Initiative.

Finally, individual LGBT Asian American Christians have played an important role in seeking equality for LGBT people with respect to civil rights. Jonipher Kwong, a gay Chinese American minister with the Unitarian Universalist Association, was the founding director of API Equality-LA. Kwong formed a faith committee within that organization to facilitate the dialogue between LGBT and Asian American communities of faith on issues of marriage equality. In 2013, Kwong played a leading role in advocating for marriage equality in Hawai'i. Following the passage of such legislation, Kwong and his husband were the first same-sex couple to be married in that state.

The QAS, API Roundtable, and NRJ websites contain additional information about LGBT Asian American Christian leaders and allies, including individuals who were not mentioned in this essay. Each of those websites contains directories of such individuals as well as historical materials about the LGBT Asian American Christian movement.

Patrick S. Cheng

See also: Essays: Gender and Sexuality; *Entries:* Wake, Lloyd K.

Further Reading

Asian Pacific Islander Roundtable, Center for Lesbian and Gay Studies in Religion and Ministry Website. http://www.clgs.org/programs/api_roundtable. Accessed July 7, 2014.

Cheng, Patrick S. *Rainbow Theology: Bridging Race, Sexuality, and Spirit.* New York: Seabury Books, 2013.

Cheng, Patrick S. "Reclaiming Our Traditions, Rituals, and Spaces: Spirituality and the

Queer Asian Pacific American Experience." *Spiritus* 6, no. 2 (Fall 2006): 234–40.

Emerging Queer API Scholars Website. http://www.eqars.org. Accessed July 7, 2014.

Eng, David L., and Alice Y. Hom, eds. *Q&A: Queer in Asian America*. Philadelphia: Temple University Press, 1998.

GRACE Website. http://www.gayasianchristians.org. Accessed July 7, 2014.

In God's House: Asian American Lesbian and Gay Families in the Church (2007). Film. http://www.ingodshouse.com/. Accessed July 7, 2014.

Law, Eric H. F. "A Spirituality of Creative Marginality." In Gary David Comstock and Susan E. Henking, eds. *Que(e)rying Religion: A Critical Anthology*. New York: Continuum, 1997, pp. 343–46.

Leong, Russell. *Asian American Sexualities: Dimensions of the Gay and Lesbian Experience*. New York: Routledge, 1996.

Lim, You-Leng Leroy. "'The Bible Tells Me to Hate Myself': The Crisis in Asian American Spiritual Leadership." *Semeia* 90–91 (2002): 315–22.

Lim, You-Leng Leroy. "Webs of Betrayal, Webs of Blessings." In David L. Eng and Alice Y. Hom, eds. *Q&A: Queer in Asian America*. Philadelphia: Temple University Press, 1998, pp. 323–34.

Masequesmay, Gina, and Sean Metzger, eds. *Embodying Asian/American Sexualities*. Lanham, MD: Lexington Books, 2009.

Network on Religion and Justice for API LGBTQ People Website. http://www.nrj-api-lgbt.org. Accessed July 7, 2014.

Queer Asian Spirit Website. http://www.queerasianspirit.org. Accessed July 7, 2014.

Shrake, Eunai. "Homosexuality and Korean Immigrant Protestant Churches." In Gina Masequesmay and Sean Metzger, eds. *Embodying Asian/American Sexualities*. Lanham, MD: Lexington Books, 2009, pp. 145–56.

"Special Issue: Queer Asian Theology." *Theology and Sexuality* 17, no. 3 (2011).

Muslims

Approaching the history and categorization of Asian American Muslims begins with questions of definition. First, who are Asian American Muslims? Where are they from? Where have they settled? How does being "Asian American" inflect and affect their practices and beliefs as Muslims in the United States, and how do their identities as Muslims influence how they understand themselves as Asian Americans?

The answers to such questions reflect challenges that Asian American studies as a field has encountered over the past two decades, in particular regarding South Asian and Arab American communities and the obfuscation of questions of religion and faith. Whereas Islam is generally associated with the Middle East and North Africa (MENA), this is a major misconception as nearly two-thirds of the global Muslim population are found in the Asia-Pacific region. According to Pew Research analysis, more Muslims live in India and Pakistan (344 million) than in the entirety of the MENA region. In addition, the largest Muslim population in the world is found in Indonesia, which is home to 12.7 percent of the world's 1.6 billion Muslims, followed by Pakistan (11 percent), India (10.9 percent), and Bangladesh (9.2 percent). Thus, for the purposes of this essay, Asian American Muslims are identified as those who hail from South, Southeast, and East Asia. While it is certainly true that

A Muslim taxi driver prays in the back of the car in New York City, New York, December 18, 2013. About six thousand Muslims live in New York City. Believing Muslims start the evening prayer with the beginning of afterglow. (Sebastian Gabriel/epa/Corbis)

Arab and Iranian Americans may also be included under the rubric of Asian American Muslims, analysis here is limited to those racially defined as "Asian" within state-sanctioned census categories. In addition, while the post-9/11 era has seen rising conversations around "the racialization of Islam/Muslims"—in which Muslims and Arabs are interpellated through associations with terrorism, and which has primarily affected South Asian and Arab communities—it is important to maintain Islam as a religious category. As such, "Asian American Muslims" also include significant numbers of converts from a variety of Asian ethnicities who have engaged and come to practice Islam through a U.S. lens. Finally, it is critical to understand that Asian American Muslims—like the broader U.S. Muslim communities themselves—are incredibly diverse, simultaneously in terms of ethnicity, nationality, denomination, class, and in regard to levels of and approaches to religious practice.

Islam in the "New World"

To understand the emergence and evolution of early Asian American Muslim communities, one must situate their presence in relation to the broader history of Islam in the United States, a history that begins in the earliest days of chattel slavery. The first Muslims in North America were African American slaves, forcibly transported to the "New World" from North and West Africa. Scholars have estimated that anywhere between one-fifth to one-third of African slaves were Muslim. Scholar Kambiz Ghanea Bassiri has noted how racism and Orientalism coalesced to enact what he calls the "de-negrofication" and "de-Islamicization" of African Muslim slaves. In the former, a claim to a Muslim identity led black slaves to be seen as "less of a negro"; Islam connoted a form of status and exoticism that at the time afforded the slave better treatment. In the latter phenomenon of de-Islamicization, African Muslim slaves downplayed or hid their Islamic identities or presented themselves as converts to Christianity in order to fare better in the face of anti-Islamic sentiment among white slave owners.

Through these examples, one sees how the early presence of Islam in the United States was circumscribed by the coupling of antiblack racism and Orientalized notions of Islam, the idea that "Islam" was simultaneously dangerous, foreign, and exotic. This intersection would continue to shape U.S. Muslim community formation in the early 20th century, when the religion (re-)emerged among black communities in the urban North. While most forms of the orthodox Sunni Islam practiced by African American Muslim slaves were destroyed through slavery, organizations such as the Moorish Science Temple, the Ahmadiyya Movement in Islam, and the Nation of Islam offered new interpretations of Islam that appealed to blacks in the urban North due to their rejection of white supremacy and associations with ideologies of Black Nationalism. Islam also offered black Americans citizenship and belonging in a religious community that both challenged and exceeded the boundaries of the nation-state. Through Islam, black Americans expressed internationalist identities, which reflected the inherently transnational, heterodox, and syncretic nature of early 20th-century Islam.

Such global identities emerged in a period of mass migration to the United States; 26 million immigrants settled in the United States between 1870 and 1920. Almost all the Muslims who arrived in the United States during that time were South Asian Muslims from British India—now India, Pakistan, and Bangladesh—who began arriving as migrant workers during the latter half of the 19th century. Almost entirely men, many settled in California's Imperial Valley, where they were employed as farm workers, while others, primarily from what is known today as Bangladesh, came through the maritime trade, initially settling in port cities like New Orleans and New York, then spreading out and moving to northern urban centers such as Detroit, Chicago, Philadelphia, Newark, and New York. These men often settled in neighborhoods of color, mainly with African and Latino Americans, with many of them marrying black and Latina American women. While some raised their children as Muslims, others did not, fearful that the religion would prevent them from assimilating into American society. As scholar and filmmaker Vivek Bald has documented, however, Bengali Muslims crafted vibrant, polycultural communities that reflected Islamic traditions and practices to varying degrees.

Mufti Muhammad Sadiq and the Ahmadiyya Movement in Islam

Perhaps one of the most influential figures in early 20th-century Islam was Mufti Muhammed Sadiq, a South Asian missionary for the Ahmadiyya Movement in Islam (AMI). The AMI was started by Muslims in the Punjab region of India (now Pakistan) in the 1880s. It offered a new interpretation of Islam that positioned the movement's leader, Mirza Ghulam Ahmad, as a *mujadid* (renewer) of Islam and preached nonviolence by urging followers to wage jihad (struggle) through the pen and not the sword. Ghulam Ahmad's interpretation of Islam was vehemently opposed by the orthodox Sunni Muslim community, due to his claim that he received prophecy from God (Sunni Muslims believe Muhammad is the final prophet, and Islamic revelation is sealed). Yet in the United States the AMI's message of continual prophecy resonated with black Americans, and over the course of the following decades hundreds, perhaps even thousands, of black Americans were recruited into their ranks, including well-known jazz musicians such as Yusef Lateef, Art Blakey, Ahmad Jamal, and McCoy Tyner.

Sadiq arrived in Philadelphia by ship on February 15, 1920. Immediately upon arrival, he was seized by U.S. immigration authorities who accused him of entering the country to preach polygamy. After demanding that he leave the country—which Sadiq refused—the officials put the missionary in jail for several weeks, from which he was eventually released on appeal. Through his imprisonment, Sadiq experienced firsthand anti-Asian and anti-Muslim racism in the United States—experiences he would mobilize in his missionary work and that allowed him to speak directly to the harsh racial realities faced by African American in the urban North. Through Sadiq, one sees the transnational nature of American Islam; the structure and knowledge propagated by the AMI deeply influenced other Muslim organizations in the United States during that time, and through the organization, African American members became closely attuned to the politics of the Indian subcontinent, with many traveling to the region to increase their knowledge of the faith. Following Sadiq's departure from the United States in 1923, a string of other missionaries from the Punjab region arrived. While some settled in the United States, most did not. However, the organization continued to send missionaries from South Asia to lead congregations, as opposed to cultivating leadership within its ranks, a structure that left many of the AMI's African American followers disillusioned with a hierarchy that excluded them from leadership roles.

While the AMI's membership increased incrementally into the 1960s, by the 1970s, African American enrollment in the group had slowed considerably, as black Americans turned instead to the political-religious teachings of the Nation of Islam and other Black Nationalist groups. Also, due to shifting immigration patterns (further discussed below), increasing numbers of AMI members from South Asia arrived in the United States in the 1970s and 1980s, often displacing and alienating African American worshippers. Indeed, such tensions between South Asians and African

Americans in the AMI were indicative of larger issues that would develop between Asian, Arab, and African American Muslims in the following decades.

From Migration to 9/11

Following the arrival and settlement of South Asian communities throughout the early 20th century, the next significant wave of Asian American Muslims arrived in the United States following the passage of the 1965 Hart-Celler Immigration Act, which reversed the immigration quotas established by the National Origins Act of 1924 and the McCarran-Walter Act of 1952. As with the broader Asian American community, the Hart-Celler Act forever altered the face of U.S. Muslim communities; according to Edward Curtis, between 1966 and 1997, approximately 2,780,000 immigrated to the United States from areas in the world with significant Muslim populations. While it is impossible to say exactly how many of these immigrants were actually Muslims, approximately 316,000 arrived from the South Asian nations of India, Pakistan, and Bangladesh during those years—which constituted a 500 percent increase from what the population had been previously.

South Asian, and thus South Asian Muslim communities, would continue to grow throughout the 1990s and 2000s, with South Asian Muslims becoming the largest ethnic group of immigrant Muslims in the United States (about one-third). The majority of South Asian immigrants are orthodox Sunni Muslims, though there are also significant numbers of Shi'ites and Isma'ilis. Though there is incredible diversity among these communities, broadly speaking, South Asian Muslim immigrants are highly educated and middle- to upper-class; while they live in almost every state in the nation, there are large concentrations of South Asian Muslim populations in California, New Jersey, and New York. During the 1970s and 1980s, in addition to establishing new houses of worship across the country, many South Asian immigrants, along with their counterparts from the Middle East, worked to build other types of Islamic institutions in which they would create religious and ethnic community. Most notably, these decades saw the emergence and development of the Muslim Student Associations (MSAs) on college campuses across America, and the Islamic Society of North America (ISNA), which would go on to become the largest Muslim umbrella organization in the United States and Canada. During this same time, Asian American Muslim communities also grew—as with the U.S. Muslim community as a whole—far more diverse, with small but significant numbers of Indonesian, Malaysian, and Chinese Muslims relocating to the United States.

While anti-Muslim sentiment was certainly present in the United States throughout the 1970s and 1980s, due to events such as the Middle East oil crisis and the Iranian hostage crisis, the attacks on the World Trade Center and the Pentagon on September 11, 2001, forever shifted the lives of many U.S. Muslims—as well as many perceived to be Muslim. Whereas anti-Asian racism—through exclusion, internment, citizenship restrictions, and so on—had certainly circumscribed the lives of Asian American Muslims until then, 9/11 brought an unprecedented level of suspicion and scrutiny to Asian American Muslims. For many of the educated, relatively wealthy members of these communities, being subjected to racialized targeting, surveillance, and at times imprisonment was a new phenomenon and led them to new levels of civic and political engagement through civil rights and advocacy organizations such as the Muslim Public Affair Council (MPAC) and CAIR (Council of American-Islamic Relations).

Despite a climate of fear and intimidation, the post-9/11 era has also led many young Asian American Muslims to craft new identities as U.S. Muslims, which have often challenged the religious and cultural traditions of previous generations. One of the primary arenas in which this has occurred is in regard to gender roles and the ways women engage Islam. For example, whereas in South Asia women rarely attend the *mosque* or participate in religious practices in the public sphere, young South Asian American women are challenging such traditions, not only by participating in *mosque* culture, but through literary and cultural expressions; examples include the work of novelists Samina Ali (*Madras on Rainy Days*), Nafisa Haji (*The Sweetness of Tears* and *The Writing on My Forehead*), and Shaila Abdullah (*Saffron Dreams*).

In addition to the increasing visibility of South Asian American Muslims and growing numbers of Muslim immigrants from China, Indonesia, and Malaysia, there have also been increasing numbers of Asian American converts to Islam, a trend that reflects Islam's status as the fastest growing religion in the United States. Perhaps the most well-known Asian American convert is Captain James Yee, former Muslim chaplain at the Guantanamo Bay Prison camp. Yee was accused of espionage and was subject to an intense investigation; however, all charges against him were eventually dropped. Yee's case became a symbol of the corruption of the U.S. government and the rampant anti-Muslim racism of the war on terror.

Sylvia Chan-Malik

See also: Essays: Islamophobia; *Entries:* Yee, James J.

Further Reading

Curtis, Edward E., IV. *Muslims in America: A Short History*. Oxford: Oxford University Press, 2009.

Karim, Jamillah. *American Muslim Women: Negotiating Race, Class, and Gender within the Ummah*. New York: New York University Press, 2009.

Lawrence, Bruce. *New Faiths, Old Fears: Muslims and Other Asian Immigrants in American Religious Life*. New York: Columbia University Press, 2002.

Mohammad-Arif, Aminah. *Salaam America: South Asian Muslims in New York*. London: Anthem Press, 2002.

Panethnic Religious Institutions

Panethnic religious life and institutions shed light on the intersections of racial and religious identity at work in the diverse ways of what it means to be Asian American and religious. Panethnic evangelical and mainline Christian churches—strongly represented by Asian Americans of East Asian descent—have distinct organizing logics around the formation of Asian American identity and community. These different mentalities have led to the formation of distinct congregational cultures; whereas evangelical congregations tend to focus on the psychological and cultural needs of their pan–Asian American religious communities, mainline congregations put an emphasis on peace and justice issues. Asian Americans of South Asian descent who primarily subscribe to Hindu and Muslim religious identities face a different dynamic of panethnicity. Whereas for South Asian American Muslims (namely, Pakistani, Bengali, and Indian), panethnicity emerges in a context of multiculturalism and multiracialism, set against the backdrop of post-9/11 politics, South Asian American Hindus (primarily Indian American) face tensions between forming panethnic identity along South Asian racial lines or more mono-ethnic Hindu lines. This essay begins by unpacking the notion of Asian American "panethnicity," which is the underlying conceptual framework for panethnic religious institutions. Then, it discusses the complex panethnic alliances and identities operating in Asian American evangelical and mainline, Hindu, and Muslim communities. For Asian American Christians, panethnicity emerges along evangelical and mainline denominational distinctions; for South Asian American Hindus and Muslims, panethnicity emerges as a stronger identity in a Muslim context compared to a primarily mono-ethnic Hindu context. Although this essay does use the common notion of panethnicity for these various communities, it is indeed important to note that the religio-ethnic worlds of Asian American Christians, Hindus, and Muslims

are not parallel to one another and do not fit neatly into a one to one comparison.

Historical Development

Asian American Panethnicity. The study of panethnic religious institutions depends, first, on understanding the notion of panethnicity. "Panethnicity" refers to the way that people of many national origins come together under a constructed collective identity, such as Hispanic American or Asian American. Yen Le Espiritu shows that panethnicity is an expanded ethnic framework that submerges ethnic distinctions—Chinese, Japanese, Korean, Indian, Pakistani—for the sake of categorization. It is dependent on the phenomenon of ethnic lumping—those of Asian descent are lumped together and characterized as possessing common characteristics. Panethnic Asian American identity is a constructed alliance and self-determined consciousness made up of subethnic groups unique to the experience of racialization in a U.S. context. It is both an externally imposed racial category and a voluntarily embraced identity and has developed as a result of both experiences of marginalization and a desire to make strategic political gains as a collective.

Lisa Lowe concludes that the term "Asian American" arose out of the "racist discourse that constructs Asians as a homogenous group." Asian immigrants had not thought of themselves as "Asian American" until those of the dominant culture began to treat those of Asian descent in similar ways. Historical examples of racism and ethnic violence reveal external pressures that helped form Asian Americans. For example, during World War II, Chinese and Korean Americans wore their ethnic clothing and "I am Korean" buttons to prevent outsiders from subjecting them to the discrimination that Japanese Americans faced with internment. The death of Vincent Chin in 1982 was also an instance of ethnic violence that resulted from ethnic lumping by outsiders. The men who killed the Chinese American Vincent Chin were angry about layoffs in the American auto industry as a result of the rise of the Japanese auto industry in the United States; they used Chin, a Chinese American, as a scapegoat for their bitterness against the Japanese. As a category of difference, primarily used to mark differentiation from the majority group, Asian American panethnic identity has emerged from experiences of exclusion and violence.

At the same time, while panethnicity is a phenomenon that those of Asian descent are subject to, it is also a politically expedient identity that has been voluntarily adopted and used to achieve collective gains such as equal housing rights and political representation in elected office. Panethnicity has become a necessary coalition and a self-determined identity through which Asian Americans have made material gains against anti-Asian sentiment, as evidenced in the protests against the hate crime committed against Chin. Furthermore, the term "Asian American" was coined during the Asian American movement in the 1960s when a panethnic coalition—primarily of Chinese Americans, Korean Americans, Japanese Americans, and Filipino Americans—was created to rally around interests of power and to fight

against oppression. The movement was marked by protests against the Vietnam War, fighting for housing rights (the International Hotel in San Francisco), and pushing for ethnic studies courses on college campuses. So panethnic Asian American identity is also embraced voluntarily for the sake of benefiting the community.

Nevertheless, even as panethnicity has been used for political empowerment, it is not an unproblematic term; it has been contested, particularly in terms of who is and is not represented. Lowe challenges the lack of heterogeneity that the term affords for including people of multiple subject positions within the term. As an umbrella category, it can mask the diversity of national origin, gender, generation, sexuality, and class represented within it. Moreover, when the term was first coined in the 1960s, it primarily referred to those of East Asian descent and excluded those of South Asian descent—namely Indian, Pakistani, Bangladeshi, and Sri Lankan Americans. Later in the 1980s, a South Asian American movement did emerge as a response to exclusion from Asian American discourses as well as from the majority culture. Along with Sucheta Mazumdar, many scholars have critiqued the term "Asian American" for this historic exclusion of South Asian Americans. The construction of the term and the phenomenon of panethnicity itself is under debate. Scholarship in Asian American studies is constantly challenging the inclusiveness and the strategic uses of the term. The historical construction of panethnicity and the contestations around the very concept undergird not only political activity and academic scholarship, but also the diverse religious lives and institutions that are formed within the pan-Asian American community.

Beliefs and Practices

Panethnic Evangelical and Mainline Churches. Russell Jeung has studied the increasing number of pan–Asian American churches in recent decades, as mono-ethnic churches have embraced other Asian groups into their communities and new church startups have used panethnic models. In his research on Asian American Christian communities, Russell Jeung has found different organizational logics between evangelical and mainline churches and their teachings on Asian American identity. Asian American evangelicals view panethnic identity as a community that is "connected by ties of friendship, not by political or economic concerns." They see Asian Americans as sharing a common generational experience. In contrast, panethnic mainline churches conceive of Asian American community within the context of racialization in the United States and focus on issues of peace and justice.

Evangelicalism has been defined in terms of the Bebbington quadrilateral (of biblicism, crucicentrism, conversionism, and activism), and 17 percent of Asian Americans subscribe to this tradition of Christianity. They increasingly attend panethnic Asian American evangelical churches that are both outgrowths of pre-existing mono-ethnic churches and new church plants. The historic evangelical church Evergreen Baptist Church of Los Angeles is an example of a church that began as a mono-ethnic Japanese American church in 1925 and then expanded into a pan–Asian American church in the 1970s. On the other hand, the Evangelical Covenant Church (ECC) is a denomination that has seen a rapid rise in the number of new pan–Asian American churches. Parkwood Community Church (Chicago) was the first Asian American church to join the Covenant denomination in 1997. After Parkwood, Grace Community Covenant Church (Palo Alto, California), New Song (multiple sites including Los Angeles), and a string of other churches followed suit. Some of these churches are increasingly multicultural, but in all instances, the leaders of these churches are Asian American. The Evangelical Covenant Church has been a good fit for pan–Asian American membership because of its open theology on issues like baptism while still maintaining a relatively conservative theology. Evangelical organizations have been popular among Asian Americans with their focus on recruiting Asian Americans. But the mainline churches have provided a perspective of the racial experiences of Asian Americans that is not often seen within white evangelical institutions.

As Jeung suggests, mainline churches have a different orientation to their understanding of church and racial identity compared to evangelical communities; mainline ministers understand panethnic Asian American identity primarily in terms of racism and marginalization. Artemio Guillermo's edited volume, for example, documents Asian American ministerial voices that decry the marginalized experiences of Asian Americans from the mainline. This stands in contrast to the psychological and therapeutic focus of ministry for evangelicals. Though the belief system that liberal mainline denominations may adopt is less clear than the Bebbington quadrilateral for evangelicalism, Jeung finds three main tenets of the Asian Americans in the mainline—the belief in tolerance, historic ties to community, and prophetic morality.

While the mainline has been more supportive of outward and explicit support of Asian American identity and leadership through forming Asian American caucuses as early as the 1970s, they have a smaller numbers in Asian American membership at 9 percent of the population. This has to do with the overall decline in mainline churches as they have not had the same growth effect as evangelical churches. The United Methodist Church at large has seen a dramatic decrease in membership throughout the recent decades. As part of this larger demographic phenomenon and the increasing success of denominations like the ECC in attracting Asian Americans, panethnic mainline Asian American churches are less visible. That being said, mainline churches have still been a place for Asian American congregations. Buena Vista United Methodist Church (Alameda, California) is a historic Japanese American, now pan–Asian American church that is engaged in its community and holds a relatively progressive theology; the senior pastor, Michael Yoshii, has been acknowledged for his activist ministry. Through caucuses like the National Federation of Asian American United Methodists, the United Methodist Church also actively sponsors programs for empowering and supporting panethnic Asian American identity.

The schism between American Christian "liberals" and "evangelicals" has a long history that dates to the early 20th century with the Scopes Trial and the fundamentalist-modernist controversy, and the vestiges of these historic legacies remain in these pan–Asian American churches. But it is also important to note that there are also more "evangelical" sections of mainline denominations and more "liberal" justice-oriented sections of the evangelicals, so the distinction between mainline and evangelical deserves some qualifications. But there are indeed overarching differences between panethnic evangelical and mainline churches, with the former primarily focused on Asian American psychology and networks and the latter focused on racialized Asian American identity. These distinctions have allowed pan-Asian American churches to develop in their own distinct ways.

South Asian American Religions— Hinduism and Islam. The above discussion of evangelical and mainline panethnic congregations primarily concerns those of Japanese, Chinese, and Korean descent. As the most religiously plural racial demographic, however, "Asian Americans" represent Hindu, Muslim, Buddhist, Sikh, and Jain traditions as well. South Asian Americans provide strong representation within these religious communities, and with increasing advances in scholarship, their experiences are being incorporated into the academic community. South Asian Americans bring a diversity of religious traditions to the wider Asian American collective as they identify as Hindu, Muslim, Christian, Buddhist, Sikh, and Jain. A post-911 political context has sharpened South Asian American, or American Desi, consciousness as they have shared the experience of ethnic lumping; at the same time, religious identity has been a marker for making distinctions among American Desis. Whereas South Asian American Muslims have formed strong panethnic alliances and identity among a multicultural, multiracial Muslim American community, South Asian American Hindus have been able to use their religious identities to distinguish themselves from their Muslim counterparts. Panethnicity has emerged as a useful identity for South Asian American Muslims to provide leadership in the Muslim community at large, whereas monoethnic Hindu (Indian) identity has allowed South Asian Americans to separate themselves from the post-911 politics.

South Asian American Hindus form panethnic alliances within their religious community, but as Hindus are largely Indian American, the panethnic religious community that develops is largely around an Indian American identity. Prema Kurien theorizes that South Asian American Hindus are mobilizing themselves largely in two camps—they choose between different religio-ethnic options by organizing around South Asian panethnic political coalitions and along Hindu, or pan-Indic lines (which include Hindu, Buddhist, Jain, and Sikh religions). While the two groups have been mobilizing around similar pressures within a U.S. context and membership is largely the same people, the two groups have different organizational logics. Organizing around South Asian American identity allows a forum for discussing explicitly ra-

cial considerations and identity politics. Organizing around Indic lines, however, affords the community the opportunity to distance themselves from an explicitly racialized South Asian identity and also allows them to distinguish themselves from the South Asian Muslim community, with whom they have historic religious differences.

In the wake of September 11, Pakistanis, Indians, Bangladeshis, Muslims, Hindus, and Sikhs have all been lumped together and a stronger sense of a "South Asian" panethnic identity has formed. But similar to the milieu of fear during Japanese American internment (and the desire of Koreans and Chinese to distinguish themselves from the Japanese), some Hindu Americans have also made concerted efforts to distinguish themselves from Muslim Americans who are mostly Bangladeshi and Pakistani. The Federation of Hindu Associations and groups like Hindu Unity, for example, have rallied along their religious identities to form agendas that distinguish them from Muslims. So organizing around a panethnic "South Asian American" identity—which includes Muslims and Hindus—provides a medium through which they could mobilize for community action. But there are also incentives, particularly in a post-911 climate, for South Asian Americans to organize around their Indic traditions. So the options for organizing a panethnic or pan-Indic community is dependent on a politics of recognition that has both strengthened South Asian American coalitions but also provided incentives for divisions based on religious lines.

At the same time that there are internal tensions among Hindus and Muslims within the South Asian American community, South Asian Americans have stood out as the primary source of intellectual and political leadership for the Muslim American community at large. Pakistani, Bangladeshi, and Indian American Muslims have come together under a South Asian American identity to exert leadership among their religious community that is also composed of African American and Arab American Muslims. The American Muslim Alliance and the American Muslim Council, for example, are led by South Asian American Muslims. Post-9/11 South Asian American Muslims have provided a political voice seeking to legitimate their place within American democracy, distinguishing themselves from Islamic extremists and arguing that the United States is a nation where Muslims can thrive. Like South Asian American Hindus, South Asian American Muslims have also prioritized domestic politics over homeland politics that would otherwise prove divisive and have been able to build coalitions together. South Asian American Muslims have proven to be uniquely positioned to provide a positive image and the religious and political leadership needed for Muslims.

In addition to exerting public leadership as a panethnic coalition, South Asian American Muslims also manage complex ties within their multicultural religion (African American, Arab American) while maintaining roots in their own communities of national origin (distinctly, Pakistani, Bangladeshi, and Indian). South Asian American Muslims not only work to establish panethnic South Asian American coalitions, but also build multinational coalitions with Arab and African American Muslims—which has not always been without tension. For example, South Asian American Muslim immigrants are more reluctant to join in on the historic racial challenges that African American Muslims may experience. Moreover, at the Islamic Cultural Center in New York City, the *mosque* is a space for various nationalities to worship, with English being the primary language that is used. But this is a unique experience within a U.S. context as South Asian American Muslims are more accustomed to ethnic and nationalistic ties to worship in their homelands. These multicultural sites of worship therefore have to balance what is at the core of "orthodoxy" and what is "cultural," and South Asian American Muslims have to make adjustments to the worship styles. At the same time, there are alternative forms of worship that South Asian American Muslims practice that preserve their national distinctions. A case study of New York City Pakistani, Bangladeshi, and Indian Muslim cab drivers showed that the cab drivers observe their ritual of prayer five times a day by using ethnic restaurants as improvised prayer spaces. Pakistani Muslims, for example, go to restaurants that are from their own ethnic origins to observe prayer five times a day. The restaurants become spaces for connecting national identity with religious identity in a larger U.S. context where *mosques* are multinational and "Pan-Islamic" spaces. Panethnic South Asian Muslim identity emerges in the midst of a cosmopolitan effort of bridging the gap between cultural distinctions under a unified Muslim identity.

Conclusion

The term "Asian American" is itself a contested identity in that it is both an imposed and voluntarily chosen identity and in that it has historically included some groups and excluded others. This essay has shown the ways that this contested notion of panethnicity nevertheless operates in heterogeneous ways within the Christian, Hindu, and Muslim lives and institutions of Asian Americans. First, Asian American Christians encounter different logics of Asian American identity depending on whether they attend a panethnic evangelical or mainline church; whereas the former is interested primarily in the psychological and communal needs of a cultural network, the latter gathers around the notion of Asian American racism and activism. Second, panethnicity faces limitations among South Asian American Hindus as this is a primarily Indian American community, but the option of choosing between organizing around race (South Asian) versus religion (Indic traditions) sheds light on the complex alliances and identities that are being built within the community. Third, South Asian American Muslims have used their South Asian panethnicity to provide leadership within the Muslim community at the same time that they are managing how to build effective alliances in a multicultural religion. The intersections between race and religion are complex and intertwined for panethnic Asian American religious institutions.

Helen Jin Kim

See also: Entries: Selma (California) Japanese Mission Church

Further Reading

Espiritu, Yen Le. *Asian American Panethnicity: Bridging Institutions and Identities.* Philadelphia: Temple University Press, 1992.

Leonard, Karen. *Muslims in the United States: The State of Research.* New York: Russell Sage Foundation, 2003.

Lowe, Lisa. *Immigrant Acts: On Asian American Cultural Politics.* Durham, NC: Duke University Press, 1996.

Shankar, Lavina Dhingra, and Rajini Srikanth. *A Part, Yet Apart: South Asians in Asian America.* Philadelphia: Temple University Press, 1998.

Politics and Religion

Rather than simply being an opiate of the masses, religion has a much more complex effect on Asian Americans' political behaviors. Like other racial groups, Asian Americans' religious beliefs and practices clearly shape their politics and spur political behavior. At the same time, American politics structure Asian American religious involvement and association. This essay first introduces how the American political framework, especially as a racialized system, establishes uniquely Asian *American* religious congregations and practices. It then examines mechanisms by which Asian American religions both support and discourage political activity.

Asian American political involvement, as theorized by political scientists, goes beyond electoral politics and encompasses a range of group solidarities, behaviors, and activities by which they have pursued their own interests. Because Asian Americans have faced a legacy of political disenfranchisement, they have resorted to seeking empowerment through a variety of means. Likewise, Asian American religious activists have used a variety of arenas to engage politically, including mobilizing at a transnational level, pursuing lawsuits, community organizing, and influencing policy through moral suasion.

The American Political Framework and Asian American Religions

As noted by sociologists and historians of religion, the United States' constitutional framework has given rise to unique religious formations and identities. By establishing the freedom of religion, it has created an open market for religious entrepreneurs to develop the most religiously pluralistic nation in the world. This same disestablishment requires faith-based institutions to attract and meet the needs of their memberships, lest they die out. The American religious marketplace, then, provides the space for Asian immigrants to bring their spiritual traditions, to practice them freely, and to recruit new adherents. Across the American landscape, in the seemingly most unlikely of places, one may now find a Hindu *mandir*, a Buddhist *wat*, or a Sikh *gurdwara*. Asian Americans are thus a major source of religious diversity in the United States, as they make up 20 percent of the Muslims, 32 percent of the Buddhists, and 88 percent of the Hindus in this country.

The political freedom to establish Asian American religious institutions also encourages cultural pluralism and distinct, hybrid identities. Immigrant congregations have long functioned as community spaces for traditional festivals and activities. They also promote the transmission of culture to the next generation. Even though Asian Americans have been subject to assimilatory pressures, their religious identities have been a guaranteed constitutional right. Indeed, certain groups of Asian Americans have preferred to identify with their religious affiliation rather than their ethnic or racial background. These individuals self-define themselves as Christians or Muslims rather than as Korean or Indonesian Americans. On the other hand, religion has provided the space for new cultural identities, such as hybridized ethnic ones or racialized Asian American ones. These new social identities, in turn, have consequences for the political affiliations of the members. For example, members of pan-Asian mainline congregations are more likely to hold more progressive political agendas as a result of their involvement in church activities.

However, because of the racialized nature of American politics, Asian Americans do not necessarily have full freedom of religion. Orientalist perceptions of Asian religions include depictions of Asian spiritual practices as foreign and exotic at best, and vulgar and intolerable at worst. In Berkeley, California and other places, neighbors have utilized public hearings and planning codes to prevent Asian Americans from associating religiously. Post-9/11, increased security measures by public and private institutions have also infringed on the religious rights of Asian Americans. Sikh American men, who wear turbans as part of their religious observance, have complained of systematic and humiliating searches of their turbans at airports. These occurrences represent what education professor Khyati Joshi terms "racialized religious oppression," in that religious observances are viewed as racial markers that are unacceptable. Ethnic studies scholar Jaideep Singh adds, "As the nation increasingly diversifies, non-white members of non-Christian religious faiths are demonized in public discourse through racialized terminology by fearful white Christians. . . . Instances of sacred site construction bring to the surface this often clandestine hostility towards an apparent 'model minority.'"

The voluntary nature of the American religious marketplace also promotes the formation of self-supporting congregations, in which members freely choose to associate, to organize and lead them, and to fund them. Because this structure is different from Asian civil societies, Asian American religious congregations take different forms, with much more lay involvement and regular participation. Besides offering places for religious practice, these congregations provide opportunities for voting and political association, for leadership development, and also for frequent schisms as ministers and lay leaders vie for power.

As Asian Americans congregate on a frequent basis, their organizational networks are primed for mobilization by political parties and interest groups. In California's 2008 election issue over same-sex marriage, proponents activated conservative Asian American churches to pass the initiative. At several rallies, Asian American Christians made up the majority

of demonstrators and speakers. In Southern California, Asian Americans who regularly attended church voted much differently from those who never attended. Of those who regularly attended church, 75 percent supported the ban on same-sex marriage, while among those who never attended, only 29 percent supported the ban. Like other religious movements, Asian American congregations have resources such as leadership, membership, and communication links that allow for easy political mobilization around particular issues.

The Effect of Asian American Religions on Politics

Voting. Religious affiliation and religiosity (degree of religious behavior) in the United States both are highly correlated to voting patterns and to political ideology. The same holds true for Asian Americans, as congregations provide both organizational and psychological resources for political participation. As stated earlier, congregations are voluntarily organized, so that they have leadership, membership lists, financial resources, communication networks, and meeting places available to be activated politically. Through participation, members learn civic skills such as voting, fundraising, and debating that enhance political participation. In terms of psychological resources, they offer the cognitive support for political engagement by providing a moral framework and sense of efficiency. By identifying right from wrong, and by empowering individuals through collective action, congregations have legitimated authority and organizing power to influence their members. Congregations help establish group solidarities around ethnicity, race, or class, which also facilitate group mobilization. Finally, religious institutions develop cultural and discursive tools, such as biblical language or prayer forms, by which leaders can motivate and encourage masses to carry on their pursuit of justice and peace.

The 2008 presidential election and statewide ballots demonstrated the role of race and religion, especially regarding the Asian American vote. Asian Americans voted for President Barack Obama by a 62 to 35 percent margin, according to national exit polls. Just as the individual Asian American ethnic groups voted in blocs, Asian religious groups tended to cluster in their presidential preference. Although Obama received majority support from most religious groups of Asian Americans, the degree of support varied significantly.

Asian Americans who consider themselves agnostics or atheists, who tend to be more liberal, favored Obama most strongly (Obama—62 percent; McCain—4 percent). Another more liberal religious group, Methodists, also heavily supported the Democratic candidate (Obama—60 percent; McCain—21 percent). Reflecting the South Asian American voting patterns, Muslims (Obama—57 percent; McCain—1 percent), and Hindus (Obama—53 percent; McCain—10 percent) also indicated similar voting preferences.

Asian American Christians supported Obama to a lesser degree, perhaps because they tend to be more ideologically conservative. Still, Asian American Catholics and Protestants were more likely to vote for Obama than their other co-religionists, especially their white ones. While opinion polls of these Asian Americans indicated a 10 percent preference for Obama over McCain, white Catholics and white Protestants both voted for McCain.

Political scientist Pei-te Lien also demonstrates how religion and religious participation significantly shape Asian American political identity and behavior in three specific ways. First, religious affiliation is highly correlated to the development of Asian Americans' ethnic identification. Asian Americans who are Hindus (27 percent) and Muslims (21 percent) are more likely to identify with the racialized "Asian American" identity, as compared to about 15 percent of all Asians. These group identifications may, in turn, affect individuals' political interests and their engagement in electoral politics.

Second, religious affiliation affects Asian Americans' political ideology. For example, Asian Americans who are Protestant (25 percent) or Catholic Christians (24 percent) are more likely to be "somewhat conservative" compared to all Asian Americans (18 percent). Third, Asian American religiosity, as measured by church attendance, correlates with greater political participation. Those who attend church more regularly are more likely to become citizens and to vote. In addition, more religious Asian Americans often are more conservative than Asian Americans in general, have greater political interest, and possess more perceived influence over local government decisions. (See Table 1.) These results support the theory that

Table 1 Religious Affiliation and Political Ideology

	Protestant Christian	Catholic	Buddhist	Hindu	Muslim	None	All
Very Liberal	4	8	6	18	8	10	8
Somewhat Liberal	27	32	21	43	50	22	28
Middle of the Road	33	24	41	17	12	35	32
Somewhat Conservative	25	24	12	14	17	15	18
Very Conservative	4	4	6	—	8	3	4
Not Sure	7	7	14	8	4	13	10

church involvement offers a greater sense of efficacy and moral framework for members.

Campaign Finance. Religion has empowered many Asian Americans to take political action, but religion can also be a significant liability in the political arena. Besides voting, Asian Americans can engage in electoral politics through lobbying, securing appointments, and making campaign contributions. In congressional and municipal elections, Asian Americans make campaign donations in amounts proportional to their representation in the overall population. However, the 1996 campaign finance scandal, infamously named the "Asian Connection," showed that being a double minority—religious and ethnic—can be a considerable liability in mainstream politics. Within the racialized political context that privileges Anglo-Saxon Protestants, Asian Americans faced mistreatment from both the media and the major political parties as being "hyperactive" in seeking influence.

When the chief fundraiser for the Democratic National Committee (DNC), John Huang, faced allegations of illegal campaign fundraising, including money laundering at the Buddhist Hsi Lai Temple, the media and politicians quickly drew upon historical stereotypes. They assumed Asian Americans were perpetual foreigners who could not be trusted. The DNC audited Asian American contributions using double standards, investigating Asian Americans who had contributed less than $2,500 but not non–Asian Americans who contributed similarly. Although some guilty convictions were made, this scandal racially stereotyped the entire group of Asian Americans.

This xenophobia continued into the investigation of Hsi Lai Temple in Hacienda

Heights, California. The Taiwanese temple became a major site for congressional investigation when the *Wall Street Journal* reported that a "luncheon" visit by Al Gore grossed $140,000 for the DNC; campaign financing law prohibits fundraising on religious property, and it was reported that the monastics at the temple had contributed about a quarter of those funds. During the congressional investigations of the temple nuns, newspapers highlighted the visible cultural gaps—congressmen in their starched suits and nuns in their brown robes, sandals, clean-shaven heads, speaking broken English.

Stuart Chandler, a researcher and advisor to Master Hsing Yun (the Hsi Lai Temple leader) at the time of the scandal, provides a contextualized interpretation of the controversy. The Buddhist concept of *chieh-yuan* (friendly relations) can shed light on what Chandler suggests may have motivated Master Hsing Yun to become friendly with American politicians. *Chieh-yuan* is a way to plant the seed of the Dharma in someone's consciousness so that it might bear fruit for enlightenment in a future reincarnation. Chandler suggests that one of the primary reasons Gore was invited to the temple was for a religious purpose, to spread the Dharma. So while Gore may have visited the temple to gain political—and possibly financial—support, Master Hsing Yun and the nuns at the temple likely had Buddhist cosmological motivations for wanting important figures to visit.

While the financial activity at the temple was illegal, understanding the religious motives in this affair does help provide a more comprehensive account than merely projecting racial stereotypes about Asian Americans as inscrutable and distrustful foreigners. The identity, citizenship, and allegiance to American ideals came into question for all Asian Americans involved. Likewise, Muslims, whether Asian American or not, have also found that their religious background has become a liability in entering the American political scene.

Homeland and Nondomestic Politics

Asian Americans' involvement in their homeland politics also dispels their stereotype of passivity and political apathy. Their interest in nondomestic issues may not necessarily decline with succeeding, acculturated generations, because of the significance of Pacific Rim economies and the internationalization of political economies. For Asian Americans, religious organizations and ideals spawned transnational movements over homeland politics. Barred from citizenship in the United States, Asian immigrants have frequently used their congregations, temples, and religious associations to mobilize around nationalist efforts. As a historical example, the role of Korean Christian nationalists in 1919 in the United States demonstrates how religion provided both the discursive and organizational resources for revolutionary aims.

March 1, 1919, marked the beginning of the Korean independence movement as Korean nationalists rose up against their Japanese colonizers. Soon thereafter, Korean American nationalists formed the Korean Congress on April 14–15, 1919 in Philadelphia to advocate for Korean independence. In the United States, Philip Jaisohn, the first Korean American to become a citizen, partnered with Henry Chung and Syngman Rhee to advocate for Korean independence from abroad. The result was a transnational movement with a Korean Provisional Government established in Shanghai.

As the United States emerged as a global power after World War I, Korean Americans were uniquely positioned to influence homeland politics. Richard Kim explains that their ties to American Protestant missionaries and their Christian rhetoric allowed them to readily appeal to Anglo-Americans. In one of their first statements to garner public awareness, the Korean Congress drafted "An Appeal to America" in which they wrote to Americans for support and sympathy for Korean independence utilizing themes of nationalism and evangelism:

> We know you love justice; you also fought for liberty and democracy, and you stand for Christianity and humanity. Our cause is a just one before the laws of God and man. Our aim is freedom from militaristic autocracy; our object is democracy for Asia; our hope is universal Christianity. (2007)

The League of Friends was also created shortly after the Korean Congress on June 16, 1919, and it similarly appealed to Christian values and rhetoric to generate wider American support and increase public awareness of human rights violations under Japanese rule.

Beyond the use of Christian rhetoric, Korean American nationalists had strong networks with Protestant missionaries who provided critical support in increasing public awareness and influencing foreign policy. The Federal Council of Churches of Christ in America supported their efforts by forming the Commission on Relations with the Orient and publishing "The Korean Situation: Authentic Accounts of Recent Events by Eye Witnesses." This publication documented the Korean human rights violations by the Japanese. Through its influence, from 1919 through 1921, over 9,700 editorials were published that were sympathetic to the Korean cause in American newspapers and periodicals. Despite their disenfranchisement, Korean Christians' religious partnerships with Protestants gave them leverage in increasing awareness for their cause.

Besides Christian congregations and associations, other Asian American religious groups have also advocated for human rights, political and religious freedom, and economic development in their homelands. For example, Janet Hoskins describes how members of a relatively new Vietnamese religion, Caodaism, have mobilized around its particular visions of social justice to pursue religious freedom in Vietnam and to help refugees adapt to their new homeland. They exemplify the transnational character of Asian American religions today, as members retain religious and political associations both in their homeland and in the United States.

Activism

As stated earlier, Asian American political involvement extends beyond electoral politics, especially since Asians have long been disenfranchised and unable to become naturalized. Asian American religions and spiritual traditions have thus encouraged members to seek social justice and ethnic interests through other arenas, such as legal redress, community organizing, and moral suasion. Congregations, in particular, provide two sources of capital: (1) bonding social capital, which enables groups to work with trust and reciprocity; and (2) bridging social capital, which connect groups to outside resources.

A sociologist of religion, Russell Jeung demonstrates how biblical language and narratives inspired Asian American evangelicals to relocate to an urban underclass neighborhood, organize their community, and eventually win a landmark housing settlement. Living with Cambodian and Latino immigrants, he found that their ethnoreligious solidarity, as a form of bonding social capital, enabled them to take collective action more easily. Despite fears of deportation or economic displacement, almost two hundred tenants joined in their lawsuit. The evangelicals who relocated to this area offered bridging social capital and access to media, legal, and political contacts. Moreover, the evangelicals' spiritual capital provided motivation to persevere throughout the three-year struggle. Jeung cites Taiwanese American Alice Wu Cardona who drew upon scriptures of home and redemption to express her religious and political commitments: "I think God has a special affinity for immigrants, especially for refugees from war, and understand the longing they feel for a home that is comfortable. We should be 'groaning inwardly as we wait eagerly' (Romans 8:23) for the hope of our redemption. I believe God has more in store for us, for our immigrants and for our imperfect world."

Employing similar concepts of social capital, political scientist Joaquin Gonzalez III specifies the terms *kasamahan* (community organization and inward-focused kinship) and *bayanihan* (outward linkages) to analyze how Filipino American religion facilitates civic engagement. He describes several case studies in which Filipino American congregations and organizations of various denominations build on these ethnic strengths to empower the community. For example, the intergenerational *kasamahan* within Filipinized churches involves a respect for the wisdom of elders and an emphasis on the shared needs of the community. Because of these ethnic bonds, university students joined to support aging Filipino veterans at San Francisco's St. Patrick Church. Together, they pray to icons of popular devotion from the Philippines, such as the Mother of Perpetual Help, the Santa Nino of Cebu, and San Lorenzo Ruiz. When many veterans were burned out of their residential hotel, altar boys and girls helped move their belongings. The community's intergenerational efforts to protest and lobby for the veterans' rights and benefits that the U.S. government denied them thus arose from the collective concern and respect that the students held for the veterans.

Filipino Americans' spiritual socialization moves them to perform hours of volunteer work both in their new homeland and in their old hometowns, which represent collective action in the form of *bayanihan*. In the Philippines, the military and police have named some people of faith as "enemies of the state" and as leaders of political opposition. By the end of 2006, 10 clergy, six lay workers, seven members of the United Church of Christ in the Philippines, and two members of the United Methodist Church had been martyred. Moved to action, ministers and students in the United States have developed national networks to end these extrajudicial killings, support human rights, and challenge American imperialism. One interfaith vigil and procession brought together not only Catholic and mainline Protestant groups, but also pastors of Filipino evangelical and independent churches. In response to their pleas, a bipartisan group of the U.S. House of Representatives urged Philippines president Gloria Macapagal Arroyal to investigate the deaths and eliminate the underlying causes of the violence. Gonzalez concludes that these two political activities are examples of the dialectical relationship between *kamasahan* prayers and *bayanihan* action:

Intergenerational *kamasahan* and passion among young and old Catholic, Independent, and Protestant Filipino migrant faithful have been transformed successfully into revolutionary actions to effectively tackle two human rights issues linked to American ascension as a global power: intergenerational *bayanihan* for veterans' benefits for Filipino World War II USAFFE soldiers, and interfaith *bayanihan* to condemn extrajudicial killings in the Philippines.

Civic Engagement

While the above cases illustrate the roles of social capital within congregations, other sociologists examine the spiritual capital of a church, which refers to the moral discourses and schemas that frame how members engage society. Elaine Howard Ecklund looks at the interrelationship between the members' social location (class, race, and ethnic background) and their moral schemas, that is, their cultural assumptions about how to contribute to society. Her first church, Grace, promotes a communal model of civic life, which deemphasizes self-focus and stresses obligations to the congregation and to American society. Korean Americans at this church distance themselves from their ethnic background and their immigrant parents' perceived clannishness, thus pushing them toward greater involvement with their broader, local community. As part of their congregational mission to evangelize others, they volunteer through church-sponsored activities to serve and proselytize the community. However, they tend to maintain a model minority image of themselves that Asian Americans' professional class standing results from their emphasis on education, self-responsibility, and hard work. In their interracial relations, then, they reinforce group boundaries of difference and have difficulties in helping "other," less privileged Americans.

In contrast, the second church, Manna, develops an "individually negotiated" model of civic responsibility, which celebrates ethnic diversity and encourages one's own personal response to God's calling. Sermons teach members to care for the needy and to emulate Jesus, who was motivated out of compassion, not obligation. In terms of understanding their racial and class positions, Manna's multiethnic discourse sees Korean Americans as "minority" Americans, thus aligning them more with blacks. They challenge the model minority stereotype and seek to learn from black civil rights movements. Surprisingly, this model fostered higher rates of volunteerism at Manna than the communal model did at Grace. Howard suggests that the individually negotiated model offers a greater freedom and range of opportunities to become engaged in civic life, leading members at Manna to volunteer more. A congregation's moral schema, therefore, facilitates or discourages political action.

Carolyn Chen's study of Dharma Light, a Taiwanese Buddhist temple, and Grace Evangelical Church in southern California, also illustrates how social context and spiritual capital determine how a religious group develops a public presence. Dharma Light practices "Involved Buddhism," orienting individuals toward cultivating merit through charitable activities. As an institution, its mission encourages group volunteer activities and world peace through interreligious dialogue. At the same time, its racial context shapes how this mission is accomplished. The temple hosts an annual "Get to Know Your Neighbors" banquet to acquaint them with this religious community. It also is a frequent financial sponsor of local public events such as free park concerts, something to which the church does not contribute. Further, Chen observes that leaders of the Taiwanese Buddhist temple get invited to public events more than leaders of the Taiwanese evangelical church, even though the church might bring in more political votes:

> By virtue of the association of Buddhism with the Far East and Christianity with the West, the Buddhists,

rather than the Christians, are the ones to be recruited and courted as the Chinese representatives at the multicultural table. . . . Ironically, because of the public perception of religious difference, those at Dharma Light feel the need to engage in mainstream American society to bargain for acceptance. Interestingly, because [of] its position as a racial and religious outsider, Dharma Light "engages in acts of public relations to both prove their Americanness and yet remain representative Chinese." (2008)

Indeed, religious affiliation and religious volunteerism are highly linked to greater community involvement. Elaine Howard Ecklund and Jerry Park found when controlling for age, gender, and education, Catholic and Protestant Asian Americans volunteer more than the nonreligious, but surprisingly, Buddhist and Hindu Asian Americans actually volunteer less than those with no religious affiliation. (See Table 2.)

Political Apathy and Avoidance

While religion in general does spur political activity, for certain issues and concerns, it can discourage engagement. Religious studies scholar Brett Esaki examined the attitudes of Asian American evangelicals regarding the ordination of homosexuals; this study included in-depth interviews of 43 Asian Americans who were identified as Bible believers (Esaki, 2009). He found that although 81 percent were privately against it, they generally avoided dealing with the issue and did not take active stands

Table 2 Religious Affiliation and Religious Volunteerism

Religious Affiliation of Asian Americans	Percent Participating in at Least One Nonreligious Organization[1]
Protestant Christian	69
Other Religion	65
Catholic	54
Nonreligious	45
Hindu	40
Buddhist	26
Total Sample	51

[1] Ecklund's and Park's data come from the 2000 Social Capital Community Benchmark Survey with 711 Asian American respondents.

against it. They steered clear of the topic because they did not believe it was significant enough to address and it was not easily resolvable, especially in discussions among non-Christians. These Christians understood that making claims based on biblical authority held no weight in the broader public sphere. Furthermore, they wanted to avoid judging others or being seen as judgmental. Esaki concludes that these Asian Americans prefer to remain harmonious with both their Christian and non-Christian peers: "Faced with a seemingly non-negotiable conflict, many Asian American Bible believers choose avoidance and try to maintain two contradictory positions—if both are held—to maintain the solidarity of the community as well as the community's foundation in the Bible."

In this case, religious and political views that are seen to be controversial or judgmental are held privately and in abeyance. Even though religious affiliation and religiosity affected the vote on California's

Proposition 8, a ban on same-sex marriage, second-generation Asian American Christians felt particularly conflicted about appearing judgmental, and therefore avoided campaigning for it. Religion does not appear to be an opiate in making the masses focus on their afterlife. Instead, for these conservative Asian Americans, their religious viewpoints run contrary to prevailing multicultural attitudes in their hometowns. Consequently, they remain reticent about their stances and unengaged in politics to sidestep appearing fractious.

Religion and Civil Society

Another type of religion, the civil religion of Asian Americans, promotes political solidarity, as well as transcendent meaning, for this group. Civil religion, as theorized by Robert Bellah, is the religious dimension of a people through which a group's historical experiences are interpreted in the light of transcendent reality.

Through a shared set of beliefs, symbols, and rituals, such as the flying of American flags to celebrate freedom on the Fourth of July, a nation becomes integrated by both meaning and purpose.

American studies professor Jane Iwamura (2007) employs the concept of civil religion to interpret the development of Japanese Americans' emergent critical faith. She asserts that annual pilgrimages to internment camps not only commemorate the historical experience of racism that shaped this community, but they also sacralize the group's mission to guard against governmental injustice. As this pilgrimage creates political awareness of the group's collective trauma, it also encourages "a spiritual healing and reconciliation that other ethnic institutions—both secular and religious—do not usually provide."

Unaligned with established religious traditions, Japanese American spiritual culture is a broadly conceived "ethnic religion" that includes a set of core values, such as homage to ancestors, interdependence, and perseverance. It informs this minority civil religion and offers an integrative, transcendent identity as pilgrims engage in memorial rites. Participants perform and embody these values as they offer flowers to the dead or dance the *Tanko Bushi*, the coal miner's dance, at these pilgrimages. In the process, they become psychically linked to those before, to each other, and to those whose rights they commit to protecting.

Iwamura thus illustrates how an ethnic community's rituals, values, and spaces can both establish minority solidarity and develop transcendent meaning. Similarly, David Kyuman Kim theorizes that the discourses of diaspora and race have become religious totems for Asian Americans, that is, moral representations of their collective ideals that draw them together. By inventing notions of home and homeland, of Asian American cultural and racial identity, Asian Americans claim both America and authenticity. Their passionate attachment to both forms of identity stems from their critical evaluation of living with ambiguous alterity and racism. He writes, "To name a people, a history, or a tradition is to work toward the articulation and expression of the sublime objects that facilitate our abilities to make meaning in the world." Just as Iwamura argues that internment pilgrimages are rituals expressing the civil religion of Japanese Americans, Kim alludes that the self-conscious invention of diasporic narratives and racialized identities by Asian Americans represent spiritual enterprises. Again, these processes are more than political pursuits, but are moral projects animating the existential and spiritual everyday lives of Asian Americans. Both ethnic and racial identities of Asian Americans thus take on religious dimensions that politically empower and encompass transformative visions of inclusiveness and justice.

Conclusion

This essay highlights four key themes at the intersection of Asian American religions and politics. First, the U.S. political and racial systems structure how Asian Americans organize, develop, and experience their religious lives. The freedom of religion in the United States fosters a thriving diversity of Asian American religious forms and practices. On the other hand, the racialization of the religions of Asian Americans exoticizes and demonizes them. Second, religion offers several resources for Asian American political engagement. It does not just provide moral suasion and community networks, but the religious schemas of Asian Americans inspire and support political activity.

Third, the study of Asian American religions and politics requires an expanded understanding of political engagement. Because Asian Americans have been and continue to be marginalized minorities, they have used their religious repertoires to empower themselves through a variety of means. Most notably, they have participated in transnational movements. Fourth, non-Christian Asian Americans are double minorities. Consequently, they are less competitive in the religious marketplace and less able to mobilize in political arenas.

Unfortunately, this essay includes less data on these double minorities, such as Asian American Muslims and Hindus. It also omits other forms of political action, such as labor organizing, multiracial coalition-building, and media work. Indeed, much more research needs to be done, given the statistically significant effect that religion has on Asian American political behavior, Instead of considering religion as the opiate of the masses, political scientists, religious scholars, and community activists should consider how religion has, and can, mobilize and sustain the masses.

Russell Jeung and Helen Jin Kim

See also: Essays: Secularization and Asian Americans

Further Reading

Busto, Rudiger. "Disorienting Subjects: Reclaiming Pacific Islander/Asian American Religion." *Revealing the Sacred in Asian America,* Jane Iwamura and Paul Spickard, eds., 9–28. Routledge, 2003.

Chen, Carolyn. *Getting Saved in America: Taiwanese Immigration and Religious Experience.* Princeton, NJ: Princeton University Press, 2008.

Ebaugh, Helen, and Janet Chavetz. *Religion and the New Immigrants: Continuities and Adaptations in Immigrant Congregations.* Walnut Creek, CA: Altamira Press, 2000.

Ecklund, Elaine Howard. *Korean American Evangelicals: New Models for Civic Life.* New York: Oxford University Press, 2009.

Esaki, Brett. "A Non-Negotiable Topic: Homosexuality and Ordination." In Brett Esaki, Russell Jeung, Helen Kim, Lalruatkima, James Kyung-Jin Lee, Tat-siong Benny Liew, Quynhhoa Nguyen, and Sharon Suh. *Asian American Bible Believers: An Ethnological Report.* Claremont, CA: Institute for Signifying Scriptures, Claremont Graduate University, 2009.

George, Sheba. *When Women Come First: Gender and Class in Transnational Migration.* Berkeley: University of California Press, 2005.

Gonzalez, Joaquin Jay, III. *Filipino American Faith in Action: Immigration, Religion and Civic Engagement.* New York: New York University Press. 2009.

Hayashi, Brian. *For the Sake of Our Japanese Brethren: Assimilation, Nationalism and Protestantism among the Japanese of Los Angeles.* Stanford, CA: Stanford University Press, 1995.

Iwamura, Jane. "Critical Faith: Japanese Americans and the Birth of a New Civil Religion." *American Quarterly* 47, no. 3 (2007), 937–68.

Jeung, Russell. "Behind the Asian American Split Vote on Prop 8: Community's Religious and Political Views May Have Been a Factor." *Asian Week*, December 2, 2008.

Jeung, Russell. *Faithful Generations: Race and New Asian American Churches.* New Brunswick, NJ: Rutgers University Press, 2004.

Joshi, Khyati. *New Roots in America's Sacred Ground: Religion, Race, and Ethnicity in Indian America.* New Brunswick, NJ: Rutgers University Press, 2006.

Kim, Rebecca. *God's New Whiz Kids? Korean American Evangelicals on Campus.* New York: New York University Press, 2006.

Kim, Richard. "Diasporic Politics and the Globalizing of America: Korean Immigrant Nationalism and the 1919 Philadelphia Korean Congress." In Rhacel S. Parrenas and Lok C. D. Siu, eds. *Asian Diasporas: New Formations, New Conceptions.* Stanford, CA: Stanford University Press, 2007, pp. 208–13.

Kurien, Prema. *A Place at the Multicultural Table: The Development of an American Hinduism.* New Brunswick, NJ: Rutgers University Press, 2007.

Lien, Pei-te, Margaret Conway, and Janelle Wong. *The Politics of Asian Americans: Diversity and Community.* New York: Routledge Press, 2004.

Nakanishi, Don, and James Lai. *Asian American Politics: Law, Participation, and Policy.* Lanham, MD: Rowman and Littlefield Press, 2003.

Okihiro, Gary Y. "Religion and Resistance in America's Concentration Camps." *Phylon* 45, no. 3 (1984): 220–33.

Prebish, Charles, and Kenneth Tanaka. *The Faces of Buddhism in America.* Berkeley: University of California Press, 1998.

Singh, Jaideep. "Racialization of Minoritized Religious Identity: Constructing Sacred Sites at the Intersection of White and Christian Supremacy." In Jane Iwamura and Paul Spickard, eds. *Revealing the Sacred in Asian and Pacific America.* New York: Routledge Press, 2003, pp. 87–106.

Suh, Sharon. *Being Buddhist in a Christian World.* Seattle: University of Washington Press, 2004.

Yang, Fenggang. *Chinese Christians in America: Conversion, Assimilation, and Adhesive Identities.* University Park: Pennsylvania State University Press, 1999.

Religion and Law

The topic of legal issues as they relate to Asian American religion encompasses a complex and difficult set of considerations. Actual legal issues rarely arise in a generic Asian American form. A church with a zoning issue will have a particular ethnic membership; the transformation of Islam into Muslim terrorism is faith specific; a church member with an immigration issue will have a specific nation of origin. Yet we seek to group these issues together into a common discussion of Asian American religion and culture. Each usage of the term "Asian American" includes a theoretical mapping of the particular legal issue onto the category of Asian American. We will examine this process of locating the law within the Asian American category in three sections.

First, what does it mean to say that a particular query or situation is *legal*? In this section we focus on three dimensions of the *legal* for Asian American religion and culture: (1) positive law, (2) constitutional law, and (3) the law as social structuring.

Second, even if we have an issue that is already enmeshed in courts, statutes, and lawyers, there is the question posed by religious studies to Asian American analyses: why or how does the issue involve *religion*? Using the example of the Sikh temple dispute in San Jose, California, we examine (1) the multiple overlapping identities for Asian Americans in addition to a religious identity and discuss (2) what being a "minority religion" means for Asian American religions. We also examine (3) the difficult notion of "freedom of religion" and (4) the racialization of Islam.

Third, we confront directly the idea of "Asian American." This discussion is in four parts. We begin with an observation that there are three dimensions to identity: ascribed identity, collective identity, and identification. Second, we note that the category of Asian American has three treatments grounded in different subject positions: racial, panethnic, and diasporic. Third, we discuss these in the context of Asian American religion and culture and conclude with a brief examination of Orientalism and religion.

Is This a Legal Issue?

Positive Law. A common understanding of law—law as an instrument—requires a short jurisprudential explanation. In legal studies and in popular discussion, the words *law* or *legal* often refer to positive law. *Positive law* can be understood both as the orders of government generally or as statutory and judicial enactments. In both approaches, positive law is separated from moral considerations. A frequent jurisprudential distinction opposes positive law and natural law. *Natural law* can be understood as law conferred by God, nature, or reason. Morality is inherent in the idea of natural law, while under positive law, law is separated from morality. Society may use positive law as a means to an

end, and if democratic processes are followed, we regard the enactment as an enforceable legal enactment. Separate and apart from legality are debates over the morality, wisdom, or efficacy of the means and the ends.

In most situations involving legal issues, we are inclined to use an instrumental view of law. Consider the list of social concerns from an early survey of Asian American religionists: (1) the privileged position of Christianity; (2) meeting legal definitions of religious organization to take advantage of benefits granted to religion; (3) access to religious education in public schools and accreditation for religiously based schools; (4) enforcement of antidiscrimination laws; and (5) institutionalization of moral beliefs such as profamily policies in state programs. If we see the question of Christian privilege as a constitutional question, then each of these situations is about laws or enactments and raises the possibility of legal redress. And in each of these situations, law is seen instrumentally—as a barrier or a means to achieve a goal. Remedies are sought through legal specialists—lawyers, judges, and legislators.

In seeing law as instrumental to solving social questions, one can easily overlook the ways in which the remedial possibilities shape the way the issues are posed or even conceptualized. Positive law defines the contours of our religious practices and therefore participates in formulating its content.

This link can be seen more clearly if we note the similarities between pastoral practices and lawyering. A commonplace observation finds the minister and the lawyer involved in critical life passages such as birth, marriage, divorce, and death. Legal considerations surround each of these moments. Around birth, the law provides such framing questions as the marital status of the parents, the financial obligations of the father, the voluntary nature of the sexual contact, and the legal permissibility of such contact.

Beyond such individual moments, the role of the law in the institutional life of churches is even more pervasive. Among the standard tools of legal practice are comprehensive encyclopedias for lawyering in particular areas. One legal treatise on religious organizations is not only lengthy—four large loose-leaf volumes—but remarkably broad and detailed. It begins with constitutional freedom of religion, then discusses the various legal forms for church organization including boards, membership, and voting. As dimensions of management and liability, the treatise discusses hiring of ministers, use of property, and church finance as well as such controversial issues as faith healing, mind control, and member discipline. In this way, the actual practice of organized religion is permeated by a fabric of positive law regulation. The limits of such legal structures may well confine the possibilities of religious practice. Nontraditional faiths or minority religions may choose to conduct themselves in an extra-legal fashion.

Constitutional Dimensions. We will provide here only a very brief overview of the constitutional law of religion. The religion clauses of the First Amendment are the first provisions of the Bill of Rights: *Congress shall make no law respecting an establishment of religion, or prohibiting the free exercise thereof.* They are known as the "establishment clause" and the "free exercise clause." The language is strong, with directives against a state religion and against state efforts to proscribe the practice of religion.

Like so many constitutional provisions, the simple language of the religion clauses has proven complex in application. Some guidelines have emerged. First, the clauses, like most of the Bill of Rights, are limitations on government—federal, state, and local. They do not directly apply to nongovernmental parties and individuals. Second, the Supreme Court has avoided trying to define religion, instead requiring "sincerely held beliefs" rather than focusing on which beliefs and practices are truly religious. Third, the Court has established a line between religious belief and religious practices. Beliefs are highly protected against government coercion while practices are subject to some forms of regulation.

The prohibition against establishing religion has several current interpretations, which include consideration of the purpose and effect of legislation on religion, and also government entanglement, endorsement, and coercion of religion. Such varied practices as prayer in government schools, evolution in the science curriculum, and municipal Christmas displays have been reviewed under the establishment clause. As with so much of the current Supreme Court's decision making, we have not been given clear guidelines of what is an impermissible establishment of religion.

The provision protecting "free exercise" has generated considerable controversy. In a widely discussed holding, the Court rejected a *strict scrutiny* approach protective of religious practices and instead upheld laws of general applicability even when the laws limit religious practices (*Employment Division v. Smith*). The decision was interpreted as limiting the free exercise of religion and was widely criticized as an ill-advised and confusing shift from past interpretations. In response, Congress enacted the Religious Freedom Restoration Act of 1993. Upon review, the Supreme Court found the law in part unconstitutional.

Alongside this confusing line of cases on the free exercise clause, the Court has also moved away from its separation of the religion clauses from other rights protected under the First Amendment. An analysis under the establishment clause or free exercise clause was distinct from freedom of speech and freedom of association. Instead of this secular–religious distinction, the Court is now inclined to combine the religion clauses and other First Amendment freedoms. This combination of ambiguous and overlapping Court decisions along with congressional enactments directed at the Court's rulings has meant little legal clarity from the Court. Even when the Court decides intensely politicized cases involving religious beliefs and same-sex marriage, abortion, or birth control, the reasoning of the Court leaves matters open for continuing debate.

For Asian American religionists concerned with how these discussions are limited to the dominant Christian discourse, the Court's ambiguous postures has made a challenge to the Christian norm twice as difficult. The intensity of the existing debates has meant that there is little cultural space to insert an objection to Christian normativity. And as a question of constitutional doctrine, the Court's overlapping and multiple approaches make it extremely difficult to craft a legal basis for such a challenge.

Law as Definition and Limit. The discussion of a legal web of regulation throughout organized religion suggested that such laws and statutes might create limits on religious beliefs. This sense of the law as frame and limit on religious practice has a stronger content if we expand our understanding of law beyond statutes and court decisions. With a broader understanding of law as legal possibility, we see encompassed within the idea of law the full range of democratic aspirations that Asian immigrants brought to the United States. Once Asians moved from sojourners to immigrants, their social aspirations took on familiar forms. Asian immigrants sought full civic participation—employment, business, family, and education. And as with other immigrant groups, religion and churches played and continue to play a crucial social role.

Much of the literature on Asian American religion and culture describes religious practice and belief in its dual roles. The ethnic church works to preserve traditional cultural practices and values. At the same time, ethnic churches function as vehicles for assimilation into American life. Within the academic discipline of Asian American studies, we see social narratives of immigration, citizenship, employment, family, resistance to discrimination and racism, and the tensions between the traditional and the new world. The aspirational dimension of these narratives is celebrated as part of our immigrant success story. These aspirations are, however, traditional secular democratic ideals.

The limitations of the secular have been the subject of grand theorizing with reference to considerations of race, slavery, and comparative religion. For Asian American religion and culture, however, the descriptions need not be so elevated. Democratic ideals and aspirations for Asian Americans have taken relatively straightforward legal goals and objectives. Barriers to citizenship were abolished. Educating our children has not only been successful, but is the subject of caricature. Employment and business long ago expanded beyond laundries, farms, and sweatshops. Voting and politics are no longer distant dreams. And diversity has been embraced by the Supreme Court as an important social value.

With these accomplishments we are coming to an end for the legal—the democratic ideal—as the aspirational for Asian Americans. The struggle to achieve basic democratic rights has largely run its course. While grand theory has raised "reenchantment" as an alternative, it is not yet clear whether Asian American religion and culture can provide a social alternative.

Is This a Religion Issue?

Religion and Multiple Dimensions of Identity. We turn next to the term *Asian American*. We examine some of the complexities of that term—the three traditions of the panethnic, the racial, and the diasporic—in the next section. If we attempt to define the Asian American, we are immediately faced with the problem that the category includes "all of the above." A hypothetical Asian American—a man, woman, or child of Asian ancestry located in an American city—embodies legal citizenship, national origin, immigrant status, gender, age, racial category, ethnic identity, sexuality—as significant identity elements. In social science terms, the category and identity for Asian American is overdetermined—the multiple dimensions make problematic any effort to determine or to define the category.

To examine multiple and overlapping identities, we consider as an example the not unusual situation of a dispute over construction of a new temple. Jaideep Singh analyzed resistance to establishing a Sikh temple in San Jose, California. In the Sikh temple case, opposition took multiple forms. In examining this opposition, we find racial discrimination—resistance to a temple with brown-skinned members. We see nativist sentiments against foreign immigrants. There was racial profiling linking temple members to the trope of the Islamic terrorist based on the visual symbols of turbans and beards on brown men. Finally, there was religious bigotry based on the temple being a "minority religion" with unfamiliar rituals and symbols. The specific venue for the conflict—local land use regulation—put the issues into a legal setting. In that context, the multiple identities make difficult a singular claim of impermissible discrimination based on religious bigotry. As a legal matter, a charge of religious discrimination is a strong legal claim and one that was pursued strategically. However strongly we may feel that religion played a crucial role in opposition sentiment, the complexities of the Asian American condition require our social analyses to be nuanced and not singular.

Minority Religions. The status of the Sikh religious community also provides a basis for examining the meaning of "minority religion." While there are multiple meanings, we will look at "minority religion" in two ways. First, the term can mean a religion of a nonwhite racial or ethnic community. A second sense is that of a religion or religious practice that is not regarded as being within the mainstream Protestant tradition. These two senses of minority religion are not, of course, exclusive categorizations but rather overlapping and at times indistinguishable.

The concept of a religion of racial or ethnic minorities has been extended by scholars backwards in history. A body of scholarship examines race or proto-race back into antiquity, including the "origins of racism in the West." Authors examine ancient Greece, Rome, and Athenian-Persian conflict. Denise Buell has identified "ethnic reasoning" in early Christianity and examined its implications for the meaning of the universalism in early Christianity. In the United States, we have the model of African American Christian churches and their vision of Christianity consolidating and flourishing since the Civil War. The investigation into antiquity, the tradition of the black church in America, and the experience of immigrant communities establishing their own churches and religious communities demonstrate the deep historical linkages between religion and racial or ethnic communities. In the case of the San Jose Sikh temple, this historical legacy means that opposition sentiments should not be narrowly parsed into religious discrimination or racial discrimination with their separate legal pedigrees. Sentiments on minority religions can be complex in their origins and their expressions.

We turn next to a focus on religious categories as the starting point for community and identity. Instead of starting with race or ethnicity, we begin with the various named religions. Using named religions derived from the "world religion" tradition, religious studies provide a very different arrangement of categories for minority religion. The modern idea of "world religions" shapes such legal formulations as freedom of religion or free exercise of religion. In that tradition, exemplified in multiple textbooks and discussions of the great religions of the world, identifying and naming a religion guarantees that religion a social position and legal rights to its practitioners.

While protective in theory, the actual treatment of religious practitioners outside of the Protestant mainstream has been marked as often by persecution as freedom and tolerance. Eric Mazur's study of the experience of Jehovah's Witnesses, Mormons, and Native American traditional practitioners outlines three strategies. Minority religious groups can establish a separate peace, accommodate their theology to political realities, or engage in sustained conflict. Two further observations are important. A crucial aspect of the first and second strategies is whether to accept the principles and values of American constitutional governance—in short, whether to accept assimilation into the legal framework. Mazur also observes that the closer the minority beliefs are to Protestant Christianity, the easier the accommodation. Mazur's analysis of possible strategies demonstrates the importance of the legal—the constitutional considerations—for minority religions. Mazur's description of possible strategies also highlights the cost of joining the world religion tradition. To participate in freedom of religion, a minority religion may be forced to choose between altering beliefs and practices or accepting nonlegal or outlaw status.

Among Asian Americans, the experiences of different ethnic groups have varied, even within the same religious tradition. Different Buddhist communities have taken divergent paths as a minority religion. Among the oldest Asian American churches, the predominantly Japanese American Buddhist Churches of America has a strong assimilationist tradition, with a visible Protestant influence on its organization and rituals. By contrast, a study of Toronto Lao Buddhists made in the 1990s notes that the community had not yet chosen a path of social engagement. Mazur's typology situates these different responses within the American constitutional order. The possibilities of worship and ritual are constrained and guided not only by the conditions of American social and economic life, but also by the constitutional and legal guidelines.

Buddhism also provides an example of how what is nominally a singular world religion can take completely different social and legal forms as a minority religion in the American context. Joseph Cheah's examination of race and American Buddhism uses Omi and Winant's theories of racial categorization to describe how American Buddhism is now divided into two distinct racial traditions. There are ethnic Buddhists—immigrants and descendants of immigrants from Asia located in or around ethnic communities. The ritual and belief of these ethnic Buddhists are largely derived from the Asian homeland. The other tradition in American Buddhism is convert Buddhism. Convert Buddhism is racially white, located in widely dispersed locales, and maintains a network of publication and communication separate from ethnic Buddhists. Cheah's study illuminates how the divide between Asian ethnic Buddhism and white convert Buddhism included not just the racial divisions carried over from American racial life, but also differences over ritual, practice, and belief within the nature of modern Buddhism. Even though both branches of American Buddhism share the Buddhist category from the world religion tradition, within America, they are both minority religions.

As adherents of a world religion, both traditions of American Buddhism are protected under constitutional freedom of religion. However, the experiences of Japanese Buddhist priests before and after Pearl Harbor or the more recent limited social outreach of Lao Buddhists in Toronto are part of an Asian American immigrant racial and political experience different from that of mainstream white America. White convert Buddhists are largely assimilated and their issues of social acceptance are different from those of ethnic Buddhists. Their experience as a "minority religion" is significantly different from those of the ethnic Asian American churches.

The two forms of "minority religion"—a religion of racial and ethnic minorities and a religion distinct from the mainstream Protestant churches—are described most clearly in the two Buddhist traditions. Their different experiences also suggest how law and legal considerations have played out differently for these different aspects of minority religion.

Freedom of Religion. A third aspect of discerning the presence of religion in legal issues is found in the idea of freedom of religion. The idea of religious freedom is a historically dense and analytically vast topic. As part of the protection of human rights, religious freedom is important to protect and defend. However, freedom of religion has also played an important role in colonial and imperial missions and also as part of efforts to impose and reinforce Christian normativity.

To show the limitations of the idea of freedom of religion, consider two examples—the opening of Japan, and attempts to nullify civil rights under freedom of religion. Jason Josephson begins *The Invention of Religion in Japan* with the arrival of American warships in 1853. He notes that the treaties forced on Japan by Perry's gunboats included a requirement that Americans be allowed the free exercise of religion including the right to erect places of worship. Josephson argues that the Japanese did not have an equivalent word for our modern conception of religion. Among

other dimensions, the Japanese did not conceptualize a general social category of religion and within that general category, specifically named members. A part of the complex events set in motion by Perry ultimately included Buddhism but not Shintō as a religion. Here, we note only that this "freedom" was imposed by force to allow the entry of Christian missionaries into Japan. While gunboat diplomacy and freedom of religion may at first glance be concepts in conflict, they are integrally linked in the history of Japanese Buddhism and the modern history of European relations with Asia.

In recent years, there has been an expansion of claims for religious freedom against antidiscrimination and health care legislation. Laws and judicial decisions prohibiting discrimination on the basis of sexual orientation, legalization of same-sex marriage, and health care legislation allowing birth control and abortion have all been challenged as infringing on religious freedom. These claims have not only been on behalf of individuals for their personal beliefs, but also for their effect on corporate and commercial practices. These cases emphasize that freedom of religion as applied is deeply infused with political and social import. The Supreme Court's failure to clarify an approach to freedom of religion or religious accommodation has generated frustration among observers. Yet even as freedom of religion is used as a high-profile political weapon against civil rights, the San Jose Sikh temple case demonstrates the importance of freedom of religion to Asian American practitioners of minority religions.

Racialization of Islam. The most compelling legal issue for Asian Americans has been the racialization of Islam and the pervasive distribution of the trope of the Muslim terrorist. In this process, even the positive aspects of world religion are reduced to an Orientalist caricature. Under the world religions approach, vast variations in religious traditions are reduced to a formal singularity—Christianity, Islam, or Buddhism. The deep histories and enormous breadth of lived practices are dissolved into a single category. The positive side of world religions is the formal granting of a level of mutual respect and tolerance. All practitioners should have a legally protected right to continue their privatized rituals and beliefs.

Since 9/11, an enormous amount of political, intellectual, and media energy has been devoted to replacing the content of the religion category of Islam with an Orientalized trope—the Islamic terrorist. World religion categories by their nature are reductionist. The inherent simplification of the world religion category of Islam was already deeply informed by European Orientalism. That simplification had already reduced the importance of the breadth of practices within Islam. After 9/11, the intense media campaign has focused on replacing any traditional or even moderately unfriendly versions of Islam with one vision—the Muslim terrorist. Older forms in the cultural content of the space reserved for the world religion category of Islam are now replaced by the terrorist. Further, freedom of religion is directly undermined. Under the guise of national security, normal levels of respect

for private worship are replaced with racial profiling and intense surveillance. This process is racialized through deemphasis of the Protestant tradition of personal interior belief and its replacement with a brown body. Instead of asking for a demonstration of sincere belief or ritual practice, the focus is on a brown body embellished with a beard and turban. By itself, the racialized body is enough to presume loss of fundamental rights of privacy and religious freedom.

This process was compressed through intense media images, op-ed commentaries, political posturing, violence against brown bodies, and requirements for public performance of Americanness rituals in school, in government, and in other public spaces. This process continues to be reinforced through an endless series of movies and television stories centering on terrorism and religious fanaticism. The breadth and scope of this continuing project of racialization means that efforts to provide an alternate American understanding of Islam and to deracialize the Asian brown body will be enormously difficult.

Law, Religion, and the Asian American Category

In this section, we focus on the Asian American category and the ways the category has been used in Asian American religious studies.

Ascribed Identity, Collective Identity, Identification. A useful distinction in identity discussions is to recognize three dimensions: ascribed identity, collective identity, and identification. *Ascribed iden-*

tities are group characteristics imposed on us. Racial stereotypes are an easily recognizable example. *Collective identity* is the effort of a social group to create itself as a group and characterize the group to others. *Identification* describes the agency by which an individual or a group moves to generate and communicate a collective identity.

Consider this simple identity statement: "I am a Buddhist." This is a personal effort at identification. I situate myself in a socially recognized group identity. For a collective identity, I regard myself as a member of the Stockton, California Jōdo Shin Shū temple in which I grew up. While I am not especially active in my Buddhist collective identity, I do participate in family rituals, usually weddings and funerals. I therefore believe that I am still a part of the Buddhist Churches of America collective identity.

There are also ascriptive dimensions. The label Buddhist and the term Buddhism that I use are largely shaped by and understood as part of the world religions tradition. Certain understandings or misunderstandings are assigned to me as part of the historical development of the category of Buddhism, as well as stereotypes and tropes attributed to Buddhism.

Within the United States, there is the further complication of race. As a Japanese American Buddhist, I am assigned to the ethnic nonwhite side rather than the white convert side of the dual American Buddhist traditions. These are ascribed social distinctions and are outside of my immediate control.

These analytic dimensions are, of course, only visible through an intellectual effort. My lived experience of Buddhism is rarely formally divided into collective, ascriptive, and identification. Yet when trying to understand and analyze identity categories, the effort to separate the different dimensions can be a useful device. This is especially true if the analysis is within an activist project where determining the possibilities of political agency may be significant.

Asian American: Panethnic, Racial, Diasporic. Within the discipline of Asian American studies, the foundational Asian American category has itself been the subject of intense and continuing scrutiny. For this essay, we observe that in the usage and analysis of the Asian American category, there are three identifiable traditions growing out of different authorial subject positions: panethnic, racial, and diasporic.

Writing in the *panethnic* tradition begins with and is grounded within an ethnic community. In this tradition, the author's subject position is American and from the interior of a community. The question of a broader Asian American grouping is a secondary element. Because legal discrimination on the basis of ethnicity or national origin is a less developed area of discrimination law, the legal plays a diminished role in these discussions. The *racial* tradition for the Asian American category is modeled on racial discrimination against African Americans after the Civil War. Discriminatory treatment of Asiatic bodies is the common theme. The author's subject position in the racial tradition is broadly American and is not limited to a particular ethnic community. Since race discrimination is a very well-developed area of legal studies, much of the work in this tradition includes law and legal history. The *diasporic tradition* has its logical starting point in the homeland. Homeland history, culture, and religion is a necessary starting point. National borders and boundaries are a foundational legal dimension. Depending on the specific analysis, international and domestic law is a part of this tradition. Related to using the homeland as a starting point is the transnational perspective. The transnational variant moves the perspective to a neutral, objective point of view, somewhere above any homeland.

A brief review of the contents of three early collections of Asian American religionists illustrates these three traditions. *New Spiritual Homes: Religion and Asian Americans*, edited by David Yoo; *Religions in Asian America: Building Faith Communities*, edited by Pyong Gap Min and Jung Ha Kim; and *Revealing the Sacred in Asian and Pacific America*, edited by Jane Iwamura and Paul Spickard, all include "Asian American" in the title. Yet the articles themselves do not reflect a strong Asian American categorization. Of the 40 articles in the three volumes, 25 are ethnic specific. The titles and the introductory discussions make clear that they wish to give content and meaning to the Asian American category. The authors of all three volumes at least mention race in their introductions as a necessary aspect of the Asian American experience.

The actual content of the articles—arguably reflecting the experience of Asian Americans studied by these authors—are more frequently ethnic rather than Asian American. Only a few of the collected authors, Russell Jeung, Rudy Busto, and David Kim, write explicitly within an Asian American categorization. Their presence in an Asian American collection is clearly appropriate. We can see their articles as being in the *racial* Asian American tradition.

The 25 ethnic-specific articles can be seen as being within the panethnic tradition. Their inclusion in books that reference the Asian American category suggests that each author is willing to accept the broad category of Asian American. Yet the content for each is based in a specific ethnicity. These articles can be seen as being in the *panethnic* Asian American tradition.

All of the authors who discuss an ethnic specific religious experience include at least some aspects of homeland culture and religious practices. A few, such as Sharon Suh's discussion of identity in "To Be Buddhist Is to Be Korean" or Timothy Tseng's history of Chinese Protestant nationalism in the United States are transnational and include important elements from a diasporic viewpoint. Those articles can be seen as being at least influenced by *diasporic* and transnational approaches to the Asian American.

This distinction of three different traditions in examination of the Asian American category is not intended to provide any preference or direction for future research. But an awareness of how we participate in the project of constructing the Asian American including its legal dimension is facilitated by understanding the importance of our subject positions and how they affect our analyses.

Orientalism. While Orientalism has been and remains an important theme in Asian

American studies, it is an analytic dimension that deserves continuing attention. As a historical question, Orientalism precedes significant immigration from Asia. We have only begun our exploration of how those understandings shaped the histories and experiences of Asian Americans. In religious studies, constructivist religious analyses (including the "invention of" scholarship) are arguably deeply implicated in the Asian religious traditions as experienced in the United States. Besides those general considerations, one of the most important legal issues for Asian American religion is the widespread acceptance of the racialization of Islam and the trope of the Muslim terrorist. It is impossible to analyze these developments without careful attention to the multiple and complex strands of Orientalism embedded deep in Western culture.

Conclusion

Since its beginnings in student strikes, Asian American studies has shared dual personalities: academic and activist. The activist personality has always had a profound influence on the direction and content of the academic work of Asian American studies. Much of that early activism was inspired by socialist revolutions in Asia. The decline of the influence of Marxist revolutionary idealism has arguably left a significant absence in activist ideologies. Further, much of the content of the investigations of Asian American studies has examined democratic ideals as the aspirational dimension for Asian Americans. Those democratic ideals have either been based on or shaped by law and legal understandings. Throughout legal studies as well as in the broader society, the use of those ideals to inspire has been the subject of increasing self-examination.

Asian American religious studies is positioned to examine and inspire in ways that are not limited by law and legal liberalism. Such projects have not yet played the leading role in Asian American religious studies. Whatever form such interventions might take, this essay should clarify that law, as presently constituted and understood, cannot play such a role.

Neil Gotanda

See also: Essays: Immigration; Islamophobia

Further Reading

Bassett, William W., W. Cole Durham, Jr., and Robert T. Smith. *Religious Organizations and the Law*. Minneapolis: Clark Boardman Callaghan, 2012.

Buell, Denise Kimber. *Why This New Race: Ethnic Reasoning in Early Christianity*. New York: Columbia University Press, 2005.

Chang, Gordon H. *Asian Americans and Politics: Perspectives, Experiences, Prospects*. Stanford, CA: Stanford University Press, 2001.

Chang, Robert. "Toward an Asian American Legal Scholarship: Critical Race Theory, Post-Structuralism, and Narrative Space." *California Law Review* 81 (1993): 1241.

Cheah, Joseph. *Race and Religion in American Buddhism: White Supremacy and Immigrant Adaptation*. New York: Oxford University Press, 2011.

Chua, Amy. *Battle Hymn of the Tiger Mother*. New York: Penguin Books, 2011.

Cook, Anthony. *The Least of These: Race, Law and Religion in American Culture*. London: Routledge, 1997.

Darian-Smith, Eve. *Religion, Race, Rights: Landmarks in the History of Modern Anglo-American Law*. Oxford: Hart, 2010.

Gotanda, Neil. "New Directions in Asian American Jurisprudence." *Asian American Law Journal* 17 (2010): 1.

Gotanda, Neil. "The Racialization of Islam in American Law." *Annals of the American Academy of Political and Social Science* (September 2011).

Hing, Bill Ong. *Defining America through Immigration Policy*. Philadelphia: Temple University Press, 2004.

Iwamura, Jane Naomi. *Virtual Orientalism: Asian Religions and American Popular Culture*. New York: Oxford University Press, 2011.

Mazur, Eric Michael. *The Americanization of Religious Minorities: Confronting the Constitutional Order*. Baltimore: Johns Hopkins University Press, 1999.

Singh, Jaideep. "The Racialization of Minoritized Religious Identity: Constructing Sacred Sites at the Intersection of White and Christian Supremacy." In Jane Naomi Iwamura and Paul Spickard, eds., *Revealing the Sacred in Asian and Pacific America*. London: Routledge, 2003.

Volpp, Leti. "The Citizen and the Terrorist." *UCLA Law Review* 49 (2002): 1575.

Wu, Frank. *Yellow: Race in America beyond Black and White*. New York: Basic Books, 2002.

Case and Statute Cited

Employment Division v. Smith, 494 U.S. 872 (1990).

Religious Freedom Restoration Act of 1993, 42 U.S.C. §2000bb et seq.

Religion, Race, and Orientalism

Asian Americans and their Asian religious traditions, beliefs, practices, and lifeways intersect with their racial profile or classification through the process of Orientalization to impact, explicitly and implicitly, their identity, their citizenship, their rights—or lack of—and their integration into American society. Religion and race are two flammable topics in American society and interact in complex and nuanced manners. The goal of this essay is to unpack these critical concepts, religion, race, and Orientalism, so as to apply them to the study of Asian religious and faith traditions, communities, and subjects in the United States, as well as to endeavor to delineate the powerful forces of religion and race within and among Asian Americans.

Religion

There are many definitions of and associations with religion. Since the 15th century, religion in the West has become implicitly universal and its characteristics appear to be natural. For example, explorers and missionaries have claimed indigenous peoples of the New World "lack" "knowledge of God" or "have . . . no religion as we understand it." Religion is also tied to belief systems, customs, rites, and rituals. Jonathan Z. Smith notes that religion, in relation to ritual practices, has become an inventory for cultural topics and ethnographic studies of particular people and their societies. By the 18th century, religion was equated with virtues that are founded on beliefs and faith in God in relation to a future, mostly metaphysical reward or punishment. Increasingly, religion became associated, or rather, interrelated with "faith," which raised issues of authenticity, credibility, and claims to ultimate truths. Over time, religion has become nested in institutions and structures that govern all aspects of religion in people's lives. In the West, the dominant conceptual model of "religion," derived from the Latin *religiō*, refers to a covenant that entails obligations between individuals and communities and their God, a mutuality that is fundamental to Abrahamic faith traditions. The etymology of "religion" is uncertain, but one possible root is *leig* meaning "to bind" and has been a subject of Christian homiletic. Critics have expressed reservations about the appropriateness of this notion of "religion" to a tradition like shamanism, for example, that is bereft of an institution or a canon or priesthood; or to Confucianism that has a canon, but without a highly structured organized institution and an ordained priesthood. While the Buddhist tradition has a canon, institution, and priesthood, it does not posit a personality—god or divinity—with whom the devotee can establish a covenant. Contemporary religious studies employ religion rather differently from theology precisely because religious studies engages with religion as an anthropological, not theological category.

Race

Although we hope that all individuals in contemporary societies "understand" race as a historical development, racial classifications, categories, and logic are deeply nested in structures of power, privilege, and knowledge. From the 15th to mid-20th centuries, European colonialists legitimated their conquest by imposing their notions of "religion" and "race" on Asians, Africans, and the indigenous people of the Americas. Race, from this perspective, is inherently biologically determined, and determined by God. As such, human values, morals, customs, language, abilities, mind, and overall civilization are determined by race, as well as God. Phenotypical differences in hair texture, skin color, and head size are evidence of the inborn biological differences of the races. Racial logic and ideas as proscribed by pseudo-scientific claims of craniology, backed by theological claims, were employed to construct a racial hierarchy that placed the "white race" at the top, and the "black" or African "race" at the bottom. Asians were classified as the "yellow" or "Mongol race." It is therefore critical that we state that we believe there is no scientific basis for racial classifications. Moreover, we recognize that racial classifications are produced and maintained, over time, in social, political, and economic contexts to reify, legitimatize, and perpetuate a racial hierarchy within our society creating inequality and discrimination. The gravest danger of "race" is that it has become "common" or rather "common sense." Racial classification and racial meaning are not questioned, but rather taken for granted as "natural" or mutually understood, or universally accepted means to make sense of human diversity. Michael Omi and Howard Winant articulate this process as "racial formation" and define "race" as a way of "making up people." Race and racial meaning are therefore constantly shifting over time. Racism and discrimination based on race are actions informed by racial ideas.

Spc. Simran Lamba, right, talks with his cousin, Megha Malhotra, left, who flew in from Boston to see his naturalization ceremony and basic training graduation at Fort Jackson, S.C., November 10, 2010. Lamba is the first enlisted soldier to be granted a religious accommodation for his Sikh articles of faith since 1984. Sikhism, a 500-year-old religion founded in India, requires its male followers to wear a turban and beard and keep their hair uncut. Army policies since 1984 had effectively prevented Sikhs from enlisting by barring those items. But Lamba was granted a rare exception because he has skills the Army wants—the Indian languages Hindi and Punjabi. (AP Photo/Brett Flashnick)

Asian Americans along with people of other racialized communities are consistently subject to racism—direct and subtle—even in the present time. Here are some major forms of racism that affect Asian Americans:

- *Institutional racism and psychological reductionism*: Racism has more to do with institutional and structural inequities rather than a set of individual attitudes. This form of racism is deeply embedded in the fabric of American society—historically and presently—as revealed by systems of white and Christian supremacy that permeate American civil society, polity, economics, and culture.

- *Race as ethnicity*: Another form of racism is equating race with ethnicity. While ethnicity refers to a person's national origins and cultural roots, race is politically defined as a result of laws and regulations enacted by the federal, state, and local governments. Race is also defined in terms of assumed physiological characteristics. Asian

Americans are often defined ethnically by ignoring the racial factors. This misinterpretation is based on a presupposition that Asian immigrants and other nonwhite Americans gradually assimilate into the dominant white population and its cultural norms. But the reality of Asian immigration as well as its "assimilation" does not follow this misreading of Asian American population. Racial minorities, whether Asian Americans or other non-European populations, do not readily integrate into the existing white racial and cultural norms and structures.

- *Model minority status and economic reductionism*: Another nefarious view of racism is the notion that economic injustices trump racial injustices. This reductionism largely stems from the impression that Asian Americans are by and large economically wealthy and thus their experiences cannot be equated with the experiences of other racial minority populations in the United States. This is perpetuated with the stereotypical image of Asian Americans as a "model minority," which developed in the late 1960s in post–World War II America. Economic reductionism is one of the major reasons why Asian Americans are often not considered a group that is subject to racism. Asian American educational and economic attainment, as represented by the stereotypical image of the "model minority," are often used as the reasons for Asian Americans' exclusion from race considerations because as a "model minority" Asian Americans are "honorary whites" or, as some argue, "equal to or better than whites" on indicators of socioeconomic success. The reality of Asian Americans is that wealth and educational attainment do not exempt them from racism—direct or subtle.

- *Subtle racism*: Direct forms of racism, such as the brutal killing of Vincent Chin during the 1980s in Detroit, Michigan, by two white unemployed auto workers, or the historic anti-Asian sentiments to drive out the Asians by white mobs are easily identifiable. Subtle racism is harder to deduce as it is coded in what appears to be harmless acts. For example, Asian Americans, regardless of their length of residence in the United States, are assumed to be "foreigners." Non-Asians will often ask these seemingly benign questions: "How long have you been here?" "Where are you from?" "You do not have an accent. Where did you learn to speak English?" While these questions appear relatively harmless, they reinforce the image of Asian Americans as "perpetual foreigners" and give evidence of the limits to the universal claims of multicultural assimilation.

Race for Asian Americans is indispensably related to their experiences of racism. Racism manifests itself in various levels of politics, in the workplace, in the media, and in everyday social encounters. The history of Asians in the United States is fraught with examples of how the United States attempted to resolve the contradictions between its economic and political imperative through laws that excluded Asians from citizenship—from 1790 until the 1960s.

Race and religion are both socially constructed, anthropological categories. Moreover, both are colonialist projects, whose ideas and practices are the foundational building blocks of a racial hierarchy and apparatus that limits power, privilege, and knowledge of racialized minority communities, both historically and in contemporary society.

Oriental and Orientalism

Orientalism is a concept by Edward Said (1979) to articulate the process and production of the "Orient" and "Orientals" or the East and its people. It is the European, or rather, Western production of its "Other." The Orient defines the Occident, the West. As such, Orientalism is a Western style of domination of the Occident over the Orient, which gives authority to the West, which envisions itself as superior in all aspects of civilization and history. More importantly, Said argues that the relationship between the Occident and the Orient is one of power—of domination, of varying degrees of hegemony because the Orient and Orientals could be *submitted*. Said says,

> Therefore, Orientalism is not a mere political subject matter or field that is reflected passively by culture, scholarship, or institutions; nor is it a large and diffuse collection of texts about the Orient; nor is it representative and expressive of some nefarious

"Western" imperialist plot to hold down the "Oriental" world. It is rather a *distribution* of geopolitical awareness into aesthetic, scholarly, economic, sociological, historical, and philological texts; it is an *elaboration* not only of a basic geographical distinction (the world is made up of two unequal halves, Orient and Occident) but also of the whole series of "interests" which, by such means as scholarly discovery, philological reconstruction, psychological analysis, landscape and sociological description, it not only creates but also maintains; it *is*, rather than expresses, a certain *will* or intention to understand, in some cases to control, manipulate, even to incorporate, what is a manifestly different (or alternative and novel) world; it is above all, a discourse that is by no means in direct, corresponding relationship with political power in the raw, but rather is produced and exists in an uneven exchange with various kinds of power, shaped to a degree by the exchange with political power (as with reigning sciences like comparative linguistics or anatomy, or any of the modern policy sciences), cultural power (as with orthodoxies and canons of taste, texts, values), moral power (as with ideas about what "we" do and what "they" cannot do or understand as "we" do). (*Orientalism*, 1979, 12)

The application of racial logic and the production of racial categories is the process of Orientalism as the "Asiatic" or

"Mongol" or "Oriental" "race" is created in U.S. history through exclusionary immigration laws and naturalization policies. Asian and Asian American religious traditions and Asian and Asian American ways of doing religion are therefore embedded with their identified and ascribed racial profiles. The history of Asian Americans from the 1840s to the mid-1960s civil rights achievements is marked by the coupling and powerful manifestations of race and religion. America was envisioned as a country for the "white race" defined by the doctrine of manifest destiny. America's expansion from the East Coast to the West Coast was understood, therefore, as part of the divine will of God. But it was God only for white men, not the indigenous, blacks, Mexicans, or Asians. The white man's burden is the task of civilizing the heathens: the indigenous Indians and the Asians, in particular the Chinese, the first group of Asian migrants to come in large numbers since the mid-1840s. The work of civilizing the heathens was squarely in the hands and "swords" of Christian missionaries who forcibly took indigenous children from their families and boarded them in missionary schools where they were stripped of their native languages, religious lifeways, and reluctantly transformed into "Westerners" and brought into "history." For the Chinese, active missionizing was coupled with immigration exclusion and denial of naturalization rights. The motto then, and regrettably, for some today: Keep America White. Economic competition in the labor market fueled much of the vitriolic contempt for Asian laborers—Chinese in particular—but it was dressed up in religious and racial

logic: America is part of God's plan; it is to be a country for free white men; and must be protected from the heathens to maintain white racial purity.

Intersection of Religion, Race, and Orientalism

Asian and Asian American religions, race, and the process of Orientalism intersect to cut and inform Asian American lives, historically and today. While Said's Orientalism has had a major impact in informing and expanding the process of how the non-European "Other" is created, it is ultimately based on a binary system that boils down to tension and conflict: the West versus East, the civilized versus uncivilized, the moral versus immoral, and ultimately the "us" versus "them." The life and historical experiences of Asian Americans cannot be easily reduced to this binary tension. Asian Americans convert to Christianity through colonial missionizing, force, or personal will, as well as identify with "America," which bespeaks an often vexing relationship with the process of Orientalism, ascribed racial identity, and religious affiliation. The forces of Orientalism maintain the stereotypical image of Asian Americans, regardless of their length of time in the United States, as "perpetual foreigners" in part due to their racially ascribed profile. The state of "perpetual foreignness" is even stronger for Asian Americans who wear their religion publicly, such as is the case for Sikhs who wear turbans, or Muslims who veil: here, race, religion, and the Oriental project intersect to cut and inform, often in harmful and negative ways,

Asian Americans and their religious cultures.

Jonathan H. X. Lee, Fumitaka Matsuoka, Edmond Yee, and Ronald Y. Nakasone

See also: Essays: Gender and Sexuality; Islamophobia; *Entries:* Yee, James J.

Further Reading

Iwamura, Jane Naomi. *Virtual Orientalism: Asian Religions and American Popular Culture.* Oxford: Oxford University Press, 2011.

Omi, Michael, and Howard Winant. *Racial Formation in the United States*, 3rd ed. New York: Routledge, 2015.

Paddison, Joshua. *American Heathens: Religion, Race, and Reconstruction in California.* Berkeley: University of California Press, 2012.

Said, Edward. *Orientalism.* New York: Vintage Books, 1979.

Smith, Jonathan Z. "Religion, Religions, Religious." In Mark C. Taylor, ed. *Critical Terms for Religious Studies.* Chicago: University of Chicago Press, 1998, pp. 269–84.

Secularization and Asian Americans

Asians in the United States are substantially more likely to be nonreligious than any other racial group. While 15 percent of Americans answered "None" to any religious affiliation, 27 percent of Asian Americans were "Nones." When those who answered "Don't Know/Refused to Answer" are added, almost 1 in 3 Asian Americans are nonreligious (32 percent).

Not only are a high proportion of Asian Americans nonreligious, but this percent-age is increasing. In 1990, 20 percent of Asian Americans were nonreligious; this number grew 60 percent by 2008. Similarly, the general American population of "Nones" grew 92.4 percent in the same period.

Individual Asian ethnic groups vary in nonreligiosity. Chinese (39 percent) and Japanese Americans (26 percent) have the highest rates of "Nones" of any ethnic group in the United States, while Korean (87 percent) and Filipino Americans (92 percent) the highest rates of religious affiliation.

What accounts for the high rate of "Nones" among Asian Americans? This essay reviews theories of secularization and possible causes of this trend within the Asian American population. It also problematizes theories of secularization as Asian American religions challenge many of the assumptions of Western sociological theories.

Secularization: Definition and Levels of Analysis

Secularization is a social condition that is related to the declining importance of religion. Theoretical debates about this decline focus on three levels: societal, institutional, and individual. On the societal level, secularization entails the rationalization and structural differentiation of society into separate spheres, such as the economy, state, and family. Religion and religious authority has become relegated to a segmented, privatized sphere, as other public sectors become more autonomous. Secularization also relates to the decreasing role and salience of religious institutions in society. As society becomes more pluralistic, people's attitudes and beliefs become more relativized. They are less likely to hold to absolute certainties, and thus the authority of religious institutions over their lives lessens. Finally, on the individual level, secularization relates to the personal beliefs, attitudes, and practices of persons. Within the United States, the number of those who identify with no religion has doubled in the past two decades, indicating shifts toward secularized identities.

Rationalization and Science

Classic secularization theories focus on modernization and the role of rationalization. Max Weber, in considering social change, observed that the rationalization of action has brought "the disenchantment of the world." The rationalization of various spheres of life, as they orient toward particular ends, differentiates them to a greater extent. The state develops bureaucracies to legitimate and administer its power over a territory, while capitalism organizes labor and capital toward greater economic gain. Each sphere also becomes increasingly autonomous as fields become specialized in personnel, knowledge, and administration. Society thus becomes secularized through the separation of church and state, through the decline of religious authority in other spheres such as the economy and aesthetics, and through the relegation of religion to the private sphere.

While religion has become more privatized, other spheres have enlarged their scope of influence in society. Science,

aimed at developing technologies to control life, provides explanations for this-worldly experiences and for nature. As science expands its field of knowledge and mastery, mysteries of the physical world become disenchanted and religion diminishes in its scope of influence and its roles. Humans no longer need to rely on gods or divine forces to explain reality or to control their environment. Consequently, people on an individual level no longer turn to religion for such functions, as scientific authority claims greater legitimacy as knowledge and truth.

Scientists and those holding scientific worldviews would therefore be much more likely to be nonreligious as they are less likely to use religious explanations for the world. Indeed, with 52 percent claiming no religion, scientists are three times more likely than the general public to adopt a secular identity. Likewise, "Nones" are more likely to believe in human evolution (61 percent) than the general American public (38 percent). As Americans attain higher levels of education, their belief in creationism also steeply declines.

In contrast to this argument, sociologists argue that despite modernity's adoption of scientific worldviews, people continue to hold religious beliefs, especially the belief in God. Empirical numbers reveal that many hold to both a belief in God and a scientific worldview. Of Americans, 92 percent believe in God or a universal spirit, and almost 80 percent believe that miracles occur.

Nevertheless, Asian Americans may indeed be more nonreligious because of their adoption of a scientific, rational worldview. They make up 14 percent of the nation's science and engineering workforce, and almost 70 percent of the doctorates earned by Asian Americans are in the life sciences, physical sciences, and engineering. In fact, almost half of Asians (47.3 percent) earned bachelor's degrees in science and engineering, in contrast to 31.6 percent of all Americans. Further, 25.8 percent of Asian Indians and 19.9 percent of Chinese Americans work in computer, science and engineering fields while only 5.2 percent of whites and 2.7 percent of African Americans do. These large percentages are due to selective immigration patterns, as the Immigration Act of 1965 favored entry of Asian professionals with scientific and technical backgrounds. They may also be attributed to the glass ceiling effect, in which Asian Americans choose certain occupational fields for upward mobility and to avoid discrimination. Like others in these fields, the large proportion of Asian Americans may come from backgrounds with science and technology and with higher levels of educational attainment.

Pluralism and Institutional Decline

Another key modern process, globalization, produces pluralistic societies, establishes a more competitive religious marketplace, and undermines certainty in religious truths. As transnational economies increase the flow of global capital, labor pools also migrate. These flows promote cultural diversity in communities with Asian migrants, as well as introducing a range of religious ideas, practices, and institutions. Pluralization can secular-

ize the United States on an institutional level in three ways. First, it introduces new beliefs and ideas that challenge dominant ideologies. Second, America's "Christian collective consciousness" disintegrates as American mainline denominations decline in their public role and their numbers. Third, minority religions that are less competitive in the marketplace similarly lose salience and adherence in the Asian American community. While some Asian religious traditions are able to secure niches in the religious marketplace, others are less able. They lose adherents, who may be more likely to reject religious affiliation.

Globalization and pluralization first establish a marketplace of ideas, even if some ideas, values, and beliefs are still accorded dominance. Not only have Asian religious traditions circulated more broadly, but new religious movements (NRMs) also have sprung up. Steve Bruce posits that increasing diversity "calls into question the certainty that believers can accord their religion." Ideas that were once universally shared may continue to be held by some and practiced in private, but their salience and public role are undermined. Indeed, those who have been raised religiously but have switched to "None" are more likely to assert that no religion is completely true.

Pluralization's second challenge is the erosion of the overall institutional influence of American religion, especially that of its civil religion. In the middle of the century, Will Herberg in 1955 wrote of America's triple melting pot, Protestant, Catholic, Jew, and of the "American Way of Life," which promoted a national solidarity and faith. However, by the close of the century, religious scholars produced books highlighting America's religious restructuring and diversity. *A New Religious America: How a "Christian Country" Has Become the World's Most Religiously Diverse Nation* is one prime example. Wade Clark Roof and William McKinney claim that secularization and America's "weakened religious culture" is religion's most serious challenge today. With a weakened religious culture and greater individualism, religion now faces what may be thought of as a "third disestablishment": an expanded pluralism in which there is less of a religiously grounded moral basis for the society. Lacking a commonly accepted faith and morality, now religious groups find themselves contending with one another to become the shaping cultural influences. Indeed, with the restructuring of American religion and its de-Christianization, mainline and even evangelical Christianity's public role have been severely curtailed and less effective in shaping American norms.

Third, although institutions compete in the open religious marketplace in the United States, some, especially ones belonging to religious minorities, are at a disadvantage in securing niches. Christian privilege structures how religion is conceived, practiced, and even experienced. For example, Khyati Joshi identifies how Western conceptions of religion—as doctrinal, congregational, and voluntary— shape how Asian Indians adhere to Hinduism in the United States. Because they are often taught Christian biblical tenets, second-generation Asian Indians seek Hindu texts to know why and what they believe more than how they might

practice it. Because the American Christian style of worship is the norm, Hindu Americans also adopt voluntary forms of congregating and preach therapeutic messages oriented toward the here and now. However, because second-generation Asian Indians do not know what they believe, or do not attend temples as their parents did, they identify themselves as nonreligious. Religious affiliation, then, is based on what one believes and where one attends church. Although Joshi argues that her subjects do practice "lived religion," they themselves claim no religion as they employ Eurocentric notions of religion.

Religious oppression also discourages affiliation and participation in minority religions, thus possibly contributing to higher rates of Asian American "Nones." Christian privilege operates to racialize Asian Americans and marginalize non-Western religions as the other. Public schools institutionalize and teach Christian holidays and narratives while Asian American students report that their ways and traditions are viewed as weird and exotic. Media messages that associate brown-skinned persons as Muslims and terrorists affect Sikhs, Hindus, and Jains alike. In addition, residents may utilize local planning codes to bar Asian American congregations from their neighborhoods.

Given the chilling effect of this institutional marginalization and Orientalism, Asian religions have difficulty securing footholds in the American religious marketplace. As minority religions, they have to orient themselves differently to the wider community than Asian American Christian ones do. Furthermore, they may not have the linguistic staffing or physical resources to transmit their traditions to the second generation. Ethnographic studies comparing ethnic Christian and Buddhist congregations indicate that the Buddhist temples have much fewer resources for religious training and youth programming than the Christian ones. Indeed, these non-Christian institutions lose many more second-generation members because of the perceived irrelevance of their ancestral traditions.

Critics of secularization theories argue that the religious resurgence in the public square signals the deprivatization, not the privatization of religion. Further, they note that the increasing diversity of the American religious landscape is evidence of the new paradigm of religion and of congregational vitality. Indeed, Asian American Christian fellowships on campus may be changing the face of American evangelicalism. However, these indicators do not account for the high rates of nonreligiousness of Asian Americans. Rather, Asian Americans have a bipolar distribution of religious affiliation, with some groups being highly affiliated and others with high numbers of "Nones." For the "Nones," lack of strong and relevant religious institutions may account for declines in the number of Asian American adherents to any religious affiliation.

Individualism and Hybridization

The freedom of religion in the United States and the religious marketplace provide spiritual options for Americans, who are increasingly shifting in their religious affiliation. More than two-fifths of Americans switch from their childhood religious affiliation. Those who are religiously unaffiliated, the "Nones," were the group that has gained the most from these changes. The Pew Research Center report in 2009 finds that two-thirds of former Catholics who have become unaffiliated and half of former Protestants who have become unaffiliated say they left their childhood faith because they stopped believing in its teachings, and roughly four in ten say they became unaffiliated because they do not believe in God or the teachings of most religions.

Additionally, many people who left a religion to become unaffiliated say they did so in part because they think of religious people as hypocritical or judgmental, because religious organizations focus too much on rules, or because religious leaders are too focused on power and money. Far fewer say they became unaffiliated because they believe that modern science proves that religion is just superstition.

While the previous two sections of this essay identified the expansion of scientific worldviews and rejection of religious institutions as major factors in increasing secularization, changes in belief are the main self-stated reason for religious switching. Even those who were raised unaffiliated switched their religious affiliation once, with 47 percent having adopted a religion in order to meet spiritual needs.

Differentiation of life spheres has led to the privatization of religion as a personal option. Pluralism has promoted an open religious marketplace, where individuals become exposed to a variety of beliefs and practices that can undermine absolute certainties. With the loss of religious authority to impose doctrines, individuals become their own authorities in matters of belief and conscience. This demonstrates that American individualistic impulses, ironically, are derived from its Protestant Reformation roots, which affirmed all individuals as equal before God. Two current forms of American individualism, utilitarian and expressive, both may reflect this individual secularization.

Utilitarian individualism involves the pursuit and maximization of one's own self-interests. With Benjamin Franklin as its primary influence, American utilitarian individualism focuses so exclusively on individual self-improvement that the larger social context hardly comes into view. Instead of being guided by religious transcendent and ethical principles, utilitarian individualists expect society, including religion, to be used for their own ends. The individual freedom to pursue one's material condition and status, by definition, entails the lessened role of religious authority, particularly the biblical tradition in the U.S. case.

Expressive individualism, on the other hand, privileges the search for personal autonomy, fulfillment, and expression. It finds its archetype in Walt Whitman, who pursued a life rich in experience, sensuality, and connection with nature. As religion's function becomes relegated to the private sphere of the individual, the ultimate meaning of church is an expressive-individualist one. Its value is as a loving community in which individuals can experience the joy of belonging. Religious institutions become therapeutic and self-oriented as they must meet such needs of their spiritual consumers. Rather than

being able to make strong ethical and moral demands, they are at the mercy, then, of catering to the emotional and expressive concerns of Americans.

Indeed, Americans now affiliate with religious traditions based on their own choice to a greater extent, which Roof and McKinney coined the "new voluntarism." They also can construct their own patchwork of religious references and practices, which Bellah et al. typified as "Sheilism." This individual approach to spirituality often parallels a rejection of organized religions as too dogmatic and intolerant. Secularization theorists suggest that such religious "bricolage" is another indicator of institutional religion's decline.

As the "Nones" grow in number, a significant proportion of them identify as "spiritual but not religious." A *Newsweek* poll found that 30 percent of Americans consider themselves within this category. Of nonbelievers, 44 percent were spiritual but not religious, while 48 percent were neither spiritual nor religious. In the Pew *American Religious Landscape Survey*, equal numbers of the total population's unaffiliated were secular unaffiliated (37.5 percent) and religious unaffiliated (37.5 percent). The religious unaffiliated stated that religion was "somewhat or very important in their lives." However, for Asian Americans, 47.8 percent were secular unaffiliated, and only 21.7 percent were religious unaffiliated. Asian Americans also had higher rates of atheists (13.0 percent) and agnostics (17.4 percent) than the rest of the population. These figures indicate that Asian Americans are more likely to be utilitarian individualists, as religion is not as salient to them.

Asian Popular Religion and Secularism

Theories of secularization beg the question of how to define religion or religiosity, especially in the Asian context. Although older secularization theories assume religion is a sacred canopy that is rupturing, the new paradigm of religion in the United States posits that religious institutions operate in an open market and mobilize more in this pluralistic environment. Religion itself is a source of identity, association, and empowerment in the United States, especially for immigrants. In its associational form, adherents join together in de facto congregationalism, where they assume lay control of the institution. Given these presumptions, religion's decline would involve drops in congregational numbers, as well decreasing salience as a source of identity, affiliation, and empowerment.

Thus, belief, belonging, and the political nature of religion have become central issues on whether secularization, or simply religious change, is occurring. For example, Hout and Fischer demonstrate that the increase in the "Nones" is largely due to a reaction against organized conservative religion's involvement in politics. Arguing against classic secularization theory and the privatization of religion, they suggest that people continue to hold to divine "belief without belonging." Similarly, Baker and Smith slice the issues of belief and belonging, and conclude that the "Nones" fall into three camps based on the intersection of belief in God and political relationship to organized religion: atheists, agnostics, and "unchurched" believers." The latter are spiritual but opposed to organized religion.

However, in the Asian context, popular religions are not primarily about belief in doctrines or even divine beings. Neither do they serve as sources of primary identity and belonging. For example, Chinese religions usually do not take the same congregational form nor serve as the same source of voluntary identity as monotheistic religions in the United States do. In contrast to Western religions, they usually have no sacred texts or religious doctrines,

Table 3 American Religious Landscape Survey, 2009

	Total Pop.	**White**	**Black**	**Asian**	**Other/ Mixed Race**	**Latino**
Unaffiliated	16	16	12	23	20	14
Atheist	2	2	< 0.5	3	1	1
Agnostic	2	3	2	4	3	1
Secular unaffiliated	6	7	3	11	7	4
Religious unaffiliated	6	5	8	5	9	8

Pew Research Religion and Public Life, "American Religious Landscape Survey," 2009.

institutional organization, hierarchical priesthood, or rites that express particular beliefs. Instead, they can be seen as syncretic, where the form of religion is a mixture of several belief systems and practices, or at least operating in a pluralistic religious landscape. Given this conceptual problem of Chinese religious belief and the diversity of Chinese religious practices, earlier scholars of Chinese popular religion not only debated why they persisted, but also whether they constituted a distinctive religion or not.

Because defining religion in a non-Western context is so difficult, few scholars have addressed secularization in China or elsewhere in Asia. Michael Syonzi identifies several problems with applying secularization and modernization theories to China. China has long had a religious marketplace before modern society, not a sacred canopy. Religious bricolage is not a new phenomenon of Western individualization, either. Instead, religion in China has been diffuse and not institutionalized. Rather, it was both public and privatized. Syonzi summarizes the primary difference between Chinese religious definitions and that of the West, noting that neither church attendance nor survey-based assessments of individual beliefs have much meaning for Chinese people, aside from Christians and Muslims. Practice, meaning participation in individual and communal rituals, is a more defining element of Chinese religion. Here again we see the mismatch of the Enlightenment-derived definition of religion with the situation in China. A more accurate measure of secularization in relation to Chinese popular religion, then, would examine decline in religious practice and ritual participation, rather than privatization of religion or religious nonaffiliation.

Another methodological problem raised by Asian popular religious practice is that of religious identity. In China, the government and scholars consider popular folk practices as superstition (*mixin*, literally, confused beliefs) or excessive sacrifices (*yinsi*). Individuals, then, rarely identify as believing or practicing such religions. In the United States, religious censuses and surveys do not offer categories for popular religious practices. Instead, mutually exclusive religious affiliations are listed, precluding the opportunity to identify with several traditions as Asians often do. As such, Asian Americans may be more likely to mark "None" or "Don't Know" on these religious surveys.

Conclusion: Secularization Theories and Asian Americans

Secularization, as well as religion, is a Western discourse of thought based on European and American models of Christianity and its relation to society, institutions, and individuals. Since the religious landscape does structure Asian American religiosity in the United States, it is shaped by the same forces of secularization, or at least religious change: modernization, rationalization, pluralism, and individualization. Each of these forces may help explain statistically significant high numbers of Asian American nonreligious. Because of selective immigration, Asian Americans are more likely to be scientists and engineers than any other Americans, and to hold a secular, scientific worldview. Asian American religious institutions, especially ones of minority religions, may be disadvantaged in the pluralistic religious marketplace. They then are less able to supply religious resources and belonging to individuals, and show a decline in adherents. Finally, Asian Americans may become increasingly individualistic in the United States and adopt utilitarian or expressive individualist approaches. They would then be more likely to identify as religious "Nones," or as "Spiritual but not religious."

However, Western secularization theories fail to fully account for the Asian American religious experience, especially those who hold to Asian popular religious practices. Instead of measuring institutional deprivatization, congregational attendance, or individual beliefs, researchers of Asian American "Nones" should consider the actual practices of how Asian Americans "do" religion, that is, their religious repertoires. A more accurate measure of religious decline for Asian Americans must include an examination of the religious rituals, practices, and orientations that they employ for spiritual purposes.

Russell Jeung

See also: Essays: Politics and Religion

Further Reading

Babco, Eleanor. *The Status of Native Americans in Science and Engineering.* New York: Commission on Professionals in Science and Technology, 2005.

Berger, Peter. *Sacred Canopy: Elements of a Sociological Theory of Religion.* Garden City, NY: Doubleday, 1967.

Bellah, Robert. "Civil Religion in America." *Daedalus* 96 (1967): 1–21.

Chaves, Mark. "Secularization as Declining Religious Authority." *Social Forces* 72 (1994): 749–74.

Chai, Karen. "Intra-Ethnic Religious Diversity: Korean Buddhist and Christians in the Greater Boston Area." In Ho Youn Kwan, Kwang Chun Kim, and R. Stephen Warner, eds. *Korean Americans and Their Religions.* University Park: Penn State University Press, 2001, pp. 273–94.

Eck, Diana. *A New Religious America: How a "Christian Country" Has Become the World's Most Religiously Diverse Nation.* New York: HarperOne, 2002.

Goossaert, Vincent. "1898: The Beginning of the End for Chinese Religion?" *Journal of Asian Studies* 65, no. 2 (2006): 307–36.

Hadden, J. K. "Toward Desacralizing Secularization Theory." *Social Forces* 65 (1987): 587–611.

Harris Poll. "Nearly Two-Thirds of U.S. Adults Believe Human Beings Were Created by God." 2005. http://www.harrisinteractive .com/harris_poll/index.asp?PID=581. Accessed July 17, 2014.

Herberg, Will. *Protestant, Catholic, Jew.* Chicago: University of Chicago Press, 1955.

Hout, Michael, and Claude Fischer. "Why More Americans Have No Religious Preference: Politics and Generations." *American Sociological Review* 67, no. 2 (2002): 165–90.

Jeung, Russell. *Faithful Generations: Race and New Asian American Churches.* New Brunswick, NJ: Rutgers University Press, 2004.

Joshi, Khyati. *New Roots in America's Sacred Ground: Religion, Race and Ethnicity in Indian America.* New Brunswick, NJ: Rutgers University Press, 2006.

Luckmann, Thomas. *Invisible Religion: The Problem of Religion in Modern Society.* New York: Macmillan, 1967.

Park, John, and Ed Park. *Probationary Americans: Contemporary Immigration Policies and the Shaping of Asian American Communities.* New York: Routledge, 2005.

Pew Forum on Religion and Public Life. *American Religious Landscape Survey.* Washington, DC: Pew Forum on Religion and Public Life, 2008.

Pew Research Center. *Faith in Flux: Changes in Religious Affiliation in the United States.* Washington, DC: Pew Forum on Religion and Public Life, 2009.

Roof, Wade Clark, and William McKinney. *American Mainline Religion: Its Changing Shape and Future.* New Brunswick, NJ: Rutgers University Press, 1987.

Ruttimann, Jacqueline. "Breaking Through the Bamboo Ceiling for Asian American Scientists." *Science* 5 (2009).

Saroglou, Vassilas. "Religious Bricolage as a Psychological Reality: Limits, Structures and Dynamics." *Social Compass* 53 (2006): 109–15.

Smith, Christian. *American Evangelicalism: Embattled and Thriving.* Chicago: University of Chicago Press, 1998.

Stark, Rodney. "Secularization, R.I.P." In William Swatos and Daniel Olson, eds., *The Secularization Debate.* Lanham, MD: Rowman and Littlefield, 2000, pp. 41–66.

Stone, Daniel. "One Nation Under God?" *Newsweek*, April 7, 2009.

Suh, Sharon. *Being Buddhist in a Christian World.* Seattle: University of Washington Press, 2004.

Swatos, William, and Daniel Olson. *The Secularization Debate.* Lanham, MD: Rowman and Littlefield, 2000.

Syonzi, Michael. "Secularization Theories and the Study of Chinese Religions." *Social Compass* 56, no. 3 (2009): 312–27.

Tamney, Joseph. "Asian Popular Religions." In William Swatos, ed., *Encyclopedia of Religion and Society.* Walnut Creek, CA: Alta Mira Press, 1998. Online at http://hirr.hartsem.edu/ency/Asian.htm.

Weber, Max. "Science as a Vocation." *Daedalus* 87, no. 1 (1958): 111–34.

Wilson, Brian. "Secularization: The Inherited Model." In Philip Hammond, ed., *The Sacred in a Secular Age.* Berkeley: University of California Press, 1985, pp. 9–20.

Yang, C. K. *Religion in Chinese Society: A Study of Contemporary Social Functions of Religion and Some of Their Historical Factors.* Berkeley: University of California Press, 1961.

Yang, Fenggang, and Helen Ebaugh. "Transformations in New Immigrant Religions and Their Global Implications." *American Sociological Review* 66 (2001): 269–88.

Spirituality

"Spirituality" is one of the more elusive expressions to have gained recent currency. Academic studies, popular literature, and common usage suggest that "spirituality" or "spiritual experience," used in contradistinction to "religion," articulates a yearning for a more authentic, intimate, and profound experience than is possible through long-established faith traditions. As an alternative to the real and perceived doctrinal, ritual, institutional, social, and other shortcomings of mainline "religion," "spirituality" is commonly understood to be a means to ultimate reality or truth and to the experience of that truth, which in turn is the basis for praiseworthy conduct. The sentiments and insights generated by spiritual exercises and experiences—both within and outside established traditions—provide meaning and support in times of personal and community crisis, and the rationale for and inspiration to respond to such diverse concerns as climate change and the environment, decolonialization and identity, elder care, and other issues.

In an attempt to lend some clarity, this essay begins with a sketch of the history and presuppositions of "spirituality," and proceeds to introduce the spiritual cultures of East and Southeast Asia and the Pacific Islands primarily through a discussion of the primal sentiments of filiality and animism, and through the immediacy of popular lore and custom, poetry and literature, and personal testimony. It concludes with suggestions for further areas of investigation. The conceptual constraints of "spirituality" will be apparent during the course of this essay.

"Spirituality:" Origin and Meaning

The Study of Spirituality traces the expression and notion of "spirituality" to 15th- and 16th-century European Christian interest in mystical experiences that were believed to lead to an overarching supra-empirical reality. Clerics pursued spirituality through established communal practices. In contrast, lay seekers cultivated their quest through personal modalities outside the established presuppositions and forms; their "private spiritualities" were concerned with personal meaning and experience. As a consequence there can be as many "spiritualities" as there are "spiritual" persons. The proliferation of spiritualities raises many academic and practical questions. One significant question concerns authenticity. To wit, how can the validity of an inner experience be ascertained?

Personal spirituality allows the individual to move beyond the confines of "reli-gion" and its institutional notions of faith and meaning, and sanctions an openness to and exploration of other faith traditions, practices, and realities. Robert Atchley notes that "spirituality" can be a herme-neutic that bridges denominations and compromises among divisive groupings. James Ellor and Melvin Kimble note that the unifying power of the expression "spirituality" was instrumental in advocating the legislative needs of older adults at the 1971 White House Conference on Aging, when out of political necessity the organizers coined the expression, "spiritual well-being," an expression that transcended denominational interests.

In 2010, Ellor wrote that prior to 1970 the person on the street would talk about religion, but few would have mentioned spirituality or spiritual needs. During the intervening years between 1970 and 1990, gerontological literature saw a shift from "religion" to "spiritual well-being" and finally to simply "spirituality." "Spirituality" also allowed for the inclusion of non-Christian faith traditions. This change was based on the growing recognition in the health services community that successful caregiving must attend to the inner life of elders from different racial and ethnic populations. On March 18, 2010, at the American Society on Aging Conference, James Ellor and Susan McFadden reported the results of their Internet survey of members of the American Society of America (ASA) and National Coalition on Aging (NCOA) on the use of "spirituality" and "religion." They found that 55 percent identified themselves as being both religious and spiritual, 33 percent said that they were spiritual, and only 2.4 percent professed to be religious (Ellor and Mc-Fadden, 2010).

A similar shift seems to have occurred in the Asian American and Pacific Islander Christian community. "Spirituality," referring to an inner reality, does not appear in *The Theologies of Asian Americans and Pacific Peoples, a Reader* compiled by Roy Sano in 1976. Interest focused on giving voice to the "experience of oppression" and "development of ethnic ministries." In *Out of Silence* Fumitaka Matsuoka used "interiority" to refer to the subjectivity of faith experience. The articles in "Racial Spirits: Religion and Race in Asian American Communities" from the 1996 *Amerasia Journal* and *People on the Way* edited by David Ng used "religion" and "spirituality" interchangeably. In 1999, David K. Yoo included in *New Spiritual Homes* a section, "Creations of Spirit," poetry and short stories to incorporate the lived experience with the intent of giving voice to the authors' ancestral traditions in light of the Bible and its tradition. I am unaware of any studies on "spirituality" in other Asian American faith traditions. I suspect, however, that the expression has been adopted and refers to the inner life of its devotees.

Explorations in "spirituality" raise many conceptual and practical questions. Let us consider the definition proposed by Ewert Cousins, the general editor of the 25-volume *World Spirituality, an Encyclopedic History of the Religious Quest*. The series focuses on that inner dimension of the person called by certain traditions "the spirit." This spiritual core is the deepest center of the person. It is here that the person is open to the transcendental dimension; it is here that the person experiences ultimate reality.

This definition presumes (1) that "spirituality" or the "spiritual experience" and the content of this experience are common in all traditions; (2) that the presence or existence of "ultimate reality" can be experienced through the "spirit"; (3) that the "deepest center of the person" is where "the person experiences ultimate reality"; and (4) that the realities of spiritual and corporeal or profane worlds are different. Perhaps the most problematic is the assumption that spiritual experience and the reality that it intuits are essentially identical for all traditions. Skeptics of this view would counter that the experience of mystics comes into being as the kind of experience of the linguistic, theological, and social-historical circumstances that govern the mystical ascent. Again, philosophical beliefs shape meditative techniques, provide specific expectations, and thus have a formative influence on the kinds of experiences that are drawn from these experiences. Thus, the respective contents of Buddhist, Christian, Confucian, Daoist, Islamic, and Hawaiian or other indigenous experiences are not the same, and perhaps even categorically different.

Further, the idea that the "deepest center of the person" is where the "person experiences ultimate reality" assumes that an individual has the capacity to experience reality and would intuitively know its validity. Such a hypothesis excludes persons with dementia, Alzheimer's, or severe brain injury. Charged with providing quality care at the end of life, activities directors in care facilities are continually imagining programs to enhance the inner life of persons with diminished cognitive capacities. However, assuming that a person can plumb his or her deepest center, the operative question is: What therapeutic value does the realization of "ultimate reality" have? In his work with terminally ill patients, Kubodera Toshiyuki observes that while both "religious care" and "spiritual care" attend to the inner needs of a person, the two are not synonymous. "Spirituality" or "spirit" is that inner foundation that sustains hope and gives meaning to a person, who may not have or has lost his or her inner supportive resources. Spiritual care is thus the attempt to assist a person to search for and discover a foundation on which an individual can draw strength and hope, and find meaning and purpose.

Both Cousins and Kubodera have proposed an intensely personal view of spirituality. A consideration of Cousins's definition would take us into rarefied reaches of mind and notions of reality. For the purposes of this essay, Kubodera's functional description of spiritual care offers some tangible expressions of the "inner life" or "spirituality" that are more readily accessible. As we shall see, the virtues or qualities associated with spirituality can arouse an individual (and a community) to cultivate his or her highest aspiration, to quicken a sense of self-identity and solidarity with the world, and to stir sentiments of gratitude and responsible action.

Asian American Spirituality

The complexities and varieties of Asian American spirituality and its subjective experience preclude a comprehensive and detailed examination. Out of practical necessity, this essay focuses on the spiritual cultures of the Ryūkyūans (Okinawans), Tais, and Hawaiians who represent the three distinct regions—East Asia, Southeast Asia, and Pacific Islands—under consideration in this essay. All share a common reverence for sentiments associated with filiality, especially a reverence for ancestors and ancestral wisdom, and the presence of innumerable spirits. Present-day East and Southeast Asians and Pacific Islanders balance traditional and modern notions of identity and spirituality, and the parallel reality of disembodied spirits.

The discovery of "man becoming a spiritual individual" emerged during the Italian Renaissance and has since spread throughout Asia and the Pacific. Interesting, as noted above, that the notion of "private spirituality" seems to have appeared at about the same time. In contrast, Alper in *Legends of the South Sea: The World of the Polynesians Seen through Their Myths and Legends, Poetry, and Art* writes that in ancient Hawai'i the individual was conscious of him- or herself only as a member of a family or community and his or her genealogy. Thus it is through *'ohana* or family that the Hawaiians, individually and communally, understood their world. *'Ohana* is the context for learning and support in Hawaiian families; and the conduit of wisdom and culture, as well as the cradle of socialization and character development. Further, the mutuality among family members established an individual's identity and responsibilities; and genealogy secured an individual's place among the generations. Similarly, it is within the family and by extension the community and world that the archetypical Asian finds primary inspiration and purpose, affirmation and hope. In short, the yearnings and aspirations of the family and a people are the primary sources of Asian American spirituality.

Ancestral Wisdom

Ancestral wisdom recalls lessons learned from the ancient need for members of a family to depend on each other for survival, and for households to cooperate with other households to undertake common projects. The Ryūkyūans children's song *Tinsagu no hana* (Balsam blossom) affectionately reminds children of their indebtedness to their parents, while reminding parents to cherish the future of their children:

> Stain the tips of your fingernails
> With the petals of the *tinsagu*
>   blossom;
> Imprint the teachings of your
>   parents
> Onto your heart.
>
> You could, if you tried
> Count the stars in the sky;
> But you can never imagine all
> The lessons of your parents.
>
> A ship sailing in the night
> Finds its bearings from the North
>   Star,
> My parents who gave me life
> Discover their way through me.

A second source of spirituality is the presence of innumerable animate and inanimate spirits that are part of Hawaiian, Ryūkyūan, and Tai spiritual cultures. The validity of this reality has been continually reinforced by the capacity of the shaman (the Hawaiian *kahuna*, the Ryūkyūans *yuta*, and the Tai *khon song*) to communicate with disembodied beings and to traverse the spiritual realms. These beliefs may appear fanciful to those bereft of a familiarity with laws of the spiritual universe and with the rhythms of the spiritual life. "Believe. Don't believe. Up to you," Chan master Tsung Tsai chides the agnostic in *Bones of the Master*; but these realities are still operative among the peoples throughout the vast Western Pacific and Southeast and East Asia regions.

These primal filial sentiments, animistic beliefs, and their ancillary rituals and customs have been overlaid and articulated through Mahāyāna Buddhist, Confucian, and Daoist ideas in East Asia; by Hindu, Theravāda Buddhist, and Islamic thought in Southeast Asia; and by Christianity in the Philippines and the Pacific Islands. Folklore, modernization, and Westernization are additional layers. The spiritualities of Asian Americans exhibit the quality of *jūsōsei* or "porously-laminated-nature," an expression the Japanese philosopher Watsuji Tetsurō (1889–1960) coined to describe the spiritual makeup of the Japanese. In the same manner, *jūsōsei* describes the composite character of Asian American spirituality. Any one layer or any combinations thereof may be the source for inspiration and more immediately, protection from unseen forces or accidents. Surviving a Bangkok taxi ride makes one a believer of the efficacy of multiple spiritualities. As an assurance against accidents, the Thai taxi dashboard altar may enshrine an array of amulets, incantations, Buddhas, royal images, monks, and even offerings to Mae Yanang, the protective water spirit. Ganesha, the elephant-headed Hindu deity, the remover of obstacles, is also popular for drivers who must navigate Bangkok traffic.

"Reflected Light" by Hilary Tham illustrates the multiplicity of spiritual layers that inform her life. Her poem makes reference to Chinese astrology and mythology, Indian Buddhist understanding of reincarnation and *karma*, the Daoist belief in the power of names, Confucian virtue, Zen Nothingness, Malayan *ronggeng* (dance), and modern ideas of justice and equality. When asked how she balances her Catholicism with her traditional Hawaiian heritage in Pat Pitzer's "Contemporary Kahuna," Momi Mo'kini Lum replied, "Very easy. My uncle taught me to bridge them, and my father taught me to blend them. I can't tell you how I do it, but I have no conflicts with it. There is only one God." Finally, Hawai'i born and raised Korean-Okinawan Debra Kang Dean acknowledges her complex genealogy:

My personal history, which is a confluence of subcultures, is the animating force that colors my actions. And the voice I have is acquired through training is, for good or ill, the bookish reciter somewhat removed from the action, attuned to the pulse of the samisen (three string lute) that guides the telling, each part must be rendered its due. (1995)

Mentoring. Generations of Asians and Pacific Islanders look to the accumulated wisdom of their parents, grandparents, and even more distant and mythical ancestors on which to pattern their lives, cherish the future of their children, relate to their neighbors, and respond to events that impact their lives.

The archetypical Asian American elder attends to his or her responsibilities by mentoring what is good and admirable for his or her children and grandchildren, and the subsequent generations of elders. This task is perhaps best articulated by the Confucian notion of filiality, a sentiment that is nurtured between parent and child. The moral and spiritual topography that it sketches are found in Book II, Chapter 4 of the *Lunyu* or *Analects*. In what is perhaps the shortest autobiography ever, Confucius (ca. 551–479 BCE) reviews his life:

At fifteen I set my heart to learning.
At thirty I took my stand.
At forty I was without doubt.
At fifty I understood the Way of
    Heaven.
At sixty my ear was attuned [to
    Heaven's ways].
At seventy I followed my heart-
    mind desires without
    transgressing the way [of
    Heaven].

The most striking feature of this life review is the role of education. Confucius saw his life as a spiritual journey that began at fifteen when he set his "heart on learning" through the age of seventy with his total resonance with the Way of Heaven. In Book XII, Chapter 1, Confucius said that mastering the spiritual topography of Heaven involves self-cultivation by learning self-restraint through the mastery of *li*, the ritual forms and rules of propriety through which individuals demonstrate respect for others and perform their respective roles in society. Even such simple ritual greetings as "Good morning" or "How are you today?" are moral acts. They acknowledge the worth of another individual. In the process of mastering *li* an individual cultivates *ren* or "humanity" in the form of "compassion" or "a loving heart." *Li* and *ren* are most effectively cultivated through xiao or "filiality," that is, "love" or "caring heart" that is nurtured between parent and child.

Confucian filiality is ordinarily understood as a child's obligation toward his or her parents; but in addition to providing for and introducing a child to the world, filiality also commits parents (and teachers) to mentor self-cultivation, and self-transformation, and self-realization. This is not special to Confucius, who by his own admission was a transmitter of ancient ideas, or Chinese culture.

A personal lesson in the journey into elderhood and the responsibilities of mentoring occurred during one of our many conversations with avant-garde *sho* (calligrapher) artist Morita Shiryū (1912–1998):

"I look forward to growing old."
"But, why?" I asked incredulously.
"I want to see how my art will mature and change."

I was 26 at the time; Morita was 58. In retrospect, my sensei (teacher), who had established an international reputation, was intensely exploring his craft as a vehicle to deepen and give form to his *kyōgai* or "spiritual dwelling place." Ordinarily *kyōgai* refers to one's socioeconomic status, but in Japanese Buddhist culture the expression denotes a spiritual and aesthetic quality that can only come from long years in the experience of being in the world. A person with profound *kyōgai* is at ease with him- or herself, and lives and relates with the world and others with complete integrity.

Morita's explorations point to the spiritual adventure of growing old that is also integral to the traditional Tai tuition of performing arts. While studying Thai music, Deborah Wong comments, "Teaching and the transfer of intangible powers are deeply linked." Malcolm Naea Chun makes a similar observation when he writes that the teacher passes wisdom along with his knowledge of medicine in traditional Hawai'i. The lifelong adventure of self-cultivation in the journey to elderhood is also the thrust of a short story, "Grandmother the Progressive," by the Thai writer Junlada Phakdiphumin, in which a grandmother mentors her granddaughters by learning from them:

Grandmother had lived a full life, passing through times of happiness and of sorrow, seeing her material fortunes wax and mostly wane through the years. She was a perfect example to us of fortitude under difficult circumstances, including bereavement: not once had Grandmother shed tears over her misfortunes. She relied on her Buddhist faith. "Impermanence," she told us, "and change—they are the only things, my dears, upon which you may depend in this life." (1996)

The narrator, a granddaughter, recalls the lessons she and her female cousins learned at the feet of their grandmother, a dowager of an old and established Bangkok family. She was the "perfect example" of the fortitude that is required to live in an uncertain world. As the narrative continues, Grandmother learns that one of her granddaughters is having difficulties with her marriage, while another is quite happy. Wanting to help the troubled granddaughter, she visits the other to discover the secret of her success. Taking to heart what she learned, she advises the granddaughter with the troubled marriage. Grandmother prided herself on being a "progressive" woman not bound to the past.

Journeying into elderhood is marked by a series of late-life celebrations that publicly demonstrate filiality, the mutual obligations between one generation and another. In the Ryūkyūs where Confucian culture has left an imprint, late-life celebrations begin with the 61st birthday that marks, according to the Chinese zodiac, the completion of one life cycle and the beginning of another. Thereafter every 12th year is highlighted. The 97th or *kajimaya* celebration is the most auspicious. (At birth an individual begins the first year of life; thus the 61st year corresponds to the 60th year according to the Western reckoning, and the 97th year the beginning of the ninth 12-year cycle.) The Japanese *beiju* or the 88th birthday, a recent innovation, has no reference to the Chinese zodiac. Rather, its significance is derived from the three Chinese characters—8, 10, and 8—that represent 88. When written vertically and compressed, the three characters form *bei* or "rice," the staple food

for life. In addition to giving elders milestones to look forward to, late-life celebrations are didactic and a form of mentoring. Grandchildren learn to respect and care for their parents by observing their parents caring for their elders.

Tai culture observes *suebchata* or ceremony for the prolongation of life on the occasion of a person's 60th birthday; every 12th year thereafter—the 72nd, the 84th, and the 96th—are marked for special celebration. This 12-year cycle is based on an archaic, pre-Indic cosmic order that was later adapted by Buddhism. In the northeast Isaan region, families sponsor *sookwan*, a ritual to reenergize a person's spirit-essence by inviting all ancestors to assist in this task. This ceremony is not limited to frail elders, but anyone who needs to have his or her life-spirit reenergized. Any person who had a significant role in an individual's life is invited to participate. The ritual can be performed by a cleric or by an elder. In neighboring Cambodia this ritual is called *bon chamran ayut*. Modern Hawaiian late-life rituals begin at age 50 and then every 10 years until age 70, then at 75, and every five years or so with a *luau* (celebratory feast). The younger person learns the meaning and mechanics of these rituals through participation and observation.

Inspiration. Ancestral exploits and wisdom inspire the decolonialization efforts of present-day Hawaiians. Thus for example, while serving as the Chief Justice of the Hawai'i Supreme Court, William S. Richardson (1919–2010) ruled in 1968 that Hawaiian land use laws should rely on ancient tradition, rather than Anglo-

American common law. This and other opinions based on Hawaiian tradition sparked a resurgence of Hawaiian pride. (Richardson's Hawaiian grandfather served as an aide to Queen Liliuokalani (1838–1917), the last reigning monarch.) Thus inspired persons such as Haunami-Kay Trask call for Hawaiian sovereignty:

In our genealogy, Papahānaumoku, "earth mother," mated with Wākea, "sky father," from whence came our islands, or *moku*. Out of our beloved islands came the *taro*, our immediate progenitor, and from *taro*, our chiefs and people.

Our relationship to the cosmos is thus familial. As in all of Polynesia, so in Hawai'i: elder siblings must feed and care for younger sibling, who return honor and love. The wisdom of our creation is reciprocal obligation. If we husband our lands and waters, they will feed and care for us. In our language, the name for this relationship is *mālama 'āina*, "care for the land," who will care for all family members in turn. (1999)

Note that she appeals to *'ohana* or family and the obligations that are incumbent on its members extend to the cosmos. Trask's statement was no doubt inspired by *Kaulana Nā Pua* ("Famous are the flowers"), penned in 1893 by Ellen Keho'ohiwaokalani Wright Prendergast (1865–1902) in protest of the overthrow of the Hawaiian Kingdom. In addition to linking the Hawaiian people to their mythological origins and subsequent generations of heroes, it also articulates the sacredness of the land with the lines:

We do not value
The government's hills of money
We are satisfied with the rocks
The wondrous food of the land

These lines gave rise to its alternative title: *Mele ai Pohaku* or the "Stone Eating" song. "Stone" refers to sacred land and sea, the bodies of the ancestors. All natural forms are believed to be manifestations of spiritual forces.

The sacredness of the land and wisdom of the ancestors also moved the citizens of Onna Village in northern Okinawa to protest the building of an urban warfare training facility on Mt. Onna. For more than 40 years the U.S. military conducted live-ammunition firing exercises that slowly destroyed the sacred mountain. Their ancestors banned the harvesting of trees; they understood that the forest that covered the mountain was the source of water and life. Reminiscent of the "Stone Eating" song, the following lines are from the opening stanzas of the Onna villagers' protest statement:

The mountain is our spiritual
     support.
If the mountain dies,
     the village perishes.
If the mountain dies,
     We shall also perish.
We would risk our lives
     to protect the mountain. (Onna
     Village, 1972)

Spirits

Spirits abound in the Ryūkyūs, Thailand, and Hawai'i. Household shrines and their accompanying mortuary and memorial rituals acknowledge the presence of ancestral spirits. Seasonal and communal festivals honor inanimate nature spirits.

Ancestral Spirits. Asian Americans together with the Ryūkyūans and Tais share the world with innumerable spirits—the animate and inanimate. The living and dead inhabit separate realms with very porous boundaries. The spirits of the dead often intrude on the corporeal to remind the living that proper funeral or memorial rites have not been performed. After death, spirits often return to their former homes. Pascal Khoo Thwe describes such a visit from his grandfather's spirit in *From the Land of Green Ghosts*. Thwe records the conversation his grandmother has with her recently deceased spouse, his grandfather:

> Is it you, La Pen? I did everything you ordered for your funeral. I hope I have been a dutiful and faithful wife to you. But this house belongs to the living, not the dead. You know that. Please go back to the grave; to your new home. Go back to where you belong. I will meet you again when I am dead. (Thwe, 2002, 93–94)

Thwe's grandfather's ghost needed only a simple reminder that he is no longer part of this world. Even under normal circumstances, death is disorienting and mortuary rituals serve to assist the spirit to adjust to his or her new life. But disoriented spirits who have been separated from their corporeal bodies from sudden and unnatural deaths often wreak havoc on the living. In Myanmar such spirits appear as "green ghosts." The Tais are also fearful of disoriented spirits. The spirits of pregnant women (*phii phrai*) are the most fearful. Two hundred years ago Mae Nak Phrakhanong, named for a district in east Bangkok, died in childbirth while her husband Maak was away at war. On his return Maak resumed his life with Nak and their child, until he was persuaded that they were indeed specters. Only the exorcism by a powerful monk was able to persuade Nak's spirit to return to her grave. In the 1999 film *Nang Nak*, Nonzee Nimibutr refashions this tale into a haunting love story. Love also inspires the spirit of Miyagi to return from the dead in the 1953 *Ugetsu*, a film by the Japanese director Mizoguchi Kenji (1898–1956). The power of love is such that it can resurrect the dead. Tang Xianzu's 1598 preface to his *Peony Pavilion* writes of Bridal Du who dies from unrequited love.

> Love is of source unknown, yet it grows ever deeper. The living may die of it, by its power the dead live again. Love is not love at its fullest if one who lives is unwilling to die for it, or if it cannot restore to life the one who has so died. And must the love that comes in a dream necessarily be unreal? For there is no lack of dream lovers in this world.

Love appears in the guise of a butterfly in ancient Ryūkyū. The following *omoro* or poem from Book XIII, Verse 965 of the *Omorosōshi* celebrates the appearance of the *unarigami* (womenfolk—sisters, mothers, and wives) on an ocean-going ship on the high seas to ensure safe passage of their *ekeri* (menfolk—brothers, fathers, husbands).

> My *unarigami*
>   has come to protect me.
> Sister *unarigami*
> has arrived to watch over me.
> She has come as a beautiful butterfly
> [to protect me],
> She has arrived as a precious
>   butterfly
> [to watch over me].
>   (*Omorosōshi*, 1972, 330)

The *unarigami* tradition recalls a remote past when the Ryūkyūs were populated by small consanguineous settlements centering on a founding family that consisted of the *niigan* (root-deity) and *niitchuu* (root-person). Believed to have shamanic powers, the *niigan*, the family matriarch, attended to the ritual and spiritual needs of the family, which included serving as a liaison between the ancestral, animate, inanimate spirits and performing rituals that ensured bountiful harvest, successful catches from the sea, and safe travel. The *niitchuu*, or the family patriarch provided for the material and physical well-being of his female partner and by extension the family, and was responsible for the secular activities of the family and the larger community.

The Vietnamese patriots also looked to their womenfolk for protection. The following passage is also a reminder of the importance of ancestors and the reciprocity between the corporeal and disembodied worlds. The following is from Duong Thu Huong's *Novel without a Name*.

> Dear sisters, you who have lived and died here as human beings: Do not haunt us any longer. Protect us. Fortify our bodies, light the way for our spirits, so that in every battle we may conquer. When victory comes, when peace comes to our country, we will carry you back to the land of your ancestors. (Huong, 1996, 1–2)

Inanimate Spirits. The Hawaiian intimacy for the land is also part of the Ryūkyūan spiritual culture. A significant rite integral to the *Umati* (festival) that occurs during the lull just before the early summer harvest is *kaa umai*, a pilgrimage to nearby village wells. At one particular site, puzzled, I asked one of the elders, Nakasone Jirō (d. 2010):

> "What are we doing here? There is no water."
> "At one time water flowed abundantly from this artesian spring. Your grandfather and our ancestors drew water; water supported their lives. We are here to demonstrate our gratitude by introducing our lineage and who we are; and ask for health and prosperity for our family."

This simple exposition sums up the Ryūkyūan spirituality. Ryūkyūans honor their ancestors by remembering what was sacred to them and by giving thanks to the spirit of water that gave them life. Their spirituality is rooted in the concrete and immediate. Like the Hawaiian "Stone

Eating" song, we are reminded that land is sacred, that land is life.

The reciprocity between humanity and the natural world is exhibited through conversations Grandma has with the plants that surround her. In "Grandma," a short story by the Tai writer Angkarn Kalayaanaphong, the plants not only initiate the conversation, they demonstrate an uncommon compassion. The kindness of plants is not strange; Tai Buddhist cosmology allows for human beings to be reborn as flowers or frogs. Grandma asks,

> Why can plants talk? In earlier days you were so quiet as to be mute. Or perhaps your compassion lies secreted deeply with you. You are able to bring forth your generosity and your magnanimous mercy so that I can feel the delight of the divine power that has revived my strength and vigor. (Kalayaanaphong, 1987, 85)

The sacredness of plants is also extended to the ordination of trees in response to the deforestation from excessive logging throughout Thailand. The symbolic gesture demonstrates that trees have the same intrinsic value as human beings.

Conclusion

The spiritual cultures of Asian and Pacific Islanders as represented by Ryūkyūans, Tais, and Hawaiians exhibit an intimacy that is rooted in sentiments nurtured by being a member of a family and community and by sharing the world with ancestral and inanimate spirits. An individual's identity is largely determined by his or her place in

the family and by his or her genealogy. The metaphor of the family is also part of Japanese Buddhist culture. Amida Buddha is referred to as *Oyasama* or "parent." Here "parent" is both mother and father. Devotees refer to themselves as "children of the Buddha." In contrast, Tais have similar but rarely used expressions, because Theravāda Buddhist culture emulates the historical Buddha as a great teacher, not "father."

The image of the parent in the form of ancestral wisdom preserved in family and popular lore or in learned treatises and formalized rituals continues to serve as models for living, preparing for the future, and recovering identity. The metaphor of the family extends to the universe, a view that is articulated by the *Western Inscription* composed by the Neo-Confucian Chang Tsai (1020–1077). The familial metaphor is warm and caring:

> Heaven is my father and Earth is my mother, and even such a small creature as I finds an intimate place in their midst. Therefore that which fills the universe I regard as my body and that which directs the universe I consider as my nature. All people are my brothers and sisters, and all things are my companions. . . . Respect the aged. . . . Show deep love for the orphaned and weak. . . . Even those who are tired, infirmed, crippled, or sick; those who have no brothers or children, wives or husbands, are all my brothers who are in distress and have no one to turn to.

Chang Tsai eloquently describes his ease in the home of his parents. Born from the heavens and the earth, he shares their nature and purpose. *Ren*, "benevolence" or "humanity" takes on different forms in human relationships; it is filial piety toward parents, respect toward elder siblings, and benevolence toward the weak and dispossessed. Moral cultivation lies in striving to fulfill one's duty as a member of society and of the universe.

The testimony of Seo-woon Jeong, a former "comfort woman," strains any credibility of Chang Tsai's vision of a moral universe. Her brutalization by other human beings diminished her belief in the rationality of human existence and human meaning. Whatever faith Ms. Jeong may have had in the goodness of humanity and such values as compassion, respect for another, humility, and common decency that were nurtured by centuries of Confucian and Buddhist education had all but vanished from the combatants. Only the image of her father and mother and the need to tell her people what had happened to her gave her the strength to survive.

Likewise Chamorro (Micronesian) poet Anne Hattori turns her prayerful thoughts to her living ancestors for strength and affirmation. In the closing lines of "Saints Nana and Tata" (Grandmother and Grandfather), she prays to "living saints . . . Nana and . . . Tata" to articulate the recovery of her Chamorro lineage and "inner foundation."

To close, Ryūkyūan, Tai, and Hawaiian spirituality is deeply rooted in primal sentiments generated by being part of a family. The familial image is of warmth and intimacy. Ancestral spirits are part of one's immediate family; and inanimate spirits are included in one's extended family. This metaphor has obvious conceptual and his-

torical limitations. Only passing reference was made to Christianity, Hinduism, Islam, or Shintō and their respective visions of reality and spiritual experiences. Others will need to explore the indigenous traditions of other parts of Asia.

Further, just as there are as many kinds of spiritualities as there are spiritual persons, there are just as many avenues where the spiritual experience can take form. Spirituality is given form through the visual, plastic, culinary, and performing arts and in the creative process itself. Chiura Obata (1885–1975), for example, expressed some of his most intense inner experiences through color and form while interned at Topaz during World War II. Spiritual fortitude is also present in the needle and appliqué work of the Hmong women refugees who escaped from Laos and settled in the United States. The plaintive plea of Kina Shōkichi for the end of war in "*Subete no hito no kokoro ni hana wo* (Blooming flowers in the hearts of all)" is an aspiration that comes from the deepest core of the Ryūkyūan people.

Finally, simply being at ease with oneself may be the most profound spiritual experience. To this end perhaps the Sanskrit *siddhānta*, meaning "a person who is fully accomplished or fulfilled" is the most fitting expression for "spirituality." It is applicable to any person who dwells in the "spiritual" experience.

Ronald Y. Nakasone

Further Reading

Alpers, Antony. *Legends of the South Sea: The World of the Polynesians Seen through Their Myths and Legends, Poetry, and Art.* Oxford: Oxford University Press, 1970.

Atchley, Robert. C. *Spirituality and Aging*. Baltimore: The Johns Hopkins University Press, 2009.

Beckwith, Martha. *Hawaiian Mythology*. Honolulu: University of Hawai'i Press, 1970.

Chang Tsai. "Western Inscription." In Wing-tsit Chan, comp., *A Source Book in Chinese Philosophy*. Princeton, NJ: Princeton University Press, 1969.

Chun, Malcolm Naea. *Hawaiian Medicine Book: He Buke Laau Lapaau*. Honolulu: The Bess Press, 1986.

Crane, George. *Bones of the Master*. New York: Bantam Books, 2000.

Dean, Debra Kang. "Telling Differences." In Garrett Hongo, ed., *Under Western Eyes*. New York: Anchor Books, 1995.

Ellor, James W. "Spiritual Well-Being Defined." *Aging and Spirituality* 9 (1997): 1–2.

Ellor, James W. "The Immerging Role of Spirituality." *Aging Today* xxxl, no. 1 (2010).

Huong, Duong Thu. *Novel without a Name*. New York: Penguin Books, 1996.

Jones, Cheslyn, Geoffrey Wainwright, and Edward Yarnold, eds. *The Study of Spirituality*. New York: Oxford University Press, 1986.

Kalayaanaphong, Angkarn. "Grandma." In Herbert P. Phillips et al., eds., *Modern Thai Literature, with an Ethnographic Interpretation*. Honolulu: University of Hawai'i Press, 1987, 80–87.

Kepner, Susan Fulop. *The Lioness in Bloom, Modern Thai Fiction about Women*. Berkeley: University of California Press, 1996.

Konstanz, Dale. *Thai Taxi Talismans, Bangkok from the Passenger Seat*. Bangkok: River Books, 2011.

MacDonald, Mary N. "Spirituality." In *Encyclopedia of Religions*. Vol. 13. 2nd ed. Detroit: Macmillan Reference, 2005.

Nimibutr, Nonzee. 1999. *Nang Nak*, 100 min. Bangkok: Tai Entertainment.

Nordyke, Eleanor C., and Martha Noyes. "'Kaulana Nā Pua': A Voice for Sovereignty." *The Hawaiian Journal of History* 27 (1993).

Onna Village Committee to Oppose the Special Forces Training Facility Construction and Live Artillery Drills. *The Mountain Dies/the Nation Prospers/the Mountain Dies/the Village Perishes*. Naha: Jono Printing Company, 1992.

Phakdiphumin, Junlada. "Grandmother the Progressive." In *The Lioness in Bloom, Modern Thai Fiction about Women*. Berkeley: University of California Press, 1996.

Pukui, Mary Kawena, E. W. Haertig, and Catherine A. Lee. *Nānā I Ke Kum—Look to the Source*. Honolulu: Hui Hanai, 1972.

Sano, Roy, comp. *Theologies of Asian Americans and Pacific Peoples*. Berkeley: Asian Center for Theologies and Strategies, 1976.

Tang Xianzu. *The Peony Pavilion, Mudan Ting*. Translated by Cyril Birch. Boston: Cheng and Tsui, 1980.

Takeuchi, Yoshinori, ed. *Buddhist Spirituality: Indian, Southeast Asian, Tibetan, Early Chinese*. New York: Crossroads, 1993.

Tham, Hilary. "Reflected Light." In Shirley Geok-lin Lim and Cheng Lok Chua, eds., *Tilting the Continent, Southeast Asian American Writing*. Minneapolis: New River Press, 2000.

Thwe, Pascal Khoo. *From the Land of Green Ghosts, a Burmese Odyssey*. New York: HarperCollins, 2002.

Trask, Haunani-Kay. *From a Native Daughter, Colonialism and Sovereignty in Hawai'i*. Honolulu: University of Hawai'i Press, 1999.

Wong, Deborah. *Sounding the Center, History and Aesthetics in Thai Buddhist Performance*. Chicago: University of Chicago Press, 2001.

Theological Construction

Theology is an imaginative construction of a comprehensive and coherent picture of humanity in the world under God in theistic religious traditions. Within the Asian American context, Christian scholars, ministers, and literary writers have been engaged in theological construction for some time. Lately, Asian American scholars of other faith traditions have joined in theological discourse because of an increasingly inclusive understanding of theology beyond the traditional theistic definition.

Historical Development

In the early stage of Asian American faith tradition-building in the first few decades of the 20th century, the theological writings appeared mainly in the newsletters and collection of sermons of the Christian churches. For example, Japanese Christian leaders who were interned in the concentration camps during World War II produced numerous reflective writings on the meaning of their faith in the difficult era. The first notable collection of Asian American theological construction appeared in "The Reader," an unpublished collection of theological reflective essays in 1972 that was undertaken by United Methodist Bishop Roy Sano, then the director of Pacific and Asian American Center for Theology and Strategies (PACTS) in Berkeley, California. The contributors to "The Reader" consisted of Christian and sometimes Buddhist persons, both ministers and lay leaders. What was noteworthy about this endeavor was the wide representation of women as the contributors at this stage of Asian American

theological constructions. Since the compilation of "The Reader," there have been numerous books and essays on theology that are written by contemporary Asian American theological religious leaders.

A sample of representative theological topics that appeared in the first wave of Asian American theological constructions during the 1960s and 1970s are:

"Sojourners: In Asian American and Biblical History"—Wesley Woo

"Cultural Heritage of Asian Americans"—Joseph Kitagawa

"The Role of Religion in Asian American Communities"

"Asian Americans: A Forgotten Minority Comes of Age"

A primary theme of the first wave of Asian American theology was the positive meaning of being a sojourner. In the past, Asian American portrayal of the term "sojourner" was as an epithet. More positive meaning can be established in light of Asian American religious leaders' sojourn experiences in the light of the pervasive activities in the world and to let this understanding define their being and behavior. Feelings of discomfort or uneasiness in U.S. society and feelings of not quite belonging can be channeled toward working for a new vision of human relatedness rather than a search for personal security and acceptance into society.

It is no surprise that the first wave of Asian Americans used the term "sojourner" to describe the history of Asian Americans. The biblical reference of the term is obvious. What is important to note by the choice of the term "sojourner" is the gnawing sense that Asian Americans live with a different yardstick from what is taken for granted as the common values and life orientations that are all around them. While the racial and ethnic experiences were first considered to be the primary source of Asian American identity, there was also a growing sense that there was something Asian American about the experience that these ethnic groups shared with each other. That "something" is the shared experience of being a sojourner, the experience of having "a stranger within." This realization led the first wave of Asian and Pacific Americans to embrace a particular kind of life orientation and value that speaks of who they are, "Holy Insecurity." Being a stranger at home means to look for ways of life that help Asian and Pacific Americans to live with basic insecurity and to find, paradoxically, the security of Christian faith in the state of insecurity. That is their interpretation of the biblical meaning of "sojourner." The following passage, which appeared in the Centennial Worship Celebration of the Japanese Christian Mission in North America (October 9, 1977), reflects the significance of the theological theme of sojourner:

> Though arriving at the end of our first century and celebrating it, we still are seekers, looking for whatever it is we are looking for. We are a pursuing church, or the pilgrim of God in the wilderness, or the dispersed like the first century Christians, or simply call it *search*—we are all on the way, together. But we are not alone, nor helpless. Our fa-

thers crossed over the Pacific for a new life in this land; they were immigrants, away from their homes. They found what the life of sojourners was like, and yet, wherever they were, they were not away from the Lord's field. They met him, and built their churches.

What Is the State of Asian American Theology Today?

What is the current state of Asian American theological construction? To respond to this question, first of all, a working definition of what it means to be Asian American is needed. The term "Asian American" is a relatively young one, just a hair over 40 years old, with its first recorded public usage occurring at the University of California, Berkeley, the gravitational center of 1960s student activism. In those days, being "Asian American" was an act of passion, a statement of purpose. The lack of a stated history and definition around the term were a source of freedom, not concern, offering a chance to build a brand-new way to be American.

Four decades later, however, the situation is more complicated: "bringing together Asian Americans has often seemed like herding cats, if those cats were randomly mixed in with, say, dogs, sheep and giraffes—a metaphor that reflects the staggering diversity of our community, which incorporates dozens of nationalities, each with multiple linguistic, religious and ethnic subsets, and a varying historical record of immigration to the U.S.," says author Jeff Yang in a recent article in the *San Francisco Chronicle*. No community has been more impacted by multiracialism, transnationalism, and panculturalism than the Asian American community. Lisa Lowe talks about Asian American cultural identity in terms of "heterogeneity, hybridity, and multiplicity." Asian Americans represent something of a beta test for the future for the meaning of peoplehood. This is the cultural context in which Asian American theology is being undertaken.

The Threefold Epistemological Scaffold of Asian American Theological Construction

In this complex and fluid context of the Asian American cultural scene today exists the current state of theological enterprise. The epistemological scaffold that describes the Asian American theological construction can be said to be threefold: (1) the translocal meaning of race, (2) the spirit of dissonance and dissent, and (3) "amphibolous" faith orientation.

Race as Translocal. For Asian Americans, our race experience is translocal. Because of the conflicting and contradicting perceptions both within ourselves (the "veil" or multiple consciousness) and placed upon us from without (a "model minority" image on the one hand and a "foreigner within" on the other), there is no fixed point of racial identity even in our own longing for a durable anchoring point. Translocality is the locus of navigating the conflicting and contradicting life orientations. Asian Americans are not at home in their own home. The "continuing material contradictions" of race is the locus from which our collective identities and values

are forged and claimed, resulting in a nomadic translocal value orientation.

The Spirit of Dissonance and Dissent. The Asian American cultural geist is dissonant with the prevailing societal milieu of America. This is to say that there is a sense of not quite fitting in to a larger cultural landscape of the United States even though Asian Americans tend to be perceived as being absorbed into the mainstream American culture. In such a setting, an emerging original culture generates deviation and dissonance with the normative culture. At the same time, the deviation and dissonance are expressed in terms of disidentification, infidelity, and dissent against the normative culture. Theresa Hak Kyung in her *Dictee*, for example, writes poorly, stutters, stops, and leaves verbs unconjugated. She adulterates the Catholic catechism by mocking the expression that human beings are created in "God's likeness" as duplication, counterfeiting, carbon copy, and mirroring. The language of dissonance and dissent points to yet another deeper epistemological significance. It is an emergence of a distinct angle of vision with a sensitivity toward pathos in life arising out of the dissonant culture.

Why was America so kind and yet so cruel? Was there no way to simplify things in this continent so that suffering would be minimized Was there no common denominator on which we could all meet? I was angry and confused and wondered if I would ever understand this paradox. (Carlos Bulosan, *America Is in the Heart*)

The juxtaposition of the publicly stated ideal of a democratic nation and Bulosan's experience of suffering, sorrow, and exclusion from the ideal is what America is all about for many Asian Americans. The movement of the geist of dissonance and dissent is ritualized and traditioned into a reliable cultural referential point within the community. Sacrality is, above all, a category of emplacement. The spirit acts as the seedbed for an alternate set of sacred conventions, a bond, a second language that hopefully brings people together.

Amphibolous Faith

For Asian Americans, faith is likely to be expressed in the domain of a myriad of conflicting and often contradictory faith traditions and cosmologies coming together, a domain where we find ourselves. The term "amphibolous faith" is particularly a theological expression embedded within Asian American Christian communities that are set within our translocal material existence coupled with the hybridization of the inherited Asian cosmological worldviews and faith traditions. Amphibolous faith is the lived material condition of the "undecidable," an "irresolute" state, the domain that becomes acute for Asian American Christians who are assumed by the dominant Christian faith communities to embrace the monotheistic claims of the historical Christian faith. And yet Asian Americans are inclined to live with nontheistic cosmologies embedded in the Asian faith traditions we inherit. When Asian Americans embrace a theistic faith, we tend to add it to the faith traditions we have been formed in. We are not likely to substitute one faith tradition for another. In other words, we cherish our formative inheritance of Asian cosmologies and faiths. Therefore we become a Buddhist Christian, for example.

Amphibolous faith is a nonsingular in vision, and disidentification as its mode is expressed particularly in its material domain. Asian Americans live amphiboly, the grammar that defies a conventional articulation—"disorienting subjects." Amphibolous faith not only defies conventional faith paradigms, but also lives in an asymmetrical domain caught between whatever is the dominant faith paradigm and the multiple other faith traditions often ignored and devalued by the dominant traditions. Amphibolous faith is truly "hybrid," not as free oscillation among chosen faith identities, but as the "uneven process through which immigrant communities encounter the violence of the U.S. State . . . the process through which they survive those violences by living, inventing, and reproducing different cultural alternatives," says Lisa Lowe. Amphibolous faith suggests that the alternative to blind belief is not simply unbelief but a different kind of belief, one that embraces uncertainty and enables us to respect others whom we do not understand. In a complex world, wisdom is knowing what we really do know so that we can keep the future open.

Major Themes in the Current Theological Constructions

The representative Asian American theological voices are still mostly confined within academic institutions. Jung Young Lee and Sang Hyun Lee treat the themes of marginality and liminality. Andrew Sung Park and W. Anne Joh revive the Korean cultural concepts of *hun* and *jeong* in their theological constructions. Joh points toward an interpretation of the cross as a place where God and humanity come together as performing a double gesture that has a subversive effect. Utilizing the Korean concept of *jeong* (a notion that helps clarify how the double gesture of the cross inspires a new relationality), Joh constructs a theology that is feminist, political, and love-centered, while acknowledging the cross as source of pain and suffering as well. Jung Ha Kim, Kwok Pui-Lan, Boung Lee, Sung Ai Yang, Kwok Pui Lan, Rita Nakashima Brock, and others are the representative women's voices today. In the biblical field Kah-Jin Jeffrey Kuan, Tat-siong Benny Liew, Frank Yamada, Henry Rietz, and others also apply postcolonial perspectives to their biblical theological interpretations.

What Are the Challenges Facing Asian American Theology Today?

A critical challenge facing Asian American theology today is the question of how the political nature of the discipline becomes institutionalized as an academic field and what the consequences of this transformation might mean. It is the issue of cultural capital associated with this new discipline. Any form of cultural or intellectual activity can gain entry into the academic field only if it produces some form of cultural capital, which can be understood on a basic level as any kind of information or knowledge that possesses some value.

Insofar as seminaries, university divinity schools, and religious studies departments are the primary institutions engaged in the reproduction and determination of the value of cultural capital, Asian American studies necessarily had to convert itself into a form of cultural capital to be institutionalized in them. At the same time, such a cultural capital needs to be accountable to Asian American faith communities. The question of how to negotiate between legitimacy in academia and accountability in faith communities is one of the primary challenges facing theological construction.

Conclusion

The expanding ethnic diversity of this century, a time when we will all be minorities, offers us an invitation to create a larger memory of who we are as Americans and to reaffirm our founding principle of equality. Let's put aside fears of the "disuniting of America" and warnings of the "clash of civilizations." As Langston Hughes sang, "Let America be America, where equality is in the air we breathe."

The creation of what Takaki terms a "larger memory" in light of the divine presence in the world is a necessary task facing Asian American theological construction. Theology is uniquely accountable to the past and to the future, not simply or even primarily to the present. Theological construction is about learning that molds a lifetime, learning that transmits the heritage of millennia, learning that shapes the future. Asian American theological communities are stewards of living tradition where learning and knowledge are pursued because they define what has over centuries made the faithful human, not because they can make us smart.

Fumitaka Matsuoka

See also: Essays: Bible and Asian Americans

Further Reading

Brock, Rita Nakashima, and Jung Ha Kim, Kwok Pui-lan, and Seung Ai Yang, eds. *Off the Menu: Asian and Asian North American Women's Religion and Theology.* Louisville, KY: Westminster John Knox, 2007.

Joh, W. Anne. *Heart of the Cross: A Postcolonial Christology.* Louisville, KY: Westminster John Knox Press, 2006.

Kim, Grace Ji-Sun. *The Grace of Sophia: A Korean North American Women's Christology.* Eugene, OR: Wipf & Stock, 2010.

Lee, Sang Hyun. *From a Liminal Place: An Asian American Theology.* Minneapolis: Fortress Press, 2010.

Matsuoka, Fumitaka, and Eliazer Fernandez. *Realizing the America of the Heart.* Indianapolis: Chalice Press, 2003.

Park, Andrew Sung. *Racial Conflict and Healing: An Asian American Theological Perspective.* Eugene, OR: Wipf & Stock, 2009.

Part 2

Entries

Afghan American Religions

Religious practices, approaches, and beliefs among Afghan Americans are quite multifaceted and can be traced to various historical moments in Afghanistan's political history. Though most Afghan Americans might identify as Muslim, there are minorities who would associate with other religious traditions, including Hinduism and Judaism. Others claim no affiliation with a recognized religious tradition. While most Afghan Americans in the diaspora in the United States would identify as Muslim, there are also many variations in how Muslim Afghan Americans integrate the philosophies and practical tenets of Islam into their daily lives. Religious traditions and practices that shape the daily dispositions of Afghan Americans today have been shaped by different groups' political and military interventions throughout Afghanistan's history, even before its establishment as an official nation state.

Afghan Americans and Religious Practice

Afghan Americans who affiliate with a particular religious tradition situate the importance and expression of their religious identities in various ways. For example, many Afghan Americans' religious rituals are shaped by certain economic and social constraints, such as their daily work sched-

ules, the neighborhoods in which they live, and the need to collect enough social, economic, and cultural capital to establish successful ways of life in the United States. For example, the way Islam is practiced and imagined as part of one's daily realities differs among Afghan Americans depending on where in the United States they reside and on their local surroundings, among other factors. Afghan Americans in Flushing, New York, have more ready access to *mosques* and religious community centers than those who reside in the midwestern United States. As opposed to those who live in an area sparsely populated with other people of Afghan descent, those who live in areas more densely populated with Afghan Americans (such as Fremont, California, often called "Little Kabul" and small communities in Flushing, New York, and parts of Virginia) have a greater chance of engaging in collective religious celebrations. The role of religion in the daily lives of Afghans also differs according to the area in Afghanistan from which they or their families emigrated. Avoiding framing secular worldviews and religious traditionalism as two polar opposites, it would be appropriate to say that those immigrants who came from the capital of Afghanistan, Kabul, understand the role of Islam in their daily lives differently than immigrants who came from a more rural area of Afghanistan, which is embedded within a different social landscape, shaped differently by

U.S. President George W. Bush prepares to sign the Afghan Women and Children Relief Act as Afghan school children and humanitarian officials watch, December 12, 2001, in Washington D.C. The legislation, passed by the U.S. Congress, will provide educational and health care assistance to the war-torn country. (Mike Theiler/Getty Images)

historical political and social processes carried out by the state.

Afghan Americans and Muslim Religious Identities and Rites of Passage

Religious identities are articulated differently in different spaces among Afghan Americans. At times, the older generation of Afghan immigrants believes that claiming a Muslim identity is seen as a critical component to being able to claim an Afghan identity. Though this kind of dis-

course automatically excludes Afghan Americans who hail from other religious traditions, it is a dominant discourse within the U.S. Afghan diaspora and continues to shape how Afghan Americans of all or no religious traditions negotiate "non-normative religious affiliations" with their Afghan identities. Some Afghan American families emphasize the practice of praying five times per day, one pillar of the Islamic religious tradition, and continue to pass on the importance of this practice to their children. At times, immigrants and their children encounter situations in which facilitating prayer five times per day becomes more challenging in a professional work environment or within a school environment. Thus, at times, people have to negotiate when they engage in prayer or may have to make up for missed prayers at another time during the day.

Many Afghan American families also take part in fasting during the month of Ramadan, another pillar in the Islamic religious tradition. The tradition of fasting calls for Muslims to refrain from eating, drinking, and any other form of worldly consumption for one month, which shifts from year to year in accordance with the lunar calendar. Some individuals make it a point to wake up early in the morning before the sun has risen to eat food that will keep them full throughout the day (often this ritual is called the *sarī*), and they will not consume anything until the sun has set, which is also based on the official time that the fast is supposed to end. Some individuals will eat a date as a way to first break their fast, a ritual that dates back to the reported practices of the Prophet Muhammad. Families may also make it a point to cook traditional Afghan cuisine most nights to break the fast along with their families. Much of the religious rituals involved in fasting and breaking the fast are, therefore, not completely related to cultivating religious piety, but also to the desire to preserve familial dynamics and interactions that take place in unique ways during the month of Ramadan. The celebration of Eid follows the month of Ramadan, which Afghan Americans celebrate in various ways. Despite the degree to which the fast is observed, Eid still emerges as an occasion for celebration even if it simply takes the form

of wishing other Muslims and Afghans "*Eid Mobārak*" ("Happy Eid") or through hosting parties at their homes. Often, Afghan families will host house parties and will serve a plethora of home-cooked Afghan food and dessert, along with music and sometimes dancing. Adults will often distribute gifts to younger people at the gathering, most of the time in the form of money.

Another way in which Afghan Americans assert their religious identity is through participating in transitional moments or what might typically be called rites of passage, such as births, weddings, and funeral ceremonies. When Afghan American Muslims witness the birth of a baby, they may engage in rituals that are designed to seal the baby's identity as a Muslim, such as having one of the parents or grandparents whisper in the newborn's ear the *shahadāh* (the phrase used to assert oneself as a believing Muslim): "*[Ašhadu 'an] lā ilāha illā-llāh, wa ['ašhadu 'anna] Muḥammadan rasūlu-llāh*" (I testify that there is no God but God, and I testify that Muhammad is His messenger.).

Funeral ceremonies (referred to in Dari as the *fātehah*) are also spaces in which Afghan Americans evoke certain aspects of Muslimness. Religious phrases might be used by those in attendance to offer their condolences to the grieving family, but these phrases are not always used based on the need to add a spiritual or sacred dimension to grieving for the individual who has passed away. People might offer words of prayer and ask that God grant the family members long lives. The funeral ceremony also features readings of passages of the Qur'an by the imam of the *mosque* in which the ceremony is held. Typically, women will sit in one room of the *mosque* and listen to recitations of the Qur'an over a loudspeaker, while men sit in a separate room and see the imam read the recitations live. At the end of the funeral, food is usually served in large portions to all attendees either at the *mosque* itself or at the home of the family member of the deceased. The idea of providing plenty of food and dessert seems to emerge as an important line along which some Afghan Americans measure the "success" of the funeral ceremony in terms of how hospitable it was to its guests.

However, the occasion of the funeral also proves, for some Afghan Americans, to serve as a collectively accessible space in which community members can engage with family and family friends, continue to reinforce bonds with Afghan social networks, and continue to assert their cultural capital as relevant within their local community. Gossip takes the form of either talking about other Afghan acquaintances or even discussing the types of fashions that those at the funeral ceremony have donned.

Weddings constitute another important rite of passage that often has religious connotations. Afghan Muslim ceremonies entail several rituals that contribute to the legitimization of the union between the bride and groom in the presence of invited family members and friends. In the religious ceremony, called the *nekāh*, either a *mollā* or someone who is considered a spiritual and legitimate religious authority to both families reads passages from the Qur'an and asks the bride and groom each three times if they are certain they want to enter into the marriage. Here, the marriage contract or *'aqd* is also signed, which stipulates the amount of the bride's *mahr* (commonly analogized to a dowry but more complex in that it does not connote a "purchasing" of the woman's hand in marriage). Another ceremony that usually takes place during the reception itself includes placing a silk sheet over the bride and groom, who are sitting next to each other, and having them look at each other through a mirror under the sheet (*morasem-e āyena mosāf*). This ritual, historically, has been and continues to be used in Afghanistan and in the Afghan diaspora to symbolize the supposed first time that the bride and groom see their faces together. At a wedding reception, the bride and groom will walk into the reception hall hand in hand, with a member of the family holding the Qur'an over their heads (assuming that at least one of the individuals identifies as Muslim) as they walk to the song "*Āhestāh Boro*" (figuratively, "Walk Slowly"). Other ceremonies might include a *khīnah* ceremony during which women guests can take packets of intricate designs of *khīnah* (also known in English as *henna*) skin dye and have them imprinted on their hands. During this ceremony, the mother of the bride also gives a *khīnah* packet to the groom. Women guests may also place a set of candles in the middle of the reception hall around which they dance, usually wearing clothing native to more rural parts of Afghanistan.

History of Afghan Religions

While this entry has primarily focused on the intricacies of the different ways that

Islam figures into Afghan American life, as mentioned in the introduction, there are numerous religious affiliations that make up the landscape of Afghan American religions. The history of religions in Afghanistan cannot be detached from the history of political systems in the Afghan state.

In the third and fourth centuries, following the move by Bactrian Greeks to cede control of Bactria to a group of Indo-European tribes called the Kushans, Kushan leadership took control of Bactria (Balkh) in northern Afghanistan. The era of Kushan rule saw the establishment of the tall Buddhist statues that were carved into a cliff at Bamiyan during the third and fourth centuries CE, but which were destroyed during the reign of the Taliban in March 2001. During the fifth through seventh centuries, several religious centers developed in Afghanistan, including those in Hadda, Ghazni, Kunduz, Bamian, Shotorak, and Bagram, which hosted Chinese Buddhist pilgrims. From the south, Hindu influence entered Afghanistan and was adopted by both the Hephthalite Huns and the Sasanians. Hindu Shahi kings ruled areas of Afghanistan, including Kabul and Ghazni, until the ninth and tenth centuries CE. In 651 CE, the Sassanian empire dissolved, while Arab groups introduced Islam as both a religious and political system within the region. While Genghis Khan, leader of the Mongols, attempted to remove Islam from Central Asia, by the end of the 13th century his descendants were also Muslim. The death of Genghis Khan saw an increase in independent localities throughout Afghanistan. The emergence of the Roshaniya in the 16th century, a group of Sufis who were inspired by a Pashtun philosopher and nationalist known as Bayezid Ansari or Pir Roshan (the enlightened one), circulated throughout Afghanistan a politically revolutionary discourse in Pashtun culture. The Roshaniya wrere considered to be part of an Ishamelite religion, which may have originated from the time of Abraham's rebuilding of the black stone temple of Kaaba in Mecca, Saudi Arabia. Following the Afghan victory over the expanding Ottoman Turks in the 18th century, Ahmad Khan Abdali, a chieftain who achieved victory in the military defeat, was crowned Ahmad Shah, Durr-i-Durran (Pearl of Pearls) or Ahmad Shah Durrani, the new ruler of Afghanistan. Durrani, over the next quarter century, consolidated his control and made his empire the second most important Muslim kingdom next to the Ottoman Turks.

The extent to which other religious traditions have found their inspiration in the landscape of Afghanistan has been an object of historical debate. Some historians have thought that references to the Afghan landscape could be found in the Rig Veda Hindu religious text, while other believed that the first identifiable mention of what is now Afghanistan can be located in the Avesta and the teachings of Zarathustra, the guiding book for Zoroastrians. Afghanistan is the reputed home of Zoraster and the Avesta, as well as Gandhara Buddhism, the Roshaniya cult, and the founders of the Bektashi, Mevlevi, and Chishti Sufi orders. Strains of mysticism and saint worship have always influenced the history of Afghanistan. Conquerors from Persia and Central Asia who returned from Hindu India slowly introduced Islam as the dominant faith. Sufism in Afghanistan relied on the premise that one had to establish a deep connection with the divine through performing mystical devotions. Leaders of Sufi groups established orders and were worshiped as saints and chieftains; shrines for these leaders continue to be present throughout the country.

The Shiite presence in Afghanistan's history has also been quite strong. The Isma'iliya subsect, who have a strong presence throughout East Africa, India, and Pakistan, have also established themselves as a recognizable minority in Afghanistan. Afghan sects of the Isma'iliya include Wakhi, Shigni, Ishkamishi, Sanaglechi, Munji, and the Pamiri, as well as some Hazara (of which there are also Imami Shiites). Some interpretations of Islam, which continue to be practiced in rural areas of Afghanistan, have been and continue to be combined with other principles of the Pashtun lineage, including *Pashtunwalī* (the codes and principles that define the Pashtun way of life). Though this festival is not limited to those who practice the Shiite religion, a special religious festival held on Nowroz (the Afghan New Year) is held at the tomb of Hazrat 'Ali, the prophet and appropriate caliph that was to succeed the Prophet Muhammad according to the Shiite religion. The tomb is said to offer Muslims a chance to achieve religious merit.

The Muslim Brotherhood made its presence known in Afghanistan in the late 1960s and early 1970s, and while the group initially challenged patriarchal structures, it eventually began to reproduce and perpetuate violent activities and political rivalries. Groups like the Muslim Brotherhood were motivated by the rhetoric of prominent Arabic thinkers such as Said Ramadan and Said Qutb. Their strain of political Islam can be traced to the revolutionary rhetoric being espoused by the era's versions of Marxism and Leninism. Burhanuddin Rabbani, who translated Qutb's texts into Dari, a dominant language of Afghanistan, helped to propagate the religious language of the Muslim Brotherhood throughout public spaces such as Kabul University. Recruits of Rabbani, including Ahmad Shah Massoud and Gulbuddin Hekmatyar, established the Jamaat-i-Islami (Islamic Society), which was responsible for many acts of violence perpetrated against women and children during the era of the Afghan civil war (1992–1996).

Religion also figures in less obvious ways in Afghanistan's history and in tribal practice. Sainthood has figured into the religious practices of Afghans, not only in Afghanistan, but also in the diaspora. Many Afghans who migrated to India in the 16th and 18th centuries constituted a trading diaspora, whose activities brought them close to other trading groups that had little familiarity with Islam or the various tribal organizations of the Pashtun ethno-linguistic group. The elite class of Afghans that emerged in India experienced different levels of success under various Mughal rulers, while they competed for influence among the Persian diaspora in India. The presence of Sufi "blessed men," about which Nile Green has written extensively, served to embody local interpretations of Islamic moral order, as they carried out miracles, and to mediate individual and group relations. The networks and connections fostered by these blessed men served as vehicles through which Afghans were able to integrate within Indian society, especially in the 15th and 16th centuries. In short, while Afghan migrants were being assimilated within the Mughal Empire in the 18th century, they also circulated tales of saints in the genealogy called *Tarīkh-e-Khān Jahānī*, which sought to present a reading of history in which the past was to be made visible at every point through tribal genealogy. These tales served to play important roles in preserving traditions of cultural memory and tribal pasts, as groups of Afghans migrated from old habitats to new ones. Saints have played important roles in Afghanistan's more contemporary history as well. The *ziarat*, or shrine, can be found throughout the country and often serves as a space where people can ask for the intercession of a certain saint with the divine, to complete a special favor. Some saints are said to cure insanity while others are said to cure dog bites, and others are used to help facilitate fertility.

Conclusion

There exists much debate among Afghan Americans about what the role of religion should be in Afghanistan. As many of those in the U.S. diaspora are part of a wave of migrants that came from the urban and more elite stratum of Kabul, their views on the role of religion in everyday life are more secularized than those migrants who are part of more recent waves of immigrants who hail from more rural areas. For the latter, religion does not necessarily fit more or less into their daily lives than those who come from Kabul, but it fits into their lives in different ways and is seen more readily within certain collective social institutions. The era

of the Taliban often serves as a reference point for many who caution against the deployment of religion for political purposes.

The emergence of the Taliban in Afghanistan in 1995 is historically seen as a particularly religiously fraught moment in Afghanistan's history. The religious practices of the Taliban cannot be properly evaluated without a more extensive examination of Afghanistan's political history. Beyond imposing a wide array of limitations on individual rights (such as depriving women of the right to go outside of the home without a male escort, or the right to attend school or work outside of the home), the Taliban disguised what were really schemes to gain political power with discourses to religiously purify Afghanistan. The preceding Afghan civil war (1992–1996) was a key period that created the gaps in political power that made the rise of the Taliban all the more possible. Some scholars have argued that the fact that none of the country's past governments have been successful in their attempts to foster a sense of nationalism among most Afghans might explain why religion has become such a potent political force throughout the country. Others have argued that the end of Marxist rule and the rise of Islamists have played a crucial role in compounding the force of patriarchal versions of Islam throughout Afghanistan and bringing back tribal leaders to power. Specifically, the government of President Burhanuddin Rabbani, which took power several years following the exit of Soviet troops from Afghanistan, is pinpointed as the beginning of the expansion of Afghan warlords throughout the rural areas, which resulted in the erosion of Afghans' political, economic, and social rights. Again, the role of religion in the Taliban regime is a paradoxical one, one that is influenced by both political desires and a rethinking of religious doctrine. James Gelvin describes this paradoxical stance well, pointing out that even the Taliban called the country it once ruled "The Islamic Emirate of Afghanistan." Gelvin points out that by using the term "Islamic," the Taliban acknowledged that yes, Afghanistan is part of an Islamic cultural sphere. On the other hand, the use of the term "emirate" indicates that the Taliban was claiming for Afghanistan sovereignty within the international state system. The Taliban even sought to represent its "emirate" in the United Nations (it never got to do so).

Today, about 80–89 percent of the Afghan population practice Sunni Islam while 10–19 percent practice Shiism, and about 1 percent practice other religions. Most of those who practice Sunni Islam practice the Hanafi version, which is one of four *madhab* (schools) of Sunni Islamic thought. While there used to be a greater Jewish minority in Afghanistan in the 1960s and 1970s, it is reported that almost all Afghan Jews fled the country during the Afghan-Soviet War (1979–1989), and that only one Afghan Jew remains in the country today. Other very small minority religious groups include Baha'is, Sikhs, Hindus, Zoroastrians, and Christians.

Helena Zeweri

See also: Essays: Muslims; Politics and Religion

Further Reading

Ahmad, Mumtaz, Zahid H. Bukhari, John L. Esposito, and Sulayman S. Nyang. *Muslims' Place in the American Public Square: Hopes, Fears, and Aspirations*. Lanham, MD: Rowman and Littlefield, 2004.

Banuazizi, Ali, and Myron Weiner, eds. *The State, Religion, and Ethnic Politics: Afghanistan, Iran, and Pakistan*. Syracuse, NY: Syracuse University Press, 1986.

Curtis, Edward E., IV. *Muslims in America: A Short History*. New York: Oxford University Press, 2009.

Fitzgerald, Paul, and Elizabeth Gould. *Invisible History: Afghanistan's Untold Story*. San Francisco: City Light Books, 2009.

Gelvin, James. *The Modern Middle East: A History*. Oxford: Oxford University Press, 2009.

Green, Nile. "Tribe, Diaspora, and Sainthood in Afghan History." *The Journal of Asian Studies* 67 (2008): 171–211.

Marsden, Peter. *The Taliban: War, Religion, and the New Order in Afghanistan*. London: Zed Books, 1998.

Moghadam, Valentine M. "Revolution, Religion, and Gender Politics: Iran and Afghanistan Compared." *Journal of Women's History* 10 (1999): 172–95.

Zulfacar, Maliha. *Afghan Immigrants in the USA and Germany: A Comparative Analysis of the Use of Ethnic and Social Capital*. New Brunswick, NJ: Transaction, 1998.

Aglipay, Gregorio (1860–1940)

Gregorio Aglipay was a Filipino secular Roman Catholic priest who led a nationalist, religious reform movement against the Spanish friars during the Philippine Revolution of 1896. The movement resulted in the birth of the Iglesia Filipina Independiente (Philippine Independent Church), a national Filipino Catholic church. Aglipay was the Independent Church's first *Obispo Maximo* (Supreme Bishop).

Members of the Malolos Congress, the constituent assembly of the First Philippine Republic, return to the Barasoain Church in Malolos City, Bulacan, where, in 1899, they drew up the constitution for the First Philippine Republic, December 8, 1929. Back row, left to right: Teodoro Sandico, Fernando Canon, Bishop Gregorio Aglipay, Simplicio del Rosario, Ignacio Villamor and Pacifico Gustillo. Front row, left to right: Santiago Icasiano, Mariano V. del Rosario, Emilio Aguinaldo (1859–1964), Pio del Pilar, and Jose Maria de la Vina. (FPG/Hulton Archive/Getty Images)

Aglipay was so closely identified with the Iglesia Filipina Independiente that colloquially it was known as the Aglipayan church. However, the Iglesia's official founder was Isabelo de los Reyes, a lawyer and prolific writer who took part in the reform movement as a propagandist. Aglipay and de los Reyes grew up in Ilocos Province and met when they were both students at San Juan de Letran, a Catholic college in Manila. Aglipay went back to Ilocos to prepare for the priesthood while de los Reyes took part in the fight against friar sovereignty through his writings. He was imprisoned for his propaganda activities in Manila, and then exiled to Barcelona, Spain, by the Spanish authorities in June 1897. In Spain, de los Reyes advocated for a separatist Filipino church.

When de los Reyes returned to the Philippines in 1901, he founded the first Filipino labor union, Union Obrera Democratica, and used it to campaign relentlessly for the creation of a national Filipino church. On August 3, 1902, in a rally of his labor union, de los Reyes proclaimed the establishment of the Iglesia Filipina Independiente and named Aglipay as the church's head without his knowledge and consent. Aglipay, who at that time viewed the declaration as precipitous, did not approve of a schism between the Filipino clergy and the Catholic Church, and therefore disavowed any involvement with de los Reyes's church. However, Aglipay changed his mind when a conference with Jesuit leaders aimed at preventing a schism failed. The Roman Catholic negotiator insulted Filipino priests in front of Aglipay by calling them "vicious and hopelessly inefficient." Convinced of the futility of reform within Roman Catholicism, Aglipay accepted the leadership of the Iglesia Filipina Independiente. On October 25, 1902, he celebrated the Iglesia's first mass in Tondo, Manila.

The schism was the culmination of the Filipino clergy's thwarted attempts to seek equality with the Spanish friars and end centuries of abuses and corruption. The Spanish monastic orders not only held unchallenged political control of the colony but also possessed a suffocating monopoly of agricultural lands and a stranglehold on the tobacco industry. To maintain their power and privileges, the friars restricted the native clergy to second-rate positions and refused to elevate them to episcopal rank by claiming that Filipinos belonged to an inferior race. To break friar sovereignty, the native clergy, headed by Pedro Pelaez, agitated for the secularization of the parishes. Unfortunately, Queen Isabella II ignored the demands of the secularization movement,

even with the support of a sympathetic Spanish archbishop.

Although the secularization movement ceased when Pelaez died during the 1863 earthquake in Manila, the native clergy continued their clamor for reform by calling instead for "Filipinization" of the Catholic Church. Three Filipino priests—Jose Burgos, Mariano Gomez, and Jacinto Zamora—emerged as leaders, inspiring not only the native clergy but also the rest of the country, particularly the intelligentsia. Aware of the growing anti-Spanish sentiment among the Filipino populace, which was attributed to the three clerics, the Spanish friars and conservative colonial government sought to carry out a program of repression and persecution. They saw their opportunity when a Filipino battalion guarding an arsenal in Cavite Province rose in mutiny when the government took away their exemption from paying tribute. The three "Filipinization" leaders were implicated in the incident and were publicly garroted in February 1872. Other priests and supporters of the "Filipinization" movement were exiled abroad.

Contrary to the expectations of the Spanish authorities, the deaths of Gomez, Burgos, and Zamora led to the intensification of nationalist fervor. The exiled liberal émigrés and Filipino students in Europe started the Propaganda Movement, which not only took up the Filipino clergy's call for secularization, but expanded the demands to include representation of the Philippines in the Spanish parliament or Cortes, equality between Filipinos and Spanish, public education independent of the friars, elimination of forced labor and sale of local products to the government, and the guarantee of basic freedoms. The most prominent member of the Propaganda Movement was the polymath Jose Rizal, a novelist, poet, journalist, ethnologist, and physician. Rizal advocated for evolutionary reform as the path to independence from Spain. He would later be executed in Manila by the Spanish colonial government, which falsely accused him of involvement in the armed revolution of 1896.

Rizal was instrumental in Aglipay's decision to become a Catholic priest. They became friends after they met as representatives of their respective colleges in fencing. Aglipay could not make up his mind to be a priest because of his own personal experience of friar persecution and the injustice done to Gomez, Burgos, and Zamora. Aglipay related to Rizal that when he was 16 years old, he and his father were jailed for failing to produce enough tobacco on their farm to fulfill the quota set by the friar-controlled tobacco monopoly. When they were released, his father sent him to his grandfather in Manila to continue his studies. Instead of dissuading him, Rizal advised him to pursue the priesthood as a moral counterweight to the friars and to work for the rights of the Filipino clergy.

Aglipay was ordained a Catholic priest in 1890 after his studies at a seminary in Ilocos Sur. He was assigned as assistant priest in various parishes scattered in five provinces on the island of Luzon. At the outbreak of the revolution, Aglipay was working in the province of Tarlac. His sympathies were with the revolutionaries but he did not actively take part in any of the uprising.

As Rizal predicted, the revolution was premature and the outcome, the Pact of Biak-na-Bato, a treaty between the revolutionary leadership and the Spanish governor general, was not favorable to the Filipino people. The leadership, headed by General Emilio Aguinaldo, agreed to voluntary exile, indemnity of $400,000 to the revolutionary army, and another $900,000 to the families of noncombatants. The terms of the pact were only partially fulfilled by both sides. The Spanish did not pay indemnity for the families of the noncombatants and the revolutionary forces did not give up their arms. Like many of the revolution's supporters, Aglipay was dissatisfied with the Pact of Biak-na-Bato because it did not achieve the goals of sovereignty for the native clergy and the Filipino people.

The governor general negotiated with Aguinaldo because Spain was anxious to avoid war in the Philippines; it was facing another war, this time with the mightier United States in 1898. It also hoped to rally Filipinos against the Americans when the war reached the colony, but Aguinaldo had returned to the Philippines having decided to cooperate with the United States in its war with Spain. Local insurgents also continued to organize and engage the Spanish in skirmishes.

Accused by his religious superiors of taking part in the insurgent efforts to form a provisional revolutionary government in Central Luzon, Aglipay was recalled to Manila where he acted as Spanish archbishop Nozaleda's emissary to the rebel forces who were holding Spanish clerics prisoners. Because of his ties with the insurgents, Aglipay was able to secure the release of the Spanish clerics, and for his service was appointed ecclesiastical governor of Nueva Segovia. Nozaleda had expected his Filipino appointee to persuade the revolutionaries to favor the Spanish over the Americans who had by then occupied Manila, but Aglipay did not get an opportunity to take sides between the colonizers. Determined to fight for religious emancipation and political independence, Aguinaldo refused to recognize Nozaleda's ecclesiastical authority and ordered Filipino priests not to accept any new responsibility from the church without the approval of his new government. He also appointed Aglipay as military vicar general. Faced with a dilemma between serving the Catholic Church and the Filipino people, Aglipay chose to honor Aguinaldo's appointment. His first acts as military vicar general were to order the Filipino clergy to organize themselves for national emergency and to create a council to ask Rome to appoint Filipino priests in all positions in the Philippine Catholic Church. In response, Nozaleda excommunicated Aglipay as a "usurper (of power) and a schismatic."

To advance "Filipinization" of the Catholic Church, Aglipay called an ecclesiastical assembly of Filipino priests in Tarlac Province to organize an independent national Catholic Church that still recognized the pope's authority. The assembly drew up a constitution but was not able to enforce it because of the looming collapse of the Aguinaldo government in the Filipino-American War. Aglipay, now regarded as one of Aguinaldo's generals, had to flee to the mountains north of Manila to wage guerilla warfare against the Americans who superseded the Spanish in a new policy of repression. When Aguinaldo was captured in May 1901, Aglipay surrendered to the Americans, who offered him amnesty.

With the end of the revolution, Aglipay resumed his plans for Filipinization of the Catholic Church. He convened another ecclesiastical assembly on May 8, 1902, in Ilocos Norte, again with the aim of asking the pope for the recognition and appointment of Filipino clergy in all levels of the church hierarchy. But before he could carry out his plans any further, Isabelo de los Reyes proclaimed the establishment of the Iglesia Independiente. The people's overwhelming response to the proclamation and the insulting reaction of the Jesuits to his overtures finally convinced Aglipay to break from the Catholic Church.

Aglipay managed the transition from Catholic orthodoxy by allowing the priests of the Independent Church to consecrate him "Supreme Bishop." Then with de los Reyes, Aglipay instituted new dogmas: the Virgin Mary was no longer venerated; the three martyred Filipino clerics—Gomez, Burgos, and Zamora—were made saints; and the vow of celibacy became voluntary. The Independent Church's beliefs were officialized in *Oficio Divino* (Divine Office), a book published by de los Reyes explaining his theology of "religious Philippinism," an amalgam of indigenous, Gnostic, and Western philosophies. Although the basis of Christian belief, Christ's incarnation, was preserved, the interpretation of his crucifixion followed the Docetic doctrine. The *Oficio* was approved by the Independent Church's Supreme Council of Bishops.

Aglipay veered farther away from Catholicism when he embraced parts of Unitarian theology as a result of a deep friendship with Unitarians, the most prominent of whom was then governor general of the Philippines, William Howard Taft. The bond between the two churches was strengthened when the Unitarians sponsored trips to the United States and Europe for Aglipay and the Independent Church's leadership. Unitarianism influenced Aglipay to renounce the doctrine of the Trinity and Christ's incarnation.

For the first few years after its establishment, the Philippine Independent Church (PIC) met with success. Its membership was estimated to be between two to four million, out of a population of eight million in 1902. However, its membership dwindled rapidly after the U.S. Supreme Court decision of 1906, which forced the Independent Church to return to the Roman Catholic Church all property that they had taken over after the revolution. Despite its appeal that the property rightfully belonged to the people whose money and labor were used to build them, Aglipay's church was stripped of all its possessions—churches, rectories, and cemeteries. The decision left the Independent Church vulnerable not only ecclesiastically, but also economically. The church's leadership failed to plan for the creation of an economic foundation that could sustain it for the future.

The Roman Catholic Church's countermeasures also weakened the Independent Church further. Shaken by the success of Aglipay, the pope promulgated sweeping changes, notably the end of Spanish sovereignty in the Philippine Catholic Church. Rome proposed reforms that created additional dioceses, provided better education for the Filipino secular clergy, and suppressed the privileges of the regular clergy and the religious orders. It sent affable and diplomatic American bishops to govern, and finally elevated a Filipino cleric to the episcopacy. With the revitalization of the Roman Catholic Church and the inroads of American Protestantism, Aglipay's church could not recover.

To rally their demoralized forces, Aglipay and de los Reyes turned to politics. The United States provided for the transition of the Philippines from a colony to independence by creating a Commonwealth government from 1935 to 1946. Thinking that they could somehow acquire political clout in the Commonwealth, Aglipay and de los Reyes formed the Republican Party, which had a nationalistic platform and included an appeal to the Supreme Court to repeal its 1906 decision. At the age of 75, Aglipay ran for president of the Commonwealth of the Philippines. Although some members of the Independent Church were elected, Aglipay was soundly defeated.

Aglipay and de los Reyes could not mount a comeback after the political debacle. Many of its members were alienated and returned to the Catholic fold. There were threats of a major split, but these never materialized while Aglipay and de los Reyes lived. On October 10, 1938, de los Reyes died. Aglipay died two years later on September 1, 1940. The two men left a vacuum in the leadership of the PIC, ushering in a period of factionalism after their deaths.

Ten years after the end of World War II and the independence of the Philippines from the United States, the PIC was characterized by internal strife and countless court litigations. Finally in 1955, the Philippine Supreme Court declared Isabelo de los Reyes, Jr., the son of PIC's co-founder, the legitimate head of the PIC. As his first major move, de los Reyes steered the PIC back to Trinitarian faith. As a result, the PIC entered into a full communion with the Episcopal Church of the United States in 1960, followed by a similar concordat with the Orthodox and Catholic churches in England and Europe. With international recognition, the PIC made the same formal agreement with other churches of the worldwide Anglican Communion. It also became a leading member of the Council of Churches in Asia and the World Council of Churches.

With the return of the PIC to Catholicity, it acquired a fresh wind of spiritual renewal and entered a period of stability. It is still considered the second largest Christian denomination in the Philippines after the Roman Catholic Church. It added new dioceses, including the diocese of the United States and Canada. However, expansion abroad has been hampered by a lack of priests and the PIC's history of poverty.

Ofelia O. Villero

See also: Essays: Catholics; *Entries:* El Shaddai; Filipino Protestants; Santo Niño

Further Reading

Scott, William Henry. "The Philippine Independent Church in History." *East and West Review* (1962): 3–13.

Vergara, Wenifredo. "Dynamics of Religious Revolution: History and Theology of the Philippine Independent Church with Implications for Renewal." DMin dissertation, San Francisco Theological Seminary, 1989.

Aikidō

Aikidō is a Japanese martial art that incorporates locks and pins, throws, and uses a wooden sword and wooden staff as training tools. Even though *aikidō* techniques can injure an attacker, the underlying philosophy of the art is to peacefully neutralize an attack with calm and graceful circular movements without causing serious harm to the attacker. *Aikidō* is not a competitive sport; there are no "fights" or "matches" or competitive tournaments. The underlying spirit guiding *aikidō* is expressed in the three Japanese characters that form its name. "*Ai*" is usually translated "harmony"; "*ki*," "life energy"; and "*dō*," "spiritual path" or "way." *Aikidō*, thus, is "The Way of Harmonizing (with) Life Energy."

This entry provides a brief history of *aikidō*, including its introduction and spread in the United States, its spiritual underpinnings, and a description of some of its techniques.

History

Ueshiba Morihei (1883–1969) founded and popularized *aikidō*. Before developing *aikidō*, he trained in several different martial arts, including *jūjitsu* (consisting of grappling and striking), *yari* (spear), and *Daitō Ryū Jūjitsu* (an art that emphasizes throwing techniques, joint manipulation, and using the opponent's force against him or her). It is this later martial art that influenced Ueshiba the most. He studied *Daitō Ryū Jūjitsu* with Takeda Sokaku (1863–1943), who conferred on Ueshiba a teacher's certificate. Many of the hand techniques and much of the nomenclature in *aikidō* is from this school.

Around 1919, Ueshiba moved to Ayabe in Kyoto Prefecture, where he began his spiritual quest as a live-in student of Deguchi Onisaburō (1860–1948), the second spiritual leader of Ōmoto-kyō, a newly formed Shintō sect. Deguchi pursued "mystical experiences" through meditation and chanting practice; and taught inner peace and potential world peace through individual virtue, an idea that Ueshiba absorbed into his *aikidō* philosophy. Ueshiba developed his martial art through hard training and he expected his students to train just as hard at his so-called "hell" *dōjō* or training hall. The bombings of Tokyo during World War II prompted Ueshiba and his wife to move to the country town of Iwama in Ibaragi Prefecture. It is here that he established the Ibaragi Shūren Dōjō, where he researched and developed his techniques, and where most of the famous *aikidō* instructors trained at one time or another. He built the Aiki Jinja (shrine) dedicated to the deities of *aikidō*. It was during this time (1942) that "*Aikidō*" became the official name of his school.

Ueshiba combined the philosophical, ethical, and spiritual aspects of the Ōmoto-kyō with the martial techniques of Daitō Ryū Jūjutsu. Just as Ueshiba separated from his teacher Takeda, students left Ueshiba to evolve their own styles. Most notable are Shioda Gōzō (1915–1944), who developed the Yoshinkan style; Tomiki Kenji (1900–1979), who created the Tomiki style; and Tohei Kōichi (1920–2011), who developed the Ki style.

The Aikikai Foundation (*Aikidō* World Headquarters) is the parent organization of different approaches to *aikidō* and is currently headed by Ueshiba Moriteru, the founder's grandson. Some of the more popular styles are the Aikikai style, taught at the *Aikidō* Headquarters in Tokyo; the Iwama style popularized by Saitō Morihiro (1928–2002) that is notable for using the *bokken* (wooden sword) and the *jo* (short staff), as well as emphasizing stable body techniques; and the Shingu style developed by practitioners from Shingu in Wakayama that is known for its large flowing movements. "Style" refers to differing philosophies and training methods. The Yoshinkan, Tomiki, and Ki styles are independent organizations.

Tohei Kōichi brought *aikidō* to Hawai'i in 1953; it was the first time that *aikidō* was seen outside of Japan. Some of Tohei's students introduced *aikidō* to the West Coast of the United States. Most notable were Isao Takahashi and Roderick Kobayashi, who helped establish *aikidō* in Southern California. Other early teachers of *aikidō* were former servicemen who had studied the art in Japan. In the early 1960s Aikikai Headquarters in Tokyo sent Yamada Yoshimitsu (b. 1938) to New York, Kanai Mitsunari (1939–2004) to Boston, and Tohei Akira (1929–1999) to Chicago as full-time instructors. They are seminal figures in spreading *aikidō* throughout the United States, Canada, and Mexico. *Aikidō* is now practiced at commercial and nonprofit *dōjōs*, high schools, grammar schools, universities, and even community recreation centers. Adult classes are normally offered in the evening and may include beginners and more advanced sessions. It is not that unusual to see 60- to 70-year-old students practicing with 20- and 30-year-olds. Women make up about 40 percent of the adult student population. Some of the most energetic students are 5 and 6 years old.

Currently the largest population of *aikidō* enthusiasts is in France, followed by the United States, and third by Japan. The greatest growth and interest in *aikidō* are in South Asia, Southeast Asia, and South America. An informal online survey revealed an estimated million and a half *aikidō* practitioners worldwide.

Spiritual Foundations

Shintō maintains that the gods are pure and humans, impure. By purifying the spirit, humans are able to get closer to the gods. Purification achieved through physical and mental *misogi*, "washings" that cleanse the "dust of impurities," is a cornerstone of *aikidō* and the other Japanese martial arts. Ueshiba believed that physical hardship experienced in *aikidō* training is a form of *misogi* that cleanses the spirit and calms the mind. Pushing oneself to the point of exhaustion, enduring great pain and discomfort, and surviving on very little sleep is essential in training.

Daily and rigorous training, enduring stress and hardship are hallmarks of traditional *aikidō* practice that awakens a bright spirit and quickens greater skills and abilities. To awaken this spirit, *aikidō* engages in special winter, summer, and New Year's training retreats. Winter and summer practices last about a week. The winter practice takes place during the coldest time of the year; summer practice occurs when the heat and humidity are at their peak. While both training retreats are most stressful and grueling, those who successfully undergo these trainings experience great joy and a feeling of accomplishment. The celebratory New Year's training is highlighted by a run up to the local shrine on its mountain perch late at night; practice continues through midnight into the New Year. Conducted in the dark, practice includes the use of wooden swords. Training ends with a run down the mountain to celebratory toasts and food.

Training also includes *kototama*, or chanting meditation. Shintō maintains that sounds create reality. Just as the Bible places great importance in the Word ("In the beginning was the Word"), Shintō believes that the vocalization of certain vowels has the power to transform the mind and relax the body. Like the other Japanese martial arts, *kototama* takes the form of the *kiai* in *aikidō*. *Kiai* is an energetic yell—*aaiiee*, made with a rising pitch—that originates from the *hara*, the lower abdomen. Voiced simultaneously with the peak moment of a physical maneuver, *kiai* is a way to focus the mind and the body. It is used in different ways in *aikidō*. The voicing of "*aaiiee*" together with an *atemi* or feint to the opponent's head or face will startle the attacker, who would normally respond by pulling back the face or head, weaken his or her grip, and slow the attack. *Kiai* is also employed to rally oneself from fatigue or exhaustion by renewing or refreshing the practitioner to better execute his or her training and counterattacks.

Training

The *aikidō* practitioner is trained to be mindful of the following four points. First the practitioner must focus on the center, the pelvic girdle region of the body that is about one and a half to two inches below the navel. This is the physical center of the body and the seat of our muscles and muscular energy. Such concentration settles and clears the mind. Second, the practitioner must extend or project his or her *ki* or energy without undue muscular tension or rigidity. *Ki* is often translated "life energy," which flows effortlessly through the body when there is no excess tension or rigidity. Third, the practitioner must employ *kokyu ryoku* (literally breath-power); however, in *aikidō*, the expression refers to the unity of the mind, body, and breath. Fourth, the practitioner must always begin with *hanmi*, a triangular stance, wherein one foot is forward and the back foot is pointed outward approximately at a 45-degree angle. This stance facilitates *aikidō* techniques, throws, and movements. This stance, inherited from the traditional sword arts, is also used with the wooden sword.

The typical *aikidō* practice begins and ends with proper etiquette. Practice begins with the *sensei* (instructor/teacher) and students assembled in neat parallel rows in *seiza*, a formal sitting posture, in which the knees are folded under the torso and the back and head are upright, facing the front of the *dōjō*. Students face and bow to an image of the founder, Ueshiba Morihei, or a scroll written with an expression that crystallizes the spirit of *aikidō*. The sensei, who sits alone, turns to face the students. They bow to each other, repeating in vigorous unison "*onegaishimasu,*" a common expression that requests a favor. In *aikidō* as in the other martial arts, the favor solicited is the honor of being allowed to practice with a partner. The favor accorded between the *sensei* and the student may seem to be asymmetrical, but it is one of mutual respect. The student asks the *sensei* to please share his or her expertise; the *sensei* in turn asks the student to please accept his or her instruction.

The formalities completed, the *sensei* rises to lead the warm-up exercises or to demonstrate a technique. After the warm-up or the demonstration, the students and the teacher bow once again to each other and repeat, "*onegaishimasu.*" Students quickly pair up, bow from a *seiza* position, and repeat "*onegaishimasu*" before commencing to practice. During practice, students alternate between being the *nage* (thrower) and the *uke* (the receiver of the technique). Practice continues until a technique is perfected. Instructions vary with different schools and/or styles and the occasion. Instruction often consists of a lecture, meditation, and physical training in unarmed techniques or the use of wooden sword or short staff. At the end of the class, as at the beginning, everyone assembles as before and bows as a gesture of respect and gratitude to an image of Ueshiba or the scroll. Subsequently, the *sensei* turns to face the students; both *sensei* and students bow to each other, voicing in unison, "*arigatō gozaimashita,*" "Thank you very much" to end the class.

Daily *aikidō* practice brings calm and tranquility. The circular movements of the art that result in the occasional effortless throws during a practice session quicken a sense of wonder and awe in both the *uke* and the *nage*. Even more amazing are those moments when both smile after a particularly effortless throw. These moments of wonder encourages the *aikidō* student to continue along the path of *aiki*, the path of the spirit. Ueshiba emphatically stated that *aikidō* is an art of the spirit and an art of peace, and the "Way" to harmony that leads to enlightenment.

Hans Goto

See also: Essays: Spirituality; *Entries:* Buddhist Meditation

Futher Reading

Stalker, Nancy K. *Prophet Motive: Deguchi Onisaburo, Omoto and the Rise of New Religions in Imperial Japan.* Honolulu: University of Hawai'i Press, 2007.

Stevens, John. *Abundant Peace.* Boston: Shambhala, 1987.

Stevens, John. *Invincible Warrior.* Boston: Shambhala, 1999.

Ueshiba, Kisshomaru. *A Life in Aikidō.* Tokyo: Kodansha International, 1999.

Aloha Spirit

"Aloha spirit" is an idea that the people of Hawai'i have a special connection to one another, the land, the culture, and the visitors. This connection is one of love, hospitality, and a forgiving, easygoing spirit or nature. Aloha spirit is significant because it is what Hawaiians believe makes Hawai'i different from U.S. states on the continent, and it is what draws thousands of tourists to its shores. *Aloha mai no, aloha aku* (When aloha is given, aloha should be returned).

Indigenous Hawaiians are very protective of the expressions "aloha" and "aloha spirit." Aloha spirit has evolved over time.

The word "aloha" is where "aloha spirit" gets its meaning. The literal translation of "aloha" depends on the *kaona* (meaning or context). "*Alo*" means to share while "*ha*" is breath, which is also life; one *kaona* can be to share one's life with another person. "Aloha" can mean a greeting or welcome, or love, such as love of the people, *aloha 'āina* (love of the land or nation), or *aloha kai* (love of the sea). In addition, "aloha" can mean caring, sharing, kind-hearted, generous, gentleness, loveable, tolerant, and is its own source of *mana* (spiritual power). Reciprocity is important. There is a cyclical nature to aloha; aloha creates aloha.

Aloha spirit is necessary for the emotional well-being of a society, and in ancient Hawai'i, aloha was necessary between husband and wife, mother and child, and *ali'i* (chief) and *maka'āinana* (commoner). An often used image of aloha between a husband and wife is the husband behind the wife, protecting her. (This is the opposite of the Western image of a clinging wife.) *Ke aloha pili pa'a o ke kāne me ka wahine* (The lasting love of man and woman). Aloha between a husband and wife assures that there is stability within the *'ohana* or family. One expression of this relationship is that wives often went into battle with their husbands, carrying food and caring for their injuries; wives also took up arms after their husbands fell, only to die beside them, like the story of Manono and her husband Kekuaokalani. After Western laws were imposed on Hawaiians, many couples did not feel the need to make their spousal commitment "official" on paper; the aloha between them was strong.

Members of Kealiikaapunihonua Keena Ao Hula at the celebration of the canonization of Father Damien at the Cathedral of Our Lady of Peace in Honolulu, Hawai'i, November 1, 2009. (AP Photo/ Lucy Pemoni)

The second relationship built on aloha spirit is that of mother and child. This relationship was important to ensure that the child grew up to be caring and respectful. There were certain foods that a mother was not allowed to eat and jobs that a mother was not supposed to do, to make certain that a "perfect" child would be nurtured. *Aloha 'ohana* (love of family) includes past family members, as well as present. *E kolo ana nō ke ewe i ke ewe* (Kinfolk seek the society of other kinfolk and love them because of their common ancestors). This aloha spirit strengthens the bonds between generations of family, even those that have passed on. The parent and child relationship is parallel to that of

mother and child. The child is raised with aloha: *Ka lei hā'ule 'ole, he keiki* (A lei that is never cast aside is one's child). Also *aloha 'ohana* can include those that become *'ohana* through a shared experience. Hawaiians who were forced to move to Kalaupapa, the leper settlement on Moloka'i Island, shared their experiences of living, surviving, and dying together. They created *'ohana*. When a cure for leprosy was discovered, many of them chose to stay in Kalaupapa and be with those people who had become their *'ohana*.

Gift-giving is another form of aloha spirit. Gift-giving is governed by an intricate system of rules that determine the timing and the type of gift, as well as the timing and type of reciprocation. One level of gift-giving is to show generosity and hospitality between people; aloha in its purest form was genuine hospitality. A baby's luau (celebratory meal) is the pure gift of aloha; it is to celebrate the aloha that the *'ohana* has for the new child. The saying, "If one has, one should give," epitomizes this purest form. On another level aloha can be more political.

The third relationship built on aloha spirit was between *ali'i* and *maka'āinana*. Aloha spirit was a trait that helped *ali'i*, who were often reserved, to relate to the *maka'āinana*. Not only did aloha spirit allow a leader to empathize, it also created the will of the *ali'i* to help their people. *Ali'i* gained political power by increasing the number of *maka'āinana* who lived and worked on their land. The way to increase *maka'āinana* was by treating them well, so others would want to join them. Since political power was tied to religious power, an *ali'i* with many loyal *maka'āinana* was thought to be favored by the gods. An *ali'i* developed his or her *mana* (spiritual power) through aloha. It was aloha that kept *ali'i* from succumbing to outside temptations and to be strong on the inside. Aloha spirit among the *ali'i* would prove to be critical once Westernization took hold.

The true test of *'ohana* is among strangers. *O ke aloha ke kuleana o kāhi malihini* (Love is the host in strange lands). Aloha and *ho'okipa* (hospitality) are intertwined because one flows from the other. When greeting a stranger, aloha comes from the host. The stranger is more than willing to reciprocate, but the host puts forth aloha and *ho'okipa*. Pretending to practice aloha and *ho'okipa* is not fulfilling. This form of aloha blended nicely with the Christian notion of love and hospitality. Christian love as brothers and sisters worked within *'ohana*, as well as between *maka'āinana*. However, when aloha was between *ali'i* and *maka'āinana* as equals, the blending of Christian love and aloha did not go as easily.

In the modern age, aloha spirit continues in various forms and it is not without controversy. Aloha feeds the activism of many indigenous Hawaiians against the experience of imperialism and colonialism. *Aloha 'āina* has been the rallying cry of various movements against military encroachment and use of Hawaiian lands. *Aloha 'āina* is the belief that the land needs to be cared for, nurtured, and protected. The movement to return the island of Kaho'olawe, also known as Kanaloa, the god of the sea, to the indigenous Hawaiians was one such movement. The only island in the Hawaiian archipelago that is named after a god, Kaho'olawe or Kanaloa was used for religious and navigational purposes until it was used for grazing by goats and target practice by the U.S. Navy.

A protest in 1976 merged *aloha 'āina* with knowledge from various *kūpuna* (elders), when young indigenous Hawaiian activists bypassed barriers set up by the Coast Guard at the risk of arrest. The Protect Kaho'olawe 'Ohana Movement led many of the protests and occupations of Kaho'olawe. In 1980, a settlement was reached with the U.S. Navy that confined the bombing and assaults to portions of the island; and Protect Kaho'olawe 'Ohana started to revitalize the other portions of the island. In 1990, the U.S. Navy stopped all military exercises and bombings on Kahoʻolawe. After clearing the island of ordinance (live ordinance is being found), the U.S. Navy officially returned Kahoʻolawe to the indigenous Hawaiians. George Helm and Kimo Mitchell, two Protect Kahoʻolawe ʻOhana activists, on one of their many protests of the bombing of Kahoʻolawe, disappeared mysteriously in March 1977; they were unable to see Kahoʻolawe's return. Bringing *aloha ʻāina* to all the islands is a goal of many who practice *aloha ʻāina*.

Another form of *aloha ʻāina* is the remembering of place names and the traditions that accompany them. Hawaiians use these place names and traditions to help perpetuate cultural knowledge about the environment, how to build their homes, irrigation systems, and the like. *Aloha ʻāina* is to have a close enough relationship with the land that you know every tree, flower, rock formation, seasons for fish or seaweed. Hawaiians on Molokaʻi Island invoke *aloha ʻāina* with the goal of being responsible stewards of the island. A form of *aloha ʻāina* for the ocean is *aloha kai*, protecting the quality of the sea and its creatures as one would care for the land.

Some members of the Hawaiian community see that aloha spirit has been coopted by the tourism industry, which is state-sponsored, or at minimum, state-supplemented. Aloha is a tourist stepping off an airplane and being given a greeting, a kiss and a *lei* (flower necklace). This kind of aloha spirit is no longer spiritual or reciprocal, but, rather, commercialized and reduced to making a profit; aloha has become an economic resource. Money is paid for aloha spirit and this money does not cover the use of limited resources nor is it equal in value to the sharing of life, culture, and history that indigenous Hawaiians give away. Aloha is reduced to its most superficial form and only found in the various luau shows.

Other members of the Hawaiian community believe aloha spirit is molding itself to the times, much as hula did over the decades. Aloha spirit is getting better because it is adapting to capitalism and commercialism. Aloha spirit is surviving by modification. Aloha Festival, now known as Aloha Week, is a community festival about promoting Hawaiian culture and keeping aloha spirit viable for the modern day. Aloha spirit practiced by indigenous Hawaiians working in the tourism industry does not have to be one of money. Those indigenous Hawaiians can practice aloha spirit as the gift of hospitality, without feeling forced by money. Practicing aloha spirit can be for your own good, rather than for the good of the tourist.

Aloha spirit is Hawaiʻi as a multiracial paradise. Hawaiʻi is the example for the rest of the world, showing how a multitude of racial groups can live and work together in peace. The upside to this is that Hawaiʻi does have something to teach the rest of the world with its multiracial population that for all intents and purposes does get along. However, that does not mean that Hawaiʻi does not have racial problems. This type of aloha spirit erases the differences and plays down the racial problems that Hawaiʻi has. Also, it has been used to argue for the dismantling of indigenous Hawaiian programs and institutions; "aloha for all Hawaiians."

Diasporic indigenous Hawaiians perpetuate aloha spirit as best they can through renaming since they are not physically a part of the ʻāina. Places of significant importance to those who live away from Hawaiʻi are often given Hawaiian place names. Aloha spirit is seen in the continuation of hula and the various *hālau hula* that teach and perform. These *haumana* (students) are of indigenous Hawaiian descent and those that are Hawaiian at heart. Hula competitions reinforce both the traditions of hula and the diasporic indigenous Hawaiian community. *ʻOhana*, Hawaiian music and concerts, *hōʻike*, and festivals are ways that the aloha spirit is perpetuated far from Hawaiʻi ʻāina, while diasporic indigenous Hawaiians live aloha through these cultural events.

Currently, aloha spirit is still a topic of debate. Aloha spirit is sometimes used as a complaint, "Where is your aloha spirit?" Aloha has also been used to excuse racial and ethnic humor, although these derogatory jokes are not in the original spirit of aloha. There are those who fear that aloha has changed so much from its original meaning that the true meaning of aloha has been lost. There are others who insist that aloha be retired and a new word used. Still others insist that aloha spirit or any form of aloha is an invention of a mythic Hawaiian past that is being used to protest any form of modernization. There are more who say that aloha cannot be defined, that it is a way of being, and that the only way one can define aloha is by doing aloha and living aloha.

Niccole Leilanionapaeʻāina Coggins

See also: Entries: Hawaiian Religion

Further Reading

Buck, Elizabeth. *Paradise Remade: The Politics of Culture and History in Hawaiʻi.* Philadelphia: Temple University Press, 1993.

Kanahele, George Huʻeu Sanford. *Kū Kanaka, Stand Tall: A Search for Hawaiian Values.* Honolulu: University of Hawaiʻi Press, 1986.

McGregor, Davianna. *Nā Kuaʻāina: Living Hawaiian Culture.* Honolulu: University of Hawaiʻi Press, 2007.

Okamura, Jonathan Y. *Ethnicity and Inequality in Hawaiʻi.* Philadelphia: Temple University Press, 2008.

Arabic (Islamic) Calligraphy

Islamic or Arabic calligraphy (Arabic *khatt*, line [of writing], script) refers to the cultivated art of writing using the Arabic alphabet, and thus ultimately an art form native to the various cultures and languages that use the Arabic script, all of which can generally be said to belong to an overarching Islamic culture. It is also practiced in non-Islamic countries where the Arabic script does not prevail (such as China or the United States), generally by Muslims, for whom reading and writing Arabic is tantamount to a religious duty.

The Arabic script, which has its origins in the much older Aramaic script, existed in earlier forms before the advent of Islam in the early seventh century CE, but it enjoyed only secondary importance in a nomadic culture whose literary culture was based not on written but on oral transmission. During the period in which the sacred poetry that formed the basis of the emerging religion of Islam was revealed to the Arab merchant-turned-prophet Muhammad over the course of 23 years, this

Qur'an (that which is [to be] recited), as it was called, continued to be committed to memory and transmitted orally, even years after Muhammad's death. However, the importance of recording in writing this religious document, understood to be the ultimate word of God, became apparent after many of those who had memorized it were killed in battle. Thus begins the history of Islamic calligraphy, for inherent in the impulse to preserve the word of the Qur'an in writing was the wish to make this writing as beautiful as possible, out of reverence for the divine message it expresses. The Qur'an itself, among the very first revealed verses, suggests the importance both of transmitting its message in general and of the use of writing specifically:

> Recite! For your Sustainer is the Most Gracious One who taught (shall teach) through the pen, taught (shall teach) mankind what he did not previously know. (Qur'an 96:4–5)

Development of the Various Scripts

Although a few styles of writing were in use at the time of the first written Qur'ans, by the latter part of the eighth century the angular, heavy, and formal Kūfī style (named after the town of Kūfah in what is now southern Iraq) had been perfected and had prevailed as the typical Qur'anic script for more than 300 years. Austere in the simplicity of its original form, kufic script evolved to become increasingly complex and ornamental, particularly as its use extended to inscriptions in various materials such as stone, tile, wood, and textile. Such developments followed divergent paths in different parts of the Islamic world, eventually leading to the development of two distinct forms: Eastern Kūfī (developed by the Persians late in the 10th century), which attained a high degree of sophistication and elegance of form, and Western Kūfī, which, though without the delicacy of Eastern Kūfī and long retaining the more conservative and static elements of the script, eventually led to the development of the graceful Maghribi (Western) script, which reached its height of beauty in the cultures of Andalusia and northwest Africa.

At the same time as these developments, various cursive Arabic scripts, whose importance would ultimately overtake that of Kūfī, were also developing and becoming increasingly sophisticated; the six major classical styles that resulted are Thuluth, Naskh, Muhaqqaq, Rayhān, Riqā', and Tawqi'. The development of the cursive styles, unlike that of the more anonymous Kūfī, is tied strongly to particular masters who reinvented, renewed, and revolutionized the calligraphic art. One of the most important of these was Abū 'Alī Muhammad ibn Muqlah (885/86–940 CE), who introduced precise rules of geometric proportion for the Arabic letters, thus redesigning and standardizing their individual shapes. Eventually, as the various scripts increased in elegance and beauty of form under the influence of ibn Muqlah and succeeding masters, they supplanted Kūfī as the script of choice for copying the Qur'an; today the majority of Qur'ans are copied in the Naskh script, though Thuluth enjoys an enduring popularity among calligraphers, being considered the most important of the ornamental scripts used for inscriptions, titles, headings, and colophons. As such it is often juxtaposed with the Kūfī script and used in the calligraphic adornment of public monuments.

Among the other important scripts in the Islamic world, Maghribi, the rounded and delicate northwest African and Andalusian successor to Western Kūfī, contrasts perhaps most distinctly against the generally more familiar forms that evolved in the far-removed centers of civilization on the Asian continent. On the opposite end of the Islamic world, however—particularly in the Persian cultural sphere of central and south Asia—a similarly unique range of styles evolved. Most established and preferred among Muslim speakers of Persian (in Iran and Afghanistan), Urdu (India and Pakistan), and to a certain extent in Turkey, is Nasta'līq, with its elegant, languorous curves that suggest an ease despite the strict rules governing its execution, and which evolved in the 15th century out of Ta'līq (hanging) script. Further styles that enjoy a broad popularity among Asian Muslims are Shikasteh, a densely written derivative of Ta'līq, and Dīvānī, an Ottoman invention of the 15th century, likewise a successor of Ta'līq.

Although the many millions of Chinese Muslims have generally adopted the scripts used in neighboring Afghanistan, a uniquely Chinese Arabic style simply called Sīnī (Chinese) has also evolved, one that shows the influence of the native brush calligraphy aesthetic. One of the most well-known contemporary calligraphers in this style is Haji Noor Deen of Shandong Province.

Art in Islam

Calligraphy can in many ways be regarded as the quintessential Islamic art form. On the religious level, without which we cannot speak of Islamic culture, it is the most appropriate art form, in part because of the primacy of the word—in this case, the divine message that the Qur'an represents, for which writing is naturally the most direct means of expression; and in part because representative art, of humans and animals in particular, have in principle (if not always in practice) long been considered taboo in Islam. This general avoidance of representative art is most characteristically shared by Judaism, although the same impulse can be seen in very early Buddhism and Christianity as well, whereby the respective central human figure was initially alluded to through symbols rather than depicted directly.

For this last reason, architecture and abstract art—expressed through the use of ornament and pattern—have also evolved as essential forms in Islam and are inseparable from a consideration of calligraphy; for calligraphy has, until relatively recently, constituted a nearly indispensable part of the aesthetic of public buildings and monuments, and ornamental pattern or illumination has long been an intimate complement to the calligraphic art itself. Indeed, the line between calligraphy and ornament is often a fine one, as writing is often employed in an almost purely ornamental manner.

Contemporary Islamic Calligraphy

Traditionally, the practice of Islamic calligraphy leaves little room for the kind of spontaneity found in Chinese or Japanese brush writing. The writing implement itself, a reed pen cut at an angle to form a hard writing tip, might not in itself have the same expressive potential that a brush does. (Nonetheless, in either case, the expression of true mastery, not only in technical proficiency but in a state of inner maturity, should affect the perceptive viewer, since the best calligraphy, as with any artistic discipline, is generally understood as a practice of improving and mastering one's own character as well as the technique and materials of writing.) As for technique, no matter how simple and natural the lines may appear, correctly executed Arabic calligraphy—unlike its east Asian counterparts—generally demands slow, deliberate movements of the pen; this is determined in part by the strict rules governing the formation of its letters, but also, of necessity, by the nature of the implements involved.

In more recent times, however, many calligraphers have increasingly broken away from the traditional forms and formal rules that have defined Islamic calligraphy for over a thousand years, experimenting with different tools, media, and techniques, so that it has become possible to write more quickly, freely, and spontaneously. Despite this, traditional methods continue to be transmitted in the time-honored manner of apprenticeship under a master, and in some places are enjoying a revival due to renewed interest in the art. The United States is home to an increasing number of masters and students of traditional calligraphic techniques; most notable among these is the internationally renowned Mohamed Zakariya, who transmits his extensive knowledge of the traditional techniques, attitudes, and context of Islamic calligraphy to those who wish to travel the classical path of learning the art; and over time, these students become teachers in their own right.

Neal Kenji Koga

See also: Entries: Islamic Canon; *Sho*, Calligraphy

Further Reading

Lings, Martin, and Yasin Hamid Safadi. *The Qur'an*. London: World of Islam, 1976.

Muhammad Asad, translator and editor. *The Message of the Qur'ān*. London: The Book Foundation, 2008.

Safadi, Yasin Hamid. *Islamic Calligraphy*. Boulder: Shambhala, 1979.

Schimmel, Annemarie. *Calligraphy and Islamic Culture*. London and New York: New York University Press, 1990.

Website of Mohamed Zakariya, www.zakariya .net, last modified 2013.

Asiamericans in the Episcopal Church

In the Episcopal Church, the word "Asiamerican" (rather than "Asian American") is the preferred term to refer to both the church people and their ministry in the context of North America. It was coined in 1973 by the late Winston Ching and other pioneers of Episcopal Asiamerica Ministry (EAM) and was first used to mean a dual-ministry to Asian immigrants and to Americans of Asian ancestry. As the term evolved, "Asiamerica Ministry" has become three-fold—ministry to Asian immigrants, ministry to Asian Americans, and the ministry of

The Reverend Allen K. Shin, the first Korean American Bishop in the Episcopal Church, center, reads prayers during his consecration ceremony as the new Suffragan Bishop of the Episcopal Diocese of New York, at the Cathedral of St. John the Divine in New York, New York, May 17, 2014. (Peter Foley/epa/Corbis)

building bridges to churches in Asia. In the Episcopal Church, Asiamerican churches are grouped into six ethnic convocations: Chinese, Japanese, Korean, Filipino, South Asian, and Southeast Asian churches.

Asian Immigration and the Episcopal Asiamerica Ministry

The Episcopal Church is one of the non–Roman Catholic churches that got involved in the Western missionary enterprise in Asia. Particularly in Korea, the Philippines, Vietnam, Laos, and Cambodia, American Protestant missions came alongside American political and military expansionism in Asia. Motivated by "manifest destiny" and "the white man's burden," American missionaries would evangelize in Asian countries, establish missionary outposts, and build missionary dioceses, hospitals, seminaries, and colleges.

Later, as Asian Christians immigrated to the United States, they would seek the familiarity of the Episcopal Church that they knew in Asia. Because the Episcopal Church is part of the worldwide Anglican Communion, Anglican immigrants from China, India, Hong Kong, Singapore, and other countries would also look for the Episcopal Church, as the equivalent of the Anglican Church.

Earliest Asiamerican Missions

In North America, the earliest recorded Asiamerican Episcopal Church dated back to 1870, when a Chinese railroad worker named Ah Foo was converted by the American Tract Society. Although he was baptized in the Presbyterian Church, for some reason he decided to serve as a lay missioner for the Episcopal Diocese of Nevada.

Fired up with zeal for the gospel, Ah Foo evangelized to his friends working on the transcontinental railroads, and in 1870 he founded a Chinese mission, the Good Shepherd Church in Carson City, Nevada. In 1874 he founded another mission in Virginia. With funds collected from his fellow railroad workers and a grant from a Caucasian sympathizer from New York, Ah Foo constructed the House of Prayer Chapel. Translating the Episcopal liturgy into Chinese, leading Bible studies, and providing pastoral care among the Chinese workers, Ah Foo grew the congregation to 150 members. Unfortunately, the chapel was destroyed in the great fire in Virginia City in 1875. The loss of the chapel and the increasing hostility of the nativists against the Chinese greatly discouraged Ah Foo. As the Chinese Exclusion Act of 1882 was being implemented, Ah Foo disbanded the congregation and left the area. The mission closed down.

The next Asiamerican mission in the United States was initiated in San Francisco in 1895, when the Rev. Masaichi Tai, the first Japanese priest ordained in the Nippon Sei Ko Kai in Japan, was sent to the United States by the Rt. Rev. John McCain, missionary Bishop of Kwanto.

The Rev. Tai started his ministry among Japanese laborers, meeting with them in his living quarters at 421 Powell Street, San Francisco. Overcome by homesickness, Tai returned to Japan in 1896 and was replaced by the Rev. Kumazo Mikami. Mikami served at Advent Episcopal Church and succeeded in evangelizing and presenting at least five candidates for confirmation in the Diocese of California. He resigned in 1899 and was replaced by the Rev. Daijiro Yoshimura, who became the first canonically resident Japanese priest in the Diocese of California and the United States.

With the assistance of Miss Mary Patterson, a former missionary in Nagano Prefecture, the Rev. Yoshimura was able to convince the diocese to supply new, larger premises, 1001 Pine Street, San Francisco. Because of her familiarity with Japanese language and culture, Miss Patterson was able to effectively advocate for the Japanese mission and to serve as a bridge between Japanese clergy and the diocese. The fledgling Japanese congregation was officially recognized as an Episcopal mission in 1902. In 1915, under the administration of Deacon Paul Murakami, the first Japanese graduate of the Church Divinity School of the Pacific (CDSP), the mission became Christ Church Sei Ko Kai, registering a membership of 25 adults and 20 children, with a budget of around $500.

Christ Church in San Francisco is the acknowledged mother church of other Japanese churches, such as St. Mary's Mission, Los Angeles, in 1907; St. Peter's Mission, Seattle, in 1912; Epiphany Mission, Portland, Oregon, in 1935; and St. George's Mission, Scottsbluff, Nebraska, in 1938.

Most of these Japanese Episcopal churches flourished for many years. In 1941, the United States joined the Pacific war following the Japanese bombing of Pearl Harbor. The Japanese Episcopal churches were abandoned as many Japanese Americans were sent to internment camps in remote places of the country. After the war, returnees from the internment camps revived their churches, but their vitality was adversely affected by the negative experiences of American war hysteria. Among those who figured as heroes among the internees was the Rev. Hiram Hisanori Kano, the Japanese Episcopal priest who ministered to his fellow Japanese in their internment camp as well as to prisoners of war from Germany.

Chinese Missions in 1900

After the untimely demise of the first Chinese mission in Nevada City in 1874, a new Chinese mission was started in San Francisco in 1905. Organized by Emma Drant, a deaconess from Hawai'i who was tutored in Cantonese, this mission grew into a sizable congregation.

In 1906, the great earthquake of San Francisco left 4,000 residents dead, over 300,000 homeless, and 80 percent of the city destroyed. The Chinese congregation evacuated to Oakland as the city underwent redevelopment. When the city's restoration was over, only half of the original congregation returned to San Francisco, while the other half remained in Oakland. The congregation that returned to San Francisco was named True Sunshine Church, and the one that remained in Oakland was named Our Savior's Church.

From San Francisco and Oakland, Chinese congregational development moved to Los Angeles (St. Gabriel's Church); Seattle (Holy Apostles Church); Manhattan, New York (Our Savior, Chinatown); Flushing, New York (St. George's Church); Brooklyn, New York (St. Peter's Church); and Boston (the Chinese mission in St. Paul's Cathedral). among other places.

Korean and Filipino Missions

The Korean Episcopal Ministry in Hawai'i was first planned in 1906, but became visible in 1907 with the establishment of St. Luke's Episcopal Parish in Honolulu, which ministered among Korean immigrants. St. Luke's Korean Ministry had its years of fecundity, but by the latter part of the 20th century had evolved into a multicultural church, like most parishes in Hawai'i. Many original Korean members of St. Luke's and their offspring also moved to the U.S. mainland and would later help establish Korean missions in California, New York, New Jersey, Virginia, Illinois, Texas, Florida, and Tennessee.

Most Filipinos who came to the United States in the early 1900s as farmworkers in Hawai'i and California were Ilocano males of Roman Catholic background. There was no attempt by the Episcopal Church to reach out to them until after the Concordat of Full Communion with the Iglesia Filipina Independiente (IFI) in 1961 and the formation of the Episcopal Asiamerica Ministry in 1973.

Establishment of the Episcopal Asiamerica Ministry

The American Immigration Reform of 1965 relatively eradicated the overt and structural racism and hostility of the Chinese Exclusion Act, the antimiscegenation laws against the Filipinos, and the Japanese internment camps. It also increased the quotas of immigrants from Asia. As the United States rose as a superpower, it became a magnet for many immigrants from Asia seeking a better future and escaping the grinding poverty in their home countries. As Asian immigrants began to settle in the United States, they sought spiritual communities. It was a perfect environment for Christian evangelism and church growth.

The few Episcopal Asiamerican churches, which were mainly Chinese and Japanese, were not only recuperating from the nightmares of their past but were also struggling to find their places in the largely white American mainstream. Meanwhile, the unparalleled positive impact of the American civil rights movement led to the emergence of advocacies among the black, Native American, and Hispanic caucuses within the mainstream Episcopal Church. The Asiamerican struggle, however, was with marginalization and the negligible number of Asian congregations.

So it was providential that in 1973, Canon James Pun was called to serve as priest of True Sunshine Church in San Francisco. He had just come from Hong Kong and understood the sense of isolation of the Asian clergy. He saw the need for a national Chinese ministry in the Episcopal Church to reach out to the increasing numbers of Chinese immigrants moving into the various parts of the country from Hong Kong, Taiwan, and China. Pun began to communicate his sense of loneliness, reaching out to other Asian clergy.

In their first meeting, in March 1973, the Rev. Canon John H. M. Yamasaki, rector of St. Mary's Japanese Church in Los Angeles and representative of Province VIII to the Executive Council of the General Convention of the Episcopal Church, affirmed the sentiment of James Pun and proposed an ad hoc committee to study the matter. It was agreed that Asian clergy should not only serve as chaplains to Asian Episcopalians, but that they should develop a strategy to enable missions and evangelism among the Asian peoples who were immigrating in record numbers to the United States. It was also imperative that a national plan to develop Asian and Pacific Island ministries be recommended to the Episcopal Church.

The members of the ad hoc committee were the Rev. Canon John Yamasaki, who took the recommendation to the Executive Council and then to the General Convention of the Episcopal Church; the Venerable Lincoln Eng, who was then rector of St. Bartholomew's Church in Beaverton, Oregon, and served as executive secretary of the ad hoc committee; and the Rev. Winston Ching, who was vicar of St. John the Evangelist in San Francisco and chair of the ad hoc committee, and who presented the proposal to the executive committee in Louisville, Kentucky, just prior to the General Convention. Other members included Mrs. Betty Lee, a lay leader from the Diocese of California; the Rev. Victor Wei, who was then the executive administrator of the Diocese of California; and Canon James Pun.

The ad hoc committee drafted and finalized the resolution and submitted it to the 64th General Convention of the Episcopal Church, which met in Louisville, Kentucky, September 29 through October 11, 1973. The resolution called for the establishment of an "Episcopal Asiamerica Ministry to deepen and strengthen the existing ministries of the Episcopal Church involved with Asian and Pacific Island peoples as well as to establish new ones." The word "Asiamerica" was invented to include both

American-born as well as foreign-born (immigrant) persons of Asian ancestry.

The response of the General Convention was overwhelming. The resolution was unanimously adopted with a corresponding initial budget of $50,000 to fund the development of Asian ministries and to hire a staff officer. At the first meeting of the Episcopal Asiamerica Ministry in San Francisco, following the General Convention, Canon James Pun declared, "I only asked for a bicycle; but they gave us a bus and hired a driver!"

The Birth of Many Asiamerica Episcopal Churches

The establishment of the national Episcopal Asiamerica Ministries enabled more intentional church planting among the Asian diaspora. With the mandate from the General Convention and funding received, Episcopal Asiamerica Ministries began to establish structures and networks to further the work of the Asiamerica ministry.

With Episcopal Asiamerica Ministries, the Episcopal Church in the provinces, dioceses, and parishes became more aware of the increasing Asian immigrant populations in their localities. Serving as an advocate for existing Asian congregations and as a resource for dioceses within Asian communities, Episcopal Asiamerica Ministries made inroads to Asian ministries throughout the country, developing and supporting new ministries and strengthening older ones.

The Rev. Albany To became the Chinese missioner in the Diocese of New York and pioneered the Church of Our Savior in Chinatown, New York City. Mitchy Ak-

iyoshi, a business executive from Japan, studied at General Theological Seminary and was ordained in New York City. She developed outreach work among Japanese business executives, their wives, and families. This work would later be known as Metropolitan Japanese Ministry, which flourished under lay missioner Ms. Kyoko Kageyama.

Several Korean priests also came to the country and established Korean churches: Aidan Koh, John Kim, Andrew Kim, and Aidan Ahn in the Diocese of Los Angeles; Andrew Shin in the Diocese of California; Paul Joo in the Diocese of Chicago; Ninian Kim in the Diocese of Long Island; Jonathan and Hilary Won in the Diocese of New Jersey; Valentine Han in the Diocese of Virginia; and many others.

In Southeast Asian ministry, the Rt. Rev. David Cochran, bishop of Alaska, retired in Tacoma, Washington. He and his wife, Mary, helped St. Matthew's Episcopal Church to welcome and sponsor the newcomers and refugees from Cambodia and Laos. Today, this congregation has become Holy Family Church in Tacoma with the Rev. Sam Lee, the first Cambodian Episcopal priest, serving as its vicar. Congregational work was also started and thrived among the Vietnamese with the Rev. Duc Nguyen in Orange Country, California; the Rev. Joseph Mai in San Diego; and the Rev. Thien Huynh in Falls Church, Virginia.

In 2005, some 700 Hmong Catholics in St. Paul/Minneapolis affiliated with the Episcopal Church of Holy Apostles, becoming the first and largest Hmong congregation in the entire Anglican Communion. In 2013, the first theologically trained Hmong Episcopalian, the Rev. Toua Vang, was ordained priest in the Diocese of Minnesota.

The Filipino American Churches

The beginnings of the Filipino Episcopal ministry in the United States were closely tied to its Concordat of Full Communion with the Iglesia Filipina Independiente (IFI) because the first Filipino missionaries who came to the United States were clergy-on-loan from the IFI. In the mid-1950s, the Most Rev. Isabelo Delos Reyes, Jr. (then Obispo Maximo of the IFI), and the Rt. Rev. Harry Kennedy (then bishop of the Diocese of Hawai'i) discussed the idea of Filipino ministry in America. In 1959, three priests were sent by Delos Reyes to Hawai'i: Timoteo Quintero, Oscar Tabili, and Justo Andres. Tabili went back home to the Philippines after quite some time; Andres moved to California and became vicar of Holy Cross Church in Stockton; and Quintero founded St. Paul's Episcopal Church in Honolulu, which has now become, under Randolph Albano, the largest congregation in the Diocese of Hawai'i and the largest Filipino congregation in the Episcopal Church.

The other IFI priests who started missions through the Episcopal Church were Sancho Gaerlan and Vito Villalon in San Francisco, Gregorio Bayaca in Los Angeles, and Eugenio Loreto in New York. Loreto would later move to Tampa, Florida, where he established the first IFI/Filipino/American parish, Jesus Christ of Nazareth. The other pioneering clergy in the Episcopal Church who came from the IFI included Fred Vergara, who founded the Holy Child Filipino Ministries in California, Nevada, and New York; Bayani Rico, who served in Daly City and Vallejo, California; Ray Bonoan and Christian Villagomeza in Tampa, Florida; and the Rev. Arsie Almodiel in Las Vegas.

The first ministry among Filipino Episcopalians started shortly after the formation of the national Episcopal Asiamerica Ministry in 1973 when Winston Ching gathered Filipino Episcopalians from various churches in the New York metropolitan area. Among those who responded to the call for a Metropolitan Filipino Ministry were Cristina Hing, Blandina Salvador, Inez Killip, Josephine Gonzales, Betty Batnag, the Sucdad family, and Alfred Pucay, who was serving as the Episcopal Asiamerica Ministry's office secretary. About the same time, the Rev. Timoteo Quintero, the IFI missionary priest serving in Hawai'i, was sent by the diocese to pursue a refresher course on Anglicanism at the General Theological Seminary. While in New York, Quintero served as seminary intern and Eucharistic minister for the Metropolitan Filipino Ministry.

Similar to the Metropolitan Japanese Ministry, the Metropolitan Filipino Ministry developed through social and religious gatherings among Filipino Episcopalians who were scattered in various mainstream Episcopal parishes in New York, New Jersey, Connecticut, and Philadelphia. The monthly Eucharist, followed by a potluck meal, was held in Good Shepherd Episcopal Church in Manhattan and became the oasis for Filipino Christians in the midst of what they felt was dry and unwelcoming fellowship in white churches. While faithfully attending Sunday masses in mainstream Episcopal parishes, they would join Metropolitan Filipino Ministry to meet fellow Filipinos, catch up with news back home, welcome new immigrants, enjoy Filipino food, and renew their cultural ties.

Being formed simply as a fellowship, there was no energy from Filipino Episcopalians to form an ethnic congregation until in 1990, when St. Benedict's mission in Los Angeles was formed. The organizer of this first Episcopalian Filipino movement was Rex Botengan. At the Episcopal Asiamerica Ministry Consultation in Hawai'i, after hearing about the establishment of the Holy Child Filipino congregation in the Diocese of El Camino Real, Botengan developed a vision of forming a Filipino congregation from among the Filipino Episcopalians scattered in various mainstream parishes in the Diocese of Los Angeles. The result of his vision was St. Benedict's Filipino Mission in Alhambra, California, which later merged with a white congregation and became, under Bishop Artemio Zabala, Holy Trinity/St. Benedict's Episcopal Church.

Following the development in Los Angeles, Metropolitan Filipino Ministry metamorphosed into two Filipino missions in two dioceses and under two Filipino Episcopal priests. Almost half of the Metropolitan Filipino Ministry members formed the initial congregation of St. John's Episcopal parish in the Diocese of Long Island under Fr. Dario Palasi, and another half formed the congregation of St. Luke's Episcopal Church under the Rev. James Kollin in the Diocese of New Jersey, leaving only a few original members for the Metropolitan Filipino Ministry in New York.

South Asians and the Episcopal Church

Similar to the start of the Filipino Ministry in relation to the Iglesia Filipina Independiente, the start of the South Asian Ministry in the Episcopal Church was also tied to the concordat and ecumenical relations, particularly with the Mar Thoma Church, the Church of South India, and the Church of North India.

The Mar Thoma Church traces its origin from the Apostle Thomas, who brought Christianity to India in 52 CE. In the early 19th century, the Mar Thoma Church in Malabar came into contact with missionaries from England sent by the Church Missionary Society, who assisted the church in Malabar with theological education, which resulted in Anglican–Mar Thoma intercommunion.

In 1979, the Mar Thoma Church requested that the Episcopal Church help provide pastoral oversight to the increasing number of South Indians who immigrated to the United States. In response to the request, an agreement was reached between the presiding bishop of the Episcopal Church and the metropolitan of the Mar Thoma Church that the Episcopal Church would provide assistance and pastoral oversight to the members of the Mar Thoma Church whenever requested. This resulted in the formation of separate but interdependent Mar Thoma churches.

While Mar Thoma is a singular denomination, the Church of South India is the result of the organic union of churches in India coming from the Anglican, Methodist, Congregational, Presbyterian, and

Reformed traditions, which merged organically in 1947. As South Indian immigrants belonging to the Church of South India immigrated to the United States, they affiliated themselves with Episcopal, Methodist, Presbyterian, or other denominations. Some, however, banded themselves into Church of South India congregations, owing allegiance to the moderator based in India.

Like the Church of South India, the Church of North India is also a uniting church, organized in 1970. Various Church of North India clergy and lay people also immigrated to the United States, affiliating themselves with the denomination of their choice. Among those who affiliated with the Episcopal Church was the Rt. Rev. Ninan George, who was a retired moderator of the Church of North India and retired general secretary of Christian Churches of Asia.

Asiamerican Episcopalians Today

At the celebration of the 40th Anniversary of the Episcopal Asiamerica Ministry in San Francisco, June 20–24, 2013, the number of Asiamerican churches and congregations in the Episcopal Asiamerica Ministry network was over 150.

There are at least four bishops of Asian ancestry who served or are serving the Episcopal Church: Richard Chang in the Diocese of Hawai'i; Johncy Itty in the Diocese of Oregon; Scott Hayashi in the Diocese of Utah; and Prince Singh in the Diocese of Rochester. There are also many Asiamerican clergy serving in mainstream white Episcopal churches as well as Latino and black Episcopal churches. Notable among them are James Kodera, Primo Racimo, Alistair So, Romeo Rabusa, Peter Tagdulang, Peter Lai, Paul Lai, Joseph Pae, and Leonard Oakes.

Another gain among Asian Episcopalians is the increase of ordained women, including Fran Toy, Ada Nagata, Ruth Casipit-Paguio, Harriett Kollin, Imelda Padasdao, Christine Lee, Irene Tanabe, Christine Pae, Arienne Davidson, Deborah Low-Skinner, Connie Lam, Vivian Lam, Winnie Varghese, and others.

Currently, the Episcopal Asiamerica Ministry Council leaders are Bayani Rico, president; Mimi Wu, vice president; Irene Tanabe, secretary; Inez Saley, treasurer. Convocation conveners are Ada Wong Nagata and Peter Wu (Chinese); Malcolm Hee and Gayle Kawahara (Japanese); Aidan Koh (Korean); Leonard Oakes and Evelina Fradejas (Filipino); Anandsekar Manuel and John Sewak Ray (South Asian); and Letha Wilson Barnard and Minh Hanh. The EAM Council is the umbrella organization that works closely with Winfred Vergara, the missioner for Asiamerica ministries and coordinator of the EAM Network.

Asiamerican Episcopalian churches are considered some of the most diverse and upwardly mobile congregations. The lesson learned in history is that church growth among Asiamerican Episcopalians is directly related to hospitality and empowerment. Where churches welcome immigrants and empower new leaders, there will be growth. Racism, lack of hospitality, and marginalization hinder the spread and growth of the Kingdom of God.

Winfred B. Vergara

Further Reading

Otani, Andrew. *A History of Japanese-American Episcopal Churches*. n.p.: A. N. Otani, 1980.

Vergara, Winfred. *Mainstreaming: Asian Americans in the Episcopal Church*. New York: Office of Asian American Ministries, 2005.

Vergara, Winfred. *Milkfish in Brackish Water: Filipino Ministry in American Context*. Manila: Filipino American Ministry Institute, 1992.

Āyurveda

Developed over centuries, *Āyurveda* is an Indian medical system that includes medical theory, doctrines, and preventive and prescriptive therapies, as well as pharmacology and surgery. Ayurvedic medicine flourished until about 1000 CE; although its influence waned under Islamic rulers and the British Raj, it has regained popularity since independence for Great Britain in 1947. This entry outlines the development, theoretical foundations, and practices of Ayurvedic medicine. We begin with a description of its three principal texts.

The expression "*āyurveda*" is a compound of *āyur*, "life," and *veda*, "knowledge." The *Āyurveda* system may have been developed as early as the fourth century BCE; however, its earliest surviving texts date from the early centuries of our Common Era. The two foundational *Āyurvedic* texts are the *Caraka-saṃhitā* and *Suśruta-saṃitā*. Both documents are *saṃitā* or compendiums of medical knowledge and theory; *Caraka* and *Suśruta* are proper names.

Caraka was a physician in the Scythian court of Kaniṣka (ca. second century CE) and the content of his compendium reflects the medical knowledge of the learning centers of Takṣaśilā, whose ruins today are situated about 20 miles northwest of Islamabad, Pakistan. In addition to medical information, the *Caraka-saṃhitā* has an Oath of Initiation, comparable to the Hippocratic Oath that new physicians promise to uphold. Its extensive philosophical reflections on reincarnation and other topics that predate the formation of the classical Hindu intellectual traditions are of great interest to intellectual historians. Commented on and revised throughout the centuries, it is used today in traditional Indian medicine. An English translation is over 1,000 pages.

The approximate date of the *Suśruta-saṃitā* is the third or fourth century CE; Suśruta was in all probability a physician from Varanasi in northeast India. The text contains extensive descriptive surgical techniques, including the removal of foreign objects, eye operations, plastic surgery, suturing, examining dead bodies, and the training of a surgeon.

Although there are other *Āyurveda* texts, they make constant reference to the *Caraka-saṃhitā* and *Suśruta-saṃitā*. In the seventh century, another important *Āyurveda* document appeared, *Aṣlāṅghṛdaya-saṃhitā* (Vāgbhaṭa's Compendium on the Eight-part Core of Medicine).

Āyuradevic texts make direct reference to the *Artharvaveda*, a work whose hymns were complied during the second millennium BCE. The Vedic tradition assumed a micro-macrocosmic correspondence between the human body and the cosmos. The human body, like that of the cosmos, is composed of five *dhātus* or elements:

Motivational speaker and author, Deepak Chopra poses for a photographer at his office in 1996 in La Jolla, CA. Chopra founded the Chopra Center for Well Being in 1995. The institution offers treatment based on the ancient tradition of Indian medicine called *Āyurveda*, which insists that medicine should be centered on the person rather than on the disease, and which takes into account the metaphysical and cosmic aspects of illness. (Paul Harris/Online USA/Getty Images)

earth, water, fire, air, and ether. Health and well-being are assured by maintaining a dynamic equilibrium of these elements through the proper knowledge and performance of rituals of sacrifice. After eight centuries the magico-religious *Āyurvedic* approach to health and healing gradually absorbed the empirico-rational approaches to medicine and healing developed by the non-Brahmanic or heterodox tradition of the Buddhists, Jains, and the now extinct Ājīvikas traditions (Zysk, 21–27). The Buddhist emphasis on direct observation, exemplified by the mediation on the decaying corpse designed to impress the truth of transiency, contrasts with the Brahmanic orthodoxy. Brahman priests rejected such exercise as polluting. Besides, they understood disease and healing to originate outside the individual, caused by *devas* or disembodied spirits.

The heterodox traditions' empiricism initiated a radical shift concerning health and healing, and diseases and their cures. Buddhist views of health and medicine are based on the Middle Way between the extremes of self-indulgence and self-denial, emphasizing the equilibrium of the mind, body, and environment. Buddhist spiritual exercises require a robust physical condition. It must be noted that neither *Āyurvedic* nor Buddhist medicine completely abandoned the magico-religious approaches to health and healing.

Medical Theory

The *Āyurveda* system is a reflection of a worldview that is crystallized in the Vedas. In the main Vedic teaching asserts that the cosmos is just one expression of *paramātmā*, the singular "absolute reality," often referred to as *puruṣa*, the "ultimate or supreme self or person." All things arise from *puruṣa* in the form of awareness or consciousness that generates matter and life. Consciousness is present in every material object from the greatest stars to the minutest cells in our bodies. *Puruṣa* gives form to itself in the guise of awareness to experience itself in life. Life, thus, is awareness; and awareness ceaselessly projects itself to evolve new and better organs of sense. The human body is thus far the best expression of consciousness in matter, after eons of development.

This seeming paradox between the identity and differences among mind, body, and *puruṣa* contrasts with Western philosophical systems that sharply distinguish between mind/consciousness and body/matter. The Vedas and the *Āyurveda* system understand mind/consciousness to include matter too. The mind, that is, consciousness, is psychosomatic in reality and in operation. Physical activity is a function of mind; and consciousness is a psychophysical operation. A person's mind-body is different from the real *puruṣa*. Since the human person is the vehicle through which *puruṣa* realizes itself, the *Āyurveda* system focuses on the physical health and well-being of the individual. This posture contrasts with the major concern of *yoga* and other Indian traditions that focus on exercises aimed at *mokṣa* or ontological liberation through the insight into *puruṣa*.

Medical Practice

As a holistic system for healthful living and well-being based on knowledge, *Āyurveda* regards a person to be both body and mind, which includes an essential spiritual component. A good physician can maintain one's health and well-being, including deliverance from disease, only with a thorough understanding of the person. A person is also understood to be an integral part of a community and the natural world. "Life" in *Āyurveda* includes the whole of living nature that impacts human health; medicine must consider the person in the context of all aspects of life. Medicine, in short, should center on the person rather than the disease.

A person's mind/body is not static. In addition to continuously balancing the self, a person is continually interacting with other beings and entities that extend to and include the entire network of life. The human body, like the cosmos, is composed of five *dhātus* or constituent parts: earth, water, fire, air, and ether. Variant combinations of these five *dhātus* result in the three *doṣas* or humors: phlegm (*kapha*), bile (*pitta*), and wind (*vāta*). These three *doṣas* pervade the body, interacting every moment. Excessiveness or insufficiency among the *doṣas* leads to the imbalance within the body and to illness. *Āyurveda* etiology is not simply limited to the imbalance of the three *doṣas*. Illness can be generated through lapses of judgment, memory, and willpower. *Karma*, including acts committed in a previous life, and demonic possession and interference are causes for illness and disease.

As a medical system *Āyurveda* comprises eight branches. These are internal medicine; general surgery; otolaryngology, including ophthalmology; pediatrics, including obstetrics and embryology; psychology/psychiatry, including psychological and dream analysis and demonology; toxicology; geriatrics; and sexology.

The *Āyurveda* physician focuses on knowing the state or condition of the relationships among the various parts of the body and mind. The goal is to restore the person to a dynamic equilibrium. To this end the physician must attempt to discern the patient's strengths, before his or her weaknesses; a patient's strength may be used to right the weakness. Since a proper diagnosis only initiates the healing process, the physician must also cultivate hope in the patient and his or her trust that the therapies will work. Strength of character and a strong mind, including determination, are essential for the healing process. Medicine is prescribed to restore balance according to body type, psychological temperament, and patient attitude; family and community relationships are also components of individual health, well-being, and any restorative therapy.

A person's physical health and personal well-being come not only from maintaining a balance within the body, but from a healthy and supportive family and community. One's health is maintained by consuming nutritional seasonal foods that are appropriate with one's *varṇa* or class, gender, and stage of life. Physical exercise, meditation, and rhythmic breathing are part of the health care routine. In addition, health and well-being necessarily include proper moral conduct and social hygiene, and being part of a small, self-sufficient community. These measures are also intended to prevent disease and for rejuvenation.

A good doctor must be thoroughly versed in the content of the above mentioned *Suśruta-saṃitā*, *Caraka-saṃhitā*, and other medical texts with regard to symptoms of diseases, pharmacology, and surgical techniques. Aiming at the restoration of the balance among the three humors, the physician takes into consideration one's body type, psychological temperament, and attitude. Family and community relationships are also considered in the therapeutic procedure. Healing is a joint exercise that includes the patient, physician, nurse, family, community, and medicine.

Development and Spread

Indian medicine and pharmacology accompanied Buddhism into Central, East, and Southeast Asia. The *Suśruta-saṃitā* and *Caraka-saṃhitā* were translated into Arabic during the eighth century; the ninth-century Persian physician Rhazes (Muhammad ibn Zakariyā Rāzī, 854–925) was familiar with these texts. The introduction of Islamic Unani medicine in the 11th century was mutually influential, especially in the area of *materia medica*. Both systems are still operative; generally, *Āyurveda* physicians treat Hindu patients, and Unani (Greco-Arabic) physicians treat Muslims.

Āyurveda physicians exchanged medical knowledge and techniques with their Portuguese counterparts during the first half of the 16th century and with their

British colleagues in the 17th century. At first the British Raj supported these native medical systems; however, due to economic pressures and hardening colonial attitudes, government support for the training of *Āyurveda* and Unani physicians was withdrawn. The training of traditional physicians was left to family apprenticeships and private colleges.

Government support for *Āyurveda* medicine has increased since Indian Independence. Today *Āyurveda* is recognized as a legitimate medical system in India. Practitioners are licensed and medical training institutionalized. Many rural people, who comprise 70 percent of the Indian population, rely on *Āyurveda* medicine for their primary health care needs. Although modernization and Western medicine challenge this ancient medical system, many persons of South Asian Indian descent living in the United States rely on *Āyurveda* prescriptions and follow its proscriptive practices, including nutrition and meditative techniques. From the second half of the 20th century, *Āyurveda* was promoted as "alternative medicine" in the West. The *Āyurvedic* Institute was established in 1984 to offer instruction in traditional *Āyurvedic* medicine and offer therapies. A quick check of the Internet displays numerous *Āyurveda* clinics, diet programs, treatments, and institutes.

Ronald Y. Nakasone

See also: Entries: Chinese Medicine; Hindu Canon; *Yoga*

Further Reading

Alphen, Jan Van, and Anthony Aris, eds. *Oriental Medicine: An Illustrated Guide to the Asian Arts of Healing*. Boston: Shambhala, 1996.

Bhishagratna, Kaviraj Junja Lal. *An English Translation of the Sushruta Samhita, Based on the Original Sanskrit Text*. 3 vols. Kolkata: Bhaduri, 1907–1916.

India: A Second Opinion. "*Āyurveda* 101." Frontline/World. PBS.org. http://www.pbs.org/frontlineworld/stories/india701/interviews/*āyurveda*101.html. Accessed July 5, 2014.

Kakar, Sudhir. *Shamans, Mystics and Doctors: A Psychological Inquiry into India and Its Healing Traditions*. Delhi: Oxford University Press, 1982.

Sharma, Priya Vrat. *History of Medicine in India, from Antiquity to 1000 A.D.* New Delhi: Indian National Science Academy, 1992.

Shee Gulabkunverba *Āyurveda* Society. *The Caraka Saṃhitā*. 5 vols. Jamanagar, India: Shee Gulabkunverba Āyurveda Society, 1949.

Tatz, Mark, trans. *Buddhism and Healing, Demiéville's article "Byō" from Hōbōgirin*. Lanham, MD: University Press of America, 1985.

Zysk, Kenneth G. *Asceticism and Healing in Ancient India: Medicine in the Buddhist Monastery*. Delhi: Oxford University Press, 1991.

B

Bala Vihar

Bala Vihar emerged as a concept or an institution as a result of the contextual needs of the modern-day devotees of Hinduism who would like to balance their faith with understanding and logic. The younger generations especially feel the need for explanations of Hindu ways of life as Hinduism carries a rich combination of ancient heritage through scriptures and contemporary reinventions of religion, which often goes unexplained but is just followed. Therefore, the modern-day Hindus struggle to find answers to their questions and to search for a comprehensive understanding of their faith to keep it alive.

Thus Swami Chinmayananda (1916–1993), being a visionary who served the society for 43 years, addressed these needs by giving lectures, interpreting scriptures, and writing books in the language that common people understand. Several *swamijis* (Hindu teachers/philosophers who lead an ascetic lifestyle, submitting to the service of God by their own calling; who wear only saffron clothes and live simply, disregarding all human attachments) have attempted the same in approaching common people, but Swami Chinmayananda is one of the prominent *gurus* of the 21st century. (A *guru* is a Hindu instructor who teaches and interprets scriptures and often lives in an ashram—a Hindu religious place where devotions are constantly taking place, where people come to live when they are committed to the ascetic life.)

Origin and Structure

Bala Vihar is one of the key institutions of the Chinmaya mission established in 1953 by the student-followers of Swami Chinmayananda. The Bala Vihars are independent units that are affiliated with the Chinmaya mission. A Bala Vihar is not necessarily an architectural organization but a fluid institution that is dynamic in nature, while carrying out the mission of Swami Chinmayananda's beliefs and values. Swami Chinmayananda is both the founder and a resource of Bala Vihar in conceptual terms, as he has written two books, *Bala Vihar I* and *II*, which are used in Bala Vihar for developing curriculum and also as resources.

Being inspired by the teachings and beliefs of Swami Chinmayananda, Bala Vihars are established as part of the Chinmaya mission for educating children at an early age in their rich Indian heritage. Swami Chinmayananda believed in and advocated for individual responsibility for a healthy society. He believed that it is possible only when each child is taught the right kind of value system, beginning in his or her formative years. He advised that children must be disciplined into the value system from a very young age so that their values will be reflected in the future society. Therefore, Bala Vihars are not just concerned about spreading Hinduism and its culture; rather the programs and curriculum are designed to instill character and values in young children facing a fast-paced society with maturity and courage. Thus Bala Vihar attempts to maintain the balance between positive traditional values and contemporary and progressive methods of education.

The nature of the Bala Vihar structure can be both institutionalized and dynamic. Bala Vihar, in other words, is quite flexible in its structure, as it can be formed and developed informally by a few like-minded families in a geographical area, while there are also many established Bala Vihars assuming an institutional structure. Therefore Bala Vihars are loose in terms of collection of data and statistics, although Bala Vihar has been emerging as a successful movement in urban cities in India, and in Western countries where there are large numbers of immigrants of Indian origin.

Bala Vihar and Its Vision

Chinmayananda strongly believed in Hindu philosophy and its positive strength for society. He believed that children must be immersed in learning Hindu philosophy, and he encouraged all Hindu parents to be intentional in imparting the Hindu value system to their children. Several Bala Vihars were established in affiliation with Chinmaya Mission all over the world. People living in urban Indian settings and Hindu families living abroad embraced them and were intentional about passing their faith to their children. Bala Vihar has

offered solutions to parents who struggle to impart the Hindu value system, which was often received by belief and not addressed and questioned by logic. Hindu parents regard themselves as unable to address the logical questions of their children who are tuned in to Western education and culture. Bala Vihar offers contextual approaches to reach out to the children with Hindu concepts, rituals, and scriptures with explanations and philosophical interpretations that are appealing to modern Hindu children. Thus Bala Vihar is a successful institution of modern Hinduism. However, Bala Vihar is neither a well-developed philosophical concept of Hinduism, nor is it a well-known institution in popular Hinduism. Most people are unaware of Bala Vihar in India as it is a fairly new concept, known only to certain cultural groups in the Hindu population.

Aim and Purpose of Bala Vihar

Bala Vihar aims to expose children from a very young age to the Hindu/Indian value system that will help them sustain their culture against the influences of the mythical or superficial understandings of alien cultures. Immigrant Hindu parents from India are passionate about teaching the Hindu value system to their children and exposing them to the rich Indian heritage and culture. This ambition gives rise to the need for resources to instruct Hinduism and its way in a structured manner, because the children of immigrants do not witness Hinduism on a daily basis. Bala Vihars and *satsangs* (devotional gatherings) offered structurally designed information about Hinduism and its culture. Immigrant parents also believe that Bala Vihars and *satsangs* provide a safe environment for immersion in Hindu culture without imposing it on the children. Thus Bala Vihar also serves as a place for socialization for children as well as their parents. Therefore, Bala Vihars offer opportunities to build a community among the students of Bala Vihar and their families through celebrations and events. In other words, Bala Vihar's prime purpose is to reproduce the Hindu-Indian environment in foreign lands and also in the urban settings of India where essential Hindu culture is on the decline.

Brief Description of Hinduism and Its Way of Life: Contributions of Bala Vihar

To define Hinduism for what it stands for has been a difficult task because of its complex nature with a multiplicity of gods, traditions, rituals, and scriptures. Hinduism has never strived to unify its concepts or to fit itself within parameters; rather it has been a way of life, a religion of dynamism instead of a religion of rigidity. Therefore the renaissance of Hinduism, with its tolerant nature, has not been institutionalized. Accordingly, Hinduism is not interested in tracing its origin or its founder. However, Hinduism is one of the strong religious belief systems existing in the world, and it can be described by its fundamental beliefs and common themes that run across the variety of its subcategories. Generally, Hinduism is passed from generation to generation not by its organized structure or instruction in Hindu schools but in families by way of the members living a Hindu life.

Hindu philosophers are often Brahmins, the priestly class, and the lay people are often distanced from the Hindu philosophy. The ordinary people from other castes receive Hinduism in the form of stories, morals, rituals, and prayers that are often described as mantras (mystical syllables or phrases) and slokas (stanza), which are simply memorized and spoken in Sanskrit as people perform devotions (*pūjā*) to the respective gods at their homes. In the temples and during the ceremonies, the priests (*pujaris*) instruct the people to perform rituals in a step-by-step process, and they trust and believe that by doing so the priests have performed devotion on behalf of the family, or for a requested person. Thus it is not a mandatory task to be a believer in Hinduism. Blind faith is aspired to out of respect and humility, while submitting to the mystery of the gods and their ways.

However, Bala Vihar brings a paradigm shift in the practice of Hinduism nowadays. Blind faith and a belief system in Hinduism are no longer appreciated by the people who are alienated from the Hindu way of life either by geographical location, living in a foreign land, or by cultural dislocation in their native land, influenced by Western culture. Bala Vihar addresses the questions of faith, the need to understand the significance of rituals, and the thrust to understand the meaning of scriptures. Bala Vihar is a contextual institution that meets the need of Hindus of the modern scientific and technological age. Although there is no rejection or movement against traditional Hinduism, most modern Hindus pay less and less attention to its depth as they cannot resonate with many of its happenings. Thus Hinduism remains in the lives of modern Hindus as a culture and not as a religion. But Bala Vihar reconnects the culture to its religion through structural instruction while engaging in logical discussion around the matters of faith.

The diaspora community of India in the Western world faces the challenge of articulating their faith, practices, and rituals, and the laypeople often do not have knowledge and resources at their disposal to articulate their faith as it happens. What is taken for granted in India, that Hinduism is a way of life, is not the same in the diaspora settings in which parents soon realize the need to address the issues of the alienation of Indian children from their cultures and of how to approach the issue effectively.

This very need has given rise to having Bala Vihar centers (or missions) established in America by immigrant parents. Today there are about 30 such centers located in major cities across the United States. These centers share the fundamental philosophy of the founder. Their programs are complementary and unique, tailored to the needs of each location.

Nature and Methods of Bala Vihar

The curriculum of Bala Vihars is designed in such a way that a child in his or her learning process may be immersed in Indian/Hindu culture so that he or she may understand the Indian heritage, culture, Hindu value system, and ways of life. Thus Bala Vihars are intentional in providing opportunities for exposure to Indian culture through celebrations, devotions, rituals, discussions, and the addressing of issues of daily life through the lens and value system of Indian culture.

In Bala Vihars the trained mission workers (*sevika* and *sevaki*) help children to make the right choices in life. The teaching methodology is often administered through games, arts, crafts, stories, and other unique techniques that ally with their learning methods in their regular schools while reinforcing spiritual and cultural values. Thus the curriculum designed for all grade levels (4–12 years) is creative and dynamic, and covers a wide range of topics from the Hindu scriptures.

Bala Vihar classes are conducted weekly either at Chinmaya mission premises or in house gatherings of devotees. The teachers are either trained missionaries or volunteers from the Bala Vihar community who are passionate about imparting Indian culture and the Hindu religious value system to the children. Using Chinmaya Mission resources, the children chant *slokas* and sing *bhajans* (devotional songs) that are used during their devotions. The classes engage in meaningful discussions rather than mere instruction. The classes often end with some kind of devotion that helps the children witness and imbibe and practice the Hindu culture through appropriate rituals. Among the many activities, chanting of praises for the gods, visiting the ashram and temples, summer camps, conducting debates, picnics, celebrating festivals, performing dramas, and dances are the crucial ones. These activities ensure immersion in Hindu culture. Bala Vihar, by giving structural instruction about Hinduism and its way of life, also addresses many myths and misconceptions of Hinduism, thus giving comprehensive understanding of its culture and traditions and their significance both then and now. This gives rise to the contextualization of Hinduism that helps the children to embrace the religion as a significant part of their lives.

Bala Vihars also engage in social outreach activities. Each Bala Vihar is an independent unit that designs its own vision, mission, curriculum, and activities, much depending on the organizers and the families that are involved. However, certain Bala Vihar units are more active in their social outreach than others. Nurturing a holistic nature in children from all aspects of life has been the aim of Bala Vihar, although most Bala Vihars concentrate on exposing children to the Indian culture and heritage, which is the prime purpose and goal of Bala Vihar.

Conclusion

The goal of Bala Vihar is to inculcate enthusiasm among children to reclaim and affirm their own Indian/Hindu identities. Bala Vihar contextualizes its methods to reach out to children in urban settings in India and in America, with approaches that are appealing and also resonate with their contexts. Bala Vihars open new perspectives to Hinduism and address many questions that often go unanswered at home and abroad.

Surekha Nelavala

Further Reading

Chinmaya Mission Chicago Website. http://www.chinmaya-yamunotri.com/. Accessed July 9, 2014.

Chinmaya Mission Palakkad Website. http://www.chinmayamissionpalakkad.com/. Accessed July 9, 2014.

Chinmaya Mission, Washington Regional Center, Frederick, MD, Chapter Website. http://www.chinmayafrederick.org/. Accessed July 9, 2014.

Kurien, Prema. "Becoming American by Becoming Hindu: Indian Americans Take Their Place at the Multicultural Table." In R. Stephe Warner and Judith G. Wittner, eds. *Gathering in Diaspora: Religious Communities and the New Immigration.* Philadelphia: Temple University Press, 1998, p. 44.

Kurien, Prema. *A Place at the Multicultural Table: The Development of an American Hinduism.* New Brunswick, NJ: Rutgers University Press, 2007, p. 50.

Baptists. *See* Morikawa, Jitsuo

Berkeley Buddhist Monastery

Berkeley Buddhist Monastery is a branch monastery of the Dharma Realm Buddhist Association, which was founded by the Chinese Buddhist monk, Venerable Master Hsuan Hua (1918–1995). Housed in a historic Nazarene church building located at 2304 McKinley Avenue in Berkeley, California, not far from the University of California campus, it opened its doors on October 27, 1994. The monastery maintains a full daily monastic schedule including morning and evening ceremonies and the noon meal offering. There are also regular Buddhist events throughout the week and open daily meditation in the morning and afternoon. In the evenings, there are lectures on the Buddhist scriptures as well as meditation classes. Ceremonies and lectures are in English and Chinese, with Vietnamese translation sometimes also available.

The monastery is also home to the Institute for World Religions, an educational and religious center for the study of Asian and Western faith and cultural traditions.

Dedicated to creating a sanctuary where one can engage in conversation on theological and buddhological principles, beliefs, and practices, the institute encourages the interfaith search for universal values in an atmosphere of cooperation and mutual respect. It aims to challenge the boundaries of our thinking and avoid attachment to narrow sectarian differences.

The Institute for World Religions was established in 1976 as a direct result of the inspiration and planning of the Venerable Hsuan Hua and the Catholic prelate Paul Cardinal Yü Bin (1901–1978). Both believed that harmony among the world's religions is an indispensable prerequisite for a just and peaceful world. They also shared the conviction that every faith tradition should affirm humanity's common bonds and rise above sectarian differences. Cardinal Yü Bin served as the institute's first director. In 1994 the institute moved to the Berkeley Buddhist Monastery. In keeping with its mission, the institute offers programs designed to bring the major faith traditions together in discourse and with the contemporary world. The institute also participates in local and global interfaith initiatives as a way to bring the principles of interfaith vision and the spiritual needs of the modern world into constructive engagement. *Religion East & West*, the institute's annual journal, is one forum for this discourse and this engagement.

As of 2013, the Reverend Heng Sure, a senior Western disciple of the Master Hsuan Hua, is the managing director of the monastery as well as the president of the board of directors of the Dharma Realm Buddhist Association. Ordained as a Buddhist monk in 1976, he has an MA in Oriental languages from the University of California, Berkeley, and a PhD from the Graduate Theological Union in Berkeley. For the sake of world peace, he undertook an over 600-mile pilgrimage along the California coast during which he bowed to the ground after every three steps. He has also been very active in a number of interfaith organizations, in encouraging a nonharming vegetarian lifestyle, and in pioneering the development of English versions of Buddhist liturgy and Buddhist-themed music employing Western musical idioms.

Ronald Epstein

See also: Entries: Chinese Temples in America; Hsuan Hua; Ullambana Assembly

Further Reading

Bhikshus Heng Sure and Heng Ch'au. *News from True Cultivators: Letters to the Venerable Abbot Hua.* 2nd ed. Burlingame, CA: Buddhist Text Translation Society, 2003.

Dharma Master Heng Sure and Dharma Master Heng Ch'au. *With One Heart, Bowing to the City of 10,000 Buddhas: Records of Heng Sure and Heng Ch'au.* 9 vols. San Francisco: Buddhist Text Translation Society, 1977–1983.

Epstein, Ronald B., in collaboration with the Buddhist Text Translation Society Editorial Committee. *Buddhist Text Translation Society's Buddhism A to Z.* Burlingame, CA: Buddhist Text Translation Society, 2003.

Vajra Bodhi Sea: A Monthly Journal of Orthodox Buddhism. San Francisco: Dharma Realm Buddhist Association, 1970–present.

Berkeley Thai Temple, Wat Mongkolratanaram

Wat Mongkolratanaram, locally referred to as the Berkeley Thai Temple, was

A group dines on Thai food at Wat Mongkolratanaram, a Buddhist temple in Berkeley, California, February 15, 2009. Some religious institutions serve food on a regular basis. Among them is Wat Mongkolratanaram, which has upset some neighbors because the Sunday Thai brunch food offering attracts lots of people. (Brant Ward/San Francisco Chronicle/Corbis)

established in 1978 when a group of volunteers formed a small temple committee and invited two visiting monks from Thailand to serve as spiritual leaders and assist with building the temple. In 1981 the temple received nonprofit status as a religious organization and established the Thai Buddhist temple and cultural center at its current Russell Street location in the city of Berkeley, California. By 2001 the temple was recognized as an official Thai Buddhist *ubosot*, or place of worship, in full accordance with Theravāda Buddhist doctrines. For nearly three decades the Berkeley Thai Temple has held a Sunday Food Offering—locally called the Thai Temple Sunday brunch—where members of the temple

prepare and serve food to visitors—Buddhists, non-Buddhists, Thais, non-Thais. Thai and Thai American Buddhists who volunteer at the Sunday brunch understand their work as an expression of *thambun*, or merit-making. Merit is the counter of *karma*, which Buddhists believe chains all living creatures in the endless cycles of reincarnation and suffering known as *saṃsāra*. Merit, as the counterweight of *karma*, may be gained primarily by supporting the community of monks and nuns, by assisting the needy, or through Buddhist meditation. Merit is also transferable. Hence, the living may perform rituals and offerings to earn merit, which may then be transferred to their beloved to assist them in the afterlife and in being reborn into the human realm. From a Thai American perspective, volunteers at the Berkeley Thai Temple engage in the religio-cultural practice of *thambun*, which, in turn, sustains the temple for the community and the livelihood of the Thai monks who reside there. In addition, the temple offers Thai language and cultural classes and programs.

The popular Sunday Food Offering came under attack in 2008 when the Berkeley Thai Temple applied to the city of Berkeley's Zoning Adjustments Board to build a Buddha Hall (*boot*) larger than the size allowed by the municipal code. The Buddha Hall would be 16 feet wide, 24 feet long, and 44 feet high (including a 14-foot spire), and the proposed sanctuary would include three Buddha statues on a raised platform. Nineteen neighbors who reside on Oregon Street gathered to protest the proposed expansion of the temple, citing that its "architecture" would change the character of the residential neighborhood. Additionally, upon discovering that the temple's 1993 zoning permit only allowed for food to be served three times a year, Oregon Street residents used this opportunity to voice their concern about the Sunday Food Offering. They cited it as "detrimental" to the health of the neighborhood and suggested that the food service be moved to a different site because it created noise, parking and traffic problems, litter in the neighborhood, and was the source of "offensive odors." The Berkeley Zoning Adjustments Board investigated the allegations, and "announced in June that the Berkeley Thai Temple had repeatedly exceeded the number of events allowed by its use permit. Although no one was able to

ascertain just how long the temple had been violating its permit, the board agreed to give the temple a chance to modify the original permit and address neighborhood concerns." Further, the board urged mediation to resolve the conflict. A *Save the Thai Temple* press release notes that "The Temple immediately responded to these concerns by undertaking extensive measures to participate in three mediation sessions with the complainants, cut its Sunday service hours in half, implement a neighborhood litter patrol, relocate the preparation of its food items, secure an exclusive parking lot from a nearby retailer, and actively reach out to its neighbors."

The temple's weekly Sunday Food Offering is well attended by upwards of 600 visitors. Some Oregon Street residents said, "We believe we have a right to reside in peace, to enjoy our residential neighborhood without a large commercial restaurant in our midst." After the initial hearing about the zoning problem, the Berkeley Thai Temple was granted a zoning adjustment. While this was good news for the temple and its supporters, at the hearing there had been accusations that the foods served at the temple were drugged. Some opponents of the temple's food service complained that they were forced to live with odors.

Some may argue that the Berkeley Thai Temple has become a victim of its own success and popularity. Those who supported the Berkeley Thai Temple and wanted to save the food service argued that there is a direct connection between saving the food service and saving the temple because 80 percent of the temple's total revenue was raised by the weekly food service. In addition, the revenue was used to support Thai language and cultural classes offered by the temple.

Unlike the challenges to the Hsi Lai Temple and the Sikh *gurdwara*, the Berkeley Thai Temple had enjoyed relative peace in the neighborhood before the plans to build a large Buddha Hall sparked the community conflict. Similar to opponents objecting to the construction of the Hsi Lai Temple and the Sikh *gurdwara*, residents on Oregon Street cited parking, traffic, noise, and crowds as their primary reasons for wanting a reduction in the food services as well as to block the construction of the Buddha Hall. The underlying racial privilege informed by an ideology of white supremacy is thinly masked as traffic and noise control, but nonetheless is revealed in comments concerning food odors or comparison of the food service to a commercial restaurant. By disregarding, either willfully or out of ignorance, the religious dimension of the Sunday food offering, opponents secularize the Thai temple community and vulgarize their activity.

Jonathan H. X. Lee

See also: Essays: Religion, Race, and Orientalism; *Entries:* Thai American Religions; Thai Buddhist Immigrant Spirituality; Theravāda Buddhism

Further Reading

Bao, Jiemin. "Merit-Making Capitalism: Reterritorializing Thai Buddhism in Silicon Valley, California." *Journal of Asian American Studies* 8, no. 2 (2005): 115–142.

Chatikul, Virada. "Wat Mongkolratanaram and the Thai Cultural Center: A Model for Intergenerational Collaboration and Thai American Leadership Development." In Jonathan H. X. Lee and Roger Viet Chung, eds. *Contemporary Issues in Southeast Asian American Studies*. San Diego: Cognella Academic, 2011.

Desbarats, Jacqueline. "Thai Migration to Los Angeles." *Geographical Review* 69, no. 3 (1970): 302–308.

Perreria, Todd LeRoy. "The Gender of Practice: Some Findings among Thai Buddhist Women in Northern California." In Huping Ling, ed. *Emerging Voices: Experiences of Underrepresented Asian Americans*. New Brunswick, NJ: Rutgers University Press, 2008, pp. 160–82.

Yahirun, Jenjira. "Thai Immigrants." In Ronald H. Bayor, ed. *Multicultural America: An Encyclopedia of the Newest Americans*. Vol. 4. Santa Barbara, CA: ABC-CLIO, 2011, pp. 2097–2133.

Bhante Dharmawara (Bellong Mahathera) (1889–1999)

Samdach Vira Dharmawara Bellong Mahathera, who was known simply as Bhante Dharma, was a Cambodian Theravāda Buddhist monk who died in Stockton, California, on June 26, 1999, a few months after his 110th birthday. Born in 1889 in Phnom Penh as Bellong Mahāthera (his full name combines his Buddhist names, his Buddhist rank, and his family name), he was a member of one of Cambodia's wealthiest and most illustrious families. Bhante attended French schools and studied law and political science at the Sorbonne in Paris. A lawyer, he served as a judge and a provincial administrator before leaving his job and his pregnant wife to spend a few months resting and meditating in a monastery. He became a monk at the age of 40 and studied Buddhism at Thai monastic universities, receiving training in the Thai Forest ascetic tradition. He later studied natural healing in Burma and India, and founded the Asoka Mission in New Delhi on land awarded by Jawaharlal Nehru, India's first prime minister. Bhante Dharma left India in 1975 for the United States, where he established Vatt Buddhikarma (Cambodian Buddhist Temple) in Silver Spring, Maryland, in 1976. He worked to settle thousands of refugees who had fled the war in Cambodia.

At the age of 90 he established Wat Dharawararama in Stockton, California. During the next 20 years, Bhante Dharmawara was deeply involved in the refugee community. He assisted in every phase of the refugee experience from finding housing and employment to helping with settling parking tickets. He was instrumental in diffusing the tensions in the aftermath of the Cleveland School massacre that occurred in Stockton on January 17, 1989. A gunman shot and killed five Southeast Asian schoolchildren and wounded 29 other children and one teacher. At the time Bhante Dharmawara was 100 years old.

Ronald Y. Nakasone

See also: Entries: Cambodian American Religions; Theravāda Buddhism; Watt Samaki

Further Reading

Cadge, Wendy. *Heartwood, the First Generation of Theravāda Buddhism in America.* Chicago: University of Chicago Press, 2004.

Prebish, Charles S., and Martin Baumann, eds. *Westward Dharma: Buddhism beyond Asia.* Berkeley: University of California Press, 2002.

Stewart, Barbara. "Bellong Mahathera Is Dead; Cambodian Monk Was 110." *The New York Times*, July 18, 1999. http://www.nytimes.com. Accessed July 10, 2014.

Bok Kai Temple

Established in 1854, the Daoist Bok Kai (variously spelled Taoist Bok Eye or Boe Ky) Temple, a religious and community center, relocated to its present location on First (or the older name, Front) and D Streets in Marysville, California, in 1869 and then was reconstructed after a fire destroyed the second temple structure in 1880. This is the only extant Daoist temple dedicated to Bok Kai, who is known as the god of water and the Northern God in the Daoist pantheon in the United States. Bok Kai was responsible for protecting the people against floods, and since 1880 Marysville has not experienced devastating floods like those of nearby Yuba City. According to professor of religion Vivian-Lee Nyitray of the University of California, Riverside, Bok Kai is a reference to Xuanming, a god associated with the north and water, and temples dedicated solely to this Daoist deity in China are rare. Bok Kai became an important deity in the Daoist pantheon in the mid-15th century when a temple was erected in his honor at the Imperial Palace in Beijing. He is included in the Daoist spiritual guardians known as the Four Saints (Sisheng), and paintings of him can be found in Daoist temples in China and Taiwan as well as in the collections of Chinese art in major U.S. museums, including the Boston Museum of Fine Arts.

According to the principles of *fengshui* (wind and water, or geomancy), an aspect of Daoism, the temple is situated on the north bank of the Yuba River near the confluence of the Yuba and Feather rivers with the main entrance facing south toward the river. This allows good spirits to enter. Daoist architectural style, in emphasizing the harmonious unity of humans and nature, creates order and equability in the layout of the buildings. The connection with nature is further developed in the attached or nearby garden that allows meditation and contemplation. Due to the 1913 Alien Land Law, the ownership of the property at one point was transferred to the Chinese Benevolent Association of San Francisco, but it is believed to be the property of the Hop Sing Tong. A train used to operate in front of the temple, making it easier for travelers to visit the temple. Today visitors come from all over the country and from abroad by car.

In recent times a levee has been built between the temple and the river so that at first the main approach to the temple is down a flight of steps from the top of the levee (instead of being level with the riverbank), but now the approach is from a park on the west side of the temple at the rear of the building. The government of the Republic of China donated the funds to erect the Memorial Gateway.

Daoist Beliefs

Daoism (also spelled Taoism) is one of China's oldest religions and philosophies, founded by Laozi (sixth century BCE), a contemporary of Confucius, in the Zhou Dynasty (ca. 770–256 BCE) and expanded by his spiritual disciple, Zhuangzi (late fourth-century BCE). The two main texts are the *Daodejing* (Classic on the Dao and Virtue) and *Zhuangzi* (Writings of Zhuangzi). Like Confucianism, the concept of the Dao (the Way; a way of thought and an everlasting principle of the origin of the universe, transcending all beings and being the origin of all transformations) is a central part of this philosophy. The Dao is used to understand nature and the universe, as well as the human body. *Yin* (female, dark, moon, etc.) and *yang* (male, light, sun, etc.), two primary elements of existence, are complementary yet opposing elements in any system, and a proper balance of these forces results in harmony and balance. *De* (Virtue) is achieved through *wu-wei* (nonaction) or that which occurs naturally and sustains the Dao. Unlike the community-centered Confucianism, Daoism emphasizes the individual, or ego, and is said to be complementary to the public community service of Confucianism. There is a saying in China that a person is privately a Daoist and publicly a Confucianist because Daoism expresses individuality and Confucianism represents the duties and obligations to the community.

The ultimate goals of the Daoists are to achieve happiness and harmony, and perhaps immortality. Meditation and physical exercise are important in maintaining balance. Painting, especially landscape painting, poetry, and the arts often derived their inspiration from Daoist beliefs. Daoists were responsible for many of the scientific and medical discoveries in China because of their interest in the relationship between humans and nature and the search for the principle underlying all things. Biology, botany, pharmaceuticals, acupuncture, and astronomy are just some of the Daoist fields of endeavors. The Daoists often phrase their beliefs in parables and sayings, for example, about how water is life to fish but death to man as it can lead to flooding and similar environmental problems. The Daoists believe that one has to follow the Dao to be a great leader; the more prohibitions you have, the less virtuous people will be; and the more weapons you have, the less secure people will be. The government that governs least is the best type of government.

In the Han dynasty (202 BCE to 220 CE), Daoism developed two major schools, one more philosophical and the other more religious. Later the religious wing divided into two major sects based on the emphasis of different concepts, and the Bok Kai Temple represents one of these sects. To combat the Indian-originated Buddhism that began to flourish in the Han dynasty, Daoism built temples and had priests and nuns to rival Buddhism. The two religions incorporated deities from each as well as often including Confucius in their pantheon of gods. Other Zhou dynasty schools of thought include the Five Elements School: (1) *metal* nourishes (2) *water*, which gives life to vegetation like (3) *wood*, which in turn feeds (4) *fire* that creates ashes to form (5) *earth*. From this the cyclical view of the development of life and history evolved. Local deities and significant historical figures became a part of the pantheon of deities. Often the Jade Emperor is regarded as the supreme deity in Daoism and he is assisted by other, lesser deities, such as the Kitchen God, who annually reports to the Jade Emperor about the good and bad behavior of a family on New Year's Eve. The Jade Emperor resides above Mount Tai in Shan-

dong Province (birthplace of Confucius), so the devoted make pilgrimages there.

China has been troubled by flooding, especially along the Huang He (Yellow River), and this gave prominence to ways of protection against floods and the accompanying famine. Bok Kai was just one of the deities that emerged to hold a prominent position in locations troubled by water problems, especially flooding.

Marysville's Chinatown and the Temple Architecture

Marysville, Yuba County's county seat, is part of the Gold Country and developed shortly after the 1848 discovery of gold at Sutter's Mill in nearby present-day Coloma. Chinese immigrants flocked to the area in search of gold while others took jobs in agriculture, laundry work, restaurant businesses, and early industries, especially woolen mills. A thriving Chinese community with a Chinatown developed and the population, at its height in 1870, was said to be over two thousand Chinese. This figure increased as weekend visitors and others visited the shops, restaurants, and theaters in town. At one time there were three Chinese theatrical troops residing there to entertain the Chinese in the region, at least three fraternal organizations (Suey Sing, Hop Sing, and Chee Kong tongs), several Chinese Christian churches, a Chinese school, a Chinese children's playground, and boarding houses. One of the fraternal brotherhoods (probably the Hop Sing Tong), associations typical of mining towns with a large Chinese population, raised money for the original 1854 temple and the 1869 relocated temple, which burned down. Using that same 1869 site, the community built the present temple using traditional Daoist Chinese temple plans that Swain and Hudson, a major construction firm, built at the cost of over $5,000, an astronomical sum for individuals earning one dollar per day.

The one-story building is divided into three parts: a central section that is the main temple, with two smaller sections to the right and left of the entrance way. The main temple, which features two red entry doors (red is the color of happiness) and two red and gold lanterns, contains one intricately carved gilt wooden altar table and then a second plainer one for offerings of incense, tea, alcoholic beverages, fruits, and flowers. The traditional altar decorations of a large, dragon-handled pewter incense burner, flanked by two pewter candlestick holders, and vases decorate the table. Fortune-telling bamboo sticks in bamboo containers and fortune-telling blocks are also on the table. A bronze engraved plaque dates from the late 1870s. By the entryway is a large bronze bell and ancient drum, both of which are still in use. Located nearby are the names of the donors for the 1880 temple construction. Both sides of the room have traditional Chinese weapons in wooden holders and silk banners, wooden engraved plaques (one pair dating to 1868), and wooden steles. At the rear of the temple is the primary altar table where the deities reside. Bok Kai, the largest figure, is in the center with a jade tablet and is flanked by six other deities: (1) Guandi, also known as Guan Yu or Guan Gong, the god of war, justice, martial arts, literature, and brotherhood from the Three Kingdoms period in the third century CE; (2) Yufeng, represent-

ing civil and military activities, including the protection of police and officials; (3) Guanyin, the goddess of mercy, who was incorporated into the Buddhist pantheon as a major bodhisattva and represents women, fertility, and mercy, especially helping people in times of need; (4) Tianhou, Empress of Heaven, also known as Mazu, who protects fishermen, overseas travelers, and coastal communities and was a historic person of the Lin (Lum) clan; (5) Huado, the god of medicine or health; and finally (6) Tudi, the god of earth. According to the local press, over 3,000 people participated in the dedication ceremony led by several Daoist priests from San Francisco.

Above the entrance to the temple in the open veranda area a skilled Chinese artist painted an exquisite mural depicting several different Daoist themes separated by environmental theme poems written in different calligraphic styles and paintings of the four seasons (fall, winter, spring, summer). Laozi, depicted as an old man, and Guan Yu, dressed as a general, are among those individuals featured in the Daoist narratives, and in one section a young boy in Western dress is depicted to represent Chinese Americans, present and future. The linear renditions of figures and attention to details, especially in the clothing, demonstrated the high skill of the artist (a point noted by the local press). Birds and flowers also are present. Many of the vibrant colors have remained through the centuries because of the rich mineral paints used. One poem describes the wind blowing through pine trees and rivers and mountains, in keeping with an appreciation of nature.

To the right (east) side of the main temple is a wing that consists of six rooms. An interior door leads to a wooden staircase from the main temple and there is an exterior door as well. A fortune-telling board with slips of paper is located near the staircase. Since roasted pigs are a major part of the celebration, there is a unique brick pig oven, which has not been used since the 1920s. There is a stove for burning spirit money and artifacts to the deities or in memory of the deceased. In one of the small rooms on the northern section there are many carved wooden sayings presented by the members of the temple. There is a room that was used to house visitors or travelers since the railroad train originally stopped in front of the temple. Chinese usually were forbidden to stay in non-Chinese hotels in the late 19th century. Another small room that has an upstairs section contains a three-wok-burner brick stove, chairs, tables, and perhaps more beds. The room also was used for gaming and other recreational activities, such as reading.

To the left (west) side of the main temple is a large room divided into two sections. There is only one exterior door. This room serves as the community meeting room and perhaps an office. Beautifully hand carved teak or rosewood chairs and tables are in the room. Built without any nails, they represent the best of 19th-century Chinese furniture in design and execution. Steles dating back to 1880 are stored here as well as other artifacts and numerous books in Chinese and English, including the priest's accounting records. The gilt sedan chair to carry Bok Kai in parades also is kept there.

This tripartite division of a temple building is typical of one of the two main sects of Daoist temple architecture. The upturned eaves and the two red wood columns with cushioned capitals by the entry temple doorway are characteristic of Song dynasty (960–1279 CE) temple architectural style. The fact that there is a public park at the west side of the building is in keeping with the Daoist love of nature and gardens.

As the economy of Marysville declined, the Chinese population decreased. Job opportunities opened in other locations after World War II so young Chinese Americans moved to places like San Francisco and Sacramento and their suburbs. As a result, the temple is only open on certain days, but on Bomb Day, Bok Kai's birthday, the temple is open with great fanfare and parades.

The Early Priest and Activities of the Temple

Yee Chow Chung (b. 1842, immigrated to the United States in 1871) served as the trained Daoist priest until his death or departure after 1920. He was married but left his wife and children in China. He kept records about astronomy as well as account books. When he died, there were no local Daoist priests to take his place because the 1892 extension of the Chinese Exclusion Act of 1882 (known as the Geary Act) had redefined priests or ministers of both Western and Eastern religions as "laborers" and therefore they were ineligible for immigration to the United States. This left the Chinese American community without a pool of Daoist priests. A lay minister probably succeeded him and eventually the care of the temple rested in the hands of a lay caretaker who often was chosen as the winner of the Bomb Day celebration that marked the birthday of Bok Kai, usually held on the second day of the second month according to the lunar calendar (late February to March in the Gregorian calendar).

Bomb Day begins with the lighting of incense and the chanting of prayers and is followed by the lighting of firecrackers and the firing of "bombs," papier-mâché bamboo-framed cylinders wrapped with newspapers and stuffed with gunpowder, one of which holds the lucky number that determines who will be the leader of the community, who will serve as caretaker of the temple, or who will appoint a representative to care for the temple. A dragon dance is part of the celebration and the original bamboo dragon frame is among the many artifacts in the Bok Kai Museum. This dragon was 150 feet long and required one hundred men to carry it. The account books for 1890 indicated that it cost $575 and the costumes worn to support it cost $480. The dragon was exhibited at the World's Fair in New York and then retired in 1937 to give way to a more modern, shorter, wire dragon frame. Bok Kai rides in a gilt wooden intricately carved sedan chair carried by human bearers. In 1880 the local newspaper reported that over 1,500 Chinese participated in the festivities. By the turn of the 20th century, the entire Marysville community participated in the celebration and in 1930 the city adopted it as one of its main tourist attractions and jointly sponsored Bomb Day with the temple administrators. According to anthropologist Dr. Paul Chace, in 2001 there were 7,000–9,000 participants lighting incense, having their for-

tunes told, partaking of the 100–200 roasted pigs and other delicacies, and watching the two hours of parades and martial arts performances. Today Marysville's Bomb Day celebration attracts visitors from all over North America and countries around the world. The other major festival is Chinese New Year and like Bomb Day, it is celebrated with an elaborate dragon dance and parade.

Structural Problems

The levee and high water table have caused structural problems to the temple. In 1947 members of the temple organized and tried to renovate and strengthen the temple building as cracks appeared. The Friends of Bok Kai organized to raise money and bring the attention of the region and nation to this treasure. In 2001 the National Trust for Historic Preservation named the Bok Kai Temple one of the 11 most endangered sites in the United States. Media attention was immediate. In 2002 the temple was listed on the state and national registers, giving it official significance in the American mosaic. The Friends sponsored lunches, lectures, and other activities to help raise funds. Chinese historical societies sponsored bus tours to Marysville. Sacred Places included the temple in its tours and donated funds for its restoration. The major contributors were the Chinese Benevolent Association of San Francisco, Rotary Club—all for general restoration—and the McBean Family Trust (for mural restoration). Getty Museum restorations helped in the project of restoring the murals. Grants from the California State Historic Preservation Office and the National

Trust for Historic Preservation also helped in the $1 million fundraising project.

Other Daoist Temples

Every major Chinese American town or city had temples, often referred to as "joss houses" by the local American population. The term derived from pidgin English from the Javanese word *deyos*, the Portuguese word *deos*, and the Latin word *dues*, all referring to "gods" in the building. Joss sticks refer to the incense sticks that were burned at the altar. The term first appeared in 1659 and by 1711 English and American writers had connected the Chinese gods or god with the term *joss*. Americans seldom distinguished whether the "joss house" was Daoist, Buddhist, Confucianist, or an organizational meeting hall (*tang* or *miao*). The Chinese are more specific and the Bok Kai Temple is called a *miao*, or temple/place of worship.

Temples in California included the Daoist Tin How Temple in San Francisco, originally built in 1852 and reconstructed in 1911, dedicated to Tianhou (Empress of Heaven), also known as Mazu. The Kong Chow temples in San Francisco and Los Angeles as well as the Mo Dai Miu (Kwan Gong) in Mendocino, a small two-room temple, are dedicated to Guan Yu (god of war, justice, literature; and protector of its followers). The Kong Chow temples also serve as a district association and clan community center. Oroville's Chinese temple consists of three different buildings, one each devoted to Buddhism, Daoism, and Confucianism. Weaverville's 1874 Daoist Temple Amongst the Forest Beneath the Clouds (Won Lim) rivals the Bok Kai Temple as a relatively large Daoist temple, but it is dedicated to GuanYu and is a California state historic park and not a functioning historic Daoist temple like Bok Kai.

Historically there were other Bok Kai temples, for example in Lewiston, Idaho. In 1875, 10 years after their arrival in Lewiston, the Chinese built the Beuk Aie Temple at the confluence of the Clearwater and Snake rivers on A and B Streets. Because A Street was eroded away by the Clearwater River, in 1888 the Chinese built a new temple to "Buck Eye" at 513 C Street, where it remained until 1959 when it was destroyed to facilitate the expansion of the local newspaper office. Another Daoist temple existed in Evanston, Wyoming, but was known only as a "joss house." Local newspapers covered the Bomb Day celebrations so it might have been dedicated to Bok Kai. In Honolulu the Daoist temple is situated in the Lin (Lum) family association building and is dedicated to Mazu or Tianhou, who is a historical person from the Lin clan. In Merced, California, a Daoist temple built in the 1880s and lasting until the 1960s was located on the second floor of a café but only some of the artifacts still remain. Other such small Daoist worship areas existed wherever there was a large Chinese American population.

Daoism experienced a decline in popularity in China as a result of the antireligious stance of the Communists in the People's Republic of China but remained vibrant in Taiwan. During the Cultural Revolution (1966–1969 or 1979, depending on interpretation), many Daoist temples in China were destroyed. After Mao Zedong's death and the ascendancy of Deng Xiaoping as China's new leader, Daoism began to flourish and spread overseas. The global concerns for the environment, pollution, dehumanization, and unrest have caused some important people to search for solutions in Daoism. As a result, there are efforts to expand Daoist associations in the United States and elsewhere in the West. New temples have been established, such as the Fung Loy Kok Daoist Temple with two branch temples in the United States and four in Canada. These temples offer a variety of activities, including the study of Daoist literature, lectures, meditation, training in traditional lion dances, cooking classes, and classes in *qigong* and *taiqi*. The nonaggressive, nonviolent, peaceful coexistence, and love of nature aspects of Daoism appealed to early and present-day American thinkers, such as Henry Thoreau. *The Tao of Pooh* taught Winnie the Pooh fans about Daoism. In some cases, there has been a unity created between Daoism and Buddhism as common ground beliefs and practices allow joint international associations to be created.

The Bok Kai Daoist Temple is one of the oldest, continuously active Daoist temples in the United States and reflects not only the Daoist architectural style but also the beliefs of one of the major religions of China.

Sue Fawn Chung

See also: Entries: Chinese American Religions; Chinese Temples in America; Daoism

Further Reading

Bokenkamp, Stephen R. *Ancestors and Anxiety: Daoism and the Birth of Rebirth in China*. Berkeley: University of California Press, 2007.

Clarke, John James. *The Tao of the West: Western Transformations of Taoist Thought*. New York: Routledge, 2000.

Kohn, Livia. *Introducing Daoism*. New York: Routledge, 2009.

Laozi. *Daodejing*. Translated by William Scott Wilson. Tokyo and New York: Kodansha International, 2010.

Little, Stephen. *Taoism and the Arts of China*. Chicago: Art Institute of Chicago, 2000.

Welch, Holmes. *The Parting of the Way: Lao Tzu and the Taoist Movement*. London: Methuen, 1957.

Zhuangzi. *Chuang-tau: The Inner Chapters*. Translated by A. C. Graham. London: Unwin, 1986.

Brahma Kumaris (Daughters of Brahma)

Brahma Kumaris (BKs) is an international nongovernmental spiritual organization headquartered at Mt. Abu, Rajasthan, India; it has over 8,500 centers in 120 countries, with regional coordinating offices in Australia, Kenya, Russia, the United Kingdom, and the United States. As a learning community, Brahma Kumaris seeks to help individuals of all ages, faith traditions, and backgrounds to rediscover and strengthen their inherent worth by encouraging and facilitating spiritual awakening and their contribution to society through spiritual education and reflective practices.

Brahma Kumaris was founded in 1936 in Hyderabad, Sindh (now part of Pakistan, but at that time part of colonial India), by Dada Lekhraj (1876–1969), who believed that the core feminine attributes—patience, tolerance, sacrifice, kindness, and love—would increasingly be recognized as the foundation on which personal growth, human relations, and the development of caring communities would emerge. Although women head the organization, there are many men in key administrative roles.

This entry provides an overview of the history, beliefs, and contributions of Brahma Kumaris. The history section traces the physical movement and development of the Om Mandali community and its spiritual unfolding; there is some overlap between these two sections.

History: Institutional Development

Lekhraj was born Lekhraj Kripalani in 1876 to a village schoolmaster. He was expected to follow in his father's footsteps, but instead entered the jewelry business and earned a considerable fortune as a diamond trader. As a businessman, a family man, and a father of five, Lekhraj maintained a highly respectable position in the community and was known for his philanthropy. A seeker of truth, he sought out learned persons for guidance. Deeply contemplative, he spent a great deal of time "talking" to his mind and endeavored to understand its behavior. On the advice of his *Guru*, he began reading the *Bhagavad-Gītā*. Commencing in 1932 he arranged *satsangs* (devotional gatherings) at his home, where passages from the Gita would be read, primarily to women and children from his *bhaibhand* caste comprised of wealthy traders and merchants, who lived in the vicinity. While reading the Gita, Lekhraj increasingly felt the presence of a great power; he also noted that attendees

were also moved. These experiences were the start of a series of progressive and more profound insights that Lekhraj and his community would come to have.

Outsiders began referring to the *satsang* as Om Mandali, a name that the community later adopted. In October 1937 Lekhraj did something quite extraordinary; he relinquished all of his wealth and property to a trust and charged eight female compatriots to administer it and promote his spiritual vision. Dada remained as advisor. Radhe (Radhi Pokardas Rajwani, 1916–1965), who had earlier instantly recognized the truth and relevance of Dada's teachings, was named the director and lead teacher. Affectionately known as Mama, she was a storehouse of wisdom and energy.

Dada's actions infuriated close relatives, who believed that women should not be accorded such responsibilities and that women should not remain celibate. Unable to quell their anger, the community moved to Karachi and changed their name to Rajsuva Ashvamedh Avinashi Gyan Yagya ("Imperishable sacrificial fire of knowledge to restore self-sovereignty through sacrificing the horse [the senses]"). The protests followed, as well as a series of court cases to—unsuccessfully—disband Om Mandali. Subsequently, the community moved into Brij Kothi, a vacant palace of His Highness Shri Brijendra Singh Ji on Mount Abu in Rajasthan. Shortly thereafter the community moved to Pokhran House (now called Pandav Bhawan), which became the first campus of the *ashram* (spiritual hermitage) Madhuban (Forest of Honey). Madhuban remains the spiritual headquarters of BKs.

During the tumultuous partition of India that commenced on August 14, 1947, the self-sufficient community devoted themselves to deepening their spiritual practice. In May 1950 Baba directed all records from Pakistan to be destroyed or buried to prevent the dissemination of misunderstanding. Many were reluctant to destroy their precious diaries, so Baba instructed that they be buried and hoped that they would be discovered during the next *kalpa* (cosmic age) cycl. The decade of the 1950s is known as the Beggary Period. It was especially difficult for those from wealthy families who had never experienced physical privation and discomfort. In 1960 the community renamed itself Prajapita Brahma Kumaris Ishwariya Vishwa Vidyalaya (Prajapita Brahma Kumaris Godly University). On June 24, 1965, Mama passed away at the age of 49. Brahma Baba passed away on January 18, 1969, at the age of 93.

At the time of Brahma Baba's passing, there were some 250 centers throughout India. Two women from the original group, Dadi Prakashmani (1922–2007) and Didi Manmohini (1910–1983), were selected as the spiritual heads and joint administrative heads; together they worked to expand Brahma Baba's vision. In 1971, centers were established in London and Hong Kong. In 1974, Dadi Janki, who had joined the organization at the age of 21 in 1937, became the main co-coordinator of service activities outside India and subsequently assumed the position of additional administrative head in London. She assumed her position as administrative and spiritual head of BKs at the age of 91 in 2007, a position she still held as of the writing of this entry (2013).

To keep pace with the growing number of members and expansion of activities, the main campus of Madhuban added other campuses: Gyan Sarovar (Lake of Knowledge), Shantivan (Forest of Peace), and the Global Hospital and Research Center that provides high-quality, modern, holistic health care services to the indigenous people.

History: Spiritual Unfolding

Dada Lekhraj together with his community experienced through their meditation practice a series of insights, which the Brahma Kumaris community freely shares with others and on which it works. The following is a brief overview of their spiritual unfolding.

While Dada was away in Kashmir between 1935 and 1936, members of the community continued to enter into trances and experienced visions. Upon his return, Dada intuited the presence of another power working within him. Shortly thereafter, he had powerful visions of paradise, destruction, and the deity Vishnu. When Dada chanted "Om" while in deep contemplation, those present frequently entered into a trance and would have visions of Dada as Vishnu, of other divine beings, and of light.

Between 1939 and 1942 an increasing number in the community experienced bodiless *samādhi*, a state in which one merges with Brahm, the spiritual abode of souls. Many reported experiencing "light upon light." The community shared their spiritual experiences. Radhe, Mama, read in classes what Dada had written. Thereafter the community stopped reading the

Gita and began recording what was being spoken through Dada. When young Sister Pushpa entered a trance, a whispering voice spoke through her. It was the voice of the Incorporeal Supreme Father, Shiva Baba (also known as Supreme Soul Shiva). Since no one had heard this voice before, it generated considerable interest. Dada surmised that the voice was of another personality who was the source of their spiritual experiences. Dada referred to this personality to be Piyu, the Beloved. Piyu is synonymous with Incorporeal Shiva Baba.

Piyu gave Dada the name Brahma and clarified his role as creator. With this revelation, the community began referring to Dada as Prajapati (Lord of the World), God Brahma. At some point during these early years, Dada felt he was indeed God Brahma, due to the intensity of the experiences that others were having through him and the power of his own insights. In the meantime, Gulzar Dadi, a young member of the community, had the first experience of *Avyakt* (angelic) Brahma in the Subtle Regions.

In 1948, speaking directly through Brahma Baba, Shiva Baba said, "*Shivohum*" ("I am Shiva") in the same whispering voice that Pushpa had heard earlier. Sometime during the 1950s the personality of Shiva Baba as a distinct incorporeal god clearly emerged. Subsequently, in 1952 the experiences of trance and meditation clearly revealed Shiva Baba and Brahma Baba to be distinct. And between 1957 and 1960 it was revealed that Shiva Baba spoke through Brahma Baba. Brahma Baba followed Shiva Baba's messages in his thoughts, words, and actions and became a concrete example for the Brahma Kumaris community.

Practices

Rajayoga meditation is the foundation of BKs spiritual practice. Like actors taking on a costume and playing their roles on the stage, each one is a soul expressing through their own physical bodies on the "stage" of the world. The soul's original nature is filled with the highest qualities of peace, purity, love, joy, and power. However, many have forgotten these spiritual truths in their addictive search for temporary physical and material happiness. This pursuit has resulted in worry, fear, and conflict. For individuals to return to their original nature, Rajayoga offers instruction in self-transformation through understanding:

- Our Consciousness and Self-Realization
- Our Home of Silence
- Our Relationship with God
- Law of *Karma*
- Reincarnation
- Eternal World Drama
- Tree of Life
- A Spiritual Lifestyle

Classes are designed to facilitate an individual's inward journey to recognize the deepest self, understand one's relationship with Incorporeal God Shiva, and appreciate the spiritual context of human existence and its contemporary relevance. Individuals are encouraged to live by the highest values that are revealed through these teachings, vision, and purpose; such a commitment will create peace and a better world.

The practice of meditation connects the inner world of thoughts, feelings, and ideas to the outer world of actions and relationships. Meditation practice builds mental, intellectual and emotional capacity. The four major pillars toward personal transformation are:

1. The study and inculcation of spiritual knowledge revealed by Incorporeal God Shiva.

2. The practice of the remembrance of the one God who is the Supreme Parent of all souls in the world.

3. The inculcation of divine virtues and application of spiritual life skills in daily living.

4. Service to others with an attitude of benevolence and awareness of the spiritual relationship between all people; such service is an opportunity to apply spiritual principles in action.

Contributions

Spiritual service in the United States started in 1976 when Sister Chandru Desai and Sister Denise Lawrence, who were serving in Toronto, Canada, drove to the United States. In 1977, the national headquarters of BKs in Great Neck, New York, was established under the leadership of Sister Mohini Punjabi. As of 2013 there are 40 centers in California, Florida, Georgia, Illinois, Maryland, Massachusetts, Michigan, New Jersey, New York, Ohio, Oklahoma, Oregon, Puerto Rico, Texas,

Virginia, and Washington. Brahma Kumaris opened Peace Village, a 300-acre retreat center in the Catskill Mountains in upstate New York, in 1991; and Anubhuti Retreat Center in Novato, California, in 2004. These retreat centers provide a place for seekers of all backgrounds to explore their spirituality through retreats, workshops, courses, and festivities. The centers are administered by people who live and work in the community and volunteer their talents and spare time. All events are offered free of charge as a service to the community. Brahma Kumaris does not raise funds; it is supported through voluntary contributions from well-wishers and those who have found personal benefit through the various courses and activities.

In the United States, Brahma Kumaris has been pivotal in organizing Call of the Time, a forum for professionals in areas of global influence; in developing the Living Values Education program; in founding Images and Voices of Hope, a venue for journalists, artists, and media professionals to dialogue; and in establishing the Point of Life Foundation for developing and participating in innovative programs for quality health care.

Brahma Kumaris also strives to promote awareness and highlight the great aspirations of the purpose and principles of the United Nations. To this end, it initiated international projects to provide people around the world with an opportunity to participate in activities of social and humanitarian concerns. Some of the projects are "The Million Minutes of Peace," "Global Co-operation for a Better World," "Sharing our Values for a Better World," "Living Values—an educational program," and "Culture of Peace." These initiatives highlight the value of spiritual development in the promotion of peace and non-violence. In 1980, Brahma Kumaris became affiliated with the Department of Public Information of the United Nations as a nongovernmental organization, and in 1983 it was granted Consultative Status on the Roster of the UN Economic and Social Council. In 1987, it was granted consultative status with UNICEF and, in 1998, General Consultative Status with the Economic and Social Council of the UN.

The Brahma Kumaris Meditation Center in San Francisco has played a significant role in the local community by offering various courses and programs and also working in partnerships with such organizations as the United Religions Initiative and the Pachamama Alliance. The meditation center is a venue for spiritual study, self-development workshops, Rajayoga meditation courses, and various other activities designed to identify and implement positive spiritual values, ethics, and understanding to help improve the quality of family, community, and professional life. The meditation center sponsors events and festivals in response to the growing levels of stress that are damaging to our communities. The director, Sister Chandru, is one of the founders of the interfaith movement in the San Francisco Bay Area and has also served on the board of the San Francisco Interfaith Center for more than two decades. Volunteers from the San Francisco meditation center feed the homeless and visit community centers, prisons, hospitals, and homes for the elderly. Volunteers lecture at schools, universities, local businesses, local organizations, and corporations on meditation, personal development, and new ways of working together in the community.

Sister Chandrika Desai

See also: Entries: Hindu Canon

Further Reading

Brahma Kumaris Website. www.brahmakumaris.org. Accessed July 9, 2014.

George, Mike. *In the Light of Meditation.* London: O Books, John Hunting, 2004.

Hassija, Jagdish Chander. *Adi Dev: The First Man.* London: BKIS, Publication Division, 2008.

Punjabi, Mohini. *Story of Immortality.* New York: Brahma Kumaris World Spiritual Organization, 2008.

Whaling, Frank. *Understanding the Brahma Kumaris.* Edinburgh, Scotland: Dunedin Academic Press, 2012.

Buddha Image

The earliest extant bas-relief narratives of the life of the Buddha sculpted at Sāñcī and Bharhut in the third century BCE only suggest his presence through images of the bo tree (*Ficus religiosa*) under which he realized enlightenment, the cushion on which he rested at the moment of the enlightenment, the *stūpa* symbolizing his *parinirvāṇa* (death), his footprint(s) signifying his being there, and the *dharmacakra* or Dharma wheel representing the first sermon. At times the Buddha is presented as part of a trident, a symbol of the Triple Jewels—Buddha (the teacher), Dharma (the teaching), and *sangha* (community)—that constitute the core of the faith.

The shift from the anionic to the iconic representation of the Buddha coincided with the rise of Mahāyāna and the spread of lay devotion (bhakti) at the beginning of the first and second centuries CE in the Mathurā and Gandhāra regions. The Mathurān image makers did not sculpt an anatomically correct human Buddha. Rather, they produced images that were composites of 32 major and 80 minor *lakṣāṇa* or marks, associated with manly beauty and heroic ideals. Thus the Buddha, a noble being and a *cakravartin* (ideal ruler), was believed to have a smooth and perfectly proportioned body; an oval-shaped face; eyebrows in the shape of the curve of an Indian bow; eyes that recall a lotus bud; ears that evoke the shape of a mango; thighs like that of a gazelle; and limbs that are smooth like a banyan tree. The triple folds of the neck are derived from a conch shell, a symbol used to call the faithful to listen to the teachings. The broad chest and narrow hips recall the lion, the patriarch of the jungle; the arms that reach to the knees and webbed fingers symbolize the Buddha's compassionate reach. The long arms enable the Buddha to embrace all beings; his webbed fingers prevent those whom the Buddha has scooped from the sea of *saṃsāra* from dribbling back in. The distended earlobes, a feature of the nobility who wore heavy ear ornaments, recall his aristocratic birth. The colored gold body emits a wondrous scent.

Buddhist lore reminds us that the future Buddha's locks curled to the right after he cut his hair, a symbol of abandoning the secular life and becoming a mendicant. He has 80 of these right-turning tufts of hair that never grew again. His curls and lotus-petal lips prompted the early British explorers to mistakenly report Buddha images to have an "African cast." The palms of his hands and the soles of his feet bear the *dharmacakra*, Dharma wheel, or *sathiya*, "swastika." Placed in the middle of the forehead, the white locks curled to the right, the *ūrṇā* emits the light of wisdom; it is depicted as a third eye in Tantric Buddhism. The Buddha image is often ringed by a halo and aureole that symbolize the Buddha's immeasurable brilliance of truth and wisdom. The Buddha's extraordinary wisdom is represented by the *ushṇīsa* or extra cranial protrusion. These features are not an afterthought, but integral parts of the representation. Artisans selectively represented only his principal features because they are too numerous.

In contrast, the Gandhāran Buddha image was inspired by Hellenic realism and tempered by Persian, Scythian, and Parthian models. Sculptors crafted Buddhist images with anatomical accuracy, spatial depth, and foreshortening. The straight, sharply chiseled Apollonian nose, brows, and mustache capture a "frozen moment." Their more realistic tradition often transformed the *ushṇisha* into a topknot or turban; the Buddha's curls were altered into wavy hair. Another obvious Mediterranean feature is the diaphanous, toga-like robe. The emaciated Buddha, an image rarely seen in Mathurā, is another evidence of Hellenistic realism.

From the close of the second century CE both the Mathurān and Gandhāran styles experienced mutual cross-fertilization. The skillful incorporation of the *lakṣānas* suggests that the Gandhāran image makers became more comfortable in incorporating native Indian notions of beauty. The result of this synthesis ennobled, refined, and purified the Buddha image that appeared in the Gupta period (ca. 320–467 CE). The soft and supple body visible beneath the thin robe swells with life-giving breath. The round face sculpted with a feeling of perfect tranquility, engaged in profound meditation, conveys in the human form a sense of the transcendent. The Gupta style became the model for Southeast Asian images.

While Southeast Asian artisans focused on the historical Buddha and events related to his life, the ideas and goals of Mahāyāna Buddhism introduced an important shift in visual and plastic representation. Central and East Asian artisans have struggled to render the celestial Buddhas and bodhisattvas and transcendental Buddha lands. The first Buddha images to enter China were probably transported in small portable shines that were molded and carved in Central Asia. These images, a fusion of Gupta and later Gandhāran styles, had a great impact on the early Northern Wei (386–535 CE) style that formed the foundation of Chinese Buddhist art. The distinctive slender and frontal figures with their cascading robes in the Wei style appear during the Japanese Asuka period (552–646 CE) in the Shaka Triad and Yumedō Kannon at Hōryū-ji (temple) in Nara, Japan. A characteristic Chinese style appears in the Tang (618–907 CE) period. The Tang style is rounder and bolder. A prime example of the classical Tang style is at the Yakushi Triad at Yakushi-ji Temple in Nara. Executed in 751, the Sokkuram Buddha in Korea is another fine example.

The Buddhist images enshrined in the temples in the United States display regional idiosyncrasies, but every image will have many of the iconographical motifs mentioned in this entry.

Ronald Y. Nakasone

See also: Essays: Arts and Cultural Production

Further Reading

Basham, A. L. *The Wonder That Was India: A Survey of the Culture of the Indian Sub-Continent before the Coming of the Muslims*. New York: Grove Press, 1959.

Coomaraswamy, Ananda K. *History of Indian and Indonesian Art*. New York: Dover Publications, 1965.

Fisher, Robert E. *Buddhist Art and Architecture*. New York: Thames and Hudson, 1993.

Mitter, Partha. *Indian Art*. Oxford: Oxford University Press, 2001.

Seckel, Dietrich. *The Art of Buddhism*. New York: Crown, 1963.

Tobu Museum of Art, at al. *Buddha: The Spread of Buddhist Art in Asia*. Tokyo: NHK, 1998.

Buddhist Canon. *See* Tripiṭaka (Buddhist Canon)

Buddhist Churches of America (BCA)

The Buddhist Churches of America (BCA) is an incorporated faith organization affiliated with the Jōdo Shinshū Honganji-ha (sect) headquartered in Kyoto, Japan. Jōdo Shinshū or Shin Buddhism was founded on the teachings of Shinran (1173–1262), a Japanese cleric active during the Kamakura period (1185–1333). The BCA

Southern Alameda County Buddhist Church, located in Union City, California, was established in 1965. Current temple membership reflects the generational and demographic shifts in the surrounding area. English, not Japanese, is the primary language of the faith. (Photo by Ronald Y. Nakasone, July 17, 2015)

administers and directs its denominational activities in the continental United States from its headquarters in San Francisco, California. This entry gives an overview of the doctrines and beliefs that guide the BCA, its history, and its institution.

Beliefs and Doctrines

Jōdo Shinshū Buddhists hold that Shinran's thoughts contained in the *Kyōgyōshinshō*, *Tan'nishō*, *Mattōshō*, and other writings crystallize the spiritual vision articulated in the *Muryōjukyō* (*Larger Sukhāvatīvyūha-sūtra*), *Kammuryōjukyō* (*Amitāyurdhyāna-sūtra*), and *Amidakyō* (*Smaller Sukhāvatīvyūha-sūtra*). The *Muryōjukyō* details 48 vows that Bodhisattva Dharmākara fulfilled to become Amida Buddha and to establish the Pure Land with the intent to save all beings. Of these 48, the 18th vow is central.

> If sentient beings hear [Amida's] name and quicken faith and joy, with even a single thought [of the Amida Buddha]; and if they offer their spiritual merit to others with a sincere heart; and if they desire to be born in [Amida's] Pure Land, they will attain birth there and reside in the stage of non-retrogression. Only those who commit the five damning offenses or slander the true teaching will be excluded.

Over the course of the development of Japanese Pure Land thought, Buddhist thinkers expanded the embrace of Amida Buddha's compassion to include all beings. The expression "a single thought" evolved to mean uttering Amida's name in the form *Namu Amida Butsu*—I take refuge in Amida Buddha. The *Amidakyō* states that sentient beings can be born in the Pure Land by simply hearing and by being sincerely mindful of Amida's name. Carrying this idea further, the *Muryōjukyō* expounds that even evil persons on their deathbeds who utter Amida Buddha's name with utmost sincerity will be received in Pure Land.

The insights from these three *sūtras* provided Shinran with the rationale for dispensing with rigorous spiritual discipline and highlighting the centrality of *shinjin*, true or sincere faith espoused by Nāgārjuna (ca. 150–250), Vasubandhu (ca. fifth century), and others. The centrality of faith assures spiritual release when the devotee appreciates his or her inadequacies and surrenders to the absolute Other Power (*tariki*) of Amida Buddha. *Shinjin*, the prime condition for birth in the Pure Land, is a gift from Amida Buddha; and the sincere utterance of the *nembutsu* is an invocation of gratitude and joy for Amida's compassion. Birth in the Pure Land is the most conducive way station for the ultimate realization of enlightenment (bodhi) or *Nirvāṇa*.

History

The Buddhist Churches of America celebrated its centennial in 1999. During the previous century the teachings of Shinran and its American institutional incarnation have had to respond and adapt to the American experience. This adventure began with the arrival of the Reverends Sonoda Shuye (1863–1922) and Nishijima Kakuryō (1873–1942) in San Francisco on September 1, 1899; this date marks the official beginnings of the BCA. Their arrival was prompted by a personal plea in 1896 by Hirano Nisaburō to the Honpa Honganji Sect headquartered in Kyoto to dispatch priests to minister to the growing Japanese immigrant community. Two years later the Revs. Honda Eryū and Miyamoto Ejun traveled to the United States to survey the spiritual needs of the Japanese community. During their visit they assisted Dr. Kaida (aka Hirakida) Katsugorō, who was in the process of setting up a medical practice in San Francisco, and others to establish the Bukkyō Seinenkai (Young Men's Buddhist Association—YMBA), the first Jōdo Shinshū Buddhist organization in the continental United States. After visiting Sacramento, Seattle, Vancouver, and other areas with sizable Japanese communities, they returned to Kyoto and recommended that priests be sent. The U.S. government census figures note that the number of Japanese immigrants had grown tenfold from 2,039 in 1890 to 24,327 in 1900.

Since most of the early immigrants were Jōdo Shinshū devotees, they naturally appealed to the Honpa Honganji authorities. In addition to serving their constituents, the leadership viewed this invitation as an opportunity to propagate Shinran's teaching to an English-speaking community. While Japanese is still integral in its rituals, in the intervening 100 years English has gradually become the *lingua franca* for conducting services and temple affairs.

Uchida Kōyu (1896–1960), who arrived in 1905 with his wife Seto, laid the institutional foundation of the Buddhist Mission of North America, the forerunner of the BCA. During their 18 years, Rev. and Mrs. Uchida witnessed the establishment of 13 temples and a number of fellowships in the western states of California, Oregon, and Washington. Temples were also established in Salt Lake City and Denver. Recognizing the growing number of temples and the administrative complexity, Uchida was officially appointed *sōchō* (bishop) in 1918. Prior to receiving this new designation, Uchida held the title of *kantoku* (director).

The sixth *sōchō*, Masuyama Kenjū (1887–1968), arrived in 1930 and quickly surmised that the Buddhist mission would require ministers who could communicate fluently in English. Shortly thereafter he established the Buddhist Society of America to reach English speakers, as well as second-generation Japanese Americans. He enlisted the assistance of Robert S. Clifton (1986–1963), Julius A. Goldberg (1908–2011), Sunya Pratt (1898–1986), and other Euro-Americans. He also encouraged American-born and educated Tsunoda Noboru (1913–2005) and Kumata Masaru (1908–1989), the first Japanese Americans to undertake ministerial training in Kyoto. The bishop created the Young Buddhist Association, moved to sponsor Boy Scout groups, encouraged Dharma (Sunday) School expansions, and promoted English publications. He left to his successor, Matsukage Ryōtai (1890–1948), 48 temples and fellowships that extended from Vancouver, Canada, to the north and New York City to the east.

The outbreak of World War II and the subsequent internment of the Japanese community along the Pacific Coast marked an important milestone in the American Pure Land experience. President Franklin Delano Roosevelt's 1942 Executive Order 1099, the Civilian Exclusion Orders, legalized the removal and relocation of persons of Japanese ancestry from their homes, farms, and businesses. U.S. authorities closed all of the Buddhist temples, and arrested and sent most of their clerics and lay leaders to various internment centers throughout the United States. Bishop Matsukage Ryōtai relocated to the Topaz Relocation Center in Utah. Government officials allowed Buddhist groups to carry on their religious activities in the centers. In 1944 a general meeting of ministers and lay leaders from the various centers and from other noninterned communities gathered at Topaz, Arizona, to adopt the articles of incorporation that officially changed the name from Buddhist Mission of North America to the Buddhist Churches of America.

Ironically, the internment provided new opportunities. In lieu of entering the internment centers, the government allowed the Japanese to settle away from the Pacific Coast states. Many found their way to such cities as Chicago, Detroit, St. Louis, New York, Philadelphia, and Seabrook, New Jersey, where they established Buddhist fellowships, many of which eventually evolved into full-fledged temples. The arrest and internment of the largely Japanese-speaking leadership thrust the younger American-born English-speaking clerics into leadership positions. After the war, great efforts were made to change the temple-related activities from Japanese to English and to nurture a new generation of leaders and devotees. English became the primary language for conducting services and other temple-related meetings. In 1954 the BCA established the Buddhist Study Center in Berkeley, California, to provide instruction in English for ministerial aspirants. The center was renamed the Institute of Buddhist Studies (IBS) in 1966; and in 1985 the IBS became an affiliate of the Graduate Theological Union (GTU).

Beginning in 1959, Bishop Hanayama Shinsho (1898–1995) and his Canadian-born successor Kenryū Tsuji (1919–2004) centralized and transformed BCA into a modern American institution through innovative educational, outreach, ministerial, and financial programs. The BCA created a scholarship fund to assist ministerial aspirants, a ministerial disability income and accidental death benefits program, a financial foundation, and other institutional reforms. Rev. Kenryū Tsuji's bishop's accession ceremony was the first to take place in the United States. On his watch the Honganji accredited the ministerial program at the Institute of Buddhist Studies. Ministerial training was now possible in English. Ordination, however, is still done in Kyoto.

Like other mainline U.S. denominations, from the mid-1970s the BCA's vitality began a slow decline, due in part to declining membership, financial difficulties, an aging clergy, and uninspiring leadership. In an attempt to reverse this decline the BCA initiated the Campaign for Buddhism in America in 1982 with the goal of raising $15 million. Funds from this capital campaign were intended to establish a more secure financial base for Buddhist education and to expand the capacity of the IBS, which was about to become part of the GTU, to improve ministerial pensions, and other programs. The campaign raised $10 million. Once again in 2003 the BCA embarked on a capital campaign, this time to raise $31 million for Buddhist education, ministerial benefits, and to secure a permanent facility for the IBS in Berkeley.

Since its mid-1970s peak the BCA has steadily lost devotees and has had to trim its administrative staff. The department of Buddhist Education and Sunday (Dharma) School that produced many innovative programs and publications was eliminated. Many temples are without ministers. The IBS's 1985 affiliation with the GTU was seen as a way to revitalize the tradition by training a new generation of ministers. It began with much fanfare; but eight years into its affiliation in 1993 the IBS began to systematically reduce its faculty and staff; it sold its newly acquired facility on Addison Street in 1997 and moved to Mountain View, California. The IBS eventually returned to Berkeley in 2006 to a newly remodeled Jōdo Shinshū Center on Durant Street. Ironically, the new facility was not designed to house its substantial Buddhist library. The IBS shares the facility with the Center for Buddhist Education that was established in 2005. Unable to sustain the BCA archives that were begun with a grant from the National Historical Publications and Records Commission, the BCA transferred its archives to the Japanese National

Museum in Los Angeles, California, in 1998.

The racial-ethnic makeup of the membership is becoming increasingly diverse. Many non-Japanese have been attracted to the faith through interest in Jōdo Shinshū teachings, in Japanese culture, and by marrying into the faith. A cursory review of the BCA's 2011–2012 directory reveals that many non-Japanese have assumed leadership roles. There are a number of non-Japanese clerics.

Administrative Structure

From its headquarters in San Francisco, the BCA oversees 61 temples and five fellowships with approximately 16,000 dues-paying members throughout the contiguous United States. Administratively, the BCA consists of eight geographical districts, six of which are concentrated on the Pacific Coast. The Mountain States District serves devotees in Colorado, Wyoming, and Nebraska. The Eastern District includes the temples and fellowships east of the Rocky Mountains. This far-flung scattering of temples is governed by a board of directors comprised of the bishop, the board president, the Ministerial Association chair, district-elected board members, board members at large, and representatives of BCA-affiliated organizations. Its annual meeting is held in February. Its 2011 budget was approximately $2,500,000.

While the BCA and the office of the bishop administer national programs, the individual temples maintain separate budgets and administrations. The individual temples support the operations of the BCA by forwarding monies based on an annual assessment of the dues-paying membership. The bishop's office appoints ministers to the local temples and mediates disputes. In addition to the overarching national organization, there are a number of affiliated organizations such as the Federation of Buddhist Women's Association, Western Adult Buddhist League, Federation of Dharma School Teachers' League, California Young Adult Buddhist League, and Western Young Buddhist League. These affiliates have local chapters.

The American Shin Buddhists in the state of Hawai'i have a separate jurisdiction and administration. The Honpa Hongwanji Mission of Hawai'i traces its beginnings to 1899. At the time of its founding, the kingdom of Hawai'i was not part of the United States. It is headquartered in Honolulu, Hawai'i. Like Hawai'i, the Canadian Shin Buddhists have a separate organization. Pure Land Buddhists arrived there in 1905. Its national headquarters is in British Columbia, Canada.

Contributions

The Buddhist Mission of North America (BMNA) and its successor organization, the BCA, have made significant contributions to American spiritual experience. In 1915, the BMNA hosted the World Buddhist Conference in San Francisco. This first international Buddhist conference in the United States was held in conjunction with the International Exposition. In 1935 Bishop Matsuyama and Rev. Shodo Tsunoda (1913–2005) traveled to Siam (now Thailand) to receive a portion of the corporeal remains of Śākyamuni Buddha from the royal family. The remains were unearthed in the late 19th century in Piprahwa in northern India. Bishop Matsukage carried the relics to the Topaz War Relocation Center. Spearheaded by the Young Buddhist Association of Hawai'i and the continental United States, BCA lobbied the U.S. Department of Defense to recognize Buddhism as a legitimate faith tradition. During World War II only Japanese American Christian ministers were allowed to accompany Japanese American combat troops. At the time the U.S. government recognized only three faith traditions; accordingly military personnel dog tags were imprinted with "C" for Catholic, "P" for Protestant, "O" for Jewish. Additionally, the Department of Defense now allows the Buddhist (Dharma) wheel on grave markers.

Ronald Y. Nakasone

See also: Entries: Higashi Honganji; Honpa Hongwanji Mission of Hawai'i; Imamura, Yemyō; Jōdo Shinshū Buddhist Temples of Canada; Obon (Urabon); Shin Buddhist Music; Shinrankai; Tripiṭaka (Buddhist Canon)

Further Reading

BCA Centennial History Project Committee. "Introduction to the 100-year Legacy." In *Buddhist Churches of America, a Legacy of the First 100 years*. San Francisco: Buddhist Churches of America, 1998.

Buddhist Churches of America. *Annual Report*, 2010.

Buddhist Churches of America. *Buddhist Churches of America, 75 Year History 1899–1974*. Chicago: Nobart, 1974.

Dobbins, James C. *Jōdo Shinshū, Shin Buddhism in Medieval Japan*. Bloomington: Indiana University Press, 1989.

Kashima, Tetsuden. *Buddhism in America: The Social Organization of an Ethnic Religious Institution*. Westport, CT: Greenwood Press, 1977.

Tuck, Donald R. *Buddhist Churches of America, Jōdo Shinshū*. Lewiston, NY: Edwin Mellon Press, 1987.

Yoo, David. 1996. "Racial Spirits, Religion and Race in Asian American Communities." *Amerasia Journal* 22, no. 1 (1996).

Buddhist Education

From its Indian beginnings Buddhism advanced eastward through Central, East, and Southeast Asia. More recently, it crossed the Pacific Ocean to Hawai'i and to the Americas with the Chinese and Japanese labor diaspora during the late 19th and early 20th centuries. It left its North and Southeast Asian homeland in the late 20th century with the refugee diaspora. The Immigration and Nationality Act of 1965, also known as the Hart-Celler Act, abolished the national origins quota system, allowing a heretofore unprecedented number of Asian Buddhists to enter the United States. Today virtually every Asian Buddhist group is present in the United States. For these newly arrived immigrant groups Buddhism is a family tradition, linked to their ethnic heritage and identity. However, as the temporal distance grows with each successive generation, the once obvious "living truths" of the faith are being progressively articulated in English and adjusted to American ways of thinking and doing to accommodate the American born and educated children, grandchildren, and great-grandchildren of the original immigrants.

This entry outlines Buddhist education in the ethnic faith community. It begins

Preschool students from the Denver Buddhist Temple Dharma school perform a Japanese dance during the 29th Annual Cherry Blossom Festival at 20th and Lawrence Streets in lower downtown Denver, Colorado. The festival, which featured Japanese and other Asian booths, food (including a beer garden), and cultural entertainment, runs from 11am and 6pm daily. (Glenn Asakawa/The Denver Post/Getty Images)

with a few observations on traditional ritual learning. Subsequently it highlights educational efforts in Hawai'i, especially the vision of Imamura Yemyō (1867–1932), who led the Jōdo Shinshū Honpa Hongwanji Buddhist Mission of Hawai'i (Hawai'i Kyōdan), and the educational efforts of Buddhist Churches of America (BCA). The 100-plus years of their educational effort offers insights into the probable path the Korean, Thai, Vietnamese, and other recently established communities will be journeying. The entry continues with brief descriptions of other Buddhist educational initiatives that in-

cludes the educational efforts of the non-ethnic or American Buddhist community. It does not discuss the academic study of Buddhism at universities and colleges.

Traditional Learning

Buddhist devotees in the United States today have a range of options to learn about their faith. First and foremost, devotees learn about their tradition by participating in rituals and festivals; by attending temple-sponsored retreats, study classes, and seminars; and through newsletters and books. Beyond the temple, for those so inclined, devotees can enroll in Buddhist educational institutions and college courses or earn advanced graduate degrees at any number of universities.

In traditional Buddhist cultures, education in the faith begins with observation and participation in rituals at home and at the temple. An intergenerational family affair, domestic rituals include daily and special services at the home altar, the periodic late life celebrations, and mortuary and memorial observances. Ritual participation involves caring for the family altar, including proper decorum and preparation of offerings. Community rituals include services that mark the major events in Buddha's life and experiences special to the community. Through the participation in the rituals—sights, sounds, movements, touch, and taste—the devotee comes to understand the essentials of the tradition. In this regard, mortuary rituals are most poignant. While the devotee many not be able to cogently articulate the metaphysical underpinnings and doctrines of the Buddha's teachings, he or she understands existentially and intuitively that life is transient, that suffering is endemic to the human condition, and that faith and trust in Buddha's Dharma or teaching is the means to overcome suffering. The Japanese sum up this traditional way of learning by saying, "You learn about your faith by observing your mother's back." How low does she bow when she approaches the altar? How sincere is her incense offering?

Participation in temple rituals educates a devotee's understanding and history of the faith and reinforces his or her cultural identity. Details vary, but all Buddhist traditions celebrate the birth and enlightenment of Siddhārtha Gautama, the historical Buddha. The Buddha's first sermon and his passing are also major services. In addition, temples often celebrate the events important to their particular temple. Thus, for example, the Japanese Jōdo Shinshū sects observe the birth (*Gotane*) and death (*Hō'onkō*) of their spiritual patriarch, Shinran (1173–1263). The Buddhist Churches of America also has a special service to commemorate its official establishment in North America in September.

Buddhist Education in Hawai'i and the United States

While observation and participation are effective in transmitting the faith in the homeland, this pedagogical method does not work well in an immigrant faith community for a number of reasons. Foremost is the increasing use of English with successive generations and attitudes wrought by the modern American experience. In an attempt to transmit and preserve the faith, the Japanese have turned to education.

During his 32-year tenure, Imamura pursued two objectives: propagation in English and the democratization of the Hawai'i Mission. Imamura understood that for Buddhism to be meaningful among the Hawai'i-born second generation Japanese and non-Japanese, who did not know the Japanese language, English needed to be the medium of communication. Thus he established the English Department in 1918. English became the medium of instruction in the Sunday or Dharma School, study classes, and seminars. At the time when the *sūtras* were rendered by linguists, Imamura called for English translations that conveyed the spirit of the Buddhadharma (Buddhist teachings) more lyrically. Increasingly, priests delivered their messages in English and many of the ritual elements have now been translated from the Japanese. To make the service experience more comfortable, he installed pews to accommodate the lifestyle of the Hawai'i-born Japanese, who no longer sat on the floor.

Believing that Buddhism could become a vital part of American life, Imamura established the Giseikai (Legislative Assembly), a legislative body of clerics and lay leaders representing each temple, who would make policy and budgetary decisions at annual meetings. This collective decision-making and administrative system departed from the traditional top-down system. In short, Imamura educated the Buddhist organization to reflect American values and institutions. The legislative system is still operative today.

The Hawai'i Honpa Hongwanji Mission continued to fulfill Imamura's educational vision by establishing in 1949 the Hawai'i Hongwanji Mission School, a kindergarten to middle school facility. Founded on Buddhist values, the school aimed to improve the English proficiency of the Japanese-speaking students and to help them navigate the Christian undertone of the American educational curriculum. Imamura's vision was further advanced when in 2001, with encouragement from then Bishop Yosemori Chikai, the Honpa Hongwanji Mission committed to create a Buddhist-inspired independent college preparatory Buddhist high school. In the fall of 2003, the fully accredited Pacific Buddhist Academy opened its doors to the first class of 14 students.

In the meantime, the Honpa Hongwanji Mission of Hawai'i established in 1972 the Buddhist Study Center that would offer programs and classes on Buddhist thought and culture and as a vehicle to distribute Buddhist resources. An essential mission of the center is to recruit and train persons interested in the Jōdo Shinshū ministry. This program is closely affiliated with the Institute of Buddhist Studies, the educational arm of the Buddhist Churches of America (BCA). The Honpa Hongwanji Mission of Hawai'i and the Buddhist Churches of America are sister organizations affiliated with the Honpa Honganji-ha Sect, headquartered in Kyoto, Japan. Established in 1949, the Institute of Buddhist Studies (IBS) affiliated with the Graduate Theological Union in Berkeley, California, in 1985. Through this affiliation, IBS offers the master of arts degree in Buddhist studies that emphasizes Jōdo Shinshū studies, programs in Buddhist ministry and chaplaincy.

In an effort to transmit the Jōdo Shinshū teachings, the BCA's Dharma School Department turned to Etsuko Steimetz (1938–1988), who developed a comprehensive K–8 Dharma School curriculum that is a systemization of the prior efforts. The graded lessons accompanied by art projects for the lower grades appear in four volumes of *Jin Shin Kyō Nin Shin, Dharma School Teacher's Guide*. In 1993, the BCA published *Iron Chain to Golden Chain, Dharma High School Readings*. As the title indicates, this publication is a collection of readings for young adults. The editor, Tsukasa Matsueda, in consultation with other Buddhist educators, selected articles that interpreted Pure Land Buddhism for the modern world. These materials are designed to assist the Dharma School teachers with their hour-long classes that are normally held concurrently with the adult service. Typically temples have a service for the children before the adult service. The work of the Dharma School Department continues through the Center for Buddhist Education (CBE) that offers a variety of Jōdo Shinshū–based learning opportunities to its members and the larger community. The CBE sponsors continuing education seminars and workshops for Buddhist clergy, lay leaders, and young people. It also offers a Jōdo Shinshū correspondence course delivered online for both BCA members and the public.

Informal inquiries and anecdotal evidence suggest that the more recently arrived immigrant Buddhist communities are experiencing educational patterns similar to that of the Japanese. For example, the first-generation Thai and Tibetan immigrant families who were born and raised with Buddhism as a family and cultural tradition, like the Japanese who arrived a century ago, see Buddhism as an essential part of their ethnic identity. The essentials of the faith are transmitted at home by the elders and at the temple. Temple leaders are finding creative ways to transmit their respective Thai and Tibetan identity to their children by establishing special summer programs and retreats. While the details differ, after the morning service of chanting and listening to a short talk by the temple priest, the children are often ushered into classrooms where they receive further instruction. Thai temples will frequently recruit language, music, and dance teachers from Thai universities for extended periods to offer instruction to im-

migrant children. The Thai Buddhist community also invites learned monks from Thailand to lecture on the faith. Understanding that the ties with the homeland will be increasingly looser, the leadership is exploring ways to adapt the faith to modern America. The Tibetan and other Buddhist communities have similar programs.

Other Educational Institutions

In keeping with the strong emphasis on education, many Buddhist organizations have established learning centers and universities to promote the faith, to train new monks and academics, and to educate the American public. The following is a random list.

Chogyam Trungpa Rinpoche (1939–1987) founded the Naropa University in 1974. While Naropa was founded by a Tibetan, Rinpoche, who was trained in the Kaguy and Nyingma traditions, the university is largely nonsectarian with a diverse student body from varying cultures, backgrounds, and faith traditions. It offers instruction on Buddhist meditative practices with traditional Western scholasticism and art. Located in Colorado, the university offers both undergraduate and graduate degrees that include contemplative psychology, environmental studies, music, religious studies, and writing and literature.

Located in Redwood City, California, the Sati Center for Buddhist Studies combines academic study with rigorous practice in meditation, primarily focusing on the Theravāda tradition. Under the auspices of the Sati Institute for Theravāda

Studies, the center offers graduate degrees: master of Buddhist studies and master of divinity in collaboration with the Institute of Buddhist Studies. Sati has a Buddhist chaplaincy training program for those wishing to become volunteer or professional chaplains in hospitals, hospices, jails, and other institutions where spiritual care is needed.

University of the West, formerly Hsi Lai University, in Hacienda Heights, California, offers a wide range of certificate, undergraduate, and graduate degree programs. Founded in 1990 by Hsing Yun of Foguang Shan of Taiwan, the university aims to "provide a whole person education in a context informed by the wisdom and values of Buddhism and facilitate cultural appreciation and understanding between East and West." With this mission, those who are enrolled in secular disciplines such as business or mathematics are required to take classes in cross-cultural relationships and Buddhist philosophy. The campus itself is alcohol and tobacco free, in concert with the values of a Buddhist lifestyle. The university opened the Nan Tien Institute in Berkeley, California, in 2011.

Dharma Realm Buddhist Association is the umbrella organization that sponsors a number of educational efforts, including the Developing Virtue Elementary School (est. 1976) and Developing Virtue Secondary School (est. 1981), the Buddhist Realm Buddhist University (est. 1976 and accredited by Western Association of Schools and Colleges in 2013), and the Institute of World Religions (est. 1976). Developing Virtue Secondary School was accredited by the Western Association of Schools and Colleges (WASC) in 2007. These institu-

tions were inspired by Venerable Master Hsuan Hua (1918–1995).

The Institute for World Religions in Berkeley, California, was the inspiration and plan of Venerable Master Hsuan Hua and Cardinal Paul Yu Bin (1901–1978), who believed that harmony among the world's religions is an indispensable prerequisite for a just and peaceful world. The institute sponsors programs designed to bring the major religious traditions together in discourse on issues meaningful to the contemporary world. The institute also participates in local and global interfaith initiatives for constructive engagement.

Barre Center for Buddhist Studies, located in Barre, Massachusetts, offers courses in Buddhist practice, history, ethics, and meditation as well as workshops, retreats, and self-study programs with grounding in insight meditation. The institute was founded in 1975 by Joseph Goldstein, co-founder of the Insight Meditation Society (IMS) with Jack Kornfield and Sharon Salzberg. In addition to regular classes the center also offers special intensive programs on topics such as Buddhist ethics, Buddhist psychology, and *vipassanā* meditation practice, as well as a self-study distance-based program.

Founded in 1992, the Namgyal Monastery Institute of Buddhist Studies of Ithaca, New York, is a branch of the Namgyal Monastery in Dharamsala, India. It was established to offer Western students a Tibetan Buddhist education in a monastic setting. Courses are taught by both ordained Tibetan monks and other visiting teachers and focus on a core program of Tibetan language, Buddhist philosophy, and *sūtra* study. The institute also offers shorter courses along with workshops and retreats. Full-time and part-time programs are officered as well as resident options.

New England Institute of Buddhist Studies (NEIBS) in Connecticut was founded in 2004. NEIBS is a nonsectarian program focusing on Mahāyāna and Shin Buddhist traditions, providing courses and workshops, seminars and training programs for the New England community. For those interested in Buddhism outside the Connecticut/Massachusetts area, the institute offers a number of distance learning courses. Courses on topics from basic Buddhism, mindfulness practice, and altar creation are offered.

Under the guidance of Khenchen Thrangu Rinpoche and Khenpo Tsultrim Gyamtso Rinpoche, in 1996 Dzogchen Ponlop Rinpoche founded Nitartha Institute for Higher Buddhist Learning in Seattle, Washington; its parent organization is Nitartha International, an educational organization dedicated to the preservation of Tibet's heritage of religious and philosophical texts. Modeled after the Tibetan monastic college system, the institute offers an intensive course of study, combining the study of core Buddhist texts and commentaries with training in analytical meditation.

These above-mentioned educational initiatives are just a sampling of the teaching institutions that Buddhist organizations have established. As increasing numbers of Buddhists enter the United States, so does the need for specialized centers. These establishments also serve those who are not born into the Buddhist faith, but are interested in Buddhism.

Christina R. Yanko

See also: Entries: Buddhist Churches of America; Hsi Lai Temple; Honpa Hongwanji Mission of Hawai'i; Imamura, Yemyō

Further Reading

Dharma School Department, Buddhist Churches of America. *Jin Shin Kyō Nin Shin: Dharma School Teacher's Guide*. 4 vols. San Francisco: Buddhist Churches of America, 1981.

Dutt, Sukumar. *Buddhist Monks and Monasteries of India, Their History and Their Contribution to Indian Culture*. London: George Allen and Unwin, 1962

Fields, Rick. *How the Swans Came to the Lake, a Narrative History of Buddhism in America*. Boston: Shambhala Press, 1992.

Matsueda, Tsukasa, ed. *Iron Chain to Golden Chain, Dharma High School Readings*. San Francisco: Buddhist Churches of America, 1993.

Seager, Richard Hughes. *Buddhism in America*. New York: Columbia University Press, 1999.

Buddhist Meditation

There is no single term in Buddhism that corresponds exactly with the English word "meditation." A wide range of contemplative Buddhist practices are rendered differently across traditions and texts, sometimes called *dhyāna, chan, zen, śamatha, vipaśyanā* (Pāli: *vipassanā*), *jñana* (Pāli: *jhāna*), *bhāvanā, samādhi, satipatthanā*, or simply "mindfulness." Meditation can encompass simple, brief exercises in attention and focused awareness, up to profound and prolonged mental training requiring years of practice under the guidance of an accomplished and wise teacher. The rich diversity of meditation styles illustrates the Buddhist idea that "84,000 methods exist because there are 84,000 different kinds of people." Thus, meditation techniques may differ due to geographical circumstances, cultural particularities, psychological dispositions, and personality types.

While the actual forms of meditation vary widely across traditions and schools, all share the same philosophical foundation, the Four Noble Truths; and all rely on a common method of training, *śīla, samādhi, prajñā*. The Buddha devised this system of study and practice after his own awakening and from his subsequent meditation on that enlightenment. Known as the Middle Way, it embraced a path of moderation that avoided the extremes of eternalism and nihilism, austerities and sensual indulgence. Wishing to share the deep understanding derived from his insight into the nature of reality, Gautama Buddha encapsulated his teaching into Four Noble Truths and the Eightfold Path. Together they provide the unifying themes and conceptual framework for all Buddhist thought.

It is important to remember that the Buddha saw himself less as a teacher of philosophy than a healer of *duḥka* or suffering—the stress, unease, anxiety that attend the ever-changing uncertainty of human experience. While still a young prince, as Siddhārtha Gautama, he observed the inexorable flow of life as it moves from birth, through aging, to sickness, until finally ending in death. Awareness of *anitya* or the transient state of affairs (the unstable, uncertain, shifting, and impermanent nature of things), he held, either consciously or unconsciously overshadows all of existence. Expressed as a disenchanted sense of burning oppressiveness in one of his early teachings, the

Fire Sermon, it was this concern and the quest for a solution to it that form the backdrop for the Noble Truths. Simply stated they are: suffering (*duḥka*) exists; suffering is caused by *avidyā* or confusion and *tṛṣna* (lit. "thirst") or craving; craving can be ended, resulting in *Nirvāṇa* or perfect happiness and liberation; and there is a *mārga* or Way to do so called the Eightfold Path. These eight ways (appropriate views, thoughts, speech, actions, livelihood, effort, mindfulness, and concentration) in turn were summed up in three interconnected types of training: *śīla*, virtuous conduct or morality, which lays the ground for *samādhi* or contemplative equanimity, which in turn gives birth to *prajñā* or insight and wisdom. Meditation falls within the second grouping, *samādhi*.

After teaching the Four Noble Truths to his first disciples in the Deer Park, Śākyamuni Buddha spoke of three stages of practice and understanding, called the "three turnings" of the Four Truths. In the first stage, one acquires a theoretical knowledge from reading, study, and learning that they are true *(pariyatti)*. Then, one pursues a direct understanding of the teachings by putting them into practice *(patipatti)*. Third, as a result of refining and perfecting one's practice, one realizes a profound awakening and becomes conscious of one's true nature *(pativedha)*—being a Buddha. This approach, beginning with a theoretical understanding that progresses to correct practice and eventually finds fulfillment in direct awakening and liberation, constitutes the essence of Buddhism. Buddhist meditation, thus, is sometimes rendered as *patipatti*, meaning the pursuit of the teaching through practice.

The goal in Buddhism is to bring one-self and others to awakening through rep-licating the enlightenment experience of the Buddha, or as the *Avataṃsaka Sūtra* says, "to walk the same path the Buddha walked." Self-effort and self-understand-ing ("self-power") is considered indispen-sable to spiritual liberation. Thus, Buddhism is by its very nature soteriologi-cal (effecting liberation), as seen in the fa-mous passage from the *Dhammapada*:

No one saves you but yourself
No one can; no one may.
You yourself must walk the Path—
Buddhas only show the way.

Buddhahood or sagehood is not, strictly speaking, transcendent. Rather it is seen as a quality with which every person is born. The concept of innate depravity is absent from the Buddhist teachings. To become a sage is simply to recover one's fundamen-tal innocence, to take over one's self com-pletely by returning to one's pristine state of mind and of heart, called "buddha-na-ture." Such activity of reclamation is called "self-cultivation." So central is this notion of "self-power" vs. "other power" (reliance on external agency) that Bud-dhism is often seen less as a religion than a transformative teaching encompassing various systems of philosophy (*prajñā*), meditation (*samādhi*), and ethics (*śīla*). Many Buddhists prefer the term *Buddhad-harma* (the teachings of the Buddha) to the term "Buddhism," in which it is often classified as a "major world religion." Moreover, this classification is disputed by some scholars because a Buddha is not a god, *Nirvāṇa* (the Buddhist goal) is not a

heaven, and a Buddha cannot save anyone through religion, as there is no self or soul (*atman*) to save. Buddhism regards itself as a system of training in conduct, medita-tion, and understanding, which taken to-gether presents a path leading to the end of suffering.

Buddhist meditation usually entails some form of settling the body, regulating the breath, and calming the mind. The re-mote preparation for this exercise is a mor-ally upright life; a more immediate preparation is the control of one's thoughts and tempering of one's emotions. An erect sitting posture is generally recommended, but Buddhist meditation can be practiced while sitting, standing, walking, and even lying down. Each form consists of specific reflective practices during which the mind temporarily withdraws from external dis-tractions and sensory stimulation by fo-cusing on a meditation topic or object of concentration. During the exercise of meditation, attention is also given to watching over one's sensations, with a view to keeping external stimuli from dominating the senses. The mind should be concentrated upon itself, to the exclu-sion of all distracting thought. Two of the more prevalent forms of Buddhist medita-tion are *vipaśyanā* and *chan* or *zen*.

Vipaśyanā has been translated as "in-sight meditation" as it entails insight into the three marks of all conditioned things: impermanence, nonself, and unsatisfactori-ness noted above. It is an abbreviation of the fuller term *śamatha-vipaśyanā*, de-scribing two poles of a contemplative pro-cess involving quieting/calming (*śamatha*) followed by insight (*vipaśyanā*). Rather than seeing them as two distinct types of meditation—*śamatha* as tranquility meditation and *vipaśyanā* as insight meditation—they work in tandem, each supporting and balancing the other. The preparatory work of pacifying discursive thoughts and emotions strengthens insight (*vipaśyanā*); and insight keeps the calm tranquility of *śamatha* from becoming dull and stagnant.

Vipaśyanā itself does not connote an altered state of consciousness, but rather a lucid and clear state of seeing, and so is better rendered as "clear seeing" or a "deep seeing" of things as they really are directly, as opposed to understanding indirectly by use of reason, argument, or learning. The scholar-monk Henepola Gunaratana described *vipaśyanā* as:

Looking into something with clarity and precision, seeing each component as distinct and separate, and piercing all the way through so as to perceive the most fundamental reality of that thing.

Śamatha-vipaśyanā employs exercises in which *satipaṭṭhāna*, "the four foundations of mindfulness," and *anapanasati*, "mindfulness breathing," are used as focusing devices for honing insight into the above three marks. *Smṛtyupasthāna* (Pāli: *satipaṭṭhāna*) or the four foundations of mindfulness are:

- mindfulness of body (or breath)
- mindfulness of feelings or sensations
- mindfulness of mind or consciousness/ mental processes, and
- mindfulness of mental phenomena or mental objects (Dharmas)

Śamatha and *vipaśyanā* were used together as a basis for developing meditative concentration (*samādhi*) and for mastering a more complete focused awareness (*dhyāna*). Then, based on *dhyāna*, one could eliminate mental defilements (*kleśa*) that impeded awakening (*bodhi*) and bring release from suffering (*duḥka*). The monk Thanisarro notes:

Although mindfulness is helpful in fostering vipaśyanā, it's not enough for developing *vipassanā* to the point of total release. Other techniques and approaches are needed as well. In particular, *vipassanā* needs to be teamed with samatha (śamatha)–the ability to settle the mind comfortably in the present–so as to master the attainment of strong states of absorption, or jhāna (dhyāna). Based on this mastery, samatha (śamatha) and *vipassanā* (vipaśyanā) are then applied to a skillful program of questioning, called appropriate attention, directed at all experience: exploring events not in terms of me/not me, or being/ not being, but in terms of the four noble truths. The meditator pursues this program until it leads to a fivefold understanding of all events: in terms of their arising, their passing away, their drawbacks, their allure, and the escape from them. Only then can the mind taste release.

The more technical and frequently used term for meditation used in Buddhist sources is *dhyāna*. *Dhyāna* simply means "stilling thoughts" or "deep concentration." It refers to the various meditative states of stillness and focused awareness the mind of the practitioner, once freed from distractions, experiences in progressive stages of depth and clarity, discernment and insight. The terms *chan* in Chinese and *zen* in Japanese are both phonetic transcriptions of the Sanskrit term *dhyāna*. *Dhyāna* is sometimes used interchangeably with the term *samādhi*, or described as a preliminary condition of entering *samādhi*—a nondualistic state of awareness arising from deep concentration characterized by purity, lucidity, and tranquility. *Samādhi* forms the cornerstone in the development of Right Concentration, the eighth element of the Eightfold Path. Prerequisites for properly undertaking *dhyāna* meditation include purity (*śīla*; moral rectitude) and the elimination of certain hindrances that disturb the mind and obstruct clear seeing or insight. The five *nīvaraṇa* are sensuous desire, *kāmacchanda*; hatred, *vyāpāda*; sloth and torpor, *styāna-middha*; restlessness and anxiety, *auddhatya-kauṛtya*; and skeptical doubt, *vivikitsā*.

If not eliminated, they hinder one-pointedness of mind, physical and mental ease, emotional stability, and the confidence necessary for deeper concentration. Both *chan* and *zen* describe a state of mind that while free of the five hindrances is not frozen. As the Sixth Chinese Patriarch, Huineng (638–713), says, "It is nowhere attached, yet everywhere engaged." As with most forms of Buddhist meditation, *chan* and *zen* is not strictly speaking a meditation style as it is a quality of mind—the ability to see events clearly in the present moment and to respond appropriately.

One of the foremost texts outlining the philosophy behind *chan* Buddhist meditation is the *Platform Sūtra of the Sixth Patriarch*. The essence of this *Sūtra* is that all beings have the Buddha-nature; all can become Buddha. The text proposes that human nature at root is the Buddha-nature. Full awakening is presented not as a future state or a distant place, but available here and now, "right within one's own mind." Thus, two main themes anchor this classic and the Buddhist theory of meditation: an immanent and universal potential for Buddhahood, and a direct approach to understanding, sometimes called "the direct teaching" as the way to realize it. Meditation has only one purpose: to activate the human potential for liberation and wisdom lying dormant but fully complete within each sentient being.

Since this inherent capacity is considered to be whole and complete, ever-present, and lacking nothing, Buddhist meditation offers no extrinsic reward or measure of achievement. Enigmatic language is often employed to express its goals and outcomes, such as "markless," "nonabiding," and "attaining nothing-to-attain." During meditation exercise, one seeks neither thought nor even understanding, but "nothing whatsoever," so that one's original nature can manifest naturally and immediately—the nature that is perfectly good. As the *Platform Sūtra* says,

> You should now believe that the knowledge and vision of the Buddha is just your own mind; there is no other Buddha. . . . Why don't you immediately see, right within your own mind, the true reality of your original nature?

Common Misconceptions

While anyone can do Buddhist meditation, even without formally becoming a Buddhist ("Taking the Three Refuges"), this does not mean that Buddhist meditation is undisciplined and antinomian, lacking formal rules, precepts, and guidelines. For example, meditation without *śīla* is enjoined in most texts as being unbeneficial and unproductive, analogized as "cooking sand hoping to get rice." Contrary to popular portrayals, Buddhist meditation is not pursued to gain psychic powers, or as a trance-like escape from reality, nor as a spiritual vision quest. Rather, contemplative practice is intended as a systematic inquiry into the nature of reality entailing self-awareness, self-discipline, dispassion, and discernment. The goal is not to "get enlightened" but rather to disentangle oneself from habitual tendencies such as craving, aversion, and delusion, which cover one's inherent bright nature. Another common misrepresentation is that Buddhist meditation is anti-intellectual or dismissive of learning. In fact, rigorous textual study, devotional rituals, and instructional classes usually complement traditional training in meditation. The Chinese scholar-monk and meditation master, Zhiyi (538–597 CE), criticized an unbalanced emphasis on "meditation alone," portraying it as an "extreme" view and practice. He insisted that theory and praxis were "like the two wings of a bird"—both were needed to fly.

Buddhist meditation does not in itself result in any lasting insight into the nature of reality, or bring about the release from suffering (*duḥka*), or the realization of the transcendent state of *Nirvāṇa*. *Nirvāṇa*, according to the Buddha, is simply the cessation of suffering, and this can occur only with the eliminations of the afflictions (*kleśa*). *Kleśa* refers to the latent tendencies and negative proclivities that cause mental and physical distress, agitation, and thus hinder practice and prevent the realization of awakening or *bodhi*. While doing meditation is generally considered necessary for awakening, it is not an end in itself, nor is it sufficient for this goal. It is merely a means to an end, and as such a skillful expedient or *upāya*.

Like all Buddhist spiritual practices, meditation is portrayed as an instrument to be used in one's quest of the Way. Once the Way is reached, the instrument should be set aside, just as the fishing net can be put away once the fish has been caught. In a famous parable, the Buddha used an analogy of a raft to describe the teaching of expediency:

> Suppose, monks, there is a man journeying on a road and he sees a vast expanse of water of which this shore is perilous and fearful, while the other shore is safe and free from danger. But there is no boat for crossing nor is there a bridge for going over from this side to the other. So the man thinks: "This is a vast expanse of water; and this shore is perilous and fearful, but the other shore is safe and free from danger. There is, however, no boat here for crossing, nor a bridge for going over from this side to the other. Suppose I gather reeds, sticks, branches and foliage, and bind them into a raft." Now that

man collects reeds, sticks, branches and foliage, and binds them into a raft. Carried by that raft, laboring with hands and feet, he safely crosses over to the other shore. Having crossed and arrived at the other shore, he thinks: "This raft, indeed, has been very helpful to me. Carried by it, laboring with hands and feet, I got safely across to the other shore. Should I not lift this raft on my head or put it on my shoulders, and go where I like?" No. He should wisely set the raft down and be unburdened.

By acting thus, monks, would that man do what should be done with a raft.

Even so, monks, is the parable of the raft Dharma taught by me for crossing over, not for retaining. The Dharma, which I speak, is like a raft. Even Dharma should be relinquished, how much the more that which is not Dharma.

Conclusion

Billed as a refuge from the stresses of the world and as an exercise to calm the mind, meditation is commonplace in the modern America experience since D. T. Suzuki (1870–1966), Suzuki Shunryū (1904–1971), and their followers popularized Japanese Zen meditation in the 1950s. Today the interested person can choose to practice the Chinese form of *Zen* or *Chan* and Korean, Mongolian, Tibetan, and Vietnamese and other Mahāyāna meditation practices. Theravāda meditation is practiced at Thai, Cambodian, Myanmarian (Burmese), and Laotian temples. *Seiza* or sitting meditation is often part of the devotional Japanese Pure Land services. After learning some of the techniques, many practice meditation in the quiet of their homes.

Martin J. Verhoeven

See also: Entries: Tripiṭaka (Buddhist Canon); *Yoga*

Further Reading

Cleary, Thomas. *Stopping and Seeing: A Comprehensive Course in Buddhist Meditation by Chih-I.* Translated by Thomas Cleary. Boston: Shambhala, 1997.

Hsuan Hua. *The Chan Handbook: Talks about Meditation.* Burlingame, CA: Dharma Realm Buddhist Association, 2006.

Huineng. *Dharma Jewel Platform Sūtra of the Sixth Patriarch.* Buddhist Text Translation Society. Burlingame, CA: Dharma Realm Buddhist Association, 2014.

Kawahata, Aiyoshi. *Universal Meditation, Key to Mental and Physical Health.* Union City, CA: Heian International, 1984.

Keown, Damien. *Buddhism: A Very Short Introduction.* Oxford: Oxford University Press, 1997.

Khantipalo, Bikkhu. *Calm and Insight. A Buddhist Manual for Meditators.* London: Curzon Press, 1984.

Kiyota, Minoru, ed. *Mahāyāna Buddhist Meditation: Theory and Practice.* Honolulu: University of Hawai'i Press, 1978.

Luk, Charles. *Ch'an and Zen Teaching.* 3 vols. Berkeley: Shambhala, 1971.

Nyanaponika. *The Heart of Buddhist Meditation.* London: Rider, 1962.

Reps, Paul. *Zen Flesh, Zen Bones.* Rutland, VT: C. E. Tuttle, 1957.

(Sramana) Zhiyi. *The Essentials of Buddhist Meditation.* Seattle: Kalavinka Press, 2009.

Burmese Americans

Since 1962 when the military regime took over Burma (Myanmar), Burmese who have immigrated to the United States have done so primarily to seek political refuge and, secondarily, economic opportunities and/or religious freedom. The term "Burmese Americans" in this entry refers not only to children of Burmese immigrants and refugees who, by the place of their birth (*jus soli*), are legally considered American citizens, but also to the conjoined diversity of both indigenous (e.g., Karen, Chin, Burman) and nonindigenous (e.g., Chinese, Indian) migrants who have resettled in the United States. After a quick overview of Burma, this entry will briefly explore the historical conditions and circumstances that have resulted in the arrival of Chinese Burmese, Indian Burmese, and the Karen to the United States. This entry will also include a section that outlines the practices, beliefs, and places of worship for Burmese American Buddhists.

With a population of over 50 million people and comprising a geographical area almost the size of the state of Texas, Burma occupies the largest land area of any country in Southeast Asia. It is a multiethnic and multireligious country, with the ethnic Burmans or the "lowland people" comprising about two-thirds of the inhabitants. The remaining one-third of the population encompasses over 130 tribal groups, divided according to linguistic origin as determined by the former Burmese military regime as having distinct ethnicities. These so-called "highland people" are grouped as follows: Shan, Kachin, Karen, Kayah, Chin, Rakhine or Arakanese, and Mon. In addition to "highland people," the Indians and the Chinese are two of the largest nonindigenous minorities in the country as they arrived in large numbers during the British colonial rule. To that effect, with many Indian and Chinese achieving prosperity through their association with the Burmese colonizers, consequently these groups have been objects of resentment by many Burmans. Comprising about 85 percent of the population, Buddhists are the dominant religious group of the country; the ethnic Indians are mostly Hindus or Muslims; and 20 to 30 percent of the Karen are Christians.

Historical Developments

The timeline of British colonial reign in Burma occurred from 1886 to 1942, which during this period introduced new ethnic tensions in part by opening the country to Indian and Chinese migrants. After Burma was incorporated into the British Indian Empire, domestic and foreign commerce was in need of civil servants and other trained personnel to support the infrastructure and the new bureaucracy. It was during this period of transition that the British introduced Indian civil servants trained as British bureaucrats into Burma. As a result, thousands of Indian professionals and peasants whom the Burmese had traditionally been engendered to despise flooded into the land of the pagodas. By the turn of the 20th century, many Burman peasants found themselves working for foreigners in their own country and, by the 1930s, Indians became the numerical majority in the city of Rangoon (Yangon), the former capital of Burma.

Ta Mwe Paw reads the Baptist Hymnal with her son Shar Eh Htoo, left, and niece Paw Ray Wah, right, on December 12, 2010, during the University Hills Baptist Church service at the Cook Recreation Center. Many of the church's congregants are refugees from Asia and Africa. The church of about 100 members moved into the recreation center in late September 2010. (AAron Ontiveroz/The Denver Post/Getty Images)

Contrary to the Indian migrants, the Chinese, particularly in the coastal regions of China, were "pushed" by acute economic and political dislocation at home and "pulled" by the British, who needed more manpower in Burma to extract teak, petroleum, and other natural resources. During this period of British colonialism, large numbers of Chinese migrants came not from the neighboring Yunnan Province but from Xiamen and other coastal areas of China. They were laborers, merchants, traders, moneylenders, small storekeepers, middlemen, and engaged in a variety of other occupations that were rarely filled by the Burmans or the Europeans. These opportunities afforded many Chinese the opportunity to establish private businesses across the country. Over the years, many Indians and Chinese became wealthy through their association with the British, which evoked feelings of anger and resentment among the Burmans. Occasionally, these feelings exploded into violence, as they did between 1930 and 1932, when there was a cycle of anti-Indian and anti-Chinese riots in southern Burma.

Moving to post–World War II, General Aung San (father of Aung San Suu Kyi), leader of the Anti-Fascist People's Freedom League (AFPFL), formed an interim government, which led to the full independence of Burma on January 4, 1948. General Aung San, however, was assassinated before Burma gained independence from the British. Therefore, U Nu, who became the first prime minister of the independent Burma, succeeded General Aung San. However, U Nu's government was preoccupied with the problems of banditry and insurgency in the countryside, the threat of secession of the Shan and Karenni from the Union of Burma, and the lack of trained Burmese professionals in the cities. These and other problems led to the involuntary surrender of U Nu's power to General Ne Win in 1958. Under his leadership, Ne Win was successful in reducing rebel activity and restoring some degree of law and order. After extending his term as a caretaker governor, Ne Win stepped down in 1960 under increased pressure from the voters for an election to restore democracy. With the pledge to make Buddhism the state religion, U Nu was reelected as the prime minister but, in 1962, when U Nu had difficulty yet again in stabilizing the country, General Ne Win staged a coup d'état with the intention of ruling the country indefinitely and, in fact, ruled Burma with an iron fist for over 20 years (1962–1988).

During his two-and-a-half decade of reign, Ne Win established his own Revolutionary Council, imposed his Burmese Way to Socialism, and implemented economic policies that called for the nationalization of all foreign and domestic businesses, including retail shops, many of which were owned by ethnic Indians and Chinese. After their means of livelihood had been taken away from them, hundreds of thousands of Indian Burmese and Chinese Burmese were expelled from the country with draconian thoroughness. As a case in point, in 1967 when the rice production suffered a dramatic decline due to the government's inappropriate management policies, Ne Win's government blamed the ethnic Chinese for the collapsed economy; violence erupted in Rangoon and other major cities across the country, and many Chinese-owned houses and stores were destroyed. After the 1967 anti-Chinese riot, many ethnic Chinese left Burma and thousands immigrated to the United States under the new Immigration and Nationality Act of 1965. Unlike the ethnic Chinese, many ethnic Indians had already been forcefully exiled from Burma prior to 1965, so those who eventually resettled in the United States were remigrants in that they immigrated to the United States by way of another country other than Burma.

The Karen group is an indigenous minority who were thought to have migrated to Burma from both the Tibetan region and from Yunnan Province of China many centuries ago. The Karen state is located adjacent to the eastern part of Burma's borders with Thailand. During World War II, Karen soldiers provided invaluable assistance to the British forces in their fight against the Japanese. For this reason, after Burma gained independence in 1948 many Karen felt betrayed and abandoned by the British who did not support the self-determination efforts of the Karen people in that they were left on their own to seek autonomy or the political rights of an ethnic nationality. Consequently, the Karen suffered tremendously at the hands of the former and coercive military regime. In fact, this recriminatory and self-presumptive military regime enforced and framed ethnic-cleansing policies that have given human rights organizations, non-Burmese governments, scholars, and activists around the world explicit confirmation of the pillage of Karen villages, the raping of women, and the use of women and children as military porters. As a result, there are hundreds of thousands of Karen refugees in Thailand. In 2006, the U.S. State Department issued waivers to the "material support" provisions in the Patriot and Real ID Act, which have allowed thousands of Karen refugees to resettle in the United States. This resettlement of Karen refugees has already changed the face of the Burmese population in the United States, bringing with them unique refugee experiences and a Burmese/Thai cultural mimesis in and related to the Karen group.

While the term "Burmese" in this entry denotes all ethnic groups living in or from Burma, it is noteworthy to point out that what the Karen and ethnic Indians and Chinese in the United States have in common is that many in these groups do not identify themselves as Burmese. This is in part due to the Burmese ethnocentric policy that grants citizenship not on the basis of nativity (*jus soli*) but on the basis of having parents who are citizens of Burma, or by being born in Burma to a Burman mother. For the Karen, their identity is formed in part by their reaction to the incursive destructibility and exploitation they suffered at the hands of the dominant and coercive former military regime.

For Indians and Chinese, the ethnonationalist policies in Burma compelled them to adopt an essentially Burmese identity for the sake of economic and political survival. After immigrating to the United States, however, many Indians and Chinese reaffirmed the cultural aspects of their ethnicity that had been lost or discarded. In other words, practices that had been suppressed to conform to dominant ideologies when living in Burma became significant to the emerging and sustaining Indian Burmese and Chinese Burmese American voice in the United States. Consequently, many Indian Burmese and Chinese Burmese in the United States identify themselves on the census form not as "Burmese" but as members of their respective ethnic group or as part of the greater collectivity to which they had previously belonged.

Beliefs and Practices

In terms of religious affiliation, almost all Burmese immigrants and refugees who have resettled in the United States are either Buddhists or Christians. However, there are a small percentage of practicing Muslims among these displaced victims and consigned settlers. For the sake of this entry, the intercultural discussion of this text will focus exclusively on the beliefs and practices of Burmese Buddhists.

The fundamental symbols constituting the core of Burmese Buddhism are commonly recognized in Buddhist literature as the three jewels of Buddhism; namely, the Buddha, *Dhamma* (Skt: Dharma), and *Saṇgha*. The Buddha (Enlightened One) is the central figure of a historical person, Siddhattha Gotama (Skt: Siddhārtha Gautama), who, by recourse to his own efforts, attained *Nibbāna* (Skt: *Nirvāṇa*). He is the Buddha, "the Awakened One," and "Siddhattha," which literally means "the one who has achieved his goal." In Theravāda Buddhism, the Buddha serves as a model for those who would pursue the path of Enlightenment. The Dharma, or the teachings of the Buddha, is found in the Buddhist scriptures, the Tipitaka (Skt: Tripiṭaka), comprising three *pitaka* or "baskets": the Sutta (Skt: *Sūtra*) Pitaka, doctrinal discourse attributed to the Buddha; the Viniya (Skt: Vinaya) Pitaka, a code of conduct given by the Buddha to regulate the life of the monks and nuns; and the Abhidhamma (Skt: Abhidharma), a set of scholarly treatises on the teachings of the Buddha. At the broadest level, the *Saṅgha* is a community of all Buddhist believers, and in a narrower sense, it refers to the monastic community. Moreover, the monastic *Saṅgha* is what most Burmese think of when the word *Saṅgha* is used, and it is regarded by the Burmese as an essential component of their Buddhism. This is patently clear in the meaning behind the Burmese word for monastery or *pongyikyaung*, as the word *pongyi* is best translated as "monks" and the word *kyaung* in Burmese literally means "school." Hence, *pongyikyaung* literally means a school for the monks or monastery.

Pongyikyaung is established not simply for the transmission of the *Dhamma* (teachings of the Buddha) but for devoting one's life to the quest of liberation (*Nibbāna* in Pāli, or *Nirvāṇa* in Skt), and to assist others in that quest. The teachers

in this school or the *kyaung* are the monks. By renouncing all that is considered permanent, a monk represents a symbol of worldly renunciation. This usually involves giving up hopes and dreams for permanence and even renouncing the idea of absolute security. In this tradition, the role of the monk is not so much to render social service to others but to demonstrate in his own life that the Buddhist ideal can be approximated if not fully attained. He embodies a model of the Buddhist ideal toward which every Buddhist must strive, even if the monk himself may not attain it. Incapable of renouncing the world, laypeople participate in that ideal through almsgiving, charity, and other forms of venerating or showing respect to the monks. Moreover, while the division of status between the monks and the laypeople is clearly distinct, the lines of demarcation between the two ways of life remain fluid. A monk may leave his monkhood for reasons that seem important without the stigma of disgrace attached to him, and a layman (married or single) may be initiated into the monkhood without having to commit his entire life to this vocation. The curriculum is ongoing since it prepares those who are willing to dedicate their entire lives, or those wanting to spend some time in this sacred space, all in the quest of *Nibbāna*. In other words, it offers the layman, who is interested in accruing merits by experiencing the life of complete renunciation, to enroll in the same school in which the monks matriculate for life. The stability of place is an important element for cultivating a discipline in the quest of *Nibbāna*, a discipline many consider to be harsh, yet, nevertheless, one that prepares a person for the life of worldly renunciation. These various functions of the monastic school or *pongyikyaung* point to a symbiotic relationship between monks and laity in the Burmese Buddhist community.

In Burmese Buddhism, the relationship between the monks and the laity is also reciprocal. The monks are teachers of the *Dhamma* and exemplars of those who strive to follow the Buddha's path. In turn, the laypeople support the monks and acquire merits for a better rebirth. This reciprocal relationship is exemplified by the morning begging rounds of the monks and the offering of food by the laypeople. Indeed, every ceremony and every merit requested on the part of the lay devotees seems to conclude with some form of *dana* (giving), such as the offering of food to the monks. Because the monks are not allowed to cook for themselves, feeding and caring for the monks are uppermost daily concerns in the minds of the lay devotees. In this way, the relation of interdependence is established between the laity and the monks: The laity is responsible for providing the basic material needs of the monks, and the monks are to be "fields of merits" for the laity.

Like other types of Buddhism in Southeast Asia, Burmese Buddhism is essentially a hybrid religious system, comprising Theravāda Buddhism and also elements of various pre-Buddhist folk religions. Even the great King Anawrahta (1044–1077 CE), who was responsible for making Burma a Theravāda country, could not successfully convert the people in his Bagan Empire through imperial edicts. It was not until Anawrahta incorporated the pre-Buddhist practice of *natcultus* into Theravāda Buddhism that his subjects began to embrace the new religion. In other words, not all of the 85 or 90 percent of Buddhists in Burmese culture adhere strictly to the tenets of traditional Theravāda Buddhism. This is seen in the Burmese Buddhists' understanding of the Buddha and his teachings: While canonical teachings of Theravāda Buddhism holds that the Buddha is inaccessible upon entering *parinirvana (final extinction)*, Burmese Buddhists, especially in times of adversity, will enlist the help of the Buddha and other supernatural agents in the hope that they will be kept out of harm's way or spared from suffering. Indeed, at the level of everyday practice, Burmese Buddhists may solicit the aid of gods, spirits (*nat*), and even the Buddha to provide protection and relief from suffering. In addition, the teachings of the Buddha (*Dhamma*) is carefully observed by Burmese Buddhists, yet certain Burmese religious beliefs and practices challenge the teachings of the Pāli canon. In direct contradiction to the concept of *ānatta* (no-self or no-soul), many Burmese Buddhists, in their everyday life, acknowledge the existence of *leip-bya* or a soul substance in every human. There are special rites and rituals in Burmese Buddhism, recited by lay leaders and monks, especially in times of unfortunate death, to ensure that the *leip-bya* of a deceased person gets a proper sendoff to the next life. Indeed, for many Burmese Buddhist believers what gets transmigrated from one rebirth to another is none other than this *leip-bya*.

Burmese immigrant Buddhists in the United States have brought with them elements of this brand of hybrid Buddhism, which does not demand from its adherents an exclusive allegiance to any one deity. This is seen most clearly in the so-called informal or popular religion that takes place within the domestic setting or private realm. On the domestic altars of Burmese American Buddhists, it is not uncommon to find religious objects representing the Buddha, gods, (Skt *arahats*), bodhisattvas, and other spiritual beings. In Chinese Burmese Buddhist homes, one can usually find on their altars a figure of Guanyin, Goddess of Mercy, one of the most widely worshipped deities in China. Having said this, in other ethnically diverse Burmese American Buddhist homes, one can find a figure of the Virgin Mary and even a picture of Jesus Christ on their altars. In essence, these casts of supernatural characters tell us something about non-normative Buddhist beliefs within Burmese American Buddhism that are reinforced in their daily devotional practice at home.

While there is no one way to pray before the home altar, most devotees begin with prostrations before the altar at least three times in honor of the Triple Gem: Buddha, *Dhamma*, and *Saṇgha*. A recitation of the Five Precepts, a litany of prayers, and the sharing of merits generally follow this. To be more precise, a litany of prayers usually consists of an intercessory prayer, asking the various supernatural beings whose figures are on the altar to intercede for the devotee. Such a reliance on various deities, including the Buddha, patently contradicts the teachings of the Pāli canon, yet it is rarely recognized as such by the devotees themselves.

Most Burmese temples in the United States are residential homes designated as temples rather than bell-shaped *zedi* or pagodas that one usually associates with Burmese temples in Burma. These home temples offer the devotees opportunities to meditate, to chant, to listen to Dharma talks, and to engage in other merit-sharing rituals. Temples are sites for celebrating commemorative rituals (e.g., the birthday of the Buddha), rites of passage (e.g., Buddhist initiation rites), and other forms of ritual. Hence, for devout Buddhists, temples become sacred sites in which they acquire merits and where the reciprocal relationship between monks and laity are nurtured and developed. Temples also function as sociocultural centers for non-Buddhists and nominal Buddhists who come to various festivities at the temples not necessarily to cultivate their spirituality but to consume Burmese food, listen to Burmese music, and socialize with friends. The idea of temples as sites of cultural preservation and enhancing co-ethnic social networks reflects the social position of Burmese American Buddhists who are both racial and religious minorities in the United States.

Joseph Cheah

See also: Entries: Theravāda Buddhism

Further Reading

Bechert, Heinz. "To Be a Burmese Is to Be a Buddhist: Buddhism in Burma." In Heinz Bechert and Richard Gombrich, eds. *The World of Buddhism: Buddhist Monks and Nuns in Society and Culture*. London: Thames and Hudson, 1984.

Cheah, Joseph. *Race and Religion in American Buddhism: White Supremacy and Immigrant Adaptation*. New York: Oxford University Press, 2011.

Fink, Christina. *Living Silence: Burma under Military Rule*. London: Zed Books, 2001.

Spiro, Melford. *Buddhism and Society: A Great Tradition and Its Burmese Vicissitudes*. Berkeley: University of California Press, 1982.

Butoh

In the aftermath of World War II in Japan, Tatsumi Hijikata proclaimed that the dances of his time and culture could not adequately respond to the suffering and darkness that surrounded him. Critiquing the forms of traditional dance and the aesthetic denial of the body present in ballet, Hijikata (1928–1986) stripped dance to its bare bones (quite literally), developed a low center of bodily gravity, and gnarled his fingers and toes. This dance form, which ascribes to an avant-garde aesthetic, isolates the slightest of muscles, gnarls the movements of the body, and is often performed in the nude with seemingly androgynous bodies powdered white, is known as *butoh*. And with the work of second- and third-generation performers, this "dance of utter darkness" is growing out of Japan and sweeping across all of Asia, Europe, and the United States.

Though the roots of *butoh* are firmly planted in Japan, the work of contemporary performing groups such as Sankai Juku, the choreography of Yukio Waguri, and the use of all female performers in Shinonome Butoh have had a great impact on the aesthetics, cultures, and spiritualities in Southeast Asia and throughout Europe, the United States, and Canada. *Butoh* is a dance form that pushes traditional boundaries and challenges the status quo. Though the body is regarded more highly in the East than in the West, the employment of nude or seminude bodies in performance is still shocking. Furthermore, these bodies are often powdered white and the performers sometimes shave their heads, giving the dancers an androgynous look, thus ascribing to both the male and female characteristics of *yin* and *yang*. As Hijikata originally intended, the "idealized" body is not highly valued in *butoh*. Unlike ballet and many other classical dance forms, *butoh* does not place emphasis on dancers attaining svelte or emaciated bodies. Rather, pedestrian and average bodies are valued.

As *butoh* is regarded as the "dance of utter darkness," contemporary *butoh* performing groups are continuing Hijikata's legacy by revaluing this notion of darkness. While darkness does stem from the repressed and suffering part of life, *butoh* is not associated with typical notions of darkness: wickedness, evil, and so on. Rather, the darkness of *butoh* is rooted in the feminine divine/spirit. With the advent of this dance form, another forerunner of *butoh*, Kazuo Ohno (1906–2010), claimed that he learned *butoh* in his mother's womb: "All dances and all of the arts come from this source." From the dark warmth of the womb all humanity finds its advent and source of life, and for this reason, *butoh* maintains the darkness intertwined in the feminine spirit. The dark feminine principle, subconscious spontaneous life, is the main metaphor for *butoh*, its aesthetic core.

Thus, the valuing of the body, the reclaiming of darkness, and the manifestation of the divine feminine have been present in a variety of ways through the work of Sankai Juku, Yukio Waguri, and Shinonome Butoh. Because Sankai Juku, Waguri, and other less well-known American *butoh* companies tour regularly throughout the United States, Asian Americans are reminded of the history and heritage of *butoh* in performances, dance classes, and workshops.

Sankai Juku is an internationally known *butoh* dance troupe co-founded by Amagatsu Ushio in 1975. In 1980, Sankai Juku performed for the first time in Europe, playing at the Nancy International Festival in France, and then that same year at the Avignon Festival. In 1984 the group made North American debuts at the Toronto International Festival and the Los Angeles Olympic Arts Festival. Since 1990 Sankai Juku has performed throughout Asia in Singapore, Hong Kong, Taiwan, Korea, Indonesia, and Malaysia. In 1985 *butoh* made American headlines when a performer from Sankai Juku plummeted to his death in Seattle, Washington during one of their most famous choreographic works. The dance involves slowly unfurling their bodies from a fetal position while suspended upside down on a cord high above the ground; the supportive rope snapped and many audience members assumed the entire stunt was part of the choreography. Sankai Juku continues to perform this piece today.

In addition to the spread of *butoh* through Sankai Juku, Yukio Waguri's choreography has had tremendous impact on the religious aesthetic of Indonesia. The Jogja Arts Festival, a center for traditional Javanese art forms, hosted several *butoh* groups including Kohzensha Dance Company and Ahiru Dance Studio. Kohzensha Dance Company was founded by *butoh* dancer Yukio Waguri. Kohzensha's five dancers, including Waguri, interpreted his work, *Transforma*, in which Waguri blended Indonesian music composed by contemporary musician Djadug Ferianto with the movements of four *butoh* dancers. In an article in the *Jakarta Post*, Asip Hasani wrote, "Waguri is known for mixing *butoh* with other dance styles, including Indonesian styles. '*Butoh* has for years been explored in Western countries. Now I want butoh to find itself in Asia,' said Waguri, who has also studied with *butoh* founder, Tatsumi Hijikata." Though *butoh* is a distinctly Japanese art form, rooted in Japanese experiences, it has truly taken hold in the West, impacting the cultures and spiritualities of Japanese Americans in ways that are deep and profound. Waguri evokes the importance of *butoh* remaining true to its roots and not becoming too Westernized.

Finally, the work of an all-female *butoh* group is also influencing Asian spiritual cultures. While Sankai Juki and Kohzensha Dance Company affirm and embody the divine feminine aspects of *butoh*, the majority of their performers are male. In contrast, Shinonome Butoh is a group of three unique female dancers formed in 1999. *"Shinonome"* is the old Japanese word that evokes the sky brazened deep orange before dawn when darkness fades away in daylight. In this vein, the dancers in Shinonome Butoh ascribe to the *butoh* notions of darkness, but add their own personal and feminist interpretation.

Butoh values the human form, reclaims the notion of darkness, and stems from the divine feminine. These characteristics are manifested in the dances of Sankai Juki, Yukio Waguri, and Shinonome Butoh. Rooted in the subversion of Buddhist, Confucian, Shintō, and Christian values in the work of *butoh's* founder, Hijikata, *butoh* found a soul in the choreography of Ohno, a devout Baptist. These two seemingly disparate forerunners also embody the *yin* and *yang butoh* holds so dear. With the death of Hijikata at a young age due to liver damage *butoh* lived on, reminding dancers and audiences of the horror of war, the value of darkness, the primacy of the human body, and the inspiration of the feminine divine. And the soul of *butoh*, Ohno, continued this legacy through the advanced age of 103, offering performances even into his hundredth year.

The rawness of *butoh* has often been attributed to the experience of living through Hiroshima. For Japanese American performers of *butoh*, whose bodies no longer dwell in the lands that inspired Hijikata and Ohno to ground their feet into the earth, squat their knees as though picking rice, and gnarl their knuckles into fists of rage against war, occupation, and violence, *butoh* harkens their hearts, minds, and bodies to their homeland, connecting their spirits with those of the past, and reminding them that even the smallest glimmer of light is better appreciated in the darkness.

Angela Yarber

See also: Essays: Arts and Cultural Production

Further Reading

Barber, Stephen. *Hijikata: Revolt of the Body*. London: Creation Books, 2006.

Blakeley Klein, Susan. *Ankoku Buto: The Premodern and Postmodern Influences on the Dance of Utter Darkness*. Ithaca, NY: Cornell University Press, 1988.

Fraleigh, Sondra Horton. *Dancing into Darkness: Butoh, Zen, and Japan*. Pittsburgh: University of Pittsburgh Press, 1991.

Hijikata, Tatsumi. *Three Decades of Butoh Experiment, A Scab and a Caramel*. Tokyo: Yushi-Sha, 1993.

Kurihara, Nanako. *The Most Remote Thing in the Universe: Critical Analysis of Hijikata Tatsumi's Butoh Dance*. New York: New York University Press, 1996.

Ohno, Kazuo, Yoshito Ohno, and Toshio Mizohata. *Kazuo Ohno's World: From Without and Within*. Translated by John Barret. Middletown, CT: Wesleyan Press, 2004.

C

Calligraphy. *See Sho,* Calligraphy

Cambodian American Religions

The Cambodian American religious landscape is primarily Buddhist, but the history of religion in Cambodia is diverse. Cambodian and Cambodian American religious culture is a blend of influences mainly from India, but also China. Therefore, it reflects an intermixing of elements from Hinduism, Buddhism, Confucian, Islamic, and indigenous beliefs that are embedded in religious practices and beliefs. Together, these influences have forged a distinctively Khmer faith that has sustained Cambodians through the war and genocide that nearly destroyed their nation in the last third of the 20th century and helped anchor diaspora communities around the world, including the largest—in the United States.

History of Cambodian Religions

Historically, Hinduism (Shiva and Vishnu cults) and Buddhism have existed together in Cambodia from the 1st century BCE to the 14th century CE. Khmer religious expression finds different influences coming from Islam and Vietnamese religions. For instance, Cambodian Muslims are descendants of the Chams, who migrated from central Vietnam after the final defeat of the kingdom of Champa by the Vietnam-

ese in 1471. Cambodian Muslims adopted a fairly orthodox version of Sunni Islam and maintained links with other Muslim communities throughout Southeast Asia. There is also a small, heterodox Islam community, the Zahidin, who practice a form of Islam similar to that of the Muslim Chams of Vietnam, but who only pray once a week on Friday and observe Ramadan only the first, middle, and last day of the month. Khmer Muslims represent a close-knit community, marrying only within their own faith community. Their total population is more than 300,000 in Cambodia, but much smaller in the United States.

Khmer Theravāda Buddhism

Theravāda Buddhism ("the Way of the Elders") is the dominant faith in Cambodia, having been the state religion since the 13th century, enduring through French colonialism until the 1950s and after, until the 1970s Communist revolution under Pol Pot. The Khmer Rouge, as the Communists called themselves, ruthlessly attempted to remove religion from Cambodian life by destroying many temples and executing many of the *Sangha*, or Buddhist communities of monks and nuns. Most of the 3,600 temples that existed in Cambodia were destroyed, and fewer than 3,000 of the 50,000 monks survived the genocide. Not until 1979, following Vietnam's occupation of the country, was religion allowed to be

Kret, one of the Cambodian community leaders, speaks to an audience of 500 during a memorial service for the seven fire victims at Glory Buddhist Temple in Lowell, Massachusetts on July 13, 2014. (Matthew J. Lee/The Boston Globe via Getty Images)

practiced publicly again. However, the rebuilding process relied heavily on Theravāda monks from Thailand.

Khmer religion is best characterized as a combination of Buddhist, Hindu, indigenous folk, and Chinese beliefs and practices. However, most Khmer are Buddhist and hence share certain basic understandings and beliefs. The most central of these is the concept of *karma* (*kam*), the belief that one's actions in previous lives and the merit (*bon*) that one has accumulated determine one's current and future life situation. This is coupled with the notion of reincarnation, the belief that every individual is at a certain stage of the rebirth process. Many Khmer will invoke their understanding of *karma* to make sense of their current lives. According to Theravāda Buddhism, life is ultimately characterized by unease (*anicca*), obfuscated by the impermanence of all things. The first of the Four Noble Truths, taught by the historical Buddha Siddhārtha, envisions life as suffering (*dukkha*) that one is expected to endure because the suffering has an end.

Khmer Folk Religious Elements

Khmer folk religion conceptualizes various spirits and souls that influence people's lives—positively or negatively. Khmer believe that there is a guardian mother spirit, an "invisible mother" (*me ba*) who protects a baby during the early years of infancy, but who can also be potentially dangerous. The invisible mother is a "spirit mother" of the baby in a previous life, who watches over her baby with much love and affection during the early years of infancy. However, many Khmer elders express ambivalence toward the invisible mother because she is potentially dangerous if the baby is left alone. Central to Khmer understanding of life is the belief that there are many nonhuman life forms cohabiting with humans; some are benign while others are frightening. Spirits of locality (e.g., mountains and villages) are called *qnak ta* ("ancestral people") and are relatively benign. Spirits of known or unknown deceased persons, ghosts of the dead (e.g., *khmoc lan* and *bray*), victims of murder, or babies who die at childbirth are potentially dangerous.

Belief and Practice in the United States

Khmer Buddhism in the United States plays a huge role in the socialization and moral education of younger Khmer Americans. The majority of Khmer Americans identify themselves as Buddhists, to the extent that ethnic and religious identities are deeply entwined. In Cambodia, Buddhist temples are places where young people, especially boys, learn moral lessons and proper respect toward elders. In the United States, many Khmer elders attribute the immorality among young Khmer Americans to the scarcity of trained Khmer monks and the shortage of temples. The life and narrative of the historical Buddha is a popular story in Khmer families. Adapting to American culture, Khmer American children fre-

quently enjoy watching Bernardo Bertolucci's film *Little Buddha* (1993), starring Keanu Reeves.

Often, because of the lack of financial resources to construct a community temple, many Khmers will construct a Buddhist shrine in private residences. Temples are important sites not only for moral education and children's socialization but also for rituals, including exorcisms and funerals. Many Khmers will perform merit transfer ceremonies on behalf of their family members who died under Pol Pot, to provide their deceased with comfort and chances for a good rebirth. In Buddhism, *karma* chains all living creatures in the endless cycles of reincarnation and suffering. Merit is the counterweight of *karma* and may be gained primarily by supporting the community of monks and nuns, or by assisting the needy, or by meditating on compassion and peace. Merit is also transferable. Hence, the living may perform rituals and offerings to earn merit, which may then be transferred to their loved ones to assist them in the afterlife and in getting reborn into the human realm. When available, a monk is preferred; however, a lay religious person may agree to perform the necessary rituals. This is not to suggest that Khmer communities are not able to produce the necessary capital to finance the construction of a temple. For instance, in 1984, about 800 Khmers in Portland, Maine, established a nonprofit organization, the Watt Samaki "Unity Temple," to raise funds for the purchase and construction of a temple. In the mid-1990s, the United Cambodian Buddhist Central Services, a large temple and community center, was established in Lincoln Heights,

Los Angeles, California. However, if the Khmer community are unable to afford the construction of a community temple, a monk or lay devotee may set up a shrine in his or her home, which becomes the de facto community temple, as is the case with an inner-city public housing community in Oakland, California. If there is no Khmer temple to be found, Khmer Americans will go to Thai, Vietnamese, or Chinese American Buddhist temples to fulfill their religious needs and duties.

Most Khmer jointly worship and perform rituals important in both Buddhism and folk traditions. There is no tension, no struggle for membership, between Theravāda Buddhism and spirits in folk belief; many times one will find shrines to local tree spirits in front of Buddhist temples, or shrines to ancestral people around a Buddhist temple. In the United States, in Khmer American communities, Buddhist temples become repositories of Khmer culture, brokers in cultural adaptation, and centers of community solidarity and Khmer identity.

Jonathan H. X. Lee

See also: Entries: Bhante Dharmawara; Cambodian Americans and Mormonism; Cham Americans; Mahā Ghosananda; Watt Samaki

Further Reading

Cadge, Wendy. *Heartwood: The First Generation of Theravāda Buddhism in America*. Chicago: University of Chicago Press, 2004.

Lee, Jonathan H. X. "Cambodian/Cambodian American Religiosity and Culture Work." In Jonathan H. X. Lee, ed. *Cambodian American Experiences: Histories, Communities, Cultures, and Identities*. Dubuque, IA: Kendall and Hunt, 2010.

Smith-Hefner, Nancy J. *Khmer American: Identity and Moral Education in a Diasporic Community*. Berkeley: University of California Press, 1999.

Cambodian Americans and Mormonism

The Church of Jesus-Christ of Latter-day Saints was founded in April 1830 in western New York. It currently has over 14 million members worldwide, including over 10,000 Cambodian American members in the United States, and about 11,000 members in the kingdom of Cambodia. The church was founded by Joseph Smith Jr., who members believe was a prophet called by God to restore the original church as organized and established by Jesus Christ. One feature distinguishing it from other Christian churches is the use of other scriptures in addition to the Bible, including the Book of Mormon, which Mormons believe was translated by Joseph Smith from ancient records containing the writings of prophets who inhabited the American hemisphere between 600 BCE to 400 CE. The book is named after the ancient prophet Mormon, the chief abridger of the ancient records. Due to their belief in the Book of Mormon as another testament of Jesus Christ, church members are often called Mormons, the church is often called the Mormon Church, and the combination of doctrine, culture, and lifestyle unique to the church is called Mormonism. While the church prefers Latter-day Saints (LDS) and Church of Jesus Christ or just "the church" to refer to the members and short name of the church respectively, church leaders and members have embraced the nickname, as evidenced by the church's recent "I'm a Mormon" public relations campaign, and use of websites such as www.mormon.org to disseminate information and share beliefs.

The church did not have a presence in Cambodia prior to the Vietnam War. However, in response to the ensuing refugee crisis, the church established the LDS Refugee Relief Fund to help refugees of any religion throughout the world. The church also sent welfare service missionaries to the Panat Nikom refugee camp in Thailand to provide humanitarian assistance to Cambodian and other Southeast Asian refugees. Service missionaries adhered to restrictions on proselytizing established by the United Nations.

Cambodian Americans first began joining the church in the late 1970s and early 1980s after arriving in the United States through refugee resettlement programs. Without any coordinated efforts, across the country large numbers of Cambodians (and other Southeast Asian refugees) began to join the church. With a rapidly increasing number of Cambodian Americans attending local English-speaking congregations (called "wards"), local church leaders felt the need to organize separate branches where the language and other needs of the Cambodian members could be more easily accommodated. Unlike wards, branches do not have strict geographical boundaries, and thus they allowed Cambodian members from across a city or larger metropolitan area to attend as a group. Members called from local wards, as well as Cambodian or other branch members, provided leadership for the branches. Leadership positions in the church are filled by unpaid lay leaders, who are "called" to serve in their respective assignments.

During the 1980s and 1990s at least 20 branches across 12 states were formed for Cambodians alone, or for Cambodians in combination with other Southeast Asian refugee groups. These include branches in the following cities and states: San Diego, Long Beach, Santa Ana, Stockton, Fresno, and Oakland in California; Lowell, Lynn, and Boston in Massachusetts; Silver Spring, Maryland; McLean and Dulles, Virginia; Providence, Rhode Island; Dallas and Houston in Texas; Philadelphia, Pennsylvania; Denver, Colorado; Seattle, Washington; Portland, Oregon; Wichita, Kansas; and Salt Lake City, Utah. These branches enabled the members to grow in their knowledge and understanding of the gospel, while also maintaining aspects of their native culture. For example, branches typically hosted Khmer New Year parties, and activities throughout the year typically involved lots of Cambodian food and Khmer music and dance. Some branches had their own Khmer traditional dance troupes and some provided Khmer language classes to help youth learn to read and write Khmer. Thus, the branches provided a safe place for church members to be Cambodian in America.

Most Cambodian branches were dissolved in the late 1990s and early 2000s, and members were integrated into their local English-speaking wards. As of 2013, only three Cambodian American congregations remain: the Long Beach Park Ward and the Oakland 10th Branch in California, and the Jordan River Branch in Salt Lake City, Utah. There are also currently 10 English-speaking wards across five states

(California, Massachusetts, Pennsylvania, Utah, and Washington) that list Khmer as a language spoken by up to 25 percent of the members.

Several factors led to the dissolving of Cambodian branches. First, refugee resettlement slowed down and came to end by 2000. Second, as Cambodian American children, youth, and young adults—who typically made up the majority of active members in each branch—shifted to English as their dominant language, there was less of a need to conduct services and instruction in Khmer. Third, high rates of inactivity led to drops in attendance at Sunday services. Fourth, reliance on leaders from outside the branch took away needed leadership from the local wards. Finally, many church leaders were concerned about the segregation aspects of maintaining separate ethnic congregations. When branches were dissolved, many members fell away. However, there were some efforts in the local wards to provide translation via portable headsets, or to provide separate Sunday school classes in Khmer mainly for the older adults.

Even in remaining Cambodian congregations, English is now the dominant language. In the Long Beach Park Ward, for example, the main worship service—called the Sacrament Meeting—is held almost entirely in English, with the exception of occasional opening or closing prayers or a talk or testimony given by older members. Translation is provided via portable headsets for those who need it. Classes for children, youth, and young adults are all taught in English. Only an adult Sunday class is taught all in Khmer. In the third hour, separate meetings for men (Elders Quorum) and women (Relief Society) are held and are usually conducted in English, but with a Khmer interpreter as needed to accommodate the older members.

When Cambodian refugees first starting joining the church, there were no Khmer materials or missionaries trained in the language. However, several full-time missionaries—young adult men and women who volunteer for 18 to 24 months of missionary service at their own expense—assigned to work with Cambodian communities learned the language through self-study and close interaction with the community. Bilingual Cambodian American members also frequently accompanied the missionaries to help translate and teach other Cambodians about the church.

As these self-taught missionaries returned home, some were recruited by 1989 to begin teaching Khmer at the Missionary Training Center (MTC) in Provo, Utah. Newly called missionaries spend two months at the MTC studying the language before being sent out to their respective assigned areas. Since 1985, over 100 Cambodian American young men and women have also served missions, some of whom were called specifically to work with their fellow Cambodian Americans. A few Cambodian Americans have also served missions in Cambodia. Since 1997, hundreds of church members in Cambodia have been called to serve missions, mostly in their own country, but at least 30 of whom served missions in the United States. Some were called to work directly within Cambodian American communities, but most were called to work with the general American population in their assigned areas. Similar to their American counterparts, these Cambodian missionaries received two months of intensive language training at the MTC to learn English. Some of their instructors were Cambodian American returned missionaries.

Early Cambodian converts to the church with strong English and Khmer literacy skills helped to translate scriptures and other materials. *Selections from the Book of Mormon* in Khmer was published in 1982, along with a few Khmer-language pamphlets, videos, and lesson manuals to support missionary work and Sunday instruction. Members also used the Khmer translation of the Bible produced by the United Bible Societies in 1954. Khmer-language resources for use in Mormon temples were created in the early 1990s, thus enabling Cambodian Americans to participate in temple worship and ordinances in their own language. However, translation work for the full version of the Book of Mormon and for other scriptures was delayed until the church was officially established in Cambodia. The full Khmer translation of the Book of Mormon was published in 2001, and in 2007 a Khmer "Triple Combination" was published containing three books of scripture—the Book of Mormon, the *Doctrine & Covenants*, and *The Pearl of Great Price*, in addition to accompanying study aids. Many other Khmer-language instructional and administrative materials have been created since 1995 with the help of Cambodian American translators, but these have been mainly for use by the growing church in Cambodia. Since the mid-2000s, most Khmer-language translation work is now done in Cambodia.

The church's semiannual worldwide General Conference is broadcast from Salt Lake City in April and October of each year, giving members an opportunity to hear talks given by the prophet, apostles, and other general authorities of the church. Five two-hour sessions across two days are translated live by interpreters into over 100 languages. Khmer translation has been provided continuously since the early 1980s by native and non-native Khmer-speaking members. Cambodian Americans, as well as church members in Cambodia, are able to view the broadcasts at their local church buildings, and audio and video archives of the Khmer translation are easily accessible via the church's website.

Anthropologists and other scholars have been puzzled about why political refugees from a predominantly Buddhist country would be attracted to the Church of Jesus Christ of Latter-day Saints. One view is that the church and its missionaries were aggressive in going after vulnerable newcomer refugees, knocking on their doors and luring them to church with promises of assistance. This view is in line with the concept of "Rice Christians," which the Merriam-Webster dictionary defines as "a convert to Christianity who accepts baptism not on the basis of personal conviction but out of a desire for food, medical services, or other benefits." While there is no denying that among early converts were those who joined in hope of economic assistance, few remained active. Church "welfare" assistance is temporary and focuses on helping individuals become self-sufficient. Faithful Cambodian American Mormons pay tithing (10 percent of their income) and other offerings, in additional to volunteering their time and energy to fulfill church leadership positions (callings). They believe that these sacrifices bring blessings into their lives.

It has also been suggested that the handsome young white male missionaries (called "elders") were especially successful in bringing in a disproportionate number of young Cambodian female converts. However, in reality, Cambodian congregations past and present are diverse in age and gender. This claim also ignores the fact that there are also female ("sister") missionaries, and even older retired couples serving missions. Also, not all missionaries are white, and many are native Cambodian Americans themselves.

Another theory is that the church represented "the white bourgeois image and values that epitomize success in the major society," and thus offered Cambodian refugees "access to white middle-class mainstream society" (Ong, 2003). However, most Cambodians in the early 1980s and 1990s attended separate branches where the vast majority of members were Cambodian or other Southeast Asian refugees. While leaders were brought in from local wards to serve in the branches, they were not all white. For example, the first branch president of the Asian branch in Lowell, Massachusetts, was African American, and one of the first presidents of the branch in San Diego, California, was a Tongan American. As branches matured, more and more leadership positions were filled by Cambodian or other Asian refugee branch members.

With the church's efforts to train Khmer-speaking missionaries and produce Khmer language materials, and the stereotypical view of white male Mormon mis-

sionaries knocking on doors, it is easy to see how scholars may come to these conclusions. However, the church did not have a coordinated preplanned effort to target Cambodian refugees. Rather, these efforts became a necessary response only after large numbers of Cambodian refugees showed interest in the church and began attending services in many different cities across the country. A review of church news reports on the formation of some of the early Cambodian branches shows similar patterns. In Long Beach, for example, one of the local church leaders described the situation leading to the formation of the Cambodian Branch:

> The missionaries were tracking and they ran into a refugee family, about six or seven of them; they came to church by themselves the first time. By the second week, that had escalated into about thirteen. . . . By the fourth week we were up to about thirty or forty; and then it jumped to seventy after the fifth or sixth week. Right now we have 350 attending. We [now] have a complete branch organization. (Jolley, 1981)

In Santa Ana, California, a Cambodian convert who had joined the church in Utah began inviting her Cambodian neighbors and friends to church, and a similar situation took place, leading to the establishment of the Santa Ana Ninth (Cambodian) Branch by 1985.

An understanding of how and why Cambodian Americans were attracted to the church and how they live their lives within the religious culture of Mormonism can be obtained through written accounts of their experiences, conversions, and testimonies. The book *Out of the Killing Fields and Into the Light* (Conrad, 2011) contains the oral histories of 12 Cambodian American Mormon converts. In addition, the Mormon.Org website contains personal "I'm a Mormon" profiles written by at least 11 Cambodian Americans. Of the 12 members in *Out of the Killing Fields*, only five described joining the church as a result of missionaries knocking on their door. Two described approaching the missionaries on their own. One described a dream in which she saw three missionaries walking along a field of grass near the ocean, wearing white shirts and name tags. "Some time later," she said, "I saw the Mormon missionaries near the beach just as I had seen them in the dream. I ran up to them and almost knocked them over with excitement." The other five members described how they were introduced to the church by other Cambodian Americans. A report on the Asian Branch in Lynn, Massachusetts, in 1992 noted that "nearly everyone here was brought into the Church by a sister, a cousin, a friend" who then introduced them to the missionaries. The efforts of Cambodian Americans Mormons to share the gospel with their family and friends is consistent with the church's emphasis on "every member a missionary."

The view that missionaries aggressively targeted vulnerable newcomer refugees suggests that Cambodian converts had no choice in the matter. However, in their written accounts these converts make it clear that it was their own conscious decision after much deliberation. Some described having attended other churches before finding what they believed to be the "true church" of Jesus Christ. The "vulnerable" charge also is inconsistent with the fact that many converts joined years after their families had settled in the United States, and that Cambodian Americans—including many born in the United States—continue to join the church each year.

Those interested in learning more about the church—called "investigators"—agree to participate in six lessons or "discussions" taught by the missionaries. They learn basic church doctrines and are invited to make commitments to read the scriptures, attend church, and keep commandments. Emphasis is placed on steps the investigators can take to find out for themselves through study and prayer to get their own personal spiritual confirmation of the truthfulness of the gospel and to ask God if they should be baptized and join the church. In their written accounts of their conversion, Cambodian Americans described finding answers to questions while being taught by the missionaries and having spiritual experiences that led to their decision to be baptized. For example, one of the converts who shares his story in *Out of the Killing Fields* is a police officer, father of four children, and a leader in his congregation. He experienced many traumatic experiences during the genocide. He noted, "Running around the jungles of Cambodia and watching people get blown to bits by land mines or shot by guards, I often wondered if there was any life after death." A friend invited him to church and introduced him to the missionaries. He recounts:

I started reading the *Book of Mormon* and praying. I was baptized in 1986 at the age of sixteen. When I was confirmed and received the gift of the Holy Ghost, I felt the Spirit strongly that what I was doing was right and that I was really being born again into a new life. The complex puzzle of my life was finally put together, and I could see the bigger picture.

Some of the converts noted they didn't fully understand the gospel when they first joined the church, or still had doubts, but through challenges and struggles their belief has developed gradually over time. (Conrad, 2011)

Mormonism entails a unique culture that sets church members apart from others in their society, whether in America, Cambodia, or any other country. The church stresses that members should be "in the world, but not of the world," emphasizing the need to be good citizens and productive members of society without pursuing the "worldly" aspects that can draw one away from God. For example, in addition to the Ten Commandments, faithful Mormons follow a law of health (the "Word of Wisdom") in which they refrain from tobacco, alcohol, coffee, tea, and illegal drugs. They dress modestly, avoid foul language, and strive to be honest in their dealings with others. They believe in the "Law of Chastity," a code of morality that prohibits sex before marriage and requires complete fidelity to one's spouse within marriage. They attend church regularly, participate in a variety of church activities, accept callings to provide voluntary service in leadership and other positions, and strive to engage in daily scripture reading and personal and family prayers to seek guidance and personal revelation to live their lives in accordance with the gospel of Jesus Christ. Adhering to these high standards of the church can be challenging, and Mormons recognize they are far from perfect. But they find comfort through their faith in Jesus Christ as their savior and belief in his atonement that makes it possible for them to repent and be forgiven of their sins.

Following baptism, new converts are "confirmed" members of the church through the laying on of hands on their heads, and they are invited to receive the "Gift of the Holy Ghost," which they believe can serve as a moral compass throughout their lives, so long as they remain worthy. Worthy male members of the church are ordained to the priesthood, which Mormons believe is power and authority from God to perform sacred ordinances and responsibilities such as baptisms, confirmations, the administration of the sacrament, and temple ordinances. Cambodian American Mormon boys between the ages of 12 and 18 may be ordained as deacons, teachers, and priests in the Aaronic priesthood and have the authority to administer the sacrament in Sunday worship services. At age 18, they may be ordained as an elder in the higher or Melchizedek priesthood. This priesthood office is required for men who choose to serve a two-year mission. While women in the church do not hold the priesthood, they also hold important leadership positions, may choose to serve missions, and help lead temple ordinances. The church emphasizes that while husbands and wives serve different roles in the family, they are equal partners in marriage and in the family.

Mormons believe that "the glory of God is intelligence," and thus great emphasis is placed on education. High school students often attend seminary—a religion class held in the early mornings before school, or through released time from school—emphasizing in-depth study of the scriptures. Many Cambodian Americans have studied at the church's Brigham Young University, with campuses in Utah, Idaho, and Hawai'i. The Hawai'i campus also has had a large number of international Mormon students from Cambodia. Cambodian American students at other colleges and universities throughout the country are also afforded opportunities for religious study and social activities through institutes of religion built adjacent to their campuses.

Mormons believe in eternal marriages and families that continue beyond the grave. Marriages performed in Mormon temples are not "till death do you part," but "for time and all eternity." The belief that "families are forever" explains the great emphasis of the church on the family. Cambodian American converts who were already married before joining the church have the opportunity to go to the temple to be "sealed" to their spouses, and also to have their children sealed to them for eternity. Only faithful members may enter the temple; thus, to have an eternal marriage, single Mormons must marry a fellow Mormon who is worthy to enter the temple. This can be particularly challenging to Cambodian Americans, given the relatively small population from which to find a potential "eternal companion." As

such, there is often a high number of interracial marriages among Cambodian Americans who marry in the temple, though this rate is not likely any higher than interracial marriages across the Cambodian American community in general. In keeping with their Cambodian culture, many Cambodian Mormons who marry in the temple also have a Cambodian traditional wedding, or at least a Cambodian-style wedding banquet at a restaurant.

Ordinances in Mormon temples are also performed for the deceased. For example, baptism is viewed as an essential ordinance required for entrance into the highest level of heaven, known to Mormons as the Celestial Kingdom. However, many people have died without ever having the opportunity to learn about Christ and his church. Through genealogy work, church members can identify the names of their deceased ancestors and then perform ordinances such as baptism for them vicariously in the temple. Many Cambodian American Mormons have participated in these "baptisms for the dead," and some have completed temple ordinances for their own deceased family members. Their belief in temple ordinances that enable the sealing of eternal families brings great comfort and joy to Cambodian American Mormons who have lost so many relatives due to war and genocide.

To conclude, the following excerpts are drawn from selected "I'm a Mormon" profiles of Cambodian Americans from the Mormon.org website, wherein they describe how they live their faith:

- An older Cambodian father who came to the United States in 1985 and joined the church with his wife and children in 1995 wrote, "We have a testimony that we have a loving eternal Father in heaven who loves us and wants us to be happy. He has blessed us with many things and continues to bless me and my family. We know that He is listening and answering our daily prayers. . . . We know that He has a plan for us and we are grateful that He has restored the knowledge of the gospel to us."

- A young college-age man who joined the church in 1999 and who is the only member in his family wrote: "Since I never had lived in a full Mormon household, I had the unique experience of living out the Mormon lifestyle alongside with my modified Cambodian lifestyle. Like any other person, my lifestyle remains the same. Since joining the Church, it has set new standards when it comes to lifestyle. Modest dressing & refraining from coffee/smoking/tea makes me have a healthy body. I still go to major Cambodian holidays as I would back in the days before I was a member of the Church, but I usually avoid the religious portions of it. . . . I live out my faith by following my standards. As a college-aged guy, I have so much stuff I can use to live out my faith proudly. Whenever I am out and about, I try to tune into the Mormon Channel, a 24-hour radio station that is on HD radio and on the iPhone, when I am driving to work or walking to an event. I also read my scriptures on my iPhone when I am at work, home, church or on the Metro rail going into the city."

- A Cambodian American woman who came to the United States when she was 10 years old in 1981 and joined the church soon after, and who is now married with two teenage children, describes how her faith has helped her despite many hardships: "My faith gave me a reason to stay positive. It gave me a reason to feel loved. I knew I had a Heavenly Father who cared for me and I trusted in him. Throughout my life my religion has guided me. I feel strength when I pray and read the scriptures. I feel peace when I attend church. I feel joy when I go to the temple with my husband. This religion brings happiness to my life. I go to church every Sunday with my family. I prepare my lesson every week for my Sunday School Class. I teach the 14 year old class. . . . I try to be a good example in everything I do. I like to help people. I enjoy reading my Book of Mormon every day. The scriptures help me to ponder and be a better person. I pray for my family, friends, our church leaders, and anyone who needs prayers. I'm so thankful for the freedom of living in this great country where I know I can pray always anytime I want and anywhere I want."

Wayne E. Wright

See also: Entries: Cambodian American Religions; Mormons

Further Reading

Conrad, P. D. *Out of the Killing Fields into the Light: Inspirational Interviews with Mormon Converts from Cambodia.* Springville, UT: Cedar Fort, 2011.

"I'm a Mormon" Profiles of Cambodian American Mormons:

- http://mormon.org/me/3HGF/Johnny
- http://mormon.org/me/9VPH/Keithsran
- http://mormon.org/me/85Z7/Morkodh
- http://mormon.org/me/35DT/Van
- http://mormon.org/me/63GJ/Cody
- http://mormon.org/me/1C9Q/SamiDara
- http://mormon.org/me/2QCW /PoamrongandIamaMormon
- http://mormon.org/me/1N8K/Khinna
- http://mormon.org/me/6F5W /TevyVarLarsen
- http://mormon.org/me/59BB/Sarith
- http://mormon.org/me/6MWK/Rosa

Jolley, J. "Splitting the Bamboo Curtain." *Ensign* (September 1981). https://www.lds.org/ensign/1981/09/news-of-the-church. Accessed July 9, 2014.

Ong, A. *Buddha Is Hiding: Refugees, Citizenship, the New America.* Berkeley: University of California Press, 2003.

Caodaism

History

Caodaism emerged within the context of French colonialism in Cochin China (the southernmost colony of French Indochina) during the early 20th century. Its founders worked for the French colonial government and had learned Asian and European forms of spirit communication. In 1920, Ngo Minh Chieu became the first disciple to receive séance messages from the Venerable Cao Dai while he was posted as a district administrator by the French colonial government on Phu Quoc Island in the Gulf of Siam. Coincidentally, five years later in Saigon, three younger servants, Cao Quynh Cu, Cao Hoai Sang (Cu's nephew), and Pham Cong Tac also received messages from the Venerable Cao Dai urging them to establish a new religion uniting Buddhism, Daoism, and Confucianism with elements of Christianity. The four men met in early 1926 and began formalizing plans to propagate the religion. On October 7, 1926, they submitted an official declaration of Caodaism to the governor of Cochin China with the signatures of 27 Caodai leaders and 247 members. They never received a reply from the governor but nevertheless proceeded with an inaugural ceremony on October 18, 1926, in Tay Ninh Province, approximately 100 kilometers northwest of Saigon, near the Cambodian border.

Philosophy

Cao Đài in Vietnamese literally means "High Palace," referring to the Supreme Palace where the Venerable Cao Dai reigns. Caodaists emphasize that their religion originated in direct séance communications from God and not through human intermediaries. They often shared with me that his representation in the form of the Left Eye is not distinguishable by race, gender, and class. As such, it encompasses teachings of tolerance that aim to create universal harmony between Western and Eastern philosophies, traditions, and rituals. Caodaists believe that the Supreme Being, the Creator, is the Great Sacred Light from which derives the universe including living beings called the little sacred light. Human beings, the little sacred light, are a part of the Great Sacred Light, the Supreme Being. By self-cultivation, human beings may become one with the Supreme Being: the little sacred light becomes one with the Great Sacred Light. All religions have the same divine origin, which is God, the Supreme Being. All religious ethics are based on love and justice. Religions are just different manifestations of the same truth.

Caodaism's pantheon of religious teachers includes Confucius, Jesus, Ly Thai Bach, Buddha, Laotzu, and the Boddhisattva Kwan Yin. Its saints include Chinese revolution leader Sun Yat-sen, French philosopher Victor Hugo, and Vietnamese poet and prophet Nguyen Binh Khiem.

Structure

The structure of the Caodai religion is organized according to the Religious Constitution of Caodaism (*Pháp Chánh Truyền*), which was given to Caodai leaders by the Venerable Cao Dai through séance messages in 1926. There are three administrative branches: (1) the Council of the Great Spirits, which is invisible and consists of saints who lived moral human lives; (2) the Legislative Body, which acts as the bridge between the human and spiritual worlds; and (3) the Executive Body, which is responsible for all administrative and missionary activities. These three boards have equal powers and must act in accordance to maintain harmony within the religion. The religious hierarchy in each branch has specified roles and limited numbers of dignitary positions. Nominations and promotions must move up the ranks and gain approval from the Vener

able Cao Dai through séances. However, since the 1975 Communist takeover in Vietnam, the Caodai congregational structure has been reorganized. The three branches of governance have been combined into a state-sanctioned Council of Governance. Moreover, as séances have been prohibited, all leadership positions must be appointed by or have approval from the government.

The Caodai Holy See (Toà Thánh Tây Ninh) is the religious headquarters built between 1932 and 1953. Located in a once deserted jungle area of the French-established Cochin China state, it has attracted thousands of new inhabitants, the faithful and nonfaithful alike, who flocked in large numbers to the religious center not only to receive religious blessings but also to seek safety from political and social unrest. According to many Caodaists, the Holy See's eclectic and colorful architecture is a manifestation of the Venerable Cao Dai's culturally multifaceted and universally encompassing teachings. Its impressive structure and design have been replicated by Caodai temples throughout the world as an extension of connection and expression of submission to the Holy See's central authority. The Holy See oversees all religious activities within the religion, from text publication to membership registration and religious ordination.

Demographics

Currently, Caodaism claims about 2.5 million followers in Vietnam, mostly concentrated in the south in Tay Ninh Province. The Communist takeover of Vietnam in

1975 forced many Caodaists to flee to other countries and transplant their religion into local societies. The United States probably has the largest number of Caodaists outside of Vietnam, which constitutes about 20,000 followers, most of whom are concentrated in Southern California. Cambodia probably has the second largest number of Caodaists outside of the homeland, mainly because of its proximity to the Caodai Holy See. According to a 2003 report by the Cambodian Ministry of Cults and Religions, Caodaism has approximately 3,000 followers in the country. Most of them attend the Kim Bien Temple in Phnom Penh. However, this number is probably fluid because of the continual flow of back-and-forth migration across the border with Vietnam. Although Caodasim has had a long history of evangelization and missionary work, nearly all Caodaists are of Vietnamese ancestry.

The Caodai Community in the United States

In 1975, when the Communist-led government of Hanoi took control of South Vietnam, many Caodaists and other Vietnamese fled their homeland. The largest number of Caodaists settled in Southern California but they were dispersed throughout the region. In 1979, through informal ties, word-of-mouth, and newspaper advertisements, a group of about five to six Vietnamese Caodaists reconnected with each other. Although there were sectarian differences among them, they were collectively motivated to revive their faith on American soil. During the same year, a Caodai digni-

tary in France introduced the group to Do Vang Ly, former ambassador of the Republic of Vietnam to the United States and member of a Caodai sect. The Caodai community decided to meet regularly at Mr. Do's home in Santa Monica and commonly referred to it as the Caodai Temple of Los Angeles. Religious life and activities gradually attracted an increasing number of Caodaists throughout southern California.

In 1983, the Caodai community decided to temporarily relocate their temple to the private home of a Caodai leader in Norwalk. The new site was much more convenient for most Caodaists who lived in Orange County. Moreover, Mr. Do was suffering from kidney cancer and several Caodai leaders felt it was inappropriate to burden him with religious activities.

Not long thereafter, the Caodai community rented a property on Marty Lane in Santa Ana. They converted the house on the land into the Caodai Temple of Orange County. The community restructured its leadership and elected Che Thuan Nghiep as its first president. Although Mr. Nghiep was originally part of the Tay Ninh group, he emphasized the need for a nondenominational Caodai movement to transplant Caodaism in the United States.

Since their arrival in the United States, many Vietnamese Caodaists yearned to build a Caodai Temple that would be architecturally similar to the Holy See in Vietnam. Mr. Do, with his personal money and financial contributions from the faithful, decided to put down a mortgage for a piece of land in Perris, a distant city in Riverside County. Meanwhile, Caodaists in Orange County did not have sufficient funding to maintain the Caodai Temple of Orange County in Santa Ana. As a result, they abandoned the temple and joined Mr. Do in Perris.

However, travels to Perris were quite difficult for many Caodaists, most of whom lived in Southern California and could not drive. As a result, a number of Caodaists requested the Caodai leader in Norwalk to reopen his home to religious activities. By the end of 1986, most Caodaists in Southern California congregated in Norwalk.

Once again, Mr. Nghiep rallied his co-religionists to purchase land to build a Caodai temple. Soon, the community had successfully collected approximately $30,000 that would be used as a down payment for a home on Ball Road in Anaheim. They converted the property into a temple and referred to it as the Caodai Temple of Anaheim. With a new structural base, the community reorganized its leadership hierarchy. Mr. Nghiep led the effort of forming the Association of Caodaists of Southern California. Members may have different roles and responsibilities but are equal in terms of authority in this organization.

During the same time, several Caodaists in southern California split off from Mr. Nghiep's group and followed Giao Huu (priest) Thuong Mang Thanh, one of the few surviving Caodai dignitaries in the United States who were ordained by the pre-1975 Holy See in Vietnam. They were followers of the Tay Ninh branch and were interested in preserving its tradition under the leadership of Giao Huu Mang. They purchased a Christian church in Westminster and converted it into the Caodai Temple of Westminter. By June 1992, they had reestablished the institutional hierarchy of the Caodai church, with the temple in Westminster as the "diocese" of all Caodai temples in California. Caodai members of the temple were visibly active in marking Caodaism on the American religious landscape, from publishing a monthly magazine to participating in interfaith dialogues and organizing the annual international youth conference.

Between December 27 and 29, 1992, a group of 500 Caodaists from different countries congregated in Anaheim to discuss visions and strategies for the development of the overseas Caodai community. The meeting ended with the formation of the Confederation of Overseas Caodaists, a nondenominational group. Moreover, plans were put in place to purchase a piece of land in Riverside to build a nondenominational Caodai temple. Members of the Caodai Temple of Westminster attended the meeting but did not want to participate in the new organization's projects, which could pose threats to their Tay Ninh base.

In sum, by the 1990s, there were three major groups among Caodaists in Southern California: the nondenominational group led by Mr. Do in Perris, the nondenominational Confederation of Overseas Caodaists under Mr. Nghiep's leadership in Anaheim, and the Tay Ninh–based group led by Mr. Mang in Westminster.

Another split occurred during the late 1990s. Among Caodaists loyal to the Tay Ninh branch in Westminster, a number of Caodaists disagreed with Mr. Mang's leadership. Most importantly, they believed that they could not genuinely maintain their

Tay Ninh traditions if their temple was housed in a Christian building. (Tay Ninh Caodaists believe that the Caodai Holy See was constructed through spiritual guidance from God. Thus, as an important part of their religious traditions, all Caodai temples must be modeled after the Holy See to genuinely reflect the teachings of God.) This group began renting a small home on Orangewood in Garden Grove with the hope of converting it into a Caodai temple that architecturally resembles the Holy See in Vietnam. This dream seemed almost unattainable during the late 1990s until May 2008, when the Tay Ninh–modeled Caodai Temple of California held its grand opening ceremony. This Caodai temple is currently the largest one in California.

In early 2009, the Confederation of Overseas Caodaists sold their land in Riverside to purchase a large apartment complex in Anaheim. The property was renovated and a large Caodai Center sign was painted on the building by 2010. The institution's main functions evolve around community and educational activities (including publishing Caodai books in English), such as meditation classes and food distribution to the homeless. Through these outreach actions of generosity and sharing, Caodaists at the center hope to attract young Caodaists and popularize the teachings of Caodaism.

Thien-Huong T. Ninh

See also: Entries: Hoa Hao Buddhism; Vietnamese American Catholics; Vietnamese American Religions

Further Reading

Hartney, Christopher. "A Strange Peace: Dao Caodai and Its Manifestation in Sydney." PhD Dissertation, University of Sydney, 2004.

Hoskins, Janet. "Can a Hierarchical Religion Survive without its Center? Caodaism, Colonialism, and Exile." In Knut Rio and Olaf Smedal, eds. *Hierarchy: Persistence and Transformation in Social Transformations.* Oxford: Berghahn Books, 2008.

Jammes, Jérémy. "Caodaism and Its Global Networks: An Ethnological Analysis of a Vietnamese Religious Movement in Vietnam and Abroad." *Moussons* 13/14 (2009): 339–358.

Cham Americans

The Cham in America or Cham Americans are residents in the United States who are ethnically Cham. The Cham are descendants of the Champa kingdom, a seafaring kingdom that occupied present-day Vietnam since the second century. Champa was heavily influenced by India and due to its coastal location held a critical position in early Southeast Asian maritime trade and international commerce. The Champa kingdom began to disintegrate after conquest by the Vietnamese beginning in 1471 and disappeared from world maps after the formation of the Vietnamese state.

History

The Cham emigrated to the United States from Vietnam and Cambodia as war refugees beginning in the late 1970s. The Cham were part of the two million refugees that left Vietnam, Cambodia, and Laos between 1975 and 1990. In South Vietnam, Cham people were recruited into the Army of the Republic of Viet Nam (ARVN) during the war. At end of the

Vietnam War in April 1975, many Cham people escaped the country due to fear of persecution after the Communist victory.

In Cambodia, the Khmer Rouge targeted the Cham ethnic minority for genocide from 1975 to 1979. The Cham are the largest indigenous ethnic minority in Cambodia; their descendants escaped Vietnamese incursions into Champa centuries earlier. The Cham comprised 10 percent of the Cambodian population, approximately 700,000 prior to 1975. The Khmer Rouge's genocidal policies toward the Cham included outright executions and massacres, banning of Islam (the main religion of the Cham), destruction of *mosques*, splitting up of families, banning of the *hijab* (Muslim scarf), forced consumption of pork upon pain of death, and banning of the Cham language and names. It is estimated that up to 500,000 Cham Muslims perished during the Khmer Rouge era, including the majority of Cham *imams* or Muslim leaders. Thousands of Cham survivors fled Cambodia due to these atrocities.

As a result of the political and violent upheavals in Vietnam and Cambodia, the Cham diaspora was further scattered to various parts of the world including Thailand, Malaysia, France, Australia, Canada, and the United States, often seeking political asylum. In the United States, the government resettled the Cham across many states so as not to strain the resources in any one area, similar to what was done for other Southeast Asian refugee populations.

as war refugees in the United States since the late 1970s. The demographic data on the population are challenging to compile due to the lack of data and research published on the Cham American diaspora. The Cham are not yet recognized as a racial or ethnic group as of the 2010 U.S. census. There is no clear estimate of the Cham population in the United States, but according to the *2006–2008 American Community Survey—Languages Spoken* report, there were 891 Cham speakers in the United States. The Cham language is classified under the Malayo-Polynesian linguistic family. First-generation Cham Americans are often multilingual in Asian languages (Vietnamese, Khmer, and Malay) and engage in transnational practices. Rough estimates of the Cham population in the United States range from 3,000 to 10,000. The United States is home to the largest Cham diaspora outside of Asia.

The Cham population, although initially distributed in various locations in the United States in the early resettlement phase, is now concentrated on the West Coast. The major concentrations of Cham people are located in California, particularly in Orange County (Santa Ana, Anaheim, Fullerton, and Pomona), Sacramento (and other cities in the Central Valley), and the Bay Area (San Jose and San Francisco). Outside of California, the largest Cham communities are situated in the Seattle and Olympia, Washington, area and total a few hundred to a thousand.

Demographics

The Cham are one of the least documented Asian American ethnicities despite living

Religion

The Cham in America are adherents of mainly Islam and Hinduism. There is a small population of Hindu Chams in America who have origins in Central Vietnam and are related to the Cham Balamon sect who adhere to a localized form of Hinduism and the Cham Bani group who follow an indigenized form of Islam. The majority of Chams in America are Muslims who migrated from South Vietnam (Mekong Delta) or various parts of Cambodia. These Muslims are followers of the Shafi'i school of Sunni Islam, which is the branch practiced in most of Southeast Asia. A few cities in Orange County (California) and Olympia (Washington), due to their large population of Cham people, boast a handful of local *mosques* that serve as a vital space where community members can gather for Friday *jumu'ah* prayer, break their daily fast during Ramadan, send their young children for Islamic lessons, and go to socialize. Cham *mosques* have demonstrated longevity as institutions as they have existed since the early to mid-1980s and continue to function today as foundations of the Cham community in their respective locations in southern California and Washington. The Santa Ana *mosque* has one of the largest Cham Muslim congregations in the diaspora with over four hundred members.

Celebrations and Rituals

Cham weddings in the United States are major social functions that attract hundreds of people and are an opportunity for the wider Cham community (both local and international) to maintain cultural, religious, and familial ties. In the early 1980s, many marriages among the Cham were often arranged by parents through their social or familial networks; that trend is now on the decline. The majority of traditional Cham weddings in America typically last for a period of three days. On the first day, the groom is welcomed by the bride's family bearing gifts. This process is followed by Islamic marriage rituals with witnesses present to legitimate the marriage contract. The second day allows the families to prepare food and make arrangements for the final wedding day. There is an informal party in the evening at the bride's (*malam nugh tagha*) and groom's respective homes to welcome their closest guests. The third day culminates in a festive celebration that brings together the bride's and groom's families and their guests to honor the newly married couple and to wish them a lifetime of happiness and peace.

There are two cultural festivals known as the *Kate* that take place annually in Northern California (San Jose and Sacramento). The *Kate* festival is a practice that dates back to the existence of the Champa kingdom to honor the Cham goddess Po Nagar and ancestors. The California Kate festivals showcase traditional Cham dance, musical performances, and costumes. These festivals are influenced by the oldest and largest *Kate* commemoration in the world, which takes place in October each year in Ninh Thuan Province, Vietnam and draws tens of thousands of people from the region.

Asiroh Cham

See also: Entries: Cambodian American Religions; Cham Muslims

Further Reading

Cham, Asiroh. "Negotiating (In)Visibility in the Cham American Diaspora." Master's thesis, University of California, Los Angeles, 2012.

Hein, Jeremy. *From Vietnam, Laos, and Cambodia: A Refugee Experience in the United States*. New York: Twayne, 1995.

Kiernan, Ben. *The Pol Pot Regime: Race, Power, and Genocide under the Khmer Rouge 1975–1979*. New Haven, CT: Yale University Press, 1996

Maspero, Georges. *The Champa Kingdom: The History of an Extinct Vietnamese Culture*. Bangkok, Thailand: White Lotus Press, 1928.

Osman, Ysa. *Oukoubah: Justice for the Cham Muslims under the Democratic Kampuchea Regime*. Phnom Penh: Documentation Center of Cambodia, 2002.

Nakamura, Rie. "Cham in Vietnam: Dynamics of Ethnicity." PhD dissertation, University of Washington, 1999.

Nguyen, Bao. *Cham American Muslim: A Triple Minority?* http://www.iexaminer.org /news/features/cham-american-muslim -triple-minority/. Accessed July 9, 2014.

Taylor, Philip. *Cham Muslims of the Mekong Delta: Place and Mobility in the Cosmopolitan Periphery*. Honolulu: Asian Association of Australia in Association with University of Hawai'i Press, 2007.

Cham Muslims

History

Ethnic Cham people descend from the kingdom of Champa, a monarchy that subsisted through 14 dynasties in Southeast Asia from 192 CE to 1471 CE. The kingdom has also been known as Lin-yi beginning in 420 CE, Hwang Wang beginning in 758 CE, and Cheng-Cheng beginning in 877 CE. The prominence of the kingdom of Champa peaked between the 9th and 10th centuries when trade with neighboring countries was prosperous. Numerous battles throughout the centuries with Vietnam and Cambodia led to the Vietnamese conquering the kingdom of Champa in 1471. The last remaining Champa land was formally annexed by Vietnam in 1832 by Emperor Minh Mang (r. 1820–1841). The former kingdom of Champa now lies in the central and southern regions of Vietnam. Three ancient sites from the kingdom of Champa remain in Vietnam, Po Nagar (Nha Trang), Panduranga (Phan Rang) and Indrapura (Quang Nam).

Although there is no longer official Champa land, Cham people survived and live on today. Cham people are known to be migratory and many Cham communities are dispersed worldwide. There have been four notable migrations of Cham people. The first migration resulted from the fall of the kingdom of Champa in 1471, when many Cham migrated to the Malay Archipelago. The second migration occurred in 1692 when the community of Imam San was developed in Cambodia. The third migration resulted from the Tây Son rebellion in the 18th century. The annexation of the last Champa land led to Cham migration in the 1830s.

During the Khmer Rouge era (1975–1979) in Cambodia, ethnic minorities were targeted and killed. Historian Ben Kiernan (2003) estimates the death toll to be 1.7 million Cambodian residents. Kiernan (2003) further estimates that approximately 35 percent of the Cham Cambodian population (approximately 90,000 out of 260,000 Cham Cambodians) were killed. The fall of Saigon in 1975 and the Khmer Rouge genocide led to the enactment of the Refugee Act of 1980, which jolted a surge of refugees to relocate to the United States. Many "Indo-Chinese" refugees, including Cham people, migrated to the United States.

Based on an analysis of historic Chinese archives, sinologist Georges Maspero (2002) estimated that there were approximately 2.5 million Cham people in his 1928 publication. In 1999, the General Statistics Office of Vietnam reported 132,000 Cham residents. In 2008, the Cambodia General Population Census reported approximately 204,000 Cham residents. The U.S. Census Bureau does not currently recognize Cham as an ethnic group. However, according to the 2010 U.S. Census 891 individuals speak the Cham language in Arizona, California, and Washington. The Cham language, which is also called Cham, is a Malayo-Polynesian language from the Austronesian language family and is spoken by Cham people. Language is therefore an important indicator of ethnic Cham people and culture. These statistics do not offer a fair representation of the Cham count worldwide as there have been documented reports of Cham people disregarding ethnic identity and primarily identifying with the Islamic religion as Muslims.

Religion

The Brahman influence in the kingdom of Champa began as early as 529 CE. The construction of Buddhist monasteries was also noted in 875 CE. Cham people were initially influenced by Hinduism, but began to practice Islam as early as the 10th century. The majority of Cham people followed Islam by the 17th century. As such, Cham in Cambodia are often referred to as Cambodian Muslims or Islamic Khmers.

Founded in the 19th century, the Imam San community in Cambodia includes a small sect of 20,000 Cham Muslims. The Imam San Cham people are often referred to as Cham Boran (Ancient Cham) or Cham Daem (Original Daem), as they only pray once a week and follow spiritual beliefs not typical in traditional Islam. Such spiritual ceremonies include the Chai ceremony that celebrates the spirits of Cham ancestors. Imam San Cham are also scrutinized by traditional Muslim followers because they celebrate Mawlid, which is the anniversary of their saint and founder, Imam San.

Cham Muslims in Santa Ana, California, are Sunni Muslims and follow the five pillars of Islam, which include: (1) *shahadah*—belief in the monotheistic God, Allah, and his last prophet, Muhammad, (2) *salah*—praying five times a day, (3) *zakat*—almsgiving, giving to the poor and needy, (4) *sawm*—fasting during the month of Ramadan, and (5) *hajj*—pilgrimage to Makkah (Mecca).

Cham Identity

Although there are few known groups of Cham people that are not Muslim, there is a significant number of Cham people that practice Islam. As such, there are reports of ethnic Cham people identifying themselves solely as Muslim and disregarding their ethnic identity. Anthropologist Philip Taylor illustrates this belief through his work with ethnic Cham Muslims in the Mekong Delta of Vietnam. As one participant declares, "To be Cham is to be Muslim." Therefore, ethnic and religious identity may be intertwined. As a result, statistics on ethnic Cham may be underrepresented as some ethnic Cham may not identify themselves as Cham.

Community and *Mosque* Development

The city of Santa Ana in Orange County, California, is home to many ethnic minorities, most pronouncedly Latinos who make up approximately 78 percent of the population. Asians make up approximately 10 percent of the population in Santa Ana, which includes a smaller number of Cham Americans. The Cham community in Santa Ana was initially formed with 15 families in the early 1980s and has grown to approximately 200 families.

Formerly known as the Indo-Chinese Muslim Refugee Association of the United States of America, the Indo Chinese Islamic Center (ICIC) was established in 1982 in Santa Ana, California, by Cham refugees of the Khmer Rouge genocide. The ICIC opened its doors as a *masjid* (*mosque*) to community members as a one-bedroom apartment, where prayer services and Qur'anic studies for school-age children were taught. Since its establishment, the ICIC has grown into a three-unit apartment complex. The ICIC continues to offer daily prayer services, Qur'anic studies, and an after-school program. Services are offered beyond the local Cham Muslim community and are also open to nonethnic Cham Muslims.

Celebrations and Ceremonies

Cham Muslims in Santa Ana, California, fast during the month of Ramadan and celebrate Eid al-Fitr (the Festival of Fast-Breaking) to mark the end of Ramadan.

Most Cham Muslim marriage ceremonies (*nikah*) take place in a three-day span, typically from Friday to Sunday. On Friday, the couple typically meets at the *masjid* with the *imam* and family members; the couple recites Arabic scripture from the Qur'an, a dowry is exchanged for the bride, and the marriage is made official. On Saturday, the couple separates and the celebratory functions are marked by gender; women and children visit the bride's home and men stay with the groom. On Sunday, the couple meets with the community for a feast to commemorate their nuptials.

Marimas Hosan Mostiller

See also: Essays: Muslims; *Entries:* Cambodian American Religions; Cham Americans

Further Reading

Cambodia General Population Census. *Demography Info by Sex*. 2008. http://celade.cepal.org/khmnis/census/khm2008/. Accessed July 7, 2014.

Chapuis, O. *A History of Vietnam from Hong Bang to Tu Duc*. Westport, CT: Greenwood Press. 1995.

Dutton, G. E., J. S. Werner, and J. K. Whitmore. "Introduction." In G. E. Dutton, J. S. Werner, and J. K. Whitmore, eds. *Sources of Vietnamese Tradition*. New York: Columbia University Press, 2012, pp. 1–5.

General Statistics Office of Vietnam. *Population as of 1 April 1999 by Ethnic Group and by Sex*. 1999. http://www.gso.gov.vn/default_en

.aspx?tabid=476&idmid=4&ItemID=1841. Accessed July 7, 2014.

Indo Chinese Islamic Center. *About Us*. 2011. http://icislamiccenter.com/about-us.php. Accessed July 7, 2014.

Kiernan, B. "The Demography of Genocide in Southeast Asia: The Death Tolls in Cambodia, 1975–79 and East Timor, 1975–80." *Critical Asian Studies* 35, No. 4 (2003), 585–597.

Kiernan, B. *The Pol Pot Regime*. 3rd ed. New Haven, CT: Yale University Press, 2008.

Maspero, G. *The Champa Kingdom: The History of an Extinct Vietnamese Culture*. Translated by W. E. J. Tips. Bangkok: White Lotus, 2002. Originally published in 1928.

Pereiro, A. P. "Historical Imagination, Diasporic Identity and Islamicity among the Cham Muslims of Cambodia." Doctoral dissertation, 2012. Retrieved from ProQuest (UMI 3546772).

Taylor, P. *Cham Muslims of the Mekong Delta: Place and Mobility in the Cosmopolitan Periphery*. Honolulu: University of Hawai'i Press, 2007.

Chamorro Spirituality

Archeological evidence suggests that the Austronesian ancestors of the Chamorro (Chamoru) people ventured into Micronesia, a vast area of approximately 3,000 islands that dot the 2.7 square miles of the north-central and western Pacific, as early as 4000 BCE and settled on the 15 Mariana Islands about 1200 BCE. After Ferdinand Magellan (1480–1521) and his motley crew chanced on the Marianas on March 6, 1521, the Chamorro people and their culture have been battered by the geopolitical whims of the colonizing Spanish, Germans, Japanese, and Americans. Even today Guam (Gua'han) is still included on the United Nations list of Non-Self-Governing Territories by the Special Committee on Decolonization of the United Nations.

Only recently have the Chamorro people systematically looked beyond their colonizers' accounts of their history and culture in an attempt to reclaim their indigenous precontact culture. In solidarity with their efforts, this entry favors the standard orthography developed by the Marianas Orthography Committee in 1971. Thus "Chamorro" is favored over "Chamoru" and "Luta" over "Rota," except in instances where the orthography is universally familiar, such as "Guam" instead of "Gua'han."

This entry provides an overview of the history, beliefs, and spiritual values of the Chamorro people. A final section outlines the history of the Chamorro experience with other faith traditions, including Catholicism, which has been the dominant religion of the Chamorro people.

History

Spanish accounts indicate that the Chamorros may have had contact with Europeans before their fateful encounter with Magellan, who named the islands Las Islas de Ladrones, or the Islands of Thieves. Magellan mistakenly interpreted the taking of whatever by the Chamorros who boarded his ships to be thievery; but for their part, the Chamorros believed that the visitors were interlopers who retrieved treasures from their land and failed to reciprocate. At any rate, perhaps because of the paucity of natural resources, Europeans largely ignored the islands until 1662, 141 years later, when the Jesuit Fr. Diego

Thesia Blas, foreground, recites the Pledge of Allegiance in the native Chamorro language of Guam, with her classmates before the start of a Chamorro class at Carbullido Elementary School in Guam, September 4, 1997. After hundreds of years under foreign control, by the Spanish, the Japanese and the Americans, the Chamorro people of Guam are on an all-out search for their identity. (AP Photo/ Norman Taruc)

Luis de San Vitores (1627–1672) established a mission and renamed the islands Las Islas Marianas in tribute to the Spanish Queen Mariana. Spain formally claimed the islands in 1667, but for the next two decades the Chamorro openly resisted colonization. In 1670 Chief Hurao rallied 2,000 warriors in an attempt to win back their homeland. During the ensuing struggle, two subchiefs, Matapang and Irao, killed San Vitores in 1672. The final battle of the Spanish-Chamorro Wars was waged on Aguiguan, a tiny island just south of Tinian. By 1699 the Chamorro population decreased from a low estimate of 20,000 to 4,000 due to war and disease.

After defeating the Chamorros, the Spanish missionaries resettled the survivors on the islands of Guam, Luta, and Saipan to facilitate administrating the land and people and to replace the indigenous traditions with Catholic faith and culture. The Spanish overlords introduced European education, culture, and agricultural methods. They also outlawed practices and institutions incompatible with Christian culture such as the indigenous spiritual leaders and healing artisans, and such institutions as *guma'ulitao* (men's houses) and the singing, dancing, and feasting associated with them. As a result much of the traditional skills such as shipbuilding and navigation were lost. Most devastating was the loss of the oral culture that preserved the memories and wisdom of their ancestors. Surprisingly, the Chamorros managed to preserve their language through *novenas* in honor of the Roman Catholic saints and songs composed by the Spanish and German religious. While the present language has a preponderance of Spanish words, Chamorro culture still continues the strong family ties, a continuing belief in ancestral spirits, and intimate connection with the natural environment, characteristics of precontact culture.

After its defeat in 1898 in the Spanish-American War, Spain relinquished control of Guam, the Philippines, and Puerto Rico to the United States and sold the present-day Northern Mariana Islands to Germany. In 1918, the League of Nations Mandate transferred administration of the Northern Marianas to Japan after Germany's defeat in World War I. At the outset of World War II Japan invaded Guam to briefly unify the archipelago. Subsequently, after Japan was defeated in World War II, the United States regained Guam and was charged with the defense and foreign affairs of the Northern Mariana Islands as part of the United Nations Trust Territory of the Pacific Islands. The Northern Marianas held referenda in 1958, 1961, 1963, and 1969 that favored integration with Guam along with the United States. But Guamanians rejected integration in a 1969 referendum, due in part to resentment toward the Chamorros from the Northern Marianas, whom they accused of collaborating with the Japanese during World War II. With a facility in Japanese, Chamorros acted as interpreters.

With the 1950 Organic Act of Guam, the island became an unincorporated territory of the United States, administered by the U.S. Department of the Interior. Those who resided on Guam became U.S. citizens. Guamanian interests are represented by a nonvoting delegate to the U.S. House of Representatives; they are not allowed to vote in presidential elections. Most Guamanian Chamorros opposed the Organic Act. In the meantime, with the approval of a 1975 referendum, the Northern Mariana Islands entered into a commonwealth association with the United States. Like other U.S. territories the Commonwealth of the Northern Mariana Islands (CNMI) is represented by a nonvoting delegate to the U.S. House of Representatives; and like the Guamanians they have no representation in the U.S. Senate. While the Chamorros on Guam and CNMI are administratively divided, their aspirations to unify the entire Marianas archipelago are being bridged through conferences, musical performances, and the arts.

According to the 2010 U.S. Census, the Chamorus are minorities in their homeland. Out of the approximately 160,000 residents of Guam, 59,000 or 27 percent claim to be Chamorro; and of the 50,000 residents of the Commonwealth, 16,000 or 37 percent self-identify as Chamorros. An estimated 93,000 Chamorros live outside the Marianas, mostly in Hawai'i and along the Pacific coast. As of 2013, Guam and the Mariana Islands expect an infusion of 8,000 military personnel and 10,000 of their dependents as part of the

U.S. realignment strategy in Asia and the Pacific.

Beliefs and Practices

Two hundred and thirty-six years of Spanish rule and Catholic proselytization have not extinguished the ancestral spirituality and practices that still animate the Chamorro people. Traditional Chamorro spirituality exhibits such shamanic features as the belief in multiple worlds, disembodied spirits, including ancestral spirits, and the shaman, who can communicate with the disembodied spirits. We begin this section with the Chamorro creation myth that grounds their worldview and their values.

The Chamorro world begins with twin siblings, Puntan and Fu'uña. Puntan instructed his sister that upon his death, she should fashion his body into the components of the universe. Subsequently Fu'uña created the sun and moon from his eyes, the rainbow from his eyebrows, and the other creatures of the world from the remainder of his body. After following her brother's wishes, Fu'uña turned herself into a rock on the island of Guam from which emerged human beings. Like their Polynesian cousins, the Chamorros trace their genealogy to the creator deities. Chamorros believe that heaven is located below the earth, and hell in the sky. In contrast to the fickle sky that constantly spawned typhoons and radiated unbearable solar heat, the cool and quiet underworld must have seemed to be a place of refuge and peace.

Cognizant that they are born from the same ancestors, and thus kin to all creation—animate and inanimate, corporeal and disembodied—*inafa' maolek* or mutual cooperation is the principal notion that guides Chamorro society and culture. *Inafa' maolek* (literally "to make," *inafa'*, "good," *maolek*), the restoration of harmony or order, is operative in the family and community. *Inafa' maolek* assumes that the original harmony had been altered by either commission or omission and must be restored. The restoration of balance is played out through the sentiments of *respetu* or respect, especially toward the elderly and other significant persons, and *chenchule'* or the exchange of gifts.

Respetu within the context of *inafa' maolek* is expressed through appropriate exchange of food, material, money, and labor, especially on the occasions of death, marriage, and other important life transitions. The value of *chenchule'* expresses respect toward the individual or family; giving does not need to be immediate, but can be done through other means. The giver expects to be similarly reciprocated when a future occasion merits it. The key is appropriateness in a timely fashion. Reciprocating with a gift of lesser value means continued indebtedness; and reciprocating with a gift of greater value creates indebtedness. If a person does not have the financial means for an appropriate gift, he or she may offer *ayudu* or help. Both *chenchule'* and *ayudu* offered in times of need are expressions of love, concern, and respect for families and persons, especially those who may not have adequate means to return the gesture.

The spirit of *inafa' maolek*, the restoration of harmony, is especially urgent when death is imminent. This critical transition period was a time to resolve problems in relationships; it was a time for forgiveness and healing. Cunningham records an instance when a dying person was carried to the home of a friend who was offered some raw fish. Those who had gathered consumed the gift. The offering and its acceptance symbolically resolved past transgressions and restored order. It is believed that the deceased should not die with guilt or hard feelings. It is also believed that if amends are not made, the spirit of the deceased is apt to wander about to take care of any unfinished work and make amends. A recent expression of *inafa' maolek* is the Inafa' Maolek, an organization founded in 1994 that seeks justice through conflict resolution.

Believing that the spirits of the ancestors resided in their corporeal remains, especially their skulls, the ancient Chamorros venerated their ancestors by burying their remains under or near their homes and preserving and placing the skulls of their ancestors on a high shelf in their homes. The skulls were the medium through which the living communicated with the ancestral spirits who inform, instruct, guide their progeny, and bring them good fortune. The living decedents exerted great efforts to remind the recently deceased that he or she was loved and respected. During the prolonged wake, family members would invite the spirit to remain with the family. While much of these indigenous practices have disappeared, modern-day Chamorros still venerate their ancestors through the pantheon of Catholic saints and holy figures and

through such Catholic rituals as Dia de los Muertos (Day of the Dead).

Communication with the ancestral spirits was facilitated by the *kakåhna* or shaman and the *makåhna*, scorer, who possessed the powers of clairvoyance and divination, and who could manipulate spirits for malevolent or beneficial purposes. The *kakåhna* and *makåhna* were also consulted for information on the condition and needs of their ancestral spirits. In addition to dealing with the spiritual realm, the *makåna* and *kakåhna* were also healers, who possessed the powers to cause or cure illness by calling upon the *manganiti* (singular *aniti*) ancestral spirits, who are ordinarily predisposed to look favorably upon their living descendants as long they meet their kinship obligations. They were also knowledgeable about medicinal plants. Catholic and Spanish colonization effectively eradicated the *makåna* and *kakåhna*; but the knowledge and practice of traditional medicine has survived in traditional healers and herbalists, *suruhanu/suruhånas* (male/female), expressions that are derived from the Spanish *cirujano* or doctor. Traditional healers were called *i åmte* in Chamorro and most were women.

Inafa' maolek is also evident in the Chamorro relationship to the natural world. They believe that everything in nature possesses an intrinsic power that should be respected. Today a person of Chamorro descent—or long-time residents of the Mariana Islands—will ask for permission in the form of a chant before entering or relieving themselves in the jungle. Not demonstrating the proper respect for the spirit of the land may result in a mysterious illness. Chamorro healers may advise the offender to return to the site where the offense occurred and ask for forgiveness from the *ante* (soul) of the enraged spirit.

Like the Samoans, the ancient Chamorro did not build temples or other identifiable venues for cooperative worship dedicated to a spiritual world. The *latte* stones—giant megalyths quarried from limestone throughout the Marianas—are believed to have been used as foundations for houses. Their indigenous spirituality continues through human relationships that are crystallized through *inafa' maolek* and expressed through the virtues of *respectu* and *chenchule.'* These relationships and virtues extend to the ancestral spirits, especially to those who have recently passed away.

Nonindigenous Religious and Spiritual Impact

Since the arrival of Fr. Diego Luis de San Vitores in 1662, Catholicism has been a pervasive, but not an exclusive influence among the Chamorro people. This section traces the presence of the nonindigenous faith traditions on the Marianas.

Supported by the Spanish government, the Catholic missions had a profound impact on the Chamorro people. San Vitores began a process of restructuring Chamorro society and life. In addition to introducing the Catholic faith, he established a school, El Colegio de San Juan Lateran; introduced new farming techniques; and implemented a policy that compelled the people to live in villages or *barrios*. The Spanish government offered only tepid support to

the Jesuit's effort, as evidenced by lack of funds to expand Plaza de España, the first mission church, or to maintain and build other churches. After the Spanish ousted the Jesuits in 1769, the Augustinian Recollects and Catalan Spaniard Capuchins cared for the missions until 1898. Under Augustinian tutelage the first native priest, Fr. José Palomo y Torres (1836–1919), emerged.

As noted, after the Spanish defeat in 1898, Guam was ceded to the United States, and the Northern Mariana Islands were sold to Germany. The United States expelled the Spanish from the islands. Initially the Augustinians were allowed to continue their work with the Chamorro people, but they too were eventually asked to leave. Fr. Palomo, the lone native priest, ministered to 10,000 Catholics. In the meantime, the Navy commander, a Protestant, facilitated the arrival of missionary groups from other Christian denominations. Overwhelmed, Fr. Palomo appealed to the Spanish Capuchins on the Caroline Islands; he also persuaded sisters from the Missionaries of the Sacred Heart, based in Baltimore, Maryland to come to Guam in 1905 to teach children. However, within three years, the U.S. commander asked the sisters to work in the naval hospital and in other nonreligious areas. Between 1911 and 1940, 17 U.S. Navy commanders assumed governorship of the island of Guam.

Meanwhile nine Capuchin friars from Capuchin Rhine–Westphalia Province were at work in the Northern Marianas Islands. Between 1907 and 1918 the German Capuchins built churches on Saipan, Luta, and Tinian. The missionaries contributed greatly to the promotion of island heritage. One notable friar, Fr. Callistus Lopinot (1876–1966), composed the first ever *Chamoru Wörterbuch*, a German-Chamorro lexicon that enabled the missionaries to communicate in the Chamorro language. However, German Capuchins and all citizens of Germany living in the Northern Marianas were expelled in 1918 by the Japanese who under the League of Nations Mandate took control of the Northern Mariana Islands.

The Chamorros were included in the Japanese imperial project. They learned Japanese and honored the Japanese emperor at Shintō shrines and rituals. During the 31-month Japanese occupation of Guam, the American Capuchins were taken prisoner and relieved of their clerical responsibilities. Once again the Chamorro Frs. Jesus Baza Dueñas and Oscar Lujan Calvo took responsibility for the spiritual needs of the people. The United States retook Guam on July 21, 1944, commencing the Americanization of the Catholic Church on Guam and the Northern Marianas. On October 14, 1965, the mission of Guam was elevated to a diocese, suffragan to the Archdiocese of San Francisco. Fr. Apollinaris W. Baumgartner (1899–1970), who led the revitalization of the church after the war, was appointed its first bishop; two months later, however, he died on December 18, 1970. The following year on May 17, the Catholic community of the Marianas greeted its first native Chamorro diocesan bishop, the Most Rev. Felixberto Camacho Flores. A second native son, Rev. Anthony Sablan Apuron, became auxiliary bishop of Agaña on December 8, 1983. The new Pacific Island Archdiocese included *suffragan* sees to the Diocese of the Caroline and Marshall Islands in what is now known as the Federated States of Micronesia and the Diocese of Chalan Kanoa in the Northern Marianas that was added later on January 13, 1985, with its native son, the Most Rev. Tomas Camacho, D.D.

At present between 80 and 85 percent of Guamanians and Northern Mariana Islanders belong to the Catholic Church. The remaining 15–20 percent of the population claim to be Protestants, Buddhists, and a range of other world religious traditions and spiritualities.

Jonathan Frank Blas Diaz

See also: Entries: Micronesian and Polynesian Traditional Religions; Pacific Islander Religious Cultures

Further Reading

Cunningham, Lawrence J. *Ancient Chamoru Society*. Hawai'i: The Bess Press, 1992.

Fischer, Steven Roger. *A History of the Pacific Islands*. New York: Palgrave, 2002.

Hezel, Francis X. *Journey of Faith: Blessed Diego of the Marianas*. Agaña, Guam: Guam Atlas Publications, 1985.

Kasperbauer, Carmen Artero. "The Chamoru Culture." *Kinalamten Pulitikåt: Siñenten I Chamoru*. Hagåtña, Guam: The Political Status Education Coordinating Commission, 2003.

Perez, Ceclia C. T. "Signs of Being: A Chomoru Spiritual Journey." MA thesis, University of Hawai'i, Manoa, 1997.

Russell, Scott. *Tiempon I Manmofo'na: Ancient Chamoru Culture and History of the Northern Mariana Islands*. Agaña, Guam: Division of Historic Preservation, 1998.

Sanchez, Pedro C. *Guahan/Guam: The History of Our Island*. Hagåtña, Guam: Sanchez, 1987.

Zamora, Fray Juan Pobre de. *The First Account of the Chamoru People.* Translated by Marjorie Driver. Agaña, Guam: MARC, 1942.

Chan, Wing-tsit (1901–1994)

Wing-tsit Chan was one of the most renowned neo-Confucian scholars (scholars in traditional Confucianism assumed the role of the priest in performing rituals), teachers, translators, and transmitters of the Way (Dao) of the last century. He was born into a family with scanty means in rural Kaiping, Guangdong Province, China. To earn money to support his family and to send his son—Wing-tsit—to school, his father worked at various times in three different countries in Southeast Asia and in the United States. His father's hard work paid off; he was able to send Chan to Lingnan College in Hong Kong in 1916. After receiving his bachelor's degree, Chan enrolled as a graduate student at Harvard University in 1924 and earned his PhD degree in 1929 by supporting himself with various odd jobs.

On his return to China, Chan received an appointment as dean of the faculty at his alma mater, Lingnan, which in 1917 had been reconstituted as a university. He held this position from 1929 to 1936. In 1935 he was a visiting scholar at the University of Hawai'i, which in 1937 offered him a regular appointment. In 1942 he became professor of Chinese philosophy and culture at Dartmouth College, Hanover, New Hampshire, where he served until his retirement in 1966. After retirement he became the Anna R. D. Gillespie Professor of Philosophy at Chatham College, Pittsburgh, Pennsylvania. He also taught part-time at Columbia University, New York.

During an academic career that spanned more than 60 years, Chan authored, edited, and translated more than 100 books, published countless articles, and gave numerous lectures. His *Source Book in Chinese Philosophy* (1963) won universal acclaim. Another influential book was *Chu Hsi: New Studies* (1989). Through his writing and teaching, Chan transmitted Chinese philosophy and culture to the West, while mainland China itself was relatively uninterested in neo-Confucianism and its ancient culture. When mainland China was inaccessible to the outside world, Chan published an annotated bibliography on Chinese philosophy, giving the world a glimpse of Chinese scholarship from 1949 to 1963. And it was also through his writings and teaching that he retransmitted the Way back to his homeland, China.

Chan's memorable translations include, but are not limited to, the following: *Reflection on Things at Hand: The Neo-Confucian Anthology compiled by Chu Hsi and Lü Tsu-Ch'ien* (1967); *Instructions for Practical Living and Other Neo-Confucian Writings by Wang Yang-ming* (1963); and *Neo-Confucian Terms Explained by Ch'en Ch'un (1159–1223)* (1986).

Chan received numerous honors during his lifetime; and a number of fellowships and a lectureship were established in his name after his death. The highest honor he received was being inducted into the membership of the Academia Sinica, Taiwan. This position is an honorary lifetime privilege without remuneration. After his death the Lingnan Foundation of Hong Kong established in 2000 the W. T. Chan Fellowship. The purpose of the fellowship is to extend "the Foundation's commitment to higher education, increased international understanding, and personal growth. . . . After their selection and orientation, each Fellow is assigned to work at a non-profit organization in the United States" (http://www.lie.org/en/Program /Linmgnan-WT-Chan-Fellowships /About). The Wing-tsit Chan Graduate Fellowship in Chinese Philosophy Fund with the East-West Center, Hawai'i, was established by the Y. S. Lee Family Endowed Fellowship Fund. The purpose of this Fellowship Fund "is to provide fellowship to assist graduate students in Chinese Philosophy and in Chinese studies at the University of Hawai'i at Manoa . . . and East-West Center" (University of Hawai'i). Chatham College in 2002 founded the Wing-tsit Chan Memorial Lecture. The first lecture was given by Tu Weiming on March 5, 2002.

Those who had worked with him and those who recognized themselves "as direct disciples" remember Chan as "the consummate scholar, teacher, mentor and friend, but, in addition, a living exemplar of the Chinese philosophical tradition" (Bloom, 1995, p. 466).

Edmond Yee

See also: Entries: Confucian Canon; Confucian Rituals; Confucianism

Further Reading

Bloom, Irene. "Remembering Wing-tsit Chan." *Philosophy East & West* 45, no. 4 (October 1995): 466–69.

Wing-tsit Chan Obituary. http://www.nytimes .com/1994/08/16/obituries/wing-tsit-chan. Accessed July 14, 2014.

Chanoyu

The traditional Japanese art form known as *chanoyu* (tea ceremony) is a popular cultural practice that attracts large numbers of followers not only in Japan but around the globe. Tea drinking first came to Japan from China around the sixth century. Many Japanese priests made their way across the sea to the great monasteries on the Chinese mainland where they studied Buddhism and there encountered the monastic practice of drinking tea. Tea drinking, acknowledged for its medicinal value, was reintroduced in the 10th century, but it did not become a widely used beverage. Finally, in the 12th century, the priest Eisai (1141–1215), who had gone to China to study Zen Buddhism, returned with seeds of the tea plant and wrote a treatise about the virtues of drinking tea. Tea drinking began to spread among the court nobles and by the 14th century was popular among the samurai, Buddhist priests, and townspeople.

Tea continued to be part of special rituals that were held in Buddhist temples. As tea drinking became more popular, it became part of the world of entertainment and was served at lavish banquets that were held in large rooms. Special tea tasting contests became the rage, complete with extravagant prizes provided by the host. From the end of the 15th century to the 16th century, a new kind of tea gathering began to emerge. This was a solemn gathering that focused not on material wealth and possessions, but that emphasized a spiritual discipline of mind and body. Spanning the 14th to 15th centuries, there were three important tea masters who each helped develop the custom of drinking tea into a spiritual discipline. Each man left his signature on the art form of *chanoyu* that we know today. Murata Shukō (1422–1502) is known for developing the quintessential size of the tea room, which measured four and a half mats in size. Shukō studied with the eccentric Zen Buddhist priest Ikkyū (1394–1481) and is credited with highlighting the use of a scroll in the tea space. Tea was inevitably connected with art connoisseurship and amassing valuable collections. Shukō dared to combine the Japanese preference for exotic and expensive Chinese wares with the more roughly shaped domestic wares produced in local kilns. Takeno Jōō (1504–1555), a linked-verse poet, helped define the aesthetic principle known as *wabi*. The term *wabi* is connected to the idea of a sublime simplicity and beauty found within the imperfect and austere. The ability to penetrate an object and understand its essence began to push tea masters beyond a superficial appreciation of the external world.

Sen no Rikyū (1522–1591) made the ultimate sacrifice to preserve the art of *chanoyu*. With his courage and creativity, he brought radical changes by challenging current notions of status and value. Rikyū made use of bamboo and plain wooden utensils and brought tea bowls made in the *raku* pottery tradition, a technique used for making ordinary roof tiles, to the height of artistic excellence. He compressed the tea room even further to one and a half mats in size and cut a small "crawling-in" space for a door so that all participants had to lower their heads to enter. Tea drinking was now a religious path connected to constant practice, contemplation, and devoted study. Rikyū paid the price for his artistic vision and was ordered to commit ritual suicide by the great warlord Hideyoshi (1537–1598).

The setting and place for holding a tea gathering reflects the contemplative nature of this art. It is common to walk along a *roji*, otherwise known as a dew-laden path, to reach the entrance to the tea room. The freshly watered path helps one purify one's thoughts and, leaving behind the superficial trappings of the outside world, the tea room represents another realm. The tea room itself is a carefully crafted structure. From the small crawling-in entrance to the careful placement of the windows that regulate the soft light, each detailed part of the room, whether it be a small hook in the ceiling or a recessed door handle in a sliding screen door, is meticulously constructed according to tradition. The mindfulness paid to the handling of tea bowls, scoops, and containers, is likewise applied to careful movements in the confined tea space. The limited space becomes limitless when the participants have coordinated their movements into a harmonious choreography. The tea room should evoke the rustic nature of a mountain hut that one chances upon while wandering the hills. Its fragile structure, which depends primarily on wood and paper, reminds one of the impermanence of life.

Chanoyu has been described as a composite art that brings to life a mosaic, which weaves together a compelling narrative. The story begins first with the hanging scroll that is carefully chosen and hung in a special alcove. Its message symbolizes the theme of the tea gathering with its calligraphy, often written in the brush strokes of a Buddhist priest. The bow in front of the scroll pays homage to the scholarly and spiritual attainments of the calligrapher and shows respect for the word or phrase, which often comes from Buddhist parables, allusions, or Zen riddles used in monastic training known as koans. The message may appear deceptively simple with set phrases such as "every day is a fine day," or "willows are green, flowers are red." Only with study and training can one attempt to understand the meaning found within layers of allusion and metaphor. Other scrolls may outline the fundamental principles of *chanoyu* with the characters for harmony, respect, purity, and tranquility. The host displays the depth of his training by assembling utensils that range in variety from the choice of the kettle to the tea bowl, the tea container, the lacquer tray for serving the sweets, and a simple sliver of bamboo that is used for a scoop. Each piece is chosen to pull the threads of the narrative together and bring pleasure to the guests.

The transient nature of life, so highly valued in Buddhism and the Japanese literary arts, is keenly felt in the tea room. The fading aroma of the incense that is used to purify the room, the sound of the whispering kettle as it comes to a boil only to be replenished with a ladle of cold water, the smooth effortless movements of the host as he purifies each utensil, reveal an art devoted to the concept of *ichigo ichi'e*, or "one moment, one meeting." This feeling of impermanence intensifies the relationships between a carefully orchestrated ensemble of people, utensils, and tea room.

An informal tea gathering to which one might be casually invited would include the preparation of separate bowls of thin tea for each guest. The more formal tea gathering, which has been planned months in advance, focuses on the preparation of a *kaiseki* meal, the placement of the charcoal in the brazier or open hearth, the serving of different kinds of sweets, and the whisking of two kinds of tea, thick and thin, and can take several hours. Vestiges of Buddhist monastic practice are ever present. The word for the tea gathering meal, *kaiseki*, refers to the warm stones monks placed in the breastfold of their robes to stave off hunger. The meal served in the formal tea gathering should never leave one feeling full. Following monastic dining customs, pickles and scorched rice served in an ewer of hot water are used by each guest to clean a set of lacquered bowls. There is an economy of conversation as participants outwardly focus on the gathering all the while directing their examination inward.

In 1906 Kakuzo (Tenshin) Okakura (1862–1913) published *The Book of Tea* in English for his patron, Mrs. Isabella Stewart Gardner (1840–1924), and her friends in the city of Boston. The Meiji Restoration in 1868 saw the opening of Japan to the West after two and a half centuries of self-imposed isolation. As Japanese statesmen, educators, artists, and writers began to venture outside of Japan in search of new ideas, they began to confront the challenge of explaining their culture to others. In his seminal work on *chanoyu*, Okakura wrote, "Those who cannot feel the littleness of great things in themselves are apt to overlook the greatness of little things in others. The average Westerner, in his sleek complacency, will see in the tea ceremony but another instance of the thousand and one oddities which constitute the quaintness and childishness of the East to him." It would be several decades later with the end of World War II that a significant number of Americans would study *chanoyu* outside of Japan.

The initial wave of Japanese immigrants to the United States occurred in the late 19th century. Most arrived as part of an immigrant labor force that found work in agricultural-related occupations. Picture brides followed a primarily male labor force, and then growing families, with more economic means and time for leisure activities, turned to the traditional Japanese arts. In Japanese American communities, the study of *chanoyu*, along with other Japanese pastimes such as flower arrangement, dance, music, and the martial arts, became a popular way for people of Japanese descent to preserve the values of Japanese culture outside of Japan. The major tea schools in Japan sent teachers and utensils and built tea rooms in community centers and Buddhist temples. Annual cultural observances, many of which were borrowed from the traditional calendar of the ancient imperial court, are a perfect way to celebrate events such as Girl's Day, Boy's Day, the summer star festival known as Tanabata, and the Japanese New Year's festival with special tea gatherings. Here in the United States the study of *chanoyu* attracts Japanese nationals living overseas, Japanese Americans, and non-Japanese participants. In 1974 the first university course on the the Way of Tea was started at the University of Hawai'i at Manoa. Just as Japanese universities often have a *chanoyu* club, American students can now participate in hosting extracurricular tea gatherings. The adaptation of the medieval principles of *chanoyu* outside of Japan presents some interesting challenges. At the same time, the peace and repose that is nurtured in the tea room has become more meaningful in a world that is increasingly driven by a fast and hurried pace.

Janet Ikeda

See also: Essays: Arts and Cultural Production

Further Reading

Hirota, Dennis. *Wind in the Pines: Classic Writings of the Way of Tea as a Buddhist Path.* Fremont, CA: Asian Humanities Press, 1995.

Mori, Barbara L. R. *Americans Studying the Traditional Japanese Art of the Tea Ceremony: The Internationalizing of a Traditional Art.* San Francisco: Mellen Research University Press, 1992.

Ohki, Sadako. *Tea Culture of Japan.* New Haven, CT: Yale University Art Gallery, 2009.

Okakura, Kakuzo. *The Book of Tea.* Mineola, NY: Dover, 1964.

Sasaki, Sanmi, Shaun McCabe, and Iwasaki Satoko. *Chadō: The Way of Tea: A Japanese Tea Master's Almanac.* Boston: Tuttle, 2002.

Sen, Sōshitsu. *The Japanese Way of Tea: From its Origins in China to Sen Rikyū.* Honolulu: University of Hawai'i Press, 1998.

Varley, H. Paul, and Isao Kumakura. *Tea in Japan: Essays on the History of Chanoyu.* Honolulu: University of Hawai'i Press, 1989.

Chinese American Religions

As the largest and one of the oldest Asian ethnic groups in the United States, Chinese in America are religiously pluralistic,

A family's prayers are sent to heaven with the scent of burning incense. Many sticks of incense are placed together in a burner at the Kong Chow Temple in San Francisco's Chinatown. The Kong Chow Temple is dedicated to the god Guandi, and is one of the oldest Chinese temples in the U.S. (Phil Schermeister/Corbis)

yet hold certain spiritual values and practices in common. According to the National Asian American Survey conducted in 2008, no religious tradition composed the majority of Chinese Americans. Instead, 19.7 percent affiliated as Protestant Christians, followed by Buddhists (13.8 percent), Catholics (1.7 percent), and other (1.0 percent). In fact, Chinese in the United States have the highest rate of all ethnic groups of having no religious affiliation, at 52.0 percent. In addition, 4.5 percent identified as agnostic/atheist and 4.1 percent said they did not know their religious affiliation. However, these latter percentages are deceptive, as many Chinese Americans venerate their ancestors and adhere to popular religious practices, and they may identify with none or sometimes more than one religion. This entry describes different Chinese American religious traditions, as well as some of the religious features that most Chinese share.

Chinese American Protestant Christianity

Chinese American Protestantism has a long history of missionary evangelism, transnational political involvement, immigrant ministries, and ethnic activism. The oldest Asian American Christian congregation is San Francisco's Presbyterian Church in Chinatown, which was founded in 1853. By the beginning of the 20th century, eight different denominations established churches among the San Francisco Chinese. Along with Bible studies and worship services, these churches developed English-language classes and other ministries to assist their members. Christian religious organizations, such as the Young Men's Christian Association and the Young Women's Christian Association, also sponsored sports and music programs to help Chinese Americans adapt.

By the 1950s, most Chinese American congregations were family-oriented and catered to the second generation in English. The civil rights movement in the 1960s and 1970s spurred a rise in ethnic activism that also shaped local congregations. As a result, many local churches helped to start denominational caucuses and social service programs, some of which became independent nonprofit organizations. For example, San Francisco's Asian Women's Resource Center and the Oakland Asian Cultural Center both were church-initiated efforts.

With the passage of the 1965 Immigration Act, the end of the Vietnam War, and the 1989 Tiananmen Square protest, Chinese immigrated to the United States from different countries in increasing numbers. This immigration has revitalized Chinese American churches, such that the number of Chinese American churches has grown from 62 in 1950 to over 1,000 by 2000.

Sociologists of religions have identified different contextual factors as to why the immigrant generation and the 1.5/2nd generation of Chinese Americans have seen large-scale conversion to Christianity. Many of the Chinese churches are now re-ceiving scholars from the People's Republic of China, who are adopting Christianity as a response to political and religious factors in China. They observe that converts often view the materialism of today's China as a reflection of its moral crisis. They become Christians not only for its spiritual beliefs, but also to reclaim traditional Chinese values. In contrast, others suggest that Chinese American college students are more likely to join Christian churches for an American group identity. Increasingly distant from Chinese traditions, but not belonging fully in mainstream America, Christians found kindred values, peer community, and ethnic identity in Chinese American or Asian American Christian fellowships.

Chinese American Buddhism

The Sze Yup Association in San Francisco, founded by immigrants from the Xinhui, Xinning, Kaiping, Heshan, and Enping districts of Guangdong, China in 1851, installed shrines on its top floor "to be as near the gods as possible." Now called the Kong Chow Temple, its chief deity is Kuan Ti (Guan Di) or Kuan Kung (Guan Gong), revered as a god of war, as well as a Buddhist bodhisattva and exemplar of Confucian virtue. Yet this temple also housed the first Buddhist shrine in the United States, as Kuan Yin (Guan Yin), the Buddhist goddess and bodhisattva of compassion, is revered there. With a plurality of gods, this temple illustrates how Chinese popular religion, or folk religion, incorporates Buddhist deities as well. By 1875 eight such temples existed, and by 1900, approximately 400 Chinese temples were established on the West Coast, with most of them hosting Buddhist shrines and altars to Chinese deities.

Like the Chinese Christian churches, older Chinese Buddhist temples have been revived and new ones built since 1965. Beyond the Buddhism integrated into Chinese popular religion, three schools of Buddhist teachings now also represent Chinese Buddhism. In the 1960s, Venerable Master Hsuan Hua sought to introduce the Dharma to the West and established what would become the Dharma Realm Buddhist Association, teaching the Pure Land form of Buddhism. This school focuses on reciting the name of Amitābha Buddha, cultivating one's single-minded vow, and the development of a strong faith in this other-power. Master Hua founded the Gold Mountain Monastery in San Francisco in 1970, and in 1976 built a large retreat center near Ukiah, California, called the City of Ten Thousand Buddhas.

The second main school of thought is taught at the Hsi Lai Temple in Hacienda Heights, California. Founded by the Venerable Master Hsing Yun, it propagates the Fo Guang Shan "humanistic Buddhism," which affirms that *Nirvāṇa* can be experienced through the cultivation of wisdom and compassion. Rather than seeking *Nirvāṇa* or pure land in another world, humanistic Buddhism focuses on the establishment of a pure land in this world.

The Tzu Chi Compassionate Relief Society, the third example of Chinese Buddhism, is a lay organization that emphasizes charitable actions. Established in 1966 by Dharma Master Cheng Yen in Taiwan, the organization established a U.S. branch in 1989. According to its organizational website, it now has over 80 offices and facilities in the United States and over 100,000 volunteers who assist in disaster relief and community service. It states, "Not only do the volunteers endeavor to promote the universal value of 'Great Love,' they also fully employ the humanitarian spirit of Chinese culture to its utmost."

Chinese American Catholicism

Catholic missionary work with Chinese in San Francisco began as early as 1856, and in 1884 Paulist fathers initiated a Chinese apostolate at Old Saint Mary's Cathedral. Immediately after the 1906 earthquake, the Society of Helpers sent sisters to meet the urgent needs in the Chinese section of the refugee tent villages. There they met Francis Low, the first Chinese Catholic convert who then introduced many friends to Catholicism. Holy Family Church became the title of the mission, which was established as a national parish for the Chinese in San Francisco.

Today about 12.3 percent of Chinese Americans, or about 300,000 individuals, are Catholic. They generally belong to personal parishes, which are established to meet particular needs of specific communities by reason of language, nationality, or liturgical rite. These parishes exhibit a "close identification between faith, ethnicity and culture" through their leadership, popular devotions, and congregational practices. For instance, Lunar New Year and Autumn Festival traditions are observed, and Chinese-language classes are often offered to students.

Chinese American Nonreligious

The percentage of Chinese Americans who affiliate with no religion is the highest rate of any ethnic group in the United States. However, this number may be inaccurate, as many Chinese Americans may identify with Chinese popular religions or venerate their ancestors, but this type of religious practice is not measured by surveys. Another reason why Chinese Americans may not identify any religious affiliation is that they may identify with more than one religious tradition. For example, they may not only venerate ancestors and deities of Chinese popular religions, but also those of Buddhism, Daoism, and even Christianity.

The accuracy of these statistics notwithstanding, many Chinese Americans do hold secularized worldviews so that they identify with no religion. About 60 percent of Chinese immigrants to the United States come from the People's Republic of China, where the government is officially atheist. Consequently, few of these households would list a religion. In addition, about one in five Chinese Americans work in the computer, science, or engineering fields, and those in these occupations are much less likely to affiliate with a religion.

Chinese Popular Religions

As stated above, many of the Chinese Americans categorized as nonreligious still hold to practices of Chinese popular religions. Here, they engage in religious acts that assume a vast array of gods and spirits, and also assume the efficacy of these beings in intervening in this world. Chinese folk religion incorporates ancestral veneration, spirits, deities, and rituals. They also include practices to influence one's luck, *qi* (life force), and *fengshui* (spatial arrangements of *qi*).

Chinese popular religious customs are best exemplified during Lunar New Year, when the majority of Chinese Americans eat special foods, display couplets for good fortune, and *bai bai* (bow in reverence) to ancestors and spirits. Some households, especially those from Guangdong, maintain taboos for blessings in the new year.

Chinese American health practices are also influenced by Chinese popular religions. The use of acupuncture, as well as the exercise of *tai chi* and *qigong*, is based on principles drawn from Chinese popular religions.

Chinese American Confucianism

Confucianism is a cultural orientation deeply embedded in China and in the lives of some Chinese Americans. As a system of ethical values, it shapes how many Chinese would answer the question about human relations, "To whom do you sacrifice?" Originating in China's pluralistic ethical-spiritual culture, Confucianism joins familial, ethical, spiritual, philosophical, educational, and sometimes political ways of life into a shared Chinese American cultural orientation. Immigrant families most strongly maintain Confucian ethical ways of life, though the American-born may also practice some Confucian values. Common Confucian practices include filial piety of children toward their parents, reverence for education, benevolence toward others, and veneration of ancestors. Many Chinese Americans also often combine Confucian influences with Buddhism, Daoism, Christianity, and Chinese popular religion.

Since at least the 19th century, Chinese Americans themselves also have debated about whether Confucian ethics were religious or secular. By the early 20th century, China's culture became more secular, so more Chinese Americans treated Confucianism as nonreligious. Chinese American Confucianism also interacted extensively with Christianity. At times, Christian conversion could "liberate" individuals from traditional Confucian family expectations, and at other times Christians fused their faith with Confucian culture. Confucianism also influenced Chinese American civic ideology and rituals in language schools and other community organizations. Further, subtle Confucian influences may contribute to Chinese American worldviews, often present in Chinese American literature.

Russell Jeung and Lisa Rose Mar

See also: Entries: Chinese Temples in America; Confucianism; Guangong; Guanyin; Taiwanese American Religions; Tianhou, Empress of Heaven; Tzu Chi Foundation U.S.A.

Further Reading

Chen, Carolyn. *Getting Saved in America: Taiwanese Immigration and Religious Experience*. Princeton, NJ: Princeton University Press, 2008.

Hall, Brian. "Social and Cultural Contexts in Conversion to Christianity among Chinese American College Students." *Sociology of Religion* 67, no. 2 (2006): 131–47.

Hsi Lai Temple. "Humanistic Buddhism." http://www.hsilai.org. Accessed July 9, 2014.

Jeung, Russell. "Second-Generation Chinese Americans: The Familism of the Nonreligious." In Carolyn Chen and Russell Jeung, eds. *Sustaining Faith Traditions: Race, Ethnicity, and Religion among the Latino and Asian American Second Generation*. New York: New York University Press, 2012.

Jin, Xuepin. "Presenting and Deconstructing: A Study of Confucianism in Chinese American Literature." PhD dissertation, East China Normal University, 2010.

Meyer, Jeffrey. "Asian American Confucianism and Children." In Don S. Browning and Bonnie J. Miller-McLemore, eds. *Children and Childhood in American Religions*. New Brunswick, NJ: Rutgers University Press, 2009, pp. 180–93.

Ramakrishnan, Karthick, Jane Junn, Taeku Lee, and Janelle Wong. *National Asian American Survey*. New York: Russell Sage Foundation, 2008.

Tan, Jonathan. "Asian American Catholics: Diversity within Diversity." *New Theology Review* 18, no. 2 (2005): 36–47.

Tzu Chi U.S.A. "Tzu Chi Missions." http://www.us.tzuchi.org/. Accessed July 9, 2014.

United States Conference of Catholic Bishops. "Asian and Pacific Presence: Harmony in Faith." New York: United States Conference of Catholic Bishops, 2001.

Want, Yuting, and Fenggang Yang. "More Than Evangelical and Ethnic: The Ecological Factor in Chinese Conversion to Christianity in the United States." *Sociology of Religion* 67, no. 2 (2006): 179–92.

Yang, Fenggang. *Chinese Christians in America: Conversion, Assimilation, and Adhesive Identities*. University Park: Pennsylvania State University Press, 1999.

Chinese Drama and Religion

Religion and drama as a field of study in the Chinese context is relatively recent, beginning in the 1980s. However, it is generally agreed that religion was the source of Chinese drama, even though the exact date of these beginnings is disputed.

Chinese drama in its embryonic form can be traced back to pre-Qin Dynasty (221–207 BCE) shamanism. But its development was rather gradual. During the Western Han Dynasty (206 BCE–8 CE) a ritual known as *nüo*, said to have power to expel pestilences and ghosts, was performed during the New Year. From this ritual the genre of *nüo* drama, with all its local variations, was subsequently developed.

During the Eastern Han Dynasty (25–220) a genre known as *baixi* (literally, 100 plays) emerged in which stories were told by acting. In the sixth century, dramatic performances integrated stories with singing and dancing. And by the time of the Tang Dynasty (618–906), dialogue was introduced. This represents a significant step in the development of drama. Another important development took place during the Song Dynasty (960–1279) when a genre known as *zaju* (variety show)—later called *yuanben* (variety show) in the Jin Dynasty (1127–1279)—appeared in northern China. A play in this genre usually consisted of four parts: a prologue, two middle acts, and an epilogue. In addition four role-types were also introduced. This genre could very well be the ancestor of the *zaju* of the Yuan Dynasty (1271–1368).

Around this time a genre known as *nanxi* (southern drama) was also well developed in southern China. The extant texts tell us that it differed from northern drama in that it is longer; several characters have singing parts; and the music is southern. This style is believed to be the forerunner of *chuanqi* (literally, transmission of the remarkable; now known as *kunqu* or *kunju*) of the Ming Dynasty (1368–1644).

In addition, China has had a long history of puppet and shadow shows. The former has existed ever since the Han Dynasty while the latter since the Tang. During the Tang there was also a genre of oral narrative literature, the *bianwen* (transformation text), which along with puppet and shadow shows also contributed to the development of Chinese drama. The *bianwen* was written in both verse and prose and was used along with drawings by Buddhist monks and others to propagate Buddhism.

The first Golden Age of Chinese drama occurred during the Yuan Dynasty with the genre known as *zaju*. Each drama consists of four acts, with one actor or actress singing throughout the entire performance. There is also an optional wedge, usually placed at the beginning of the play, or sometimes between the acts. The songs were written rhymed verse while the dialogues were delivered in prose.

The second Golden Age took place during the late Ming period in which a genre known as *chuanqi* came into prominence. Unlike Yuan *zaju*, Ming *chuanqi* is notable for its colossal length, ranging from 17 to 50 or more scenes, excluding the prologue.

Besides Yuan *zaju* and Ming *chuanqi*, other forms of drama also flourish in China. It is estimated that about 360 regional/local genres exist today. Yuan *zaju* is no longer performed due to most of the musical scores being lost. Ming *chuanqi* is still on stage worldwide, though it has seldom been presented in its entirety since the mid-18th century.

Throughout the long centuries of evolution, an intertwining occurred between religion and drama. This intimate relationship can be seen in language, themes, concepts, authorship, functions, aesthetics, and troupe selection of deities as protectors. To illustrate the relationship between religion and drama, we will use a few traditional dramas for a systematic analysis of how religious drama functions. Specifically we will point out how the playwrights derived theoretical underpinnings to enhance the aesthetic qualities of their works within the contexts of Confucianism, Daoism, and Buddhism. However, it is important that we first focus our attention on the *nüo* genre.

Nüo Drama

Nüo is the first genre of Chinese religious drama and carried its own distinctive characteristics. Strictly speaking it is not a single drama, but a series of performances that constitutes the whole. A *nüo*, with local variations, generally consists of three main parts with subdivisions as illustrated by the *nüo* of the Tujia ethnic people, who are scattered throughout the Hunan and Hubei provinces. Each performance begins with a ritual of shamanism called *kaitan* (open the altar), by inviting the divinities from Confucianism, Daoism, and Buddhism to come to drive away ghosts and pestilences.

The performance proper is known as *kaidong* (open the cavity) in which the upper and lower cavity dramas are performed. These plays are both religious and secular. The final part of the performance is called *saotan* (sweep the altar) during which all divinities are sent back to the heavenly realm. The performance usually lasts two to three days or longer.

Religious Drama: Function

Religious drama has at least four main functions: entertainment, affirmation, challenge, and moral education.

Entertainment. One of the functions of literature is to entertain. Religious drama, as part of the literary genre, is no exception, but it entertains more than just the mortal audience. In the Chinese context it amuses the divine as well. This aspect is clearly seen at temple fairs. On such occasions, if the drama is performed within the temple compound, the temporary stage is constructed in the central courtyard facing the main temple where the chief deity resides and presides. The dramas selected for performance are purely religious in nature and affirm the tradition. On the other hand, religious plays that do not make it into the temple courtyard during a temple fair or festival are usually critical of a given tradition.

Affirmation. In Buddhism the transformation text story *Mulian Jiu Mu* (*How Mulian Saves His Mother*) is renowned. This plot is simple: Mulian is a disciple of Buddha, but his mother is a mean and avaricious woman. In death she is condemned to the deepest hell with incessant hunger because her neck has been narrowed to the point where she can hardly take in any food. Mulian, out of filial devotion, repeatedly descends into hell to save her.

Based on this story a repertoire of Mulian drama was developed. This play or a variation of it is usually performed at the Yulanpen (Festival of the Hungry Ghosts), which falls on the 15th day of the Seventh Moon according to the lunar calendar.

In this play we see an affirmation of the Buddhist tenet of *karma* and the propagation of filiality, which was originally derived from Confucianism.

Challenge. But not all Buddhist plays affirm Buddhism (nor do all the Daoist or Confucian plays for that matter affirm their respective traditions). Some of them actually challenge the very tenet of the tradition. For example, *Sifan* (*Longing for Worldly Pleasure*) is a single-scene play possibly derived from the no longer extant drama *Niehai Ji* (*Tale of the Sinful Sea*) of the *chuanqi* genre. It is used to critique the Buddhist concept of celibacy or suppression of desire, which in the mind of the playwright is against human nature. It features a young nun tormented by sexual desire. She attempts to control it, but the harder she tries the worse her desire gets. In the end she runs away from the nunnery looking for a suitable mate.

Similarly some dramas affirm one school of thought while challenging another within a given tradition. The Ming *chaunqi, Mudan Ting* (*The Peony Pavilion*) by Tang Xianzu (1550–1617), is a case in point. It portrays a 16-year-old maiden longing for love. Unfulfilled, she dies but returns to life when her desire is met.

This simple tale carries a heavy philosophical/religious burden, however. The Confucian school of *Lixue* (school of principle), which began in the Song dynasty, had by the time of the Ming dynasty become rigidly influenced by Buddhism and was advocating the elimination of desire while ignoring *qing* (love/passion) in human life. Under the influence of another Confucian school known as *Xinxue* (school of heart/mind), which insisted on the importance of human feelings, the playwright using this drama challenged the school of principle while affirming the school of heart/mind within the neo-Confucian tradition.

The theme of love/passion as a challenge to Confucianism, Buddhism, and Daoism was developed in *Yuzan Ji* (*The Jade Hairpin*) by Gao Lian (dates unknown) of the Ming dynasty. Set at a Daoist nunnery, it features a tale of an illicit love affair between a young Confucian scholar and a beautiful maiden from a fallen noble family. Yet the ritual of the heroine's becoming a member of the Daoist order is Buddhist, reflecting the principle of the unity of the three teachings, Confucianism, Daoism, and Buddhism. And yet with one stroke of the brush the playwright challenged the concept of suppressing *qing* (as advocated by the three teachings) and lifted up the issue of liberating feminine sexuality in the society.

Education. The moral didactic function of Chinese traditional drama is well known. A play may be Confucian, Daoist, or Buddhist in nature, but its teaching of morality and virtue is derived from Confucianism as illustrated by *How Mulian Saves His Mother* mentioned above. Sometimes a play such as *Yiwen qian* is also used to promote the teachings of a tradition.

Furthermore the Confucian moral social order is usually affirmed by the playwrights, including those who are critical of some aspects of the tradition. The author of *Yuzan Ji*, though critical of one aspect of the three teachings, is a case in point.

Religious Drama: Aesthetics

The matter of aesthetics in traditional Chinese drama can be examined from a variety of perspectives. But if it is viewed from a religious standpoint, its empty stage, certain movements of dramatis personae, and the grand reunion scene are based on concepts found in both Buddhism and Daoism.

Emptiness as Aesthetics. The traditional Chinese stage is empty, though occasionally a chair or two plus a small table may be found on stage. But these few items may represent a bridge or a mountain or something else. In other words, they are changeable according to the symbolic needs of the moment. On the other hand, emptiness is considered aesthetic, because it is not limited by space and time. Its versatility allows the performers to name the space and fill in the time and scenery as the plot develops.

The theoretical basis is derived from the Buddhist notion of emptiness while the performers' filling in the scenery through the embellished language in the arias or dialogues is based on the Daoist concept

that everything is birthed from nothingness. The intermingling of these two concepts draws the mind of the audience into participating in the performance, and gives the audience a sense of oneness with the story unfolding on stage.

Movement as Beauty. Singing and dancing simultaneously is a defining characteristic of Chinese traditional drama. A number of such movements are derived from the ancient shamanic rituals while others such as *longtao* (actor playing a walk-on part on stage) follow the Daoist *Taiji Tu* (Diagram of the Great Ultimate). In other words, the walk-on movement on stage is done according to the complementary bipolarity pattern of yin and yang as laid out in the *Taiji Tu*.

Grand Reunion as Karmic Aesthetics. Traditional Chinese dramas, be they comedy or tragedy or a combination of the two, always conclude with a reunion or a wrong righted at the end, giving rise to the speculation that there is no tragic play in the Chinese repertoire. This may not be true. For example, *Dou E Yuan* (*Injustice Done to Dou E*), a Yuan *zaju*, is a tragedy (but some scholars also consider it to be a combination of comedy and tragedy). Dou E is accused of murder and executed, but her soul continues to seek justice, which is granted when her father, now a high official, discovers the wrong done to her.

This way of resolving the plot of a drama is considered aesthetic in the Chinese tradition. The theoretical underpinning of this sense of aesthetics is the Buddhist concept of *karma*.

Modern Drama

Since the literary movement of May 4, 1919, China has also developed a genre of spoken drama, due to Western influences. The plays in this style, reflecting the spirit of the time, are generally devoid of religious sentiment, if not straightforwardly against religion. These playwrights consider religion to be superstitious. This movement together with the Cultural Revolution (1966–1976) also dealt a heavy blow to traditional dramas, as both these literary and cultural movements were antitraditional. However, since 1978 with the economic reform in mainland China, traditional plays have made a significant comeback, with troupes touring to perform on Western soil as well.

The American Scene

With the exception of the *nüo* and the *zaju*, many forms of drama continue to be staged in America not just for the Chinese, immigrants and native-born alike, but the general population as well. For example, in 1930 Mei Lanfang's (one of the most famous Peking opera master performers playing the *dan* role in the 20th century) tour of America caused a tremendous sensation in this country. And in 1997 the entire *Mudan Ting*, which when so performed requires at least 21 continuous hours, was staged in New York for seven nights of performance. The nine-hour abridged version of this poetic opera was staged at four University of California campuses in 2006, with every performance completely sold out. Preceding the performance was a two-day symposium held on the campus of the University of California at Berkeley.

Chinese drama is also studied at colleges and universities that offer Chinese language and literature as major subjects of academic inquiry. In addition there are formal and informal dramatic societies in the United States, such as the East Coast–based Evergreen Kunqu Society, the Eight Harmony Guild on the West Coast, as well as *piaoyou* (literally, ticket-friends, i.e., amateur groups) groups that gather together in private homes for singing and discussion.

Edmond Yee

See also: Entries: Confucianism; Daoism

Further Reading

Dolby, William. *A History of Chinese Drama.* New York: Barnes and Noble Books, 1976.

Chinese Medicine

Historical Developments

Chinese medicine can mean several things. Chinese medicine can be understood as an indigenous medical system that was developed within the framework of Chinese culture. The medical tradition has roots in Chinese cosmology, Daoist cultivation methods, and Confucian social ethics. Chinese medicine is also a dimension of Chinese culture that focuses on practices that heal, maintain, balance, and improve the human body. This broader understanding of Chinese medicine includes not only healing by professional practitioners (e.g., herbalists, acupuncturists, bone setters, and ritualists; see section on Beliefs and Practices), but also a wide range of practices that common people do to maintain

Many first generation Chinese Americans rely on traditional Chinese medicine to stay healthy and cure illnesses. Traditional Chinese medicine shops are usually located in Chinatown communities. Traditional Chinese doctors are also seen there. This shop is located in Vancouver, Canada. (Leszek Wrona/Dreamstime.com)

their health. In today's world, where Western science and biomedicine are considered advanced and authoritative, Chinese medicine can also mean an integration of medical systems tailored to the social, economic, and cultural needs of the Chinese people. Since this entry focuses on Chinese medicine within the Asian American context, we will address mostly the first two understandings of Chinese medicine: Chinese medicine as a traditional medical system, and Chinese medicine as a dimension of Chinese culture.

History of Chinese Medicine in the United States. For as long as the earliest

Chinese ethnics had been in the United States, the home remedies, herbal formulas, food therapy, acupuncture, bone setting, and other healing techniques had always been part of life in the Chinese American community. Although there were records of Chinese medicine practitioners advertising in English-language newspapers in major cities in America as early as the 1890s, during the earlier eras when Chinese ethnics were frequently targets of racial discrimination, Chinese American practitioners served patients mostly within the Chinese enclave.

The opening of the People's Republic of China (PRC) in the 1970s and the ensuing diplomatic relationship between China and the United States marked the beginning of a new phase for Chinese medicine in America. Along with the American public's increased interest in Chinese culture, news media coverage on the efficacy of acupuncture also brought Chinese medicine into mainstream consciousness. The politicking by enthusiastic patients and practitioners led to state certification and licensure of acupuncturists, first in Nevada (1973), then California (1974), and many other states followed.

Coinciding with the heightened receptivity of the American public toward Chinese medicine, the People's Republic of China also actively exported a standardized form of Chinese medicine that highlights the national identity of China's traditional medical theories while eliminating the "contaminations" from China's long history of superstitions and lack of scientific logic. The PRC government called this new system Traditional Chinese Medicine (TCM; hereafter specified as PRC-TCM) to differentiate it from Chinese medicine that could be understood as any practice of medicine (which can include Western biomedicine as well) provided within the Chinese context. "Traditional" pays tribute to the power of the antiquity and cultural authenticity of China's indigenous medicine, offering a contrast to the authority of Western biomedicine. Ironically, PRC-TCM and other traditional healing techniques are not the main modes of medical services in the PRC today; they are only supplemental to Western biomedical diagnoses and treatments there.

In response to the rapidly growing popularity of Chinese medicine in mainstream America, the National Center for Complementary and Alternative Medicine (NCCAM), a subsidiary of the National Institute of Health established in 1991, devotes resources and funding to defining Chinese medicine and verifying the effectiveness of Chinese healing methods. NCCAM defines Traditional Chinese Medicine (TCM) as a medical system that "originated in ancient China and has evolved over thousands of years," and within the American context, as a medicine that is complementary to "conventional medicine" (or Western biomedicine). Several major medical schools and medical research centers also have conducted clinical trials and evidence-based research on the efficacy of Chinese medicine, mostly on acupuncture treatments.

In sum, the Chinese medicine in America today is shaped by the Chinese medical tradition, the development of medicine within the Chinese enclave in America, the politicized redefinition of Chinese medicine by the government of the PRC, and the defining and regulatory powers of the National Institute of Health, state medical boards, and licensing agencies.

Education and Knowledge Transmission. Before there were schools for Chinese medicine in the United States, earlier Chinese American practitioners of Chinese medicine were trained as apprentices of already-established practitioners. Some medical families only trained within the bloodlines to preserve their heritage formulas and techniques. Other masters sought capable students and transmitted knowledge through long-term master-disciple relationships. When the state medical boards first licensed acupuncturists in the 1970s, many of these home-schooled practitioners were given the first licenses; some of these senior practitioners are still practicing today.

After the opening of the PRC in the 1970s, the influx of immigrants from China also brought practitioners who were trained by their state medical schools. Unlike practitioners trained under traditional apprenticeships, state-trained practitioners were trained in a range of programs—some were trained in the new PRC-TCM system, some were trained to integrate Chinese and Western medicines, and others were only trained in Western biomedicine.

Currently, 34 states in America regulate their acupuncturists. Many states that certify or license their acupuncturists now require completion of graduate-level programs in TCM or other Asian medicine. The curricula of the TCM programs in America typically incorporate PRC-TCM with additional courses on Chinese medical language, counseling, clinic administration, and so on. Based on student demands and faculty interests, some schools also offer courses such as Chinese medical classics and Chinese medical history to enrich the cultural aspect of the medical education.

Furthermore, the National Certification Committee for Acupuncture and Oriental Medicine (NCCAOM) administers standard examinations in acupuncture and Chinese herbology, which are required by most states. California and Nevada administer their own licensing exams. Although acupuncture is also used in other medical systems—it has been used in traditional Japanese, Korean, and Vietnamese healing, and also utilized by some European and American healers who do not use Chinese medical theories—exams offered by NCCAOM and the states of California and Nevada focus exclusively on TCM theories and applications.

Beliefs and Practices

Basic Understanding of the Human Body. In the traditional Chinese conception of the cosmos, a shared life energy, or *qi*, makes and fills all living entities within it. Humans, as part of the cosmos, are made with and sustained by this *qi*. *Qi* inside the human body circulates through 14 invisible pathways (or meridians), each meridian correlated with the functions of an organ in the body. When there is a blockage in one of these pathways, the functions of the correlating organ are compromised. Along these meridians are points that correlate with specific aspects or functions of the organ—these are the acupuncture points. Stimulating the acupuncture points bring about healing because they help regulate specific organ functions.

The "organs" in Chinese medicine are not just the physiological organs. Each organ represents a set of bodily functions, which may or may not directly correspond with how Western physiology understands the functions of the physiological organ. For example, in Chinese medicine, the function of the liver is to produce blood; in Western physiology, blood is produced in the spine. The discrepancy is rooted in the fact that the liver in Chinese medicine is first understood in terms of a set of functions, and the physiological liver does function to store glycogen, synthesize plasma protein, and decompose red blood cells, all very important aspects of blood production. Some of the organs in Chinese medicine do not have physiological form. The triple burner (*sanjiao*), which has no physical form, is an organ responsible for the digestive aspects of metabolism.

Chinese medicine conceptualizes health differently from Western biomedicine. Biomedicine considers one healthy if there are no symptoms of illness and the vital measurements fall within the average range of the population in general. In Chinese medicine, health is defined by the state of balance within the individual, where the dynamics between organ functions are equalized and harmonious. This inner state of health is reflected in the patterns in one's pulse, the smell of one's breath, the tone of one's voice, the manner of one's actions, and the colors and textures of one's tongue, face, ears, palms, and fingernails. A practitioner of Chinese medicine pays close attention to subtle signs and patterns in the patient to identify where the imbalances are and what treatments to use to recalibrate into the state of balance.

Acupuncturists. Acupuncture treatments involve inserting very thin, sterilized, disposable needles into acupuncture points on the human body. There are more than three hundred standard acupuncture points, and several hundred extra points that acupuncturists can use depending on the conditions of the patients. Some acupuncturists also apply electrical stimulation and moxibustion (burning a small ball of *moxa*, a type of dried herb) on the inserted needles.

As mentioned before, practitioners of Chinese medicine are licensed or certified as acupuncturists in most states in America. However, acupuncturists in America often use more than just acupuncture in their clinics. For some practitioners, even though they are legally recognized as acupuncturists, acupuncture is not even the main mode of healing they use in their clinics. In most states, licensed or certified acupuncturists can also prescribe Chinese herbal formulas, use Chinese massage techniques, and utilize other forms of non-Chinese naturopath therapies such as homeopathy.

Herbalists. Within the Chinese context, herbal therapy is actually more popular than acupuncture. In many Chinese American families, herbal concoctions and soups are familiar ways of healing and nourishing. Resident herbalists at the Chinese herb shops can make diagnoses and prescribe formulas; besides brewing customized concoctions from raw herbs, barks, and minerals, there are also manufactured teabags, powders, and pills for common conditions.

Beyond herbal medication, food therapy is also an important aspect of Chinese herbology. On the general level, there are diet rules for eating certain food items that are most appropriate for each season. On the therapeutic level, an herbalist can identify the specific composition and current condition of each person, and prescribe diet rules that can most benefit the health of the individual. For example, a person with a cold and weak composition would benefit from consuming foods with warming qualities, such as ginger, cinnamon, and lamb meat, and should avoid foods with cooling qualities, such as melons, tomatoes, and crabs.

Bone Setters, Massage Therapists, and *Qigong* Practitioners. The bone setters and massage therapists are the physical therapy specialists in Chinese medicine. Mostly dealing with musculo-skeletal problems, some bone setters and massage therapists use their hands in place of needles to stimulate acupuncture points and meridians. Some practitioners practice *qigong* (exercises that cultivate and control one's *qi*), and use their *qi* as a tool to heal. Without touching the patients or touching very lightly, *qigong* healers can infuse *qi* into acupuncture points, use *qi* in place of manual force to manipulate musculo-skeletal conditions, or use *qi* to penetrate directly into internal organs. Some practitioners use *qigong* in conjunction with bone setting and massage, so that the manual therapy is more effective, and because less physical force is used, the patients also experience less pain.

Ritualists. Historically, ritual therapy (*zhuyou ke*) was also a specialization in Chinese medicine. Besides Daoist healers who specialize in rituals, there are some practitioners who usually use acupuncture, herbs, and other manual therapies, but also have small rituals as part of their healing repertoire. Such small rituals include chanting mantras to help make healing more effective, reciting incantations and burning talismans to drive away illness-causing spirits, or sometimes even chan-

neling deities to provide healing. Ritualists are not common among the practitioners in America, and many practitioners, especially those from the PRC, speak vehemently against those techniques that they consider to be superstitious.

Emily S. Wu

See also: Entries: Āryudeva

Further Reading

Acupuncture.com. www.acupuncture.com. Accessed July 9, 2014.

Barnes, Linda L. *Needles, Herbs, Gods, and Ghosts: China, Healing, and the West to 1848*. Cambridge, MA: Harvard University Press, 2005.

Cassidy, Clare M. "Chinese Medicine Users in the United States: Part I. Utilization, Satisfaction, Medical Plurality." *The Journal of Alternative and Complementary Medicine* 4 (1998a): 17–27.

Cassidy, Clare M. "Chinese Medicine Users in the United States: Part II. Preferred Aspects of Care." *The Journal of Alternative and Complementary Medicine* 4 (1998b): 189–202.

Chinese Medicine Directory. http://www.chinese-medicine-directory.com/. Accessed July 9, 2014.

National Center for Complementary and Alternative Medicine. http://nccam.nih.gov/. Accessed July 9, 2014.

Scheid, Volker. *Currents of Tradition in Chinese Medicine: 1626–2006*. Seattle: Eastland Press, 2007.

Unschuld, Paul U. *What Is Medicine?: Western and Eastern Approaches to Healing*. Berkeley: University of California Press, 2009.

Wu, Emily S. "Utilization of Spiritual Capital among Practitioners of Traditional Chinese Medicine in the San Francisco Bay Area." PhD dissertation, Graduate Theological Union, 2010.

Chinese New Year

The date for the beginning of Lunar New Year was not fixed in antiquity. It changed with each new dynasty. In his study, *Festivals in Classical China*, Derk Bodde offers five different dates for the beginning of the year. However, since 105 BCE it has been made permanent: the first day of the first moon according to the lunar calendar.

The term for "year" also varied from dynasty to dynasty in ancient China. For example, during the reigns of the legendary emperors Yao and Shun it was called *zai*. From the 21st to the 16th century BCE during the Xia Dynasty it was called *sui*, which was changed by the Shang Dynasty (16th–11th century BCE) to be called *si*. But the character *nian* adopted by the Zhou dynasty (11th century to 771 BCE) has been used since then, with the exception of a short period from 744 to 758 during the Tang Dynasty (618–907 CE) when it was once again called *zai*. Like the various terms used for "year," the term for "the first day" of the year also varied ranging from *shangri* (the first day) to *zhengzhao* (the first morning), with five other terms in between. Later the term *yuandan* (the first day) was adopted.

Lunar New Year Parade in New York City, February 21, 2010. Chinese New Year is one of the most celebrated holidays for Chinese and Chinese Americans. Festive parades and community fairs are held in communities big and small. The biggest celebration in the United States is held in San Francisco, California. (Joshua Haviv/Dreamstime.com)

New Year customs and rituals as we know them today are also the result of a long evolution. There were eliminations and preservations, as well as additional new elements acquired, throughout the centuries. Furthermore, the practice of such customs and rituals varied from place to place though there are also shared elements among various locales.

The New Year

The Chinese New Year, as a concept germinated in the Zhou Dynasty and formalized in the Han, is a time of intense religious activities such as making sacrifices to ancestors, household gods, exorcism, merriment and visitations among families and friends. In traditional China at the imperial court, this was also a period of political activities, involving foreign nations, feudal lords, ministers and the emperor himself.

The New Year also marks the sending away of the old and the welcoming of the new; both require a series of ritual acts or ceremonies before the arrival of the first day of the New Year.

The Sweeping. On the 24th day of the 12th moon, homes are swept clean. Some ethnographers such as Goran Aijmer have argued that such sweeping is both for exorcism—sweeping away pestilences and bad luck from the old year—and for preparation for the visit of ancestors in the new.

The Stove God. Each traditional Chinese household has a Stove God (Kitchen), who is supposed to watch over the family's deeds, good and bad. This god returns to heaven to report on the family's behavior to the Jade Emperor, a deity in the Daoist pantheon, on the 24th day of the 12th moon. The return involves the removal of the image, made of paper, from the kitchen where the spirit niche is placed. On the last day of the year a new image is pasted in the old place, to mark that the Stove God is returning from heaven on the first day of the New Year at dawn.

There are various stories about the origin of the Stove God. The custom of the Stove God's returning to heaven first appeared in writing in a fourth-century work, *Baopuzi neipian juan zhi liu* (*Inner Chapters of the Master Who Embraces Simplicity*, V. 6) by Ge Hong (283–343), a Daoist master.

New Year's Eve

New Year's Eve or *chuxi* was a time of anxiety and anticipation. Families in traditional China were anxious to make sure that all pestilences and ghosts were kept out of the house in order to ensure a healthy and auspicious coming year. To achieve this aim, the Chinese performed (and some continue to do so) the following ritual acts.

Door Gods. The origin of using door gods or *menshen* to keep away pestilences and ghosts began in the former Han dynasty. On New Year's Eve, the images of Shen Shu and Yu Lu, carved on peach wood along with a rope made of reed, were hung on the doors. Shen Shu and Yu Lu were transcendental brothers, as one of the stories goes, who lived on a beautiful mountain. They used a rope made of reed to catch harmful ghosts and feed them to the tigers. Subsequently as the story gained popularity, people would hang images of the brothers and a rope on their front doors to keep ghosts and pestilences from entering their homes. Sometime during the third century, their images were no longer carved but written on peach wood.

Shen Shu and Yu Lu remained popular until the Tang dynasty when Zhong Kui, another ghost catcher, replaced them as a door god. Then Zhong was replaced by Qin Chiong and Yuchi Gong, the two founding generals of the Tang dynasty.

Expelling Ghosts and Pestilences. Hanging door gods could only keep pestilences and ghosts from entering the home, but could not keep them away from the house. So beginning in the former Han Dynasty, the ritual act of expelling ghosts and pestilences or *zhu nüo* was performed, accompanied by drums. The origin of this act was derived from shamanism. The performers would wear colorful masks and dance during the ritual in hopes that undesirable elements would be frightened away. The ritual was discontinued at the Qing court (1644–1911), but not among the people. Moreover a genre of religious drama called *nüo* evolved from this ritual and continues to be popular among some Chinese today.

Firecrackers. The origin of setting off firecrackers or *bianpao* on New Year's Eve into the New Year was rooted in the Han Dynasty. Before powder was discovered, the ancient Chinese set bamboos over a fire to heat them up so they would crack and make noise to frighten the evil ghosts away. Later firecrackers would

serve as celebratory signs of welcoming the gods.

Staying up All Night, Giving Money to Children, and Decorating the Money Tree. The custom of staying up all night on New Year's Eve or *shousui* first began during the Southern-Northern dynasties (420–589) and reached its height during the 7th to 10th centuries. On this night, families would gather for a celebratory reunion dinner and stay up all night in order to send the old year away and to welcome the new.

On New Year's Eve, children were given cash strung together in the shape of a dragon on a colored string and placed by the foot of the bed. This custom is called *yasui qian*. It is possible that the practice of giving money to children in a red envelope during the New Year might have derived from this custom.

The money tree refers to the auspicious omen of putting pine and cypress branches into a vase and decorating them with old copper coins, shoe-shaped gold or silver ingots, and pomegranate flowers. This custom continued to be practiced in the first half of the 20th century by some Chinese, but now it may not be observed any more.

Chunlian. Pasting spring couplets or *chunlian* on both sides of doorposts began toward the end of the Tang Dynasty and became very popular from the Northern Song Dynasty (960–1127) until today. Initially as the custom developed, people wrote auspicious characters or short sentences on peach wood on which the images of the door gods were painted. Later the auspicious sentences were written or printed on red paper. The custom of spring couplets also gave birth to the practice of writing parallel couplets for other occasions, such as weddings, birthdays, funerals, and so forth.

First Days of the New Year

Yuandan. The first day of the New Year called for religious activities as much as celebration and merriment. Families in traditional China would set off firecrackers at dawn to frighten away the bad ghosts. Thereafter heads of households would gather the family members together to offer sacrifices to ancestors, before offering toasts and eating peach soup. Later sacrifices to other gods also took place during the New Year. Today some of these customs are no longer practiced by some Chinese, especially urban dwellers.

Then everyone would put on fine new clothes and begin *bainian*; that is, calling on relatives and friends. This was done either in person or by placing a calling card in a designated receptacle or by bowing at the front door of those to whom such visits were paid. If calling was done in person, then there was an exchange of gifts between the calling party and those whom they called on. Today the custom of calling on relatives and friends in person continues. With the development of technology such calling is also done electronically nowadays.

Designated Days. The first six days of the New Year were traditionally designated to six domestic animals, chicken, dog, pig, lamb, ox, and horse, in that order. The idea was that these animals along with human beings ushered in the New Year. Therefore the animals were not to be butchered on their designated day. The seventh day was specially set aside for humanity and the eighth, for grains. If the weather was clear during the eighth day, it was believed that everything that year would flourish; otherwise, calamity would occur. However, by the time of the third century, the taboo of not killing chickens on the first day was no longer observed.

Today with the exception of the seventh day, which continued to be observed into the last century by some in "cultural China," these designated days may no longer be observed.

The Lantern Festival. The Lantern Festival or *yuanxiao* now occurs on the 15th day of the first moon, but historically the length of this festival varied from Dynasty to dynasty, ranging from three to five days, that is, from the 14th to the 16th or the 14th to 18th. But in the Ming Dynasty (1368–1644) it lasted for 10 days, from the 8th to the 18th, and then in the Qing Dynasty (1644–1911), it reverted back to five.

This festival that originated in the Han Dynasty was religious in nature and dedicated to the worship of Taiyi, the highest god. In offering sacrifices to Taiyi, the ceremony on the 15th was the most solemn. The ceremony began in the evening, and with lanterns brightly lit, lasted throughout the night.

The religious nature of this festival was gradually replaced by merriment and entertainment, such as enjoying riddles written on the lanterns. Among the hosts of activities on this occasion during the Ming period, the most striking was the introduction of dragon and lion dances.

Elimination and Continuity

When the Republic of China was founded in 1911, the government adopted the solar calendar and eliminated the official celebration of the New Year, but the festival continued among the population. When the People's Republic of China was established, the New Year Festival was renamed Spring Festival or *chunjie*. It is a major festival in China today. The holiday spirit in many respects rivals that of bygone days. Outside of mainland China, the New Year is celebrated worldwide by the Chinese and some non-Chinese alike.

Chinese New Year in the United States

The Chinese in the United States have been celebrating their New Year ever since their arrival on American soil over a century and a half ago. Initially the celebration took place in the bachelor quarters, but gradually with the arrival of women, it became a family festival again.

The first modern public celebration in the form of a parade took place in San Francisco, California, in 1953. The event was a fusion of Chinese and American cultures, as exemplified by the participation of St. Mary's Chinese Girls Drum and Bell Corps, which was organized in 1940 and continues today. Even before the first parade was arranged, this was the school that organized the first Lantern Festival among the Chinese in North America.

There was a fourfold reason behind this public display of cultural fusion: Cold War politics; celebration of "American democratic practices and [defusion of] anti-Chinese American sentiment aroused by the Korean War (1950–1953)"; revitalization of "Chinatown business"; and as a means of unifying "non-Communist Chinese Americans."

Conclusion

Chinese New Year customs and rituals have been evolving ever since antiquity and will, no doubt, continue to change. Thanks to modern medicine and advanced sciences, the fear of pestilences and evil ghosts is no long present. The religious aspect too has faded into the background. As the tradition encounters other cultures and contexts, people adjust the celebration to meet the needs of the day, as the first modern parade in America has shown. Perhaps it is due to this adaptability of the people that the tradition is constantly renewed and revitalized and continues to live as long as there are Chinese people on this Earth.

Edmond Yee

See also: Entries: Chinese Drama and Religion; Dragons; Duanwu Festival

Further Reading

Aijmer, Goran. *New Year Celebrations in Central China in Late Imperial Times*. Hong Kong: The Chinese University Press, 2003.

Bodde, Derk. *Festivals in Classical China: New Year and Other Annual Observances during the Han Dynasty 206 B.C.–A.D. 220*. Princeton, NJ: Princeton University Press, 1975.

Eberhard, Wolfram. *Chinese Festivals*. New York: Henry Schuman, 1952.

Yeh, Chiou-Ling. *Making an American Festival: Chinese New Year in San Francisco's Chinatown*. Berkeley: University of California Press, 2008.

Chinese Temples in America

Like immigrants the world over, Chinese immigrants to America during the early 19th century brought with them their religions and religious institutions. Chinese temples reflect the religious diversity and unity of Chinese religiosity, which blends Confucian, Buddhist, Daoist, and folk religious beliefs and rituals into a temple. There are Chinese Buddhist temples, Chinese Daoist temples, Chinese Confucian temples, and Chinese popular religious temples. Chinese and Chinese Americans will visit all these varieties of temples based on the ritual calendar, personal need, and community holidays and festivals.

In China, a temple—be it a Buddhist (*si*) or Daoist or popular temple (*miao*)—is a community center where people meet to discuss politics, seek medical advice, celebrate major festivals, and hold meetings; more importantly, the temple serves as a Chinese school. These multiple functions of the temple can also be seen in immigrant Chinese communities in the United States, both historically and today. Material evidence found in the temples today speaks to these multiple functions, and they remain centers for community solidarity. As a community temple, it is managed by a local committee, which might or might not have a resident priest. The priest might be an ordained Daoist specialist or a local religious specialist, such as a medium or shaman.

By the early 21st century, however, most of the historic Chinese temples in California are seeing their role in the Chinese community decline, as new generations of American-born Chinese have moved away. Today, temples are either fully operated by the city and maintained as historic landmarks and museums (e.g., Oroville's Chinese Temple, originally built in 1863), maintained by the state of California (e.g., Weaverville's Joss House, founded in 1874), or they are established as nonprofits under local community and board supervision (e.g., Hanford's Taoist Temple of 1893, Auburn's Joss House of 1909, and Mendocino's Temple of Kwan Tai of 1852). Still other temples remain under full Chinese ownership and are still actively used as places of worship (e.g., the Kong Chow Temple of 1857 and the Tien Hau Temple from 1852 in San Francisco's Chinatown). A final type, represented by the Bok Kai Temple in Marysville, originally built in 1854, is a temple owned and operated by the Chinese community, which may donate the temple to the city or state as a means to finance its restoration, but without fully relinquishing it entirely. These temples are all registered as city, state, or national landmarks, except for the two fully functioning temples in San Francisco's Chinatown—the Kong Chow Temple and the Tien Hau Temple.

The Mendocino Temple of Kwan Tai, the Kong Chow Temple, Auburn Joss House, and Hanford's Taoist Temple are all dedicated primarily to the red-faced god of war, literature, and social harmony—Guandi. The Tien Hau Temple in San Francisco's Chinatown is dedicated to the goddess of the sea, also known as the Empress of Heaven. The Bok Kai Temple is dedicated to the Dark Emperor of the North, also known as the True Warrior Zhenwu. Each year in early spring the Marysville community celebrates the Bok Kai festival, which has the distinction of being the oldest continuous parade in California. These historic temples are vibrant reminders of the bittersweet historical circumstances and conditions of life in America for Chinese immigrants as they were generally built in Chinatowns, ghettos on the periphery of "white societies." The Mendocino Temple of Kwan Tai was renovated by the descendants of the Hee family. One of the descendants commented that as a little girl she was embarrassed by the little red temple because it reminded her of how different she was from her peers. The majority of the religious artifacts on display at these temples all date back to the late Qing period (1644–1911). However, there are Chinese American elements in them as well. For instance, at the Hanford Taoist Temple, there is a display of an "unhewn log," which is a symbol used in the *Dao dejing* (*The Classic Book of Integrity and the Way*) to illustrate the ideal state of being. This is unique to Hanford and is not replicated in Daoist temples in China, Taiwan, Hong Kong, or Singapore.

Interestingly, there is continuity in the role that these historic temples play in their respective local communities—they remain sites of community unity even as they have lost their daily worshippers.

Moreover, recent changes in immigration polices, which have allowed large new contingents of Chinese immigrants to come into the United States since the 1960s, have provided fertile ground for new Daoist and Buddho-Daoist temples to be established, such as the Ma-tsu Temple U.S.A. in San Francisco, or a Sino-Southeast Asian temple association dedicated to Guandi, the Teo Chow Association, located in major cities throughout California, Texas, and New York.

As a result of modernization and the forces of globalization, Chinese religious temple organizations have become transnational, reflecting Chinese/Chinese American transnational lifeways and subjectivities. Recent developments of Taiwanese Buddhist temples offer the best example of new forms of transnational Chinese temples. The Hsi Lai Temple, the largest Buddhist monastery in North America, completed in 1988 at a cost of $26 million, is situated on 15 acres of a hillside at Hacienda Heights in Los Angeles, near "Little Taipei," a rapidly growing community populated by mostly Taiwanese Americans. Hsi Lai is a satellite community of the mother temple, Foguangshan, "Buddha Light Mountain," located at Kaohsiung (Gaoxiong) in southern Taiwan. Foguangshan was founded by Master Xingyun, who is the 48th patriarch of the Linzhi school of Chan (Zen) Buddhism. Foguangshan has branches across the United States located in Denver, New York, San Francisco, San Diego, as well as in other major cities worldwide. Hsi Lai Temple has also established Hsi Lai University (University of the West), offering undergraduate and graduate degrees in education, business administration, and most importantly, Buddhist studies.

Another global Buddhist organization has left an influential footprint on the American religious landscape, the Tzu Chi Compassion Relief Society (Ciji Gongdehui), a worldwide network with centers throughout Europe, Latin America, Southeast Asia, and North America. The headquarters of Tzu Chi Compassion Relief Society in the United States is located in Los Angeles. Tzu Chi Compassion Relief Society has established itself in the new American religious landscape through the promotion of social services, primarily through its free clinic program. Dharma Master Zhengyan, along with a group of 30 followers, founded Tzu Chi Compassion Relief Society in Hualian, Taiwan, in 1966. Currently, Tzu Chi Compassion Relief Society is the largest civil organization in Taiwan. In 1993, the Tzu Chi Compassion Relief Society Foundation established its Free Clinic in Alhambra, California. The clinic is a general health care facility providing medical assistance to financially disadvantaged residents in Los Angeles. It incorporates traditional Chinese healing with Western medicine and Buddhist philosophies of compassion to serve clients without regard to age, sex, race, class, or religious affiliation. In addition to these two major global Taiwanese Buddhist communities, there is Zhuangyen Monastery located at Carmel, New York, and serving New York, New Jersey, and Connecticut. Another major center is the Jade Buddha Temple associated with the Texas Buddhist Association in Houston, Texas.

A politicized and transnational Chinese Buddhist community that originates from mainland China is also making a great impact in America: Falun Gong, or Falun dafa. Falun Gong is a new Chinese Buddhist movement founded by Li Hongzhi in 1992. In the late 1990s, the Communist Party of China banned Falun Gong, which drove Falun Gong participants into exile. They have resettled in Taiwan, the United States, and Europe and have successfully established a global network of chapters and temples and grown in membership despite their suppression. They have also established themselves as a global human rights case against China's suppression of religious freedom. Falun Gong participants hold regular demonstrations in front of Chinese embassies worldwide.

The life and vitality of Chinese temples in America depends on whether or not Chinese Americans continue to practice their heritage traditions. As evident from historic Chinese temples, descendants of the immigrant population who established Chinese temples do not continue to venerate or perform rituals at the temples. Instead, the temples become historic landmarks and symbols of a once lively yet vanished Chinese cultural influence. In this way, Chinese historic temples become more akin to Confucian temples known as *wen miao*, "temples of culture." However, in places where new immigrant Chinese resettle, such as Chinatown communities, historic Chinese temples remain relevant and maintain religious and ritual traditions, as is the case with the Tien Hau Temple and Kong Chow Temple. Moreover, changes in immigration policies during the 20th century and the impact of war have diversified the Chinese population in America, which reflects the new diversity of Chinese temples that have been established since the 1980s, as is the case with Taiwanese temples and Sino-Southeast temples.

Jonathan H. X. Lee

See also: Entries: Bok Kai Temple; Chinese American Religions; Ching Chung Taoist Association of America; Daoism; Hsi Lai Temple; Taiwanese American Religions; Tianhou, Empress of Heaven; Tzu Chi Foundation U.S.A.

Further Reading

Huang, Chieng-Yu Julia, and Robert P. Weller. 1998. "Merit and Mothering: Women and Social Welfare in Taiwanese Buddhism." *The Journal of Asian Studies* 57, no. 2 (1998): 379–96.

Lee, Jonathan H. X. *Auburn's Joss House: Preserving the Past for the Future (The Auburn Chinese Ling Ying Association House)*. Auburn, CA: The Auburn Joss House Museum and Chinese History Center, 2004.

Lee, Jonathan H. X. *Hanford's Taoist Temple and Museum (#12 China Alley): The Preservation of a Chinese-American Treasure*. Hanford, CA: Hanford Taoist Temple Preservation Society, 2004.

Lee, Jonathan H. X. *The Temple of Kwan Tai: California Historic Landmark No. 927—Celebrating Community and Diversity*. Mendocino, CA: Temple of Kwan Tai, 2004.

Lin, Irene. "Journey to the Far West: Chinese Buddhism in America." *Amerasia Journal* 22, no. 1 (1996).

Ching Chung Taoist Association of America

Historical Developments

Daoism is one of the oldest religious and philosophical traditions in China, dating back to as early as the fifth millennium BCE. The Ching Chung Taoist Association of America (CCTAA) is an orthodox, lineage Daoist temple located in San Francisco's Chinatown. Established in 1978, the temple community has approximately 1,000 members on its registry and about 60 disciples who actively participate in the daily operations of the association and in performing regular religious ceremonies. The association traces its lineage to Ching Chung Koon (Azure Pine Monastery) in Hong Kong—now officially registered as Ching Chung Taoist Association of Hong Kong (CCTAHK)—which in turn traces its lineage to the True Dragon Sect of the Quanzhen (Complete Perfection) school from Northern China. Although connected by a shared lineage, the CCTAA and CCTAHK are completely separate in their organizational operations.

Ching Chung Koon in Hong Kong was established in 1949 by Master Hau Po-woon (1912–1999). A Daoist master from the famed Zhibao Tai community in Guangzhou, Guangdong Province, China, Hau eventually established two temples in Hong Kong—one in Kowloon, and another in New Territory. Besides providing worship and ritual services, Ching Chung Koon also offered charitable social services, which over the years expanded to several free medical clinics, senior homes, and schools (preschool through high school).

Through a sand divination—a Daoist practice where deities possess the body of gifted disciples to write on a tray of sand, and the celestial scripts are interpreted and recorded, usually with other community members as witness—in 1978, Ching

Chung Koon's guiding deity, Lü Dongbin, instructed the Ching Chung Koon community to establish a temple in the United States. The Reverends Wilson C. Lee (Daoist name: Li Dazhi; 1931–2005) and Lily L. Wong (Daoist name: Wang Feiqiong; 1933–2002), who were husband and wife and both senior disciples of Hau, were entrusted with the mission. The Lee family immigrated to San Francisco the same year and first started as a home shrine. The San Francisco temple at 532 Grant Street was established in 1979 and was officially open to the public in 1981. The home community in Hong Kong shipped a full cargo container of shrine furniture, statues of deities, and other important ritual accessories made by in-house craftsmen. In 1996, the temple relocated to its present location, a larger space than the previous location, at 615 Grant Street. The husband and wife team was dedicated to replicate, as much as possible, all the religious services that were available in the home community in Hong Kong.

The Lee Family

Wong and her family lived close to the Kowloon temple and worshiped deities in the temple regularly. She started regular temple worshipping when she was about 10 years old, but did not become an official disciple until she was 28 years old. She was a 16th-generation disciple, and the only one in the Wong family to become a disciple. Her husband followed her lead into the religious community, and eventually became a 20th-generation disciple.

Counting from the establishment of Ching Chung Koon in Hong Kong in 1949,

every passing year marked a new generation of disciples. Unlike lay parishioners who only pay respect to the deities and make occasional donations to the temple, disciples are required to study texts from the Daoist canon, make bodily and spiritual cultivation part of their daily lives, and learn how to perform official ritual services.

Both Wong and Lee were trained to independently officiate rituals, but Lee was recognized as the leader of the San Francisco Ching Chung community until his death in 2005. With the assistance of his wife and son, Lee also assisted in the establishment of Hong Kong CCTAA's Canada branch in Vancouver, British Columbia, in 1989 (registered as Ching Chung Taoist Church of Canada).

Their son, Jefferson H. Lee (Daoist name: Lee Dancheng; born 1963), was a godchild of Hau. The younger Lee spent much of his childhood in the Hong Kong temple with his godfather, and was later also officially ordained as a disciple (31st generation). He was in his teens when the Lee family immigrated to the United States, and he participated in the founding of the San Francisco community. After the death of his parents, he became in charge of the San Francisco temple. While he assisted in the performance of rituals when his father was alive, he pointed out that it was the spirit of his deceased mother who stayed behind to assist in temple rituals when he became the head of the community. It is a customary duty in this lineage that when an ordained master passes on, his or her spirit stays with the community for seven additional years to guide and assist the next community leader. He expects that when it comes to his time to pass on, his spirit will also stay in the temple shrine for seven years to assist the next community leader.

Fluent in English, Cantonese, and Mandarin, the younger Lee devotes his weekends to serve the CCTAA community and educate the general public about Quanzhen Daoism. During the week, he works full time as a funeral director. He attributes his entry into the funerary business again to family tradition—his uncle established the first funerary parlor in Hong Kong. When he attended a relative's funeral in San Francisco in the early 1990s, the lack of understanding of proper Daoist death rituals motivated him to enter a mortuary school and attain a state license for funeral direction. His funerary career has been a success. At one point, he worked for a large funerary corporation and managed 25 mortuaries and several cemeteries. Currently, he works with a smaller, noncorporate mortuary that has close connections with the Chinese and Japanese communities in San Francisco.

The younger Lee is married and has two sons. Neither of his sons is planning to carry the family torch by becoming an ordained Daoist priest or a funeral director.

Beliefs and Practices

CCTAA's roots in Quanzhen Daoism can be easily identified by their worship of three prominent masters in the Quanzhen lineage—Lü Dongbin (one of the Eight Immortals and central guiding deity of the Quanzhen lineage), Wang Chongyang (founder of the lineage, 1113–1170), and Qiu Chuji (Wang Chongyang's disciple who started the Dragon Gate Sect and brought the Quanzhen school to prominence in the Yuan Court, 1271–1368). From this historical lineage, CCTAA inherited a rich literature on philosophy, alchemy, talismans, rituals, and bodily cultivation. After the People's Republic of China opened its door to the outside world and before his death in 1999, Hau also traveled extensively throughout China to visit Daoist masters and continued to reaffirm and expand the content of the religious repertoire of his association.

After the death of Hau, CCTAHK maintained its legitimacy by closely connecting to the Chinese Daoist Association, a government-sanctioned organization that regulated Daoist communities in the People's Republic of China, including Baiyun Guan in Beijing. Many of the beliefs and practices of CCTAHK have been adjusted to be more consistent with the Baiyun Guan interpretations. The Lee family remains orthodox in their teachings and ritual practices—the CCTAA maintained the teachings, ritual procedures, and religious wardrobe that were originally transmitted by Hau.

The younger Lee explains that the religious vocation of an ordained priest is only part of a long series of administrative training. As Daoist disciples who are on the path to eventually join the celestial bureaucracy, he, his parents, and other disciples consider the opportunities serving as administrators of the religious institution in the human world as prerequisite to becoming a member of the community of deities who govern over all aspects of human affairs. When the disciples leave the human world (not only after their physical deaths but also after the seven years of service in the temple as spirit mentors), they will go to a destination called Langhan Gong (Temple or Palace of Esteemed Favor), where they continue their administrative training and mobilize further upward on the chain of celestial commands.

The Lees have been invited to perform public Daoist rituals in Chinese ethnic communities in the United States and Canada. Besides performing Daoist death and funerary rituals upon request, both father and son have officiated at public rituals at dragon boat festivals in both Toronto and San Francisco. Like most other Chinese Daoist and Buddhist communities, CCTAA also performs community rituals for Lunar New Year, birthdays of guiding deities and past masters, ancestral memorials on Qingming Festival—a festival that takes place in the spring—and offerings to ancestors and hungry ghosts in lunar July. Introductory rituals are also performed for new disciples who officially join the lineage to study rituals and commit to become core members of the community. Other problem-solving rituals for individuals and households can also be performed for members and nonmembers upon request, where CCTAA would charge fees to cover for the cost of offerings and other materials necessary for the rituals.

Official ritual performances only happen a few times in the year. Members of the CCTAA community, whether they are disciples or not, visit the temple shrine to pay respect to the deities. There is no requirement for community members to worship at any regular interval. The temple shrine is also open for public visits and worship. Worshippers, especially CCTAA members, usually bring fruits, sweets, or flowers as their offerings to the deities. All worshippers are expected to pay respect to the deities with lighted incense sticks. Worshippers who request blessings or guidance are expected to burn paper money to show additional appreciation toward the deities.

In the early years of its establishment, there were a few CCTAA members who were able to perform sand divination as a way to channel messages from the deities to the community members. In recent years, occasions for sand writing have diminished. Instead, the younger Lee receives messages from the deities in his dreams and sometimes also during waking hours. He claims that sometimes he would have a sudden urge to write things down, or observe his own fingers becoming restless and wanting to hold a pen, and as he holds a pen in his hand, deities would channel their messages through automatic writing. Other times a message would appear in his mind, and he would know that it was a message from the deities; the messages are often fleeting and he would have to write them down as soon as possible. These messages are the deities' direct guidance to the community, as directives for community-level decisions, or forecasting important happenings for individual members, or as orders for specific tasks to be done.

Although generally not a charitable organization, CCTAA tries to support its members and sometimes the larger Chinese ethnic community in times of need. Donations made by members and shrine visitors not only fund the daily operations of the organization, but also supplies for an emergency fund in case a funeral or other rite needs to be performed with the family of the deceased, or ill or troubled persons are unable to pay for the ritual offerings and materials. Outside of ritual needs, the emergency aid is generally available only for the organization's members, and the assistance is available not only in terms of monetary funding, but also in terms of access to personal connections and resources through the social networks of CCTAA's registered members.

Emily S. Wu

See also: Entries: Chinese Temples in America; Daoism; Daoist Canon; Daoist Rituals; Ghost Festival/Zhongyuan Festival

Further Reading

"Ching Chung Taoist Association of America." In Louis Komjathy, ed. *Daoist Organizations in North America.* http://www.daoistcenter.org/organizations.pdf. Accessed July 9, 2014.

The Eight Immortals of Taoism. Translated by Kwok Man Ho and Joanne O'Brien with an Introduction by Martin Palmer. New York: Penguin Books USA, 1991.

Choy, Wilbur W. Y. (1918–)

Wilbur W. Y. Choy, a bishop of the United Methodist Church, was born in Stockton, California. He is the son of Lie Yen Choy and Ida Lee. His father was born in the United States and educated in China; his mother was born in Guangdong, China. Both parents came to the United States just before World War I. The family lived in Stockton, California, where his father was principal of the Chinese Language School and also engaged in farming and in business.

Choy married Grace Ying Hom of San Francisco on September 26, 1940. They had four children, Randolph, Jonathan, Phyllis, and Donnell. Grace died in 1977. Choy married Nanci Adachi-Ogawa in 1982.

As a child, Choy attended the Chinese Methodist Mission, which later became the Chinese Christian Center. He received an AA degree from Stockton College in 1944 and a BA from the University of

Gov. Ronald Reagan takes his oath of office as 33rd Governor of California with his left hand on the 400-year-old Bible of Padre Junipero Sera, which is held by California Senate Chaplain Rev. Wilbur Choy. (Bettmann/Corbis/AP Images)

the Pacific in 1946. Although he was trained to be an architect and worked as a draftsman, he turned to the ordained ministry and received an MDiv from the Pacific School of Religion (PSR), Berkeley, California, in 1949, where he became the first Asian American student body president. Later, he received a DD from PSR (1969) and an LHD from the University of Puget Sound, Tacoma, Washington, in 1973.

Choy was ordained a deacon in 1947 by Bishop James C. Baker and an elder in 1949 by Bishop Donald Harvey Tippett. He served as an associate pastor at the Chinese Methodist Church, Stockton, from 1943 to 1949, and as its pastor from 1949 to 1954. After that church was merged with the Clay Street Methodist Church and became St. Mark's Methodist Church, Choy became the pastor (1954–1959) of its racially mixed congregation. He was the first Asian American clergy in the California-Nevada Conference to be appointed to a white congregation as an associate pastor (Woodland Methodist Church, 1959–1960, Woodland, California), and pastor of another white congregation (Oak Park Methodist Church, Sacramento, California) from 1960 to 1969. The Chinese United Methodist Church, also in Sacramento, was added to the appointment from 1968 to 1969. While at the Oak Park church, a member of the congregation and a prominent state senator, Albert S. Rodda, had Choy appointed the first Asian American chaplain of the California State Senate. In that capacity, Choy prayed at the 1967 inauguration of Ronald Reagan as governor of the state.

Choy was appointed district superintendent of the Bay View District (1969–1972) and was elected as the first Asian American bishop of the United Methodist Church in 1972 in Seattle, Washington. He was assigned to the Seattle Area, covering Washington and Northern Idaho, for two quadrennia, 1972–1980, and to the San Francisco Area, covering Northern California and the northern portion of Nevada, 1980–1984. Choy retired in 1984.

On the Council of Bishops, Choy served on the Committee of Relational Concerns and was assigned as a representative to the World Methodist Council, where he became a member of the Executive Committee. He also represented the United Methodist Church at the Conference of Chinese Christian Churches in North America. Choy served as vice president of the United Methodist General Board of Church and Society and was the chair of the Division of General Welfare. He was a trustee of the PSR and the University of Puget Sound, Tacoma, Washington.

Although Choy was a pathfinder as the first Asian American preacher and teacher in many settings, and member and officer in numerous organizations, he continued his ties with Chinese people in the United States and abroad. Choy is also remembered for launching many other people into leadership roles. In order to diversify clergy leadership in the Pacific Northwest Conference, he brought United Methodist clergy from the Philippines to be appointed pastors. He was among the earliest bishops to appoint clergywomen to his cabinet and to the conference staff. In addition, when Choy was the district superintendent of the Bay View District, he gathered in 1972 an ecumenical group of Asian American clergy who were interested in developing an Asian American perspective in theology and reshaping theological education. The group was organized that year as the Asian American Center for Theology and Strategies, the first of its kind among Asian Americans.

Roy I. Sano

See also: Entries: United Methodism

Further Reading

Coudal, Mary Beth. *Asian American, Pacific Islander, and Asian Church Leaders Share the Gift of Diversity with the United Methodist Church* (http://gbgm-umc.org/global _news/full_article.cfm?articleid=6130).

Guillermo, Artemio R. *Churches Aflame: Asian Americans & United Methodism.* Nashville, TN: Abingdon Press, 1991.

National Federation of Asian American United Methodist Churches (nfaaum.org).

Church of Jesus Christ of Latter-day Saints (LDS). *See* Mormons

Classical Indian Dance

For wherever the hand moves, there
  the glances follow;
Where the glances go, the mind
  follows;
Where the mind goes, the mood
  follows;
Where the mood goes, there is the
  rasa.

(Nandikeshvara, *Abhinaya Darpana*)

In Hindu performance theory, the word *rasa* is an aesthetic concept also used in culinary arts and is appropriately translated as "flavor." *Rasa* refers to the "essence," the "taste" of a dance or a dish of *tandoori* chicken. It refers to the heart of the performer, the spirit imbued in the movements, the way in which the divine is embodied and invoked through the dance. According to Susan Schwarz (2004), Vasudha Narayanan maintains that "the performers of music and dance, the transmitters of the religious tradition, speak for Hinduism. We should listen to them." In India the concept is not so much religion *in* dance as it is religion *as* dance; though the nuance is slight, Hinduism teaches us that dancers have a role in performing the divine into being. As such, the oldest Hindu texts, the Vedas, Upanishads, and Puranas, include important references to dance.

Additionally, the *Nātyaśāstra* (*Natyashastra*) is essentially a Hindu source book on dramaturgy compiled sometime between the second century BCE and the second century CE. Aesthetic theory certainly existed prior to the *Natyashastra*, but it provides us with precise descriptions and guidelines for movements, facial expressions, and mudras or *hastas* (hand gestures), which are particular, prescribed, and incredibly intricate. In the Hindu context, the practicing of these movements and gestures was used as a comprehensive aid to learning virtue, proper behavior, ethics, and morality of the divine realm.

Furthermore, Shanta Serbjeet Singh believes that dance is the "ultimate metaphor" of India's worldview, that is, "it holds up the clearest mirror to the Indian vision of life on earth" (Rowell, 1992,

Members of the Jayamangala School of Music and Dance perform at the Greenbelt Community Center as a part of the Artful Afternoon series. The school of Indian music and dance is located in Greenbelt, Maryland. (Katherine Frey/The Washington Post/Getty Images)

180–81). The seven most commonly acknowledged classical Indian dances are *Bharatanatyam, Odissi, Kathak, Kathakali, Kuchipudi, Manipuri*, and *Mohiniyattam*. The classical distinction awarded to these particular forms is an indication that they were traditionally performed in temple worship, and according to Shovana Narayan, in the Indian context "classical" denotes adhering to principles of the *śāstras* and an inherent sprit of Sanskritization. The sheer quantity of dances and the intricate precision of their movements and gestures are designated as divinely inspired activity. Where the gods and goddess are dancers, the human followers are sure to be dancers, as well.

According to Prathibha Prahlad (2009), to speak about *Bharatanatyam* is to "enter into a philosophical discourse on ethics, aesthetics and social reality all at once"

(11). The historical evolution of this dance form is fairly controversial and is characterized by some radical changes over time. The antiquity of this dance is attested in sculptural evidence found in temples that illustrate dancing girls from as early as the second century BCE. Yet, the origins of *Bharatanatyam* stem from three interrelated sources: Lord Shiva, the *Nāṭyaśāstra*, and *devadasi*.

First, it is believed that *Bharatanatyam* is possibly the dance that Shiva danced. Ramanathan notes that Shiva's dance as Nataraja is not only symbolic of the cosmic dance, but representative of an entire philosophy of life embedded in *Bharatanatyam*. The origins of *Bharatanatyam* are also found in the *Nāṭyaśāstra*. The *Nāṭyaśāstra* contains 37 chapters of exhaustive material on every aspect of the performing arts: technique, presentation, and even appreciation. It is believed that the ancient beginnings of *Bharatanatyam* are evident in this text.

In addition to Lord Shiva's dance as Nataraja and the dramaturgy of the *Nāṭyaśāstra*, many scholars purport that *Bharatanatyam*'s roots are found in the hereditary population known as the *devadasi*. The word *devadasis* is translated as "servant of God," but *dasi* can be further rendered as "consort" or "spouse," as the female dancer was viewed as literally married to a deity. The *devadasi* practiced a traditional and classical dance known as *Sadir* in Tamil Nadu and *Karnatakam* and *Dasiattam* in the Karnataka and Telugu districts. The dancers were dedicated to the temple, and therefore to the deities, at a prepubescent age and were understood to have an intimate physical relationship with the divine, thus making the dancer's body a living icon or an embodiment of the sacred; if the dance were seducing the divine, worshippers would consider contact with her body quite powerful. *Devadasi* traditionally trained their entire lives and were literate, educated, and financially independent women, whose sexuality was a lively part of their identity. However, bills prohibiting the dedication of girls to temple service in such manner were introduced in several south Indian states, first in Mysore in 1910, then in Travancore, and finally in the Madras presidency in 1927.

A second example of Indian classical dance is *Kathak*. *Kathak* originated in the Indus-Gangetic belt where Brahmins recounted stories based on Hindu mythology until they reached the point of ecstasy, which manifested itself through the medium of dance. It is believed that attainment of *ānada*, or spiritual bliss, is the ultimate goal in Hinduism and that the best way to work toward *ānanda* was through the embodied practice of *yoga*. Within this framework, the practice of *Kathak* was considered to be one of the highest forms of *yoga*.

Kathak derives from the word *kathakar*, or storyteller, and *katha*, or story. It has always been taught by members of the highest caste. However, the arrival of Islam in northern India necessitated a shift in *Kathak* since the traditional Hindu stories highlighted in the dance referred to a multitude of deities, the worship of icons, and understood the dancer as a living icon. So, mystical and devotional elements of Hinduism, namely bhakti, combined with the mystical elements of Islam, namely Sufism. To this end, under the reign of Akbar in the 16th century, *Kathak* was no longer confined to Hindu myths, but began to include contemporary and social themes. Because *Kathak* evolved by bridging two disparate religious traditions—Hinduism and Islam—it cannot be described as "secular" entertainment. Susan Schwartz (2004) believes that it is more appropriate to assert that *Kathak* "transcended particular religious affiliations, it did so by reaching for and attaining *rasa* in its most elemental sense, as an experience of transformation of a spiritual nature, not confined by ideologies or theologies" (56).

In addition to *Bharatanatyam* and *Kathak*, there are several other classical Indian dances worth noting. First, *Kathakali* is described as "embodied doing." It is much newer than other classical Indian dances, stemming from the 16th to 17th centuries.

Originally only performed for the gods, *Kathakali* is performed by males of the highest caste and is most distinct because of its costuming, particularly the heavy headdress. The performer is the lens through which the divine reality manifests itself.

Odissi is another manifestation of classical Indian dance. The earliest known depictions of *Odissi* dance come from the Udaygiri caves of *Orissa* in northeastern India. The technique is structural and sculptural and its roots are found, like *Bharatanatyam*, as performed by female *devadasi* in temples. Typically the music is soft and lilting and the movements are more sensuous, as seen in the traditional stance, *tribhanga*, where the torso is moved in a direction opposite to the head and hips.

Kuchipudi is another form of classical Indian dance, which was originally performed by male dancers of the Brahman caste. In the 16th century Siddhendra Yogi believed in *bhakti yoga*, or sweet love and devotion to God. He had an arranged marriage from a young age, but had to wait for his bride to grow into maturity, so while she matured he devoted himself to music and songs to Krishna through *madhura bhakti* (sweet devotion). When the ferry boat driver did not arrive to take him to his bride's wedding, he decided to brave the waters and swim. There was a torrential downpour and Siddhendra Yogi cried out to Krishna to save him, promising that if he lived he would devote his life to singing and dancing Krishna's glory. He was saved and the *Kuchipudi* dance was revealed to him in a moment of enlightenment.

Yet another example of Indian dance is *Manipuri*. *Manipuri* is most associated with Krishna and Radha through *raslila*. *Raslila* literally means "dance of divine love," combining *rasa*, "essence" and *lila*, "play." In 1926 Tagore formalized the dance. The women's movements are rounded and soft and the men's movements are similar to martial arts, often done with drums or spears.

A final example is *Mohiniattam*, which literally means "dance of the enchantress," from *mohini*, meaning "charming, seductive women" and *attam*, meaning "dance." The dance was developed in the mid-19th century for women, who were not allowed to dance in *kathakali*. The hands are clenched and usually held at the stomach or left side of the waist.

While all of these forms of Indian dance flourish in India, many are also present in the United States. Most major cities offer classes in *Bharatanatyam* and *Kathak*; even smaller cities and fitness centers offer fusion classes and Bollywood classes. Though Bollywood is certainly not a classical Indian dance, it utilizes similar movements, such as stomping, mudras, exact head postures and facial expressions, and very precise hand gestures. Where there are large Indian populations, cultural centers, restaurants, and studios offer classes in various classical Indian dances for children and adults as a way of preserving the culture. For example, this writer first witnessed classical Indian dance when Pallavi Bhowmilk performed *Bharatanatyam* solos at an interfaith aesthetics conference in Berkeley, California. Bhowmilk performs and teaches classical Indian dance in the San Francisco Bay Area.

The primary way most Western audiences have witnessed classical Indian dance in the United States is with the fame of *Kathak* dancer Akram Kahn. An English dancer of Bangladeshi descent, Kahn's background is rooted in classical *Kathak* training, which he often blends with modern/contemporary dance. Kahn partnered with prima ballerina Sylvie Guillem to perform *Sacred Monsters* throughout the United States. For many, this was a first glimpse at *Kathak* or any classical Indian dance.

Angela Yarber

See also: Entries: Indian Festivals

Further Reading

Anand, Mulk Raj, ed. *Classical and Folk Dances of India*. Bombay: Asia, 1963.

Prahlad, Prathibha. *Bharatanatyam*. Austin, TX: Wisdom House, 2009.

Rowell, Lewis. *Music and Musical Thought in Early India*. Chicago: University of Chicago Press, 1992.

Schwartz, Susan. *Rasa: Performing the Divine in India*. New York: Columbia University Press, 2004.

Singh, Shanta Serbjeet, ed. *Indian Dance: The Ultimate Metaphor*. Chicago: Arts Media, 2000.

Venkataraman, Leela, and Avinash Psricha. *Indian Classical Dance: Tradition in Transition*. New Delhi: Lustre Press, 2002.

Yarber, Angela. *Embodying the Feminine in the Dances of the World's Religions*. New York: Peter Lang Press, 2011.

Confucian Canon

The Confucian canon is always open, resisting permanent fixation and closure. The formation of the canon was evolutionary and complicated, involving scholarly establishment and political authority. The sources of the canonical texts were diverse and rich, with some of the material dating back to the Shang Dynasty (16th–11th centuries BCE). Unlike the canons of Buddhism and Daoism, which were (and are) read and studied mainly by the professional religious, the Confucian canon traditionally played an extremely important role in the formation and development of Chinese culture and in education. Kings and emperors turned to the canon for their political authority and legitimacy. But no one has ever claimed it to be divinely inspired, though Dong Zhongshu (ca. 179– ca. 104 BCE) of the Former Han Dynasty (206 BCE–8 CE) attempted to interpret the texts theologically. But such an attempt was short lived.

The Role of Scholars

As is true in all religious and spiritual traditions scholars often played a key role in the formation of canons. The Confucian tradition, with its present canon consisting of nine books divided into two divisions—the Four Books and the Five Classics—is no exception. During the early stage of canonical formation, traditionally Confucius was credited for editing the Five Classics, the core works in the canon, and "authored" portions of some of them, such as the Ten Wings (Ten Appendices) in the *Book of Change*. But scholars now are rather skeptical about Confucius' role as the author of any part of the texts of the Five Classics; they are willing to acknowledge his role as an editor whose chief contribution was to collect and edit the ancient texts into the precanonical classics.

The Five Classics—*Shu Jing* (*Book of History*), *I Jing* (*Book of Change*), *Shi Jing* (*Book of Poetry*), *Chun Qiu* (*Spring and Autumn*), *Li Ji* (*Book of Rites*)—became the established canon during the early reign of Wudi (r. 140–87 BCE) of the Former Han dynasty with its capital located in ancient Chang'an. Subsequently an imperial university was founded in 124 BCE along with five doctoral chairs to study the newly established canon. The importance of this university can be judged by its enrollment, which at one point reached 30,000.

Toward the end of Wudi's reign, around 90 BCE, another set of the classics written in the ancient script was found, giving rise to the controversy between the modern script text and ancient script text schools. These two set of texts not only represented two editions, but also two interpretations. The erudite at the university possessed the modern script texts, but the ancient script texts had more chapters heretofore unknown along with variant versions of sentences and paragraphs. The ancient script texts then were not recognized by the state, giving rise to the question of which edition was authentic.

But the controversy in the Han period went beyond the matter of authenticity. It involved honor, privilege, and an attractive stipend, which the occupants of the modern script chairs enjoyed. Meanwhile the experts in the ancient script tradition sought state recognition. Their petitions were all blocked by the modern script scholars. In the year 51 BCE by imperial decree a convention was called to resolve the issues. Several new chairs were established but none was awarded to the scholars of the ancient script.

However, the ancient script scholars did achieve their goal, albeit very briefly, during the reign of Wang Mang (r. 9–23 CE), the prime minister of the Han emperor Ping (r. 1–5 CE) and usurper of his throne. When the dynasty was restored to the house of Liu—the capital was moved from ancient Chang'an to Luoyang, hence the beginning of the Later Han Dynasty (25–220 CE)—the ancient script texts and their experts were once again relegated back to their former state. During the reign of Emperor Zhang (r. 76–88 CE), again a lover of the ancient texts, four lectureships were set up for the study of the ancient script texts.

Toward the end of the Later Han Dynasty in 175 CE and again between 240 and 248 CE the canonical texts were engraved in stone to ensure their correctness for posterity. This version, along with other noncanonical Confucian writings, is now housed in the Stele Forest Museum in Xi'an, China.

At the end of the Former Han Dynasty, the country was plunged into great political upheaval and turmoil. The nation was divided and in 317 CE the modern script edition of the classics was lost in the chaos. In 581 CE the country was once again unified under the short-lived Sui Dynasty (581–618 CE). After the founding of the Tang dynasty (618–906 CE), the ancient script classics became state sponsored.

The Confucian canon in 836 CE was expanded from the Five Classics to include the following works: *Zhou Li* (*The Rites of Zhou*), *Yi Li* (*The Book of Rituals*), *Xiao Jing* (*The Book of Filiality*), *Lun Yu* (*The Analects*), *Meng Zi* (*The Mencius*),

Er Ya (*The Dictionary of Terms*), *Gongyang Zhuan* (*The Commentary of Gongyang*), and *Guliang Zhuan* (*The Commentary of Guliang*).

For the next three centuries the canon remained unchanged. The major reformation of the Confucian canon occurred in the Southern Song dynasty (1127–1279 CE) under the leadership of Zhu Xi (1130–1200 CE), who was the most important figure in the revival of Confucianism in the history of China. Born in 1130 into a family of scanty means, he received his *jinshi* degree (the highest degree one could earn in imperial China) in 1148. Preferring studies and writing to officialdom, from the day he received his *jinshi* degree until the day he died in 1200, Zhu served at court for only 46 days, lecturing on the *Daxue* (*The Great Learning*), a book in the present canon. He was a prolific writer, authoring, compiling, and annotating almost 100 books during his lifetime while existing on a temple guardianship—an insignificant position from which he received a small stipend.

Zhu restructured the canon by elevating the now Four Books—the *Daxue*, the *Lun Yu*, the *Meng Zi*, and the *Zhong Yong* (*Centrality and Commonality* or *the Doctrine of the Mean*)—over the Five Classics. Of these four books, the *Daxue* and the *Zhong Yong* were originally chapters in the *Li Ji*. He further incorporated the canon into his comprehensive educational curriculum, which continued into the early 20th century. He maintained that for students to understand *li*, a concept articulated by Zhu, they should master the Four Books in the above order first before studying the Five Classics. Once the students gained an appreciation for the Confucian way, they would be in a position to study history.

During his lifetime Zhu was often criticized for being unorthodox. Thus, the canon did not receive official sanction until the Yuan Dynasty (1271–1368 CE). Once sanctioned, the number of books in the Confucian canon has remained the same.

The Role of Political Authority

The scholars alone in any faith or spiritual tradition would not and could not have been able completely to facilitate the process of canonization without help from the political authority, be it governmental or ecclesiastical. The development of the Confucian canon was no exception. The political authority of the government played a key role along the way, forming a symbiotic relationship.

In the history of China, the period from 475 to 221 BCE was known as the Warring States. The designation of the period itself suggests political divisions and wars. But in 221 BCE the country was unified under the Qin State. Thus the short-lived Qin Dynasty (221–207 BCE) was born. To rule the nation after such a long period of division, the Qin Court engaged the service of the Legalist School—one of the philosophical schools developed during the Warring States period. Under the influence of legalism the Qin Court suppressed and persecuted the Confucian school by burning its books and burying its scholars alive.

After the Former Han Dynasty was founded in 206 BCE, the country experienced unprecedented centuries—except for the brief interruption by Wang Mang as noted above—of *pax sinica*, economic growth, and territorial expansion. The imperial court, however, also retained some of the Qin policies against the old aristocracy. However, Emperor Wudi (r. 141–87 BCE) became the key figure in strengthening the government bureaucracy, in finding ways to control the officials, and in locating talented bureaucrats to manage the ever-expanding empire. He saw the Confucian notions of the moral basis of superior-subordinate relations as a tool to achieve his aims. Thus he became a patron of Confucian studies.

Confucianism, with Wudi's patronage, now became a state ideology, and the Five Classics and the other Confucian writings became a dominant force in the spiritual, political, and intellectual lives of the Chinese. But when the curtain fell on the Later Han Dynasty in 220 CE, Confucianism stumbled as well and was not to be revived until the Song dynasty (960–1279 CE).

Centuries of division and chaos followed the fall of the Han Dynasty. The country, however, was once again unified in 581 CE under the short-lived Sui dynasty (581–618 CE). The house of Li succeeded the house of Yang and founded the Tang dynasty (618–907 CE). Tang China, like Han China, also experienced unprecedented flourishing in culture, literature, commerce, foreign relations, and so forth. Daoism and Buddhism dominated the spiritual and intellectual lives of Tang China, while Confucianism and Confucian scholars undergirded the government apparatus and functions. The need for scholars to manage the bureaucracy was immense. Thus in 836 the canon

was expanded to 13 books as mentioned above.

As mentioned above, Zhu Xi's philosophy was under constant attack during his lifetime. The canon he devised did not received official sanction until 1313 during the Yuan Dynasty. The Mongols, founders of the dynasty, appreciated neither the Chinese nor the Confucian culture. The Confucian scholars were relegated to a social position just one notch above that of the beggars who occupied the bottom stratum in the social hierarchy. Moreover, the Mongols, being nomadic people, were illiterate. And yet they needed educated persons to help them govern the country. Thus in 1313, two years before the government reinstated the examination system, the canon devised by Zhu Xi was accepted as the standard texts that all aspiring candidates should master.

Characteristics and Importance of the Confucian Canon

The Confucian canon is anthological and encyclopedic. Topics therein range from philosophy to history, instructions on government, records of battles, literature, politics, kingly proclamations, rituals, spiritual cultivation, education, flora and fauna, daily life, life of the hereafter, and so forth.

The canon's importance was well and long acknowledged in traditional East Asia and some parts of Southeast Asia and in Europe in the 18th century. It had considerable influence on the thinking of the French and German intelligentsia plus a circle of theological thinkers. And the canon's influence on the Chinese and within cultural China is beyond question, as Laurence G.

Thompson, a 20th-century leading scholar on Chinese religions, states, "The Confucian Canon occupies a position in Chinese culture comparable to that occupied in the West by the Bible plus the major works of Greek and Roman literature."

Modern Period

With the fall of the Qing Dynasty (1644–1911 CE) along with the elimination of the imperial examination system in the early 20th century, China ushered itself into modernity. The role of the Confucian canon has also been diminished. The People's Republic of China, founded in 1949, simply ignored it altogether until after China began economic experiments in 1978. Since then the importance of Confucian studies has been on the rise again. Meanwhile, Confucian studies continue to play a key role in Taiwan under the government of the Republic of China and in Hong Kong in the Confucian academies and universities as well as in other nations in East Asia and some countries in Southeast Asia. In fact, American scholars of Confucian persuasion have argued that the economic achievement of the four little dragons—Taiwan, South Korean, Singapore, and Hong Kong—was pretty much due to Confucian influence.

The Role of the Canon in Asian America

The precise role the canon plays in the lives of Asian or Chinese Americans is difficult to identify without a comprehensive survey or an in-depth study. But it is safe to say that most likely it is not read by many, except the few educated elite. However, some of the concepts found in the canon continue to play a key role in the everyday life of the common folks. This is very evident in their notion of family solidarity and mutual support, in their actualization of the concept of *xiao* (filiality), in their performance of family rituals, and in their pursuit of education, just to name a few.

In recent years when interreligious dialogues are in vogue, Confucianism and its Asian American specialists have also taken their rightful places at the table in America and elsewhere.

Furthermore, Confucian studies also occupy an important position at some public and private institutions of higher education. One can actually get an advanced degree in Confucian studies from the departments of languages and literature, philosophy, or history at these institutions of higher learning.

Edmond Yee

See also: Entries: Confucian Rituals; Confucianism

Further Reading

Henderson, John B. *Scripture, Canon, and Commentary: A Comparison of Confucian and Western Exegesis*. Princeton, NJ: Princeton University Press, 1991.

Tu, Wei-ming. *Confucianism in an Historical Perspective*. Singapore: The Institute of East Asian Philosophy, 1989.

Confucian Rituals

Confucian rituals are rich and elaborative. They have an inner logic and a structure through which personal behavior as well as social and familial interactions are expressed. The Confucians always acknowledge that their rituals are created by people, and the ritual texts are meant to be manuals and guides, flexible enough to be modified to meet contextual needs. Some of the ritual books date back to antiquity while others were written throughout Chinese history. It is safe to say that these rituals are no longer performed in their entirety in either China or the United States, but elements of them can still be seen in America among the Chinese and other Asian Americans whose motherlands were influenced by Confucianism.

In this entry we will describe the ancient ritual texts, point out major developments in the history of the Chinese Confucian world, and highlight the elements that are still being practiced in America among the Chinese.

The Ancient Ritual Texts

By no later than the Later Han dynasty (25–220 CE), there existed three officially recognized ritual texts: the *Yi Li* (*The Book of Ceremonies and Rites*), the *Zhou Li* (*The Rites of Zhou*), and the *Li Ji* (*The Book of Rites*). Neither the *Yi Li* and the *Zhou Li*, however, were popular among the people, because, first, the *Yi Li* is extremely difficult to understand, even among scholars; second, the *Zhou Li*, which offers an idealized description of the offices and personnel of the Zhou dynasty (11th century–771 BCE), can hardly be considered a manual on rituals, but rather a book that deals with constitutional laws and government.

The *Li Ji*, in its original 49 chapters or in the present 47 chapters, has been influential in Confucian circles. It is concerned with a variety of topics ranging from personal life and daily interactions with others to rituals for every aspect of human existence, including the life hereafter. For example, its opening chapter states that the foundation for all social behaviors (rituals) is based on "reverence or respect." Its last chapter (i.e., chapter 47 in the present edition) deals with the four regulations of mourning garments. Chapter 9 offers the idealized concept of "Universal Harmony." This statement was inscribed in front of the United Nations (UN) building in New York City by the Republic of China, and not removed until after October 25, 1971, when the People's Republic of China took over the seat at the UN.

Even today the *Li Ji* continues to influence the Confucian world and beyond through the two chapters *Daxue* (*The Great Learning*) and *Zhongyong* (*Centrality and Commonality or the Doctrine of Means*). Zhu Xi (1130–1200 CE) extracted these two chapters to form two independent books that are now part of the Confucian canon. The *Li Ji* also influenced subsequent ritual texts, including Zhu Xi's influential *Family Rituals*.

Historical Development

Some scholars established new or modified existing rituals to meet their needs, while others were ordered by imperial decrees. One such decree is *Da-Tang Kaiyuan Li* (*Rituals of the Kaiyuan Period of the Great Tang*) that was issued in 732. Confucian scholars, notably Zhang Zai and Sima Guang among others in the Song dynasty (960–1279 CE), also wrote their own rituals. However, it was Zhu Xi's *Family*

Rituals that has been most influential and continues to be significant in the Chinese community in the United States today.

Believing that the ancient rituals were too complicated and expensive, Zhu Xi settled on four family rituals: the capping ceremony, weddings, funerals, and sacrifices. Chapter 1 of *Family Rituals* introduces the general principles of ritual; chapter 2 deals with capping and pinning ceremonies; chapter 3 lays out the ceremony for weddings. Chapter 4 is about funerals. Chapter 5 consists of ceremonies for various sacrificial rites.

Confucian Rituals in the United States

The coming of age ceremonies of capping and pinning are no longer performed in the United States. Traditionally young men were capped between 15 to 20 years of age; and the pinning ceremony was for girls as young as 15 who were not engaged. If a girl is not yet pinned, the pinning ceremony may take place when she becomes engaged. These ceremonies are no longer performed because U.S. laws—not family ceremonies—determine when a person becomes an adult.

At the present traditionally minded Chinese families in the United States continue to observe some ritual elements detailed in *Family Rituals*, such as the presentation of gifts. The gifts, of course, differ from those of centuries past. Likewise the groom's welcoming of the bride is still observed, but today's groom fetches his bride in a limousine rather than on horseback.

The sitting arrangement at the wedding banquet has not changed. The closest relatives to the bride and gloom sit close to the head of the table. Through this structural arrangement the families continue to assert their solidarity.

Traditional Chinese American families observe a "tea ceremony" in which the bride offers tea to her in-laws. While this practice is not detailed in *Family Rituals*, it is likely that the offering of tea replaced the serving of wine.

The elaborate and lengthy funeral ceremony marks the actual separation between the living and the deceased. The Chinese American community has discarded many of the elements found in Zhu Xi's funeral ceremony, some for practical reasons. For example, Zhu's funeral ceremony includes a "calling-back" ritual in which a servant goes up to the roof with the garment of the deceased, calls the person by name, and says "So and so, come back!" three times. Thereafter the garment is thrown to the ground where a second servant retrieves the garment and places it over the body of the deceased. If the person is not revived, then he or she is deemed dead. Today in America, death is determined by a physician or some legal authority.

Other elements of the traditional ritual are observed. Most notably, hemp garments are often worn by the immediate family of the deceased as a symbol of mourning; incense is offered; the image or picture of the deceased is carried as part of the funeral procession; paper money is burned and scattered (this practice is not found in *Family Ritual*, but Zhu Xi was not against it); food is offered; and a limousine is used as a carriage for the soul.

Offering sacrifices to the ancestors is very important in Chinese culture. It makes little difference whether a person is a Buddhist, a Daoist, or a Confucian, because the Chinese believe that life and death constitute a continuum. The living depend on the ancestors to dispense wisdom and advice to guide them in their daily existence, and the dead depend on the living to supply them with nourishment.

The sacrificial rite practiced by Chinese Americans is most evident during the Qingming Festival. Traditional families offer food, wine, freshly cut flowers, incense, paper money, fruits, and so forth to the ancestors at their grave site. After the visit, sacrificial offerings are carried back home and shared, thus communing with the ancestors.

Sacrifice to Confucius

Besides the above-mentioned rituals there is a communal ritual called Sacrifice to Confucius. This ritual was first observed in 195 BCE during the Former Han Dynasty (206 BCE –8 CE). This ritual was first offered to Confucius, but in 72 BCE this ritual included his 72 disciples. In 76 BCE, music, in addition to the three sacrificial animals—ox, sheep, and pig—were introduced. And in 178 CE a statue of Confucius was placed in front of the sacrificial altar until 1469 CE, when a spirit tablet of the master was used instead.

The latest revision of this ritual took place in 1968 in Taiwan. It now consists of 34 steps accompanied by animal offerings, dance, music, and songs along with the use of incense and candles.

This ritual that honors Confucius was suspended in 1949 with the establishment of the People's Republic of China. The last known ceremony on mainland China was performed in Hunan Province in 1956, until 1978 when the ritual was officially resumed. This ceremony continued without interruption in Taiwan. The Koreans have conducted this ritual semiannually ever since antiquity.

It is uncertain as to when the Chinese community first organized a Sacrifice to Confucius ceremony in the United States. But in Northern California the sacrifice has been observed uninterrupted since 1981. The ceremony takes place on or around September 28, the master's birthday, each year.

While the ritual has been modified, the following elements continue to appear: a procession, a painting of the master hanging in front of the sacrificial altar, dancers holding feathers, performers singing songs, offerings (now fruits and cakes instead of the traditional three animals), and music as well as a recessional. In addition, the current ceremony has added students reading the *Rules of Disciples* and an outstanding teachers award ceremony.

The annual sacrifice is organized by a committee committed to pay respect to the master and to promoting Confucian values. The ceremony usually takes place in a school (though one year it was held in Golden Gate Park in San Francisco) and is open to the public.

Edmond Yee

See also: Entries: Confucian Canon; Confucianism; Qingming Festival

Further Reading

Ebrey, Patricia Buckley, trans. *Chu Hsi's Family Rituals: A Twelfth-Century Chinese Manual for Performance of Cappings, Weddings, Funerals and Ancestral Rites.* Princeton, NJ: Princeton University Press, 1991.

Legge, James, trans. *Li Chi, Book of Rites.* New York: University Books, 1967.

P'ian, Rulan Chao, "Music and the Confucian Sacrificial Ceremony." In Lawrence E. Sullivan, ed. *Enchanting Powers: Music in the World's Religions.* Cambridge, MA: Harvard University Press, 1997.

Confucianism

Confucianism, a misnomer created by the Jesuit missionaries in the 16th century, has no counterpart in its native China or East Asia, where the term *Rujia* (school or family of scholars) is the common designation for this tradition. *Rujia* signifies a genealogy, but it is also a scholarly tradition, a political system, a code of ethics, a worldview, a way of life, and a spiritual tradition with a strong emphasis on humans' capacity for self-transcendence. But unlike Greek humanism, which places humans above all things, Confucian humanism is not devoid of the transcendent. Likewise the term Confucianism may lead people into thinking that the tradition was founded by a man known in the West as Confucius (551–479 BCE), which actually is a Latinization of the Chinese phrase Kong Fuzi or Master Kong, an honorific form of address to the man named Kong Qiu. He was not the founder of the tradition nor was he given that honor. However, for the sake of the readers who are familiar with the terms "Confucius and Confucianism," they shall be so used in this entry.

History and Formation

The origin of Confucianism is lost in the mist of antiquity, though some scholars argue that its genesis can be traced to the Shang (1766–1122 BCE) and the Zhou (1122–246 BCE) dynasties. The form of Confucianism, as first inherited, advanced, and transmitted by Confucius, that we have today is the result of many centuries of evolution shaped by scholars, especially Mengzi (371–289 BCE), Xunzi (ca. 310–211 BCE), and those of the Han (208 BCE–220 CE), Song (960–1279), and Ming (1368–1644) dynasties.

Confucius: The Master. Confucius was born in Qufu, Shandong Province. By the time he was born his family's fortunes had fallen from aristocracy to that of commoners. There are many stories surrounding his birth; one states that he was born in a cave, which is well preserved today, at the foot of Mt. Ni. His father died when he was young. His mother brought him up and served as his first teacher. He may not have been a diligent student when he was young, for he did not become serious about learning until age 15. From that point on he became a lifelong learner and teacher as well as an occasional holder of minor posts in government. But he was not a very successful official.

At the age of 56 he gathered some of his disciples and began traveling from state to state seeking a prince to employ his political philosophy in government. At the age of 67, after finding no one to accept his ideas and ideals, he returned with his disciples to his native land and began a career as the first private teacher in China until he died at the age of 72. After his death his disciples split and formed schools of their own based on different aspects of the teaching of the master.

Yu Wen, 23, is a teacher of Mandarin at the Confucian Cultural Institute in Mexico City. During the last day of classes for the 2011 school year, she drilled students with flash cards of household objects. (Keith Dannemiller/Corbis)

Lun Yu (*The Analects of Confucius*), an exposition of the life and ideas of Confucius was most likely written by the second generation of his disciples. In this book we not only see Confucius in action, sense his aspirations, his fears, his joys, and so forth, but also experience his creative transformation of some feudal concepts of the past. He revolutionized, for example, the concepts of the *junzi* (profound person) and *ren* (love, humaneness, or benevolence) by infusing a moral dimension into them.

Mengzi and Xunzi: Defenders and Advocates. Mengzi and Xunzi were defenders and advocates of the Confucian persuasion during the Warring States years (475–221 BCE), a chaotic period in Chinese history in which there were six major schools contending for supremacy. On the surface Mengzi and Xunzi appeared to be quite different, with Mengzi being called the idealist while Xunzi was the rationalist. Their theories on human nature certainly seem to set them apart, with Mengzi advocating that human nature is good while Xunzi insists that it is evil and that goodness is the result of conscious activity. Mengzi here is emphasizing that human beings have the capacity of becoming good while Xunzi emphasizes human behavior, but in the end they both agree on the perfectibility of human beings through education and self-cultivation leading to self-realization.

Qin and Han: Setback, Triumph, and Decline. After the long period of war and division, China was finally unified under the Qin Dynasty (221–207 BCE). The Qin emperor favored legalism and ordered the burning of the Confucian classics and the burying alive of the scholars.

After the Han Dynasty consolidated its power during the reign of Wuti (r. 140–88 BCE) and at the urging of Dong Zhongshu (ca. 179 BCE –ca. 104 BCE), a noted Confucian scholar, Confucianism was accepted as the state ideology and has been the foundation of Chinese thought ever since. With the political deterioration of the Han Dynasty toward the end of the second century, followed by disunity, the upsurge of neo-Daoism, and the wide spread of Buddhism, Confucianism declined from the third through the sixth centuries.

Tang and Song Dynasties: Revival. After the long period of disunity, China was once again unified under the Sui Dynasty (581–618), which was succeeded by the Tang Dynasty (618–907). The intellectual and spiritual life of Tang was dominated by Buddhism and Daoism alternatively; Confucianism remained in the service of the government, however. By mid-Tang there were already signs of a Confucian revival with the publication of an essay titled *Yuan Dao* (*The Origin of the Way*) by Han Yu (768–824). The revival culminated in the Song dynasty. The masters of Northern Song, especially the two Cheng brothers, and Zhu Xi (1130–1200) of the Southern Song were the architects of the revival, with the latter being the most important figure in the entire movement.

The two Cheng brothers, Cheng Hao (1032–1085) and Cheng Yi (1033–1108), though at the time they did not realize it, initiated two schools of thought in the Confucian tradition subsequently known as the Cheng-Zhu school or *lixue* (school of principle), and the Lu-Wang school or *xinxue* (school of heart/mind). The school of principle was completed by Zhu Xi while the school of heart/mind did not reach its pinnacle until the person of Wang Shouren (1473–1529), better known as Wang Yangming, of the Ming Dynasty.

Zhu Xi was born into a poor family in Fujian Province. He began his education at an early age and spent more than 10 years studying at different Daoist and Buddhist schools before turning to Confucianism. Zhu, following the work done by Cheng Yi, built his metaphysical system based on the early cosmologies developed by other Northern Song masters. He maintains that there is *li* (abstract principles or laws) in every category of things and that *li* is eternal, existing before heaven and earth came into being. Thus when an individual thing comes into existence, *li* is inherent in it, making it what it is and constituting its nature. So it is true with human beings. Hence human nature is nothing more than the *li* of humanity. In other words, nature or human nature is *li*. This line of thought was not without challenge, which, during the Song dynasty, came from Lu Jiuyuan (1139–1193), culminating in the work of Wang Yangming.

Ming Dynasty: Challenge. Wang Yangming, a noted philosopher, scholar, poet, statesman, and general, was born into an illustrious scholarly and official family in

Zhejiang Province. He, like Zhu Xi, also came under the influence of Daoism and Buddhism before returning to the Confucian persuasion. When he was young he followed the teachings of the Cheng-Zhu school. Later in life he realized that the Cheng-Zhu school's method of spiritual cultivation, which is to extend one's knowledge through the investigation of the principles of things, was not the way to acquire truth and knowledge. They are acquired, as it were, through the recapturing of one's heart/mind or *xin*, for the heart/mind is principle or *li*. Hence there is nothing outside of the heart/mind.

Confucianism in Modern Times. Both schools flourished side by side until the early 19th century when Western colonial powers and Protestant Christianity entered China. Faced with the assault of colonialism and the relentless attack of Christian missionaries and some Chinese intellectuals themselves, Confucianism once again declined. However, the resilience of Confucianism has never allowed it to disappear. In fact, many elements in practice have always been implicitly hidden or explicitly carried out in China and beyond. By the mid-20th century there were signs of yet another revival led by Confucian scholars in Taiwan, Hong Kong, and to a certain degree scholars in the West. Since the 1980s Confucianism has been on the rise again, not only in China proper but in many parts of East and Southeast Asia as well. But modern Confucianism is not an exact replica of the traditional Confucianism; rather it is a transformed system for the sake of engaging modernity in the arenas of contemporary politics, economics,

education, family, and religion by offering the world, according to Xinzhong Yao, its "moral and spiritual values," and by serving as a counterbalance to a "right-based morality" with an ethic that emphasizes responsibility. Thus the traditional *shuyuan* (academy/institute), once considered centers of intellectual and spiritual activities, are on the rise again in East Asia. The government of the People's Republic of China itself has decided recently to establish 100 Kongzi Shuyuan (Confucius Academy or Institute) worldwide to teach Chinese culture and language. No doubt Confucianism is one of the subjects that will be taught.

Confucianism as a Spiritual System

Confucianism, as a spiritual system, worshiped Di (the Supreme Being) or Shangdi (the Lord-on-High) as the highest spiritual being and moral authority in the Shang and early in the Zhou dynasties. As the tradition evolved the worship of Tian (heaven) gradually supplemented and replaced that of Di and Shangdi as the Supreme Being. This change came about as the Zhou Dynasty slowly consolidated its political power. It is most likely that Di, Shangdi, and Tian are the same deity, but were called by various names by people from different regions. Even though the Confucians worship Tian, they do not rely on Tian for transcendence. In Confucianism transcendence is achieved through self-cultivation.

Confucianism has a canon consisting of the Five Classics and the Four Books. Each book represents a different vision. It also observes, since the Song Dynasty, four family rituals: capping, wedding, funerals, and sacrificial rites. Parts of some of the rituals, especially the sacrificial rites, continue to be observed by Asians and Asian Americans who continue to be under Confucian influence.

Confucians believe that each person has two souls: the *hun* and the *po*. Upon death the *hun* soul ascends to heaven and the *po* soul remains with the corpse. They further believe that life and death constitute a continuum; hence the necessity of performing sacrificial rites to the deceased ancestors with whom they form a symbiotic relationship.

Obviously not all Asians or Asian Americans claim to be Confucians. However, no matter which tradition, Eastern or Western, East Asians may profess themselves to follow, they seldom cease to be Confucians. For thus is the way of life in the Confucian world.

Confucianism in North America

H. G. Creel in his 1949 book *Confucius, the Man and the Myth* argued that the American Revolution was indirectly influenced by Confucianism. Whether Creel was right or wrong is a matter of debate. What we do know is that Confucianism was washed onto the North American shores by the waves of immigration from China as early as 1848. These immigrants brought the tradition with them and built temples in honor of Confucius, as attested by the now defunct temple in Stockton, California. By no later than the end of the 19th century, some major universities in America began offering Confucian studies in their language, philosophy, or history departments. Today the number of such institutions is on the increase. And as previously mentioned the Chinese government itself has decided to establish 100 Kongzi Shuyuan worldwide; a number of them have been established from coast to coast in North America. The Chinese American community likewise has been offering sacrifices to Confucius from time to time since the 1920s, and such sacrifices now have become an annual ritual ever since 1982.

But the recognition of the importance of Confucius and Confucianism goes beyond academia and the Asian community. For example, in the year 2000 the governor of the state of California signed a law designating the birthday (September 28) of the master as Confucius Day. And on October 28, 2009, the U.S. House of Representatives overwhelmingly passed a resolution (H. Res. 784) honoring the 2560th anniversary of the birth of the master and recognizing the invaluable contributions he made to philosophy and social and political thought. It was further pointed out that Confucianism has had a tremendous influence on Japan, Korea, Vietnam, and the cultures of a number of Southeast Asian nations. Moreover, it has likewise made quite an impact on numerous American scholars as well as contributed to the multicultural reality of America. Such impact and contribution, in addition to those just mentioned above, have significant meanings in the fields of science, law, medicine, engineering, music, art, and so on.

How is Confucianism practiced in America by the Chinese and the people who have been influenced by it? Being a defused spiritual tradition, it is practiced within the family. We can see this practice through parts of the wedding and ancestral sacrifice rites observed by the family, the family's emphasis on the ethical realm in the members' daily life, as well as its insistency on solidarity through the realization of the concept of filiality.

Edmond Yee

See also: Entries: Chinese Drama and Religion; Confucian Canon; Confucian Rituals

Further Reading

The Analects. Translated by D. C. Lau. Hong Kong: The Chinese University Press, 1992.

Fung Yu-Lan. *Short History of Chinese Philosophy*. Edited by Derk Bodde. New York: The Free Press, 1948.

Tu Wei-ming. *Confucianism in an Historical Perspective*. Singapore: The Institute of East Asian Philosophies, 1989.

D

Daoism

Daoism has been called the most misunderstood of the major religions of the world, and thus understanding its role in Asian American religious culture is not easy. Like Hinduism and Shintō, it has no founder, credo, or single sacred text. Unlike Buddhism or Christianity, it is not a missionary faith, and thus has never found the need to express its teachings succinctly to outsiders.

Portrait of Lao-Tzu, Chinese philosopher from the 6th century BC. Drawing by Sesshu Toyo (1420–1506). Japanese civilization, Muromachi period, 15th civilization. (DeAgostini/Getty Images)

Traditional Chinese Daoism is the indigenous religion of China and takes as its goal the realization of the Dao (perhaps better known as Tao), which means "way" and refers to the formless reality that forms all things. "Realizing the Dao" can be expressed through ritual, philosophy, biospiritual cultivation, or moral action. Historically, Daoism is the sum total of several lineages or denominations, most based on textual revelations. Many of these lineages incorporate the teachings of previous groups. Thus Daoism's canon of sacred text is open.

Daoism is different from Chinese popular religion and in fact often defines itself in opposition to popular religion and local cults (and in some ways has manifested as a minority, elite religion). By the same token, "being a Daoist" is not simply a matter of accepting traditional Chinese cosmologies, theories of the body, or practicing longevity techniques. Nonetheless, there has been much mutual influence between Daoism and all these Chinese cultural practices.

Today, there two main forms of Daoism: Zhengyi (Orthodox Unity), with married clergy acting as priests for the community, is most common in Taiwan and Southeast China; and Quanzhen (Perfect Truth or Complete Realization) is monastically centered and is prevalent in the rest of China and, in a nonmonastic form, in Hong Kong. There are also several sublineages within each tradition.

Daoism in America has two separate aspects: as part of Chinese American religiosity, and as "Popular Daoism," a new American religion, a hybrid created by Chinese immigrants who took on the role of "Daoist masters" and their American disciples.

Chinese Immigrant Daoism

The first recorded migration of Chinese people to the U.S. mainland was in 1848, the year gold was discovered at Sutter's Creek in California's Sacramento Valley. By 1854, an estimated 13,000 Chinese lived in the United States, most working as gold miners or railroad workers, and in 1860, the first year accurate statistics were kept, 34,933 Chinese were reported living in the continental United States. In 1880, that number had tripled to 105,613.

The Chinese brought their religion with them but not in the same way as other immigrants to North America did. Unlike Italian Catholic or Japanese Buddhist immigrants, the Chinese were not accompanied by missionaries, nor were they supported by ecclesiastical structures that created branch churches in the new land. Unlike Jews in America, the Chinese did not set up independent temples as centers of learning. Rather, for the Chinese in America, organized religion remained in the hands of companies representing the interests of immigrants from particular clan villages or geographical areas in China. In San Francisco, for example, the six main companies (or lineage associations), known as the "Six Families," were in charge of funeral arrangements, financial security, and protection against outsider malefactors. They were also quick to build temples. What is generally considered to be the oldest temple in San Francisco's Chinatown, the Tianhou Temple, was built by the Sze Yap Company in 1852, located on the fourth floor of a narrow building on a one-block street.

By the time of the 1882 Chinese Exclusion Act, there were uncounted Chinese temples across the western United States, probably numbering in the hundreds. Chinese temples were not just prevalent in San Francisco and other urban centers but in small towns as well. They were built and still exist in the towns of Marysville and Oroville in the Sacramento Valley, which had a large percentage of Chinese inhabitants.

Did Daoism exist in any form in early Chinese America? The standard answer, which can be found in any description of temples in Chinatowns, is that Daoism existed in a blended, popularized form. Mariann Kaye Wells described the temples as "alloyed with some Taoist and Buddhist gods and beliefs." But using the stricter definition of Daoism presented in the introduction, with Daoism understood as opposed to and not equivalent to popular religion, there is no evidence that any Daoists were part of early Chinese America. As Daoist scholar Louis Komjathy put it, "the 'syncretic' or popular nature of the early Chinese temples makes it unlikely that individuals specifically identifying themselves as 'Daoists' inhabited the United States during the early phases of Chinese immigration." It seems unlikely that a Daoist religious professional, often tied to a particular location in China, would choose to emigrate.

By contrast, those in charge of the Chinatown temples were neither religious professionals nor monastics but, in a sense, paid volunteers. A Daoist priest or temple custodian, who sold the incense and the candles, might or might not assist the worshipper, strike the drum and gong to announce him or her to the gods, or help in the divination procedure. He was not necessarily a cleric in the Western sense, and in America, at least, his position was purchased by him for the year, either outright or at a public auction. Even the gods enshrined in the temples were not Daoist. Tianhou, for example, made the transition from semihistorical figure to local deity to Empress of Heaven not because of the petitions of Daoists but rather by imperial decree, since the government often "standardized" local cults to maintain better control over them. The gods and apotheosized figures one sees in Daoist temples in China (the Three Purities, the Eight Immortals, Zhang Daoling, or Wang Chongyang, for example) were not, so far as can be determined, visible in these temples. Thus, we know of no individual that identified himself or herself as a Daoist during the first century of the Chinese life in America (1849–1950).

Since the 1960s, several temples more readily identified as Daoist have opened in North America; most of these are offshoots of Hong Kong–based popular Quanzhen Daoist temples. A prominent example is Ching Chung Taoist Association in San Francisco, which is a branch temple of Qing Song Guan (Green Pine Temple), one of the most prominent Daoist temples in Hong Kong (they also have branches in Canada and Australia). For 25 years, the leader of this temple was the Rev. Wilson C. Lee (1931–2005). Lee was born in Guangdong, trained in Hong Kong, and arrived in America in 1981. Lee was kept busy with liturgical duties but also functioned as a public exponent of Daoism. He often performed traditional Daoist ceremonies for public events in the Bay Area, and occasionally in other parts of the United States and in Canada.

Notably, Lee rededicated the 19th-century Chinese temples of Tianhou in San Francisco's Chinatown and the "joss house" in Weaverville in the mountains of Northern California. One might see these actions of reconsecration of popular religious sites by a particular sectarian movement with interests in promoting its own version of Daoism as parallel to the process of local temples being taken over and "standardized" by larger organizations, a hallmark of Daoism in China for centuries.

Some Taiwanese sectarian movements founded in the early 20th century, such as Yiguandao and Tiandao, have branches in North America, and these temples sometimes promote themselves as being Daoist. But in general, among the religious preferences of Chinese Americans, Daoism would be ranked far behind Christianity, Buddhism, and nonaffiliated.

Popular American Daoism

From the 1850s on, Americans writing on the topic of Chinese religion—from Paul Carus to Thomas Merton—might have theoretically benefited from first-hand research without leaving the United States by visiting Chinese temples and talking with Chinese Americans about their religious life. These writers never did. The only Anglo-Americans who described Chinese temples in America in the 19th and early 20th centuries were popular journalists looking for good stories. Instead, the narratives of the American discovery of Chinese religion and of Chinese religions in America, which occur roughly simultaneously, run parallel yet rarely meet for over 100 years. When they do meet in a series of cultural encounters, Popular American Daoism is born. One of the earliest examples of these cultural encounters I have found is a short film made in 1948. The art film *Meditation on Violence*, directed by the well-known avant-garde filmmaker Maya Deren, is probably the first American recorded image of Chinese martial arts, and was apparently shown in universities and art theaters throughout the country. The film opens with a title card stating it is "based on traditional training movements of the *wu-dong* and *shaolin* schools of Chinese boxing." The sole actor is Chao-Li Chi, a young, well-built Chinese man, bare-chested, wearing a white scarf around his waist. To the sounds of Japanese drumming, he performs a loose interpretation of *taiji*, then kungfu, and finally a sword form. The whole effect is stylized and theatrical. Deren, in her explanatory notes to the film, links the movements of *taiji* to the *Yijing*'s hexagrams.

Is this the symbolic birth of Popular American Daoism (even though Daoism is never mentioned)? It is certainly an example of a creative collaboration between two educated intellectuals. Deren brought her financial resources and artistic and metaphysical temperament. Chi brought the skills he acquired growing up in a privileged home in China, along with his desire to be a creative artist, mitigated by racial limitations imposed on him by being Chinese in America.

Chao-Li Chi was still teaching *taiji* as of the early 21st century and does not call himself a Daoist master. But in 1970, he helped found one of the first Daoist organizations in North America, the Taoist Sanctuary of North Hollywood, California, along with Dr. Khigh Dhiegh and Master Share K. Lew.

Masters and Institutions

The 1970s saw the birth and growth of exclusively American Daoist organizations led by Chinese masters. This development was due mainly to the 1965 changes in the immigration laws of the United States and Canada, which brought more Chinese to North America. A handful of these immigrants were experienced in various Chinese religio-physical techniques and eager to teach these skills to willing Americans. At approximately the same time, young North Americans' search for spirituality outside traditional institutions (often called "the new religious consciousness") led them to embrace teachers and practices from Asia. Thus, the situation was ripe for the creation of Popular American Daoist masters and organizations.

The immigrants who became Daoist teachers came from the well-educated and privileged classes of China who experienced a sense of displacement and of loss, a feeling of belonging to a nation and a culture that no longer existed as they remembered it—not just the land of China that they left but the social, educational, and cultural nexus of the Qing Dynasty literati, which was torn by civil war, invasions, revolutions, and communism— which was an important factor in creating Popular American Daoism.

Daoism in America revolves around the figure of the teacher. If we compare American Daoism to American Buddhism (not the first or last time this comparison has been made in this study), we find that Buddhism in North America has carried over its institutional forms from Asia to a vastly greater extent. This statement is not meant, of course, to underestimate the importance of the personality of the Asian Buddhist monk; teachers such as Shunryū Suzuki, Chogyam Trungpa, and of course the Dalai Lama have influenced the very identity of American Buddhism. But American Buddhism also has created a series of institutions (*zendōs*, monasteries, and temples) that maintain the continuity and permanence that American Daoism cannot match.

The first American Daoist organization officially recognized as a tax-exempt religious institution in the United States was the Taoist Sanctuary, founded in North Hollywood, California, in 1970. However, the founder of the sanctuary was not Chinese—though he often played one on TV (most famously as the Red Chinese agent Wo Fat on *Hawai'i Five-0*). Khigh Dhiegh was of Anglo-Egyptian descent and was born Kenneth Dickerson in New Jersey. Nonetheless, his Taoist Sanctuary was the first comprehensive Daoist organization in America, teaching *taiji*, martial arts, the *Daodejing*, and the *Yijing*, and conducting seasonal Daoist rituals (albeit invented by

Dhiegh himself). Dhiegh brought to the sanctuary teachers who were from China, including one who had been trained at the Daoist mountaintop monastery in Guangdong, China. The Taoist Sanctuary currently operates in San Diego, directed by Bill Helm, a former student of Dhiegh's.

In 1976, three students of the Taoist Sanctuary, studying Chinese medicine in Taiwan, met a Chinese doctor whom they invited to the United States. Hua-Ching Ni settled in Malibu, California, opened a shrine called the Eternal Breath of Tao, and began teaching classes privately in a venue he named the College of Tao. Over the years, Ni-sponsored organizations have multiplied. His private acupuncture clinic was known as the Union of Tao and Man. He also founded Yo San University of Traditional Chinese Medicine in 1989, an accredited degree-granting college. His sons, Maoshing and Daoshing, now head both the clinic and the university while Master Ni lives in semi-seclusion.

A Thai-born Chinese named Mantak Chia moved to New York City in 1979 and opened the Taoist Esoteric *Yoga* Center, later renamed the Healing Tao Center. Today, Chia attracts an international clientele to his Tao Garden in Thailand, while the Healing Tao USA is headed by Chia's former student, Michael Winn. Chia's classes and books are best described as a popularized, streamlined system of *qigong* based on Chinese internal alchemy (*neidan*). Moy Lin-Shin founded the Taoist Tai Chi Society (TTCS) in 1970 in Toronto. These are some of the major institutional forms of Popular American Daoism. They all teach practices through a combination of weekly classes and yearly or seasonal retreats or seminars. What all these practices have in common is that they can be performed individually, not collectively, as a modular part of a daily regimen. This may well be inevitable in the American context.

Each practice has been radically recontextualized in North America: the *Daodejing* and the *Yijing* entered the American scene through the field of Sinology, which never imagined these texts would be construed as modern practice. Once *taiji* was in common circulation in the early 1970s and linked to the philosophy of the *Daodejing* and the *Yijing*, spiritual practice groups could offer courses in the study of these two texts as well as in *taiji*, linking them by a common vocabulary (*qi*, *yinyang*).

Elijah Siegler

See also: Entries: Bok Kai Temple; Chinese American Religions; Chinese Drama and Religion; Chinese Temples in America; Ching Chung Taoist Association of America; Daoist Canon; Daoist Rituals; *Fengshui*; Ghost Festival/Zhongyuan Festival; *Taiji Quan*; Tianhou, Empress of Heaven; *Yinyang*

Further Reading

Clarke, J. J. *The Tao of the West*. London: Routledge, 2000.

Komjathy, Louis. "Tracing the Contours of Daoism in North America." *Nova Religio* 8, no. 2 (2004): 5–27.

Siegler, Elijah. "'Back to the Pristine': Identity Formation and Legitimation in Contemporary American Daoism." *Nova Religio* 14, no. 1 (2010): 45–66.

Towler, Solala. *A Gathering of Cranes: Bringing the Tao to the West*. Eugene, OR: Abode of the Eternal Tao, 1996.

Wells, Mariann Kaye. "Chinese Temples in California." Master's thesis, University of California, Berkeley, 1962.

Daoist Canon

Throughout the history of Daoism, there had been attempts to canonize its texts, but the results had never been standardized across all sects. Rather than being a single selection of central texts, the *Daozang* collections include most, if not all, Daoist-related textual materials of their times, and categorize them for easier referencing.

While texts serve as important references for Daoist ritual experts, self-cultivators, and religion scholars, and while some textual materials are deemed sacred (especially talismans and written chants that are used as key tools in rituals), for most Daoist adherents, especially the lay followers, texts are not central to their religiosity. The lineage Daoists often transmit their religious knowledge secretly from one generation to the next, each sect with its own selection of religious texts. Furthermore, the lay worshippers are most familiar with a genre of texts called "moral books" that are available in folk Daoist temples. These moral books include some texts and chants that are included in the *Daozang* collections, but mostly consist of vernacular stories with moral lessons and health tips.

First *Daozang*

The earliest *Daozang*, compiled in the fifth century, included about 1,200 scrolls. The first and probably the most influential attempt to index and categorize Daoist texts was initiated by Lu Jingxiu (406–477 CE), a founding father of the Shangqing (Supreme Purity) sect. Lu promoted active integration of Daoist, Confucian, and Buddhist theories and practices, but also emphasized the need to clearly identify and categorize texts that are specifically Daoist in their authenticity, orientation, and content. Fashioned after the Chinese Buddhist canon index *Zhong jing mulu* (circa 375 CE) (*The Index of Numerous Sūtras*), the Daoist textual materials were divided into three main categories. The *Dongzhen* (*Cavern of the Realized*) collection consists mostly of texts on spiritual meditation methods and discussion. The *Dongxuan* (*Cavern of the Mysterious*) collection consists mostly of texts on instructions for communal rituals to align with the cosmos and communicate with deities. And finally, the *Dongshen* (*Cavern of the Spirit*) collection includes invocations and magical formulas, as well as philosophical writings by respected Daoist sages and masters such as Laozi and Zhuangzi. Later *Daozang* compilations maintain these three basic categories.

By the sixth century, four supplementary categories were added: the *Taixuan* (*Great Mystery*), the *Taiping* (*Great Peace*), the *Taiqing* (*Great Purity*), and the *Zhengyi* (*Orthodox Unity*). The *Taixuan* texts are mostly meditation texts that were not already included in the *Dongzhen* collection. The *Taiping* category supplements more charms, rituals, and liturgy to the *Dongxuan*. The *Taiqing* collection adds biographies and writings by non-Daoist masters and thinkers to the Cavern of the Spirit category. Finally, the *Zhengyi* includes additional rituals and charms, especially but not exclusively those used by the Celestial Masters sect.

Ming Dynasty *Daozang* (1445 CE)

By the 15th century, the *Zhengtong daozang* (*Authentic Dangzang*) and *Wanli xudaozang* (*Wanli's Supplemental Daozang*) included 1,476 books and 5,485 scroll chapters, and amounted to a total of about 6 billion characters of texts. Until 2004, the Ming Dynasty *Zhengtong daozang* and *Wanli xudaozang* together were considered as the most comprehensive and authoritative Daoist canon. There are two complete collections of the Ming dynasty *Daozang* preserved today—one housed in the Baiyun Guan, the national Daoist head temple in Beijing, and the other in the library of the Kunai-chō (Imperial Household Agency) in Japan.

Modern Chinese *Daozang* (2004 CE)

The latest major attempt to update the canon was the *Zhonghua daozao* (*Chinese Daozang*) published in 2004, a collaborative effort by the Zhongguo daojiao xiehui (The Chinese Daoist Association), Hua Xia Publishing, and the Zhongguo shehui kexue yuandaojia daojiao yanjiu zhongxin (Center for the Study of Taoism of Chinese Academy of Social Sciences), all of them state-run or state-regulated by the government of the People's Republic of China. Because institutional Daoism declined in the Qing Dynasty, this modern *Daozang* was the first major update of the *Daozang* since the Ming Dynasty.

The modern *Daozang* includes the core collection of the Three Caverns and the

Four Supplemental Categories. In addition, the canon includes later texts in Daoist theories by major sects, non-Daoist discussions on meditation, standardized rituals and liturgies, and biographies of Daoist sages and masters.

Daozang in Asian America

There are only a small handful of Daoist masters in North America trained by the major sects in canonical texts and rituals. Laypeople who worship popular Daoist deities at home shrines or in community shrines do not have much exposure to the *Daozang*, nor do they regularly reference the collection. This is true not only in the Chinese American community, but also in Chinese societies globally. The few lineage Daoist priests in Chinese America who were trained in *Daozang* literature use texts in classical Chinese. English translations of the *Daozang* texts are far and few, and are mostly used by religion scholars rather than virtuoso Daoist practitioners.

In American academe, the study of Daoism is a relatively new specialization in the discipline of religious studies. The American Academy of Religion, the largest national conference for religions scholars, now has a Daoist Studies section, indicating the growing interest in academic inquiries in Daoism. On the other hand, the current trend in Daoist studies still primarily focuses on the analysis of texts from antiquity to the Ming Dynasty. The focus on classical textual sources makes the *Daozang* more important to these scholars than the canon is in the contemporary religious communities.

Edmond Yee

See also: Entries: Ching Chung Taoist Association of America; Daoism; Daoist Rituals

Further Reading

Boltz, Judith M. "*Daozang* and Subsidiary Compilations." In Fabrizio Pregadio, ed. *The Encyclopedia of Taoism*. Vol. 1. London: Routledge, 2008, pp. 28–33.

Daoist Canon Online. James Miller of Queens University, Canada, and Louis Kamjathy of University of San Diego. http://www.daoist studies.org/. Accessed July 10, 2014.

Schipper, Kristofer Marinus, and Franciscus Verellen. *The Taoist Canon: A Historical Companion to the Daozang*. Chicago: University of Chicago Press, 2004.

Zhengtong Daozang Translation Project. Norman Gaundry of University of British Columbia, Canada. http://www.dztransla tion.com/index.html. Accessed July 10, 2014.

Daoist Rituals

The Daoist tradition has a rich history of rituals. As religious professionals, Daoist priests have always played important roles in providing ritual services to lay communities for seasonal worship, exorcism, funerary rites, and installation of statues and shrines for households and neighborhoods. Some Daoist ritualists also perform healing for the sick and the injured.

The Daoist canon and other texts that were passed down within the institutional lineages make up a rich repertoire of rituals on all scales—from large community-based festivals to talismans for healing small physical discomforts. Direct transmissions of ritual procedures from deities and disembodied worthies through human

The Rev. Tim Yao, a Daoist monk, blesses two dragon boats from Hong Kong at Battery Park, New York City. The boats took part in the Hong Kong Dragon Boat Festival at Flushing Meadows-Corona Park, Queens. (Robert Rosamilio/NY Daily News Archive/Getty Images)

channels are also respected sources of ritual knowledge.

Communicating with Spirits

There are three important categories of disembodied spirits that Daoists worship and communicate with—deities, ghosts, and ancestors. Besides deities who were born in the celestial realm, some humans are promoted to become deities after death as a reward for their exceptional moral character or spiritual cultivation. These Daoist rituals, for the most part, are performed as means to pay respect to, conjure, exorcise, and communicate with these spirits.

For the practicing Daoists, the spirits are very much part of the human community. Deities and ancestors are revered, and rituals through which to pay respect to them are performed regularly by the Daoists. However, unless they are part of the core disciples and administrative staff at a temple community, the lay Daoists visit the temples only on major ritual days, at challenging times when they must petition to the deities, or when they visit the deities as they would visit their elder relatives. The temples are typically open to the public, and worshippers can drop in any time to offer some incense, food, spirit money, and prayers.

In the celestial realm, the deities constitute an administration that oversees all affairs in the cosmos, with the ranks mirroring the human world. Especially when the human administrations fail, the celestial bureaucracy serves as the alternative and more authoritative administration to appeal to.

One of the most common rituals that is practiced by lay and ordained Daoists (and also some syncretists who do not self-identify as Daoist) is to submit written petitions to the deities. Depending on the issues of concern, one would seek the deity/deities that have jurisdiction over the matter at hand. When the affair at hand is serious or if it is in a more communal scale, then a priest can be hired to perform a ritual and submit the petition more formally.

Major Temple Rituals

There are two aspects to communal Daoist rituals: the *zhai* rituals for purification and the *jiao* rituals for offering. Usually, the *zhai* and the *jiao* are performed as parts of a series of ritual festivity. The following are a few important occasions in Daoist temple communities when these rituals are performed:

1. The first type of such occasions is called the *La* days. *La* rituals can be traced to the ancient Chinese practice of offering the first cut of their seasonal hunt to Heaven, Earth, and ancestors. There are five *la* days in the year: *Tian la* (Lunar January 1, or the New Year), *Di la* (Lunar May 5, or *Duanwu* Day), *Daode la* (Lunar July 7), *Minsui la* (Lunar October 1), and *Houwang la* (Lunar December 8, or the *Laba*). For the few days prior to the *la* days, Dao-

ist priests and dedicated practitioners would start practicing the *zhai* purification preparation: fast or eat a vegetarian diet (vegetables and without the five spices: garlic, onion, shallot, chive, and scallion), meditate, or even go into a period of seclusion. Lay practitioners would also abstain from sexual activities. On the actual *la* days, those who gather for the rituals would bathe and purify themselves with incense before attending the communal *jiao* ritual, where food and wines are offered to Heaven, Earth, and ancestors, along with appropriate ritualistic announcements and chants.

2. A second type of occasion takes place on the birthdays of deities and guardians. The deities, again, are highly cultivated or empowered disembodied spirits who staff the celestial administrative hierarchy. Guardians are often not directly responsible for human affairs, but oversee the functions and operations of astrological elements such as stars, constellations, and zodiacs (including the cyclical patterns of days, months, and years). Other guardians are responsible for natural elements and phenomena, such as wind level, rainfall, changes of seasons, harvest, and so on. Celebrations of the birthdays of key (and high-ranking) deities such as the Five Emperors (of the five directions) and the main deities worshipped by each temple community are the highlights of their activity calendars. Depending on the available resources and preferences of each individual temple community, celebrations or at least offerings of food and gifts to

deities and guardians on their birthdays could take up almost every day of the year. High-ranking deities are treated with formal rituals and sometimes theatrical and musical entertainments, while lower ranking deities and guardians are often treated with homemade dishes or specific food items tailored for the attributed personalities and preferences of these spirits.

3. A third type of occasion is for the ancestors and wandering ghosts; both categories are disembodied spirits with no administrative roles. Many families have home shrines where they pay respect to their ancestors daily. Since ancestors are considered very much active participants (through the ancestral tablet as their proxy) of a family or clan community, they are included as part of most festivities throughout the year, when the descendants would pay respect and offer food to them. Solar April 5 is the Qing Ming Festival, a day when the descendants not only pay respect to the ancestral tablet but also go to their grave sites (and sometimes a family tomb or cemetery) to sweep the graves and offer food and wine there. The Daoist temples would also perform rituals for community members in honor of their ancestors. On Zhongyuan Day (Lunar July 15), ancestors are worshipped more elaborately again, followed by individual household and communal ritual offerings to the wandering ghosts, who are disembodied spirits of those who do not have descendants taking care of them ritually and materialistically. For the entire month of Lunar July, wandering ghosts are released from the underworld to roam freely in the human world, occasionally causing problems. The temple communities would perform *jiao* rituals to feed and appease these wandering ghosts.

Instilling Spirits

When a shrine, whether a communal, temple, or household one, is set up with one or more deities for worship, the statues and paintings must be ritually instilled with the proper spirits. *Kaiguang*, which literally means "opening up with light," involves chanting and evoking the spirit of the deity or guardian, and painting the eyes and dotting cinnabar paint on the forehead of the statue. Daoist ritual experts, some going by classical textual sources, others by channeling deities who instruct them in the process, are hired to perform the spirit instilling.

The shrine or temple sites are first ritually cleansed and consecrated, and the spirits of the deities and guardians are invited to reside in the statues and paintings that represent them. Every visual representation of disembodied spirits, even as part of the temple or shrine architecture or carved on ritual tools, must be instilled with the correct spirits—not doing so would risk having unknown and possibly evil spirits take residence in them. Since regular worship empowers the spirits, evil spirits also gain power if they are worshipped.

Another event where the instillation of spirits is important is the dragon boat races during the Duanwu Festival. The dragon boats, when they are properly instilled with the spirit of the dragon god, represent the deity in energetically blessing, irrigating, calming, and appeasing the rivers that could potentially flood during the monsoon season. Accompanied by chants and deliberate ritual gestures, Daoist priests carefully paint the eyes on the dragon heads to instill the dragon god spirit into them.

Healing and Exorcism

The Daoist tradition, especially through the track of immortality cultivation, has a rich repertoire of healing methods. Besides healing through herbal concoctions and diet, physical treatments such as acupuncture, moxibustion, cupping, and other manual manipulations, Daoist priests (and sometimes a type of healer called *zhuyou*) specialize in healing through exorcism. Through chants, written petitions, talismans, and ritual gestures, deities and guardians in charge of fighting and regulating ghosts (broadly defined by spirits that could range from wandering humanoid spirits, to energetic bugs, to nonspecific ill sensations) are invited to help get rid of the illness-causing spirits.

Exorcism is also performed for haunted houses, as well as roads and sites where accidents and even deaths happen more frequently than normal.

Death and Funerary Rituals

Funerary rituals are extremely important in Chinese culture. When a person dies, he or she must be properly transitioned, through proper ritual, to become an ancestor who will be memorialized, worshipped, and included as a member of the clan or family.

In the ritualistic Daoist framework, death is not the end of life, but disembodiment of the spirit as a result of death is considered a crisis in a person's existence. This is different from the philosophical Daoist (such as Zhuangzi) perception, which considers death not as a crisis but simply returning to nature. In the context of lineage Daoism, however, Daoist priests perform rituals to ensure that the spirit of the deceased is guided, maintained, and instilled onto physical objects, lest the spirit wander away in confusion and not receive proper worship by the family later on.

Upon the death of a person, the spirit of the newly deceased is ritually transferred to a temporary worship tablet, usually made out of paper with the name of the deceased written on it. In the cases of accidental death when the Daoist ritual specialist cannot perform the proper spirit transfer ritual immediately, a spirit pole (a long bamboo pole with leaves on top, sometimes with strips of white cloth tied on top too) is used to call for the wandering spirit of the deceased to take temporary residence on the pole. The ritualist would chant, accompanied by the family members of the deceased, to call the name of the deceased until they have retrieved his or her spirit. Then the retrieved spirit would be transferred to a temporary tablet, and worship would be performed for it until the burial.

The dead body and the temporary spirit tablet are worshipped at home or a funeral home for 49 days (in contemporary practice, sometimes with an expedited schedule that could take as little as a week). After 49 days, the family would consult with a Daoist priest or a divination/astrology specialist to choose a burial site and burial date that is most beneficial for the entire family. During the burial, the dead body (sometimes in the form of already cremated ashes) is placed in the grave with the proper ritual. Also, a permanent worship tablet, usually made with wood, would have the name of the deceased carved on it and the spirit instilled in it, so that the family could pay respect to it at home. If the family already has an ancestral tablet that they pay regular respect to, then the family can also add the name of the newly deceased onto the back of the existing tablet. The spirit of a deceased person that does not properly reside in a ancestral tablet and is not worshipped properly is considered a wandering spirit, and it is expected to cause chaos and misfortunes for the entire family or clan.

Daily Household Rituals

Families that worship Daoist deities at home have shrines that display the statues (again with proper spirits instilled) of the deities of their choice, usually alongside the ancestral tablet. Sometimes Buddhist bodhisattvas (most commonly Guanyin) and the Buddha are also worshipped on the Daoist home shrines. Folk Daoists typically consider Buddhist and Daoist deities and enlightened beings part of the same Daoist pantheon.

Daily rituals performed at home shrines are usually simple—offerings of water, incense, and sometimes fresh fruits and flowers are considered sufficient. On special cultural and religious holidays, the food offerings can become much more elaborate,

and paper money of the netherworld and effigies are burned as additional offerings.

Most lay Daoist worshippers communicate with the deities by simply saying their wishes as they offer lighted incense to them. Some especially devout practitioners also practice daily chanting of selected classical Daoist scriptures.

Daoist Rituals in Chinese America

In Chinese American communities, the most common practices of Daoist rituals are in the form of home shrine worship and annual sweeping of ancestral graves. For example, some Chinese American families in Monterey, California, even though they are predominantly Christian and fifth- and sixth-generation descendants since their pioneer ancestors established homes there, perform sweeping and offer food at the local cemetery for their ancestors on Qingming. In San Francisco, California, where the city's population is 20 percent Chinese ethnic, lineage-trained Daoist priests are available to perform a wide range of rituals—most of the ones listed earlier in this entry. However, besides the few metropolitan cities with large Chinese ethnic communities (Honolulu, Dallas, Houston, Chicago, New York City, Newark, Washington, D.C., and Seattle among them), there are very few formal Daoist temple communities in North America. Daoist ritualists are sometimes requested to travel and perform proper community rituals—most notably when a foundation is being laid for a new building, to practice exorcism for haunted locations, and to make ritual preparations for dragon boat races.

Emily S. Wu

See also: Entries: Ching Chung Taoist Association of America; Confucian Rituals; Daoist Canon; Ghost Festival/Zhongyuan Festival; Qingming Festival

Further Reading

Daoist Studies. http://daoiststudies.org/. Accessed July 10, 2014.

Dean, Kenneth. *Taoist Ritual and Popular Cults of Southeast China.* Princeton, NJ: Princeton University Press, 1993.

Kohn, Livia, and Arnold D. Roth. *Daoist Identity: History, Lineage, and Ritual.* Honolulu: University of Hawai'i Press, 2002.

Komjathy, Louis. *The Daoist Tradition: An Introduction.* London: Bloomsbury Academic, 2013.

Lagerwey, John. *Taoist Ritual in Chinese Society and History.* New York: Macmillan, 1987.

Saso, Michael R. *Taoism and the Rite of Cosmic Renewal.* Pullman: Washington State University Press, 1990.

Schipper, Kristofer Marinus. *The Taoist Body.* Berkeley: University of California Press, 1993.

Silvers, Brock. *The Taoist Manual: An Illustrated Guide: Applying Taoism to Daily Life.* Honolulu: Sacred Mountain Press, 2005.

Disciples of Christ. *See* Kagiwada, David

Dragons

The dragon is perhaps the most extraordinary and auspicious creature born from the Chinese imagination. It has a camel-shaped head, pearl-studded forehead, deer-like horns, rabbit-like eyes, bull-like ears, a snake-like neck, hawk-like claws, and a razor-sharp, sword-shaped tongue. In addition to the carp-like scales covering its body, the creature has scales aligned in reverse along the back side of the flowing black beard. To touch in any way one of these backside scales leads to death. Moreover, with its shape-shifting abilities, the dragon can transform itself from the infinitely large to the infinitesimally small and can magically become invisible. The dragon also has the capacity of bioluminescence that can be modulated to highlight the brilliance of its serpentine form.

Dragons are everywhere, but they are most content to be in their palatial abode deep in the ocean. The ancients reported seeing dragons soaring to the heavens in spring and watching them entering the ocean to their watery abode in autumn. However, when Japanese farmers plead for rain (*amagoi*) for their parched rice fields, the dragon king has responded by rising with a great rush. Witnesses reported being buffeted by strong gusts of wind and seeing thick mist rising from the water surface before the dragon broke to the surface. The great speed at which the great creature ascended to the sky created dark rain-laden clouds in its wake that spread wide and thick.

The dragon is a symbol of greatness. A person of great ability or daring is said to be like a dragon. The scholar who successfully passed the Chinese imperial examination was said to have "leaped through the dragon's gate." The sage Confucius referred to the old master Laozi as being like a dragon. The dragon was the emblem of the emperor, who was the only person permitted to have the image of the five-talon dragon on his robes.

In Chinese mythology, it is believed that Chinese people are descendants of the dragon. As such, the dragon is the most popular Chinese zodiac symbol and is heavily used in folk art. An example of dragon folk art is seen in the Nine Dragon Wall in Chicago Chinatown. (Timehacker/Dreamstime. com)

The dragon motif is ubiquitous in cultures that belong to the Chinese cultural sphere. It can be found climbing on the pillars of Daoist and Confucian temples, and even curling around the columns of commercial buildings in Chinatowns across the United States. It inhabits the ceilings of Buddhist temples and perches on incense burners. It graces the roof of Shuri-jō (castle) in the old Ryūkyūan capital of Shūri. It appears in blue on Ming ceramic wares and is printed on Chinese restaurant menus. It has inspired the dragon boat race associated with the Duanwu Festival in Asia and in the United States that gener- ally takes place in fall. The dragon also plays a prominent role in the Chinese New Year parades in the United States. But mostly, it lies hidden, waiting to quicken the imagination.

Ronald Y. Nakasone

See also: Entries: Chinese New Year; Duanwu Festival

Further Reading

Joya, Mock. *Things Japanese.* Tokyo: Tokyo News Service, 1958.

Plopper, Clifford H. 1935. *Chinese Religion Seen Through the Proverbs.* Shanghai: Shanghai Modern, 1935.

Duanwu Festival

The Duanwu Festival (Duanwu Jie) is traditionally celebrated on May 5 on the lunar calendar, which is usually around mid-June on the solar calendar. In much of Asia, especially in the southern regions, this is the time when the weather gets hotter and the rainy season starts, when infectious diseases become more frequent. Therefore, the main theme of the practices associated with Duanwu is the driving away of illnesses, demons, social injustice, and bad luck. Duanwu is also most popularly associated with dragon boat races and the making and eating of rice dumplings wrapped in bamboo leaves.

House Cleaning and Small Rituals

Historically, plagues often break out during the humid lunar May month. Many of the small rituals that are practiced on Duanwu clearly serve illness prevention and healing functions. One important health-promoting practice is house cleaning. After the house is carefully swept and cleaned, water infused with flower of sulfur is sprinkled inside and outside the house. Families would also hang fresh or dry mugwort (*ai-cao*) and calamus (*changpu*) bunches outside the door to keep illnesses, insects, demons, and bad luck at bay.

People, especially young children, bathe in mugwort and other medicinal herb–infused baths on this day. Small embroidered pouches, which are stuffed with fragrant, insect-repelling herbs, are given to children to hang around their necks. Adults drink wine infused with flower of sulfur, which is also believed to protect the body from in-

vasions of illness, demons, and worms. In the popular folk story *The Legend of the White Snake*, Xu Xian's beautiful wife Bai Suzhen accidentally drank some sulfur-flower wine, which reverted her back to her true form of a giant white snake.

Ancestral Worship and Commemoration of Martyrs and Exemplary People

Ancestral worship with home-cooked dishes and rice dumplings is part of the ritual practices for Duanwu. Since ancestors are considered an integral aspect of communal life in Chinese society, the ancestors are worshipped on Duanwu just as they would be included for all traditional festivities throughout the year.

One unique aspect of Duanwu customs is the commemoration of historical and fictional figures who sacrificed their lives for patriotism and social justice. At least four famous martyrs throughout history are linked to Duanwu and commemorated on this day. Wu Zixu (ca. 490–470 BCE) was a respected politician who warned his king of the invasion by their neighboring kingdom. Rather than listening to Wu's advice, the king gave Wu a sword to self-execute and dumped his remains into the river. After Wu's death, his prediction came true, and his home kingdom was seized.

Another patriot who was linked to Duanwu and became most representative of the festival was Qu Yuan (340–278 BCE). Qu, a poet-politician, was known for his intelligence and integrity, but his king repeatedly ignored his counsel and brought the kingdom to decline. By the time he was in his 60s, he had already been exiled twice. In a state of complete disillusionment about the fate of his homeland, he drowned himself in the Miluo River (*Miluo jiang*) on lunar May 5, 278 BCE.

Two women are also often commemorated on Duanwu. Cao E was a young girl from the Eastern Han Dynasty (23–220 CE) who drowned in a river attempting to save her father. And Qiu Jin (1875–1907 CE) was a recent addition who was admired for her courage in revolting against the Qing imperial government.

Finally, the ghost-buster deity Zhong Kui is worshipped twice a year, once on lunar New Year's Eve, and again on Duanwu. Most likely a fictional character, Zhong was said to be a Confucian literatus from the Tang Dynasty (618–907 CE) who excelled in the official examinations for prospective government officials. When Zhong was summoned to court, the emperor denied him recognition because of his disheveled appearance. In angry protest, Zhong killed himself on the spot. The Jade Emperor of the Daoist pantheon took pity on his spirit and included him in the celestial administration based on his moral merits. From then on, Zhong was given the responsibility of finding and arresting demons that are on the loose.

The stories of the individuals commemorated on Duanwu exhibit a few characteristics (but don't necessarily have all of them): (1) They were considered morally exemplary by being patriotic, sometimes by providing honest but unwanted advice to their superiors, other times by protesting against unjust regimes; (2) they died tragic deaths, such as by committing suicide or as a result of torture; (3) their deaths took place either by or in a river, or happened on lunar May 5.

Qu Yuan, the River God, and Dragon Boat Race

Qu Yuan is by far the person most popularly commemorated on Duanwu. After his suicide, people who lived by Miluo River reportedly rowed boats in an attempt to find his remains. When they could not recover the remains, they wrapped rice and meat in bamboo leaves and threw those dumplings into the river in hopes that the fish would eat those instead of Qu's body. Some sources speculate that it was for the retrieval of the remains of Wu Zixue, who predated Qu by almost two centuries, that this custom was initiated. Popular folklore attributes these attempts to be the precedent of dragon boat races.

Since lunar May marks the rainy season in the central and southern regions of China, it is also a time that is prone to floods. Considering the long recorded tradition of the worship of the river god by shamans (*wu*) and occasional human sacrifice to the rivers, the boat racing and offering of food to the river could have already been a custom before Wu Zixue or Qu Yuan. The heads of the dragons on the race boats, for instance, were identity totems of ancient tribes in the central regions. Furthermore, in the Daoist pantheon, the dragons are deities that rule over rainfall, water bodies, and underground mines. An important ritual in dragon boat racing, even as a secular, competitive sport, is to instill the spirit of the dragon in the race boats by painting in the eyes of the dragon head. Religiously and symbolically, racing dragon spirit–embodied boats in a river confirms the jurisdiction of the dragons over the river. Furthermore, racing these boats along the river currents serves as blessings to cleanse the river of malignant creatures and patterns, protecting people from floods, drowning, and other water and weather–related disasters.

Today, the dragon boat race is practiced as part of the Duanwu festivities in the Chinese world. Also, rather than throwing rice dumplings into the rivers, they are used as part of the table offerings for the ancestral and deity worship on the day, and shared among family and friends. Even for those who do not practice the worship rituals, eating rice dumplings and watching the dragon boat races (whether in person or on TV) are central to—if not synonymous with—the Duanwu festivity.

Dragon Boat Race in the Asian American Context

In the Chinese American community, Duanwu is not as widely celebrated as the Lunar New Year, Qingming (Clear and Bright), or Zhongqiu (Mid-Autumn Festival). Dragon boat racing has been separated from the rest of the traditional festivity and promoted as a sport. In fact, the sport of dragon boat racing has become so popular in the past two decades that local, regional, and international leagues have been formed. Annual competitions take place in several major cities around the United States.

For example, dragon boat racing has been promoted by the California Dragon Boat Association as a sport that "enhance[s] bonding and interaction among different ethnic and cultural groups locally, nation-

ally, and internationally." Far from being limited to Chinese Americans, participants are widely multiethnic and multicultural. It has been popular as a recovery sport for breast cancer survivors, and also has been embraced as a team-building sport for corporate offices and medical professionals.

Furthermore, as dragon boat racing is taken out of its cultural context, the festivity has transformed in orientation as well. Rather than having dragon boat racing as part of the Duanwu festivity in lunar May, there are now Dragon Boat Festivals that take place in September. With boat racing as its central event, the festivals are mostly devoid of the traditional Duanwu practices. For instance, since 2006, the San Francisco Dragon Boat Festival has been sponsored by Kaiser Permanente, a major health insurance provider and hospital group. The annual festival has very little cultural content, but focuses heavily on the promotion of community health and health education.

Emily S. Wu

See also: Entries: Chinese New Year; Dragons

Further Reading

Barker, Pat. *Dragon Boats: A Celebration.* New York: Weatherhill, 1996.

Storm, Kimberly Ann. "The Survivor Sistership Dragon Boat Team: A Phenomenological Study of Breast Cancer Survivors." Unpublished EdD thesis. Saint Mary's University of Minnesota, 2008.

White, Paul, Thomas Shou, and Qingge Zhao. *The Legend of White Snake; and, Liang Shanbo and Zhu Yingtai (The Butterfly Lovers).* New York: Better Link Press, 2008.

E

Eid al-Adha, Festival of Sacrifice

The Eid al-Adha or Eid al-Kabir (the greater festival) in Arabic is known as the Festival of Sacrifice. It is also called Eid e Qurban in Persian or Bakar Eid in Urdu or Kurban Bayrami in Turkish. It is celebrated on the 10th day of Dhu al-Hijjah, the last month in the lunar calendar, on which *hajis* or pilgrims have finished their religious rituals with a sacrifice in the valley of Mina. *Hajj* or pilgrimage is obligatory for each Muslim who can afford to make a ritual visit to Mecca at least once in his or her life. Muslims who have not performed the pilgrimage observe the festival at the same time that pilgrims sacrifice on this day. Islam adopts the old Arab custom of sacrificing not only for pilgrims, but also for all Muslims as *sunna* or the prophetic religious act. This ritual is obligatory for all Muslims who can afford to buy a sacrificial animal (cow, camel, goat, sheep, or ram) that meets a fixed age and is free from certain imperfections. The sacrificer can retain one-third of the animal; the rest is given to relatives, friends, neighbors, and the poor and needy.

The Eid lasts four days. The Eid begins with the *salat al-eid*, the communal prayer of the festival, which is common to the festival of breaking the fast after the end of Ramadan. Women are also allowed to attend the prayer, though it is not obligatory. Muslims can perform it any time after the sun completely rises to just before the time of noon prayer. The prayer is then followed by the *khutbah* or sermon. The prayer is performed until sunset of the 12th day of Dhu al-Hijjah and the sacrifice may be made until sunset on the 13th day of Dhu al-Hijjah.

Another essential element of the Eid is the recitation of *Tashrik Takbir* ("God is the greatest. God is the greatest. There is no god but God. God is the greatest. God is the greatest. All thanks are due to God") after obligatory prayers throughout the four days of the Eid. Traditionally, Muslims sacrifice animals to distribute to the needy of the community. The Muslims dress up in their new or finest clothes. Women cook special cuisine. They give presents to children. They send greeting cards to one another. They visit and congratulate family and friends. They also visit the cemeteries.

Origin of the Festival

Islam was considered to be the religion of pure monotheism already propagated by Abraham. Abraham was associated with the Kaaba and the rituals of the pilgrimage because he built the Kaaba in Mecca together with Ishmael and performed the first paradigmatic pilgrimage. Then, they spread the pure monotheistic faith. The festival commemorates Abraham's will-

Imam Masud Tariq-Towe embraces a member of his congregation following a prayer service to celebrate the first day of Eid al-Adha at the proposed site of a community space named Park51 in New York, October 26, 2012. (Lucas Jackson/Reuters/Corbis)

ingness to sacrifice his son, whom Muslims believe to have been Ishmael rather than Isaac, unlike Jewish and Christian traditions. Since neither Isaac nor Ishmael is named in the narration of the *Qur'an* (37:99–113), some early Muslim scholars determined Isaac was the intended victim of sacrifice. But the view of Ishmael as the intended victim is the established idea based on the Qur'anic textual evidences (11:71, 51:28–29, 37:99–113).

Observation of the Festival in the United States

Since the Muslim Eids do not get official recognition as legal holidays to be observed by Muslims in offices and schools, *mosques* take on an important role in celebration of these festivals in the American context. Although *mosques* (houses of worship) or Islamic centers help Muslims maintain their Islamic identity, many Muslims in America attend the *mosque* for the Eids, whether or not they attend the *mosque* regularly. Like the Eid al-Fitr, the Eid al-Adha is a time of great celebration and enjoyment for both American-born Muslims and Muslim immigrants in America. These Muslims buy sacrificial animals of which part is eaten and the rest given to the needy, or donate money to a Muslim charity that will provide the meat of sacrificed animals to those who are in need. The festival remains a religious and family occasion for many Muslims in America in general, but some Muslims invite their non-Muslim friends and neighbors to their festival celebrations to acquaint them with Islam and Muslim culture.

Hatice Yildiz

See also: Essays: Muslims; Entries: Islamic Canon

Further Reading

Firestone, Reuven. *Journeys in Holy Lands*. Albany: State University of New York, 1990.

Hadda, Yvonne Yazbeck, and Adair T. Lummis. *Islamic Values in the United States: A Comparative Study*. New York: Oxford University Press, 1987.

Mittwoch, E. *"Id al-Adha."* In Bernard Lewis and V. L. Menage, eds. *Encyclopedia of Islam*. Leiden: E. J. Brill Luzac, 1971.

Paret, R. "Ibrahim." In Bernard Lewis and V. L. Menage, eds. *Encyclopedia of Islam*. Leiden: E. J. Brill Luzac, 1971.

Smith, Jane I. *Islam in America*. New York: Columbia University Press, 1999.

Tabari. *Prophets and Patriarchs: The History of Al-Tabari*. Edited by William M. Brinner. Albany: State University of New York, 1987.

El Shaddai

El Shaddai is a Catholic charismatic movement that is highly popular in the Philippines. It claims to have eight million members, drawn largely from the poorer sectors of Philippine society. The numbers increase to 11 million when its followers, those who are not affiliated formally with El Shaddai but take part in its mass rallies and prayer meetings, are counted. El Shaddai also has chapters in countries with large Filipino diaspora, including the United States, Canada, Hong Kong, Taiwan, Japan, Malaysia, Singapore, Thailand, Korea, New Zealand, Australia, Israel, the United Arab Emirates, Italy, and Germany. It has a growing presence in many cities in the United States and Canada, particularly in New York, San Francisco, Daly City, Los Angeles, San Diego, Seattle, New Jersey, Portland, Anchorage, Toronto, Vancouver, and Calgary. Its ubiquity in Filipino American communities is masked because it is usually affiliated with a local Roman

Filipino Christian evangelist Brother Mike Velarde addresses foreign correspondents based in the Philippines during a forum, May 3, 2006, in Manila. Velarde, founder of the Christian charismatic movement El Shaddai and a crucial backer of past presidents, opposed the moves by lawmakers and then-Philippine President Gloria Macapagal Arroyo to change the country's constitution through the People's Initiative and termed it illegal. (AP Photo/Bullit Marquez)

Catholic parish, although El Shaddai follows its own schedule and charismatic activities separate from the parish.

El Shaddai grew out of a radio program hosted by its founder, Mariano "Mike" Velarde, beginning in 1981. As a real estate developer, Velarde was forced to purchase a radio station, DWXI, in a land deal. Together with a friend, Velarde used the radio station for evangelization. He ran his own gospel program once a week, surprising himself when he kept receiving letters and visits from his listeners who provided him with testimonials that his radio broadcast healed them of their illness and suffering. His radio program was entitled *To God Be the Glory*, but upon seeing the booklet *El Shaddai: The God Who Is More Than Enough*, written by American Pentecostal preacher Rev. Kenneth E. Hagin, Velarde changed the title of his program to *El Shaddai*. He explained to his followers that El Shaddai is one of God's biblical names and its translation in English is "God Almighty."

Hagin's influence goes deeper than a change in the title of Velarde's radio program. Hagin wrote about his dramatic spiritual conversion in 1934, when God revealed himself to him by curing him of a congenital heart ailment and blood disease. Likewise, Velarde claimed that he experienced God's miraculous power when Jesus appeared to him the night before he was scheduled to have surgery for an enlarged heart. The next morning his doctors had to cancel the surgery because their patient no longer had the disease.

El Shaddai's first prayer rally occurred when Velarde invited his "prayer-partners," as he called his first listeners, to a "Thanksgiving" mass outside DWXI, where a few thousand people showed up. Encouraged by the initial response, Velarde instituted prayer and healing rallies, drawing more and more prayer-partners until the assemblies regularly reached 500,000 to a million people. The events were later held at several places in Metro Manila like Rizal Park and the Cultural Center of the Philippines, which could accommodate huge crowds. DWXI and prayer and healing rallies became the cornerstones of the Catholic charismatic movement, officially registered as El Shaddai DWXI Prayer-Partners Foundation International, Inc. Velarde's formal title as El Shaddai's head is Servant Leader, but he is popularly known as Brother Mike.

Learning from the success of DWXI, the El Shaddai foundation has extended its presence on the airwaves, buying radio and television time for an average of two hours every day at nearly every major city in the Philippines. It also broadcasts its programs in cities in the United States, Hong Kong, and Indonesia. Media savvy, the foundation offers live radio and video streaming of its programs and special events, almost all of which feature Velarde preaching.

El Shaddai has not bypassed the print media. It publishes *Bagong Liwanag* (New Light) magazine and *Miracle* newsletter three times a year. Predominantly written in Tagalog, the magazine contains "healing messages" from Velarde and testimonials from those who have been physically healed or delivered from their vices. *Miracle* newsletter, written in English, is circulated to El Shaddai's chapters worldwide and has the same basic content as the magazine but with news updates on the different chapters and testimonials from followers residing abroad. Velarde's experiences and teachings have also been collected in books that are published and distributed by the El Shaddai foundation. Some publication titles are *How to Win Your Battles All the Time*; *El Shaddai's Miracle Assurance Policy against Sickness, Famine and Bankruptcy*; and *El Shaddai's Miracle of Seed-Faith*.

Although it describes itself as Catholic, El Shaddai preaches and practices a version of "prosperity theology" that is heavily influenced by Pat Robertson's *700 Club*. Prosperity theology, also known as "health and wealth gospel," views physical health and economic prosperity as the will of God for Christians. Healing and wealth are promised to believers, and their opposites—illness and poverty—are manifestations of a broken faith, which can be overcome through virtuous acts such as "positive confession" and the donation of money. Prosperity theology sees the relationship with God as contractual; God is faithful and just, but to claim his blessings of health and prosperity, believers must fulfill their end of the bargain by confessing their faith and giving money to Christian ministries. It teaches that followers speak out loud the positive changes that they expect to happen in their lives as a way of claiming God's provisions and promises.

Although El Shaddai does not preach a codified set of tenets or complex doctrines related to prosperity theology, it shares three main features with other members of the prosperity movement: healing, positive confession, and prosperity. From its beginnings as a radio program with DWXI, El Shaddai has always emphasized healing messages and the cure of physical ailments by the Holy Spirit. In his mass rallies, Velarde encourages his audience to "shout out" their beliefs, name what they desire, believe in it, and "confess it." To elicit financial blessings from God, Velarde urges members and believers to tithe 10 percent of their income to El Shaddai or donate an unspecified amount, called a love offering, if one cannot afford to tithe. El Shaddai calls the tithe and love offerings "miracle seed of faith offerings," and sees these not as thanksgiving for miracles and favors but a way to induce material rewards from God.

Tithes and love offerings are submitted in envelopes together with prayer requests, which are pieces of paper on which a petition is written as a prayer. Before the prayer requests are sent to El Shaddai headquarters, Velarde or a local preacher and the crowd present during meetings and mass rallies "pray over" them to incur God's blessings. Aside from prayer requests, rally participants hold up other objects representing their petitions such as wallets, passports, savings books, and job applications.

El Shaddai followers believe that pray overs by Velarde bring better results. Thus, Filipino members residing abroad send their prayer requests and seed-of-faith offerings to El Shaddai's headquarters in Metro Manila to be prayed over by Velarde.

As a manifestation of El Shaddai's tremendous growth, it was able to build a mega-church in 2009 on a 25-acre property owned by Velarde. Officially called "House of Prayer," the building has a capacity of 16,000 seats, with an additional standing room that can accommodate 25,000. There is also more space outside for an overflow crowd. The building was inaugurated in time for Velarde's 70th birthday.

Through El Shaddai, Velarde's influence is keenly felt in Philippine politics as he actively backs and endorses political candidates, like ousted Philippine president Joseph Estrada. His latest involvement was the organization of a "White Vote" movement to endorse six senatorial candidates for the May 2013 elections who opposed the Reproduction Health Law, which guarantees universal access to contraception, fertility control, sexual education, and maternal care. It was passed by Congress and signed into law by President Benigno Aquino III in 2012.

Ofelia O. Villero

See also: Essays: Catholics; *Entries:* Aglipay, Gregorio; Filipino Protestants; Santo Niño

Further Reading

Wiegele, Katharine L. *El Shaddai and the Transformation of Popular Catholicism in the Philippines.* Honolulu: University of Hawai'i Press, 2005.

Episcopal Church. See Asiamericans in the Episcopal Church

Estrella, Julia Keiko Higa Matsui (1940–)

Julia Keiko Higa Matsui Estrella, a retired social worker and community organizer, is a second-generation Okinawan Japanese

born and raised in Hawai'i. She is the second daughter of Kyozo Matsui from Hiroshima, Japan, and Matsuo Higa, a native of Nakagusuku, Okinawa. Estrella is known for her work in giving voice to the needs and the rights of minorities and other underrepresented people through her efforts in the United Church of Christ (UCC), the Pacific and Asian American Center for Theologies and Strategies (PACTS, 1987–1995), and volunteer work.

In 1974, together with Mary Tomita (1919–2009), who were both members of the Sycamore United Church of Christ of El Cerrito, California, Estrella rallied the Asian and Pacific Islander members from different congregations of United Church of Christ denominations throughout the country to establish the Pacific Islander and Asian American Ministries (PAAM) as a Special Interest Group at the 10th General Synod in 1975. PAAM today continues to address institutional racism and injustice within the denomination and to support and strengthen minority clergy and lay leadership at the local churches.

In a 2010 interview with Eiko Kosawa of the Center for Hegemony Studies, Estrella reflected on her acts of civil disobedience and her "arrests" as an important political tool to bring public awareness to racial discrimination and other social injustices. Early on in the interview Estrella states that "civil disobedience" is a misnomer; protests that rectify injustice should be more correctly termed "civil obedience," because such acts are of a higher order of justice. In concert with this belief, in 1974 Estrella and the city of Berkeley (California) councilwoman Ying Lee Kelly, the first Asian American person elected to the council, were arrested for advocating divestment from the apartheid country of Union of South Africa. They were among a group of approximately 50 others on the University of California, Berkeley campus. At the time Estrella was an intern for Ying Lee Kelly to fulfill a requirement for her master's in social work degree at the University of California at Berkeley.

In 1993, while serving as the director of the Pacific and Asian American Center for Theologies and Strategies (1987–1995), Estrella was arrested a second time for protesting the U.S. military testing of missiles ("Star Wars") on sacred Hawaiian lands on Kaua'i. She was arrested a third time on March 28, 2006, for demonstrating against the city and county of Honolulu's decision to begin the nighttime closure of Ala Moana Park to the homeless. While the civil and military authorities did not pursue her first two arrests, the Honolulu Police Department charged Estrella and Sinea Utuloa Langi with criminal trespass in the second degree. The American Civil Liberties Union of Hawai'i defended Estrella and Langi for lawfully exercising their constitutional rights to protest. The city and county of Honolulu dropped all criminal charges.

Estrella was especially active in advocating for minority rights and causes during her tenure as director of PACTS. In an especially significant project Estrella, together with Martha Dayang of Hui Kakea Pono and others, successfully lobbied the UCC to apologize to the Hawaiian people for its participation in the 1893 overthrow of the Hawaiian Kingdom. In 1991 the General Synod of the UCC directed Rev. Dr. Paul Sherry to apologize to the Kanaka Maoli (Native Hawaiian). The apology was delivered on January 17, 1993, on the 100th anniversary of the overthrow. After returning to Hawai'i in 1995, Estrella became active with Micronesians United, an advocacy group for Micronesian immigrants, on health, housing, and educational issues.

Ronald Y. Nakasone

See also: Entries: Pacific and Asian American Center for Theologies and Strategies

Further Reading

Ikuta, C. Nozomi. *New Conversations*. Cleveland: United Church Board for Homeland Ministries, 1999.

Kosawa, Eiko. "A Conversation with Julia Estrella." 2010. http://www.hegemonystudies.org/journeytojustice/page/3/. Accessed October 18, 2013.

Nakashima-Brock, Rita. "Asian Protestantism." In *Encyclopedia of Women and Religion in North America*. Bloomington: Indiana University Press, 2006, pp. 498–505.

Pacific Islander Asian and American Ministries United Church of Christ. http://nationalpaam.org/. Accessed July 9, 2014.

Zikmund, Barbara B. *Hidden Histories in the United Church of Christ, Vol 1*. New York: United Church of Christ Press, 1984.

F

Falun Dafa/Falun Gong

On May 13, 2012, the 20th anniversary of his first public speech promoting Falun Dafa, better known as Falun Gong, the new religious movement's founder and leader, Li Hongzhi, gave a speech to a packed audience of his disciples in New York. Those in attendance had traveled from around the country and across the world to get a glimpse of, hear a teaching from, and simply be in the presence of Master Li. The contents of Li's speech reflected upon the enormous shifts of fortune experienced by the movement in its brief history as well as looked forward with predictions of greater changes yet to come, changes that would affect not only Falun Gong and its practitioners, but the whole world and indeed the entire cosmos.

Li Hongzhi first gave a lecture series on Falun Dafa to the public from May 13 to 22, 1992, in a rented auditorium of a high school in Changchun, Jilin Province, China. The lecture series began on the date to which Li Hongzhi would, in 1994, officially change his birthday—a date that coincided with the celebration of the birthday of the Buddha in the altered year of Li's birth, 1951, according to the lunar calendar. Li claims to have, by this change, corrected the year and day of his birth, which had originally been recorded as July 27, 1952. The initial workshops given by Li in May 1992, which were sponsored by the Changchun City Somatic Science Research Society, saw over 350 people sign up for participation. Subsequent workshops at the Changchun Army Club and the Provincial Party Commission drew some 800 attendees. Between June 1992 and March 1993, Li gave nine lecture series in Beijing.

Li would soon begin to distinguish between the broader world of *qigong* in China at that time—with the number of schools and techniques numbering in the hundreds—and the unique nature of Falun Gong. In 1995, his nine-day lecture series was edited into his second book, *Zhuan Falun*, or *Turning the Law (Dharma) Wheel*. In that book, and in numerous other writings that would follow, Li drew connections between the teachings and practices of Falun Dafa and a variety of teachings and practices known most widely from Daoist and Buddhist traditions. Li even went beyond Chinese religious history, saying that the supposed founders of Buddhism, Daoism, and Christianity (Sakyamuni, Laozi, and Jesus, respectively) had taught not to establish religions, but to "guide cultivation practice." Finally, however, Li declared that the teachings that he presented in his system of Falun Gong go beyond all previous teachings.

Li Hongzhi's teachings build mainly on the long history in China of transforming oneself through the cultivation of *qi*, but he distinguishes his Falun Dafa from these

Members of Falun Gong, or Falun Dafa, assemble in Times Square, New York City, and strike a harmonious meditative pose during a celebration of the birthday of their spiritual leader. (Laurence Agron/Dreamstime.com)

qi-based methods, and from the *qigong* craze of his own time in China, by asserting that his cultivation practice transforms the self/body through the accumulation of *gong* and the elimination of *qi*. More will be said on the matter of *gong* and *qi* below, but here we must take notice of the significance of Li's ever-growing reference to and deployment of overtly religious language and symbolism in the early years of Falun Gong to the fate of the movement in Mainland China.

The Communist government of the People's Republic of China recognizes only five religions that citizens may freely practice: Daoism, Buddhism, Islam, and Catholic and Protestant Christianity. In the 1980s and 1990s, however, a social space was opened up by the party allowing for the teaching and practice of various forms of *qigong*, which involve numerous practices centered on breathing and bodily movement aimed at the achievement of physical and mental health and well-being. The allowance of what would become the aforementioned *qigong* craze of those decades was conditional on the separation of such practices from any religious elements that might have been traditionally intertwined with them, most notably in relation to Daoist and Buddhist teachings. As the new *qigong* schools grew increasingly religious in their rhetoric, Falun Gong chief among them, such movements drew increasing criticism in widely published newspapers, magazines, and television news broadcasts.

From as early as 1996, just a year after the publication of *Zhuan Falun*, Falun Gong found itself the target of several such reports in the Chinese media. Whenever such a report would appear, the growing ranks of the Falun Gong faithful would rapidly rouse a response, mobilizing through means of modern social networking groups of protesters, who would show up at the sites of the offending newspaper offices or television stations, demanding retractions of media denunciations of the group. One such protest, now widely documented, was held in late April 1999 and would eventually lead to the outlawing of Falun Dafa in mainland China. In that instance, some 10,000 members of the movement chose to surround the headquarters compound of the Chinese Communist Party in Beijing to petition for specific demands. While those gathered dispersed after one day following a reportedly initially reassuring dialogue with party members, within three months of the incident, on July 21, 1999, Falun Gong would find itself outlawed in China, a move apparently inspired by a fear of the group's ability to rapidly mobilize such prominent groups of protesters and its certainly exaggerated claims of 100 million followers in China. However, the ban on Falun Gong was officially reasoned as due to the group's and its leader's overstepping the boundaries of religious freedom by engaging in illegal religious activities. Li Hongzhi, however, had left China in 1995, ultimately relocating to New York in the United States, where he remains in exile from his homeland to this day.

From New York, in the intervening years, Falun Gong has built up an impressive headquarters for global media outreach, including the newspaper and website *The Epoch Times* and the New Tang Dynasty Television station. While both organizations deliver a wide fare of news stories from around the world, each also gives extensive attention to mainland China's anti–Falun Gong campaigns since 1999, just as each is generally critical of the Chinese government. *The Epoch Times* has even issued a small book entitled *Nine Commentaries on the Chinese Communist Party* [CCP], which likens the CCP to a "giant, evil possessing spirit" that is destined to soon perish due to its persecution of Falun Gong.

The New York–based television station, New Tang Dynasty TV, is related to Falun Gong in a fashion similar to the *Epoch Times*. Falun Dafa has never operated as an institution in which individuals can be said to have "membership," and no records of "members" are kept. Since early on in China, however, Falun Dafa has proclaimed 100 million practitioners, a number that it now touts as being a "worldwide" tally, but this claim is surely an immense exaggeration, to say the least. Still, in large American cities, such as San Francisco, Los Angeles, or New York, as well as others around the world, there may be hundreds and even thousands of practitioners, while the movement may also have at least a presence in smaller towns where one might never suspect them. In those places where they have a significant presence, like major American cities, one often finds members in front of the Chinese embassy, both proselytizing for Falun Dafa and protesting the Chinese Communist Party over the continued outlawing of

Falun Gong in mainland China and what practitioners understand to be an ongoing "persecution" of adherents in that country.

Falun Gong Fundamentals: Teachings

According to the practitioners, acceptance of Li's teachings is usually due to a combination of the persuasiveness of Li's writings and teachings as well as the almost universally reported experience of the supernatural power of Li through the healing of illness and/or injury. That is to say, Li's authority is granted legitimacy by virtue of his audience's culturally determined hopes of an enlightened and supernaturally gifted teacher who will transform their lives, their selves, and their world. This raises the significance of the aforementioned incident in which Li changed his birthday to coincide with that of the Buddha. It is also suggestive, to say the least, that the title of Li's central scripture, *Zhuan Falun*, translates to the equivalent of the Buddha's first sermon, "Setting in Motion the Wheel of the Dharma."

Practitioners' hopes are reinforced through the teachings of Li Hongzhi, who presents himself as a Buddha figure who has descended to earth from "higher levels" of the cosmos—indeed, the highest of innumerable levels—to save human beings in the age of the end of the Dharma, which is characterized by worldwide social degeneration. Li claims also that he has dispatched to each individual practitioner one of his innumerable *fashen*, or "law bodies," which exist in another dimension, and that these serve each cultiva-tor as a guide in both their practice and their daily lives, constantly arranging the student's cultivation by ensuring that the cultivator will meet trials to overcome in life, thereby transforming their *yeli*, or *karma*. By eliminating *karma* and cultivating *de*, or virtue, Master Li's students are guided toward self-perfection. These goals are achieved through daily performance of five physical exercises as well as daily reading of *Zhuan Falun* and Master Li's numerous other texts. These activities serve to aid cultivators in their primary endeavor to raise the level of their *xinxing*, which is elevated in direct relation to the practitioner's accumulation of what Li calls *gong*.

The theory behind the production of *gong* is complex and involves an effort by Li to redefine some central concepts found variously in Buddhism, Daoism, and *qigong*. For *gong* "is developed through the transformation of the substance called virtue [*de*], and through the cultivation of *xinxing*." In Falun Dafa, virtue is a white physical substance that attaches to and surrounds the body in another dimension. This substance exists in relation to another, *karma*, which "is a type of black substance that surrounds the human body. It has physical existence in another dimension and can transform into sickness or misfortune." These two substances, virtue and *karma*, according to the teachings of Li, are the twin sources of pleasant and painful experiences in this life, respectively. One develops *karma* from committing negative acts, speaking negative words, or thinking negative thoughts just as, conversely, positive thoughts, words, and deeds result in the storing up of virtue, which in turn is transformed into *gong* once one has eliminated all of one's *karma*.

From *karma* and *de* to one's *xinxing*, one is obliged to transform these various aspects of oneself by means of the Falun Gong practices, discussed below. Aside from such formal practices, however, Li also teaches that one is cultivating oneself in every moment of one's life. Li teaches, for example, that a process of transformation takes place "after a conflict," referring to his understanding that people can transfer virtue and *karma* to one another while interacting in the course of everyday life. If, for instance, one were to shout insults at another, then virtue would flow from the insulter to the insulted and a reverse exchange of *karma* would take place. Naturally, then, it is the intention of Falun Gong practitioners to rid themselves of *karma* and to obtain for themselves virtue and subsequently *gong*. The significance of the teaching in Falun Dafa is that suffering hardships and tribulations in the midst of living a "normal life in society" is the primary mechanism for progressing toward enlightenment and developing *xinxing* and *gong*.

Indeed, members of Falun Gong report that while they used to get upset often, and used to "have many problems," Falun Gong cultivation has allowed their negative reactions to daily frustrations to cease and given them a calm determination to both endure hardships and to be kinder in their interactions with others. As mentioned above, most practitioners also reported the supernatural healing of illness or injury, which they also attributed to the practice, and there was much discussion, if little admission, of practitioners having

developed supernatural powers, which are said to be, like healing, something of a side effect of the principal practice of raising one's *xinxing*. Aside from the potential for change lying within each moment and interaction, there are more formal elements of Falun Gong practice, to which we now turn.

Falun Gong Fundamentals: Practices

For practitioners in North America, and indeed around the world, there are today four main components to Falun Gong practice: (1) clarifying the truth, (2) sending forth righteous thoughts, (3) the daily performance of the five physical exercises, and (4) the daily reading of Master Li's teachings. The practice known as clarifying the truth arose mainly as a response to the Chinese Communist Party's persecution of the movement since 1999. Engaging in this aspect of practice might mean volunteering to spend time at the entrance of popular tourist sites or the Chinese Embassy, if you happen to live near one. At these sites are displayed posters declaring both Falun Gong's "goodness" and its teachings of *Zhen, Shan Ren*, or "Truthfulness, Compassion, Tolerance/Forbearance," as well as other placards depicting images of tortures allegedly carried out by the CCP against mainland Chinese practitioners. Volunteers also engage passersby in conversation if possible and hand out literature that might either be the teachings of Master Li or the aforementioned *Nine Commentaries on the Chinese Communist Party* put out by *The Epoch Times*. Viewing Falun Gong as the repository of

Chinese civilization's millennia-long history of self-cultivation technologies, and the Chinese Communist Party as the enemy of that history and its modern incarnation in Falun Dafa, practitioners' of Chinese descent around the world may find their identities are reinforced as the standard-bearers of traditional Chinese culture, struggling against forces that would see that culture destroyed.

Another way that practitioners wage this ongoing battle with the Chinese Communist Party is through the world-traveling stage production *Shen Yun*. The costume and dance extravaganza began in New York in 2006 and today has three touring companies covering East and Southeast Asia, Europe, and the Americas. Promoting the production and selling tickets has become one of the principal activities of Falun Gong adherents around the world, as they believe the show itself serves to "clarify the truth" of the situation between Falun Gong and the CCP. Indeed, aside from providing an artistic platform to make a political and religious statement, practitioners believe *Shen Yun* can have a supernatural benefit in the lives of those who attend its performances.

Shen Yun claims to revive the 5,000-year-old Chinese civilization. In a series of 22 scenes, Chinese cultural heroes from throughout history are displayed triumphing over evil with their superior virtue, continuing a battle begun in the earliest emanations of time between the forces of heaven and the demonic forces led by an evil red dragon. In the end, though, the audience will also witness a recreation of the persecution of Falun Gong practitioners in mainland China. As actors portraying Falun Gong adherents suffer beatings by actors portraying Chinese police officers, the world seems about to end. Indeed, in the 2012 version of the show, projected on a screen backdrop to the stage, the audience sees a comet explode in the sky, threatening all life on earth at the very moment that Falun Gong seems to have been eradicated in China by the police. In the final moments, though, a Buddha figure appears in the sky and with his giant palm he forestalls the comet, saving the planet and revivifying the Falun Gong practitioners who now rise to the heavens, becoming buddhas and goddesses themselves.

Another important practice for adherents of Falun Gong is that of "sending forth righteous thoughts," which first appears in the writings of Li Hongzhi in 2001 and involves 15 minutes of meditation observed each day at 6 a.m., noon, 6 p.m., and midnight. One day a practitioner expanded on the significance of this practice, saying to me, "Because practitioners develop supernormal powers, doing 'sending forth righteous thoughts' really has enormous power to rectify the *Fa* and eliminate problems." "Rectifying the *Fa*" refers to the rectification of the universe by the *Fa* (Dharma), or Dafa (Great Dharma), taught by Li Hongzhi, which he says he is carrying out throughout the incalculable dimensions of the cosmos—a project in which his followers contribute through performance of the Dafa practices.

The remaining practices are (1) *liangong*, or daily performance of the five physical exercises of Falun Gong, and (2) *xue fa*, or daily reading of Master Li's writings. To these third and fourth elements of Falun Gong practice we must add the already discussed cultivation of one's *xinxing* in daily life. Practitioners will often gather in local parks or at the home of an adherent to collectively do the slow, often perfectly still, Falun Gong exercises and to read together from *Zhuan Falun* and Li's other works. If a group is large enough and its members dedicated enough, practitioners might meet for this type of activity early every morning, or perhaps just once a week. When adherents gather to read and reflect upon the teachings of Master Li as a group, they call these meetings Fa Study. Large versions of these events, called Experience Sharing Conferences, which can attract thousands of Falun Gong practitioners, take place around the world. Master Li has appeared on a semiregular basis at conferences taking place in North America over the last several years, notably at the 20th anniversary Fa Teaching in New York with which we began this entry.

"Experience sharing" is an essential part of *Fa* Study, and refers to the reflections on their lives and practice that individuals make to the group, after the recitation of Li's writings that formally composes Fa Study. That practitioners regularly engage in these national and international conferences helps one to understand, in part, how the maintenance of uniformity in both belief and practice among practitioners, both throughout Taiwan and around the world, is achieved. However, within these national and international meetings, practitioners themselves are concerned with the most mundane matters of everyday life. At these meetings, as at more regular, local *Fa*

Study meetings, people speak of the tests that arise in the course of everyday life. Some report trouble with their spouses, or children, or parents; often practitioners have family members who do not understand their allegiance to Falun Dafa. People speak of suffering illness, injury, as well as fears and doubts surrounding every problem that modern life affords. Again and again in my fieldwork experience, practitioners testified that it was their practice and study of Falun Dafa that ultimately delivered them from these tribulations, which, they always concluded, had been arranged by Master Li for them to make progress in cultivation. Always the illness or injury faded, as did the uncomfortable situations that arose in relationships with family, friends, co-workers, and strangers alike.

The Social Practice of Self-Cultivation

The cultivation of the self, then, inevitably involves relationships with others, and typically a great many of them. Falun Gong practitioners perceive their lives in particular ways, structure them through various imaginative acts, and perform the narratives of their lives accordingly, especially in the communal *Fa* Study. In Li's teachings, they are given models for behavior, often being exposed to explicit stories about how to triumph in various modern, everyday situations.

Troubles in life can do as much to reinforce Li's teachings as triumphs. Daily difficulties are sent by Li and so he declares that practitioners should be thankful when they find themselves being verbally abused or in some other seemingly negative or demeaning situation. Again and again Li maintains that sufferings of all kinds are necessary for practitioners to make progress. One may suffer social embarrassment, verbal or physical abuse, financial difficulties, conflict in one's relationships, and so on. Any and indeed every experience one has in one's everyday life can be explained according to Dafa. When things go badly in practitioners' lives, it is due to tests sent by Li. If practitioners overcome such trials through perseverance, and if circumstances improve, it is interpreted as Li having rewarded one for having passed the test.

Therefore we can say that Falun Dafa practice does indeed transform practitioners and their worlds, in that it transforms their *perception* of themselves and their worlds. Practitioners perform these transformations through their collective practice, reinforcing their understanding of Li's teachings as well as their perception of the truth of those teachings. By sharing with one another stories relating the experiencing of Li's power and the power of the practice of Dafa in their lives, practitioners give one another an extended repertoire upon which to draw in legitimating, either to themselves, to one another, or to others who are not adherents, the practice in which they are engaged.

Life for the Dafa practitioner is an opportunity to better oneself insofar as it is through Dafa that one endeavors to practice self-cultivation. Li's teachings revive and revise millennia-old teachings from Chinese tradition and, moreover, Li makes these "traditional teachings" relevant to the modern lives of his audience, and goes even further to identify his followers as the maintainers of traditional Chinese culture. This may be attractive to Chinese Americans and members of the worldwide Chinese diaspora, but the movement has now attracted followers of diverse backgrounds from around the world. The teachings of Li that are read during *Fa* Study spur the assembled practitioners to reflect upon both these traditions and their own merits in attempting to practice and uphold them, and further makes the merits of those traditions real for the group in that they see the teachings reflected in their own daily lives, week after week, as they attend to this method of *Fa* Study. Indeed, *Fa* Study can be said to consist of the twin activities of reflection upon the master's teachings and the reflection upon one's efforts to practice those teachings in everyday life. Through this practice, and the others discussed above, practitioners of Falun Dafa firmly believe that they not only transform themselves, but that they aid their master in transforming the world.

Ryan J. T. Adams

See also: Entries: Chinese American Religions; Daoism

Further Reading

Li Hongzhi. *Falun Fo Fa: Essentials for Further Advancement.* 3rd translation ed. New York: Universe, 2000.

Li Hongzhi. *Falun Gong: Principles for Perfect Health and Enlightenment.* Gloucester, MA: Fair Winds Press, 2001.

Li Hongzhi. *Zhuan Falun.* Taipei: Yih Chyun, 2002.

Li Hongzhi. "Fa Teaching Given at the NTDTV Meeting." Talk given on June 6, 2009. falundafa.org.

Ownby, David. *Falun Gong and the Future of China*. New York: Oxford University Press, 2008.

Palmer, David A. *Qigong Fever: Body, Science and Utopia in China*. New York: Columbia University Press, 2007.

Penny, Benjamin. *The Religion of Falun Gong*. Chicago: University of Chicago Press, 2012.

Fengshui

Historical Developments

Fengshui, also known as geomancy, is an ancient Chinese art of selecting ideal locations. Since the beginning of recorded history, *fengshui* masters, also known as geomancers, have used principles derived from accumulated wisdom to find locations for building villages and towns.

The literal translation of the term *fengshui* means wind (*feng*) and water (*shui*). The oldest existing record of the term appeared in the *Book of Burial* by Guo Pu (276—324 CE):

> *Qi* (life force) dissipates as it rides the wind, and stops only by the presence of water. The ancients try to coalesce [the *qi*] so that it would not dissipate, and to control it so it would stop at will. This is why they call [the craft] wind and water (*fengshui*). (Pu Guo and Cheng Wu, 1983; translation by contributor)

Humans, as part of the cosmos, were believed to survive best when they tune in to the natural rhythms of nature, manifested in the observable flow of *qi* and water. As natural phenomena, *qi* and water are similar in that they are evasive yet pervasive, and can be nurturing or destructive. The ability to read, interpret, and even manipulate *qi* and water helped the ancient Chinese find locations that were safe and comfortable for building their dwellings.

By the Han Dynasty, the geomancers had integrated cosmology, numerology, and other complicated calculations into their craft. There were detailed specifications for finding sites for building palaces, temples, businesses, residences, and graves. As the civilization advanced, *fengshui* theories shifted their main objective from ensuring human survival to maximizing human prosperity. Proper *fengshui* for a palace ensures the safety and prosperity of the reigning family and the entire empire. Temples and businesses flourish with the help of beneficial *fengshui* as well. When the *fengshui* of a residence is synchronized with the owner of the household, the entire family is supposed to enjoy harmonious relationships and prosper both in terms of procreation and wealth. Graves as the residence for the deceased are carefully located and constructed, so that beneficial *fengshui* can help cultivate the energy of the whole family through the remains of the ancestors. The descendants, by the vibration of blood relations with the ancestors, can then prosper in all aspects of their lives.

Today, *fengshui* practices are readily observable in some Chinese American businesses and homes. For as long as Chinese ethnic communities have existed in the United States, members of the community with *fengshui* knowledge have always been consulted for selecting auspicious

Fengshui literally means "wind" and "water" and is the Chinese art of geomancy. It is believed the *qi* (or *chi*), meaning "energy" flows through space, as well as the universe and the human body. The goal is to keep the cosmic energy flowing, therefore, placement of furniture and interior design become important elements in the practice of *fengshui*. Illness and misfortune can occur if energy is not flowing into an area, or if too much energy is stuck and not circulating. The *fengshui* compass is used to determine placement of doors, windows, furniture, and so on for optimal circulation of cosmic energy. (Bokgallery/Dreamstime.com)

dates and locations for important events and new establishments. Starting in the 1980s, several Chinese American geomancers established schools to disseminate the craft not only to Chinese ethnics but mainstream Americans as well. These masters simplified the traditional system to accommodate language and cultural barriers. The new generation of *fengshui* consultants trained by these masters interpret the traditional principles with understanding of the mainstream American lifestyle and sense of aesthetics. Many of the consultants are not Chinese ethnics, but have been successful in serving their non-Chinese clients who are unfamiliar with Chinese culture.

Beliefs and Practices

Very rarely do *fengshui* practitioners exclusively use only one approach and completely avoid the others. While different orientations of *fengshui* practices may have been attributed to founders from specific geographical regions, the applications of the methods themselves have never been confined to locality. *Fengshui* as a system of knowledge has porous and often shifting boundaries alongside conventional wisdom, astrology, and divination. The following are some major systems or methods that are commonly utilized by geomancers.

Compass System. In the early Han Dynasty, diviners known as *kanyu jia* used astrology and numerology as means of controlling and manipulating *qi* on the cosmic scale. They were able to determine auspicious times and directions, and developed a form of cosmography that eventually transformed into *luopan* or the *fengshui* compass. The compass system inherits much of the *kanyu* mentality and the compass, but operates on a smaller, more local scale of human dwellings and graves. In short, whereas the *kanyu jia* were more concerned about controlling the *qi* on the level of the whole universe by astrology and numerology, the compass system of *fengshui* uses similar methods to match people with cosmologically compatible residences and graves.

There are two major divisions in the compass system. The San He subsystem uses 10 Heavenly Stems and 12 Earthly Branches as the basis of its calculations and analyses, while the San Yuan subsystem uses the 8 trigrams and 64 hexagrams of *Yi Jing* (also known as the *Book of Changes*). Either way, the shared goal is to determine the auspicious times and directions for orienting features of a building or a burial site. Notice that both space and time are addressed; lucky and unlucky sectors of a house actually change from month to month and year to year. Taking the birth year of the head of the household, the geo-

mancer uses formulas to find the most ideal directions for placing doors and entrances, crucial features of the house (especially the master bedroom, kitchen, and bathroom), and even furniture (especially the beds). For a gravesite, the gravestone must face the exact direction that is most auspicious. The calculations are extremely tedious and complicated, which can partially explain why geomancers have the reputation of being quasi-elites in Chinese societies, especially back in the imperial times. Even though they were typically not literati, the mastery of *fengshui* math places geomancers in a somewhat higher position than other service professions such as servants, performers, and courtesans.

Form System. The form system focuses on observing physical characteristics of the landscape. It determines the nature of the *qi* of a site by looking at the shapes and positions of hills, valleys, and watercourses. When a plot of land is being considered, whether to build a residence or a burial site, the geomancer looks at the plot in relation to the topography around it. Shapes of geographical features are classified by the five phases—metal, wood, water, fire, and earth. Depending on the client's birth year (which also has a designated phase among the five phases), the geomancer is able to determine whether the specific landscape is suitable for the client.

The constructive and destructive cycles of the five phases are critical to the form analyses. The ideal environment should have a landscape with characteristics of phases that are constructive or at least not destructive to the client's phase. For example, metal creates water in the constructive cycle, so it is suitable for those born in water years to live close to a hill with metal characteristics, which would look soft and round with gentle slopes. However, since metal destroys wood in the destructive cycle, those born in the wood years should avoid living close to the same hill. Today, in cities where the landscapes are mostly man-made, buildings and other architectural structures are also examined using the theory of the five phases.

Besides determining the five phases in surrounding topography, the form system also considers the four animal guardians around a site. The topography around a site is divided into four directions and assigned to four animals—Black Tortoise, Green Dragon, Red Bird, and White Tiger. The most ideal site faces south, with the surrounding hills cradling it like an armchair; the highest hill should be at the back where the Black Tortoise is; slightly smaller hills on left and right to balance the Green Dragon and the White Tiger; and the smallest hill in the front for the Red Bird. When the hills are not in the preferred proportions, the protecting powers of the four guardians are compromised.

Ritualistic System. Geomancers have the reputation of being quasi-literati in Chinese society. Chinese literature on *fengshui*, whether based on information provided by Chinese geomancers or authored by them, emphasize the abstract, amoral principles of the compass and form methods. Some see the particular orientation as a strategy to counter the urban legends about begrudging geomancers hiding harmful ritual objects in their clients' houses. As holders of special knowledge

that can dramatically affect the fortunes of a household (in the case of a residence) or even the entire clan (in the case of a grave), the geomancer is both respected and feared at the same time. To build a reputation as professionals who are both nonsuperstitious and moral, it is important for geomancers to elevate their own image from quasi-literati to literati. Moral Confucian literati would avoid talking about gods, ghosts, and the like, while modern, "scientific" (informed and influenced by Western science; in other words, educated) literati would never be caught being superstitious. The market competition is fierce between geomancers, and a trustworthy image is extremely important for a successful career in Chinese geomancy.

To complicate the matter further, there are also the Daoist priests, who sometimes competed with geomancers professionally. Imagine a community working on building a local temple. Should people hire a geomancer and look for a site auspicious for building a temple? Or should people hire a Daoist priest who can make the site auspicious by performing rites? Rather than using the compass and form principles, the Daoists incorporate their system of divine bureaucracy and magical rituals into techniques suitable for geomantic adjustments. Exorcisms to drive away ghosts and *sha* (evil forces) are often performed, and talismans (paper charms) are used to counter the inauspicious impact of the environment.

Popular *Fengshui* Schools in the United States

Today Chinese Americans are often not just bicultural but also transnational; they often travel, work, and have homes on both sides of the Pacific. The newest information on *fengshui* and access to respected geomancers are readily available. Local Chinese American geomancers are able to educate themselves with knowledge produced in the Chinese context, and sometimes popular geomancers are invited from overseas.

Aside from the traditional systems that are popular in Chinese communities, there are Americanized *fengshui* schools created with mainstream Americans in mind. Master Lin Yun (1932–2010), the founder of Black Sect Tantric Buddhism, invented a convenient system that relies mostly on the cultivated spiritual power of the practitioners and small rituals referred to as "transcendental cures." While the principles of the compass and form schools are still incorporated in the Black Sect system, complicated calculations are not emphasized. The majority of professional *fengshui* consultants in the United States, especially the non-Chinese ethnics, practice either the Black Sect system or modified versions of it.

Also influential in America are Lilian Too and Eva Wong, who simplify the traditional compass and form methods for the American audience and publish introductory *fengshui* books in the English language.

Emily S. Wu

See also: Entries: Chinese American Religions; Daoism; *Yinyang*

Further Reading

Bruun, Ole. *Fengshui in China: Geomantic Divination between State Orthodoxy and Popular Religion*. Honolulu: University of Hawai'i Press, 2003.

Kennedy, David. *Fengshui for Dummies*. Foster City, CA: IDG Books Worldwide, 2001.

Rossbach, Sarah, and Yun Lin. *Living Color: Master Lin Yun's Guide to Fengshui and the Art of Color*. New York: Kodansha International, 1994.

Too, Lillian. *The Complete Illustrated Guide to Fengshui*. Dorset: Element, 1996.

Walters, Derek. *The Fengshui Handbook: A Practical Guide to Chinese Geomancy and Environmental Harmony*. London: Thorsons, 1995.

Wong, Eva. *Fengshui: The Ancient Wisdom of Harmonious Living for Modern Times*. Boston: Shambhala, 1996.

Filipino Protestants

The 350 years of Spanish colonial rule in the Philippines resulted in a predominantly Roman Catholic Christian country. It was only after the Spanish-American War, when the United States acquired the Philippines from Spain with the 1898 Treaty of Paris, that Protestantism gained a foothold. Protestant missionary activity came hand in hand with U.S. colonial rule. In 1898, Bishop James Mills Thoburn of the Methodist Episcopal Church urged Protestant churches in the United States "to enter in the name of the Lord and give the people of the Philippines a pure Gospel." In the same year, Dr. George Pentecost reported to the U.S. Presbyterian General Assembly, "God has given into our hands . . . the Philippines Islands . . . [and] by the very guns of our battleships, summoned us to go up and possess the land." Presbyterian, Baptist, and Methodist leaders met in New York to strategize ways of introducing Protestantism to the

The Rev. Canon Raynald Sales Bonoan, Diocesan Canon Missioner to the Asian American community in the Diocese of Southwest Florida, in Safety Harbor, Florida, July 7, 2014. Fr. Bonoan was born on December 16, 1954, in the Philippines to the late Bishop Emerson Bonoan and Alicia Sales and was raised in the Episcopal Seminary community of St. Andrew's in Quezon City where his father was a professor. (Douglas R. Clifford/ZUMA Press/Corbis)

Philippines. The result was a comity agreement of the missionary enterprises, dividing up territory and converts. Only one Protestant church would be established in each area. In 1901 the Protestant denominations established the Evangelical Union to coordinate activities that laid the foundations for an indigenous religious movement. After an initial period of resentment toward American missionaries, Filipinos gradually accepted Protestant Christianity.

The Japanese occupation from 1942 to 1945 prompted the formation of the Evangelical Church in the Philippines that combined 13 denominations to better deal with the diverse Protestant groups. In 1948 the Christian Church (Disciples of Christ), the Philippine Methodist Church, and the United Evangelical Church (composed of the Presbyterian and Congregational Churches) formed the United Church of Christ in the Philippines (UCCP). The UCCP was established during a time of economic bankruptcy and rebuilding from the ravages of war.

Filipino Migration

Economic hardships and joblessness continued and worsened after the end of World War II. The situation forced many

Filipinos to seek employment abroad. This labor diaspora was facilitated by labor export systems that Spanish colonial administrators had established and that was adopted by U.S. military governor-generals and commonwealth administrators, and the subsequent Philippine government. Eleazar Fernandez notes, "The diaspora (*diaspeiro*—scattering of seeds) of people has intensified at an alarming rate in the era of globalization. Among the top diasporized people in the world are Filipinos. They are now scattered in 192 countries."

The United States is home to the largest group of Filipinos working and living outside the Philippines. Terrence Valen, director of the Filipino Community Center in San Francisco, California, identifies four periods or waves of Filipino migration. The first wave began during the American colonial era, a period spanning the 1900s to the 1940s. The Hawaiian Sugar Planters Association recruited a number of Filipino agricultural workers, who in turn encouraged others to join them. California agricultural interests recruited agricultural workers. Filipinos went to work in Alaskan canneries and for the U.S. Navy as mess cooks and compartment cleaners.

The second wave of migration spans the years between 1946 to 1960. Filipinos who were recruited by and enlisted in the U.S.

Table 4

Census-Defined U.S. Urban Areas	Number of U.S. Filipinos*	Percent Filipinos in the Urban Area
Daly City, CA	33,649	33.3
Vallejo, CA	24,451	21.1
Honolulu, HI	45,818	15.7
Stockton, CA	21,133	7.2
San Diego, CA	76,738	5.9
San Jose, CA	53,008	5.6
San Francisco–Oakland, CA	42,417	4.9
Long Beach, CA	20,964	4.5
Virginia Beach, VA	17,481	4.0
Las Vegas, NV	19,042	3.3
Los Angeles, CA	122,787	3.2
Sacramento, CA	13,468	2.9
Seattle, WA	15,757	2.6
Chicago, IL	29,664	1.1
Newark, NY-NJ-CT	123,254	0.9

This does not include undocumented residents and people who are not officially counted.

Army during World War II and veterans were given preference for visas to the United States. As a result many chose to move to the United States. The third wave spans the years from 1965 to 1990. Filipino professionals, especially nurses, doctors, and engineers, immigrated to the United States. At the same time, family-based immigration policies opened pathways for U.S. Filipinos to petition their families to come and join them. Overlapping the third wave, a fourth wave of immigration resulted from the 1970 Philippine Labor Export Program and other government policies that actively encouraged Filipino workers to work and establish businesses abroad. Most of the migrants currently residing in the United States are the result of this program. Some who overstayed their tourist, student, or guest worker visas are undocumented.

The U.S. Census of 2010 shows the U.S. urban areas with the largest concentration of Filipinos, over 10,000 in population (U.S. Census Bureau).

Beginnings

In light of the intensifying rate of Filipino migration and its pastoral responsibility, the United Church of Christ in the Philippines (UCCP) started sending missionaries to the United States. The first missionary commissioned by the UCCP was the Rev. Dr. Ben Junasa. In May 1956, Rev. Junasa arrived in Hawai'i and gathered a team that consisted of the Reverends Angel Taglucop, Serafin Chaves, and Erasto Arenas to start a Filipino ministry in areas with a heavy concentration of Filipinos. The team made Honolulu their first home base.

In the 1970s, the United Church of Christ, USA, started recognizing the Pacific Asian American ministry initiatives. This resulted in the election of Asian American members into leadership roles. The Board for Homeland Ministries elected Rev. Angel Taglucop. In his capacity, Rev. Taglucop alerted the conference minister of the Northern California/Nevada Conference, the Rev. Mineo Katagiri, to the growing Filipino population in the San Francisco Bay Area, many of whom were members of the United Church of Christ in the Philippines and were ready to become part of the United Church of Christ in the United States.

In 1979, Katagiri invited Rev. Erasto Arenas, who was at that time assisting Rev. Taglucop to establish a church in Hawai'i, to develop a ministry among the Filipino community in the Bay Area. Salvador Arenas, Rev. Arenas's brother who lives in San Bruno, California, immediately rallied former members of the UCCP Tambo, Parañaque, where Rev. Arenas once served. With the support of a core of enthusiastic devotees, Rev. Arenas quickly laid the foundation for a church. The historic first worship service of the first Filipino American United Church of Christ in the United States took place on August 16, 1979, at St. John's UCC on El Camino Street, a rented space. It was attended by 41 adults and children. The church grew rapidly. In just two and a half years, the congregation was able to move to its current church building at 461 Linden Avenue. The congregation continued to grow, and after 15 years, the church sanctuary was filled to capacity during worship services.

Growth and Expansion

In 1980 Rev. Arenas, with the help of other Filipino clerics, organized the Council for Filipino Ministries (CFM) in the Northern California/Nevada Conference for the express purpose of organizing and establishing congregations in areas with large Filipino populations. From San Bruno, the Filipino churches under UCC spread to the greater San Francisco Bay Area, across the state to the south, to some eastern and northern states, and to Canada. The Cosmopolitan Evangelical UCC in San Jose was established in January 1980 under the leadership of the Rev. Serafin Chavez. The Eagle Rock Fil-Am UCC in Los Angeles was organized in January 1982 by Rev. Angel Taglucop and Rev. Erasto Arenas. The Fremont Fil-Am UCC was organized in September 1982 with the Rev. Manuel Tabujara as the organizing minister. In 1983, the Filipino-American UCC in Vallejo was organized by Rev. Angel Taglucop. The Sunnyvale Fil-Am UCC was organized in February 1986 by the Rev. Federico Ranches. A split of the Fremont Church gave birth to the Filipino-American Evangelical Church in January 1989 with Rev. Manny Tabujara as pastor. In 1994, the church in San Diego was organized with Rev. Alex Achacoso as pastor. And in 1995, a Filipino-American church was founded in Sacramento with Rev. Socrates Herrera as pastor. The Filipino-American UCC in Detroit, Michigan was organized as well as in Winnipeg, Manitoba, Canada. Unfortunately, the churches started in Salinas and Stockton did not survive. The latest church to be organized is the Faith Community Church in Oakland, now pastored by the Rev. Bladimer Paeste. As of this writing, approximately a thousand members in the Northern California/Nevada Conference alone are served by the Filipino American churches.

The CFM of Northern California, under the current leadership of the Rev. Dr. Reynaldo Desenganio, the moderator, remains active and meets regularly. It has shifted its purpose and task to promoting a closer relationship between and among churches in the council, and to providing direction to the Filipino ministries within the UCC. The council also serves as ministry partner with the conference on cultural matters. CFM holds fellowships and joint celebrations, usually on Thanksgiving and Christmas. It conducts educational and advocacy programs. And it also responds to needs in the Philippines such as helping calamity victims through fundraising.

Consultation and Ecumenical Cooperation

Twenty-nine years after the founding of the first Filipino American church under the UCC, a historic consultation gathered former UCCP church leaders serving in the United States in Fremont, California, between June 30 and July 1, 2008. The general secretary of the UCCP and a staffer from its national secretariat, together with other key leaders of the UCC, both from the Northern California–Nevada Conference and from the national church staff, were also present.

The consultation listened to the struggles and deepest spiritual needs of the diaspora Filipinos in the United States. The participants identified two primary concerns. The first is the pain of separation from life in the homeland and the sense of rootlessness, loneliness, and "invisibility." The predicament of being uprooted and the need to establish new roots create a confusion and ambivalence in the newly arrived immigrants. The consultation underscored the need for a new way of understanding and interpreting identity and belonging. The diaspora is not simply "neither" (in-between) and "in-both" (in both worlds), but "in-beyond"—an emerging identity out of the interweaving of roots and wings and of memory and imagination.

A second but related struggle is dealing with the complex effects of the longtime colonized-colonizer relationship between the homeland and the new land. A remnant colonial mindset persists in many Filipinos in the homeland and coming to and living in America reinforces it. This ambivalence often manifests in a disdain for anything Filipino and in lack of self-esteem and self-respect. This attitude blinds diasporic Filipino to their new homeland, thus preventing any efforts to make it a better place.

The consultation also highlighted the efforts of those clerics who established the first congregations. It affirmed their efforts to address the issues of a people scattered, separated from families and friends in the homeland, and struggling to integrate. The clergy and church nurtured the sense of closely knit family, a key feature in Filipino culture. The consultation challenged former UCCP pastors serving different denominations to sustain and increase the growth of existing congregations, not only numerically, but also holistically. The consultation recommended the formation of an organization of former UCCP church workers now serving or living in the United States for mutual support and sustained collaboration on shared Philippine concerns and U.S.-based ministries. The following were identified as possible areas of cooperation: educational exchanges, including training on evangelism and church development strategies; sharing materials and resources; developing community ministries; advocating for health and environmental justice; supporting education for children; partnering with faith and other organizations; fostering ecumenical relations; facilitating visits/exchanges (e.g., young people or organizations visiting the Philippines for study/exposure); supporting education, particularly of potential pastors.

One pressing concern that the consultation addressed was the spate of extrajudicial killings, abductions, and torture in the Philippines that targeted journalists, civic leaders, and human rights activists, including clergy and church lay leaders. Twenty-six church workers were victims of these human rights abuses between 2004 and 2007 alone. The participants were reminded of UCCP minister Andy Pawican who was shot dead on May 21, 2006, for supporting farmers in Pantabangan, Nueva Ecija. The consultation urged everyone to make human rights and peace a priority and tasked a committee to draft a resolution to urge an end to the killings.

Marma C. Urbano

See also: Essays: Catholics; *Entries:* Aglipay, Gregorio; El Shaddai; Santo Niño

Further Reading

Arenas, Erasto. *Brief Pictorial History of the First Fil-Am UCC, San Bruno, California.* 2013.

Deats, Richard L. *Nationalism and Christianity in the Philippines.* Dallas: Southern Methodist University Press, 1967.

Sitoy, T. Valentino, Jr. *Several Springs, One Stream: The United Church of Christ in the Philippines.* Vol. 1. Quezon City: UCCP, 1992.

First Chinese Baptist Church, San Francisco

When gold was discovered in California in 1849, a large number of Chinese from various districts near the city of Guangzhou came to the United States through the port of Hong Kong. Home Mission Boards in the major denominations saw this as a God-given opportunity to reach the Chinese. The Presbyterians were the first to come to San Francisco's Chinatown, establishing work in 1853. Congregationalists and Methodists followed in 1878.

The First Chinese Baptist Church in San Francisco was organized in 1880 by Dr. J. B. Hartwell, a Southern Baptist missionary who had served in China. After several years, the work was turned over to the Northern Baptists (now American Baptist Churches of the U.S.A.).

The church was first located in Chinatown in a rented storefront on Washington Street across from Portsmouth Square. In 1888, through the support of the American Baptist Home Mission Society, the work was moved to a permanent location on the corner of Waverly Place and Sacramento Streets.

Missionary Janie Sandford came in 1884, the first of a long line of missionaries to serve the church. The missionaries worked with women and children and taught English to adults. The first Chinese pastor was the Rev. Tong Kit Hing, who came in 1886. He and those who followed him were responsible for Sunday worship, evangelistic outreach, and pastoral care. Trained in China, these early pastors generally did a tour of duty of several years here in the United States, after which they returned to China.

In 1906, a group of church members, feeling that the church should be independent from the control of the Home Mission Board, left to form the Chinese Independent Baptist Church. The same year, the church building was completely destroyed by the earthquake and fire. For the next two years, the congregation met in Oakland, a city across the bay. A denominational-wide effort raised $10,000 to construct a new building, completed in 1908. A third story was added to the church building in 1930.

In reaching out to the Chinese, the Home Mission Society had hoped that eventually the churches they established would become self-supporting. However, continuing discrimination against the Chinese limited their employment opportunities: working in laundries, restaurants, and domestic service were the main avenues of livelihood for many. The term "Chinaman's chance," which came into use during this period, meant you had no chance at all in terms of making it in America.

In the early part of the 20th century, the Chinese population in the United States fell dramatically. In 1882, when the Chinese

Diana Ming Chan, left, teaches Victor Lee, center, and his wife, Teresa Furia-Lee, fan movements at the First Chinese Baptist Church during Chinese New Year weekend celebration in San Francisco's Chinatown, January 25, 2004. (AP Photo/Jeff Chiu)

Exclusion Act was passed, the Chinese population in America stood at 132,000. By 1920, it had dropped to 60,000. Outreach to the Chinese felt the impact of that change.

In the early 1930s, a young child named James Chuck (1929–) made initial contact with the church when he was sent by his parents to the church-sponsored nursery school. His parents had come to the United States in the late 1920s under business papers. Chuck was born in Oakland, California, but soon after the family moved to San Francisco, where they lived in a one-bedroom apartment. At that time, many of the Chinatown families lived in rooming houses with a shared kitchen and bath.

His father found work as a cook in a Chinatown butcher shop, and also held a second job at night making noodles for a Chinatown teahouse. His mother found work as a seamstress in one of the many Chinatown sewing factories.

After attending nursery school, Chuck continued in the Sunday school, belonged to a club for boys, attended the Chinese-language school sponsored by the church, participated in the youth program, was baptized, and took an active part in the life and mission of the church.

In the 1930s and 1940s, there were few Chinese doing anything important: there were no Chinese policemen, judges, or public officials; and only a few professionals whose practice was largely limited to Chinatown Chinese. Vocational choices available to Chinese were very limited.

World War II was a turning point for the Chinese. Employment opportunities opened up for the Chinese in Bay Area shipyards. Because China was an ally in the war effort, American society gradually saw Chinese people in a new light. Following World War II, many more opportunities for work opened up to Chinese Americans, but some discrimination continued in housing and other areas through the 1950s and early 1960s. Some church members reported that they were unable to buy homes in some of the new housing developments.

When Chuck graduated from the University of California at Berkeley in 1950, he began seminary studies at Berkeley Baptist Divinity School to prepare himself for the Christian ministry. While he was in the seminary, the church called him to join the church staff as youth director. Upon his graduation in 1953, in response to the increasing number of English-speaking young people in the church, the church called him to be the English-speaking pastor. When the Chinese-speaking pastor left for New York to start a new work in 1954, Chuck was called to be the pastor of the entire congregation, becoming the longest-serving pastor of the church until his retirement in 1991. He was followed by Dr. Jeff Sharp, who had been a missionary to Hong Kong and spoke fluent Cantonese. After his term of service, he was followed in 1998 by Dr. Don Ng, an American-born Chinese who grew up in Boston and who served for many years on the staff of Edu-

cational Ministries, American Baptist Churches in the U.S.A.

In 1955, the National Council of Churches convened a meeting at the First Chinese Baptist Church to bring together pastors and lay leaders of Chinese churches from all across the country to discuss a study that they had commissioned regarding the status of Chinese churches in America. At that time, there were about 80–90 Chinese congregations in the country, almost all related to one of the mainline denominations. Fifteen of these congregations were in San Francisco and the East Bay. At the meeting, there was tension between the old guard Chinese-speaking pastors and an emerging group of younger pastors who felt that more attention needed to be paid to the American-born English-speaking constituents.

In the beginning of the 1950s an increasing number of Chinese were able to find jobs following their graduation from college: as teachers, accountants, engineers, and so on, some working for the government, others in the private sector. Because of this, the church was able to become financially self-supporting in 1955. The congregation assumed the salary of the one missionary who was still assigned to the church. The Home Mission Society, which held the deed to the church property, deeded the property to the church, stipulating only that if the property were ever sold, the $35,000 or so that they had invested would be returned to them.

The next couple of decades would be a period of transition for the congregation. The church people began to assume responsibility for all phases of the church's life and mission: in time, the ongoing program of the church would include English classes; church school for children, youth, and adults; leadership training programs; fellowship groups; Youth Camp; Family Camp; a six-week Day Camp; retreats; and short-term missions.

Prior to the 1950s, most church members lived in Chinatown and were able to walk to church. This began to change in the latter part of the 1950s, when long-time members and young married couples began to move out of Chinatown proper. As a result, many church activities were concentrated on Sunday. The several adult fellowship groups met monthly on Saturdays, usually at the homes of members.

Beginning in the 1960s, a major change in the immigration laws allowed a large number of Chinese to immigrate to the United States. Ministry to these new arrivals, some of whom had church backgrounds, revitalized many Chinatown churches. First Chinese Baptist Church responded by adding a Chinese-speaking pastor to the staff. A Cantonese service was initiated, together with various programs for children, youth, and adults. The church program evolved into two parallel tracks, one for the English speaking, and the other for the Chinese speaking. Keeping the church united under these circumstances was a constant challenge for church leadership.

In 1978, a group of Chinese-speaking church members felt led to start a new church focused specifically at new immigrants. The new church—San Francisco Chinese Baptist Church—rented facilities about half a mile away in the North Beach area. The congregation has since grown, and in 2012 moved out to a new location in the Sunset district of San Francisco.

In 1998, a group of English-speaking young adults felt led to start a new church in the Sunset District of San Francisco. They called their new church Sunset Ministry. They too have evolved into an active, thriving congregation.

Even with these departures, the congregation at the First Chinese Baptist Church remained strong. Over the years, the congregation has sent forth about a dozen or so people into Christian ministry. In 2005, the church celebrated its 125th anniversary with the completion of a major renovation and retrofit of the church facilities, and reaffirmed its commitment to stay in Chinatown.

In the first decade of the 21st century, the church initiated a project to preserve and to share the life stories of persons connected with the church. Those participating in the project were asked to talk about parents, growing up, schooling, work, marriage and family, and faith and values. Their stories, together with photographs, were published in three volumes under the title *Chinatown Stories of Life and Faith:* the first in 2002, the second in 2008, and the third in 2012. Collectively, the three volumes give a richly textured account of how the church showed them a new way to live, provided a place for them to belong, and gave them a vehicle for witness and service.

Now in its second century of service and witness, First Chinese Baptist Church in San Francisco remains an active and vital congregation, bringing the good news in an ever-changing environment that Jesus Christ can bring healing and wholeness to human life.

James Chuck

Further Reading

First Chinese Baptist Church Website. http://www.fcbc-sf.org/. Accessed July 9, 2014.

Fujinkai (Buddhist Women's Association)

Fujinkai or the Buddhist Women's Association has been a part of Japanese American religious communities since the arrival of Japanese immigrants to Hawai'i and the United States. Fujinkai was founded by Takeko Kujo, daughter of the head abbot of Nishi Hongwanji in Japan in the last decades of the 19th century. Buddhist missionaries to Hawai'i and the United States established women's organizations at each Buddhist temple. They were often led by the wife of the Buddhist priest or other prominent women in the community. Christian congregations established women's associations, which were also called Fujinkai. All adult or married women were de facto members of Fujinkai. Members of these organizations were responsible for the day-to-day functioning of the temple—housekeeping, fundraising, child care, and education. Although they served in traditionally domestic roles, they were not simply adjuncts to male temple leaders. Their work was critical to the life and development of Japanese American religious institutions.

The first Buddhist Women's Associations were founded in Hawai'i when Japanese immigrants were recruited to work on sugar and pineapple plantations. Nearly 40 temples were founded between 1898 and the outbreak of World War II in 1941; each temple had a women's association, usually led by the wife of the temple priest. Fujinkai in Hawai'i was led by the wife of the pioneering Bishop Yemyo Imamura, who served in Hawai'i from 1903 until his death in 1932. Kiyoko Imamura oversaw these local chapters as the president of the Hawai'i Fujinkai. In addition to raising six children, she was "the right hand of her husband," as well as a poet and teacher at the Japanese language school.

Fujinkai offered an avenue for women's leadership in an otherwise male-dominated hierarchy. Members of the Fujinkai were responsible for some of the most important functions of temple life: fundraising, preparations for community celebrations and holidays such as Obon, Sunday schools and day care, and the upkeep of the temple. Their work was particularly important in smaller rural communities and plantation towns where the Buddhist temple served as the center of community life. Members of the Fujinkai also provided spiritual and moral support for families and children, and an opportunity for women's spiritual growth and religious devotion.

Women were not necessarily relegated to domestic or traditionally female roles in these religious organizations. The wives of Buddhist priests served as missionaries alongside their husbands. Shigeo Kikuchi, the wife of Rev. Chikyoku Kikuchi, was responsible for the Buddhist Temple in Naalehu, Hawai'i when her husband was interned during World War II. As a community leader, she often interacted with military authorities and worked to protect the community from harassment. In the absence of a priest, she organized farewell services for Nisei soldiers. Shigeo distributed *nenju* (prayer beads) and told them,

"When you are lonely or when you're in trouble, repeat '*Namu Amida Butsu.*'"

Organizations like Fujinkai were important for Nisei who faced extraordinary pressures to assimilate to the culture and norms of American life without challenging traditional Japanese values and family structures. This problem was particularly acute for women whose roles were limited by patriarchal norms of both Japanese and American culture. Although Fujinkai retained many traditional practices, over time, women used this organization to exercise leadership in a way that was not possible in the larger community or society. Fujinkai was an important avenue for leadership for Nisei women and girls who were negotiating the boundaries between traditional Japanese values and more relaxed American customs. Women in patriarchal societies and institutions were ostensibly relegated to inferior roles. But as women's associations became more powerful and began to exercise more control over the everyday functions of churches and temples, women naturally and seamlessly carved out an arena for leadership that demonstrated their intelligence and abilities.

Membership in Fujinkai declined along with Buddhist congregations after World War II. However, Buddhist Women's Associations have expanded their mission and outreach and are organized internationally by the World Federation of Buddhist Women's Associations. Chapters from Japan, Hawai'i, Buddhist Churches of America, and Buddhist Churches of Canada and South America meet quadrennially. Fujinkai conferences are the largest gatherings of Jōdo Shinshū Buddhists in the world and promote international cooperation between Japanese and Japanese American Buddhist communities.

Lori Pierce

See also: Entries: Buddhist Churches of America; Honpa Hongwanji Mission of Hawai'i

Further Reading

Densho Encyclopedia. "Fujinkai." http://encyc lopedia.densho.org/Fujinkai/#cite_note -ftnt_ref4-3. Accessed July 9, 2014.

Hawai'i Federation of Buddhist Women. "History of the Buddhist Women's Associations of Hawai'i." http://encyclopedia.densho .org. Accessed July 9, 2014.

Iwamura, Jane Michiko. *Kaikyo: Opening the Dharma. Memoirs of a Buddhist Priest's Wife in America.* Honolulu: Buddhist Study Center Press, 1998.

Kikuchi, Shigeo. *Memoirs of a Buddhism Woman Missionary in Hawai'i.* Honolulu: Buddhist Study Center Press, 1991.

Matsuura, Shinobu. *Higan: Compassionate Vow. Selected Writings of Shinobu Matsuura.* n.p. English edition, 1986.

G

Gedatsu-kai

Gedatsu-kai, or Gedatsu Church of America as it is known in the United States, is a syncretic spiritual tradition drawing on elements of Japanese Buddhism, Shintōism, and the folk mountain religion Shugendō. It recognizes a "Universal Life Force" called *Tenjinchigi* and emphasizes respect and gratitude toward all things, particularly ancestors, to bring peace and happiness. In the United States, Gedatsu-kai has centers in Honolulu, Sacramento, and Los Angeles.

Beliefs and Practices

The primary goal of Gedatsu (to undo) -kai is to help all beings achieve peace through spiritual awakening. It teaches that peace and happiness come by overcoming self-centeredness so we can see things in their true state. The ultimate true state of things is *Tenjinchigi* (god of heaven and earth) or the Universal Life Force. *Tenjinchigi* is a creative principal that generates, interrelates, and sustains all things. *Tenjinchigi*, then, is the primary sacred object of Gedatsu-kai and orients its basic teachings and practices.

Gedatsu-kai teaches that spiritual practice is present in all aspects of daily life, which is a constant means to test our character. Good character will manifest itself in three ways: (1) by living in daily gratitude to the five sources of life: country, parents, teachers, society, and all things; (2) by paying respect toward ancestors, particularly by observing the ritual of *amacha kuyō*; and (3) by expressing reverence for *Tenjinchigi*.

These forms of respectful gratitude are embodied in various practices. The primary practice is *amacha kuyō*, the daily ritual of pouring *amacha* tea on wood plaques with the names of souls and spirits related to one's family. This cleanses the souls and spirits and lets them be at peace. *Amacha kuyō* is performed at home. There are two other versions of *amacha kuyō*. One is done at the church by pouring *amacha* on a *stūpa* (a vertical stone memorial with Buddhist roots; originally *stūpas* housed relics of the Buddha). The *stūpa* represents spirits and souls generally rather than those connected to one's family. *Amacha* may also be poured on the ground or in the ocean as a means to console spirits that may be connected to those particular places.

In addition to the *amacha* rituals, reverence is also expressed by offering water, rice, salt, and *sake* before three altars in a Gedatsu-kai church. The central altar is dedicated to *Tenjinchigi* and is enshrined in a Shintō-style altar. On the left side is an altar dedicated to *Gochi Nyorai* or the "Universal Buddha of Five Wisdoms." These are inseparable from *Tenjinchigi*. The difference is that *Tenjinchigi* represents the essence or substance of the Universal Life Force while *Gochi Nyorai* represents the different ways *Tenjinchigi* is actively expressed in different contexts. *Gochi Nyorai* is enshrined in a Buddhist-style altar. Third, on the right side is an altar dedicated to Gedatsu Kongo, the founder, and this is enshrined in a Buddhist-style altar.

Gedatsu-kai also practices two kinds of meditation, *hiho* meditation and *goho shugyō*. In *hiho* mediation the practitioner sits up straight, holds a *hiho* amulet in the palms, and concentrates on breathing. Through this she or he is aligned with the Universal Life Force. In *goho shugyō* the practitioner holds a *goho* amulet before an altar and chants reverence to the name of Gedatsu Kongo. Through this she or he may receive messages from spirits, particularly regarding sprits that may be causing illnesses or problems. In addition to these the core text and source for the main prayers for Gedatsu-kai is the Buddhist scripture the Heart *Sūtra* (*Prajñāpāramitā Hṛdaya*).

Finally, Gedatsu-kai celebrates various festivals throughout the year, such as sun, moon, and water festivals as well as the Buddhist festivals of Higan and Obon, which commemorate ancestors. Of particular note are the Taisai festivals held every spring and fall. These are a gathering of all the Gedatsu-kai members. During Taisai there is a special service called *Saito Goma* at which members burn wood plaques expressing gratitude.

History

Gedatsu-kai was founded in 1929 by Okano Seiken, posthumously named Gedatsu Kongo (1881–1948). Its presence in America began with Ine Kiyota, a first-generation Japanese immigrant to America. In 1937, on an extended visit back to Japan, she converted to Gedatsu-kai. Then, with the outbreak of the war she was detained at the Tule Lake internment camp, which was unique because it held Japanese Americans who did not take a vow of loyalty to the U.S. government. While in the camp, Kiyota actively shared Gedatsu-kai with others. It attracted followers not only for the practical benefit it offered of being able to fix problems by communicating with spirits, but also for its social benefit of uniting people of Japanese ancestry by employing traditional cultural and spiritual elements (Ishii, 164–66).

The next stage in Gedatsu-kai's growth was in 1950 when Takeo Kishida moved to the United States. Gedatsu Kongo had put Kishida in charge of Gedatsu-kai at his death and Kishida decided to focus on establishing Gedatsu-kai in America. During this time churches were established in San Francisco, Sacramento, and Los Angeles. Kishida also undertook the task of systematizing the beliefs and practices of Gedatsu-kai, basing it "on the Japanese mountain religion known as *Shugendō*". As Kenji Ishii observes, this formalization of beliefs and practices changed the face of Gedatsu-kai from a more casual opportunity for first-generation Japanese to participate in cultural and religious activities they would be familiar with to a more self-conscious identity of what made Gedatsu-kai unique. Up to now, the organization has maintained a modest presence in California as well as a branch in Honolulu.

It publishes a monthly newsletter, *Gedatsu Companion*.

Peter L. Doebler

See also: Entries: Buddhist Churches of America; Shingon; Shintō

Further Reading

Earhart, H. Byron. *Gedatsu-Kai and Religion in Contemporary Japan: Returning to the Center*. Bloomington: Indiana University Press, 1989.

Ishii, Kenji. "Transformation of a Japanese New Religion in American Society: A Case Study of Gedatsu Church of America." In Kei'ichi Yanagawa, ed. *Japanese Religions in California: A Report on Research within and without the Japanese American Community*. Tokyo: University of Tokyo, 1983, pp. 163–95.

Kiyota, Minoru. *Gedatsukai: Its Theory and Practice*. Los Angeles: Buddhist Books International, 1982.

Ghost Festival/Zhongyuan Festival

The Zhongyuan Festival is a Daoist event celebrated on the 15th day of the seventh moon (normally August according to the present solar calendar). The genesis of this festival is lost in the mist of antiquity. Some sources maintain that the Buddhist Ullambana Assembly influenced its birth, while others claim that both the assembly and the festival benefited from mutual development and influence. And others maintain that the two festivals are rooted in Chinese folklore.

In the Chinese tradition, the seventh lunar month is known as a ghost month. At the beginning of the month, the gate of the netherworld is swung open to let the ghosts out to be reunited with their living descendants; the gate is closed at the end of the month. However, some became ghosts unjustly; they will wander about and cause havoc in the mortal world. To pacify these disoriented ghosts, they are offered food

A Chinese woman burns paper money (also known as joss paper) to the deceased and ancestors at a street to mark the Zhongyuan Festival, also known as the Ghost Festival on August 18, 2005, in Kunming of Yunnan Province, China. The Ghost Festival, Chinese equivalent to the Western Halloween, falls on the 15th day of the lunar calendar. During the festival, people make offerings to their ancestors and homeless-hungry ghosts. This practice is observed by many first generation Chinese Americans. Food offerings made to ancestors are eaten by the living family members after the ritual because they are considered to be blessed. (China Photos/Getty Images)

and netherworld paper currency. These offerings were subsequently formalized by the Daoists, who performed rituals and made offerings to the ghosts in hopes of releasing their souls (*chaodu*) from suffering.

The Beginning of the Tradition

Both Daoism and Buddhism began to flourish in China toward the end of the fourth century. There is evidence suggesting that sometime during the Six Dynasties (229–589 CE), people had already begun to observe the Zhongyuan Festival. And by the Tang Dynasty (618–907 CE), both the Daoist Zhongyuan Festival and the Buddhist Ullambana Assembly had become major popular events celebrated at temples and monasteries, as well as in residences of some wealthy persons.

The Theme of the Tradition

While the theme of the Ullambana Assembly is filial piety (*xiao*) toward parents, with a collateral motif of making offerings to the *Sangha* (Buddhist monks), the theme of the Zhongyuan Festival is humanity or humaneness (*ren*) toward the ghosts, and rituals are performed to release them from suffering. Filial piety and humanity are major Confucian virtues.

The Name of the Festival

Daoism recognizes three seasons— Shangyuan (the beginning), Zhongyuan (the middle), and Xiayuan (the last)—and each is celebrated with a feast. Each season is presided over by a celestial officer who carries out the Jade Emperor's verdicts of punishment or reward. The officer of the Celestial Realm (Tianguan) presides over the Shangyuan season and bestows prosperity; the officer of the Terrestrial Realm (Diguan) governs the Zhongyuan season and grants forgiveness for wrongdoings; and the officer of the Water Realm rules the Xiayuan season and delivers people from disasters. These officers can also withhold their gifts and create disaster in the sky, on the earth, and in the water.

The Shangyuan season begins on the 15th day of the first moon (normally February of the present solar calendar), the Zhongyuan season on the 15th day of the seventh moon, while the Xiayuan season is on the 15th day of the 10th moon (normally November of the present solar calendar). The Zhongyuan season occurs during the ghost month in which people both celebrate the return of their deceased relatives and ward off unwelcome wandering ghosts. Sometime during the course of history, people felt the month-long event was too long and decided to hold the festival only on the 15th day of the month. Hence the observance merged with the Zhongyuan Festival, which in turn became the official designation of the ghost month in the Daoist tradition. Since the Buddhist Ullambana Assembly is also observed on the 15th day of the seventh moon, sometimes the designations of the two events become interchangeable.

The Way of the Festival

In traditional China the 15th day of the seventh moon initially was a time for the Daoists to offer sacrifices at the ancestral graves, a ritual similar to that of Qingming, and to worship the officer of the Terrestrial Realm, who on this day would appear on earth to judge the good and the bad. Subsequently the ritual of the release of souls from suffering was added to the occasion.

The ritual was divided into public and private realms. Public rituals, supported by temple funds and private donations, were conducted in temples. A tall pole with a hanging lantern on it would be erected as a signal to the wandering land ghosts that the feast was about to begin. To notify the water ghosts, temples would float lighted lanterns on rivers and other watery bodies. Private rituals, which took place in people's residences, were strictly private affairs.

Generally the content of the sacrifice, accompanied by burning incense, consisted of a variety of meat and fish dishes, as well as other delicacies. Paper currency and paper clothes were also burned as offerings. However, in traditional Fujian Province, on the east coast of China, the ritual of the release of souls took place over seven days, during which time people readied a small boat for the going-out-to-sea ritual. Before departing, the boat was loaded with sacrificial food and 20-plus male and female servants made of paper. In front of the altar were two wooden barrels. Both priests and monks chanted Daoist scriptures and Buddhist *sūtras*, followed by taking some cloths soaked in pig, dog, chicken, and cow blood as well as other loathsome ingredients and tossing them into the barrels. After covering the barrels, a piece of paper with the seal of the priest on it was placed on each, signifying a ritual sealing of all pestilences and undesirable ghosts. Accompanied by drums and music, the barrels were carried to the Heavenly Bridge and were placed on the boat. However, on the way, should someone touch the barrels, it was believed that person would die. The boat floated out to sea with the ebbing tide, symbolically sending all pestilences and ghosts away.

Zhongyuan Festival in the United States

The Zhongyuan Festival is observed by all sects of Daoism in the United States. The rituals performed may vary, depending on the schools to which the different sects belong. Generally the chanting of scriptures by the Daoist priests for the purpose of releasing the souls from suffering is the essential element shared by all temples.

At the Ching Chung Taoist (Daoist) Association of America, for example, the ritual of scripture-chanting is a seven-day event. Each day a different scripture is chanted. On the first day, the priests and priestesses chant the scripture for six to seven hours, but from the second through the seventh days, the daily chanting lasts 12 hours. In addition there are also morning and evening services (i.e., *zaochao* and *wanchao*). The entire festival is open to the public.

Edmond Yee

See also: Entries: Ching Chung Taoist Association of America; Obon (Urabon); Qingming Festival; Ullambana Assembly

Further Reading

Wong, Eva. *The Shambhala Guide to Taoism.* Boston: Shambhala, 1997.

Guangong

Guangong, a native of Hedong Prefecture (now Yuncheng City, Shanxi Province), was a hero toward the end of the Eastern Han Dynasty (25–220) when the empire was divided by three contending powers. Guan belonged to the Shu faction led by Liu Bei, a fallen scion of the Eastern Han Dynasty. The other two contenders were Cao Cao and Sun Quan. His surname was Guan, his given name Yu, and his style Yunchang, changed from the original Changsheng. Of his family and his early childhood little was known. When he became an adult he ran into some unknown trouble in his village, forcing him to flee to Zhuo County in You Prefecture (now Zhuo County, Hebei Province), where he met Liu Bei and Zhang Fei. The three became sworn brothers and loyal comrades-in-arms.

His official biography in the *Sanguo zhi* (Annals of the Three Kingdoms), volume 4, *juan* 36, gives no date of his birth but states that Guan died in the 24th year of Jian'an (219) during the reign of Emperor Xian of the Eastern Han Dynasty. The date of his birth (June 24, 160), was not determined until the Yuan Dynasty (1271–1368) and was confirmed during the early Qing dynasty (1644–1911). He married two women, though we do not know when, and had two sons and a daughter. His wives and children were captured twice by two different warriors.

By 184 the very foundation of the Eastern Han Dynasty was undermined by factional struggles at court, culminating with the revolt of the Yellow Turbans. From Liu Bei's biography we learned that Liu and his men along with other warlords eventually quelled the rebellion. Liu was accorded an official position. He in turn appointed Guan to guard the city of Xiapi and to execute the duties of a prefect. For the first time Guan attained officialdom.

After pacifying the Yellow Turbans, the warlords continued to fight among themselves. Territories were conquered and reconquered. Alliances shifted too, according to military might and political power. But

Guangong, also known as Guandi is a popular god in Chinese religions. Guangong is the deified image of a famous general in the Three Kingdoms Period (220–280 CE) in Chinese history. He is generally venerated as a God of Literature and War, in addition to wealth in business. As such, many Chinese-owned businesses in the United States will house an altar to Guangong behind their cash register or at the front entry. He is a popular subject of Chinese folk art, as seen in the large paper-cut Profile of Guangong created by Gao Xiaodong. Gao created the paper-cut in Hejin, a city of north China's Shanxi Province, June 4, 2009. (Xue Jun/Xinhua Press/Corbis)

Guan stood fast by his lord and sworn brother, Liu. In 200, Cao's forces defeated Liu and captured Guan. Cao treated him well by granting him the title of general-in-charge of a group of 25 chariots.

Shortly thereafter Yan Liang attacked Cao, slaying two of his generals before Guan decapitated him. Thereupon Cao conferred upon him the title of Tinghou of Hanshou, a rather low rank, and gifted him liberally in hopes that Guan would remain in his camp. But Guan was untouched and refused the gifts. Shortly thereafter Guan took leave of Cao without bidding him farewell in person but instead leaving a letter behind. Cao was advised to send an army after him, but knowing where Guan's heart belonged, he refused. Guan reunited with Liu after spending not more than six months in the Cao camp.

In 208, Liu's forces retreated to the south with Cao in pursuit. Liu split his forces into two with Guan leading a naval force of several hundred ships and he himself commanding the rest. They were to meet at Jiangling. This was also the year when the famous Battle of the Red Cliff occurred between the Cao forces and the united forces of Sun and Liu. Guan was not a major planner before the battle, but his naval force obviously contributed to the defeat of Cao's forces. After the battle the dust finally settled, and Jingzhou, a strategic place between the north and the south, was once again in Liu's hand. Liu appointed Guan prefect of Xiangyang.

In 211, Liu moved to Yizhou, leaving Guan and the others behind in Jingzhou. In the following year when trouble occurred in Yizhou, Liu ordered a large contingent of his forces to come to his aid. Guan re-mained behind. In 214 Guan was made governor-general of Jingzhou, which became a symbol both of his success and downfall. This was the highest official position Guan ever held. His biography states nothing about his administrative ability as a governor-general, but from the attention both the Cao and the Sun camps paid to Jingzhou, we can deduce that Guan must have been a good administrator.

Jingzhou was a strategically important place for both Liu's and Sun's state policies. Thus in 215 conflicts surfaced between the two powers. Liu sent Guan south to defend the territory. At the same time, both Liu and Sun were aware of the increasing strength of Cao in the north. Instead of doing battle they sued for peace. Guan played a key role in the negotiations.

In 218, Liu attacked Hanzhong. In the following year Guan led his army to attack Fancheng. He was successful initially. Meanwhile Sun, on behalf of his son, sent an emissary to Guan asking for his daughter's hand. Guan's refusal angered Sun.

While Guan was busy battling around Xiangyang and Fancheng, both Sun from the south and Cao from the north attacked Guan's forces. Sun's forces captured Guan's wives and some of their children in addition to a large number of soldiers. Along with his eldest son, Guan Ping, Guan was captured when they retreated to Linju and both were decapitated at Zhangxiang. Sun, to please Cao, sent Guan's head to him. Cao buried Guan in Luoyang with a rite befitting a duke. In 260, the title of *Zhangmu hou* (Marquis of Military Awe and Dignity) was posthumously conferred on Guan.

Popularization of a Hero

The beginning of Guan's popularization coincided with the rise of his worship in the late Tang Dynasty (618–907). It reached its height through narrative and dramatic literature during the Yuan and Ming (1368–1644) dynasties.

Guan in Narrative Literature. The two historical narratives that gave birth to the far-reaching popularization of Guan are the *Sanguo zhi pinghua* (*The Annals of the Three Kingdoms: A Popular Tale*), based on the *Annals of the Three Kingdoms* published in Yuan, and *Sanguo yanyi* (*The Romance of the Three Kingdoms*), a late Yuan and early Ming masterpiece. In *Sanguo zhi pinghua* Guan was depicted as a static character lacking charisma. But in the *Sanguo yanyi*, he is depicted as a dynamic character whose exploits are greatly romanticized and expanded. For example, Guan's biographer described in one short paragraph how Guan after his capture by Cao Cao returned to the Liu camp without bidding farewell in person. But under the brush of Luo Guanzhong (ca. 1330–1400), the author of *Sanguo yanyi*, this short paragraph was embellished and expanded into four chapters. In addition to these two major works, there are also shorter pieces telling of Guan's exploits.

Guangong in Dramatic Literature. The Yuan and Ming dynasties represent the golden age of Chinese drama. During this period and to a lesser degree in the Qing dynasty as well, playwrights composed numerous dramas in different genres depicting the historical conflicts of the Three Kingdoms. Out of this corpus there are about 50 known dramas with Guan as the hero or in which he plays a part. Some of these dramas are quite close to the historical account of Guan while others have been embellished to show his heroic acts and his qualities of loyalty (*zhong*) and rightness (*yi*).

For example, Guan Hanqing's (ca. 1300) *Dandao Hui* (*Meeting the Enemy with a Single Sword*) is a case in point. The basic plot is derived from Lu Xiao's biography, which tells the story of Guan and Lu meeting each other face-to-face to settle the issue of Jingzhou with the soldiers from both sides staying 100 steps behind. But the playwright also went beyond the basic history by introducing two characters into the drama to show the audience Guan's heroic actions through their eyes and his ability as a negotiator-strategist.

Deification of a Hero

After Guan died, Liu Bei constructed a tomb containing his personal effects and offered sacrifices to him in Chengdu (now in Sichuan Province). But this was not the genesis of belief in Guan. The belief in Guan most likely began in Jingzhou in central China where he died. However, he was not initially treated as a god, but as a ghost (because of the circumstances under which he died) who might return to avenge the wrong done to him.

By the mid- to late-Tang Dynasty, the people in Jingzhou believed that Guan was the god who guarded wealth against poverty. Up to this point he was still a local deity. His becoming the object of national belief and worship had to do with Buddhism and Guan's purported theophany—or divine manifestation—to the Dharma master Zhiyi (538–597) of the Tiantai school of Buddhism. This is said to have happened at the site of the not yet built Jade Spring Monastery in Henan Province and on two other occasions. While the claim of theophany cannot be substantiated by historical evidence, it is generally agreed that the widespread worship of and belief in Guan had to do with Buddhism deifying him and making use of the theophany myth. But when this happened and when the Buddhist action merged with the Guan belief in Jingzhou is a matter of debate.

By the end of the Tang Dynasty, the belief in Guan was firmly established and worship of him took shape during the Song and the Yuan dynasties. At the same time, in Buddhism Guan was worshipped as the Guardian of Dharma at the Inspection Altar; in Daoism he was worshipped as the one who, while esteeming tranquility, had achieved a higher degree of purity. During the Ming and Qing periods, Guan became a sage in Confucianism.

Beginning in the Song Dynasty, some emperors would confer titles of honor upon Guan, culminating in the Qing Dynasty, which conferred four honorary titles upon him.

There are three reasons for people believing in and worshipping Guangong: (1) the qualities of loyalty and courage of the historical Guan Yu; (2) sacrifices offered to him by the people in Jingzhou; (3) Buddhist deification of him and incorporation of this popular belief into their system.

The worship of Guangong takes place in his temples. But when the first temple was built is a matter of debate. Tradition has it that Cao Cao was the first to build a temple for him shortly after Guan died. What we do know is that by the time of the Ming and Qing dynasties his temples were all over China.

The American Scene

The worship of Guangong continues to be popular among the Chinese worldwide. During the Cultural Revolution (1966–1976) in China a large number of his temples were destroyed, but since then the rebuilding process has begun. In Taiwan alone today there are 348 temples; most of them were built after the establishment of the Republic of China in 1911.

There are also temples dedicated to him in North America and elsewhere outside of mainland China. Several historic Chinese American temples honor him and are specifically dedicated to his worship, such as the Mendocino Temple of Kwan Tai, and Marysville's Bok Kai Temple. The temples are independent entities. There is no overarching institution linking them together or overseeing them.

To the merchants he is the god of wealth. His image or statue can be seen in many Chinese and Vietnamese American shops and other business establishments all over the United States today. The merchants believe that Guan's qualities of trustworthiness (*xin*) and rightness (*yi*) may symbolically suggest to the customers that because they worship Guan, they themselves have such traits. Besides residing on altars in Chinese and Vietnamese American businesses, he may also be enshrined in their homes.

The story of the Three Kingdoms continues to be romanticized and popularized today. For example, on October 23, 1994, the Central TV Station in Beijing began broadcasting a television drama of 84 episodes titled *Romance of the Three Kingdoms*. More recently China produced two movies covering the Battle of the Red Cliff. Young Chinese Americans are introduced to the Chinese epic *The Romance of Three Kingdoms* via a high-tech transmission as exemplified by *Dynasty Warriors*, a series of tactical action video games created by Omega Force and Koei. The game is based on *The Romance of Three Kingdoms*, known in Japanese as *Shin Sangokumusou*. *The Romance of Three Kingdoms* and its heroes—Guangong, Liu Bei, and Zhang Fei—thus have become part of the cultural literacy of Chinese American youth through video games. In addition to the popular shows there have also been academic conferences and symposia on Guangong studies. Thus the old hero may have died but he will not fade away in the hearts and minds of the Chinese.

Edmond Yee and Jonathan H. X. Lee

See also: Entries: Bok Kai Temple; Chinese American Religions; Chinese Temples in America; Daoism

Further Reading

Adler, Joseph. *Chinese Religions*. London: Routledge, 2002.

Lee, Jonathan H. X. *Auburn's Joss House: Preserving the Past for the Future (The Auburn Chinese Ling Ying Association House)*. Auburn, CA: Auburn Joss House Museum and Chinese History Center, 2004.

Lee, Jonathan H. X. "Contemporary Chinese American Religious Life." In James Miller, ed. *Chinese Religions in Contemporary Societies*. Santa Barbara, CA: ABC-CLIO, 2006.

Guanyin

Guanyin's Origin Myth

The concept of the bodhisattva is a very important one in Mahāyāna Buddhism. Bodhisattvas are compassionate divine beings who are dedicated to the universal awakening, enlightenment, and/or salvation of all sentient beings. They exist as guides and providers of succor to suffering beings and offer everyone an approach to meaningful spiritual life. Avalokiteśvara is the most popular and important of all the Mahāyāna bodhisattvas because of his many unique virtues, especially his compassion for all sentient beings and his deep involvement in their welfare. He took a vow that he would not attain final *Nirvāṇa* until all sentient beings are delivered and saved from suffering, or rather, saved from *saṃsāra*, the cycle of death and rebirth characterized by suffering. According to Mahāyāna tradition he is to look after the benefit of humankind during the *Bhadrakalpa*, between the death of the historical Gautama Buddha and the advent of the future Buddha Maitreya.

It is generally agreed that the cult of the Bodhisattva Avalokiteśvara originated in the northwestern borderland of a unified India. In Buddhist mythological texts it is narrated that once upon a time, Amitābha (Bodhisattva Unlimited Light) while in meditation emitted a white ray of light from his right eye, which brought Padmapani Avalokiteśvara into existence. Amitābha blessed him, whereupon the bodhisattva uttered the prayers *Om Mani Padme Hum*, thus Avalokiteśvara is regarded as the spiritual "son" of Amitābha. Avalokiteśvara's

The Guanyin altar at Tzu Chi U.S.A. headquarters. For Tzu Chi, Guanyin's teaching on compassion is a guiding principle of everyday life. Guanyin is the most venerated female sacred in all of Asia, and Chinese, Japanese, Korean, and Vietnamese immigrants naturally brought her with them when they came to the United States. But her presence has also reached beyond the immigrant communities to enter the lives of countless European-Americans. (Courtesy of Jonathan Lee)

connection to Amitābha, his spiritual father, is so intimate that the bodhisattva carries a small Amitābha image on his crown. This iconographic clue clearly indicates this bodhisattva as Avalokiteśvara who otherwise would look no different from other bodhisattvas. Some scholars suggest that Avalokiteśvara came into existence as a result of Sakyamuni Buddha's compassionate gaze, therefore explaining the name, which means "He Who Looks Down from on High." Avalokiteśvara plays the role of

saving all sentient beings from their afflictions during the *Bhadrakalpa*. He is the bodhisattva possessed of all the qualities of the Buddha—especially his compassion and skill-in-means, *upāya*. He is the eternal outpouring of the compassion that is wisdom and the wisdom that is compassion. The idea of compassion or *karuṇā*, which was an ancient Buddhist concept, was thus concretized in the person of the bodhisattva who would sacrifice everything, his own personal happiness and his own merit, for suffering humanity. More importantly, with Avalokiteśvara the Buddhists obtained what they had previously lacked—a personal savior whom they could invoke and in whom they could take refuge.

Avalokiteśvara, like Buddha, is possessed of *upāya*, skillfulness or skill-in-means. He may employ various means and assume various forms to deliver the Buddha Dharma to various grades of people and/or creatures according to their inclinations and capacities for understanding. The popularity of Avalokiteśvara in India is attested to not only by the literature concerning him, but also by the large number of his iconic forms that have been discovered, and by the testimony of the Chinese travelers who visited the great Buddhist centers, such as Xuanzang, who recorded the popularity of Avalokiteśvara's veneration at Mathura, Nalanda, Kanauj, and many other places.

Avalokiteśvara Becomes Guanyin

Bodhisattva Guanyin (Perceiver of Sounds), or Guan-shih-yin (Perceiver of the World's Sounds), is the Chinese name for the Indian-based Mahāyāna Bodhisattva

Avalokiteśvara (He Who Looks Down from on High). Guanyin is the best-known Buddhist "deity" in China, and by extension, Chinese America, where, for at least the last thousand years of Chinese religious history, she has been generally depicted and represented in the feminine form. The Indian Avalokiteśvara was not originally depicted popularly and/or represented in female form. Usually he was depicted as a handsome young prince in India, Tibet, Southeast Asia, and even in China before and during the Tang Dynasty (618–907). Guanyin's female form became popular during the later Tang Dynasty and the Song Dynasty (960–1279), as evident by literary, epigraphic, and artistic artifacts. Scholars of Chinese Buddhism argue that the making of Guanyin in China is an example of the "domestication" or the Chinese "transformation" of Avalokiteśvara.

The process of domesticating Avalokiteśvara in China can otherwise be viewed as the "sinification" of the Indian Avalokiteśvara. Although this differentiation is useful, I suggest another perspective, introducing the concept of examining the gender "transformation" not so much as a "transformation" or "domestication," but as the "popularization" of the female image of Avalokiteśvara. This creation of a female Guanyin was revolutionary! The Chinese had taken a male deity, albeit an androgynous one with "feminine" attributes such as compassion, and turned this around to create a female deity. From there, they created entirely new representations of the deity in statues, depicting her with gentle femininity. After the female Avalokiteśvara/Guanyin was established, increasing centralization and consolidation

of China under the Tang and Song dynasties underscored the importance of having a national religious structure. Popular Daoism and popular Buddhism offered an umbrella structure under which they were able to absorb ancient local deities—both female and male—by incorporating them into their respective celestial pantheons. As this occurred, Guanyin's already diverse sources of origin took on Daoist and even shamanistic hues, making her identity as a purely Buddhist deity in China somewhat inaccurate. Guanyin's success in China is a direct result of her ability to transcend barriers of specific nomenclature. This is also the case in Guanyin's American experience. Guanyin can be found not only in Chinese Buddhists temples, but in Japanese Buddhist home shrines, on Vietnamese American restaurant altars, in non-Asian women converts' homes, and in neo-pagan shrines as well.

Guanyin in America

Long before the first Chinese gold miner or laborer migrated to the United States in the late 1840s, Guanyin devotion in China, Korea, Japan, and Vietnam was well established. Dating back to the early 19th century, there is material evidence of Guanyin veneration among the first waves of Chinese immigrants to the United States. Guanyin is found on the altars of historic Chinese Buddho-Daoist temples throughout California's gold mining towns (i.e., Oroville, Weaverville, and Auburn, California), as well in San Francisco's Chinatown (i.e., Tianhou Temple). Like migrants the world over, the Chinese brought their religious rituals and beliefs with them.

The veneration of Guanyin developed in America (and Europe) as several cultural and political forces converged: feminism, 19th-century geopolitical events in Asia since World War II, and the immigration of Buddhist teachers to the West. When China became Communist in 1949, many Chinese monks escaped to Hong Kong, Taiwan, Singapore, and the United States. Similarly, while most Tibetan lamas escaped to India, some came to the United States when Tibet was occupied by China in 1959. With the end of the Vietnam War in 1975 and the arrival of new immigrants from Vietnam and other Southeast Asian countries since the 1980s, people in America have been exposed to many forms of Buddhism as well as the different names and identities of the bodhisattva.

From 1848 to 1965 the veneration of Guanyin was limited to Asian immigrants. The liberalization of immigrant policy after 1965 parallels the changing mainstream attitude and belief in American culture. This period witnessed a spiritual search among Euro-Americans who were disenchanted by Judeo-Christian spiritualities. Their gaze was focused on Asia, primarily on India and China—Hinduism, Buddhism, and Daoism. The initial reaction to Guanyin veneration was not very positive because non-Asian converts approached Buddhist practices with a "reformation style" focus that emphasized quiet seated meditation (i.e., *zazen*), a nonritualistic and nondevotional style of Buddhist practice.

As more non-Asians converted to Buddhism, and as more and more Asian immigrants began to openly practice Guanyin Buddhism in America, coinciding with the rise of the feminist movement—expressed in goddess worship and neo-paganism—Guanyin veneration became more popular. Similar to the process by which Guanyin veneration developed in China, Guanyin was popularized in America through publications that focused on Guanyin devotion and rituals, as well as through material representations of Guanyin from mundane garden art, to new depictions of Guanyin as a mother goddess to the world.

The way Avalokiteśvara became Chinese is slightly different from the way she became American. Locally produced art and representations played a key role in the Chinese transformation of Avalokiteśvara. In America, Guanyin did not become "American." Instead, Americans appropriated her in their religious practice because she represents an available source of cosmic compassion. Changes in the social consciousness of people in the 1960s through 1990s also played an important part in the transplantation of Avalokiteśvara veneration in the United States outside of Asian/Asian American communities.

Guanyin in the Lives of Asian Americans

Today, Guanyin is the single most popular deity in all of Asia and Asian America, where she is worshipped in her many manifestations as Kannon or Kanzeon by Japanese/Japanese Americans, Kwanse'um by Koreans/Korean Americans, and Quan-am by Vietnamese/Vietnamese Americans. Among Tibetans, the Dalai Lama is believed to be the living personification of Avalokiteśvara. Guanyin altars are located in the homes of Buddhist Chinese, Japanese, Korean, Vietnamese, Tibetan, and some Indian American families. Many elderly Chinese and Vietnamese grandmothers will wear a jade pendant of Guanyin as a way to ward off evil and as a reminder to be compassionate to all sentient beings they encounter. Newly married young female devotees of Guanyin will visit her temple to request a baby, ideally a son. Vietnamese refugees, and Sino-Cambodian and other Sino-Southeast Asians make offerings to Guanyin at their homes and at community temples to create merit for family members and loved ones who died during the Vietnam War. For early and new immigrants, Guanyin provides security and comfort during the immigration and relocation process.

Guanyin's Compassion and American Religious Pluralism

Guanyin's compassion is without limits and is universal, for she reaches out to anyone who calls her name in times of turmoil and hopelessness. This perquisite of "calling" her name may be related to another iconographic change related to Avalokiteśvara/ Guanyin: the transformation of the emphasis from "looking" related to Ava*lok*ite, to "hearing" related to Guan*yin*, where "*yin*" means sound. This switch in emphasis and role to the "one who listens to the world's sounds" or "observer of the world's sound" indicates that Guanyin will listen to anyone's cries, prayers, wishes, and calls. The "sight" to "sound" transformation may have been a smooth one facilitated by the *Lotus Sūtra* where it simply states that anyone who utters or calls her name will be assisted by her constant virtues. This easy access to her catalyzed her rise to fame and

popularity. Today her influence is not limited to Asians only.

One of the leading voices on religious pluralism in America, Diana Eck, argues that the way in which Americans of all faiths and beliefs can engage with one another to shape a positive pluralism is one of the essential questions—perhaps the most important question—facing American society today. The rise of the Avalokiteśvara/ Guanyin veneration in the United States in the recent decades speaks to a model of religious pluralism that is not only idealistic but is also meaningful. However, there is a considerable amount of work that still must be done to achieve meaningful diversity in American society. In the post-9/11 atmosphere, as a result of racist Islamophobia and Arabophobia, meaningful religious diversity is at risk. All Arabs are racialized as Muslims, and all Muslims are racialized as Arabs who are, by extension, "terrorists" and therefore "evil." The continued suggestion by conservatives and birthers that President Barack Obama is a Muslim bespeaks the power of the voice of white racist, antidiversity, antireligious pluralism in contemporary American politics and society. Meaningful religious pluralists believe and insist that Americans recognize themselves to be a pluralistic people, that there are diverse and legitimate alternative ways of being American. The creative appropriation and expressions of Guanyin's compassion in America is not a sign or signal of American pluralism, but rather of its possibilities.

Jonathan H. X. Lee

See also: Entries: Chinese American Religions; Chinese Temples in America; Taiwanese American Religions; Tianhou,

Empress of Heaven; Tzu Chi Foundation U.S.A.

Recommended Reading

Banerjee, Radha. *Ashtamahabodhisattva, The Eight Great Bodhisattvas in Art and Literature*. New Delhi: Abha Prakashan, 1994.

Blofeld, John. *Compassion Yoga: The Mystical Cult of Kuan Yin*. London: George Allen and Unwin, 1977.

Boucher, Sandy. *Discovering Kwan Yin Buddhist Goddess of Compassion: A Path toward Clarity and Peace*. Boston: Beacon Press, 1999.

Hurvitz, Leon. *Scripture of the Lotus Blossom of the Fine Dharma (The Lotus Sūtra)*. Translated from the Chinese of Kumarajiva. New York: Columbia University Press, 1976, chapter 25.

Palmer, Martin, and Jay Ramsay with Man-Ho Kwok. *Kuan Yin: Myths and Prophecies of the Chinese Goddess of Compassion*. London: Thorsons, 1995.

Yü, Chün-fang. *Kuan-yin, the Chinese Transformation of Avalokitesvara*. New York: Columbia University Press, 2001.

Gurdwara

A Sikh site of worship is known as a *gurdwara*. There are currently nearly 200 *gurdwaras* in the United States, in at least 34 states, with several located in each major urban center in the country.

From Punjabi, *gurdwara* translates to "the portal to the *Guru*" or "the abode of the *Guru*." This name is indicative of the fundamental attribute of a *gurdwara*, the presence of the *Guru Granth Sahib*, the Sikh holy scriptures. These sacred sites serve as the spiritual centers for local Sikh life in South Asia, and wherever Sikhs have set-tled throughout the world. The external indicator of the presence of a *gurdwara* is the bright orange *Nissan Sahib*, or Sikh flag, which flies above the building at all times.

Guru Nanak, the founder of the Sikh faith, called upon his followers to establish a *dharamsal* in which to congregate and worship, wherever they lived. These structures later came to be called *gurdwaras*, after the installation of the *Guru Granth Sahib*—the eternal *guru* of the Sikhs—in these sites.

These institutions have played a significant role in shaping the lives of Sikhs by providing a site in which to inculcate the Sikh religious ethos in community members. During the many difficult times in the history of the Sikh minority, these religious centers have been a source of strength and inspiration for the community. They served as repositories for the faith, allowing for the maintenance of communal life when the community was weakened and dispersed. Within these institutions, Sikhs have found a sense of identity, cooperative spirit, and peace in an otherwise stormy outside world where they are usually a distinct, tiny minority. Inside the walls of a *gurdwara*, Sikhs learn of their faith's message of emancipation from the cycle of life, death, and rebirth, and from the invidious divisions of this world: race, class, caste, gender, wealth, and so on. For Sikhs, their sovereignty over their *gurdwaras* has always been central to their conception of their own freedom.

In a *gurdwara*, during Sikh religious activities, all congregants are seated on the floor, usually with their legs crossed. When a Sikh enters the main hall of a *gurdwara*, she or he first bows her or his

Sikhs gather to pray at the Sikh Temple Gurdwara Sri Sachkand Sahib in Roseville, California, August 6, 2012. (Max Whittaker/Reuters/Corbis)

head before the *Guru Granth Sahib* in acknowledgment of the knowledge contained in its pages. The *Guru Granth Sahib* is the focal point of the *gurdwara* and any religious functions that may be occurring, serving as the eternal living guide of spiritual and practical wisdom for Sikhs. The worshipper then joins the congregation by taking a seat on the floor.

While men usually dominate religious services and *gurdwara* committee membership, this cultural disposition contradicts Sikh scripture, which explicitly acknowledges the equality of women. As in all other things, Sikh women are granted the same rights as Sikh men to conduct religious ceremonies. Sikh communities throughout the world continue to struggle to live up to the profoundly advanced message of gender equality espoused by their *gurus* five centuries ago.

Services in the *gurdwara* consist of singing sacred hymns and reciting prayers from the *Guru Granth Sahib*. The singing of hymns is often accompanied by musical instruments, usually a harmonium and *tabla* (drums). Although Sikhs have no priestly class, the religious services can also include an exposition (*katha*) by the *granthi* (*gurdwara* caretaker who often leads services and prayers) about the random selection chosen daily (*hukam)* from the *Guru Granth Sahib*, or any other member of the congregation. On occasion, the religious service is supplemented by lectures or poems highlighting important aspects of Sikh history and theology. Services are concluded with *ardas*, a daily prayer from the assembled congregation, which seeks God's blessings for peace and prosperity for all humanity, and specific blessings for the Sikh *panth* (community). Notably, Sikhs who were martyred for the sake of the *gurdwaras* are remembered in the *ardas*. After the religious service, *Karah Parshad*—a sweet concoction made from equal parts sugar, butter, and flour—is distributed to the congregation.

Not only does a *gurdwara* serve as a site for religious worship and congregation, but it also functions as a site for marking the important ceremonies in the life of a Sikh, from naming ceremonies for a newborn, to marriages, *amrit* ceremonies (initiation into the *Khalsa*), and final rites. The local *gurdwara* is a site of much festivity when celebrating the anniversaries of the birth of one of the Sikh *gurus*, or of the *Khalsa* (*Vaisakhi*).

This sacred site also can serve the very secular functions of a community center, a school, temporary accommodations for Sikh pilgrims or non-Sikh travelers, a medical clinic, and a base for local charitable activities. The *gurdwara* often serves the local community by feeding many of the destitute in a region. Among the aspects of the Sikh faith and ethos exhibited by a *gurdwara* is the fact that service (*seva*) is rendered to all who ask—regardless of religion, caste, race, gender, social position, or other aspect of their personal identity—without any effort at proselytization. *Seva* is a religious duty of every Sikh, and the *gurdwara* is usually where young Sikhs get their first opportunity to learn about the importance of this sacred, community-building activity. As such, the *gurdwara* serves as a training ground for social service.

All are welcome in a *gurdwara* regardless of any earthly affiliation—as long as they cover their heads, remove their shoes, wash their hands, and are not inebriated. Sikhs visit *gurdwaras* in line with the divine directive of the *gurus* to join the *sangat*, the assembled body of women and men meeting in religious congregation in the presence of the *Guru Granth Sahib*. For Sikhs, it is essential to participate in such congregations to grow spiritually by being in the company of other devotees, who can provide moral and spiritual support through their own example.

Visitors to a *gurdwara* are fed in the *Guru ka Langar*, or free community kitchen—a Sikh institution open to all, and supplied through the charity of the congregation. *Langar* embodies some of the fundamental principles of the Sikh faith. Both *seva* and the profound egalitarianism of the vision of the Sikh *gurus* are given radical, concrete expression in this sacred Sikh institution. It was established by *Guru* Nanak as a way to both feed his fledgling religious congregation and to demonstrate conclusively the Sikh notions of service and equality.

Langar was a weapon employed by the *Guru* to annihilate caste divisions among his followers. In a *langar*, all are served a communally prepared and served meal regardless of caste, necessitating an interaction between castes eschewed in the pollution-obsessed eating rituals of Hindus. In fact, the *gurus* adopted the practice of refusing admittance to their court until a person had partaken of the *langar*, regardless of the social standing of that person. Pauper and emperor alike had to submit to the equalizing symbolism of the Sikh institution of *Guru ka Langar* before being allowed to see the *guru*.

The *langar* is supplied and maintained through *seva* from the congregation. They volunteer to supply, cook, and serve the food, as well as clean up. The work of sustaining *langar* is done by a volunteer army imbued with the sacred duty inherent in their task. *Langar seva* offers Sikhs an opportunity to serve their community through their labor, while simultaneously engaging in worship by serving God's creation.

While Sikh theology forbids sanctification of any particular site or geographical feature (i.e., river, mountain, rock), most Sikhs hold a very special place in their hearts for Harimandir Sahib, known among non-Sikhs as the Golden Temple. Located in Amritsar, Punjab, and recognized as the site of Sikh spiritual authority, it sits opposite the Akal Takht, the site of Sikh political sovereignty.

In addition to its beauty and historical significance to Sikhs, Harimandir Sahib itself symbolizes the universality of the Sikh faith. Its foundation stone was laid by a Sufi saint, Mian Mir, at the invitation of the fifth Sikh *guru*, *Guru* Arjan Dev. The *gurdwara* complex was placed on a lower level than the surrounding land, inviting all to enter in one of its four entrances. The existence of four entrances, one facing each direction, differs markedly from the lone entrance of traditional Indian temples, symbolizing the welcome extended to all by a *gurdwara*, regardless of the person's earthly background.

Harimandir Sahib has historically served as the primary source of inspiration and direction for Sikhs, the base of Sikh religious and political activities for centuries. The site is not only a reminder of the deeply meaningful and often painful history of the Sikhs, but a link to the present, as the epicenter of contemporary Sikh affairs. All of the major Sikh religious and political movements have emanated from Harimandir Sahib, and many thousands of Sikhs have given their lives as martyrs to defend it.

In the diaspora, the *gurdwara* has taken on entirely different significance, because it is often the only Sikh-operated institution available to serve the needs of the local Sikh community, geographically dispersed as it may be. As such, in the diaspora, the *gurdwara* has become a de facto center not only for Sikh religious life, but also for the social, political, and economic needs of a small migrant community, which experiences societal discrimination both as a result of its racialization and its non-Christian belief system.

Early diasporic *gurdwaras* also aided pioneer Sikh migrants in their passage to North America in the early 1900s. The *gurdwara* in Hong Kong, for example, offered a place for migrants to the United States and Canada to stay until they could board the ship to their destination. While there, these new migrants were educated on what they would encounter and need to survive in the often hostile climate of North America.

The first *gurdwara* in North America was built in Stockton, California, in 1912 and was the site of tremendous social and political activity for the pioneer generation of South Asians to North America. From this *gurdwara*, Sikh Americans worked together with Muslim and Hindu migrants to challenge the white supremacist attitudes and laws that permeated the United States at the time, as well as struggle for independence for their homeland from Britain.

In a fervent attempt to cling to the most salient aspects of their religio-historical identity, Sikhs have built a *gurdwara* wherever they have migrated. In the diaspora, the *gurdwara* structure has often been pragmatically modified to contend with the difficulties of local zoning laws and communities, particularly in areas with a small Sikh population. As such, many *gurdwaras* are modified structures built for other purposes or congregations. Increasingly, as they have established strong families and communities, Sikhs throughout the United States have sought to autonomously construct their sacred space by building new structures that reflect the Sikh sacred architectural tradition. Contemporarily, in many parts of the United States, this has become a source of conflict, as Sikh Americans—and other non-Christian congregations of color—have experienced vociferous community opposition to the construction of their sacred sites. Despite this often bigotry-laden opposition, the Sikh American communities throughout the nation continue to construct temples to serve the needs of the rapidly growing Sikh communities in the United States.

Jaideep Singh

See also: Entries: Sikh American Legal Defense and Education Fund (SALDEF); Sikh Canon; The Sikh Foundation; Sikh Gurus

Further Reading

Dhillon, Gurdarshan Singh. *Researches in Sikh Religion and History*. n.p.: Sumeet Prakashan, 1989.

Jensen, Joan. *Passage from India*. New Haven, CT: Yale University Press, 1988.

La Brack, Bruce. *The Sikhs of Northern California: 1904–1975*. New York: AMS Press, 1988.

Singh, Jaideep. "The Racialization of Minoritized Religious Identity: Constructing Sacred Sites at the Intersection of White and Christian Supremacy." In Jane Naomi Iwamura and Paul Spickard, eds. *Revealing the Sacred in Asian and Pacific America*. New York: Routledge: 2003, pp. 87–106.

Singh, Patwant. *Gurdwaras in India and around the World*. Delhi, 1992.

H

Han

Han is an expression coined by Korean *minjung* (downtrodden) theologians in the 1970s. Broadly defined, *han* is the unbearable and festering pain caused by intrapersonal, interpersonal, economic, sociopolitical, and cultural repression and oppression that is manifested through profound physical, mental, and spiritual pain, frustration, despair, or broken-heartedness. This intense suffering is totally consuming, inhabiting even the unconscious self. *Han* can be likened to a black hole that is created when a star collapses to "singularity"; its gravitational force is so strong that everything, even light, is swallowed.

Structure of *Han*

Korean theologians identify three causes of *han*: individual, collective, and structural. Individual *han* is the result of an individual's experience of oppression that is often connected to collective and structural oppression. Individual *han* appears as lingering traumatic memory of childhood abuse. Recent research strongly suggests that such experiences impact not only emotional and mental well-being, but physical development of the brain and even its DNA. Jerald Kay of Wright State University's School of Medicine reports that abused children are inclined to suffer

from depression, drug abuse, and other chronic ailments as adults. Studies also indicate that abused children have a more active amygdala, the fear center of the brain. A heightened sense of fear can lead to hypersensitivity to possibly fearful situations; it can also result in indifference. In addition, because of the less enhanced connections between the left and right hemispheres, the more rational left brain has less control of the more emotional right brain.

At its collective level, *han* is the collective consciousness and unconsciousness of victims, such as the ethos of cultural inferiority complex, racial lamentation, racial resentment, the sense of physical inadequacy, and national shame. However, *han* can be described as a festering wound generated by unjust psychosomatic, social, political, economic, and cultural repression and oppression. It entrenches itself in the soul of the victims of sin and crime, demonstrated by diverse grief-stricken responses such as those of the survivors of the Nazi holocaust, the Palestinians in the occupied land, the racially discriminated-against, battered wives, the molested, the abused, and the exploited. It is a wound festering in a victim's heart. At its structural level, *han* is a chronic sense of helplessness and resignation before powerful monopolistic capitalism, pervasive racism, tenacious sexism, and oppressive classism.

Causes of *Han*

There are several possible causes of *han*.

1. **Moral evil**. Sin may cause *han*. When we sin against others, deeply hurt them, and do not do anything about it, the hurt may turn into *han*. We can sin against ourselves and our own sin may produce *han* when we do nothing about it. Self-inflicting injuries can cause *han*. An extreme case is suicide.

2. **Natural evil**. Natural evil such as hurricanes, tornadoes, and earthquakes can trigger *han* in their victims.

3. ***Han.*** *Han* can cause *han*. Parental *han* can cause *han* in children. For instance, parental genetic diseases can produce children's *han*.

4. **Unknowable variables**. Job's *han* is not caused by sin, *han*, or anything else. It is a religious, spiritual *han*.

Han and Sin

Where sin is committed, *han* arises as its corollary. The victims of sin develop *han*. They bear excruciating agony and humiliation under oppression, exploitation, abuse, mistreatment, and violation. If their situations do not allow them to change such conditions, they further deepen their *han*.

Sin causes *han* and *han* produces sin. Sin is of perpetrators; *han* is of victims. The sin of perpetrators may cause a chain reaction via the *han* of victims. Sometimes *han* causes *han*. Furthermore, unattended or unhealed *han* gives rise to evil. This evil can regenerate *han* and sin. Also, sin and *han* collaborate to engender evil. They overlap in many tragic areas of life.

Han is frozen energy. *Han* can be resolved either negatively or positively. When it explodes negatively, the person of *han* seeks revenge and destroys others (evil). When resolved positively, *han* can be the energy to change sinful situations and *han*-causing elements, cutting off the chain of the vicious cycle of sin, *han*, and evil.

Although for convenience we have divided the sin of perpetrators and the *han* of victims, most people experience both sin and *han*. This does not mean that we belittle the difference of *han* between perpetrators and victims, but point out the complex entanglement of sin and *han*. Many people who are victims in one aspect of life are perpetrators in another. The notion of *han* may help us transcend a one-dimensional approach to the problem of the world from the doctrine of sin. With the perpetrator-oriented doctrine of sin alone, the Christian doctrines of sin and salvation that are helplessly trapped in an ego-trip need to be liberated. To liberate Christian doctrines for perpetrators alone, we need to pay attention to victims' *han*. So, we will see whether Jesus grapples with the content of *han* in his ministry.

	Personal	Collective
	Active / passive	Active / passive
Conscious	Will-to-revenge / resignation	Corporate will-to-revolt/collective despair
Subconscious	Bitterness / helplessness	Racial resentment / racial lamentation

Han and Jesus

The primary reason for Jesus's coming into the world was to bring good news to the afflicted and the sinned-against. Jesus said, "Those who are well have no need of a physician, but those who are sick; I have come to call not the righteous but sinners" (Mk 2:17). Here, "sinners" are not all sinners.

There were two types of sinners in Jewish society at that time. One was a publicly recognized criminal against civil laws. The other was a person in a lowly and socially unacceptable occupation. We can differentiate the latter type of so-called sinner into two categories. One is the sinner of dishonorable occupation. The other is the sinner of low status such as the sick or the poor. Jesus's followers in general were the disreputable, the uneducated, and the ignorant, whose religious ignorance and moral behavior were problematic to their access to salvation, according to the public view of the time. They were publicans and sinners (Mk 2:16), prostitutes (Mt 21:32), or the sick. They were simply called "sinners" (Mk 2:17; Lk 7:37, 39).

The sinners of the first category were involved in despised occupations. Some examples were herders, tax collectors, and publicans. Others were sinners because of the unclean or ill-smelling nature of their jobs (e.g., butchers, tanners, coppersmiths). They were alienated and could not partake in worship.

The sinners of the second category were the sick people who could not fulfill the duties of the law. As we have seen in Job, the theology that treated sickness as the consequence of sin was widespread in Judaism (Ps 73; Jn 9; Mk 2:5). Thus, the blind, the lepers, the mentally disturbed, and the hemorrhagic were particularly regarded as either unclean or cursed by God. The sick were not transgressors, but those who were condemned by the religious leaders.

Most poor and powerless people were called "sinners" by the religious leaders because poverty prevented them from observing the Sabbath or the law of purification. The *'amm ē hā-'āreṣ* were the uneducated and the ignorant, whose lack of religious knowledge and moral practice stood in the way of their entrée to salvation. During the Babylonian exile, the cream of society was taken as captives; the common people including the Samaritans were left behind. These people were called the *'amm ē hā-'āreṣ*, the people of land. From the time of Ezra, the term was used to designate a low class of people who were ignorant of the law. Rabbinic Judaism used the term to refer to the poor and the powerless, who were despised and marginalized.

Jesus came into the world to take their infirmities and bear their grief (cf. Mt 8:17). He had compassion for the crowds "because they were harassed and helpless" (Mt 9:36). He proclaimed the good news for these heavy-laden. In Jesus's eyes, the righteous were the actual sinners who had to repent of their sin of self-righteousness, religious persecution, and ostentation. In contrast to the religious leaders and scribes, Jesus invited the *han*-ridden—the despised, the sick, and the poor—to his rest: "Come to me, all you that are weary and are carrying heavy burdens, and I will give you rest" (Mt 11:28). Their burden was double: public contempt and the hope-lessness of attaining God's salvation. They were not in fact sinners, but were the sinned-against and marginalized by the oppressive religious leaders and their legal system. They were *han*-ridden.

This implies that these so-called "sinners" needed solace, healing, and liberation, not repentance. Jesus used all his measures, including miracles, to heal the wounded of their suffering, oppression, and affliction. Contrary to our present theology that is basically engaged with sinners' sin and salvation, Jesus's teaching centered on comforting the sinned-against, healing the wounded, giving voice to the voiceless, that is, liberating them from their *han* while confronting the oppressor. Jesus was the friend of the *han*-ridden.

Andrew Sung Park

See also: Entries: Korean American Religions

Further Reading

Barth, Amy. "Abuse Leaves Its Mark on Victim's DNA." *Discover* (January/February 2010): 62.

Kim, Bock, ed. *Minjung Theology*. Singapore: The Christian Conference of Asia, 1981.

Lamb, Kevin. "Lasting Effects of Abuse." *Dayton Daily News*, June 25, 2002, C1.

Hawaiian Religion

'Imi Loa (Purposeful Search)

Hawai'i continually gives birth to its religion through *'imi loa*, the purposeful search and deep and profound inquiry into *Akua*, the Divine. Emerging from a free-flowing communal imagination, this search has been tethered by the introduction of *palapala* or writing in 1821 and with it, Euro-American forms of knowledge, conceptualization, and transmission. To focus solely on texts is to ignore the wisdom of the ancient proverb: "'*A 'ohe pau ka 'ike i ka hālau ho'okahi*"—Knowledge does not spring forth from only one source. Hawaiians see *Akua* revealed in relationships, things, and events—a smile from an elder, family, trees, places of ritual worship and celebrations, sunrise, dance, the community's successes and failures, even a video conference with a friend an ocean away.

On Being Hawaiian

Before contact with outsiders, Hawaiians knew themselves to be Kanaka Maoli or human, not a specific ethno-cultural group among many. Oral traditions recount how *Akua* guided their forebears from their legendary homeland of Kahiki, across vast stretches of open ocean to what is now known as the Hawaiian Islands. Their population soared to over three-quarters of a million by the turn of the 18th century. In addition to establishing an ecologically sustainable aquacultural and agricultural society through the use of stone and wood, the Kanaka Maoli society created a hierarchical polity headed by the *ali'i*, male and female chiefs. They were supported by an ecclesiastical bureaucracy of *kahunas* or priests, who upheld and governed through *'Ai Kapu*, a system that detailed what was sacred, what was forbidden, and what was appropriate be-

A native group conducts a ceremony on the Kahoolawa Island Reserve in Hawai'i. This small island was once used by the U.S. Navy for bombing practice. Hawaiian groups fought and got it back. It is now under the care of Kahoolawe Island Reserve Commission while the U.S. Navy cleans it up. In 2003 it was returned to the state of Hawai'i. (Karen Kasmauski/Science Faction/Corbis)

havior. In this system everyone and everything had a role and a place.

The chiefs of Hawai'i under Kamehameha I (1758?–1819) coined the expression "Hawaiian" to identify those persons who resided within the kingdom. The contemporary Hawaiian community consists of (1) national subjects of the Hawaiian kingdom that include the Kanaka Maoli and those who became naturalized citizens during the kingdom period; (2) former subjects of the kingdom who became citizens of other states, but still maintain cultural ties to Hawai'i; and (3) those individuals who are recognized by the first two groups to belong to the Hawaiian cultural fold. Multiethnic and multinational, "Hawaiian" thus refers to those persons with genealogical ties to the ancient Kanaka Maoli and with *'āina*, the land, which is Hawai'i.

Cosmological Anthropology

Akua animates *ola* or the physical life of a newborn by infusing *ea* or life essence through its *ha* or divine breath. Thus a Kanaka Maoli is both a physical and spiritual being. Physical life consists of the mutual indwelling of *kino* or physical body, *kino wailua* or soul, and *'uhane* or spirit. *Kino wailua* and *'uhane* are different forms of *mana* or life-energy that existed before the emergence of physical life and will exist after the death of a person.

At the end of corporeal life, the *kino wailua* and *'uhane* that once dwelled in a person return to the spiritual world. The *'uhane* bridges the *kino* with the spiritual world. The reality of such a world is confirmed by reports of those who have experienced *wailua* or astral travel. These travelers describe visiting familiar places and seeing sights and hearing conversations while their bodies are at rest.

Akua

Akua or the Divine appears in different forms; among them are: *"Ka 'Ekahi, Ka Hā, Ke Kanahā, Ka Lau, a me Ke Kini Akua"*—the One, the Four, the Forty, the Four Hundred, and the Multitudes. For some Hawaiians there is only *Ka 'Ekahi* or *'Io*—the One. 'Io is the One above all; the One in which all other divine personalities are but aspects. Other Hawaiians acknowledge *Ka Hā*, the four male deities of (1) *Kū*, god of war; (2) *Kāne*, god of fertility and procreation; (3) *Kanaloa*, god of the ocean; and (4) *Lono*, god of peace and agriculture. Each of these gods has charge over a specific, but sometimes overlapping aspect of the natural world. And each is known through its respective *kinolau* or bodily manifestations.

Associated with the upright, firm, and erect, *Kū* is known by the flowering evergreen *'ōhia lehua* (*Metrosideros polymorpha*) tree and the coconut tree, *niu* (*Cocos nucifera*); he is also associated with the *puka-mai-ka-lā* or sunrise. Kāne is known through such jointed-stemmed plants as kava or *'awa-a-Kane* (*Piper methysticum*), the *maile* vine (*Alyxia olivaeformis*), taro or *kalo* (*Colcocasia esculenta*), and sea-weed, *limu-kala* (*Sargassum echinocarpum*). His jointed nature is also seen in *uila-ma-ke-ha'i-ka-lani*, lightning. He is present in *ka-wai-ola*, fresh water. Kanaloa, the god of ocean-dwelling life, is associated with the *palaoa*, the sperm whale (*Physter macrocephalus*) and octopus, *he'e* (*Octopus* spp.); he is also linked with the sandalwood tree, *'aoa* (*Santalum* spp.), and banana plantain, *mai'a* (*Musa paradisiaca*). Lono is the god of peace and agriculture; he is known through musk fern, *laua'e* (*Phymatosorus grossus*), reef triggerfish, *humuhumunukunukuapuā'a* (*Rhinecanthus aculeatus*), hopbush, *'a'ali'i* (*Dodonea viscosa*), candlenut, *kukui* (*Aleurites moluccana*), sweet potato, *'uala* (*Ipomoea batatas*), and black-haired pig, *pua'a* (*Sus scrofa* subsp.). Performers of sacred rituals fashion these *kinolau* or bodily manifestations of *Akua* into their regalia.

Normally the chiefs interacted with the four major *Ka Hā* deities and the *maka'āinana* or commoners focused their devotion to the forty *Ke Kanahā* or minor deities who manifest specific aspects of the four principal *Ka Hā*. Some believe that the *Ke Kanahā* designate separate and distinct patrons of the daily activities and vocations. For instance, fishermen pay homage to *Ku'ulakai*, the guardian of good fishing and safety on the ocean. Others turned to *Ke Kini Akua* (the great multitude of gods and goddesses). Some honor patrons of their occupations. Dancers pay homage to Laka, goddess of the hula. Others honor elemental deities such as *Kamapua'a*, the boar god; *Pele*, the fire goddess; *Poliahu*, the snow goddess, and *Māui*, who introduced fire. In addition, *'ohana* or extended family honors their *'aumakua*, ancestral god or guardian spirit.

Hawaiian interaction with *Akua* is very pragmatic. The collective and multiple generations of experience confirm and strengthen their relationship with *Akua* and its varied manifestations. However, when the virtues associated with *Akua* do not conform to lived experience, the Hawaiians readily adjust their understanding and relationship with *Akua*. This changing relationship can be seen in the production of *ki'i* or crafted images to symbolize *Akua*. When their understanding of *Akua* changes, a new *ki'i* is created and the old ones destroyed.

'Ai Kapu (Eating Restriction) and Mana (Divine Power)

'Ai Kapu means "eating restriction" and as a governing system it detailed the appropriate relationships among chiefs, priests, commoners, *Akua*, and *'āina* or land. *'Ai Kapu* regulated sacredness and its associated privileges that are demonstrated in and through natural and supernatural manifestations of mana, divine power. As the corporeal manifestations of *Akua*, high-ranking chiefs possessed great mana by virtue of their genealogical links to the gods and mythic origins of creation. Chiefs manifested their mana through beneficent deeds, good governance, and military victories. When dictated by *kapu* or restriction, genealogy may accord a female chief a status higher than even the highest ranked male chiefs.

Ancient Hawai'i was governed through *'Ai Kapu* tenets: (1) men and women were not to prepare food nor dine together; (2) the chiefs, as the corporeal manifestations of *Akua*, were sacred; and (3) whatever actions the chiefs performed toward the land and the commoners were *pono* or doing what is right by *Akua*.

'Ai Kapu required that the males and females prepare their meals separately and dine separately to ensure that the respective sexes would receive the mana appropriate to their sex. Pork, for example, a bodily form of the god *Lono*; banana, a bodily form of the god *Kanaloa*; and the coconut, a bodily form of the god *Kū*, were restricted to men.

As the corporeal manifestations of *Akua*, the chiefs observed strict *kapu* concerning their person, food, drink, travel, and shelter. Commoners were not to come into personal contact with high chiefs unless bidden to do so. Should a commoner not afford proper respect, that person would be severely punished and even put to death. Lesser trespasses could result in expulsion from the community, amputation, and beatings. Violating a *kapu* was a transgression against the holder of the mana or divine power, be it a person, place, object, or relationship. An individual could avoid punishment for violating a *kapu* by seeking refuge at a sanctuary maintained by a kahuna called *pu'uhonua*. Chiefs could also be a *pu'uhonua*, if they possessed mana equal or superior to the holder of the mana that was violated.

Priesthood, Politics, and Power

Six centuries before Kamehameha I unified the islands, the priest Pā'ao introduced the *Kū* tradition together with its ecclesiastical bureaucracy that became dominant in the chiefdoms of *Maui Nui* and Hawai'i.

Together with the priesthood of *Lono*, the *Kū* priesthood exerted power from the *Puʻukoholā Heiau* on the northwestern coast of the island of Hawaiʻi and other state *heiau* or temples. The *Kū* order held ascendancy for eight lunar months and the Lono priesthood for four. The rule of Lono began with the *Makahiki* season that began with the rising of the star constellation *Makaliʻi*, also known as the Pleiades, in October-November until it set in February-March. During *Makahiki* the people made offerings to *Lono* and other gods associated with fertility and harvest. They harvested their crops, rested, and competed in games that challenged the body and mind. War was prohibited. Both institutions would remain in power until Liholiho, Kamehameha II (1797–1824), dismantled all the ancient priestly institutions.

As befitting the god of war, the *Kū* tradition supported the selection of chiefs who manifested their mana through victory in warfare in addition to pedigree. The victor reaped the mana of the defeated chiefs by offering them as sacrifices to *Kū*. In contrast, in the western chiefdoms of Oʻahu and *Kauaʻi* where the *Kāne-Kanaloa* and *Lono* traditions were prominent, the selection of the highest chiefs weighed astronomical signs and considered geopolitical factors in addition to genealogy.

Kahuna (Priest) and *Heiau* (Temple)

In ancient Hawaiʻi, political and ecclesiastical authorities were interwoven. The chiefs provided the kahuna with food, housing, and a *heiau* to perform rituals. The priests in turn validated their patrons' right to govern as sacred intermediaries,

and worked to delegitimize their competitors. Power shifts and political maneuvering did not fundamentally change the system outlined by *ʻAi Kapu*; chiefs were chiefs, priests were priests, and commoners were commoners.

The *heiau* served as venues for state and community ritual and learning. The state *heiau* were predominately dedicated to the deities of *Kāne, Kanaloa, Lono*, and *Kū*. The state *heiau* were often situated in a strategic geographical location—a hilltop or bluff that projected political power and reaffirmed the divine connection between the chief and *Akua*. A prominent example of such an effort is *Puʻukoholā Heiau* in Kohala, Hawaiʻi. Kamehameha I ordered it to be constructed to unite the chiefdoms of the Hawaiian Islands. In addition to being venues of devotional rituals, the *heiau* functioned as vocational training and research centers. In the 16th century Chief Kakuhihewa established *Keaīwa*, a healing *heiau* in ʻAiea, Oʻahu to increase availability and access to medicinal herbals. The massive Kaneiolouma Heiau at Poʻipu, Kauaʻi served multiple purposes, including training in the military arts and aquaculture.

Men usually performed the rituals at the state *heiau*. They made offerings of and wore *kinolau* or the bodily manifestations of the particular deity who was being honored. Human sacrifice, normally of persons of chiefly rank, was performed only at a state *heiau*. Commoners participated in state rituals for the *Makahiki* celebrations and in time of great communal hardship, or in preparing for large-scale projects. Women were for the most part barred from involvement in state rituals.

But the feminine presence was ubiquitous. The crescent symbol of *Makaiwa*, the Nine Guiding Stars, a symbol of *Hina*, the moon goddess, was a prominent architectural feature of the state *heiau*. Additionally, women produced almost all of the ritual artifacts such as the smooth flatsedge *makaloa* (*Cyperus laevigatus*) and the thatch screwpine *lauhala* (*Pandanus tectorius*) mats, and paper mulberry *wauke* (*Broussonetia papyrifer*a) tapa cloth. For their part women had their own *heiau* and rituals that barred male participation.

As centers of learning the state *heiau* directed the epistemic framework used by all Kanaka Maoli by standardizing vocabulary and definitions. These centers passed on the knowledge of fishing, agriculture, aquaculture, hunting, soldiering, navigation, astronomy, healing, and all manner of skills. The kahunas also generated new knowledge through research and experimentation. Commoners established *heiau* dedicated to vocational patrons and in close proximity to their respective workplaces to ensure rain, bountiful harvest, good hunting and fishing, and increased fertility. Families built *heiau* to their *'aumakua* or ancestral spirits near their homes.

Devotional Expression

The hula or sacred gesture, *mele* or song, *mo'olelo* or story, and *oli* or chant are forms of *pule* or devotional expressions that honor *Akua* and the chiefs. Additionally, these performances transmit the ideals and values of the community by recounting the sacred relationship between the cosmos and the Kanaka Maoli, the feats of the gods, chiefs, and ancestors. The 2,000-line *oli*, the *Kumulipo* (translated as "Source of Life"), details the origin of the universe and the place of humanity within it. The opening lines read:

O ke au i kahuli wela ka honua
O ke au i kahuli lole ka lani
O ke au i kuka'iaka ka lā
E ho'omālamalama i ka mālama
O ke au i Makali'i ka pō
O ka Walewale ho'okumu honua ia
O ke kumu o ka lipo i lipo ai
O ke kumu o ka Pō i pō ai
O ka Lipolipo, o ka lipolipo
O ka lipo o ka Lā, o ka lipo o ka Pō

At the time that turned the heat of
   the earth
At the time when the heavens turned
   and changed
At the time when the light of the sun
   was subdued
To cause light to break forth
At the time of the night of Makali'i
Then began the slime which
   established the earth
The source of the deepest darkness
Of the depth of darkness, of the
   depth of darkness
Of the darkness, in the depth of the
   night,
It is night, so was night born.

The *Kumulipo* continues with the unfolding relationship between the sky and earth, earth and ocean, ocean and land, land and plants, plants and animals, animals and *Kanaka Maoli*, and *Kanaka Maoli* and *Akua*. Each animate being and inanimate thing has a place in relation to all other beings. The *Kumulipo* reinforced the relationship between *Akua* and the chiefs, who in turn used it to justify their divine responsibility to govern. The *oli* was the linguistic medium that expressed the *'Ai Kapu*, the rules and conventions that organized Kanaka Maoli society, polity, and spiritual life. A composite work, the *Kumulipo* was revised and reworked over the ages. It was first written down in the 19th century to link the elected *mō'ī* (monarch) Kalākaua (1831–1891) to *Akua* through an ancestral line of chiefs.

Believed to be infused with mana or divine power, only the highest-ranking *kahunas* or priests were entrusted with interpreting, producing, and performing the *oli*. As keepers of the sacred chant, priests staged rituals to commemorate the agricultural *Makahiki* celebrations and other events at *heiau*, and at a *wahi pana* or sacred site such as Kilauea, an active volcano and the home of the *Akua* Pele, and Mauna Kea, the tallest mountain in Hawai'i, which is the realm of the *Akua*, the place in which Wākea or Skyfather and Papa or Earthmother met to give birth to the islands, home of many sacred sites dedicated to the *Akua* and the *'aumakua*, and a central place in Hawaiian religion.

Redirection of 'Ai Kapu

The arrival of Captain James Cook (1728–1779) in 1778 and the subsequent influx of foreigners greatly challenged the *'Ai Kapu* system. When a Kanaka Maoli broke a *kapu* or restriction, he or she could be punished or forced to seek refuge. However, foreigners often avoided *kapu* by fleeing onto a ship or by seeking protection from the military forces of their nation. The inability of the chiefs to punish foreigners who broke *kapu* under the *'Ai Kapu* undermined its viability. Moreover, the chiefs disregarded the eating restrictions to sample new cuisine and dine with foreigners of the opposite sex. Such violations did not go unnoticed by the Kanaka Maoli citizenry. Traditional Hawaiian society was further challenged when traditional healing practices were unable to stem the diseases that foreigners introduced. By the mid-19th century over 90 percent of the Kanaka Maoli population succumbed to such common afflictions as the common cold, taking with them centuries of cultural knowledge.

Under the *'Ai Kapu* system, the chiefs had responsibility for the kingdom and its people. Kamehameha I responded to the new sociocultural and political reality, but he still operated under the old paradigm. He saw Christianity as a potential source of mana or divine power to reinvigorate Hawaiian society. He sent a letter on February 25, 1794, through Captain George Vancouver (1757–1798) to King George III (1738–1820) asking for Anglican ministers to be sent to the islands so the chiefs could learn about and evaluate Christianity. In that same letter, Kamehameha also ceded the Hawaiian kingdom to Great Britain. From that point on, Kamehameha I and his chiefs recognized King George III as their liege and lord. Kamehameha I died in 1779, before the arrival of the Anglican ministers, and the task of judging the value of Christianity would be left to his successors.

The chiefs understood that the *'Ai Kapu* needed to be changed, and they debated how and what changes needed to take place. In 1819, Kamehameha II (1797–1824) and his regent stepmother Ka'ahumanu (1768–1832) fundamentally reordered the *'Ai Kapu* by dining together outside of the customary times. They bypassed the authority of state priesthoods and violated the *'Ai Kapu* system. In so doing they asserted their *kuleana* or responsibility as chiefs to ensure the survival of the Hawaiian people and culture in a new global reality.

Ka'ahumanu and Kamehameha II broke with the traditional *'Ai Kapu* order in consultation with and assistance from Hewahewa (?–1837), the ranking state kahuna. Keōpūolani (1778–1823), wife of Kamehameha I and the highest ranked *ali'I*, also lent her mana. Her rank and mana were such that even though her husband and her son were the political heads of the Hawaiian kingdom, they deferred to her as a corporeal *Akua* in matters under her province. Later Kamehameha II ordered the dismantling of all of the *heiaus* and the burning of all *ki'i*, crafted images of the *Akua*.

Not all chiefs agreed. Kekuaokalani (?–1819), a cousin to Kamehameha II and to whom Kamehameha I had given the sacred *ki'i* of Kū, the war god, made a final attempt to preserve the old system. Kekuaokalani lost to Kamehameha II's army at Kuamo'o on the island of Hawai'i (1819). As was customary within the *'Ai Kapu*, the people followed the edicts of the victors.

Adoption of Christianity

The American missionaries who arrived in March 1820 were led by Rev. Hiram Bingham I (1789–1869) of the American Board of Commissioners for Foreign Missions. They were not the religious instructors Kamehameha I had requested from King George III. Nonetheless, the missionaries set about transcribing the Hawaiian language into written form and taught it to the chiefs. For the next four years, the chiefs evaluated the value of Christianity. A month after Kamehameha II set off to Great Britain to confirm the 1794 ceding of the Hawaiian kingdom, Regent Ka'ahumanu formally declared Christianity to be the new state religion by ordering the observance of the Sabbath on December 21, 1823. The Christian religion thus became part of the foundation of the new legal system for the Hawaiian kingdom. On April 13, 1824, Ka'ahumanu met in council with the chiefs to ensure that writing and the Christian Gospel would be extended to the commoners. She also proclaimed laws that prohibited murder, theft, and fighting. The adoption of Christianity as the new state religion along with the adoption of a constitutional government allowed Hawai'i to become the first non-European country to be recognized as a sovereign and independent state in 1843.

Contemporary Practice

Contemporary religious practice is as varied as those under the *'Ai Kapu*. To survive, the Kanaka Maoli adapted, at great cost, to the radical sociopolitical and ideological changes that transpired since their first contact with foreigners. The chiefs are no longer the governing authority, the old priesthood does not hold sway, and most of the *heiau* lie in ruins or are in disrepair. With the decline of the state *heiau* and supporting priesthood, traditional religious instruction has all but ceased. The once unified system of governance, economy, and religion led by the chiefs and the priesthoods has been passed to the modern *hālau* or schools and the *'ohana* or the extended family.

Hālau include those of dance, martial arts, farming, outrigger canoeing, civic engagement societies, philosophy, and many more. Schools primarily honor the *Akua* under whose aegis their discipline falls. The school's rituals often include the use of the appropriate *kinolau* or bodily manifestations of their patron *Akua*. *Lono* is honored in those engaged in competitive disciplines, such as *kukini* or running, *he'enalu* or surfing, *papa-hōlua* or sledding, *mokomoko* or wrestling, *hākōkō* or boxing, *uma* or hand-wrestling, *'ō'ō* or spear-throwing, *moa-pahe'e* or dart-throwing, *'ulu-maika* or rolling-disks, *mo'okūauhau* or genealogy-recitation, *'ōlelo-no'eau* or proverbial-sayings, *'ōlelo-nane* or riddles, and *kōnane* or Hawaiian checkers. *Hālau* often cooperate to organize *Makahiki* celebrations that revolve around the agricultural cycle, even though many Hawaiians no longer cultivate the land and participate in harvest. When multiple *hālau* or *'ohana* sponsor large events, they will cooperate on the principle of *pono* or doing what is right and drawing from the mana or divine power of both the venue and those who gather for the event.

As in the past, some observe the protocol of leaving an offering when passing from one *Akua* domain to another, seeking permission to enter into a place or event, requesting blessing for undertakings, honoring someone or something, offering thanksgiving, and requesting safety. Blessings are often offered before constructing a building or beginning a new venture. Other religious protocols are associated with important life transitions including births, birthdays, graduations, marriages, and death. Some Hawaiians still deflesh the bones of their deceased and secret them in the mountains or sand dunes of their *'ohana* as respected *iwi kupuna* or bones of the ancestors. Others will deposit the cremated remains of their loved one in the realm of Kanaloa, the ocean.

A few Hawaiians tend the grounds of *wahi pana* or sacred places; others have rebuilt and maintain the *heiau*. Still others maintain *ahu* or stone altars and *ahu lele* or stone altars with wooden scaffolding and raised platforms; many continue to place *ho'okupu* or offerings before sacred sites and on their home altars. During the solstice, some participate in *huaka'i* or pilgrimage to different *wahi pana* and adorn themselves with the *kinolau* or bodily manifestations of the *Akua* at celebrations and ceremonies. Still others will ensure that their mana or divine power is not used by others by burning their personal items, including hair and nail clippings. Some use ti, *ki* (*Cordyline fruticosa*) leaf, *'umeke* or bowl, *Kane-i-ka-wai-ola* or fresh water found on the leaves of taro plants after rainfall, and *pa'akai* or dried sea salt to bless and honor, or for exorcism. Some simply use *pa'akai* for personal ritual purification.

Some vocational practitioners understand that creating leis, quilts, and hats, weaving mats and nets, or making clothes are a form of *pule* or prayer. Crafting the *kāhili* or noble standards made of feathers, and leis and *niho palaoa* or whale-tooth pendant with *pule* emanates mana. Those who practice *lua*, a form of martial arts, recognize that their practice is *pule* as well.

Hawaiians ask their *'aumakua*, guardian spirits, for protection and guidance. An *'aumakua* can manifest itself in the form of animals and plants; these include the green sea turtle or *honu*, the shark or *mano*, the lizard or *mo'o*, and the spider or *lanalana*. *'Aumakua* can also manifest itself as an inanimate object. Members of a family recognize their *'aumakua*, no matter what form it chooses.

The *'aumakua* are both gods and relatives, who are the intermediaries between the physical and the corporeal worlds. The family *'aumakua* is a source of strength in times of weakness or sickness; they issue warnings of danger, offer guidance at moments of confusion, inspire performances, and encourage the arts and sciences. When a fisherman has a bountiful catch, a craftsman produces a fine piece, or a scientist discovers new knowledge, credit is often given to the *'aumakua* for interceding with *Akua* to release mana for the success. The *'aumakua* is also a corrective beacon for those whose behavior is offensive or whose actions are detrimental to the family well-being.

Conclusion

The *Kanaka Maoli* community weathered its encounter with foreigners and their alien ideas that challenged the viability of the old *'Ai Kapu* order and the traditional forms of Hawaiian religion. They adapted and reimagined their religion, became a modern society with a constitutional monarchy, and were recognized by other independent and sovereign states. The structures of this new Hawaiian religion have been bequeathed to this and the future generation of *Kanaka Maoli*. Imbued by mana, Hawaiian religion and cultural imagination continues to evolve. From birth to the rejoining with the spiritual source, a Hawaiian practicing his or her religion lives as *ola* (physical being) that is attuned to *Akua* (the Divine), the *'āina* (the land), *'aumakua* (the ancestors), the future generations, and each other.

Anthony Makana Paris

See also: Entries: Micronesian and Polynesian Traditional Religions; Pacific Islander Religious Cultures

Further Reading

Beckwith, Martha Warren. *Hawaiian Mythology*. Honolulu: University of Hawai'i Press, 1970.

Johnson, Rubellite Kawena. *Kumulipo: Hawaiian Hymn of Creation*. Vol. 1. Honolulu: Topgallant Publishing, 1981.

Kanahele, George S. *Kū Kanaka, Stand Tall: A Search for Hawaiian Values*. Honolulu: University of Hawai'i Press, 1986.

Kauanui, J. Kēhaulani. *Hawaiian Blood: Colonialism and the Politics of Sovereignty and Indigeneity*. Durham, NC: Duke University Press, 2008.

Kepelino. *Kepelino's Traditions of Hawai'i*. Translated by Martha Warren Beckwith. Honolulu: Bishop Museum Press, 2007.

Silva, Noenoe. *Aloha Betrayed: Native Hawaiian Resistance to American Colonialism*. London: Duke University Press, 2004.

Valeri, Valerio. *Kingship and Sacrifice: Ritual and Society in Ancient Hawai'i*. Translated by Paula Wissing. Chicago: University of Chicago Press, 1985.

Young, Kanalu G. Terry. *Rethinking the Native Hawaiian Past*. New York: Garland, 1998.

Henepola Gunaratana (1927–)

Henepola Gunaratana, a Sri Lankan Theravāda cleric, was born on December 7, 1927, in the small village of Henepola. He became a novice (*samanera*) at the age of 12 and a full-fledged monk (*upasampadā*) at 20. After completing his studies at Vidyalankara College and Mahā Bodhi-affiliated Buddhist Missionary College, he was sent to India as a representative of the Mahā Bodhi Society to work among the poor in Sanchi, Delhi, and Mumbai. Subsequently, Henepola Gunaratana spent 10 years in Malaysia working with the Malaysian Sasana Abhivurdhiwardhana Society, Buddhist Missionary Society, and Buddhist Youth Federation. He also served as the rector of the Buddhist Institute of Kuala Lumpur.

At the invitation of the Sasana Sevaka Society to serve as the general secretary of the Buddhist Vihara Society of Washington, D.C., Henepola Gunaratana came to the United States in 1968. Twelve years later he was elected president of the society. During this interval, he earned a BA, an MA, and a PhD from the American University. He offered courses in Buddhist thought and culture at a number of universities, including American University, Georgetown University, University of Maryland at College Park, and other universities.

In 1985 Henepola Gunaratana founded the Bhavana Society, a retreat center located in High View, West Virginia, to offer programs for long and intensive meditation practice. Affectionately referred to as Bhante G ("Bhante" is an honorific for Theravāda clerics) by his students, Henepola Gunaratana continues to lead *vipas-sanā* retreats, lecture, and write as of 2014. He has authored a number of books. Some of the most popular are *Mindfulness in Plain English, The Path of Serenity and Insight*, and *The Four Foundations of Mindfulness in Plain English*.

Ronald Y. Nakasone

See also: Entries: Sri Lankan American Religions

Further Reading

Cadge, Wendy. *Heartwood: The First Generation of Theravāda Buddhism in America.* Chicago: University of Chicago Press, 2004.

Seager, Richard Hughes. *Buddhism in America.* New York: Columbia University Press, 1999.

Twarkov, Helen. "Going Upstream: An Interview with Bhante Henepola Gunaratana." *Tricycle* 4, no. 3 (1995).

Hezhen (Nānai) Shamanism

The ancestors of the approximately 5,000 Tungusic-speaking Hezhen, who reside in China, and the 15,000 Nānai, as they are known in Russia in scattered settlements in the central Amur Basin, coined the expression *sămén*, from which "shaman," "shamanism," and "shamanic" are derived. The Hezhen and Nānai are closely related to the Manchus, who conquered China in the 17th century. While the Manchu are being quickly assimilated into Chinese culture, the Hezhen and Nānai still continue to practice their ancient shamanic culture. The smallest of the 55 ethnic groups officially recognized by the current Chinese government, the Hezhen people continue to observe and reinforce their shamanic traditions through the recitation of *imakan* or epic sagas, *talunku* or myths and legends, *syoxuli* or children's stories, and *jarinku* or folk songs. Many of these performances are accompanied by the *mukingi* or mouth organ, and drum. Of these four genres, the *imakan* offers the richest insight into their shamanic traditions.

Hezhen Culture

Living in the frigid forests of eastern Siberia and Manchuria, the Hezhen and Nānai cultures are based primarily on hunting and fishing, leading lives intimately tied to the rhythms of the changing seasons. Their great reverence for nature is projected in a belief that phenomena possess a divine spirit. In addition to venerating the sun, moon, stars, and other celestial bodies, they hold fire, rivers, mountains, animals, and plants to be sacred. The hawk is believed to be especially replete with spiritual energy and has a ubiquitous presence in the *imakan* epics. Families and entire villages venerate their deceased ancestors, whom they trace to animals. Some Hezhen trace their ancestry to fish. Like their Ainu cousins, who live in northern Japan and southern Sakhalin Island, other Hezhen believe that they are descendants of bears. Researchers have reported the presence of three carved totem pillars lined along the outside west wall of a shaman's home. In addition to the forest, flowers, and grasses, the Hezhen people venerate the tree on whose trunk they would often carve the likeness of a human face or the image of an animal. These images often become the focus of their aspirations and yearnings.

The Hezhen people honor the presence of a divine spirit in animate and inanimate phenomena, but as hunters and fisherfolk they regularly take the lives of animals. Therefore every year before the hunting and fishing season commences, the menfolk participate in a great ritual of thanksgiving (*xunjini*) by reciting the following prayer: "To all honorable spirits who protect us from disease and calamity, please allow us to take lots of fish and game." They place abundant quantities of liquor and dishes of fish, meat, and fowl on a raft that is sent adrift on the river as ritual offerings. If the offerings quickly disappear into the river, it is a sign that the gods are pleased and the people can expect to be amply rewarded. If the offerings linger, it is an omen that the gods are unhappy and it will be a bad year. These and other rituals are performed by a shaman, the intermediary between the people and the gods, who pleads for blessings for a bountiful harvest, good fortune, and protection from a number of diseases, including smallpox. The shaman also conducts private rituals of gratitude, especially if he or she has successfully cured a person of disease or exorcised a demon spirit. One such ritual is the *tarikaidani*. For this ritual, the family brings offerings of a live fowl and pig to the shaman's home. The shaman leaps three times before proceeding outside to the west wall of the house, where the fowl and pig are slain and their blood drunk. The shaman continues to dance and chant until the meat is cooked and offered as a sacrifice.

The Hezhen shaman assumes different titles that reflect his or her specialization. For example, a *baceren* or *iceren* shaman exorcises evil spirits and treats a number of diseases. The *xurilan* or *xan'lan* shaman performs rituals that can cure minor illnesses; the *axa mafa* shaman specializes in quelling smallpox. The most powerful shaman is *dakasulukakachi*, who can traverse the spiritual realms, retrieve wayward spirits, and restore life. The adventures of such a journey are recounted in the epic saga *Site Mergen*.

Site Mergen

The 1,680-line oral poem *Site Mergen* is an ancient epic saga that recounts Site's birth and childhood, his performance of a ritual that allows him to journey to *bunio* (the underworld) to retrieve the wayward spirit of his mother, his battles, and his founding of a new era. *Site* means "child." *Mergen* means "hero" and "wise" in Manchu, qualities needed for good leadership. The following is an outline of the narrative. The only documented version of *Site Mergen* was collected by this author in the late 1990s from a Hezhen tradition-bearer named You Jinliang, who related the saga in the Hezhen and Chinese languages.

Synopisis of the *Site Mergen***.** Childless for close to 13 years, Donson Mergen and his wife Sinfen Dedu (*Dedu* is a suffix affixed to the female's name that indicates a young woman), sacrifices a boar's head to the gods in the hopes of being rewarded with a child. A year later they are blessed with twins, a girl and a boy. The family lives happily for five years, but while out on a hunt, Donson chances on Kesyen Dedu, who invites him into her home. Saying that she has been searching for him, Kesyen reminds Donson that they were

husband and wife in a former life; she offers him liquor laced with an evil potion and urges him to kill his present wife and children. Donson returns to Sinfen Dedu and beats her to death. Unable to summon the courage to kill his five-year-old twins, Cinleke and Site, Donson barricades the children in the house and returns to Kesyen Dedu. The siblings manage to free themselves. Distraught and without any clue as to the whereabouts of their father, the siblings set off to locate their father. They chance on their father and Kesyen, who immediately orders a maidservant, Saken Dedu, to kill the children. The maidservant turns out to be their mother's sister and helps the children escape.

During their escape the siblings are pursued by a *busyuku*, a demon-spirit. (As we shall see later, *busyuku* refers to the spirit of the deceased, and the gatekeeper of *bunio* or the underworld.) Through a series of magic maneuvers they evade capture until they finally meet Mudoli Mergen, who promptly slays the demon. The children live with Mudoli for the next 10 years. Cinleke Dedu eventually grows up to become Mudoli's wife. When Site grows up, he builds a boat and the three make their way to the children's original home, where they find their childhood dwelling and their mother's remains. Site vows to locate and retrieve their mother's spirit. In the following passage Site instructs his sister and her husband of their ritual responsibilities during the nine days he is away.

> [I] have gathered all of Mother's
> corporeal remains;
> Elder Sister, Elder Brother-in-law,
> [I] must ask you to please

Offer incense thrice a day [and];
Beat the drum thrice a day.
[Please] rest my body on a table
[and] in a cool place,
while [I am] journeying to *bunio* to
    locate Mother's spirit;
[I] shall return in nine days.
Xelila xelila xelei xelilala xelei
Mother made me a shaman (*sămén*).
Unbao Mafa [and] Shinbeao Mama
    please honor [my request].
Please hitch four large yellow-
    colored dogs to a sleigh [that]
will send me directly [to the
    underworld].
Please place in [it] my sacred hat,
    costume, waist-bell, sword, drum,
    and protective mirror
So I can leave immediately.

This passage reveals much of the Hezhen world and the shaman's powers and responsibilities. The sleigh and other sacred paraphernalia are symbols of the Hezhen shamanic world and the shaman's power. The drum represents the universe; its beating symbolizes the shaman's cadence in his or her journey to spiritual realms. The costume signifies waves; the bell refers to wind and thunder; the hat and mirror stand for the light of the sun, moon, and stars; the bird perched on the hat symbolizes the shaman's capacity to freely traverse the different worlds; and the sleigh is the vehicle that enables travel to these realms. The immensity of these realms is represented by the number nine. Another important symbol, not mentioned, is the shaman's staff or "shaman's tree." The staff is understood to be the "tree of the universe." Tree roots represent the earth; the trunk, the middle realm; and the flared top (branches), the seven spiritual realms.

Site's shamanic power is a gift from his mother; but he requires the assistance of his sister and her husband to offer incense, to beat the drum, and to care for his body while he is journeying. He calls on Unbao Mafa and Syenbiao Mama, his guardian deities, to ready a sleigh and to equip it. Thus prepared, Mudoli Mergen and Cinleke Dedu sound the drum and rattle the waist bells. Shortly thereafter Site retires to the ground and enters into a trance. Together Mudoli Mergen and Cinleke Dedu carry his body indoors and place it on a table in a cool place.

Site's spirit leaves his body and boards the sleigh. The journey begins. Along the way he receives directions from a cuckoo, nightingale, and owl who remember seeing a distraught *busyuku* or spirit of a woman crying with each step on its way to Sanyin, the river that separates the realm of the living from *bunio*, the underworld. The nightingale recalls the spirit lamenting, "I died, but it was not a good death; I left two children at home." The owl, who also remembered seeing the distraught spirit, tells Site to hurry, she may not have reached the entryway to *bunio*. Urging the sleigh dogs on, Site sees in the distance a *busyuku* (gatekeeper) next to the Sanyin River. He approaches and inquires, "Have you seen a *busyuku* pass by here? Do you know where my flesh and blood may be? Please answer truthfully. I want to take her spirit back with me." The *busyuku* looked intently at Site and began to sing.

Xelila xelila xelilala xelilala xelilala
    xelele xelelei

You have just found your mother.
There are few humans as good as
  you.
Your mother is at an aunt's home.
I will take you to her immediately.

Straight away after meeting his aunt and mother, Site kneels to the spirit of his aunt and announces that he will take his mother's spirit back; he lifts her on his back and begins the homeward journey. On the ninth day Mudoli Mergen and Cinleke Dedu, shortly after beating the drum, notice Site stirring and emerging from his trance. After ingesting some nourishment, Site begins to chant and dance around his mother's remains in an effort to reunite her spirit with the corporeal remains. After two weeks of continually chanting and dancing, he asks his brother-in-law to lift the fish-skin blanket covering his mother's remains and report its condition. Mudoli Mergen observes that flesh seems to be covering her bones. After his brother-in-law's report, Site continues to chant and dance over and around the remains for the next 12 weeks. At the end of each two-week sequence Site asks Mudoli to lift the blanket covering his mother's remains and to describe his mother's condition. Each time he lifts the blanket, he reports the progressive restoration of the mother's body. At the end of the sixth 14-day sequence Site asks,

How is my mother? There was
  much laughter.
[Site] began dancing again for
  another two weeks.
Once again the brother-in-law lifted
  the blanket [and] saw that Mother
  was up and laughing.

Site Mergen asks his older sister to
  bring Mother some clothes.

The rescue of and the restoration of Sinfen Dedu's life is viable within the framework of the Hezhen belief that humans possess three distinct and eternal spirits. The first is the *olen*, a spirit that animates sentient—plants and animals—life; it separates from the body at death. The second spirit is *xanin*. Associated with thought and memory, this spirit can leave the body for short periods of time, for example during dreaming. It is for this reason that the maidservant who rescues Cinleke and Site as they flee from Kesyan Dedu can say, "I will protect you in my dreams." The third spirit, called *fuiang'gu*, has the capacity to appear in a future life. The Hezhen believe that after death, a person's spirit, accompanied by the god of death, returns to the site where it separated from its corporeal body. A man will return after seven days and a woman after nine to be reborn as another human or plant form.

The Hezhen believe it is important to dispatch the *olen* (practices vary, within a week or 100 days or a year or three years) at the end of the mourning period. Normally the family will commission a shaman to perform *dakasurudani*, a ritual that properly sends the spirit of the deceased to *bunio*. On the appointed day, the family gathers and burns the belongings of the deceased and fills a sleigh with food and clothing the spirit will need in the afterlife. The shaman asks the spirit to accept these gifts and is reassured that a divine hawk will guide the way. Unless this ritual is performed, the Hezhen believe that the spirit of the deceased will turn into a demon-spirit. In *Site Mergen* the *olen* or the spirit of Site's mother was not accorded a proper send-off and was an unhappy *busyuku*.

The Nānai, the Russian relatives of the Hezhen people, hold to a variant belief of the three spirits. They hold that the three spirits are *omiya*, *elugeni*, and *honia*. *Omiya* refers to the spirit that resides in the person from before birth into childhood; this spirit is called *omiya gaske*. The *ergeni* refers to the spirit that is with a person from one year old until death. In *Site Mergen, ergen*, the root of *ergeni*, means "life" and "breathe." At death the spirit is called *xanin*. *Honia* refers to "spirit" and "shadow." To the Hezhen people death is thought to be like a shadow, a pale reflection of life.

Through his extraordinary shamanic powers, Site Mergen reunites the three spirits that formerly resided within his mother. Such reunion is possible because the spirits, believed to be eternal, have simply left the body. Moreover the third spirit, *fuiang'gu*, possesses the capacity to appear in a future life.

The narrative continues. After Site retrieves his mother's spirit and restores her to corporeal life, Site, his sister, and her husband seek revenge. They set out to locate and kill their father and Kesyen. After some difficult battles and just as Site is about to strike his father, Mudoli Mergen intervenes. Mudoli explains that Donson was poisoned and tricked by Kesyen Dedu and thus not responsible for his actions; besides, killing one's father is a grave offence. Site pursues Kesyen Dedu and is about to slay her, but she escapes by transforming herself into a hawk. She returns as

a hawk to strike Site, but a powerful hawk appears to vanquish her. The hawk that rescues Site is a symbol of the supernatural power of the shaman's divine spirit; the hawk, always the symbol of a female shaman, is the incarnation of Syanken Dedu, who later becomes his wife. Finally, the battle between Kesyen Dedu and Syanken Dedu in their hawk incarnation signals the presence of "red" shamans, who use their powers for evil purposes.

Conclusion

Set in the harsh landscape of Siberia, typical of other Hezhen epics, *Site Mergen* recounts the birth and experience of becoming a shaman. Powerful Hezhen shamans are known to lose their parents at an early age and experience much suffering. Site Mergen is atypical, however, in that he is male in a society where shamans are female. But he receives his extraordinary shamanic powers from his mother and is aided by other female-protector shamans. Elements of the Tungusic shamanic tradition observed by the Hezhen and Nānai people have some parallels in certain cultures in the northwest area of North America. Most notable is the intercession of a female spiritual protector. Throughout *Site Mergen*, Site and his sister are rescued by a female shaman. The female-protector appears as the *unarigami* in Ryūkyūan (Okinawan) culture. In traditional Ryūkyū the sister (more expansively, womenfolk) is the spiritual guardian of her brother (more expansively, menfolk); and during the Ryūkyū kingdom this relationship expressed itself in dual-sovereignty polity. The king ruled under the spiritual direction of the *kikoeōgimi*, supreme priestess, an office reserved for a close relative.

Only a few speakers of the Hezhen language exist in China today and the traditional lifestyle is rapidly giving way to modernization. While efforts are being made to revive and sustain the *imakan* tradition, such an attempt should be made within the context of the shamanic culture.

Yu Xiaofei (Yamada Aki)

See also: Essays: Spirituality; *Entries:* Chinese American Religions; Hmong Shamanism; Shamanism, Modern

Further Reading

Balzer, Marjorie Mandelstam. 1997. *Shamanic Worlds, Rituals and Lore of Siberia and Central Asia.* New York: Armonk, 1997.

DuBois, Thomas A. *An Introduction to Shamanism.* Cambridge: Cambridge University Press, 2009.

Holm, David. *Recalling Lost Souls, The Baeu Rodo Scriptures, Tai Cosmogonic Texts from Guangxi in Southern China.* Bangkok: White Lotus, 2004.

Higashi Honganji

Jōdo Shinshū Buddhism's second largest denomination, called Higashi Honganji, has nine temples in the United States. Higashi Honganji, whose formal name is Shinshū Ōtani-ha, traces its roots to a samurai battle in 17th-century Japan, the effect of which more than 400 years ago split the powerful Honganji organization in half, creating two giant temples just blocks away from each other in the city of Kyoto, which due to their location resulted in the names *"Nishi"* (West) and *"Higashi"* (East) Honganji. Over the years,

Higashi has become known for its influential and progressive thinkers who helped interpret Jōdo Shinshū in the modern era and eventually to the Western world.

Near the end of the 16th-century, Honganji had followers throughout Japan and a fortress-like headquarters in Osaka surrounded by a town of supporters that symbolized power and influence. The temple stood at the site where Osaka Castle stands today. In 1570, military leader Oda Nobunaga (1534–1582), in an attempt to conquer other warlords and unify the country, launched a battle against Honganji, whose followers rushed to its defense, resulting in a 10-year standoff. After Oda was assassinated by one of his own generals, his successor, Toyotomi Hideyoshi (1536–1598), negotiated a truce with Honganji's abbot, who agreed to leave the compound, a move his eldest son Kyōnyo (1558–1614) opposed. A new temple was built in Kyoto, where a younger son eventually became abbot. The next ruler, Tokugawa Ieyasu (1542–1616), in a move that further weakened Honganji's political influence, offered Kyōnyo his own temple just east of his younger brother's temple. Higashi Honganji temple in Kyoto today is one of the largest wooden structures in the world and one of Japan's largest Buddhist temples. The denomination claims a membership of about 5.5 million followers in Japan.

Shortly after Japan ushered in the modern era in the 1860s, leaving behind centuries of feudalism, Japanese immigrants began venturing west, initially finding work in the fields of Hawai'i. Higashi ministers from Japan traveled to the islands and established the denomination's first temples in the early 1900s, several in

Buddhist monks and practitioners attend the annual dusting at Nishi Honganji Temple on December 20, 2014, in Kyoto, Japan. The dusting is conducted in the traditional way, by blowing the dust out of the hall with big fans while others raise the dust by hitting the tatami mat with bamboo branches. (The Asahi Shimbun/Getty Images)

rural areas in new Japanese communities. Many of those temples closed in the following decades as those workers and communities disappeared. Today five Higashi temples remain on the islands of Oʻahu, Hawaiʻi, and Kauaʻi.

Japanese immigrants continued to move westward, establishing other communities on the West Coast, particularly in the San Francisco Bay Area and Los Angeles. Unlike its Nishi counterpart, the Higashi denomination made no concerted effort to establish temples on the mainland United States, although priests were sent to Brazil, which today has two dozen temples. In the United States, Higashi's development was characterized more by serendipity.

In Los Angeles, Nishi minister Izumida Junjō (1866–1951) switched to the Higashi denomination after a dispute with temple leaders. In 1904, he founded a temple that eventually became the first Higashi temple in California and later the central temple of Higashi Honganji's North America District. The temple is located in Los Angeles's Little Tokyo district. In Berkeley, California, a single Nishi Honganji temple served a vibrant Japanese community during the early 1900s until a rift occurred among members over its Japanese-language school. In 1926, a group of families left to start a temple headed by a Higashi minister, making it Higashi's second mainland temple.

Today in addition to Los Angeles, Berkeley, and Hawai'i, Higashi temples are also found in the Southern California cities of West Covina and Newport Beach. Membership ranges from 400 families at its largest temple in Los Angeles to much fewer at its smallest temples.

While all Jōdo Shinshū denominations trace their teachings to the 13th-century priest Shinran, the way those teachings were interpreted vary. Fundamental Jōdo Shinshū teachings are rooted in Pure Land Buddhist *sūtras* which are full of arcane and abstract concepts and references that primarily focus on a symbolic Buddha named Amida that resides in the Pure Land, a place of peace and bliss, having vowed to save all living beings. The core expression of worship is reciting the name of this Buddha. Consequently, over the centuries, Jōdo Shinshū seemed to incarnate into a form increasingly dissimilar from the original Buddha's teachings, resembling more a form of prayer and deity worship.

A reformation of Jōdo Shinshū thought occurred at the turn of the 20th century led by Kiyozawa Manshi (1863–1903), a Higashi scholar whose controversial career includes teaching, protests, expulsion from the organization, reinstatement, founding the Higashi denomination's first university, illness, poverty and the tragic deaths of his wife and two sons. An early student of Western philosophy, Kiyozawa vehemently spoke out against the denomination's emphasis on fundraising while sacrificing spiritual study and practice. At one point, he adopted an extremely harsh lifestyle, only wearing Buddhist robes, living a threadbare existence, and eating a subsistence diet that ultimately contributed to his contracting tu-

berculosis. However, he came to see the fallacy of belief in a "self," instead describing ultimate reality as "power beyond self." His writings and focus on spiritual understanding through personal experience using the language of Western rationality set the tone for a number of subsequent Higashi teachers, several of whom became influential in their own right, such as Akegarasu Haya (1877–1967), Kaneko Daiei (1881–1976), and Soga Ryōjin (1875–1971). That philosophical lineage influenced the founders of the Chicago Buddhist Temple and the Maida Center for Buddhism in Berkeley, California.

While Higashi Honganji follows a progressive interpretive approach to teaching Jōdo Shinshū, it adheres to traditional rituals in ceremony and services. Such practices may be found at its American temples, evident in an emphasis on ritualistic chanting of Buddhist *sūtras* and reciting melodic poems of Shinran, performed by priests wearing traditional Japanese-style robes.

In the United States, the temples served dual roles since their founding as spiritual centers and as de facto preserves for Japanese language, food, and culture where Japanese immigrants could feel welcome. Temples typically sponsored clubs specializing in flower arranging, *bonsai*, martial arts, Japanese poems, singing, and so forth. As each succeeding generation became more "Americanized" and in many cases intermarried with other races and ethnicities, and as non-Japanese people joined the temples, much of the Japanese culture aspect faded or disappeared, especially the Japanese language. Still, some clubs remain, Japanese food commonly is served, and certain activities continue to be popular such as summer bazaars and the *Obon* dance, a kind of Japanese group folk dance.

The most important function of the Higashi Honganji temples remains spiritual. They continue to be places where people go for services, weddings, and funerals, and to listen to Buddhist teachers. Though relatively small in number, Higashi Honganji in the United States represents a denomination of the largest Japanese Buddhist sect and an influential force in the development of Buddhist thought.

Ken Yamada

See also: Entries: Buddhist Churches of America; Honpa Hongwanji Mission of Hawai'i; Jōdo Shinshū Buddhist Temples of Canada

Further Reading

Ama, Michihiro. *Immigrants to the Pure Land: The Modernization, Acculturation, and Globalization of Shin Buddhism, 1898–1941.* Honolulu: University of Hawai'i Press, 2011.

Andreasen, Esben. *A Brief Introduction to Shin Buddhism: A Personal View.* Kyoto: Shinshu Ōtani-ha, 2004.

Haneda, Nobuo, trans. *December Fan: The Buddhist Essays of Manshi Kiyozawa.* Kyoto: Higashi Honganji, 1984.

Rogers, Minor L., and Ann T. Rogers. *Rennyo: The Second Founder of Shin Buddhism.* Fremont, CA: Asian Humanities Press, 1991.

Saito, Gyoko, and Joan Sweany, trans. *Shout of Buddha: Writings of Haya Akegarasu.* Chicago: Orchid Press, 1977.

Hindu Canon

Encompassing a vast range of beliefs, practices, and festivals, Hinduism evolved from centuries of cultural and spiritual development; it was not established by a single person or a founding event. The expression "Hinduism" is relatively new. It was only in the 12th century that the expression gained currency. Invaders from Afghanistan and Persia (Iran) referred to the region east of the Indus River as Hinduš, the Parsee (Farsi) equivalent of the Sanskrit "Sindhu." Thereafter, the term "Hindu" was used to describe the inhabitants from the northwestern provinces of India. Today the region is called Hindustan. Nearly a millennium earlier, when Alexander the Great invaded the Punjab region of northern India in 327 BCE, the indigenous population was known as the Vedic people, that is, those who followed the practices prescribed in the Vedas.

This entry provides an overview of the more significant documents of the Hindu canon, its history, central ideas, and its use in the South Asian community in the United States.

Vedic Scripture

The British archeologist John Marshall (1876–1958), who in the 1920s was responsible for the large-scale excavations of Harappa and Mohenjo-daro, claimed that the beginnings of Hinduism can be traced to the culture and spiritual traditions of the Indus Valley (Harappan) civilization that flourished between 2300 and 1500 BCE. He identified what he believed to be features of the Indus Valley religion: a cosmic male god (Puruṣa) and a mother goddess (Aditi); the veneration of animals and plants; and symbolic representation of the phallus (*liṅga*) and vulva (*yoni*). However, due to the scarcity of additional evidence, his assertions have been much debated. For example, Marshall identified a cross-legged seated figure with a horned headdress on what is known as the Paśupati seals to be an early depiction of Shiva. But some scholars have speculated that the figure may be a mythological "lord of the animals" that is common to Eurasian Neolithic hunting societies. Some have speculated that the ancestors of the Tamil of southern India were the Indus Valley people, thus preserving the spiritual heritage of Harappa and Mohenjo-daro, which found its way into the Brahmanic tradition.

Be that as it may, the spiritual culture of the Indus Valley civilizations was profoundly impacted by Aryans who entered India about 1500 BCE from Eurasia. These invaders possessed an oral tradition of sacred hymns that is collectively known as the Vedas ("knowledge"). The four Vedas are the *Rig-*, *Sāma-*, *Athar-*, and *Yajurveda*. Tradition holds that the sages (*rṣi*) in deep meditation "heard" (*śruti*) the first sounds (*om* or *aum*) of the universe that led to its creation. The Vedic hymns are thus articulations of the cosmic vibrations or cosmic breath that were intuited by the sages, and preserved and transmitted by Vedic priests. Fittingly, *om* is the first letter (or sound) of the Sanskrit alphabet.

More properly, the Vedas are referred to as *samhitā*, "that which is heard." Since the articulation of this "cosmic harmony" (*rta*) through speech (*vāc*) impacts the cosmos, Vedic verses have been transmitted orally in an effort to transmit the correct cadence, pitch, and pronunciation. The correct articulation of words (*mantra*) in connection with Vedic sacrifice has the power to control the gods. "Brahman (ultimate reality) is the word," and "the Brahmin (priest) is the keeper of the lord" (*Rigveda*, X: 125). The preoccupation with ritual in the Vedas is rooted in the belief that action (*karma*) or even inaction has an impact. It is through the proper knowledge of performance of rituals of sacrifice (*yajña*) that humanity comes to know the truth of, participates in, and manipulates the cosmic rhythm. Rituals give form to what the Vedic sages believed to be the nature of the universe and its creation: Life entails the devouring of life. This reality was most apparent in fire, which must constantly be fed to be sustained. The continually "devouring" fire is the nature of creation and its creator, both of which are personified in Agni, who represents all that burns, or devours. The universe is fire and offering (*soma*). The hearth fire, the very image of the cosmic fire, is evidence that humanity has captured and can tame the cosmic fire. Fire is an essential element in Vedic sacrifice (Daniélou, 67–8). Devotees recreating this belief offer rice and ghee.

Hymns recited at Vedic rituals, including the annual Soma New Year rite, highlight the preparation, offering, and consuming of *soma*, a sacred drink. Another important ritual is the kindling and the veneration of fire, a necessary feature in ritual. Instruments for the performance of the sacrificial ritual, the Vedas were crystallized in their present form by 1000 BCE and written down about 500 BCE. Within the Hindu context, oral transmission has always been considered superior to the written word.

The *Rigveda*, the oldest Veda, consists of 1,028 hymns that pay tribute to the Vedic *devas* (gods) and the exploits of a few contemporary tribal leaders. The most important *devas* are Agni, the "fire deity," who receives offerings and transports them to the gods; *ādityas*, a group of seven or eight nature *devas*; Uṣas, the most prominent goddess, who is the patron of poets; and Sūriya, the *deva* of the sun. Indra, the leader of the *devas*, is instrumental in the early stages of creation; Vishnu and Shiva also appear, but not as the great *devas* of later Hinduism. *Devas* are not the "personification" of natural phenomena, but expressions of their mysterious and sublime powers. The Vedic *ṛṣi* intuited and gave form to the actuality of the physicality of fire, or sun, or water, and their underlying vitality. Like the Japanese Shintō *kami* that resides in nature, "*deva*" embraces both the physical and "spiritual" realities of natural phenomena.

The *Sāma Veda* is a compilation of extracts from the *Ṛigveda* with the instructions for recitation; the *Atharveda* contains an assortment of sacrificial formulas, poems used for healing, magic, quickening love and affection, and sorcery. It also has hymns for important life milestones. The most recent, *Yajurveda*, is a collection of prose *mantras* and expositions of their use in ritual sacrifice.

In contrast, the Brāhmaṇa texts are concerned with the sacred power of the *mantra*; they stress the correct knowledge of the meaning and performance of rituals that include such rites of transition as birth, marriage, and death. Āraṇyaka or "wilderness or forest text" discusses the more unorthodox and "dangerous" ideas that were to be learned and discussed away from the usual ritual sites. Because of their metaphysical discourses, some scholars considered these "forest texts" to be part of the

Upanishadic texts that were composed between 800 and 400 BCE. The Upanishads contain the speculations by a number of Vedic teachers concerning the nature of the world, the nature of humanity, and their place in the world. These speculations were prompted in part by shifting political and economic orders that weakened the authority of the Brahmanic priests and doubts concerning the efficacy of Vedic rituals. The Upanishadic period was a time of great intellectual ferment within the tradition that gave rise to Buddhism, Jainism, and other schools of thought that sought an alternative to Vedic ways of thinking, being, and doing.

The Upanishadic texts articulate this shift by questioning the efficacy of the knowledge of and proper performance of ritual detailed in the Brāhmaṇa texts. One important change is the internalization of ritual and personal responsibility; this shift is accompanied by a rethinking of the ideas of *saṃsāra* (transmigration of an individual's *ātman* [life-force, soul] through successive lives), "passage" or "transmigration," rebirth, and *karma*. Vedic cosmology posited continual and routine rebirth. At the end of one corporeal life, an individual would be blissfully reunited with his or her ancestors. But the length of such reunions was determined by the "amount" of one's ritual that he or she had performed in the prior corporeal existence. Once the efficacy of these actions expired, one would be reborn, hopefully and preferably back into one's own clan. In a break from the idea of continual rebirths and the union with Agni, Indra, or Brahman, and through knowledge of and performance of ritual sacrifice, the

Bṛhadāraṇyaka Upaniṣad linked liberation, or *mokṣa*, and transmigration with the efficacy of personal responsibility. The support for such an idea is linked to *karma*, the law of cause and effect. The law guarantees that actions committed in the past manifest themselves in the present and will impact the future. *Karma* thus ensures that good or evil action will reap its appropriate consequences, even through successive lives. The efficacy of *karma* established the rationale for an ethical and moral basis to challenge the Vedic notions of rebirth and *mokṣa*, the notions of caste, and the Brahmanic priests who had a monopoly on the knowledge and performance of the Vedic rituals. These ideas established the basis for the subsequent developments of Indian thought, including Buddhism and Jainism.

The Vedic canon concludes with the *Kalpa Sūtras*, which include the *Śrauta Sūtras*, *Gṛhya Sūtras*, and *Dharma Sūtras* that systematically detail proper ritual and behavior. The *Śrauta Sūtras* concern themselves with rituals, procedure and decorum; the *Gṛhya Sūtras* deal with domestic rituals. The *Dharma Sūtras* are concerned with Dharma, "proper behavior" or "right conduct"; many of the rules enumerated in these texts overlap with those listed in the *Gṛhya Sūtras*. The *Dharma Sūtras* link the notion of *karma* and *saṃsāra* with personal conduct. Conduct is linked to *mokṣa*, liberation from samara, to specific stages of life, sex, social status, and caste. One who conducts his or her life according to his or her Dharma can anticipate a better rebirth. Conversely, one who violates his or her Dharma will be reborn as a lesser state. Among the many *Dharma* texts, the *Manavadharma Śāstra* or *Manusmritī*, *the Code of Manu* (ca. 200 BCE–200 CE) is probably the most important.

The Code of Manu enumerates the duties of each of the four *varṇas* or castes: *brāhmaṇa*, *kṣatriya*, *vaiśya*, and *śūdra*. The *brāhmaṇa* caste is responsible for teaching and studying the Vedas and performing its rituals. The *kṣatriya*, or warriors, are responsible for protecting and administrating the country; the *vaiśya* are to engage in trade and farming. The *śūdra* are to serve the other three *varṇas*. The separation of society into four classes is already mentioned in the *Ṛigveda* (X.90). But the motivation for this distinction seems to have been to distinguish the Vedic people from other people they encountered as they advanced into the subcontinent. Only later did the *brāhmaṇa* class, in an attempt to preserve their priestly prerogatives and maintain social and political stability, limit access to knowledge and performance of Vedic sacrifice. The Vedas and the *Code of Manu* do not link the *varṇas* to lineage or pedigree, but to a person's role or function in the community (Quigley, 2003). By the time the *Code of Manu* was being complied, the *varṇa* system had become very complex. *Dharma* texts identify numerous *jātis* or subclasses. Today there are some 4,000 *jātis*.

The Epics

Originating during a period after the Vedic literature, the *Itihāsa* ("history") is the collective expression for the *Ramāyaṇa* and *Mahābhāratha*. Related are the Purāṇa ("ancient books"), of which 18 are usually accepted as the *Mahāpurāṇas* that are the scriptures of the major Hindu traditions.

Itihāsa-Purāṇa are often referred to as the fifth Veda, the sacred text of the common people who had no access to the four Vedas and thus were unable to reap the benefits of their insights. The exploits of heroes and heroines, gods and goddesses, men and women that appear in these epics are part of the living tradition of Hinduism. The epics and their numerous renderings in the many Indian vernaculars are vehicles for transmitting the traditional Hindu values, morality, and faith.

In addition to reflecting on the interests and concerns of the *kṣatriya* or warrior aristocracy, these epics are a compendium of the Indian understanding of the creation and destruction of the universe. The epic lists the genealogies of kings, heroes, sages, and demigods, the laws for ruling a kingdom, and how a common man should live. The most famous epics are the *Ramāyaṇa* and *Mahābhāratha*. The 700-verse *Bhagavad-Gītā* is part of the *Mahābhāratha*. Many modern scholars regard the *Mahābhāratha* to be an exposition of Dharma (duty or "what is right") and its application; and the *Ramāyaṇa* an affirmation and illustration of *Dharma*. The *Ramāyaṇa* (Rama's journey) consists of 24,000 verses in seven books (*kāṇḍas*) and 500 cantos (*sargas*) that tell the story of Rama, whose wife Sītā is abducted by Rāvaṇa, the king of Lanka (present-day Sri Lanka).

The 100,000 stanza *Mahābhāratha*, an epic of the Kurukṣetra War, relates the fates of the rival Kaurava and Pāṇḍava princes, who struggle for the throne. In brief, King Vicitravīrya had two sons, Dhṛtarāṣṭra and Pāṇḍu. According to custom, the older, Dhṛtarāṣṭra, should succeed his father; but since he was born blind, his brother was made king. Pāṇḍu died after a short reign, leaving five minor sons. Dhṛtarāṣṭra succeeded his brother and the five Pāṇḍu brothers grew up with their cousins. Dhṛtarāṣṭra considered the five Pāṇḍava brothers to be the rightful heirs, but his oldest son Duryodhana claimed the throne and attempted to kill the rival princes. This initiated a series of events that culminated in an 18-day battle.

The *Bhagavad-Gītā* is inserted in the *Mahābhāratha* just before the climactic battle of the Kurukṣetra War. Arjuna, the third Pāṇḍava brother, is consumed with self-doubt concerning the righteousness of engaging his kinfolk and teachers in war. He is posed to attack his teacher, Drona, and his mentor, Bhishma. Krishna (Kṛṣṇa), who as an avatar of Vishnu (Viṣṇu) has taken the guise of a charioteer, explains the necessity and inevitability of the war; he extorts Arjuna to fulfill his duty as a *kṣatriya*. By fulfilling his responsibility as the leader of his clan, he is exercising *karma marga* (path of action).

Moreover, Krishna explains that since the self (atman) is eternal and thus indestructible, Arjuna should not grieve over the imminent deaths of his kinfolks, friends, and teacher. Moreover, actions when undertaken with a spirit of detachment are sacrificial acts, and without karmic consequences. Actions performed without any attachment to the action or concern for its results lead to *mokṣa* (spiritual liberation). (See the entry on *Yoga*.)

Let your concern be with action alone and never with the fruits of your action. Do not let the results of action be your motive, and do not be attached to inaction.

Firmly fixed in *yoga*, Oh Dhanaṃjaya, perform your actions, renouncing attachments, indifferent to success or failure. This balanced indifference (*samatva*) is called *yoga*. (*Bhagavad-Gītā*, 2:47–48)

Arjuna's action (*karma mārga*) is his path to *mokṣa* (liberation). Krishna continues to describe the three other spiritual paths. Liberation can be realized through *jñana mārga*, the study and cultivation of intellectual understanding into one's identity with Brahman. *Mokṣa* can be achieved through *bhakti mārga*, the devotion and faith to one's personal deity; and through *rāja* or *dhyāna mārga*, the cultivation of meditation to gain insight into the *Atman* that resides within the self. Krishna also discourses on the nature of and attributes of Brahman, the supreme reality.

The *Ramāyaṇa* relates the adventures of Rama, who faithfully observes the Dharma (duty) as a son, a prince, and a husband. Rama accepts a 14-year exile and the loss of his throne to honor a promise his father, King Daharatha, made to install Bharata, a son he fathered with Queen Kaikeyi. As the oldest, the throne is rightfully his; even his half-brother Bharata agrees. Sītā decides to join Rama, demonstrating her devotion and duty as a wife. They are accompanied by Lakṣmaṇa, the loyal younger brother. While in exile in the forest, Rama subdues many demons, pacifying the wilderness for the many ascetics and hermits. One day Rama and Lakṣmaṇa wound a demon princess, who had tried to seduce Rama. She returns to her brother Rāvaṇa, the 10-headed ruler of Lanka, who in retaliation devises a plan to abduct Sītā, after hearing of her incomparable beauty. Rāvaṇa kidnaps Sītā and takes her to his kingdom. While in captivity, Sītā remains faithful to Rama, spurning all of Rāvaṇa's seductive advances. In the process of locating and saving Sītā, Rama solicits the help of Hanumān, the monkey king, who has the power of flight, because his father was the wind. He locates Sītā in Lanka. Thereupon Rama and Lakṣmaṇa cross over from the tip of India to Lanka via a causeway made up of Hanumān's monkey army. After a series of battles Rama defeats Rāvaṇa and his army. After rescuing Sītā, they return to Ayodhya, where Bharata vacates the throne. We learn at the end of the narrative that Rama is an avatar of Vishnu.

Both the *Bhagavad-Gītā* and *Ramāyaṇa* explore the challenges of observing one's duty or Dharma in the face of competing concerns. Arjuna realizes *mokṣa* by fulfilling his duty as a warrior. Rama, Sītā, and Lakṣmaṇa are exemplars of Dharma. Hanumān is revered as the loyal follower. Both epics are retold time and again in the subsequent centuries in the many vernacular languages of India and more recently on television, video, and film. The heroes and heroines and their exploits of the *Bhagavad-Gītā* and *Ramāyaṇa* are part of the common lore of present-day South Asian culture and their overseas communities in the United States and elsewhere. The Vedas, Upanishads, and *Itihāsa-Purāṇas* are still part of a living tradition. Vedic hymns are still recited at weddings, funerals, and daily devotions. Their ideas and narratives have inspired philosophers, poets, artists, and ordinary persons. In an effort to retain and pass on their culture, many families place images of their spiritual and cultural heroes in shrines at home. Some will light a lamp; place offerings of flowers, fruits, or cooked food before the shrine; and recite chants they may have learned. At the beginning of events, *slokas* (verses) devoted to removing obstacles are chanted.

Vedic verses are chanted at the rites of transition; its *pūjās* (ritual worship) are integral to the life of Indians in the homeland and in the United States. The stories and lessons embodied in the great epics guide the paradigms on which children are taught to behave and relate to the world. While adjustments are made to accommodate to life in the U.S. context, the perennial insights continue to be passed on through family rituals and participation at communal rituals at a nearby ashram.

Amba Raghavan and Ronald Y. Nakasone

See also: Entries: Hindu Education

Further Reading

Daniélou, Alain. *The Myths and Gods of India: The Classic Work on Hindu Polytheism.* Rochester, Vermont: Inner Traditions International, 1985.

Flood, Gavin, ed. *The Blackwell Companion to Hinduism.* Oxford: Blackwell, 2003.

Klostermaier, Klaus. *A Survey of Hinduism.* Albany: State University of New York, 1989.

Radhakrishnan, Sarvepalli. *The Bhagavadgītā.* New Delhi: HarperCollins India, 1993.

Sargeant, Winthrop. *The Bhagavad Gītā: Twenty-fifth Anniversary Edition.* Albany: State University of New York Press, 2009.

Sharma, D. S. *A Primer of Hinduism.* Chennai, India: Sri Ramakrishna Math, 2010.

Hindu Education

Hindu education in the United States can mean forms of education, formal or otherwise, for Hindu Americans who may not necessarily be Asian Indians, or other Americans who trace their ancestry to South Asia. It may also refer to forms of education, rituals, or practices that may not be directly associated with mainstream Hindu religious and cultural practices, with *yoga* being the most notable example. It could also mean a process of understanding the spiritual, cultural, or religious practices adhered to by converts to religious movements that had some presence in America, notably the Vedanta Society, the Self-Realization Fellowship, Transcendental Meditation, or the Rajneeshi movement. In a somewhat similar vein, the recently established Hindu University of America offers instruction in scriptures, *yoga*, and meditation.

Hinduism in America is primarily seen as an immigrant religion, with occasional offshoots being traceable to efforts of visiting religious leaders. The nomenclature "Hinduism" is considered problematic largely due to the association of the word with the caste-based social practices of inequality and discrimination, following which many practicing Hindus may self-identify differently. A recent Pew Research Center survey found that among American Hindus, while 53 percent self-identified as Hindus, 19 percent saw themselves as Vaishnava Hindus, 10 percent considered themselves Shaivite Hindus, 3 percent identified themselves as Hare Krishna, and around 2 percent were Vedantists. Forms of instruction inspired by Hindu practices are often called differently, keeping in view the sensibilities involved. Suffice it to say, there is more to "Hindu education" than education merely for Hindus.

The evolution of Hinduism as a self-sustained tradition capable of attracting prominent converts has been in accordance with the geopolitical transformations of the predominant sending country, India. With the passage of the 1965 Immigration and Naturalization Act, urban university-educated professionals migrated from all over India, with significant overrepresentation of Gujarati, Punjabi, and Malayali language speakers. Although Asian Indian Hindus form a religious majority in India (~ 80 percent), they constitute a miniscule minority (~ 0.4 percent) in America. They are more likely to practice in-house religion by worshipping at a household altar or shrine and engage in daily prayers, meditation, and fasting. They also attend local centers of worship like Hindu temples or cultural associations. For them, obligations to family and community ties are almost coterminous with religiosity. This is consistent with historian Padma Rangaswamy's observation in a Chicago survey that the form of the transplanted religion depended on the religious group, the part of India from which the immigrants arrived, and outlook toward religious issues.

Among the mostly theologically unlettered first-generation immigrants, this leads to a rejection of perceived threats from the dominant culture like unfettered promiscuity, lack of family values, religious and spiritual ignorance, and lack of respect for elders. The marginality of the immigrant social experience presupposes

a realignment of religious and ethnic affiliations. New ethnic boundaries are formed and older ones renegotiated. Many distinctions based on caste, cuisine, language, and place of origin, which are salient markers of ethnic boundaries in India, give way to mutual acceptance and association. By affirming a semblance of collective identification, Asian Indians tend to project a pan-Indian basis for ethnicity. In this, the dominant Indian religion Hinduism acts as a fulcrum on which multiple ethnic identities are negotiated.

Cultural self-identification tends to encompass both the physical as well as the metaphysical. At the metaphysical level, religion-centric spirituality, which emphasizes the spiritual as a cultural given, emphasizes a moral superiority of the South Asian civilization, to be used as a tool to counter the "degeneracy" of an alien cultural milieu. At the physical level, it means imparting religious instruction in summer camps and Sunday services, which are partly inspired by evangelical practices. Ethnographic scholarship suggests that organizational aspects of American religion like congregation-style worship, potluck luncheons, Sunday religious schools, and emphasis on social service are adopted; other rituals that are more contextual in India are overlooked. English is often the language of social occasions and the medium of instruction in Sunday camps.

Religious organizations serve as places for nonreligious social contact and group formation. This often creates awareness about shared ethnic identities and possible ethnic boundaries. Immigrant religious organizations play salient roles in developing multiple and shared notions of ethnicities. In doing so, these organizations become both repositories and conveyors of cultural capital. While they offer instruction in regional Indian languages to the second generation, they also help immigrants to associate with one another in nonreligious activities like volunteering, charitable work, organizing food drives, blood donation activities, and other community-related activities. For children of minority immigrant groups, being part of a collective provides a basis for self-introspection. As most of these children attend better schools than their parents, where the majority of the students are whites and whiteness remains the normative standard of social acceptance among peers, being "young, brown, and Hindu" can be a source of identity crisis.

Hindu religious organizations indicate varying levels of adaptation. Subethnic religious associations like Bala Vihars and *satsang*s are the social spaces that foster ethnic pride. Usually located in the precincts of religious and cultural associations, Bala Vihars are educational associations for children and *satsang*s are local worship groups. Depending on the location and the place of origin of the majority of the first-generation immigrants, the Bala Vihars gather on weekends or Sundays and impart instruction in a combination of Sanskrit with other languages like Tamil, Hindi, Gujarati, or Bengali. In a typical Bala Vihar, a child might be asked to memorize the 10 names of Krishna. *Satsang*s impart weekend sessions in religious texts like the *Bhagavad-Gītā* or the *Ramāyaṇa*. Schools of music like the local Thiagaraja societies offer instruction in Carnatic vocal or instrumental music to Tamil- or Telugu-speaking immigrants and their children. Other schools of music offer instruction in Hindustani classical music.

Children of Indian origin understand very early that in a predominantly white society, acquiescence to dominant norms and mimicry of dominant behavior ensures greater social acceptability. However, the identity crisis is averted to a large extent by participation in religious schools like the Bala Vihars. These micro-level subethnic organizations teach children about their religion and culture. These organizations require steady commitment from adults, who invest their time, energy and money in imparting religious education to their children. They adopt practices like Sunday religious worship, potluck luncheons, congregation-style following, and emphasize strong academic achievement among their children. Parents look after the health, academic progress, and extracurricular achievements of their children. These micro-organizations are mostly region specific, language specific, and often last until the children get ready to attend college. By resorting to ethnic pride, these institutions help to negotiate the ethnic identity crisis faced by children. Children grow up knowing about the heritage, culture, and religion of the country of their parents. In the process, they become assertive and confident about their identity as brown-skinned Indian Americans.

In many Hindu religious associations, there have been undercurrents aimed at creating a pan-Indian Hindu "Great Tradition," which borrows from Orientalized notions of a great past. In these institutions, women are the primary reproducers of culture and ethnicity. Contrary to the egalitarian and pluralist ideals of a Western liberal society, the duties of priesthood and temple management are usually the preserve of upper-caste rich men. While Hinduism has many different schools, and the practices of reproducing religion differ considerably among subethnic groups, a global pan-Hindu ethnocentric identity often works to bridge that divide. In promoting the agenda of a global pan-Indian Hindu identity, many Hindu organizations often question the idea of the pan-Indian secular identity of earlier Hindu groups, and also that of most Muslim, Christian, and Sikh groups.

Since the mid-1980s, the politicization of the Hindutva movement has posed significant challenges to the secular and multicultural ethos of the Indian American community. The Hindutva associations help second-generation fellow ethnics to take more pride in their Hindu American identity, as compared to their Indian American identity. Hindu nationalism in the United States is a reaction to perceived or real ethnic victimization. It is also a good example of what Benedict Anderson called "long-distance" nationalism. What makes it interesting is its religious basis for affirming cultural nationalism. This dichotomy was reflected in the California textbook controversy in 2005 when two groups related to the Hindu right in India, the Vedic Foundation and the American Hindu Education Foundation, reacted strongly to the portrayal of Hinduism and Indian history in sixth-grade history textbooks. The major points in contention were the supposedly "equal" status of women in ancient India and the denial, among others, of the religious origins of the caste system

and the Aryan invasion theory. While those arguing in favor of revision argued for a more idealized vision of an imagined great past, by ignoring the persistent reality of social discrimination in contemporary India, scholars, human rights groups, Dalit and Christian groups, and others opposed any changes. The state Board of Education rejected the suggested major revisions on monotheism, women's rights, the caste system, and migration theories, although the last would be treated as disputed.

In many college campuses, religious organizations and students' associations have promoted an ethnocentric basis for association to Indian students, many of whom often contribute monetarily to the activities of the Hindu right in India. Hindu right-wing groups operate on college campuses, on the Internet, and have extensive social networks. Their activities include voluntary participation, funding activities, and religious and cultural instruction. College campuses are often the sites in which the ethnic identities are reformulated. As both interfaith and pluralist groups and right-wing Hindu groups seek the membership of the second-generation Indian Americans, there is no fixed trajectory to indicate their spiritual loyalties. For the second-generation Indian ethnic, the choice is often between genteel multiculturalism and militant Hindu cultural nationalism. It is also between brown-skinned pan-South Asianism and assertive ethnocentric Hinduism.

This entry began by questioning the use of the expression "Hindu education in America." As the varieties of Hinduism and the uses of alternative nomenclatures to refer to Hindu practices enrich American life, so will forms of education. Hindu education is more than forms of instruction for immigrant Hindus from India or those who trace their ancestry to South Asia. The contributions of other forms of education for mainstream Americans, through *yoga*, meditation, and spiritual practices, and their contributions to American religious and cultural life requires another essay with a different name.

Amitava Ray

See also: Entries: Hindu Canon; Hindu Temples in America

Further Reading

Bhalla, Vibha. "The New Indians: Reconstructing Indian Identity in the United States." *American Behavioral Scientist* 50, no. 1 (2006).

Brettell, Caroline. "Voluntary Organizations, Social Capital, and the Social Incorporation of Asian Indian Immigrants in the Dallas–Fort Worth Metroplex." *Anthropological Quarterly* 78, no. 4 (2005).

Khandelwal, Madhulika. *Becoming American, Becoming Indian: An Immigrant Community in New York City*. Ithaca, NY: Cornell University Press, 2002.

Kurien, Prema. "Religion, Ethnicity and Politics: Hindu and Muslim Indian Immigrants in the United States." *Ethnic and Racial Studies* 24, no. 2 (2001).

Leonard, Karen, Alex Stepick, Manuel Vásquez, and Jennifer Holdaway, eds. *Immigrant Faiths: Transforming Religious Life in America*. Walnut Creek, CA: AltaMira Press, 2005.

Prashad, Vijay. *The Karma of Brown Folk*. Minneapolis: University of Minnesota Press, 2000.

Purkayastha, Bandana. *Negotiating Ethnicity: Second-Generation South Asian Americans Traverse a Transnational World*. Piscataway, NJ: Rutgers University Press, 2005.

Rangaswamy, Padma. *Indian Americans*. New York: Chelsea House, 2006.

Williams, Raymond, ed. *A Sacred Thread: Modern Transmission of Hindu Traditions in India and Abroad*. Chambersburg, PA: Anima, 1992.

Williams, Raymond. "Swaminarayan Hindu Temple of Glen Ellyn, Illinois." In James Wind and James Lewis, eds. *American Congregations*. Vol. 1. Chicago: University of Chicago Press, 1995.

Hindu Temples in America

Migrant Hindus in the United States have constructed temples in their new communities to transplant their religious faith. A place of worship becomes a vehicle to express the particular group identity in a pluralistic society. The temples become important centers for performing rituals and also interacting with friends and relatives. Hindus gather at temples during important festivals and holidays. In addition, many non-Hindus from other ethnic and cultural communities are welcome to attend services at Hindu temples, both in America and in India.

Hindus in the United States and India generally go to a temple for *darshan*. Among Hindus, *darshan* is understood as a way of "touching God with your eyes" or "perceiving or knowing God" or "focusing on God." Hindu temples always have divine icons (*vigrahas* or *murthis*) or symbols of different deities made either of black stone or metals (*pancha loha*) installed in the innermost sanctum of the temple called *Garbha Gruha*, which the devotees are not allowed to enter. The larger stone idol set permanently in stone

A Hindu priest lights a candle at Nebraska's only Hindu temple, May 14, 2004, in Omaha, Nebraska. The temple is a source of pride for the Hindu community. (AP Photo/Nati Harnik)

food offerings (*Neivedyam*), and offering of oil/camphor lamp (*arati*), with the priests chanting/reciting sacred mantras while performing these rituals.

Temples can be large, with complicated architectural designs, or very small, with just a room over the icon of the presiding deity. Larger traditional temple buildings have tall towers (*gopurams/shikharas*), which vary in architectural style depending on their geographical location. Most North Indian temples have beehive-shaped (Nagara-style) *gopurams*, and South Indian temples have pyramid-shaped (Dravida-style) *gopurams*. Also, there are some temples that have the hybrid design known as (Vesara-style) *gopurams*. The traditional temple structure is built by architects trained in temple building scriptures (*Agama Shastras* and *Vastu Shastras*), and they are invited to build such temples in the United States.

Although temples are sacred and divine places of worship for Hindus, it is not mandatory for a Hindu to visit the temple on a regular basis or during his or her whole life. Unlike other organized religions, it is not necessary for a Hindu to perform rituals such as marriage or naming of a child in a temple. Many Hindus go to a temple on auspicious occasions or on religious festivals or holidays. Older people also go on pilgrimages (*thirthayatras*) to visit sacred lands with temples (*divyadesams*). Modern-day temples have evolved from simple places of worship into institutions engaging in several social, cultural, and religious activities and philanthropic or charitable services. These institutions play a significant role in the lives

is called the *Mula Murthi*, and the smaller metal idol, which is transferrable, is called the *Utsava Murthi*.

These icons are believed to have divine powers and are worshipped by Hindus with daily *pūjās* and temple rituals performed by a priest (*pujari*) who has specialized training in religious mantras. Priests performing *pūjās* in temples in the United States usually come from India, are knowledgeable about different *pūjā* practices, and often speak several Indian languages, which makes them capable of serving all types of devotees. *Pūjās* and rituals include sacred bathing of the icon (*Abhishekam*), decoration (*Alankaram*), of Hindus in the United States and serve the needs of their community.

Establishing sacred sites similar to those in the homeland resulted in a proliferation of Hindu temples in the United States. The icons of gods and goddesses, along with architectural design, are replicated as closely as possible. There are "330 million" deities in the Hindu pantheon. Consequently, Hindu immigrants have erected temples dedicated to many gods. The Council of Hindu Temples in North America was established in 1984 to give uniformity for temples in their style of functioning and management. There is at least one Hindu temple in each state of the United States. The construction of Bharatiya Temple in Detroit was finished in July 1981. The Hindu Temple of Greater Chicago was built in the 1970s and later expanded, and a temple dedicated to Lord Rama was opened in 1981 in Lemont, Illinois. Some notable temples in the United States include Ganesha Temple of Flushing, New York; Malibu, California's Sri Venkateswara Temple; a temple in Pearland, Texas, dedicated to Sri Meenakshi; and the United Hindu Temple of New Jersey.

Some of the temples retain their connection with and draw inspiration from temples in India. The famous Tirupati temple situated in Chittoor District, Andhra Pradesh, India is dedicated to Lord Venkateswara. It is a template for many such temples constructed in the United States. In the 1970s, the temple was replicated in Pittsburgh. The Tirumala Tirupati Devasthanams, who manage the affairs of the temple in India, supported construction of many such temples in the United States.

This organization supplied artisans as well as priests. It is estimated that 150,000 persons visit the Pittsburgh temple annually. The temples also publish books and periodicals on Hinduism. The temple authorities involve themselves in charitable works. The Hindu temples sometimes face difficulties in getting trained priests from India because of immigration problems. Many times the chief priest of a temple does not give necessary support to the new entrants. There are also disputes among the persons managing the temples.

Hindu temples in the United States provide an opportunity for immigrant Hindus to learn about Hindu philosophy and scriptures in the American context and help them cope with life problems and develop solutions consistent with Hindu values. Unlike traditional orthodox temples in India, temples in the United States encourage people to ask constructive questions about their tradition and thus develop new ways of thinking about it. They often provide the much-needed link to Indian culture and traditions for Indians and their children who are living in the United States and help develop a strong sense of Indian identity and values through special religious and cultural programs or events for all ages. The temples have become the embodiment of cultural and religious identity for Hindu immigrants. The varied activities of the diaspora community in these temples generates interest in Hinduism itself. The Hindu temple is not an ivory tower for American Hindus only; it endeavors to mingle in the mainstream of American tradition. In several American Hindu temples, prayers were organized in January 2009 to seek divine blessings for the administration of President Barack Obama.

Geetha A. Mandayam, Patit Paban Mishra, and Jonathan H. X. Lee

See also: Entries: Hindu Canon; Hindu Education

Further Reading

Hanumadass, Marella L. *A Pilgrimage to Hindu Temples in North America.* Oak Brook, IL: Council of Hindu Temples of North America, 1994.

Kurien, Prema A. *A Place at the Multicultural Table: The Development of an American Hinduism.* New Brunswick, NJ: Rutgers University Press, 2007.

Mehra, B. "Hindu Temples and Asian-Indian Diasporic Identity in the United States." *Detroit Monographs in Musicology* 40 (2004): 93–102.

Panchapakesan, Krishnamurti. *Bharat Rekha in America: A Study of Hindu Temples in USA.* Topeka: Kansas Medical Publishers, 2005.

Hindustani Classical Music

Indian classical music, with its intricate melodic and rhythmic systems reflecting a profound metaphysics of sound, developed from ancient Vedic sources and over time has produced two distinct subgenres—the Hindustani (or North Indian) tradition practiced in present-day northern India, Pakistan, and Bangladesh, and the Karnatic (or Carnatic) tradition in southern India. While the two continue to share many similarities, the traditions began to diverge as early as the 13th century due to influences introduced in northern India by Muslim rulers. While both traditions continue to thrive and grow in South Asia,

American audiences have been exposed far more extensively to Hindustani music over the past century, due to the efforts of a number of Indian master musicians, most famous among them sitar virtuoso Ravi Shankar (1920-2012). Hindustani music will accordingly be the focus of the current discussion.

Over the course of the 20th century, Hindustani classical music went from being virtually unknown in the United States to being widely recognized and appreciated. Among its earliest ambassadors in the West was Hazrat Inayat Khan (1882–1927), a Sufi teacher and musician whose ensemble, the Royal Musicians of Hindustan, toured the United States and Europe for several years beginning in 1910. While Inayat Khan conceived of his mission to the West primarily in spiritual terms, hoping to introduce Americans and Europeans to a more profound way of living through exposure to the inspired music of India, his performances did not typically have the reception he hoped, being more often treated as thrilling exoticism from the "mystic East" at a time when such Orientalist fantasy was much in vogue. It was not until mid-century that Hindustani classical music began receiving more serious attention from American audiences in its own right. One important event in this shift was the recording of the first long-playing record of Hindustani classical music, *Music of India: Morning and Evening Ragas*, featuring master sarod player Ali Akbar Khan (1922–2009). At the beginning of the album, famed violinist and conductor Yehudi Menuhin, a sincere admirer of Hindustani music who had invited the sitarist to the United States, acted as guide for

American listeners, introducing Khan and the other musicians and explaining the basics of raga form. Khan's renown was furthered by live concerts as well as an appearance on American television the same year; 12 years later he opened the Ali Akbar College of Music in the San Francisco Bay Area, which continues to teach Hindustani classical music using traditional teaching methods of oral transmission. However, it was Khan's direct contemporary, Ravi Shankar, who was most responsible for igniting the popularity that Indian classical music has enjoyed in the United States since the 1960s. His virtuosity and versatility in solo performances as well as his many collaborations with other musicians—among them Yehudi Menuhin, George Harrison, and John Coltrane—helped to make the rich Hindustani classical music tradition familiar to a far wider American audience, a trend that has only continued with the growing popularity of world music in recent decades.

However, this popular success can obscure the deeper significance attributed to music in Indian spiritual contexts, within which it is not considered mere entertainment—though it may be that as well—but ultimately is seen as a means for uniting the individual soul with the divine. The earliest known Indian treatise discussing music is a Vedic text dating from approximately the fourth century CE, the *Natyashastra*, concerning aesthetics of dance, theater, and music. The *Natyashastra* introduces the important aesthetic concept of *rasa*—flavor or effect, and by extension, aesthetic emotion—and describes eight major categories of human emotion that underlie musical compositions and other art forms—the *rasas* of *shringar* (divine or human love), *karuna* (sadness, compassion), *vira* (heroism), *hasya* (laughter, comedy), *raudra* (anger), *bhayanaka* (fear), *vibhasa* (disgust), and *adbhuta* (surprise). To these, another *rasa*, *shanti* (peacefulness), was later added for a total of nine widely accepted *rasas*. Of the nine, only *shringar*, *karuna*, *vira*, and *shanti* are typically employed in music, and of these *rasa shringar*, with its focus on longing for union with the human or divine Beloved, features more frequently than the others.

While North Indian classical music was initially grounded in Vedic and Brahmanic traditions (from which arose what we now term Hinduism), the introduction of Persian and Sufi influences, especially under Mughal rule starting in the 16th century, led to a new phase of musical enrichment and development. While some musicians patronized by Muslim rulers maintained their original affiliation with Hindu practices, others converted to Islam, leading to ongoing interreligious musical collaboration that can still be seen in the tradition today. The affinities between Hindu and Sufi mystical understandings of music likely eased the way toward this merging of musical cultures.

Hindu tradition teaches that in the beginning was the unheard, unstruck sound—*anahad nada* or *anahata* in Sanskrit—the creative matrix from which the manifest universe arose and to which all must ultimately return. This unstruck sound is held to be ever-present, though only perceivable to the inner, spiritual ear during profound states of meditation. This primordial vibration, with which all creation resonates, is associated with the divine as creator and is called *Nada Brahma*—literally "the sound of God" or "sound as God." (Brahman—understood as the creative matrix from which all arises—is distinct from Brahma, the creator god within the Hindu *trimurti* [trinity] of Brahma, Vishnu, and Shiva.) All of nature is understood to partake of this vibrational quality and to seek harmony with it. In his autobiography, *My Music—My Life*, Ravi Shankar explained: "Our tradition teaches us that sound is God—*Nada Brahma*." Shankar goes on to say that musical sound and the musical experience are steps to the realization of the self. As such, Hindus view music as a kind of spiritual discipline that raises one's inner being to divine peacefulness and bliss. The highest aim of Hindu music is to reveal the essence of the universe it reflects, and the ragas are among the means by which this essence can be apprehended. Thus, through music, one can reach God.

Likewise, Sufi tradition attributes mystical properties to sound, especially in the form of music. Hazrat Inayat Khan discusses the continuities between Hindu and Sufi conceptions of music, noting that the Vedanta speaks of *Nada Brahma*, the Sound-God, the sound that is God, of which all things are made. Sufis call it *sawt-e-sarmad*, the sound that intoxicates man. Before this world was, all was in sound, God was sound, we are made of sound.

The qualities of sound prized in Hindustani classical music and the structure of the raga form itself reflect the relation between the vibrational ground of being and the universe of form that emerges from it.

Philosopher Ananda Coomaraswamy (1877–1947), whose writings helped further American interest in Indian aesthetics and spirituality, described the deep resonant sound of the *tanpura* (alternate spellings: *tambura, tamboura*)—the droning stringed instrument that "is heard before the song, during the song, and continues after it" and that creates the raga's felt ground of vibration—as "the timeless Absolute, which as it was in the beginning is now and ever shall be." From this foundational sound, the musicians draw forth the raga itself, which Coomaraswamy likened to the variety of Nature, emerging from its source and returning at the close of its cycle. The harmony of that undivided ground with this intricate pattern is the unity of spirit and matter. Expressive qualities of the human voice are preserved even in instrumental performance through the preference for instruments capable of mimicking vocal flexibility, able to slide from one note to the next. Richness is also added through the presence of sympathetic strings on instruments such as the sarod or sitar, which resonate with the struck tones, as well as drone strings that are strummed as the raga intensifies in tempo and rhythm.

A raga, frequently translated as "color" or "passion," is a melodic mode within which a melody is largely improvised within the constraints of an intricate set of strict guidelines. These guidelines determine the selection of notes allowable within the specific raga, the distinctive heart phrase that recurs throughout its performance, and the characteristic phrase fragments that the soloist skillfully weaves into his or her improvisations. They also serve to ensure that the raga maintains its distinctly individual character despite never being performed the same way twice. Each raga is associated with a particular aesthetic emotion (*rasa*), and most are associated with the energy and mood of a particular time of day or night, with some considered specific to particular seasons as well. Traditionally, a raga would never be played at the wrong time, as this would detract from its unique beauty, so closely aligned with the particular feelings at that part of the day.

During the improvisational first segment of a raga, the *alap*, the soloist slowly develops the raga's characteristics, introducing and embellishing upon its notes one by one, accompanied only by the drone of the *tanpura*. These characteristics remain recognizable throughout the performance of the raga, which can last for hours. The form moves from this initial phase into the greater intensity of the second section, the *gat*, in which the rhythmic cycle—or *tala*— is introduced by the percussionist playing the tabla (a paired set of hand drums). Within the *gat*, the soloist's improvisation—which during the *alap* had been free of the structure of fixed rhythm—becomes constrained by the demands of the *tala*. The tablist, in turn, must constantly adjust the rhythmic patterning to follow the lead of the soloist, and a complex and lively interplay between the two musicians begins.

While this partnership between performers is clearly crucial, Indian aesthetics also emphasizes the important partnership between musician and listener—and the need for deep empathy as well as knowledge on the part of the latter—if a performance is to be successful. Both playing and listening to a raga is meant to be a visceral and potentially transformative experience, mirroring and inducing a state of reabsorption in the divine. This intimate communion and union is a theme echoed by the many-layered experience of human relationships invoked within Hindustani musical practice: reverent communion of the musician with the music he or she plays, intimate interplay between musicians, engaged partnership between musician and listener, and, frequently, the use of *rasa shringar* with its evocation of human and divine love. As music itself is understood as a mirror of and bridge to divine union, so are the many forms of human intimacy that are evoked and incorporated in the experience of the raga. Ideally, then, through the sensory experience of music and of the relational states it engenders, the musician and listener both may be swept into a state transcending the everyday world, to taste the bliss of dissolving into the sound that is God.

In addition to the two forms of Indian classical music, there are a variety of folk styles (e.g., Rajasthani folk, Sufi, Baul, etc.) due to the ethnic diversity, each with distinct regional flavor. The compositions are different from region to region, not just because of the diversity of the population, but also the diversity of the subjects/issues. The instruments used are rustic and primal. For example, in the eastern region of India, the Baul folk tradition was prominent during pre-independence India. Baul singers were basically mendicant ascetics with almost no material possessions and would eat only when offered food; these singers traveled through rural India singing about the freedom struggle and spreading awareness of the freedom movement among the masses. The only "instrument" they possessed was an "Ektara," one string on a piece of bamboo that was attached to a dried gourd shell. The Ektara is tuned to the scale in which the singer would sing and is used mainly as a percussion instrument as opposed to a melodic one. The Baul sings very loudly and fully for people to be able to hear him from within their houses as he passes by them.

In the last couple of decades with the increase of people of Indian origin, many local bands emerged in the San Francisco Bay Area, in the suburbs of Boston, in Calgary (Canada), and other locales with a South Asian presence. In addition to fellowship, these bands are trying to keep their musical tradition alive by integrating the sounds of folk instruments like the Ektara with Western instrumentation. Some bands have performed at international music festivals, raising awareness of Indian music. Part of their motivation is to pass on to their children and grandchildren their musical tradition.

Colette L. Walker

See also: Entries: Shin Buddhist Music

Further Reading

Berendt, Joachim-Ernst. *The World Is Sound: Nada Brahma: Music and the Landscape of Consciousness*. Rochester, VT: Destiny Books, 1983.

Coomaraswamy, Ananda K. *The Dance of Śiva: Essays on Indian Art and Culture*. New York: Dover, 1985 (1924).

Danielou, Alain. *Ragas of Northern Indian Music*. Philadelphia: Coronet Books, 2010.

Farrell, Gerry. *Indian Music and the West*. Oxford: Oxford University Press, 1997.

Hirlekar, Hema. *Nuances of Hindustani Classical Music*. New Delhi: Unicorn Books, 2010.

Khan, Ali Akbar, and George Ruckert. *Classical Music of North India: The First Years of Study: The Music of the Baba Allauddin Gharana As Taught by Ali Akbar Khan at the Ali Akbar College of Music*. Saint Louis: MMB Music, 1991.

Khan, Hazrat Inayat. *The Mysticism of Sound and Music*. Boston: Shambhala, 1996.

Lavezzoli, Peter. *The Dawn of Indian Music in the West: Bhairavi*. New York: Continuum International, 2006.

Neuman, Daniel M. *Life of Music in North India: The Organization of an Artistic Tradition*. Chicago: University of Chicago Press, 1990.

Ruckert, George E. *Music in North India: Experiencing Music, Expressing Culture*. New York: Oxford University Press, 2004.

Saxena, Sushil Kumar. *Hindustani Music and Aesthetics Today: A Selective Study*. New Delhi: Sangeet Natak Akademi, 2009.

Sen Chib, Satyendra K. *Companion to North Indian Classical Music*. New Delhi: Munshiram Manoharlal, 2004.

Wade, Bonnie C. *Music in India: The Classical Traditions*. Englewood Cliffs, NJ: Prentice-Hall, 1979.

Hmong American Religions

The Hmong are an ethnic minority population with origins in Southern China and Southeast Asia. While the exact origins of the Hmong are shrouded in time, it is believed that they originated in China where they have lived for at least 2,000 years. The largest Hmong population in the world, close to 2 million, still live in southwestern China, centered in the provinces of Hunan, Guizhou, and Yunnan. Hmong oral history, however, tells of a time almost 300 years ago when war and persecution by the Han

Mua of St. Paul, Minnesota describes his imprisonment in Laos to the media, July 12, 2003, at the Beaver Lake Lutheran Church in Maplewood, Minnesota. Mua, a U.S. citizen of Hmong origin, was freed through diplomatic negotiations after a month in custody, along with two European journalists. At rear from left is the Rev. Peter Rogness, bishop of the St. Paul Area Synod of the Evangelical Lutheran Church in America; NengFue Lee, and Mua's wife, Sue. (AP Photo/Janet Hostetter)

Chinese ruler caused many Hmong to emigrate and settle throughout the countries of Southeast Asia including Burma, Laos, Thailand, and Vietnam, where they favored the high mountain areas that were not as densely populated and where they could practice traditional slash and burn agriculture and establish autonomous villages.

Hmong village life centered around the family and the clan and society was patriarchal and patrilocal, although descent was traced through the mother. The Hmong, whose name in the Hmong language simply means "human being," are a fiercely independent people who value freedom and who have managed to maintain Hmong culture and tradition through centuries of minority status and oppression. The traditional religion of the Hmong people is animism, the belief that spirits inhabit the natural environment who can affect human beings for good or ill, and who must be propitiated to maintain a proper balance. Most Hmong in the United States are from Laos due to a shared history of conflict and cooperation during the wars in Southeast Asia in the mid-20th century. The remainder of this entry will focus on Hmong experience in Laos and later the United States.

Traditional Religious Beliefs and Practices

In traditional Hmong animistic belief a Hmong home is protected by six main "house spirits." In order of importance, these spirits are located in the home altar, the center post of the home, the hearth, the stove, the door to the home, and the bedroom. These "tame" spirits protect the family from the encroachment of the spirits of disease and death and from the "wild" spirits believed to live beyond the village or home. They also help to ensure prosperity, including, in a village context, good crops and healthy livestock. The "door spirit" is particularly important for this, and some homes celebrate an annual festival for the door spirit to welcome prosperity into the home. Each house has an altar in recognition of the spirits and to enable communication with the ancestors.

Each village has a shaman, who can be either male or female, to assist in communicating with the spirits in difficult or especially important situations. These sha-

mans are "chosen" by the spirits—usually through a period of severe illness from which the individual recovers once he or she agrees to become a shaman and begin learning the rituals.

Shamans assist families at times of important family transitions and events and during illness. When a shaman is summoned to assist with an illness, he or she will typically enter into a trance to communicate with the spirits. Sitting on a bench facing the house altar, the shaman invokes her or his "teacher spirits" to appear and offer instruction on curing the person. The shaman will shake a ritual rattle with one hand while chanting and beating his or her thigh with the other. The shaman's assistant beats a gong in time with the chanting. The bench is transformed into a "spirit horse," which the shaman "rides" in the trance to meet and communicate with the spirits that are understood to be causing the illness. During the trance, the shaman will ask for the sacrifice of a pig or chicken to calm the offended spirit. The purpose of the sacrifice is to send the animal's spirit to the spirit world in place of the ill person's spirit, so that the ill person's spirit can return and recover. The animal's spirit is also expected to protect the individual from future harm or illness. Some of the blood of the sacrificed animal may be wiped on the clothing or feet of the ill person. Paper "spirit money" is then burned as an offering. The shaman may still need to fight off the evil spirits. This may include jumping as well as rolling around on the floor and groaning or shouting. When all becomes quiet, the shaman's helper will touch him or her gently on the back to conclude the trance state. The shaman will throw the "divining sticks" to determine the outcome of the contest. The shaman will thank the "teaching spirits," the family will thank the shaman, and they will share a meal together. A special ceremony is also held once a new baby is three days old. This "soul calling" (*hu plij*) asks the child's souls to come and reside within the body. Hmong traditionally believe that each individual has three souls. After the ceremony is completed, strings are tied on the child's wrists to connect the child's souls to the body. Later in life, if an illness is believed to be caused by a "lost soul," a similar ceremony can be performed to lead the person's soul back to his or her body.

While still a distinct minority faith, Christianity has a strong presence among the Hmong of Laos. Twenty percent of Hmong in Laos were estimated to be Christian in 1998. While the 1991 Constitution of the Lao People's Democratic Republic guarantees religious freedom and the equality of citizens of all faiths, by the government's own admission, this policy has not always been equally enforced. There is still a cultural/political preference for Buddhism, and Christians have sometimes suffered persecution.

Changing Practices and Realities in the U.S. Context

Recent studies have found that 75 percent of Hmong people in the United States continue to practice the traditional faith, but increasingly many of the younger generations have converted to Christianity. At least 50 percent have now converted to Christianity. Additionally, the younger generation who are more adept in English and acculturated to American society have supplanted the traditional leadership roles of elders. Marriage and funeral rites have changed as well, with less frequent payment of a bride price and "bride capture" marriage. Funeral ceremonies are sometimes varied in an attempt to accommodate differing religious beliefs of family members. But nowhere have changes been as dramatic as regarding the role of shamans in healing. With the Hmong arrival in the United States and their exposure to Western health care, traditional healing practices have often come into conflict with mainstream U.S. medical practices. Hmong community members and organizations have played a vital role in "bridging" the gap in cultural understanding between communities, making Hmong more comfortable in modern medical settings and helping to devise ways that particular traditional healing rituals can occur in a hospital setting.

In tandem with an additional large influx of Hmong from 2004 to 2006, the California Endowment funded nine Hmong serving organizations in the population center of the Central Valley, from Fresno to Sacramento, as the Hmong Health Collaborative, to advocate for their health needs. As part of the work, hospital staff in the region were trained in Hmong traditional healing practices and 55 shamans underwent weeklong training in hospital policies and procedures, toured medical facilities, and met medical staff. Working with hospitals, policies were developed that allowed shamans to have access to patients and a specific list of rituals that would be allowed. The Hmong Health Collaborative developed a "Shaman Handbook" with all the information about hospital procedures for shaman access to patients, allowed rituals, and the contact information for each trained shaman. Medical staff and Hmong patients now have a concise guide to assist them in working together.

At the same time, many Hmong are becoming more acculturated to Western medical practices and will now often add this care to whatever traditional remedies they may try. This is not a new phenomenon for the Hmong who, even in Southeast Asia, were known to have a pragmatic approach to illness. While illnesses believed to have a spiritual cause require the presence of a shaman, the Hmong believe that some illnesses do not have a spiritual cause. For these conditions, many different "cures" may be tried, including herbs, "cupping" and "coining," and the tying of strings or amulets—continuing until something is found that works. Many Christian Hmong also continue to use these traditional practices, with the exception of the services of a shaman, in addition to Western medical care. Another key area of change since arrival in the United States is traditional funeral practices. It is believed that it takes three days for the deceased's spirit to make the full transition from this world to the spirit world. Upon death, one of the individual's souls goes to heaven, one remains with the body, and one is reincarnated. Relatives were expected to keep vigil with the deceased during this time. In Laos, funeral rites were slightly different for each clan and subclan. However, some common elements included the maintenance of the body of the deceased in the family's home for two days. On the third day the body would be taken outside the family home, a cow sacrificed to allow the person's spirit to return to the place where

they were born, and the body buried. In the United States, however, the body can only be housed at the funeral home, which necessitates an expensive 72-hour rental of the funeral home. The body must also be embalmed. At the time of the funeral, the "spirit guide" (*Txiv Taw Kev*) comes to perform rituals to lead the spirit of the deceased back through all the places she or he has lived to the place that they were born, to pick up their placenta (*Tsho Tsuj Tsho Npaug*), which traditionally is buried beneath the central post of the house where the person was born. It is the placenta that ultimately enables the deceased to go to the spirit world, where her or his ancestors live. A contingent of people also come to help facilitate the funeral, including the *gasu* (*Kav Xwm*), clan leader and funeral supervisor, Kheng player (*Txiv Qeej*), younger male relatives (*Txiv Cuab Tsav*), women (*Niam Ua Mov*), and cooks, *chu ka* (*Tshwj Kab*). A contingent of people, including unmarried women and two to three men, form the *chu ka* (*Tshwj Kab*) who come to cook food for the family and all the mourners over the three days. The *gasu* (*Kav Xwm*) comes to perform the *Hi See* (*Hais Xim*), bowing before the deceased with incense to ask for blessings for the living and also to wish the deceased good luck in the next life. The Kheng (Hmong flute) player (*Txiv Qeej*) and "drum hitter" (*Txiv Nrnas*) come to perform a ritual dance to assist the deceased to the spirit world as well. Unlike in Laos, in the United States, the family must buy animals to slaughter and the cow must be slaughtered in a specialized slaughterhouse, and the *gasu* (*Kav Xwm*) clan leader must go to oversee the slaughtering. Some of the animal's meat is then reserved for him. Because of the cost of the animals, as well as burial and rental of the funeral home, Hmong funerals in the United States have become quite expensive. While Christian and non-Christian Hmong generally both have three-day funerals, some Christian Hmong will carefully decide which rituals of a traditonal funeral to be present for and which ones not.

The Hmong have shown a remarkable ability throughout their history, as a minority and stateless people, to maintain and pass along their important cultural traditions. That pattern continues today, despite the changes that life in America has brought to the Hmong community.

Sophia Dewitt

See also: Entries: Hmong Shamanism; Laotian American Religions

Further Reading

Hmong Health Collaborative. *Shaman Spiritual Hospital Handbook: Shaman Handbook for Hospital Staff and Families.* Fresno, CA: Hmong Health Collaborative, 2010.

Lewis, Paul, and Elaine Lewis. *Peoples of the Golden Triangle: Six Tribes in Thailand.* New York: Thames and Hudson, 1984.

Lipson, Juliene G., Suzanne L. Dibble, and Pamela A. Minarik. *Culture and Nursing Care: A Pocket Guide.* Duluth, MN: Regents of the College of St. Scholastica, 1996.

Moua, Vayong. "Hmong Christianity: Conversion, Consequence and Conflict." Northfield, MN: St. Olaf College, 1995. Online at http://www.miaoupg.com/hmong.htm.

Vannasopha, Mahā. *Religious Affairs in Lao P.D.R.: Policies and Tasks.* Vientiane: Department for Religious Affairs, Lao Front for National Construction Central Committee, 2005.

Hmong Shamanism

Hmong Americans, an ethnic group that has deep roots in many parts of Laos, fought alongside the Americans during the Vietnam War and were eventually forced out to resettle as refugees, with the largest number settling in the United States and smaller numbers in France, Australia, and Canada at the end of the war. Many have since converted to the dominant religious affiliations in the United States while many still retain the traditional practices and are still actively engaged in the practice of shamanism.

There are two main subgroups that have resided in the United States, one of which is the Hmong who speak the Green dialect, *Hmong Njua*, and the other who speak the White dialect, *Hmong Daw*. The two main distinctions between these two groups are the traditional dress of the women and their linguistic distinction, though the two dialects are mutually intelligible. The current estimate of Hmong population in the United States is about 300,000 with the majority residing in California, Minnesota, and Wisconsin.

Cosmology and Worldview of the Hmong

The Hmong's worldview or cosmology can be understood in the sense of time and space: time in the sense of present, past, future, and day-night time; space in the sense of *Sau ntuj* (Upper Realm), *Nplaj teb* (Earth), and *Dlaab teb* (Spirit World). This complex system of space and time defines the cycle of the human soul and spirit. The realms are not perceived as isolated and fixed; rather, they are fluid, alive, inhabited,

Wang Pao Yang, a Hmong shaman, shows a large metal ring in his right hand and rings on his fingers which he uses during spiritual healing ceremonies for people who are very sick, September 2, 2009, at his Fresno, California home. The Hmong Health Collaborative is trying to improve access to hospitals in the San Joaquin Valley for spiritual healers like Yang. (Eric Paul Zamora/Fresno Bee/ MCT/Getty Images)

and interconnected through birth, death, and the renewal progression that an individual passes through during his or her life course.

The Hmong believe in the existence of more than one soul, though how many in particular has been a controversial matter as it depends on whom one speaks to. A *Plig* or soul is the spirit that resides in the body keeping the individual healthy and alive. What is agreed upon is that a soul can exist

inside and outside of the body. When a soul is viewed to have been separated from the body, it is generally believed that the soul has been lost, resulting in a state known as *Poob Plig* or "lost soul." What follows is a *Hu Plig* or soul calling ceremony that would be performed by a shaman to recall the lost soul, though it is common for the head of household to perform this task if he or she knows the procedures.

For the Hmong, a healthy body goes beyond the individual, as it plays relevant purposes within the sociopolitical function of the community. In other words, the individual understands his or her meaning and identity through the practice of memberships within the community. In this sense, the individual comprehends that interrelationship and intercommunication with others outweigh singular achievements when functioning as a collective membership.

The Hmong's worldview has its own rationality and inner reasoning in comprehending the judgment of time, space, and nature around them. The culture and tradition has profound implications in explaining the mysteries of life and the meaningful activities of their society. The highly developed spiritual system and worldview of the Hmong is an active process that is constantly being transformed and shaped though time and space, though what remains are the profound sacred meanings that rest just beneath the layers of their tradition and culture practices.

Initiation and Instruction—Practice, Role, and Healing

An individual does not decide to become a shaman. To become a shaman, one has to be called upon through special visitations of the spirits. In this way, the shaman is viewed to be genuine and have authenticity. Often, a shaman begins his or her career in sickness, usually during youth. Symptoms may include shivering, stiff jaws, shaking of the arms and legs, or even illness such as epilepsy. Shamans tend to describe their experiences as having experienced and overcome critical forces of death and disease.

Traditionally, the practice of shamanism is exclusively a male's entity, however, there are also female shamans in the United States with some having profound reputations within the Hmong American community. A shaman that has gained prestige and profound reputation within the community may be called upon to perform regularly, though he or she may respectfully deny the request.

The shaman's role is not typically sought due to the fear of evil spirits and ruthless omens, though once committed, he or she would begin the training through apprenticeship to a more knowledgeable shaman for a few years. Given the oral tradition, there are no written books or manuals regarding the practice of shamanism, hence, the mode of instruction is guided by oral and participatory learning. During this transition period, the novice shaman learns the sacred chants, personal mnemonics, and procedures of the shamanic rites from the experienced shaman. The absence of books and manuals provides the opportunity for the novice shaman to explore the practice of shamanism from a variety of approaches as well as for personal uniqueness.

Having overcome death and illness, the Hmong shaman has been reinvigorated by the experience, has witnessed life and death, knows the way, and hence, is capable of assisting and going there again on behalf of others. These profound trainings and experiences allow the shaman to engage in creating a moral worldview that provides an existent, yet interpretive framework for dealing with the sick individual. Through this perspective, the shaman is able to stimulate belief in a philosophical, yet accessible way. The shaman is more than a healthy social centerpiece within the community as he or she is also an active agent of cultural knowledge in performing and exercising the core beliefs of the culture.

Hmong Shamanism and Health Care Professionals

While it has been three decades since the arrival of the Hmong, their shamanism practice still functions as a vital constituent in many communities. In the last two decades, health care professionals were ignorant of the practice of shamanism, which resulted in a great deal of miscommunication and misunderstanding. One classic case is that of Lia Lee in Fadiman's (1997) *The Spirit Catches You and You Fall Down*, in which there were astounding miscommunication and miscomprehension of both cultural perspectives regarding the implication of epilepsy. Nevertheless, recent research in the medical field has documented that health care professionals are becoming sensitive and receptive in finding approaches to mutually engage both sides.

Though these ceremonies and rituals carried out by the shaman are spiritual, behind them are profound emotional and psychological meanings for individuals who acknowledge and believe them. Researchers have contended that the shaman's role is comparable to that of a minister or priest who mediates personal concerns through interventions, such as prayer or offering individuals psychological and emotional support.

With the compromise of the two systems, many Hmong have felt that their tradition of shamanism is being acknowledged and appreciated in the health care system. While some have converted to other religions and have rejected the practice of shamanism, many individuals have yet to relinquish the tradition. Many still recognize shamanism as an active-dynamic form of religious healing and consider it to be greatly valuable and effective.

Yeng Yang

See also: Entries: Hmong American Religions; Shamanism, Modern

Further Reading

Capps, L. Lisa. "Ua Neeb Khu: A Hmong American Healing Ceremony." *Journal of Holistic Nursing* (2010).

Cha, P. Ya. *An Introduction to Hmong Culture.* Jefferson, NC: McFarland, 2011.

Conquergood, Dwight. *I Am a Shaman. A Hmong Life Story with Ethnographic Commentary.* Minneapolis: Center for Urban and Regional Affairs, University of Minnesota, 1989.

Helsel, Deborah, Marilyn Mochel, and Bauer Mochel. "Chronic Illness and Hmong Shamans." *Journal of Transcultural Nursing* (2005).

Helsel, Deborah, Marilyn Mochel, and Bauer Mochel. "Shamans in a Hmong American Community." *Journal of Alternative and Complementary Medicine* (2004).

Hoa Hao Buddhism

Hoa Hao Buddhism is an indigenous religion of Vietnam. It was established in 1939 in southern Vietnam, when the country was still a French colony. Its name derives from the village in which it was founded, also the location of the religion's Holy Land. The religion's founder was Prophet Huynh Phu So, whom followers believe is one of two living Buddhas in Vietnam. Prophet So continued the fundamental Buddhist teachings and traditions established by the first living Buddha in Vietnam—the Healing Buddha of Tay An—who led a form of Buddhism known as Buu Son Ky Huong Buddhism in 1849 in southern Vietnam.

Philosophy and Rituals

Similar to Buu Son Ky Huong Buddhism, Hoa Hao Buddhism emphasizes simplicity, purity, and harmony in rituals and practice. As Prophet So had preached, the essence of Buddhism is not be attached to elaborate pagodas and ceremonies involving statues, gongs, and bells, which are often found in other forms of Buddhism. Instead of spending financial resources on these extravagances, Prophet So had taught that the money should be directed to helping the poor and supporting social programs.

In line with this philosophy, Hoa Hao Buddhism emphasizes home worship as the center of religious devotion. The idea is that even farmers can continue to work and participate in daily life activities while practicing the faith. Many Hoa Hao Buddhists have simple in-home altars at home. To represent their purity, they offer only fresh water, flowers, and incense on their altars. They do not use food as is often the case for many other branches of Buddhism.

To convey its simplicity, purity, and harmony, Hoa Hao Buddhism is represented by the color brown. Adherents believe that it symbolizes the Buddhist spirit because brown is a combination of all other colors. The religion's flag is simply rectangular and brown, bearing no characters or pictures. Its insignia is round and brown, with a picture of a white lotus and four initials, P.G.H.H. (*Phat Giao Hoa Hao*, which is Vietnamese for Hoa Hao Buddhism).

Demographics

During its early years of establishment, Hoa Hao Buddhism grew rapidly in popularity. In 1966, the total number of Hoa Hao followers was estimated at over two million people or 10 percent of the population of South Vietnam. In provinces such as Chau Doc, An Giang, Kien Phong, and Sadec in South Vietnam, Hoa Hao Buddhists accounted for 90 percent of the population. In other provinces, this proportion varied from 10 to 60 percent.

Today, the Hoa Hao Buddhist population is either the largest or the second largest indigenous religion of Vietnam, following Caodaism. According to Vietnamese official records, there are approximately 1.3 million followers of Hoa Hao Buddhism. However, followers have claimed that their population is as great as 3 million.

Outside of Vietnam, the largest Hoa Hao Buddhist concentration (approximately 3,000 members) is in Orange County, Southern California, also the home of the largest number of Vietnamese outside of Vietnam. Other large concentrations reside in Los Angeles, San Jose, Sacramento, and San Diego. Altogether, there are approximately 5,000 Hoa Hao Buddhists in California. Although Hoa Hao Buddhists openly welcome non-Vietnamese to their religion, as of today, nearly all adherents are Vietnamese and only a handful are non-Vietnamese.

History

Since its founding, Hoa Hao Buddhist followers experienced many periods of persecution as different political factions competed for control and power in Vietnam. Beginning with the French, Hoa Hao Buddhists were seen by the colonial government as nationalist and a threat to its rule. In particular, relations with Communists were strained ever since the Viet Minh allegedly mass murdered hundreds of Hoa Hao Buddhist followers in September 1945 and allegedly killed their prophet two years later.

With the fall of Saigon in 1975, Hoa Hao Buddhism became severely repressed by the new antireligion government. The religion's properties were confiscated, religious practices and teachings were prohibited, and its managerial structure was abolished. It was not until 1999 that Hoa Hao Buddhism became an officially recognized religion of Vietnam. Today, it is one of six official religions of the country. However, despite the recognition, Hoa Hao Buddhism continues to be under the close scrutiny of the Vietnamese government. For example, visitors to the Hoa Hao Holy Land must obtain temporary residence permits issued by authorities.

The 1975 Communist takeover also forced many Hoa Hao Buddhists to flee to other countries. In their new homes, Hoa Hao Buddhists have transplanted their faith and continued to lobby for religious freedom in Vietnam.

The Hoa Hao Buddhist Community in the United States

As Hoa Hao Buddhists arrived in the United States beginning in 1975, they slowly rebuilt their community. In 1978, they established their first temple (Hội Quán) in a rented building in Long Beach, California. It was here that they held the first annual Grand Ceremony (Đại Lễ) in commemoration of the birth of Prophet So. There were more than 100 Hoa Hao Buddhists in attendance. A year later, Hoa Hao Buddhists began reprinting religious books. As their community grew and expanded, they began publishing *Tập Sản Đuốc Từ Bi* (*The Torch of Compassion Magazine*) in 1981, and even religious radio broadcasts in 1994. In 1987, as the community expanded, Vietnamese Hoa Hao Buddhists moved the temple to a home in Santa Ana that members had purchased with donations.

Today, California has three Hoa Hao Buddhist temples. In adition to the one in Santa, there are temples in San Jose and Sacramento. There are also temples in Washington, D.C., Houston, Dallas, At-lanta, Seattle, Philadelphia, Pittsburgh, Richmond, Chesterfield, New York City, Boston, Chicago, and Pensacola.

Hoa Hao Buddhists in the United States are primarily concerned with preserving and spreading their religion and lobbying for religious freedom in Vietnam. They have institutionalized weekly scripture classes for the youth, whom they see as important for sustaining the religion in a new country. They have also continued to popularize their religion through magazine publications, DVDs, the Internet, and other popular mediums.

Hoa Hao Buddhists also dedicate their lives to speaking against religious suppression in Vietnam. By organizing with other Vietnamese religious groups and forming the Interfaith Alliance, for example, Hao Hao Buddhists have made presentations to politicians in Washington, D.C., about the Vietnamese government's atrocities toward the faithful, from house arrests to the destruction of properties. Hoa Hao Buddhists in the United States have also mobilized their homeland campaigns across borders, working with co-religionists in other countries, including those in France, Canada, and Australia.

Thien-Huong T. Ninh

See also: Entries: Caodaism; Vietnamese American Buddhists; Vietnamese American Catholics; Vietnamese American Religions

Further Reading

Hoa Hao Buddhist Church. *Brief Description of Hao Hao Buddhism*. Santa Fe, California: Hoa Hao Buddhist Church Overseas Office, 1996. http://www.hoahao.org. Accessed July 10, 2014.

Nguyen, Huynh Mai. *The Little Girl of Hoa Hao Village*. 2007. http://www.nguyenhuynhmai.com. Accessed July 10, 2014.

Nguyen, Long Thanh Nam. *Hoa Hao Budhism in the Course of Vietnam's History*. Hauppauge, NY: Nova Science Publishers, 2003.

Honpa Hongwanji Mission of Hawai'i

Honpa Hongwanji Mission of Hawai'i (HHMH) is a Buddhist organization affiliated with the Jōdo Shinshū Honganji-ha (Nishi Hongwanji) sect centered in Kyoto, Japan. Its 35 temples throughout the state of Hawai'i, base their spiritual life on the Jōdo Shinshū (True Pure Land) teachings of Shinran (1173–1262). HHMH serves as the central administrative hub of Nishi Hongwanji temples in Hawai'i from its headquarters in Honolulu. This entry provides an overview of HHMH with emphasis on its history and contributions to Buddhist education and to society.

Beliefs and Practices

The Jōdo Shinshū school of Buddhism (Shin Buddhism), of which HHMH is a part, arose through the insight and experience of Shinran and is a sectarian development within the larger tradition of Pure Land Buddhism, based on the *Muryōjukyō* (Larger *Sukhāvatīvyūha-sūtra*), *Kammuryōjukyō* (*Amitāyurdhyāna-sūtra*), and *Amidakyō* (Smaller *Sukhāvatīvyūha-sūtra*).

Pure Land Buddhist teachings emphasize the Mahāyāna Buddhist ideal in which salvation for oneself cannot be separated from that of others. Hence, in the mythological story of Bodhisattva Dharmākara becoming Amida Buddha through the fulfillment of 48 aspirations or "vows"—described in the *Larger Sukhāvatīvyūha-sūtra*—the salvation of all beings is the fundamental condition for Dharmākara's own acceptance of Buddhahood. The content of the 48 vows is epitomized by the 18th vow, which voices the aspiration that all beings everywhere will reach enlightenment when, hearing and thinking about the name "Amida," they awaken aspirations to be born in Amida's Pure Land and are thus assured of birth in that land in the next life. In the Pure Land tradition, aspirants are encouraged to recite the *nembutsu*, that is, to say the name of Amida Buddha (*Namo Amida Butsu*) as the means to actuate Amida's saving power and thus guarantee birth in the Pure Land. Even ordinary people who are unable to live virtuous lives or perform difficult Buddhist practices can achieve birth in the Pure Land and ultimate enlightenment through the easy practice of reciting the *nembutsu*.

Shinran, however, brought a unique perspective to this view. Based on his own experience, he realized that the desire to recite the *nembutsu* (or to perform any practice) to save himself remained an expression of human self-centeredness and ego. He realized that true and real "birth" occurs when one awakens to oneself as a being filled with blind passion, totally lacking in virtue and unable to save oneself. Only then is one able to hear the *nembutsu* as Amida's voice calling out, assuring salvation. The practitioner thus awakens faith in the reality of already being saved though Amida's Vow. In his personal insight, Shinran inverted the ordinary view of religion and re-envisioned the act of religious practice, particularly that of reciting the *nembutsu*, as a sign of salvation—and an expression of gratitude for that salvation—rather than as a means to an end.

This insight had radical implications for society in that the attainment of salvation became a matter of "grace" rather than something earned. Thus, religious or state authorities could no longer use fear of punishment in the afterlife as a means to threaten people or to enforce conformity. Existentially, for ordinary people, Shinran's teaching removed anxiety about the next life since, for the adherent of Shin Buddhism, trust in Amida's saving power was the central focus of his life. Total reliance on Amida meant that one felt accepted "just as I am," and that life could be lived with gratitude and joy. Thus, for Shin Buddhists, there is no act or practice that need be performed.

However, in the historical development of Shin Buddhism in Japan, institutionalization brought with it a large degree of conformity with generally accepted religious rituals in Japan, most of which catered to the respect for ancestors and to the family piety that were the norm in a Confucian society. As a result, the tradition of obligatory memorial observances at prescribed days and years after the death of a family member became a mainstay of Shin Buddhist life for most people, as well as the main financial support of the temple, just as it was in every other Buddhist sect. Even today, the performance of these rituals is a large part of the occupation of temple ministers and of the involvement of temple members.

In HHMH, the fulfillment of family ritual obligations still forms a large part of the work of each temple, though the numbers of members who most value and request such observances have been diminishing as the older generations have passed away. At the same time, the younger generations who have rekindled an interest in Buddhism, as well as non-Japanese persons who have been attracted to Shin Buddhism, are not satisfied with family piety and are seeking a spiritual path that can help them understand and find meaning in their lives in this confusing modern world. The teaching of Shinran, which emphasizes self-acceptance and appreciation of life as it is, is finding a truly receptive audience today amidst the disturbing uncertainty of these times. For HHMH, this has been an opportunity to share Shinran's message of hope through various educational programs and by responding to the needs of society in new and creative ways.

Historical Developments

The arrival of Buddhism in Hawai'i began with the need for cheap labor to work the booming sugar plantations of the 1870s and 1880s. Recruiters searched for workers in Japan, where crop failures and problems of modernization beset Japan at the time of the Meiji Restoration in 1868. An early group of migrants arrived in Hawai'i in 1868, the first year of the Meiji period (*Gannenmono*). However, Japanese immigration formally began in 1885 with an agreement between the Japanese and Hawaiian governments. They were designated *Kanyaku Imin*, which means contract immigrant (laborer). Reportedly, over 200,000

Japanese came to Hawai'i between 1885 and 1924, when limits were placed on the numbers permitted entry. The immigrants were mainly single males who intended to make their fortunes in Hawai'i, fulfill their contracts, and return home to live on their savings. However, many workers could not afford to return and so established roots in Hawai'i. They were largely Buddhist in background, from areas in western Japan where the Nishi (West) Hongwanji branch of the Jōdo Shinshū Buddhist school was strongest.

The immigrants repeatedly requested authentic clergy from the mother temple. As a minority group, they experienced various forms of discrimination and Christian evangelism. Nevertheless, they held on to their traditional customs, faith, and loyalties. The Nishi Hongwanji responded in 1889 by sending Rev. Kagahi Soryu (1855–1917). While his visit was short, Kagahi established Dharma centers (*fukyojo*) in Honolulu and in Hilo on the island of Hawai'i. He perceived that the people of Hawai'i, apart from the Japanese, would not accept Buddhism, and suggested to the Hongwanji in Japan that the Christian God should be equated with the Eternal Buddha, since Christianity was the dominant religion. This view was quickly rejected and Kagahi never returned to Hawai'i.

Other Buddhist denominations followed the Hongwanji. The Higashi (East) Hongwanji, sister branch of the Nishi Hongwanji, arrived in Hawai'i in 1899. By 1930 there were approximately 170 temples of all sects in Hawai'i, 70 of which were reputedly established by the Nishi Hongwanji Sōchō Bishop Yemyō Ima-

mura (1867–1932). There are now about 35 remaining Nishi Hongwanji temples in Hawai'i.

Satomi Honi (1853–1922) assumed leadership of the mission in 1898. He established a Shin Buddhist temple on Fort Street in downtown Honolulu where he started the Fujinkai (later Buddhist Women's Association). Yemyō Imamura succeeded him in 1900. Imamura's contributions and influence as a Buddhist and community leader in Hawai'i were wide ranging. He was suited for this role, receiving a high level of education in the Hongwanji, including a broad understanding of religion together with knowledge of English. He was also inspired by his association with the famous modern educator Fukuzawa Yukichi (1833–1901), the founder of Keio University, who stressed the study of English. Further, Imamura participated in the Hanseikai (Society for Self-Reflection), a reform and temperance movement, and was editor of the *Hanseikai Zasshi* (magazine).

With his strong interest in education, cultural enlightenment, and religious reform, Imamura, confronting community opposition, embarked on a mission to implant Buddhist roots deep in the soil of Hawai'i. Imamura began the Young Men's Buddhist Association in 1900, cooperating with the YMCA in its citizen's education campaign, promoting democracy and the wartime food conservation effort. In 1902 Imamura established an independent elementary school, Hongwanji Fuzoku Shogakko, to counter the anti-Buddhist environment of the zealous minister Takie Okumura's (1865–1951) Nuuanu Nihonjin Shogakko. In 1907, Imamura opened the Hawai'i

Chugakko (Junior High School) to provide a higher level of education.

The purpose of these schools was to teach English and Japanese to the youth and also to Americanize them. Okumura's approach to Americanization was to convert the students to Christianity, maintaining that this was the only basis for democracy and good citizenship. Imamura taught loyalty as American citizens, while retaining Japanese culture, values, and relationships. Establishing the Giseikai or Legislative Assembly in 1908, HHMH itself became more democratic, following the example set earlier by Hongwanji in Japan. In addition, Imamura called for justice and equality in the face of discrimination by the dominant society. While educating the youth in Buddhism and extolling democratic ideals, he exposed the hypocrisy of a "democratic" society that claimed that only Christians could be good citizens.

The Hongwanji schools flourished as a result of Imamura's effectiveness in mediating and ending the 1904 sugar strike, instigated by a cruel overseer. Stressing Buddhist principles of gratitude and compassion, Imamura persuaded the workers to return to work, leading the planters to view Buddhism more favorably as a force for peace and stability. As a result, the planters donated land for temples and Imamura became the recognized leader of the Buddhist community. During the 1920 sugar strike, Imamura sided with workers who were evicted from their homes and suffered financially. Earning only 77 cents a day, they were asking for a wage increase to improve their living conditions. Imamura and other Buddhist clergy attempted to convince the

sugar planters to accept the workers' demands, and thereby earned the planters' ire. This situation resulted in later efforts to limit or abolish language schools (an attempt that failed in the U.S. Supreme Court), to restrict immigration, and to support intensive efforts at "Americanization."

In 1917, as a result of a gift of land to Hongwanji by Mary Foster (1844–1930), an ardent Buddhist, Imamura constructed the Honpa Hongwanji Hawai'i Betsuin. The building had an eclectic architecture that combined Western, Indian, and Buddhist elements to suggest the universality of Buddhism. He termed temples as "abodes of light and love." Light is a symbol for wisdom and temples were to be centers for education. He set up what he called "Education Homes," where English was taught to first-generation (Issei) immigrants and Japanese to the second (Nisei), to avoid divisions in families over language and matters of citizenship. In 1921, Imamura and Thomas Kirby initiated the Hongwanji English Department. In 1924 they engaged the assistance of Ernest (Kaundinya-Shinkaku) Hunt and his wife Dorothy (Shinkoh), who were the first Caucasian priests, to compose the first English service book, *Vade Mecum*, for use by Nisei youth.

Through immigration, the Hongwanji quickly became the largest religious body and the largest Buddhist sect in Hawai'i. Imamura's progressive leadership set the direction for Hongwanji's future, integrating both the Japanese immigrants and Buddhism itself into Hawaiian society. He introduced pews and pulpits in temples, assembled *gatha*-hymn books, and even installed a pipe organ, the first in any Buddhist temple, at the Hawai'i Betsuin in 1918. In addition, the first Hawai'i Betsuin choir was organized. In 1929, inspired by the visiting Chinese monk Tai Xu, Imamura established the nonsectarian International Buddhist Institute to spread Buddhism.

Tragedy struck the Hongwanji with the sudden death of Imamura of a heart attack in 1932. Major changes came with the appointment in 1935 of the fourth bishop, Gikyo Kuchiba (1883–1955). In the midst of economic depression and dissatisfaction with Hunt's stress on Theravāda Buddhism's ethical teachings, Kuchiba sought Hunt's resignation, though the English ministry was continued.

With the onset of the war in 1941, Issei Japanese and their citizen Nisei children found their loyalty and patriotism under great suspicion. However, those suspicions were dispelled with the valor of the highly decorated Japanese American 100th Battalion and the 442nd Regimental Combat team, which fought bravely in Europe. Some 374 youth of the Hongwanji died, unrecognized by the military as Buddhists. It was not until after the war—and partly due to the exemplary service of these solders— that Buddhism was finally recognized as a religious identity by the military.

During the war, ministers were incarcerated in concentration camps under martial law and soldiers occupied temples. Services were carried on largely by laypeople, thereby limiting the efforts of the temples. With the end of the war in 1945, the members of the HHMH set about reestablishing their closed temples and reorganizing for a new era. In this new era, laypeople assumed more control of tem-

ples, initially electing bishops from among the clergy. The English language was emphasized. At this time, the Hongwanji Mission School was established and the YMBA (now YBA) was reactivated. A new hymn book, *Praises of the Buddha*, replaced the *Vade Mecum* and English services and Dharma schools increased. In 1954–1955 the *Shinshu Seiten* (*Shinshu Sacred Texts*), an English anthology of Pure Land and Shinran's writings, was published by Yamamoto Kosho, sponsored by the HHMH. However, demographic changes also affected Hongwanji and other Buddhist sects. Membership in neighboring islands decreased as people moved to O'ahu and Honolulu. In 1965 under Ohara Shojitsu (1897–1979), lay study groups and radio broadcasts were initiated. Most outstanding was the construction of the new Hongwanji Mission School building.

In 1967, Rev. Kanmo Imamura (1904–1986), the son of Yemyō Imamura, became the first elected Nisei bishop in Hawai'i, after a dedicated ministry in Berkeley. Education became a focus for Imamura with the opening of the Buddhist Study Center adjacent to the University of Hawai'i in 1974, on the occasion of HHMH's 85th anniversary. It was intended to be a student center to carry on research and translation, as well as ministerial training. Soon after, for health reasons, Kanmo Imamura resigned and returned to Berkeley. On the occasion of the 100th anniversary of the Hongwanji in Hawai'i, a new and modern Buddhist Study Center facility was opened.

With changing demographics, marked by the passing of the first generation and the aging second generation, HHMH temples witnessed a decline in membership, largely through attrition, while few new members were added. Further, the third (Sansei), fourth (Yonsei), and fifth (Gosei) generations have shown little interest in the temples. This was partly due to the growing success and respect enjoyed by Japanese Americans (due both to the bravery of the Nisei veterans and to greater political participation in the Hawaiian community after statehood in 1959). Thus, the youth have had greater mobility to develop their lives without depending on temples for encouragement and social recognition. On the other hand, the growing acceptance of Buddhism in contemporary Western society has encouraged rediscovery and renewal of declining ethnic traditions.

Despite an aging and declining membership, the HHMH developed new congregations in Kailua, in Mililani, a new community with younger families, and in Kapolei, an emerging community in west O'ahu. In 1989, becoming aware of the reality of an aging community, the farsighted leaders, Mrs. Shimeji Kanazawa and Mrs. Rose Nakamura, organized an interfaith volunteer organization called Project Dana. *Dana* is a Buddhist concept meaning "selfless giving," and Project Dana serves to aid the increasing numbers of those in the community who find themselves as caregivers of parents and spouses, providing volunteer help to aid them in surmounting the difficulties of this role. The effort has grown throughout the islands, has spread to the mainland, and has been nationally recognized.

The Hongwanji Mission School is a respected Buddhist elementary school, but offered instruction only to the eighth grade. With the launch of the Pacific Buddhist Academy in 2003, HHMH now has an accredited Buddhist school system.

Growing recognition of the importance of education for the future of the HHMH, as well as for the spread of Buddhism, has given rise to lecture programs such as the Futaba Annual Memorial Lecture, a meditation program, and the Dharma Light Project, an adult educational program, providing courses in Buddhism for members and the general community. These programs are centered at the Honpa Hongwanji Hawai'i Betsuin, but they serve a much wider segment of the HHMH, as well as the general community.

The development of HHMH's social awareness and involvement has recently became evident though the success of Pacific Buddhist Academy students and Junior YBA youth in gaining legislative approval for an annual Peace Day commemoration. Further, the public support of HHMH for civil union legislation represents a significant turning point in its political involvement with—and in relation to—the general society.

Through its 120-year history, influenced by the progressive spirit of Yemyō Imamura, the HHMH has shown flexibility and adaptability in meeting new challenges. The title of Ruth Tabrah's book marking the 100th centennial commemoration, *A Grateful Past, a Promising Future*, remains an apt description of Hongwanji's path in history.

Administrative Structure

The HHMH is headquartered in Honolulu on the island of O'ahu. The organization comprises 35 temples divided into five geographic districts (Honolulu, O'ahu, Kaua'i, Maui, Hawai'i). The 2011 Annual Report numbers the total dues-paying membership at 5,081. HHMH is governed by the bishop and the board of directors, comprised of board president, Ministers' Association president, board members elected by the local districts, and representatives of affiliated organizations. This is augmented by the bishop's advisory board (*Sanmu*), the district ministers' associations chairpersons (*Kanji*), and the district counsels. Various standing committees support and advise the bishop and the board. The Annual General Assembly (*Giseikai*) is held in February. The annual budget for 2011 was $1,290,744.00.

The office of the bishop oversees statewide programs and is responsible for assigning ministers to local temples. District programs are administered by the local district councils. Each individual temple is governed by its own board of directors, chaired by a temple president.

Contributions

HHMH has made significant contributions to the spiritual life of the Hawaiian Islands and the well-being of society. Yemyō Imamura's views on democracy, religious equality, and pluralism were way ahead of their time and paved the way for the current diversity and mutual respect among religions that is characteristic of Hawai'i today. Moreover, his willingness to intervene in the sugar strikes of 1904 and 1920 set a precedent for Buddhist social engagement and involvement in society.

HHMH's contribution to Buddhist education in America is demonstrated by its development of the Hongwanji Mission School and Pacific Buddhist Academy, providing the only accredited K–12 school system in the West based on Buddhist teachings and values.

In recent years, HHMH has made serious efforts to reach out to and participate in the general society through Project Dana, which provides welcome aid to caregivers, and through Peace Day, which educates the public on issues of peace and social justice. Further, HHMH's engagement in society has been expressed in its recent Giseikai Resolution in support of civil unions, which takes a decisive stand on the issue of equality, fairness, and individual rights.

Alfred Bloom and Richard Tennes

See also: Entries: Buddhist Churches of America; Buddhist Meditation; Higashi Honganji; Imamura, Yemyō; Jōdo Shinshū Buddhist Temples of Canada; Obon (Urabon); Shin Buddhist Music

Further Reading

Ama, Michihiro. *Immigrants to the Pure Land: The Modernization, Acculturation, and Globalization of Shin Buddhism, 1898–1941.* Honolulu: University of Hawai'i Press, 2011.

Bloom, Alfred. *Strategies for Modern Living: A Commentary with the Text of the Tannisho.* Berkeley, CA: Numata Center, 1992.

Hawai'i Federation of Honpa Hongwanji Buddhist Women's Associations. *Hosha: A Pictorial History of Jōdo Shinshū Women in Hawai'i.* Honolulu: Honpa Hongwanji Mission of Hawai'i, 1989.

Honpa Hongwanji Mission of Hawai'i. *Annual Report: From January 2011 to December*

2011. Honolulu: Honpa Hongwanji Mission of Hawai'i, 2011.

Williams, Duncan Ryuken, and Tomoe Moriya, eds. *Issei Buddhism in the* Americas. Urbana: University of Illinois Press, 2010.

Hsi Lai Temple

Hsi Lai Temple (Hsi Lai means "coming west," implying that the Buddha Dharma is coming to the West), located in Hacienda Heights, California, is one of the largest Buddhist monasteries in America. Its founding can be traced back to the visionary Dharma master Xing Yun of the Foguan (Buddhist Light) Mountain Monastery in southern Taiwan, the biggest monastery on the island today, with more than one million followers, and branch temples, schools, and local associations in five continents.

The Founder

Xing Yun (1927–) was born into a family with scanty means in Jiangdu County, Jiangsu Province, Republic of China, at the time when the country was facing internal problems and external threats. His surname is Li and given name is Guoshen. He spent his childhood with his maternal grandmother who was a devout Buddhist. His father disappeared without a trace on a business trip when he was young, and he left home to become a Buddhist novice at the age of 12 at the Qixia (Dwelling on Evening Glow) Monastery in northern Jiangsu Province. He received his Buddhist name, Wuche (Thorough Awakening), and style, Jinjue (Awaken Now), from his Dharma master, Zhikai (dates unknown). But later he changed his style to Xing Yun (Starry Cloud) after settling in Taiwan. The Qixia Monastery belongs to the Linji Chan School and Xing Yun is the 48th successor of his lineage.

During his first 10 years as a monk, he attended different Buddhist institutions of education, but did not become a student at any regular school. In fact, all his life he never had any formal schooling and received no diploma from any educational institution. Perhaps it is for that reason that he always pays great attention to education as his activities in Taiwan and in America as well as elsewhere indicate. He became a self-taught scholar and calligrapher, conversant in the secular and sacred affairs of the present and the past.

After World War II, the Chinese civil war resumed with vigor on mainland China. The Communist Party's army swept across the country like an unstoppable prairie fire; the Nationalist Party's army kept withdrawing farther and farther south, until it had retreated to the island of Taiwan in 1949. Xing Yun joined the Ambulance Corps organized by a group of Buddhist monks and reached Taiwan in the same year. He was a homeless 23-year-old monk. As the Ambulance Corps was withdrawing with the Nationalist Party's army, he was suspected of being a Communist spy and was jailed for a short period of time.

After wandering from monastery to monastery, he finally settled in Yilan County, south of Taipei, where he began teaching the Dharma. Life in Yilan was not easy. He was not conversant in the local dialect and knew next to nothing about the Yilan culture. But he gradually overcame these difficulties, was accepted, and became a respected Dharma master. In addition to teaching the Dharma, he eventually organized a kindergarten and was involved in literary activities in Yilan. In 1965 he began construction of the present-day Foguan Mountain Monastery and became its first abbot until his retirement in 1986. Since then he has been traveling the world spreading the Dharma to all five continents.

Xing Yun has an ecumenical and inclusive heart-mind with regard to other faith traditions. He insists that all faiths should live together in harmony, because all faiths aim for the same goal through different routes. In fact, he maintains that it is perfectly fine for anyone to believe in two faith traditions.

Traditional Buddhism is hierarchical; monks rank higher than nuns and the clergy higher than the laity. But Xing Yun has ploughed a new furrow by insisting that everyone is equal regardless of his or her roles or functions.

Education, as previously mentioned, and charitable work are also important. Thus under his leadership Foguan Mountain Monastery has established educational institutions for the clergy and the laity as well as charitable organizations to help those who need assistance.

For his work in Taiwan and elsewhere Xing Yun has received numerous awards and honors. But as the Chinese saying goes, "a tall tree catches the wind." Xing Yun has been subjected to criticism, gossip, and rumors. However, he has survived without much of a scratch and is now recognized as one of the eminent Buddhist monks of our time.

History

Hsi Lai Temple (registered with the state of California under the name International Buddhist Progress Society) has a brief history. It traces its beginning to Xing Yun's first trip to America as one of the representatives of the Taiwan Buddhist delegates that attended the American bicentennial celebration in 1976. Two years later he entrusted US$50,000 into the hands of two of his disciples—Ci Zhuang and Yi Hang—and sent them to America to secure a piece of property so they would have a venue to teach the Dharma. Upon arriving in Southern California, the two disciples were discouraged by the high price of real estate. But Xing Yun encouraged them to stay and they subsequently purchased a church building in Maywood, California, as the headquarters of the International Buddhist Progress Association and as a temple where they could teach the Dharma.

Soon the two Dharma masters discovered that they were in need of a bigger place to accommodate the large number of worshippers and practioners. Thus, the White Pagoda Temple was built in Maywood. The White Pagoda Temple would soon prove to be inadequate. Plans were developed for a much bigger temple to be built in South Bay in the greater Los Angeles area, but the society could not acquire land in that city. Finally, with the help of some devotees, the current site was secured. But applying for a building permit proved to be a formidable task, with opposition coming from the city officials and its residents. Finally, after a number of public hearings and numerous meetings, permission to build was granted.

The groundbreaking ceremony took place in 1986 and the temple was completed in November 1988.

Practice

Hsi Lai, as previously mentioned, belongs to the Linji Chan lineage but it also embraces other major schools of Buddhism, especially Xing Yun's brand of Humanistic Buddhism. Xing Yun traces his idea of Humanistic Buddhism back to Sakyamuni Buddha, who was born, grew up, and became enlightened in this human world, and above all he also realized *Nirvāṇa* here on earth. So instead of practicing the Dharma in remote forests, Xing Yun teaches that followers of the Buddha should incorporate Buddhism into the totality of their daily lives. He discourages his fellow Buddhists from practicing traditional asceticism; instead he insists that they should carry their faith in their everyday life with all its joys, sorrows, challenges, demands, and responsibilities in fulfilling their life-goals and in serving others.

Hsi Lai's mission is to provide a center for spiritual culture in America; a place for Westerners to learn about Buddhism and to promote cultural exchanges, East and West. Today Hsi Lai provides a variety of programs, both in Chinese and English, to its members and the community. It lends its facilities to the community's civic activities. Its conference rooms are available, free of charge, to the city for meetings and other gatherings.

This temple along with its founder likewise founded in 1991 the University of the West in Rosemead, California. The university is accredited by the Western Association of Schools and Colleges and offers bachelor's and master's degrees in a number of fields, including a Buddhist chaplaincy program, and a PhD degree in Buddhist studies.

Edmond Yee

See also: Entries: Chinese Temples in America; Taiwanese American Religions

Further Reading

Lin, Irene. "Journey to the Far West: Chinese Buddhism in America." David Yoo, ed., *New Spiritual Homes: Religion and Asian Americans.* Honolulu: Univerity of Hawai'i Press, 1999, 134–168.

University of the West. www.uwest.edu/site/. Accessed October 25, 2013.

Hsuan Hua (1918–1995)

Hsuan Hua, a native of China, is widely recognized in the Chinese Buddhist community as one of the great enlightened monks of the 20th century. He was born into a peasant family in a small village south of Harbin in Manchuria (Dongbei) in northeast China. His lay name was Bai Yushu and he was also called Yuxi. When he formally became a Buddhist in his mid-teens, he was given the Dharma name Anci (Peace and Compassion), and after becoming a monk, he was also known as Dulun (Liberator from the Wheel of Rebirth). Upon granting him the Dharma-seal of the Weiyang Chan Buddhist lineage, Elder Chan Master Xuyun (1840–1959) bestowed upon him the Dharma-transmission name Hsüan Hua (Xuanhua—To Proclaim and Transform).

Childhood

Master Hsuan Hua was the youngest of eight children and was strongly influenced by his Buddhist mother. As a child he followed her practices of eating only vegetarian food and reciting the Buddha's name. At the age of 11, after seeing a dead baby lying on the ground, he realized the universality of death and rebirth and that all is impermanent. Although at that time he made up his mind to become a monk, he agreed to his mother's request to delay his going forth into the monastic life until after she passed away. The following year, with his parents' permission, he traveled widely looking for an authentic and wise spiritual teacher.

When Master Hsuan Hua was 15, he began his formal education in a tiny village school. At age 16 he began to give lectures on Buddhist scriptures to interested local villagers, almost all of whom were illiterate. Assisted by a photographic memory, he was extremely diligent in his studies so that he was, in the space of two and a half years, able to memorize the Four Books and the Five Classics of the Confucian tradition. During that period he also studied and memorized many works on traditional Chinese medicine, astrology, divination, physiognomy, and the scriptures of the great religions, including the Hebrew scriptures and the New Testament. At age 17 he founded a free school in which he alone taught around 30 children and adults from his poor peasant community.

Laying the Foundation

Origins of Master Hsuan Hua's Mission to the West. The Venerable Master taught all beings without regard to path of rebirth, country, ethnic origin, religion, and so forth. There are two countries, however, where he had special affinities in this life: China and the United States. Although the majority of his disciples are Chinese, history will probably remember him primarily for his work in bringing the teachings of the Buddha to the people of the West.

The story of his mission to the West begins in rural Manchuria at his mother's grave site. Master Hsuan Hua, then in his late teens or early twenties, was observing the Chinese filial practice of three years' mourning. As a novice Buddhist monk, he did it in a uniquely Buddhist way by building a meditation hut of sorghum thatch and sitting in continuous meditation there. One day he had a vision of Venerable Master Huineng (638–713 CE), the sixth patriarch in China of the Chan (Zen) Buddhist lineage, walk into his hut. The patriarch spoke with him for a long time. Master Hsuan Hua remembered him saying:

> The five [Chan] lineages will divide into ten to teach and transform living beings: a hundred and then a thousand, until they are endless, . . . countless like the sands of the Ganges . . . the genuine beginning [of Buddhism] in the West.

That was part of the Sixth Patriarch's instruction to Master Hsuan Hua in which he told him that he should leave China and spread the Dharma in the West. Afterwards Master Hsuan Hua got up to accompany the patriarch out of the hut. Only after the patriarch had disappeared did Master

Hsuan Hua remember that the patriarch had left this world long ago.

Despite knowing from this initial vision of the sixth patriarch that he would eventually go to the West to propagate the Dharma, Master Hsuan Hua had little contact with Westerners until he moved to Hong Kong in 1949. There he had his first substantive experiences with Western culture.

After his Dharma-lineage predecessor, Venerable Chan Master Xuyun (1840–1959), passed away and Master Hsuan Hua completed the proper ceremonies in his memory, he felt that conditions had ripened for pursuing his Dharma mission in the West. Several of his lay disciples from Hong Kong had already gone to the United States to study.

In November 1960, Master Hsuan Hua went to Australia to investigate the conditions for the growth of Buddhism there. He spent a difficult year there and then returned to Hong Kong briefly. In 1958 a branch of the Buddhist Lecture Hall had already been established in San Francisco by his disciples there. In response to their invitation, Master Hsuan Hua decided to go to San Francisco and arrived there early in 1962. At the small Chinatown temple, he lectured on the *Amitābha Sūtra*. During that period various Americans who were interested in Zen, such as Richard Baker, former abbot of the San Francisco Zen Center, visited Master Hsuan Hua.

In the fall of 1962 the Cuban missile crisis broke out. Wishing in some measure to repay the benefit that he had received from living in the United States, and seeing clearly the catastrophic threat imposed by the missiles in Cuba, the venerable master embarked on a total fast for 35 days, during which he took only water. He dedicated the merit of his sacrifice to the ending of the hostilities.

The Monk in the Grave Period. In 1963, because some people who attended his lectures in Chinatown were not respectful of the Buddha's teachings, he left there and moved the Buddhist Lecture Hall to a first-floor flat on the corner of Sutter and Webster Streets on the edge of San Francisco's Fillmore District and Japantown. Master Hsuan Hua's move marked the beginning of a period of relative seclusion during which he called himself "a monk in the grave." It lasted until 1968. He later continued to refer to himself in that way and wrote the following poem:

> Each of you now meets a monk in
>   the grave.
> Above there is no sun and moon,
>   below there is no lamp.
> Affliction and enlightenment—ice is
>   water.
> Let go of self-seeking and become
>   apart from all that is false.
> When the mad mind ceases,
>   enlightenment pervades all.
> Enlightened, attain the bright
>   treasury of your own nature.
> Basically, the retribution body is the
>   Dharma body.

It was at that Sutter Street location that Master Hsuan Hua first started having regular contact with young Americans who were interested in meditation. Some came to his daily public meditation hour from seven to eight every evening, and a few

Americans also attended his *sūtra* lectures. He lectured there on the *Amitābha Sūtra*, the *Diamond Sūtra*, the *Heart Sūtra* with his own verse commentary, on his own commentary to the *Song of Enlightenment*, and also on portions of the *Lotus (Dharma Flower) Sūtra*.

In July 1967 Master Hsuan Hua moved back to Chinatown, this time relocating the San Francisco Buddhist Lecture Hall in the Tianhou Temple, the oldest Chinese temple in America. There he lectured on the *Verses of the Seven Buddhas of Antiquity* and the "Universal Door" chapter of the *Lotus (Dharma Flower) Sūtra*.

On Chinese New Year's Day in 1968, Master Hsuan Hua made two important pronouncements to a small gathering. First, he predicted that in the course of the year the lotus of American Buddhism would bloom. At that time there was still little outward sign of the influx of young Americans, which would begin that spring.

Second, noting the great fear among large segments of the community that there would be an earthquake in the spring of that year, he declared that as long as he was in San Francisco, he would not permit earthquakes large enough to do damage or cause injury or death to occur. Every subsequent Chinese New Year he would renew his vow. When the San Francisco earthquake of 1989 occurred, Master Hsuan Hua was out of the country in Taiwan.

In the spring of 1968 a group of students at the University of Washington in Seattle wrote to Master Hsuan Hua and requested that he come to Seattle to lead a week-long meditation session. Master Hsuan Hua had Nancy Dana Lovett, a disciple, write for him to Ron Epstein, another disciple who was a member of the Seattle group, to tell the group that he could not come to Seattle, because if he left San Francisco, there would be an earthquake. He suggested that they come to the Buddhist Lecture Hall in San Francisco instead. The group went and that spring both a Buddha-recitation session and a Chan (Zen) meditation session, each a week long, were held. About 30 people attended.

The 1968 *Shurangama Sūtra* Summer Lecture and Cultivation Session. At the conclusion of the spring sessions, Master Hsuan Hua suggested to several of the participants that a three-month lecture and cultivation session be held during the summer months. About 30 people decided to attend. During that 98-day session, Master Hsuan Hua lectured on the *Shurangama Sūtra* twice a day, and near the end of the session three and even four times a day, to explain the entire *sūtra*. The lectures were also open to the general public. The session itself started at six every morning and officially ended at nine in the evening. In addition to the *sūtra* lectures, the schedule consisted of alternate hours of meditation, study, and discussion, so there was very little free time.

Although those who attended were of varied ages and backgrounds, the majority were young Americans of college age or in their middle or late twenties. Most had had little or no previous training in Buddhism; however, several had studied Buddhism at the undergraduate level and some at the graduate level. A few had also had a little previous experience with meditation. The handful who had some competency in Chinese provided translations, which started out on a rather rudimentary level and became quite competent during the course of the summer.

Events of special note that took place during the session included two refuge ceremonies, at which most of the regular participants became formal disciples of Master Hsuan Hua, and a precept ceremony late in the summer in which almost all the disciples took vows to follow moral precepts of varying numbers, including some or all of the five moral precepts up to the 10 major and 48 minor bodhisattva precepts. One participant took the vows of a novice monk. Master Hsuan Hua's teachings that summer especially emphasized the moral precepts as a foundation for the spiritual life. In this way he used them as an effective antidote against the proclivities of the popular culture of the time for drug experience and sexual promiscuity.

Five Americans Become Monastics. Soon afterwards four other Americans, three of whom had also participated in the summer session, also became novices. In December 1969 the five, three men and two women, received full ordination as Buddhist monastics at Haihui Monastery near Keelung, Taiwan, and became the first Americans to do so. They were *Bhikshus* (monks) Heng Chyan, Heng Jing, and Heng Shou, and *Bhikshunis* (nuns) Heng Yin and Heng Chih.

Master Hsuan Hua's Plan for American Buddhism. With the founding of a new American *Sangha*, Master Hsuan Hua was then ready to embark on a remarkable program for building American Buddhism. Master Hsuan Hua has explained that his life's work lay in three main areas: (1)

bringing the true and orthodox teachings of the Buddha to the West and establishing a proper monastic community of fully ordained monks and nuns (*Sangha*) here; (2) organizing and supporting the translation of the entire Buddhist canon into English and other Western languages; and (3) promoting wholesome education through the establishment of schools and universities.

Establishing a Buddhist *Sangha* in the West

The First Ordination Ceremonies in the West. Because of the increasing numbers of people who wished to leave the home-life to become monks and nuns under Master Hsuan Hua's guidance, in 1972, at Gold Mountain Dhyana Monastery in the Mission District in San Francisco, Master Hsuan Hua decided to have the first formal, full ordination ceremonies for Buddhist monks and nuns in the West. He invited virtuous elder masters to preside with him over the ordination platform. Five monks and one nun received ordination. In 1976, 1979, 1982, 1989, and 1992, subsequent ordination ceremonies were held at the Sagely City of Ten Thousand Buddhas, which is located near Ukiah, California, about 110 miles north of San Francisco, and progressively larger numbers of people received full ordination. Over 200 people from countries all over the world were ordained under him.

Master Hsuan Hua as Reformer. Master Hsuan Hua was determined to transmit the original and correct teachings of the Buddha to the West and was outspoken about not infecting Western Buddhism with corrupt practices that were widespread in Chinese Buddhism. While encouraging his disciples to learn the ancient traditions, he cautioned them against mistaking cultural overlay and ignorant superstition for the true Dharma. He encouraged them to understand the logical reasons behind the ancient practices.

Among the reforms that he instituted were the following: he reestablished the wearing of the precept sash (*kashaya*) as a sign of a member of the *sangha*; he emphasized that the Buddha instructed that monks and nuns not eat after noon and encouraged his *sangha* to follow the Buddha's practice, which he himself followed, of eating only one meal a day at noon; he also encouraged them to follow his example in the practice of not lying down at night, which was also recommended by the Buddha. In the early days at Tianhou Temple in San Francisco's Chinatown, some of the disciples, to train themselves in this practice, found appropriate-sized wooden packing crates abandoned in the streets and modified them so that they could sit in them at night and keep themselves from stretching out their legs. Master Hsuan Hua also criticized the current Chinese practice among many Buddhist laypeople of taking refuge with many different teachers, and he himself would not accept disciples who had previously taken refuge with another monk.

Some of Master Hsuan Hua's American disciples were initially attracted to Master Hsuan Hua and Buddhism because of their interest in extraordinary spiritual experiences and psychic powers. Many of them were trying to understand remarkable experiences of their own, and many with special psychic abilities were naturally drawn to Master Hsuan Hua. Clearly recognizing the danger of the popularity of the quest for special experiences in American culture, Master Hsuan Hua emphasized that special mental states can be a sign of progress in cultivation but can also be very dangerous if misunderstood. He taught about the Buddha's monastic prohibitions against advertising one's spiritual abilities and made clear that spiritual abilities in themselves are not an indication of wisdom and do not ensure wholesome character.

Generally speaking, Master Hsuan Hua was concerned with the pure motivation of those who left home under him and did not want the American *sangha* to be polluted by those who had ulterior, worldly reasons for leaving the home-life. To that end he established these fundamental guidelines for monastic practice:

Freezing to death, we do not
    scheme.
Starving to death, we do not beg.
Dying of poverty, we ask for
    nothing.
According with conditions, we do
    not change.
Not changing, we accord with
    conditions.
We adhere firmly to our three great
    principles.
We renounce our lives to do the
    Buddha's work.
We take the responsibility to mould
    our own destinies.
We rectify our lives as the *Sangha's*
    work.
Encountering specific matters, we
    understand the principles.

Understanding the principles, we
apply them in specific matters.
We carry on the single pulse of the
patriarchs' mind-transmission.

In addition he summarized the standards of conduct that he upheld throughout his life for all his disciples, both monastics and lay people, in his Six Great Guidelines: not contending with others, not being greedy, not craving illicit gratification, not being selfish, not seeking personal advantage, and not lying.

One of Master Hsuan Hua's more remarkable endeavors in the area of monastic reform was his attempt to heal the 2,000-year-old rift between the Mahāyāna and Theravāda monastic communities. He encouraged cordial relations between the respective monastic communities, invited distinguished Theravāda monks to preside with him in monastic ordination ceremonies, and initiated talks aimed at resolving areas of difference.

Founding of the Sino-American Buddhist Association and the Dharma Realm Buddhist Association. Master Hsuan Hua felt that one of the marks of decay of proper monastic practice in China had been the gradual shift of emphasis from large monastic training monasteries to small individual temples, each with one or two monks or nuns free to do more or less whatever they pleased. To ensure that tendency for laxity of practice did not take hold in the West, Master Hsuan Hua wished to unite all his *sangha* members and laypeople under a single organization, one that could both help to maintain uniform pure standards of conduct for members of the *sangha* and discourage the making of offerings to individuals instead of to the *sangha* as a whole. To strengthen the central organization and in recognition of his growing number of American disciples, in December 1968 the Buddhist Lecture Hall was expanded into the newly incorporated Sino-American Buddhist Association. As that organization became more international in scope, in 1984 the name of the organization was officially changed to the Dharma Realm Buddhist Association.

Monasteries and Temples Founded by Master Hsuan Hua in the West. With the large influx of Americans wishing to study the Dharma, the small Tianhou Temple was quickly outgrown, and in 1970 the association moved to a large three-story brick building, which was remodeled to become Gold Mountain Dhyana Monastery. In 1976 Master Hsuan Hua established the Sagely City of Ten Thousand Buddhas, which now encompasses about 700 acres of land at Wonderful Enlightenment Mountain near Ukiah in northern California. Among the many other temples, monasteries, and retreat centers established by Master Hsuan Hua in the West are Gold Wheel Monastery in Los Angeles, Long Beach Monastery in Long Beach, California, Gold Buddha Monastery in Vancouver, Gold Summit Monastery in Seattle, Avatamsaka Monastery in Calgary, the Berkeley Buddhist Monastery and Institute of World Religions, and the Administrative Headquarters and International Translation Institute, both in Burlingame, California.

Explaining the Buddha's Teachings and Translating the Buddhist Canon

What Master Hsuan Hua Taught. In retrospect, the vigor, depth, and breadth of Master Hsuan Hua's efforts in teaching in the West are extremely remarkable. In his early days of teaching Westerners, he often had little or no help. He cooked, taught them to cook, sat with them in meditation and taught them to sit, entertained them with Buddhist stories, and taught them the rudiments of the Buddha's teachings and Buddhist courtesy and ceremony. He gave lessons in Chinese and in Chinese calligraphy, and taught the fundamentals of the pure Buddhist lifestyle.

As his Western students progressed in their understanding and practice, he did not slack off in the least. He continued not only to lecture daily on the Buddhist *sūtras*, but to give various other classes. He lectured on the four major Mahāyāna Buddhist *sūtras*, completing the *Shurangama Sūtra*, the *Lotus (Dharma Flower) Sūtra*, and the *Avatamsaka Sūtra*, and finishing a substantial portion of the *Nirvāṇa Sūtra*. He also lectured on the *Heart Sūtra*, the *Diamond (Vajra) Sūtra*, the *Sixth Patriarch's Platform Sūtra*, the *Earth Store Sūtra*, the *Song of Enlightenment*, and a host of other Buddhist works.

He also trained a whole staff of translators and taught many disciples how to lecture on the *sūtras* themselves. In almost every formal teaching situation, to train his disciples, he would first ask them to speak and only speak himself after they had had the opportunity.

Master Hsuan Hua's teaching methods included yearly *sūtra* lectures and cultivation sessions modeled on the first *Shurangama Sūtra* session. He laid down vigorous standards for meditation and recitation sessions, giving frequent instructional talks during the sessions. He explained the importance of the Buddhist teachings about repentance and encouraged the bowing of the Great Compassion Repentance, the Great Repentance before the Ten Thousand Buddhas, and other repentance ceremonies.

Much of Master Hsuan Hua's most important teaching took place outside of his formal lectures. For Master Hsuan Hua, every situation was an opportunity for teaching, and he paid little attention to whether the recipients of instruction were formal disciples. For him every worldly encounter, whether with disciples or politicians or realtors, was an opportunity to help people become aware of their faults, change them, and develop their inherent wisdom. Master Hsuan Hua was always open, direct, and totally honest with everyone in every situation. He treated everyone equally, from the president of the United States to little children. Everything he did was to benefit others and never for himself.

Traveling to Spread the Dharma in the West. Whenever and wherever he was respectfully invited to speak about the Buddha's teachings, Master Hsuan Hua always tried his best to oblige, even if it was at the cost of his own physical well-being. In addition to his almost continual traveling in the United States and Canada to lecture and several major trips to Asian countries, Master Hsuan Hua also visited South America and Europe.

In 1973, Master Hsuan Hua traveled to Brazil, Argentina, Paraguay, and other countries in South America. His main purpose was to establish affinities with the people, and so he spent much time while there reciting the Mantra of Great Compassion and transferring the merit accrued by his recitation to the local people.

In 1990, at the invitation of Buddhists in many countries of Europe, Master Hsuan Hua took a large delegation there on a Dharma tour, knowing full well that, because of his ill health at the time, the rigors of the trip would shorten his lifespan. However, as always Master Hsuan Hua considered the Dharma more important than his very life. Among the countries visited were England, France, Belgium, Germany, and Poland.

The Buddhist Text Translation Society and *Vajra Bodhi Sea*. In 1970, Master Hsuan Hua founded the Buddhist Text Translation Society with the eventual goal of translating the entire Buddhist canon into English and other languages of the West. Master Hsuan Hua saw clearly that reliable translations into English with readable and understandable commentaries were essential to the understanding and practice of the Buddhadharma by Westerners. To date the Buddhist Text Translation Society has published hundreds of volumes, and the work of translating Buddhist scriptures, many with Master Hsuan Hua's own commentaries, is ongoing.

Also in 1970 Master Hsuan Hua founded *Vajra Bodhi Sea, a Monthly Journal of Orthodox Buddhism*. It has been published continuously ever since. Initially in English, it now appears in a bilingual Chinese-English format.

Promoting Education

Master Hsuan Hua felt that one of the weaknesses of Buddhism in China was that it did not give high priority to education and failed to develop a widespread network of Buddhist schools and universities. To begin to remedy that situation in the West, the venerable master founded Dharma Realm Buddhist University, primary and secondary schools, and developed financial aid programs for needy and deserving students.

Master Hsuan Hua taught that education is the best national defense. He counseled that in elementary school children should be taught filial respect, in secondary school love of country and loyalty to it, and at the university level students should learn not only professional skills but a sense of personal responsibility for improving the world they live in.

Master Hsuan Hua balanced tradition with educational innovation. He pioneered what he called the development of each individual's inherent wisdom, and he was always ready to employ new ways of teaching. For example, he wrote several songs in English himself and encouraged his disciples to use that medium for teaching the Dharma.

Dharma Realm Buddhist University. In 1976, Master Hsuan Hua established Dharma Realm Buddhist University with its main campus at the Sagely City of Ten Thousand Buddhas. Its main goals are to provide education to all the peoples of the world by explaining and propagating the Buddha's teachings, developing straightforward minds, benefiting society, and enlightening all beings. The university is currently seeking full accreditation for its undergraduate and graduate degree programs. In his final instructions, Master Hsuan Hua indicated that his disciples should pay special attention to the fulfillment of his vision for the university.

Over the years many well-known professors from American universities, including Edward Conze, Padmanabh Jaini, David Ruegg, Henry Rosemont, Jr. and Jacob Needleman, to name just a few, came to pay their respects to Master Hsuan Hua and to listen to his teachings. He was also invited to lecture at various universities, including Stanford University, the University of California at Berkeley, the University of Washington, the University of Oregon, the University of California at Los Angeles, the University of California at Davis, the University of Hawai'i, and San Francisco State University.

Saṇgha and Laity Training Programs. In 1982, Master Hsuan Hua established the Saṇgha and Laity Training Programs. The Laity Training Program emphasizes Buddhist studies and practice for laypeople in a monastic setting with an emphasis on moral discipline. The Saṇgha Training Program emphasizes religious practice, monastic discipline, and temple management. Through these programs Master Hsuan Hua has been able to train fully qualified and committed staff for the various programs and activities of the Dharma Realm Buddhist Association.

Developing Goodness and Instilling Virtue Schools. At the suggestion of Carol Ruth Silver, who was then a San Francisco

supervisor, Master Hsuan Hua founded Developing Goodness School in 1976. In addition to nurturing the roots of goodness and virtue in young children, the school was devoted to quality education. It promoted a bilingual Chinese-English curriculum and taught the fundamentals of both Western and Chinese cultural heritages. The founding principal, Terri Nicholson, and her staff taught the first classes in the furnished basement of the International Institute for the Translation of Buddhist Texts on Washington Street in San Francisco. The school moved to the Sagely City of Ten Thousand Buddhas in 1978. Instilling Virtue Secondary School opened its doors in 1980, and a separation into boys' and girls' schools occurred in 1981.

Master Hsuan Hua's Ecumenical Teachings. In consonance with his universal vision, Master Hsuan Hua often said that Buddhism was too limiting a label for the Buddha's teaching and often referred to it as the teaching of living beings. Just as he was critical of sectarian divisions within Buddhism as not being in the true spirit of the Dharma, he felt that people should not be attached to interreligious distinctions either, that it is important for people of all religions to learn from the strengths of each religious tradition. To make that vision a reality, he invited his good friend Paul Cardinal Yu Bin, the Catholic cardinal of Taiwan, to join him in establishing a World Religions Center at the Sagely City of Ten Thousand Buddhas and to be its first director. He suggested that the cardinal be a "Buddhist among the Catholics" and that he himself would be a "Catholic among the Buddhists." Unfortunately the cardinal's untimely death delayed the plans for the center, which in 1994 opened in Berkeley as the Institute for World Religions.

Master Hsuan Hua also directed Dharma Realm Buddhist University to host a World Religions Conference in 1987 at the Sagely City of Ten Thousand Buddhas. Also in 1987 Master Hsuan Hua gave a major address at the Third International Buddhist-Christian Dialogue Conference in Berkeley. In 1975 Master Hsuan Hua was invited to give a eulogy at Grace Cathedral in San Francisco for Avery Brundage, who had been president of the International Olympic committee. In 1989 Master Hsuan Hua was invited to the Quaker Retreat Center at Pendle Hill, Pennsylvania, to give a series of talks, and in 1992 he was the guest speaker at the yearly Vedanta Society gathering at Olema, California.

Hsuan Hua's Enduring Legacy for the West

Throughout his life the venerable master was widely known for his selfless humility and his compassion for all living beings. He worked tirelessly and without regard for his own health and welfare to dissolve the boundaries of ignorance that obstruct true self-understanding. He constantly worked for peace and harmony throughout the world on all levels, between people, between species, between religions, and between nations. Although his mission has been to the Dharma realm, in this brief account we have tried to focus on his contributions to Buddhism in the West. In this light, we conclude with a brief overview.

When the first Chan (Zen) Buddhist patriarch, Bodhidharma, came to China (late fifth or early sixth century CE), although Buddhism had arrived several centuries earlier, most people in China were still confused about the central meaning of the Buddha's teaching and could not distinguish what was true from what was false, what was superficial from what was essential. Patriarch Bodhidharma cut through that confusion and taught people to illuminate their own minds, see their true natures, and become Buddhas. Venerable Master Hsuan Hua came to the West about a hundred years after Buddhism's first introduction here. When he arrived there was much genuine interest but also tremendous confusion and misunderstanding. Teaching that Buddhism flourishes only in countries where the *sangha* is strong and pure, Master Hsuan Hua established a reformed monastic community and emphasized the importance of moral precepts for both monastics and laity. Understanding the practical and pragmatic nature of the American character, he emphasized vigorous and proper meditation practice in the spirit and lineage of Patriarch Bodhidharma, so that the eternal truths of the Buddha's teachings could be directly and personally experienced. Seeing clearly the dangers of widely prevalent wrong notions about the Buddha's teachings, he explained the major Buddhist scriptures in a clear and simple manner while bringing out their contemporary, practical relevance. Then he worked to make those teachings available in English so that they would be accessible to Westerners. And finally, he chose to live and teach in the West so that every day he provided a living, breathing manifestation of the true meaning of the Buddha's teachings. In that way he touched and profoundly transformed the lives of countless beings and led them to the path of Buddhist enlightenment.

Ronald Epstein

See also: Entries: Berkeley Buddhist Monastery; Ullambana Assembly

Further Reading

In Memory of the Venerable Master Hsuan Hua. 3 vols. Burlingame, CA: Buddhist Text Translation Society, 1995–1996.

Records of the Life of the Venerable Master Hsüan Hua. Vols. 1 and 2. San Francisco: Committee for the Publication of the Life of Ch'an Master Hua, 1973, 1975.